THE

LIVES AND TIMES

OF

THE CHIEF JUSTICES

OF THE

Supreme Court of the United States.

BY

HENRY FLANDERS.

IN TWO VOLUMES.

VOL. I.

JOHN JAY—JOHN RUTLEDGE

PHILADELPHIA:
J. B. LIPPINCOTT & CO.
1874.

PREFACE.

THIS volume was announced as in press several months ago. Unavoidable circumstances have postponed its publication until now. The author trusts, however, that the public have been gainers by the delay.

He has endeavored to consult every accessible source of information that could serve to illustrate the character of the men whose lives he has undertaken to write; or throw light upon the times in which they acted. He need not say to the student of American history, that the American Archives, by Mr. Peter Force, are an invaluable repository of authentic documents; that they let in a flood of light upon the obscure passages of our history, and upon the characters of our public men. He is happy to acknowledge that he is greatly indebted to that work for any value that may be ascribed to his own.

He is also, in common with his countrymen, under great obligations to the unwearied industry and acknowledged abilities of Mr. Jared Sparks. His researches have been of incalculable service to historical science. The notes appended to the writings of Washington and Franklin elucidate whatever is of public or private interest, during the period over which those writings extend, and to which they relate. To say nothing of the other numerous and valuable works which bear his name, those notes and illustrations alone would insure to Mr. Sparks a durable fame.

The author's particular thanks are due to Mr. William Jay for the polite manner with which he submitted to his use his own labors, together with the important testimony of Lord St. Helen's, respecting the negotiations at Paris, in 1782 and 1783.

He must also express his obligations to those of the descendants of Rutledge, who have been so good as to put him in possession of facts, elsewhere unattainable, respecting their distinguished ancestor. He has thus been enabled to elucidate passages of his life that have hitherto rested in fable.

To those of his friends, who have either supplied him with new facts, or pointed out new sources of information, he begs, in this public manner, to return his sincere thanks. He would do injustice to his own feelings, did he fail to mention, in this connection, Mr. Lloyd P. Smith, of the Library Company of Philadelphia. He has, with unfailing politeness, assisted the author's researches, and given him the full benefit of his extensive bibliographical knowledge.

It has been the author's careful endeavor to state facts with precision, and suppress or extenuate nothing that the public were entitled to know. He trusts that the day has passed when exaggeration can supply the place of truth, and empty eulogy take the place of authentic information. It is believed that the reader will find in the following pages the political history of his country fairly related, and the character of its public men delineated without improper bias.

CONTENTS.

THE LIFE OF JOHN JAY.

CHAPTER I.

CHAPTER II.

1754—1764.

CHAPTER III.

1764—1774.

CHAPTER IV.

1774.

CHAPTER V.

1774.

CHAPTER VI.

1774—1776.

CHAPTER VII.

1776.

CHAPTER VIII.

1776—1777.

CHAPTER IX.

1777—1778.

CHAPTER X.

1778—1779.

CHAPTER XI.

1779 — 1782.

CHAPTER XII.

1782—1784.

CHAPTER XIII.

1784—1789.

CHAPTER XIV.

1789—1794.

CHAPTER XV.

1794—1795.

CHAPTER XVI.

1795—1801.

CHAPTER XVII.

1801—1829.

LIFE OF JOHN RUTLEDGE.

CHAPTER I.

CHAPTER II.

1739—1761.

CHAPTER III.

1761—1764.

CHAPTER IV.

1764—1774.

CHAPTER V.

1774.

CHAPTER VI.

1774.

CHAPTER VII.

1774—1775.

CHAPTER VIII.

1775.

CHAPTER IX.

1775—1776.

CHAPTER X.

1776—1778.

CHAPTER XI.

1778—1782.

CHAPTER XII.

1782—1783.

CHAPTER XIII.

1783—1791.

CHAPTER XIV.

1788.

CHAPTER XV.

1789—1795.

CHAPTER XVI.

1795.

CHAPTER XVII.

1795—1800.

THE

LIFE OF JOHN JAY.

CHAPTER I.

HIS ANCESTRY.

THE year 1685, memorable for the revocation of the Edict of Nantes, found Pierre Jay, the first of his family of whom we have any distinct information, a thriving merchant in the old town of Rochelle. A Protestant in his principles, he could not fail to discover, from the temper of the times, that expatriation from his native land, or the adoption of a worship which he abhorred, was the distressing alternative presented to him. But that virtue which is founded on religion, and that fortitude which derives its support from the same exalted source, are seldom allured from the path of duty by the suggestions of interest, or the desire of repose. The steadiness and fidelity with which the Protestants of France adhered to their denounced and despised creed, amid all the violence of persecution, stands, and will for ever stand, a testimony to their moral greatness and to the innate worth of human nature itself.

Louis XIV., regardless of the wise and tolerant maxims of the illustrious Colbert, whose great abilities reflected lustre upon his reign, had long resolved to extirpate from his dominions the religion of dissent. The penal laws against the Protestants, which were in force anterior to the Edict of Nantes, were revived and executed with unsparing severity. And to render effectual the work of intolerance, new ones were devised, of the most rigorous and cruel character. The ordinance which formally revoked the Edict of Nantes, was announced on the 22d of October, 1685. But for months previous to that fatal act, religious freedom had been struck down. Every means that bigotry could suggest to overcome the conscience and subdue the wills of the recusants, arbitrary power had freely employed. Their churches were demolished, their pastors banished, their schools prohibited, and the peace, security, and happiness of their families destroyed. The *dragonnades* were revived. In the summer of 1685, troops were introduced into Rochelle and quartered upon the Protestant inhabitants. Dragoons were placed in the house of Mr. Jay, 'to live and act at their discretion.'[1]

[1] The subject of our biography left behind him an unfinished history of his ancestors, written in the latter part of his life. Several extracts from that history, written in a very chaste and pleasing style, are inserted in the memoir of him by his son, Hon. William Jay. *Vide* Life of J. Jay, vol. i., pp 1–9. From these extracts the facts stated in the text have been chiefly derived. It will not be inappropriate to quote in this place one or two passages *in extenso*. They will explain the circumstances under which Mr. Jay wrote, and, at the same time, illustrate the serious and reflective turn of his mind. He thus commences his narrative :—

'You have often expressed a wish that I would reduce to writing what information I have respecting our ancestors. I was pleased to find that you desired it, and have often regretted that a succession of affairs more immediately important constrained me from time to time to postpone it. My life has been so much a life of business, that idle time has not been among my burdens. In this place of peace and retirement, which a kind Providence has provided for me in my declining years, I for the first time enjoy the sweets of rest and tranquillity. Leisure hours begin to increase, and I purpose to employ some of them in giving you the information you request.

The persecution had become too intolerable to be borne. The future disclosed nothing but additional calamity, and Mr. Jay determined to abandon a country which, like an unnatural mother, no longer protected her own offspring. His family at this time consisted of his wife, a daughter of Mons. François, a merchant in Rochelle, and three children, viz., two sons and a daughter. The eldest son, Augustus, was born on the 23d day of March, 1665. At the age of twelve, he was sent to England to be educated. He remained in that country six years. He was then recalled by his

---

'When and where we were born, and who were our progenitors, are questions to which certain philosophers ascribe too little importance. It becomes us to be mindful that the great Creator has been pleased to make men social beings; that he established between them various relations, and, among others, those which arise from consanguinity; and that to all these relations he has attached particular and corresponding duties. These relations and duties promote the happiness of individuals and families; they pervade and harmonize society, and are subservient both to public and personal welfare.

'How fleeting, how forgetful, how frail is tradition! There are families in this State who are ignorant even of the names of the first of their ancestors who came to this country. They know not whence, or why, or how they came. Between those days and the period of our Revolution, the field for biography has become barren. Little has been written, and of that little much has been lost by the destruction of papers during the war. The time, however, is approaching when this barren field will be cultivated by genius and by pride; and, under the auspices of obscurity, (ever friendly to fiction,) become fertile in fables. My faith in the generality of historical relations of every kind has been gradually declining for these thirty years. On various occasions I have seen accounts of events and affairs which I knew to be incorrect. Not a few of the common and current opinions respecting public men and public transactions are common and current mistakes, designedly countenanced by demagogues to promote party or personal purposes. The time, however, will most certainly come when the world and all that therein is, will be purified in a refiner's fire. It will then be of little importance to us whether our ancestors were splendid or obscure, and whether events and characters have been truly or partially represented, or not represented at all.'

father, and sent to Africa, but to what part, or for what purpose, is now unknown. At the time of which we speak, he was still absent. Mrs. Jay, and her remaining children, were secretly withdrawn from the house and placed on board a vessel which Mr. Jay had engaged for the purpose. Favoring gales, and a good Providence, attended them. They set sail without being discovered, and were safely landed at Plymouth, in England.

Mr. Jay remained behind, doubtless to settle his affairs and 'save what he could from the wrecks of his fortune.' But the absence of his family provoked investigation. As might have been anticipated from the arbitrary proceedings of the time, he was arrested and thrown into prison. The friendly interposition, however, of influential Catholics, with whom he was closely connected, soon enabled him to regain his liberty. But he had no assurance of security for the future, and he determined to effect his escape. Several vessels in which he was interested, and one, of which he was sole owner, were now looked for in the harbor of Rochelle. He instructed a pilot, 'on whose good-will and attachment he relied, to watch these vessels, and to put the first of them that came in immediately at anchor, at a place agreed upon between them.' Fortunately, his own vessel, freighted with his own cargo, (principally of iron,) was the first to arrive. He was notified of this happy circumstance by the "faithful and friendly pilot," and, with his aid, got on board the ship without discovery, and was carried to England.

The ship and cargo, 'some articles of value' which he sent over with his family, together with some additional property brought over by himself, were the only means he saved from the estate he had accumulated in France, and which was immediately seized when his departure became known. 'No part of it afterwards came to the use of either himself or his children ' His pecuniary situation, however, was comfortable, and, removed from the storms and agitations that afflicted his native country, his remaining life, although doubtless saddened by exile, by separation from kindred and friends, appears to have passed on, with one or two sharp interruptions, smoothly and happily to the close.

It is not known how long Augustus remained in Africa after the flight of his family. It could not, however, have been long. On his return to Rochelle, unapprised of the misfortunes that had befallen his parents, he found himself amidst the consuming fires of persecution, which were now raging with increased violence. Loyal to the religion of his fathers, but one course consistent with safety was presented to him, viz., to escape from the country. Aided by the kindness of friends, he got safely away, in a vessel bound to Charleston, in South Carolina, a State which afforded an asylum to numbers of his persecuted countrymen, and, in turn, was enriched by the acquisition of such a people. 'Augustus very properly reflected that his parents had two younger children to provide for, and that it became him to depend on his own exertions. It was his first intention to settle in South Carolina.' The climate, however, proved injurious to his health, and he determined to go elsewhere. He went to Philadelphia, which he found in such an infant state, that he thought it advisable to go to New York. Here he fixed his residence. 'His first employment was that of a supercargo, and he continued in it for several years. His parents found themselves relieved from anxiety about his welfare, and with great satisfaction observed his industry and promising prospects.'

In the year 1692, Augustus was led by 'certain commercial affairs at Hamburg,' to take passage on board a vessel bound for that city. 'The vessel was captured by a privateer from St. Maloes, and carried into that port. He, with other prisoners, was sent to a fortress about fifteen miles from St. Maloes. He was in that fortress when the news of the battle of La Hogue arrived there. Orders were thereupon given that the prisoners should that evening be put and kept in close custody. By negligence or accident, the prisoners became informed of this order.' Augustus determined, if possible, to effect his escape. He made the attempt, and was successful. Making his way to Rochelle, 'he was kindly received and secreted' by his aunt Mouchard. 'Through her address and management,' he obtained a passage on board a vessel bound for Denmark, whither he safely arrived. Returning from that country, 'he went to Holland, and from thence to England, to visit his father and sister. Much to the grief and loss of the family, his mother had lately died, and he found his father and sister deeply affected by it.' His younger brother too, a youth of adventurous character and military tastes, had preceded her to the grave about two years before. He died of wounds received at the battle of the Boyne, where he served as a volunteer in a regiment of French refugees, embodied in the cause of a Protestant king, whose triumph on that field confirmed to Englishmen their political and religious liberties.

'Painful as it must have been to his sensibilities to leave his father and sister amid the sorrows arising from such bereavements, the affairs and engagements of Augustus constrained him to return speedily to America. Bidding them what proved a last adieu, he sailed for New York. Here, in the year 1697, he was happily married to Ann Maria, a daughter of Mr. Balthazar Bayard. The ancestor of this gentleman was a Protestant professor of theology at Paris in the reign of Louis XIII., who abjured his country in preference to his religion, and took up his residence in Holland, whence several of his grandchildren removed to America — Mr. Balthazar Bayard being one of the number.

Henceforth, the life of Augustus Jay abounded with blessings. Successful in his business as a merchant, happy in his domestic relations, beloved and respected by the citizens of his adopted city, he seems to have realized the aspiration of the poet, and 'crowned a youth of labor with an age of ease.' To the praise of his filial piety it should be mentioned, that 'he had no sooner found himself settled and his prospects fair, than he represented the prosperous state of his affairs to his father and sister, and earnestly pressed them to come over and participate in it. But his father thought himself too far advanced in age to undertake the voyage, and no considerations would have prevailed on his excellent daughter to leave him.' Augustus Jay died at New York, in the year 1751, at the advanced age of eighty-six.

He left four children; three daughters and a son. The son was born in 1704, and, in honor of his grandfather, named Peter. Destined to what had hitherto been the hereditary profession of his family, he was placed at an early age in the counting-house of Mr. Peloquin of Bristol in England, who had married, after the death of her father, his aunt, the sister of Augustus Jay. Returning to his native country in 1728, he soon after married Mary Van Cortlandt, the daughter of Jacobus Van Cortlandt. The maternal grandfather of this young lady was Frederick Philipse, "whose family, originally of Bohemia, had been compelled, by Popish persecution," to abandon their country and seek refuge in Holland, whence Frederick came to New York. 'Thus had the subject of our memoir the honor to be descended in three instances from ancestors who chose to abandon their country rather than their religion.'

Peter Jay was a judicious and successful merchant.

Eschewing politics, he devoted himself assiduously to his business. 'When little more than forty years old,' he had earned a fortune sufficient, with 'the property he had acquired by inheritance and marriage,' to enable him to gratify his taste for rural life, and retire from the dusty thoroughfares of trade, to the freshness and repose of the country. Two of his children had been deprived of sight by the small-pox, a disease, at that period, of formidable character, but which, thanks to the progress of medical science, and the beneficent discovery of Jenner, is now little dreaded. 'It was thought that the two little sufferers could be brought up more safely and advantageously in the country than the city.'

Thus prompted by inclination and paternal affection, Peter Jay purchased a farm at Rye, on the shores of Long Island Sound, about twenty-five miles from New York, and fixed his residence there in the early part of the year 1746. Here Mrs. Jay and himself, surrounded by their children, to whose education they now devoted themselves, and enjoying the healthful and animating pursuits of the country, never had occasion to regret their seclusion from the busy world from which they had retired. Their home, amid all the trials and 'sharp incommodities' which beset their age, was cheered and adorned by the habitual exercise of those domestic virtues which beget and impart social happiness. Both 'were actuated by sincere and fervent piety; both had warm hearts and cheerful tempers; and both possessed, under varied and severe trials, a remarkable degree of equanimity. But in other respects they differed widely. He possessed strong masculine sense, was a shrewd observer, and admirable judge of men; resolute, persevering, and prudent; an affectionate father, a kind master, but governing all under his control with mild but absolute sway. She had a cultivated mind and fine imagination; mild and affectionate in her temper and manners, she took delight in the duties as well as the pleasures of domestic life, while a cheerful resignation to the will of Providence during many years of sickness and suffering, bore witness to the strength of her religious faith. So happily did these various dispositions harmonize together, that the subject of this memoir often declared, that he had never, in a single instance, heard either of his parents use towards the other an angry or unkind word.' They were both singularly exempt from ambition or aspiring wishes, and content 'along the cool sequestered vale of life' to keep "the noiseless tenor of their way.'

CHAPTER II.

1745—1764.

HIS BIRTH AND EDUCATION.

JOHN JAY, the first Chief Justice of the Supreme Court of the United States, was born in the city of New York, on the 12th day of December, 1745. He was the son of Peter and Mary Jay, and the eighth of a family of ten children. The sketch of his ancestors which we have given in the preceding chapter, presents a pleasing instance of unassuming but heroic virtue, flowing with its original purity from one generation to another, and in all its course meeting with no obstruction, and sullied with no stain. And we shall see that he whose career we are now to trace, did no discredit to the examples which adorned and illustrated the line from which he sprung. In honor and virtue he was their equal, while his ability and public service, by attracting attention to his lineage, have made their merits known to the world.

While still an infant, he was removed with the family to the country place which Mr. Jay had provided at Rye. The influence of natural scenery upon character has been often remarked. We shall not dwell upon it here. We may observe, however, that he whose boyhood has been familiar with natural objects, who has passed that formative period of existence amid the repose and expansive influences of the country, has just cause to congratulate himself upon so happy a circumstance. His after-life will bear witness to the benefits derived from it. In all his conduct, in vigor of intellect and promptitude of action, he will generally assert a superiority over him who was bred up amid the conventionalities and artificialities of the town. He will have a higher relish and keener appreciation of life. He will be less governed, in his conduct and opinions, by the semblance of things. He will be likely to *go through the world like a substance and a force, not like a formula of one.* Our American public life is full of examples which illustrate the correctness of these observations. We deem it fortunate, therefore, that the childhood of John Jay was passed in the country, in communion with nature—that he was a natural product, and not the growth of a hot-house.

He was taught the rudiments of knowledge by his mother, who snatched sufficient time from the pressure of domestic concerns, to instruct her children. He made good progress under her tuition, and was prepared, when eight years old, to enter a grammar school. As a child, he was remarked for his serious and studious disposition. 'Johnny is of a very grave disposition,' observes his father, 'and takes to learning exceedingly well. He will soon be fit to go to a grammar school.' He was at this time in his seventh year. In the following year, the hopes and favorable anticipations of the father seem to have gathered strength. In a letter to his uncle, Mr. Peloquin of Bristol, he modestly says, 'I cannot forbear taking the freedom of hinting to you that my Johnny gives me a very pleasing prospect. He seems to be endowed with a very good capacity, is very reserved, and quite of his brother James's disposition for books.'

It is interesting to observe how the characteristics of the boy manifest themselves in the life of the man. Contemporary with this reserved and studious lad, whose conduct gave his parents such a *pleasing prospect,* there was growing up in another country, under very different auspices, and subjected to a very different training, one of those great original natures that appear, at long intervals, upon the earth to rouse mankind from the torpor of despotism or luxury, to shake and thereby purify the moral elements of society. Gabriel Honore Mirabeau was quite another man from John Jay; a great and irregular genius, *the broad, burly mutineer of the world,* one of the most extraordinary men of his extraordinary times.

The father of young Mirabeau, 'the tough old Marquis,' like the father of young Jay, did not fail to discern the qualities of this elder lad of his, nor to give utterance to the impressions which they made upon him. 'This creature,' he says, 'promises to be a very pretty subject. Talent in plenty and cleverness, but more faults still inherent in the substance of him.' 'Only just come into life, and the extravasation of the thing already visible! A spirit cross-grained, fantastic, iracund, incompatible, tending towards evil before knowing it, or being capable of it.' 'A high heart under the jacket of a boy; it has a strange instinct of pride, this creature; noble withal; the embryo of a shaggy-headed bully and kill-cow that would swallow all the world, and is not twelve years old yet.' 'A type, profoundly inconceivable, of baseness; sheer dull grossness, and the quality of your dirty, tough-crusted caterpillar, that will never uncrust itself or fly.' 'An intelligence, a memory, a capacity that strike you, that astonish, that frighten you.' 'A nothing bedizzened with crotchets. May fling dust in the eyes of silly women, but will never be the fourth part of a man, if by good luck he be anything.' 'One whom you may call ill-born, this elder lad of mine; who bodes, at least hitherto, as if he could become nothing but a madman: almost invincibly maniac, with all the vile qualities of the maternal stock over and above. As he has a great many masters, and all, from the confessor to the comrade, are so many reporters to me, I see the nature of the beast, and doubt we shall ever do any good with him.'[1]

Observe in what a different strain he writes from Peter Jay. The one is describing, inconsistently and angrily to be sure, an eager, turbulent, impetuous, magnetic nature, full of life, impatient of restraint, pressing on to its objects, exultant, and defiant in its strength. The other, a calm, reflective being, intent on duty, anxious for the right, never *irregularly great,* but always equal to whatever station is assigned him, and attracting the regards of men by the integrity of his life, the justness of his views, and the elevation of his aims, rather than by the exhibition of rare and strange powers. Jay was animated by virtuous, Mirabeau by aspiring sentiments. The one or the other character will challenge our admiration or engage our affections, just in proportion as our mental and moral qualities are assimilated to theirs.

In his eighth year, Mr. Jay sent 'Johnny' to the grammar school at New Rochelle, a village but a few miles distant from Rye. The inhabitants were mostly of French extraction, and spoke their native tongue. He had thus an opportunity, at the most receptive period of life for that kind of acquisition, to become familiar with a language, which was to be of almost indispensable importance to him, in his subsequent diplomatic career.

---

[1] Carlyle's Miscellanies, Art. Mirabeau.

The first separation of a lad from the paternal homestead — the first breaking up of his earliest associations — is one of the sharpest trials to which childhood is subjected. Whoever has read, (and who has not?) Lamb's Essay upon Christ's Hospital Five and Thirty Years ago, will remember how pathetically he describes his sufferings and loneliness whilst an inmate of that celebrated school. As he retraces the impressions, and revives the recollections of his boyhood, he touchingly observes: O the cruelty of separating a poor lad from his early homestead! The yearnings which I used to have towards it in those unfledged years! How, in my dreams, would my native town, (far in the West,) come back, with its church, and trees, and faces! How I would wake weeping, and, in the anguish of my heart, exclaim upon sweet Calne in Wiltshire!'

If John Jay has left us no such picture of his feelings while under the roof of the Rev. Mr. Stoope, pastor of the French church at New Rochelle and principal of the grammar school there, we know enough of the treatment to which he was subjected to be at no loss to conjecture that he experienced them.

The Rev. Mr. Stoope was a Swiss gentleman of peculiar, but not uncommon character. Curious and all-intent upon his studies, particularly the mathematics, careless of money, utterly improvident, he seems to have been as heedless of the practical affairs of life as one of Aristophanes' philosophers.[1] The parsonage went to decay;

---

[1] Sublime in air,
Sublime in thought, I carry my mind with me,
Its cogitations all assimilated
To the pure atmosphere in which I float:
Lower me to the earth, and my mind's subtle powers
Seized by contagious dulness, lose their spirit;
For the dry earth drinks up the generous sap.
The vegetating vigor of philosophy,
And leaves it a mere husk.

THE CLOUDS, Scene II.

the larder was left unsupplied; the boys shivered with cold, and were scantily provided with food; but whatever domestic ills might befall, the absorbed mathematician worked out his problems, enjoying the pleasures of the mind, notwithstanding he might suffer from the wants of the body.

Mistress Stoope was, in all respects, a contrast to her husband. The entire management of the household devolving upon her, and forced by his negligent habits to be doubly careful, the prudence which she was compelled to exercise, and which, under other circumstances, would doubtless have amounted to no more than a commendable economy, assumed, in her situation, the harsh and repulsive aspect of penuriousness. Her temper, too, seems to have grown somewhat testy under the pressure of domestic trials, and, if the boys were not always well fed, they could seldom complain that they were not well scolded. It is easy to perceive, that from the combined effects of negligence on the part of the husband, and excessive frugality on the part of the wife, little John Jay had rather a comfortless time of it during the three years that he remained with Parson Stoope. In after-life he was accustomed to mention, that in winter he contrived to prevent the snow from drifting upon his bed, by closing the broken panes of glass with pieces of wood. His chief source of amusement appears to have been in roaming about the woods and fields.

We cannot say whether he made much progress in his studies during this period, nor are we concerned to know that he did. Early mental development is apt to be at the expense of physical strength; and the overtasked mind of childhood soon loses the vigor and spring of its faculties. How often are those confident hopes which early intellectual pre-eminence inspire, utterly disappointed when the hero of the school enters upon the arena of life! The fault is not in his stars, but in a vicious system of education, which unnaturally excited, and thereby enfeebled, his powers. We deem it fortunate, therefore, that John Jay, at the age of eleven, notwithstanding the hard and rugged life that he had led during the three previous years, returned to his father's house at Rye in robust health; that excessive application had neither impaired his body, nor unduly stimulated his mind. He was now placed under the instruction of a private tutor, and continued his studies with him until he was prepared for college. This is not the place to criticise that mode of education. We may observe, however, that in the practical affairs of mankind, 'book-learned skill,' without the support of a high and dauntless character, carries with it but little weight, and inspires but little respect. United, their power challenges and receives universal homage. That education, therefore, which developes and brings into activity, not merely the intellectual qualities, but those which underlie and are superior to them, such as give 'an erect countenance, a firm adherence to principle, a power of resisting false shame and frivolous fear,' qualities "that assert our good faith and honor, and assure to us the confidence of mankind," is obviously the most desirable. And herein consists the advantage of a public school over private instruction. It is an admirable discipline for a boy. It tries and improves his courage, arouses and strengthens every manly quality of his being, inspires a love of justice, and sends him out into the world with a spirit, intelligence, and sense of honor that fit him to play a useful part in the drama of life. We do not say that this is invariably the result, but the natural tendency of that sort of education. It is not book-learning alone that the ingenuous youth has acquired, but that knowledge, so vastly important, and yet so little considered, which comes from communion with many and various minds, or, as it has been aptly termed, 'the knowledge which boy receives from boy.'

The life and career of Mr. Jay furnish, perhaps, the best answer that could be made to these observations; but a single example cannot outweigh the general voice of experience. Besides, the effect of his early and solitary mode of education was doubtless counteracted by his subsequent removal to college.

In 1760, in his fifteenth year, he entered Columbia (then King's) College, as a freshman. That institution, the *alma mater* of many distinguished scholars, was then in its infancy. In its origin, the object of zealous and persistent, and, in some respects, merited opposition, it outlived the storm that rocked its cradle and endangered its existence, and, after a century of eminent usefulness, still exhibits the vigor of youth, mildly tempered with the dignity of age.[1]

---

[1] The people of New York, devoted to commerce, and far in advance of their Eastern neighbors in point of opulence, were, for a long time, very far behind them in all that concerned the means and diffusion of education. It was not until the year 1732, that any public measure was adopted for the encouragement and support of a public school, and then, because it had become apparent that a school could not be maintained from the voluntary contributions of the inhabitants. It was in the latter part of that year, that the Assembly made provision for the endowment of a free school, wherein were to be taught the Latin and Greek languages, and the practical branches of the mathematics. This school, which was to be under the charge of Mr. Alexander Malcolm of Aberdeen, the author of a treatise upon book-keeping, was established by a bill drafted by Mr. Philipse the Speaker, and brought in by Mr. De Lancey. The preamble excited a good deal of merriment. It ran thus: 'Whereas, the youth of this colony are found by manifold experience to be not inferior, in their natural geniuses, to the youth of any other country in the world: therefore be it enacted,' &c. Smith's History of New York, vol. II, p. 3. So late as the year 1751 there were but fifteen persons in the province, out of orders, who were academics. The population was multiplying. Wealth increased; but along with the march of material prosperity, the means of education did not keep pace. The public attention was at length thoroughly aroused to this subject, and the

The reputation which a young man earns at college for scholarship and talent, is a very uncertain indication of future eminence. Facility in the performance of college tasks implies neither originality, comprehensiveness, nor grasp of mind. Memory, attention, and industry go much further in the exercises of the schools than the highest genius without them. The latter is apt to work by irregular methods. It forgets the prescribed task, while contemplating the masterpieces of the poet and orator, or accompanying the historian over vast tracts of time, searching out the source and pursuing the march of empire, or, with the metaphysician, diving deep into the mysteries of being, —— seeking to ascertain and define its laws. College honors neither bespeak nor con-

---

endowment of a college became an object of general interest. For this purpose, the sum of £3443 was raised by means of successive lotteries. In November, 1751, the Assembly passed an act establishing King's College, and vesting the fund which we have mentioned in a board of ten trustees. Seven members of the board were of the Episcopal church, two of the Dutch, and the remaining member was an English Presbyterian. This inequality in the representation of the different sects aroused a feeling of hostility to the incipient institution. It was increased a thousand-fold when, in the year 1754, the trustees applied to the Governor for a charter, containing provisions which placed the college on a sectarian basis. One provision was, that none but an Episcopalian should be made President. Another was, that the Book of Common Prayer should be used for its religious exercises. The application of the Trustees for a charter of this nature, although it comported with their wishes, was precipitated by the offer of a tract of land, by Trinity Church, upon condition that the charter should contain the obnoxious provisions. Their application, after considerable delay, was at last successful, and the charter was granted. It now became necessary to obtain an act of the Assembly, transferring the funds of the old institution to the officers of the chartered one. The dissenting sects, whose means had been contributed for a college to be established, as they supposed, upon a free and liberal basis, determined to prevent a sectarian triumph, by defeating the proposed transfer of the college funds. In this they were partially successful. In 1756, the Assembly appropriated one-half of the funds for the erection of a jail and pest-house : the other half went to the college.

fer intellectual pre-eminence. A great man is essentially a self-made man. 'His arena is not a closet, with Greek manuscripts, but the wide world.' The discipline which fits him for his high destiny is severe and stern, and properly developes character as well as mind.

We shall not seek, therefore, to find in the college course of young Jay the prognostic of his future celebrity. The details of his college life, however, although meagre, are, nevertheless, highly honorable to him. He was studious and persevering. Whatever faults he had acquired by his previous mode of life, he endeavored to overcome. An indistinct articulation exposed him to the raillery of his comrades. He at once set about remedying this defect. By incessant care and attention, he got rid of it. He read in a hurried and confused manner. By daily practice in reading aloud, he soon obtained a ready command of his voice. He applied himself vigorrously to the art of composition, an art to which both himself and his compatriot, Mr. Jefferson, were so largley indebted for the influence which they exercised upon the minds of their countrymen. He seems to have pursued all his studies with equal steadiness and resolution, and graduated, crowned with the highest honor that the college could bestow.

During the last year of his college course, having fixed upon the law as his future profession, he read, in the original, the immortal work of Grotius, *De Jure Belli et Pacis*.[1] That he mastered at the immature age of eigh-

[1] Whoever is unfamiliar with the Lectures of Sir James Mackintosh, on the Law of Nature and Nations, has yet to read one of the finest pieces of composition in the English language. From the twentieth to the twenty-sixth pages of that work, is a memorable passage, in which Sir James employs all the graces of diction to do homage to a great character, and commemorate the value of his labors. After the perusal of that passage, the reader will be prepared to appreciate, at their proper rate, the attempts which are frequently made to disparage the genius and learning of Grotius.

teen, the endless details and principles of that abounding and, in some respects, astonishing production, is what we do not assert, nor demand of others to believe. But the desire and resolution to read such a work, at such an age, bespeak capacity, and capacity ambitious of excellence. Nor could he have concluded the perusal of it, without finding the boundaries of his knowledge enlarged, and the faculties of his mind strengthened and improved.

A few weeks before the close of his college life, he was unexpectedly involved in a difficulty with the faculty, which resulted in his rustication. It was a small matter — the breaking of a table in the College hall — a piece of mischief which young Jay witnessed, but did not join his fellow-students in committing. The noise of the demolition reached the ears of the President, Dr. Cooper, who suddenly made his appearance among the surprised offenders, but not in time to discover them in the act. Upon interrogation, the young rogues, with the exception of Jay and one other, stoutly denied that they broke the table, or knew who did. Jay and his truth-telling comrade admitted that they knew the authors of the mischief, but refused to disclose their names. This natural and manly conduct, in the eyes of college magnates, was a high and grave offence. The professors were assembled, and the contumacious students summoned into their presence. Jay justly contended that there was nothing in the college statutes, which he had subscribed, requiring him to play the invidious part of an informer, and that his refusal to do so could not be construed into an act of disobedience. But college professors are not always the nicest judges of 'the fine strains of honor,' and this defence was deemed invalid. He and his companion were accordingly suspended. This undeserved punishment seems to have made as much impression upon Mr. Jay, as the 'ribald invective' of Weddeburn upon the mind of the philosophic Franklin. His son mentions, that he retained among his papers, to the day of his death, a copy of the statutes, which he had so truly but ineffectually expounded. The sense of injustice, however, may be borne. No wound is inflicted upon the conscience, and no stain upon the character. He who suffers in the cause of truth, or justice, or honor, commands the respect of his fellows, and preserves his own. That youth who is so insensible to all honorable sentiments as to turn informer against his companions, merits universal contempt. He discovers a spirit of infinite baseness. He deliberately violates that implied faith, which is the bond of union, among the inmates of a public institution, and barters away his honor, and the confidence and esteem of his associates, generally with no higher motive than to secure the favor or friendship of the college officers. Base, dishonorable, or criminal conduct on the part of a student, absolves his comrades from the common bond, and, in such a case, they must be guided by the dictates of duty. It is not necessary to dwell upon extreme cases.

At the expiration of the sentence of rustication, Jay resumed his position at College. On the 15th day of May, 1764, he received his degree of Bachelor of Arts. He was appointed to speak the Latin Salutatory, an appointment from which he probably derived more pleasure than from all his subsequent honors.

CHAPTER III.

1764—1774.

HIS LEGAL STUDIES AND EARLY PRACTICE AT THE BAR.

We have already seen that Jay, before the completion of his college course, had fixed his choice of a profession. But there was existing, at that time, a very unusual and peculiar obstacle to his study of the law in New York. The members of the bar, to prevent inroads upon their practice, had made an agreement not to receive into their offices, as clerks, any young men who intended to pursue the law as a profession. We should naturally suppose that a bar resorting to such a contrivance to secure the legal business of the province, must have been composed of the 'inferior, unlearned, mechanical, merely instrumental members of the profession.' Ability is generally conscious of its powers, fearless, ready for conflict, and invites, rather than avoids, a generous rivalry. Incapacity, on the contrary, is timid, illiberal, unmanly, and dreads competition. But I find among the lawyers of this period, high and eminent names—men who were an honor to their profession, and ornaments to the State. The sagacious and untiring Alexander, the father of Lord Stirling, had died but a few years before. The estimable and accomplished William Smith, the Historian of the Province, had been elevated to the post of Chief Justice but the previous year; while still at the bar were the irascible and impetuous, but honorable and sincere, William Livingston, the younger Smith, John Tabor Kempe the Attorney-General, John Morin Scott, and Benjamin Kissam.

Prevented by the agreement which we have mentioned, from acquiring a legal education in his native province, Jay's father made preparations to send him to London as soon as he should leave college. But before the time arrived for his departure, the bar of New York, prompted by a consciousness of their unmanly conduct, or by the odium which it excited, abandoned their exclusive and invidious policy.

This obstruction being removed, Jay lost no time in sitting down to the study of his future profession. In two weeks after leaving college, we find him installed in the office of Benjamin Kissam, Esq., as a student at law. If Mr. Kissam was not the most learned nor the most brilliant member of his profession, he certainly was one of the best and most genial of men.

He lived with his students on terms of free and familiar intercourse. While absent at Albany in the summer of 1766, attending an important capital trial, he wrote to Jay, requesting 'some account of the business of the office.' The unfledged barrister replies in a style 'free enough in all conscience.' He returns a playful and ambiguous answer to the question addressed to him, and then proceeds, in rather a vague strain, to give him 'the news of the town.' 'Things remain here,' he says, 'if I may speak in your own language, pretty much *in statu quo.* Some, with reluctance, shuffling off this mortal coil; and others solacing themselves in the arms of mortality. The ways of men, you know, are as circular as the orbit through which our planet moves, and the centre to which they gravitate is self: round this we move in mystic measures, dancing to every tune that is loudest played by heaven or hell. Some, indeed, that happen to be jostled out of place, may fly off in tangents, like wandering stars, and either lose themselves in a trackless void, or find another way to happiness; but, for the most part, we continue to frolic till we are out of breath; then the music ceases, and we fall asleep. It is said you want more soldiers. I suspect Mr. Morris was lately inspired by some tutelar deity! If I remember right, he carried a great many *flints* with him. Good Lord deliver you from battle, murder, and from sudden death. Pray, how do all these insignia of war and bloodshed sit upon Sam. Jones' lay stomach? I wonder how he can bear to see Justice leaning on an officer's arm, without getting a fit of the spleen; or behold the forum surrounded with guards without suffering his indignation to trespass on his stoicism. I dare say he is not much pleased with such unusual pomp of justice, such unprecedented array of terror; and would rather see the court hop calmly along upon her own legs, than walk tolerably well with the assistance of such crutches. God bless him! I wish there were many such men among us; they would reduce things to just principles.'

Mr. Kissam at once replies to this facetious sally of his young friend, and in a tone that proves him to have been superior to that unamiable, professional pride which is too apt to be the distinguishing mark of a barren or uncultivated heart. 'I have just now received,' he says, 'your long letter of the 12th inst., and am not a little pleased with the humor and freedom of sentiment which characterise it. It would give me pain if I thought you could ever suspect me capable of wishing to impose any restraint upon you in this high and inestimable privilege of friendship. Because I can see no reason why the rights of one relation in life should destroy those of another, I detest that forbidding pride, which, with formal ceremony, can stalk over the social rights of others, and elevate the soul in a vain conceit of its own dignity and importance, founded merely in some adventitious circumstance of relative superiority. Take this, therefore, if you please, as a *nolli prosequi* for the heinous crime of writing a free and familiar letter to me; with this further, that whenever you transgress in the other extreme, you must not expect to meet with the same mercy.' Jay, who remained four years in Mr. Kissam's office, and thus had an opportunity to observe and know him intimately, and afterwards often came in contact with him at the bar and in social intercourse, was accustomed to say that he was 'one of the best men he ever knew, and one of the best friends he ever had.' As a lawyer, his rank among his cotemporaries of the New York bar, 'if not first, was in the very first line.'

The study of the law ninety years ago, was a rugged and laborious task. The path to the profession had not then been smoothed and illuminated. Blackstone's Commentaries, the first of a long line of treatises upon every branch of legal science, were not published until the latter part of the year 1765. If, however, we have the advantage of our ancestors in the more attractive style and method of modern treatises upon the law, they had a compensation in the narrower compass of professional study. For commercial and insurance law is, to a great extent, a modern growth. The leading principles were transplanted by Lord Mansfield from the general maritime law and the jurisprudence of the Romans, and, under the fostering care of succeeding judges, they have become a part, and a most beneficent and indispensable part, of our legal system. The common law, admirable as it is in many respects, for an agricultural people, and for the protection of personal rights, is not sufficiently flexible and comprehensive, to embrace the diversified wants of a commercial nation.

When Jay began his legal studies, Bracton, Britton, Fleta, Glanville, and Coke-Lyttleton, were the fountains whence the student was to seek the originals, and, as it were, the elements of the law. Unless his mind was peculiarly constituted, the quaint style, the metaphysical subtleties, and critical niceties, leading, at the first view, to no intelligible result, which characterise the works we have mentioned, were calculated to discourage and disgust him at the outset. James Otis was accustomed to say that Blackstone's Commentaries would have saved him seven years' labor poring over and delving in black-letter.[1] Lord Eldon, however, was an advocate of the old mode of legal study. In this, as in all things else, he was opposed to innovation. In a letter to a young friend who was about to begin his preparation for the bar, he advises him to find time to read Coke on Littleton again and again. 'If it be toil and labor to you, and it will be so, think as I do when I am climbing up to Swyer or to Westhill, (high grounds at Encombe, commanding extensive views,) that the world will be before you when the toil is over; for so the law world will be, if you make yourself complete master of that book. At present, lawyers are made good, cheap, by learning law from Blackstone and less elegant compilers. Depend upon it, men so bred will never be lawyers, (though they may be barristers,) whatever they call themselves. I read Coke on Littleton through, when I was the other day out of office, and when I was a student I abridged it. To a chancery man, the knowledge to be obtained from it is peculiarly useful in matter of titles. If you promise me to read this, and tell me when you have begun it, I shall venture to hope that, at my recommendation, you will attack about half a dozen other very crabbed books which our Westminster Hall lawyers never look at. Westminster Hall has its loungers as well as Bond-street.'[2]

The object of the student is, to make himself familiar with the principles of legal science. To say, therefore, that because these principles are reduced to order and system; that they are spread out before him in an

[1] Tudor's Otis. [2] Twiss' Life of Lord Eldon, vol. i., p. 387.

elegant and attractive form, so that while he adds to his knowledge, he improves his taste; to say that a man so bred will never be a lawyer, is to assert what is contradicted by common observation, and what is repugnant to common sense. To put into the hands of a beginner Coke on Littleton, or one of the older law-writers, full as they are of undigested learning and abstruse refinements, is about as sensible as to encumber the soldier of the present day with the mailed armor that clad the warrior of the middle ages. Lord Eldon would reverse the injunction of the apostle, and even to the babes of the law, give strong meat instead of milk, their natural food. That the books recommended by his lordship would be serviceable at an advanced period of the student's progress, may be admitted. They may throw light upon doubtful or obscure points of professional learning. They may induce habits of reflection, and patience of research. They may render the understanding acute, but they will fail, of themselves, to enlarge its horizon. There is, however, another view of this subject, and too important to be overlooked. It is this: that, while the scholastic refinements and subtleties of the elder law-writers, their perplexed and abstruse speculations, their rude and undigested learning, must necessarily exercise the mind, their powerful tendency is to exercise it in one direction, and disproportionately develope one power at the expense of others. They do not call into action the higher faculties. The imagination and the feelings remain dormant. The result is a sort of *numb rigidity of intellectual life.* The tendency which we have mentioned may doubtless be counteracted by reaching and inciting to activity those faculties which, otherwise, would remain unemployed, by parallel, but dissimilar courses of study. But if this cannot be done, and professional dexterity is not the end of life, then it would be better for the student, rather than follow Lord Eldon's advice, to bury his lordship's favorite books 'certain fathoms in the earth, and deeper than did ever plummet sound.' Who doubts, if Lord Eldon had ameliorated the effect of his legal studies, by extending his ideas to the regions of philosophy and poetry, that he would have had greater comprehension and elevation of mind, that he would have been a better man and a less inveterate tory?[1] With most men, however, authority is more imposing than reason. We propose, therefore, to put in opposition to the authority of Lord Eldon, a very high American authority. We propose to cite the opinion of Mr. Webster. 'A boy of twenty,' says Mr. Webster, 'with no previous knowledge of such subjects, cannot understand Coke. It is folly to set him upon such an author. There are propositions in Coke so abstract, and distinctions so nice, and doctrines embracing so many distinctions and qualifications, that it requires an effort not only of a mature mind, but of a mind both strong and mature, to understand him. Why disgust and discourage a young man by telling him he must break into his profession through such a wall as this?' 'Acting upon these views,' says Mr. Everett, "even in his youth Mr. Webster gave his attention to more intelligible authors, and to titles of law of greater importance in this country than the curious learning of tenures, many of which are antiquated, even in England. He also gave a good deal of time to general reading, and especially to the study of the Latin classics,

[1] 'It cannot escape observation, that when men are too much confined to professional and faculty habits, and, as it were, inveterate in the recurrent employment of that narrow circle, they are rather disabled than qualified for whatever depends on the knowledge of mankind, on experience in mixed affairs, on a comprehensive connected view of the various complicated external and internal interests which go to the formation of that multifarious thing called a State.' —Burke: Reflections on the French Revolution.

English history, and the volumes of Shakspeare. In order to obtain a wider compass of knowledge, and learn something of the language not to be gained from the classics, he read through attentively Puffendorf's Latin History of England.'[1]

What method Jay adopted in the study of the law is wholly conjectural. The first volume of Blackstone's Commentaries must have made its appearance in this country as he was entering upon the third year of his studies, and we may fairly suppose that he abandoned black-letter law for the more attractive pages of that elegant compiler. Be that as it may, we have contemporary authority that he was a diligent student, and his after career furnishes evidence that he now laid the basis of a competent stock of professional learning. His law was adequate to the exigencies of his practice, and sufficient to enable him, in his judicial capacity, to pursue legal investigations with honor to himself and benefit to the public. His mind, like the mind of Chief Justice Marshall, was happily fitted to suggest and 'comprehend arguments drawn *a priori*, from the spirit of laws, and the natural foundations of justice.'

It was, I think, the observation of George III., that lawyers did not know so much more law than other persons, but that their superiority consisted in knowing where to look for it. Possibly his majesty might have formed this opinion from an estimate of the acquirements of his chancellors, Loughborough and Erskine. At any rate, a little reflection, or a more extensive acquaintance with the gentlemen of the long robe, would have led him to a different result. But even if the observation were generally true, it would by no means materially derogate from the distinction of the profession. For to be familiar with the sources of knowledge, to know the appropriate

---

[1] Works of Daniel Webster, vol. i., xxviii.

place of the most dissimilar principles, and to be able, from previous study, to comprehend their limits, bearings, and relations, is a great power, and essentially the foundation of legal education.

This consideration will explain how Jay and the lawyers of the ante-Revolutionary period, (whose business was wholly interrupted by that event, and whose thoughts thenceforward were occupied with political, diplomatic, or military pursuits,) upon their return to the bar, or elevation to the bench, at the close of the contest, at once rose to eminence in their respective spheres. They knew where to apply for the requisite knowledge, and with minds quickened and enlarged by the important scenes through which they had passed, they gained in one direction infinitely more than they lost in another.

Mr. Kissam had in his office at this time another student of the same age with Jay, the son of an opulent Quaker merchant, who, tiring of a mercantile life, had by perseverance and the friendly interposition of Mr. Kissam, who had formed a favorable estimate of his talents, obtained the reluctant consent of his father to study the law. This was the celebrated Lindley Murray, who afterwards won an honorable distinction by his grammar, and the love of the virtuous by the purity of his life, and the unpretending excellence of his religious writings.

In his autobiographical letters addressed to Miss Frank, he alludes to this period of his life, and thus refers to his fellow-student: 'The celebrated John Jay, Esq., late Governor of New York, was my fellow-student for about two years. His talents and virtues gave, at that period, pleasing indications of future eminence: he was remarkable for strong reasoning powers, comprehensive views, indefatigable application, and uncommon firmness of mind. With these qualifications, added to a just taste in literature, and ample stores of learning and knowledge, he was happily prepared to enter on that career of public virtue by which he was afterwards honorably distinguished, and made instrumental in promoting the good of his country.'

This testimony to the youthful talents, virtues, and industry of Jay, is interesting and valuable. It comes from a man of grave and serious character, who retraces, in the evening of his days, the impressions of earlier life, and, uninfluenced by political or social ties, expresses the judgment which he formed of the character of his fellow-student from a daily observation of it, during a period of two years. We cannot but regret that Mr. Murray did not pause a little longer over this period of his life. He could have told us with what feelings he and his friend Jay witnessed the assembling of the stamp-act Congress, and the impressions which the proceedings of that day made upon them. Descending to particulars, and considering the eminent services which his fellow-student subsequently rendered to his country, and the space he filled in the eyes of his countrymen, he might have amused a vacant hour and gratified a natural curiosity, by giving us some account of his youthful habits.

The society of New York at that day, if not characterized by that elevation of sentiment, refinement of manner, and general culture which belong to older and less commercial communities, was frank, friendly, and social. The prejudice of race, from intermarriage, social contact, and identity of interest, had worn away, and the descendants of the Dutch, Huguenots, and English, constituted a harmonious population. An injurious influence, however, was exerted on the manners and habits of society in New York by the number of adventurers whose residence was merely temporary, and who resorted thither for the purpose of accumulating fortunes, with which they hoped to purchase pleasure or distinction in the metropolitan cities of Europe.[1] New York, at this time, 'was the capital of the central province, and the head-quarters of the standing forces in America; having a septennial Assembly, a royal council, ships of war anchored near its wharves, and within the town itself, a fort, mounting many heavy cannon.'[2] The English officers were naturally a marked feature of the society of the place. Colden, the Lieutenant-Governor, was a man of learning, fond of social intercourse, and lived in a style suited to his position. Unpopular as a magistrate, partly from zeal for what he deemed the prerogatives of his office, and partly from several instances of real or fancied duplicity in his conduct, he had, nevertheless, some very attractive qualities as a man. His house was the resort of such scientific and literary characters as the province, at that time, could boast, who found him possessed of congenial sentiments, and devoted to congenial pursuits.

That Jay found sources of amusement and instruction in a society thus constituted, may be naturally supposed. His spirits, at this period of his life, were gay and unchecked by austere views of life and its aims. He had an observant eye, and an ingenious mind. 'Chill penury' did not cloud his prospect, nor 'freeze the genial current of his soul.' He was happily fitted, both by nature and fortune, to impart and receive pleasure from the friendly collisions of social intercourse.

In 1768 he was admitted to the bar, and formed a partnership with Robert R. Livingston, who was afterwards the Chancellor of New York, during a period of twenty-four years. This connexion, however, continued but a short time. The professional business of the Province at this period, was not of a very important character. Since the celebrated trial of Zenger for libel,

---

[1] Grahame's History of the United States, vol. iv., p. 135. Mrs. Grant's Memoirs of an American Lady.

[2] Bancroft, vol. v., p. 331.

in 1735, no cause of peculiar public interest had occurred.[1] The most fruitful sources of professional employment, so far as I can ascertain, were the collection of debts, by suit or otherwise, and the prosecution of suits of ejectment. There was, besides, the usual amount of 'municipal litigation' and 'obscure contention.' Mr. Kissam writes to Jay, who is attending the November Term of the Circuit Court at White Plains, the year after he came to the bar, and requests him to take charge of his business. 'One cause,' he says, 'is about a horse-race, in which I suppose there is some cheat; another is about an eloped wife; another of them also appertains unto horse-flesh.' 'There is one writ of inquiry.' 'As to the cause about Captain's Island,' he goes on to observe, 'this, tell Mr. Morris, must go off; because, as you are concerned against me, I can't tell where to find another into whose head the cause can be infused in the miraculous way of inspiration; and without this, it would be rather too intricate for any one to manage from my short hints.'[2] Causes of this nature were not calculated

[1] An exception should be made perhaps with respect to the case of Forsey *vs.* Cunningham. That case involved the question whether an appeal lay from the verdict of a jury to the Governor and Council, who exercised a well-established jurisdiction as a Court of Errors. The court was willing to grant a writ of error, but refused to permit an appeal to be taken. Colden granted an order to arrest all further proceedings in the cause. The Chief Justice Horsmander disregarded it, and perfected the judgment; but the clerk refused to seal the execution. The conduct of Colden in this affair subjected him to a good deal of odium, and was disapproved by his council.

[2] This letter of Mr. Kissam evinces his appreciation of the talents of his quondam student, who, it would seem from the language of Mr. Kissam, had as much readiness in discovering the 'points' of a cause from a few 'broken hints,' as some of his contemporaries of the Irish bar. Curran, it is said, was accustomed to find out what his client's defence was, from listening to the opening argument of the plaintiff's counsel. The following is Mr. Kissam's letter:

'NEW YORK, 6th Nov., 1769.

'DEAR JACK: When you consider that all the causes you have

to tax very heavily the resources of the bar, or add to the distinction of the profession. But whatever the character of professional business at this time, whether more or less important, Jay from the first obtained a respectable share of it. He was not condemned, like so many illustrious names in the profession, to wait year after year, suffering the pangs of deferred hope, until some lucky accident varied the prospect, and placed him in the line of employment. He seems never to have known the want of money, and could not, in after life, from any experience that he ever had, have appreciated Hazlitt's admirable essay on that subject.

It is a common notion, that young men who are dependent upon their own resources are more likely to

---

hitherto tried have been by a kind of inspiration, you will need only a small degree of enthusiasm to be persuaded that my lameness is a providential mercy to you, by calling you to action again. If it was not for you, or some other such apostolic lawyer, my clients would be left in the lurch this Court, as I am afraid I cannot attend myself. But, sir, you have now a call to go forth into my vineyard; and this you must do, too, upon an evangelical principle — that the master may receive the fruits of it. All I can tell you about the causes is little more than to give you a list of their titles; but this is quite enough for you. . . . . . . There will probably be some of my old friends who may inquire after me, and perhaps some new ones will want to employ me; will you be kind enough to let them know that you will take care of any business for me. I ask these favors from you, John, with great freedom. I wish you good success with my consignments, and hope they'll come to a good market. If they don't, I am sure it will not be the *factor's* fault; and if my clients' wares are bad, let them bear the loss. You will see my docket, with memoranda to direct what is to be done. If my leg is better, perhaps I may see you on Wednesday; but it is very uncertain. When Mr. Morris is not against me, I am sure he will be with me; and you may call on him for that purpose with as much freedom as if I had a perfect right to command his service. I know the goodness of his heart, and his friendship for me will make him embrace every opportunity to serve me with pleasure.

'I am your humble servant,

'BENJAMIN KISSAM.'

make a figure in life than those who have not the stimulus of necessity to urge them to exertion. Wealth undoubtedly, in the hands of the young, unless very happily constituted, leads to idleness and dissipation, and, in the generality of cases, is an effectual bar to all arduous enterprises. Poverty, on the other hand, is feeble, and instead of being an incentive to exertion and economy, is apt to induce indolence and profusion. There are, indeed, conspicuous examples to the contrary, but exceptions prove the universality of the rule. But the case is widely different with narrow or moderate means. Here a wise economy may be exercised. The possessor is not driven to despair. He is not reduced to shifts. He can bide his time. He is urged to action, but has an opportunity to choose the mode and season. His soul is not debased by perpetual strife with the petty cares and pressing wants of the day. This was the happy condition of some of the most distinguished characters in the law, of such men as Hardwicke, Mansfield, Camden, Eldon, and the major part of our eminent American lawyers and magistrates.

The youth of Jay was fortunate. Looking to his profession as the road to independence and honorable distinction, he had no 'low-thoughted cares' to impede his studies or check his aspirations. When he came to the bar, he at once obtained practice. His ardor in a favorite pursuit was unrepressed by baffled wishes and deferred hope. He set out on his professional career with spirits full of activity and full of energy. It is true, no great and memorable opportunity occurred to him to establish, by a single forensic effort, his professional fame. No cause of public concern, such as Henry had, when he pleaded against the clergy, Otis when he denounced writs of assistance, or Adams when he defended Captain Preston, illustrates any part of his professional life. Nor do we mean to insinuate that he would have risen to the height of a great occasion, and signalized it by any such displays of oratory as characterized the efforts we have mentioned. It was not by strains of eloquence that he rose to distinction; and the same may be said of every one of his successors upon the bench, with the exception, perhaps, of John Rutledge.

His career at the bar served as a preparation for that higher and more distinguished career in the service of his country which linked his name with the history of his times, and will carry it down, in unbroken connection, to the latest generations. He was but twenty-three when admitted to practise in the courts. His active professional life did not extend over a period of six years. But during that time he was coming in contact with men and things. He was learning the sentiments of his countrymen and forming his own. He was familiarizing himself with public affairs. His mind was employed. His faculties were developing and strengthening under the discipline of business. So that if he did not secure the honors of his profession at a bound, he did more — he fitted himself for the most eminent usefulness in several of the highest departments of the public service.

As Jay's practice increased, it naturally happened that he was occasionally brought in contact with Mr. Kissam. It is related that on the trial of a cause where they were engaged upon opposite sides, Mr. Kissam, being puzzled by some point made by his antagonist, observed that he had brought up a bird to peck out his own eyes. 'Oh, no,' replied his quondam pupil, 'not to peck out, but to open your eyes!' A similar anecdote is told of that great lawyer, Jeremiah Gridley, whose fame is as imperishable as the granite hills of his native New England. Referring to Adams[1] and Otis, he was accustomed to

[1] Adams did not study with Gridley, but was admitted to the bar on his motion.

observe that he had reared two young eagles who were one day to peck out his eyes.

In the latter part of the year 1770, the lawyers of New York established a club called the Moot. The professed object of this association was 'social conversation and the mutual improvement of each other.' The members agreed to meet, as appears from their by-laws, 'the first Friday of every month.' 'The party politics of the province' were strictly inhibited as a subject of discussion. Embracing nearly all the lawyers of the New York bar, and certainly the most prominent of them, the opinion of the Moot upon any controverted point of law carried with it great weight. It is said that it was regarded with respect by the judges, and had an influence upon their decisions. Jay was a member, and among the youngest members of this club.

His application to business and study at this period was too intense for his health. If he did not, according to the first branch of Lord Eldon's advice to the young Grants, 'live like a hermit,' he seems to have acted upon the spirit of the second, and 'worked like a horse.' By the advice of his physician, he took lodgings six miles from town, and for several months rode in every morning on horseback, and returned in the evening. The exercise proved beneficial, and his health was restored.

Fortunate as a lawyer, respected as a man, Jay now added to the sources of his happiness by a felicitous marriage. We find this event announced in Rivington's New York Gazette for May 5th, 1774. 'Last week was married John Jay, Esq., an eminent barrister of this city, to Miss Sally Livingston, third daughter of William Livingston, Esq. The ceremony was performed at the seat of the young lady's father, near Elizabethtown, in East Jersey.'

We have had occasion, incidentally, to mention Mr. Livingston in the preceding pages. He had now retired from the bar, and fixed his residence in New Jersey, in whose affairs he was destined to act a conspicuous part. Mr. Livingston was no ordinary man. He was of a fearless and uncompromising character. He had an utter abhorrence of bigotry. His ardent feelings and earnest nature, when roused by any act of tyranny or injustice, lent ten-fold force to the natural weight of his talents, and made him, in the arena of controversy, a bold and powerful champion.

The marriage of his daughter to Mr. Jay was propitious to the happiness of both. Their lot, however, forbade uninterrupted domestic enjoyment. The troubles of the time soon summoned Mr. Jay to the service of his country. The pleasing prospect of professional eminence and fireside felicity was overcast. During the long period of twenty-seven years, he was constantly employed at home and abroad in the public service. As our narrative proceeds, it will be seen that Mr. Jay finally retired, with a wearied spirit, from the cares of office, to enjoy undisturbed the pleasures of domestic life. Man proposes, but God disposes. The day of repose, of uninterrupted happiness, so fondly anticipated, so eagerly embraced, had scarcely dawned, when Mrs. Jay was removed forever from his sphere.

CHAPTER IV.

1774.

HIS POLITICAL CAREER.

WE are now to survey Jay on the field of politics. A great crisis had arisen in the affairs of the colonies. A revolution in the sentiments and feelings of the people was being rapidly accomplished. 'The close affection which grows from common names, from kindred blood,' and long association, was hastening to decay and dissolution. The controversy had now lasted, with short and beguiling intervals of repose, nearly ten years. The passage of the stamp-act in 1765, had roused a flame of resentment and opposition from one end of the country to the other. The spirit and vigor manifested by the colonies on that occasion procured its repeal. The reception of that intelligence produced unbounded joy and rejoicing. But the repeal, accompanied as it was by the declaratory act, 'was but the guiling shore to a most dangerous sea.' For the surrender of the right of taxation in a particular instance and on an emergent occasion, was of little moment, so long as the germinating principle of mischief was cherished and preserved. If 'a right of taxation was necessarily involved in the general principle of legislation and inseparable from the ordinary supreme power,' and that was the prevailing opinion among the jurists and statesmen of England, then it only remained for Parliament to exercise the right whenever the times seemed propitious, or the occasion favorable. Upon the question of strict right and parliamentary power, Chatham and Camden stood opposed to nearly the whole body of the legal ability of the kingdom. In little more than a year after the repeal of the stamp-act, the hopes of future harmony which that measure had inspired, were suddenly dissipated. The passage of the bill imposing duties on tea, glass, paper, &c., early in the year 1767, re-opened the fountain of discontent and controversy, and issued in war and revolution. The measures and counter-measures, the menaces of coercion, and the threats of resistance, the suspension of assemblies and the calling of conventions, the agreements of non-importation, and all the changes and agitations that occurred in the interval between the passage of the tea act and the Boston Port Bill, belong to the province of history. We shall not pause here to survey that extensive field.

The Boston Port Bill became a law on the 31st day of March, 1774. When the intelligence reached the colonies, it produced a deep sensation. It was perceived by the more sagacious minds, that unless prompt, vigorous, and united opposition to the policy of the mother country should induce a change of measures, an appeal to the sword would inevitably ensue. The intensest excitement everywhere prevailed. 'The cause of Boston is the cause of all!' became the signal cry of patriotism in all the colonies. Submission or resistance was the only alternative that seemed to offer. It was at this gloomy, clouded hour, that Jay first appeared upon the field of politics. What had been his previous views, with what sentiments he had observed the accumulation of that menacing cloud which now 'blackened all the horizon,' does not appear. But at this imminent, perilous crisis, neutrality, if desirable or desired, was hardly possible. 'It was a time for a man to act in.' Mr. Jay was fully sensible of the alarming crisis that had arrived in the public affairs. He was opposed, however, to precipitate action. In fact, while viewing the acts of the ministry as aggressive, unconstitutional, and dangerous to the rights and liberties of his countrymen, his sentiments as to the measure and mode of redress were of the most moderate tone. He had not risen 'to the height of the great argument.' He was seeking reinforcement from hope, not resolution from despair. He was eminently a man of prudence and caution. He was not sagacious of the future. His watch, unlike Talleyrand's, did not go faster than his neighbor's. He seldom placed himself in the van of events. No fiery, burning zeal dwelt in his bosom. But when he assumed a position, the solid ground was not more immovable. He performed his duty under all circumstances with steadiness, resolution, and undiverted attention. But neither his opinions nor conduct were in the smallest degree the result of impulse or enthusiasm. His perceptions were strong rather than quick. He was more remarkable for logic than intuition. Thus constituted, we might naturally infer that he would embrace the views of the moderate party, rather than those of more eager and impetuous characters. As the contest proceeded, however, his spirit rose with the spirit of his countrymen, and he advanced steadily but cautiously on the course he now adopted.

When intelligence of the passage of the Boston Port Bill reached New York, a letter was immediately despatched to the Boston Committee of Correspondence by Isaac Sears, 'a creature of much spirit and public virtue,'[1] and that bold, ardent, sincere, and indefatigable champion of the popular cause, Alexander M'Dougall, recommending the most vigorous measures as the most effectual, and assuring them of the sympathy and support of the people of New York.[2] This letter added that a

[1] Gen. Charles Lee to Washington. Life of Gouverneur Morris, vol. i., pp. 82, 83.

[2] This letter was written on behalf of the Committee of Vigilance of New York. It was published in the Boston Gazette, but without the

public meeting would be called to give effect to their sentiments. A publication was accordingly issued, calling upon the citizens of New York to meet and consult on the measures proper to be pursued in consequence of the late extraordinary and very alarming advices received from England. This meeting was held on the 16th day of May, 1774. The result of its deliberations was the appointment of a Committee of Fifty, to correspond with the other colonies on all matters of moment. Gordon says that the committee was appointed against the concentrated opposition of the tories; but in this he is mistaken.[1] The irregular energy displayed by the Sons of Liberty in opposition to the stamp-act, had shown what course of action might be anticipated if they were permitted to take the lead on the present occasion. The ministerial party dreaded the ascendency of the popular classes, and apprehended less mischief from the obnoxious acts of Parliament than from the unrestrained impulses of their own countrymen. They believed with Voltaire, that 'when the populace meddles with reasoning, all is lost.' But the impetuous and patriotic zeal engendered by the news of the Boston Port Bill rendered it prudent to disguise these sentiments. Hence, the efforts of the tories, as Gordon terms them, were directed, not against the appointment of the committee, but to dissolve the old committee, and secure a majority of their party upon the new one.[2] They came pre-

signatures. When it reached New York, the boldness of its tone, and the unqualified character of its pledges, roused in the ministerial party both indignation and alarm. After the appointment of the Committee of Correspondence, it was publicly announced that this letter did not emanate from them nor express their sentiments.

[1] Gordon's History, vol. i., p. 238.

[2] Lieutenant-Governor Colden, who writes to the Earl of Dartmouth, June 1st, 1774, referring to the appointment of the committee, says, 'The men, who at that time, (i. e., the time when the news of the Boston Port Act arrived in New York,) called themselves the Committee—

pared with the list of a committee favorable to their views. This was discovered by the vigilant Sears, who immediately proposed that all lists should be removed from the table, and nominations be made from the meeting. This proposition was carried, but the result was not favorable to the popular party. While several of the most earnest and active of their leaders were placed upon it, others were excluded, and their opponents secured the majority. On the 19th another meeting was held at the Coffee House to sanction the proceedings of the meeting of the 16th. The committee nominated on that occasion was approved, together with the addition of another member, Mr. Francis Lewis.[1] The adherents of the ministry were uncommonly elated at this result, and flattered themselves that they had gained an important triumph. Rivington, the proprietor of the Gazette bearing his name, wrote to his friend Henry Knox, afterwards General Knox, but then a bookseller in Boston, assuring him that no non-importation or non-exportation agreement would be adopted either in New

---

who dictated and acted in the name of the people—were many of them of the lower ranks, and all the warmest zealots of those called the *Sons of Liberty*. The more considerable merchants and citizens seldom or never appeared among them, but I believe were not displeased with the clamor and opposition that was shown against internal taxation by Parliament. The principal inhabitants being now afraid that these hot-headed men might run the city into dangerous measures, appeared in a considerable body at the first meeting of the people after the Boston Port Act was published here. They dissolved the former committee, and appointed a new one of fifty-one persons; in which care was taken to have a number of the most prudent and considerate people of the place. Some of them have not before joined the public proceedings of the opposition, and were induced to appear in what they are sensible is an illegal character, from a consideration that if they did not, the business would be left in the same rash hands as before.'—Force's American Archives: Fourth Series, vol. i., p. 372.

[1] Mr. Lewis was a member of the popular party. His addition to the committee, however, still left his friends in a small minority.

York or Philadelphia. 'The power over our crowd,' he adds, 'is no longer in the hands of Sears, Lamb, and such unimportant persons, who have, for six years past, been the demagogues of a very turbulent faction in this city; but their power and mischievous capacity expired instantly upon the election of the Committee of Fifty-one; in which there is a majority of inflexibly honest, loyal, and prudent citizens.'[1] Colden, the Lieutenant-Governor, who had now reached his eighty-seventh year, but whose faculties retained all the vigor of their prime, saw the discomfiture of his old enemies the *sons of liberty* with a satisfaction too real to be dissembled. He did not live long enough to learn from experience that revolutions never go backwards, and that those who represent, whether consciously or not, the cardinal ideas of their time and country, rise superior to obloquy and move on to certain triumph.

The day following the meeting of the 19th, Gouverneur Morris, then a young man of twenty-two, self-confident, daring, ambitious, contemptuous, 'flown with insolence' and scorn of the masses of his countrymen, writes to his friend Mr. Penn of Philadelphia, and from his letter we may gather the sentiments that animated the party to which at that time he belonged.[2] 'The port of Boston,' he says, 'has been shut up. These sheep,' (the people,) 'simple as they are, cannot be gulled as heretofore. In short, there is no ruling them; and now, to leave the metaphor, the heads of the mobility grow dangerous to the gentry, and how to keep them down is the

[1] Life and Times of Gen. Lamb, p. 91. See also as to the views and feelings of the citizens of New York at this period, Force's Am. Archives, supra, pp. 299–302, notes.

[2] It is perhaps superfluous to add, that Mr. Morris subsequently became one of the most earnest and zealous champions of the independence of his country, and rendered various and valuable service to the public cause.

question. While they correspond with the other colonies, call and dismiss popular assemblies, make resolves to bind the consciences of the rest of mankind, bully poor printers, and exert with full force all their other tribunitial powers, it is impossible to curb them. But art sometimes goes further than force, and therefore to trick them handsomely, a committee of patricians was to be nominated, and into their hands was to be committed the majority of the people, and the highest trust was to be reposed in them by a mandate that they should take care, *quod respublica non capiat injuriam*. The tribunes, through want of a good legerdemain in the senatorial order, perceived the finesse, and yesterday I was present at a grand division of the city, and there I beheld my fellow-citizens very accurately counting all their chickens, not only before any of them were hatched, but before above one-half of the eggs were laid. In short, they fairly contended about the future forms of our Government; whether it should be founded upon aristocratic or democratic principles. I stood in the balcony, and on my right hand were ranged all the people of property with some few poor dependants, and, on the other, all the tradesmen, &c., who thought it worth their while to leave daily labor for the good of the country. The spirit of the English Constitution has yet a little influence left, and but a little. The remains of it, however, will give the wealthy people a superiority this time; but would they secure it, they must banish all schoolmasters and confine all knowledge to themselves. This cannot be. The mob begins to think and to reason. Poor reptiles! it is with them a vernal morning; they are struggling to cast off their winter's slough; they bask in the sunshine, and ere noon they will bite, depend upon it. The gentry begin to fear this. Their committee will be appointed, they will deceive the people, and again forfeit a share of their confidence. And if these instances of what with one side is policy, with the other perfidy, shall continue to increase and become more frequent, farewell aristocracy. I see, and I see it with fear and trembling, that if the disputes with Britain continue, we shall be under the worst of all possible dominions. We shall be under the dominion of a riotous mob. It is the interest of all men, therefore, to seek for reunion with the parent state. A safe compact seems, in my poor opinion, to be now tendered. Internal taxation is to be left with ourselves. The right of regulating trade to be vested in Great Britain, where alone is found the power of protecting it. I trust you will agree with me that this is the only possible mode of union.'[1]

Mr. Jay was a member of the Committee of Fifty-one, and his political life began with that appointment. He was of those who favored moderate courses. We shall see, however, as we trace his career, that he gradually advanced with the current of opinion, and took his position among the most resolute of those who opposed the ministerial pretensions. The committee held their first meeting on the 23d day of May. An answer to the Boston Committee, who had recommended the general adoption of a non-importation and non-exportation agreement, until the act for blocking up their harbor was repealed, first demanded their attention. To any measure involving a suspension of trade, the majority of the committee were strongly opposed. But some step must be taken. The public expectation must not be disappointed. A congress had been proposed. The idea was in the minds of the people. 'Some think,' says Mr. Van Schaack, a young lawyer of honorable character, in a letter to a friend written two days before the meeting of the committee, 'there should be a Congress of deputies from all the colonies, to consider of some general plan of

[1] Life of Morris, by Sparks, vol. i., pp. 24, 25

measures.'[1] Gordon asserts that the representatives of the popular party in the committee insisted upon a Congress, and that their opponents acceded to the proposal rather than provoke popular violence, but with the expectation of preventing the very measure which they formally recommended.[2]

The committee appointed Alexander M'Dougall, Isaac Low, James Duane, and John Jay a sub-committee, to prepare the draft of an answer to the Boston Committee. The letter drawn up by them was approved by the general committee, and immediately despatched to Boston. It is supposed to have been the production of Mr. Jay. It undoubtedly expressed the sentiments of the majority of the citizens of New York. It relieved them from any immediate apprehensions of a non-importation or non-exportation agreement. The merchants had a lively recollection of the last one, from which they had seceded, and thereby dissolved it. They treated the question as one of policy, and could not discover the wisdom of hazarding the freedom of their own port by indulging any romantic sympathy for the people of Boston. 'People in town,' says Van Schaack in the letter from which we have just quoted, 'are somewhat divided in sentiments as to what steps it will be most expedient to take. A non-importation agreement has been mentioned, and

---

[1] Life of Van Schaack, pp. 16, 17.

[2] Gordon's History, vol. i., p. 238 'The whigs in it,' (the committee,) says Gordon, 'insisted that there must be a Congress. The violence of Captain Sears' temper, and his influence over the populace, induced the tories to fall in with the proposal of one, rather than be exposed to the dangers of a mob; but they expected that they should prevent it. A letter was sent to the Boston Committee with a recommendation to them to appoint time and place. They approved of a Congress, but declined making the appointments. The York Committee considered the answer; and it was carried to write to them afresh upon the subject. The tories were caught; for having agreed to the motion for a Congress, they could not hinder it by all their contrivances.'

some have even gone so far as to propose entirely to stop our exports to the West Indies. These measures are chiefly espoused by the mechanics. The merchants insist that we ought not precipitately to enter into either of these plans; that a non-importation will draw down the vengeance of Great Britain upon us, and that will probably bring about the shutting up of our own port; that if we are deprived of our exports, we shall be ruined; that our produce will lie upon hand, and many articles, particularly flaxseed, being of a perishable nature, will be a total loss upon those who cannot bear it; that our tradesmen will be without employ, our merchants be incapable of making remittances, and, in short, all ranks and denominations of men be irreparably injured.'

The defence of a people's rights is no holyday affair. It involves sacrifices and perils. 'This is the road that all heroes have trod.' The question for the citizens of New York at this crisis was, whether in support of a great cause they would put to hazard their interests, their repose, and possibly their safety. A portion of the population were eager to assume that position, and that portion, too, upon whom a suspension of trade would bear most heavily. We mean the tradesmen and mechanics. Their ultimate losses might be less, but their present distresses would be greater.

The committee were not prepared to second their views. In their letter to the Boston committee, they observe: 'While we think you justly entitled to the thanks of your sister colonies for asking their advice on a case of such extensive consequences, we lament our inability to relieve your anxiety by a decisive opinion. The cause is general, and concerns a whole continent, who are equally interested with you and us; and we foresee that no remedy can be of avail unless it proceeds from the joint act and approbation of all. From a virtuous and spirited union much may be expected, while the feeble efforts of a few will only be attended with mischief and disappointment to themselves, and triumph to the adversaries of liberty. Upon these reasons we conclude that a Congress of deputies from the colonies in general, is of the utmost moment; that it ought to be assembled without delay, and some unanimous resolutions formed in this fatal emergency, not only respecting your deplorable circumstances, but for the security of our common rights. Such being our sentiments, it must be premature to pronounce any judgment on the expedient which you have suggested. We beg, however, that you will do us the justice to believe that we shall continue to act with a firm and becoming regard to American freedom, and to co-operate with our sister colonies in every measure that shall be thought salutary, and conducive to the public good.'

At this stage of the controversy, if we may rely upon cotemporary testimony, there were but few minds in the colonies that contemplated separation from the mother country as a thing either necessary or desirable. The public expression of such a sentiment would have been received with reprobation. The boldest measure that the popular party now advocated, was non-importation and non-exportation. They thought it was suited to the exigency of the occasion, and likely to procure a redress of their grievances. By declining to adopt it, the committee lost the confidence of the most active and earnest portion of their constituents. The proposal of a Congress did not compensate the loss of their favorite measure. As that measure, however, would naturally engage the attention of the Congress, the question was obviously important, who should represent New York in that body. The action of the committee in regard to it was looked for with a lively interest. But it was a question which the majority of the committee were by no means anxious to press to an immediate decision. They delayed it as long as they could. On the 4th day of July, however, they met to determine it. It was moved by Theophilact Bache, and seconded by John De Lancey, that the committee nominate five persons to meet in a general Congress, at the time and place which should be agreed on by the other colonies, and that the freeholders and freemen of the city and county of New York be summoned to appear at a convenient place, to approve or disapprove of the persons thus nominated. This motion was carried. Captain Sears then moved, and was seconded by P. V. B. Livingston, 'an old man, extremely staunch in the cause, and very sensible,'[1] that Isaac Low, James Duane, Philip Livingston, John Morin Scott, and Alexander M'Dougall be the nominees. Scott and M'Dougall were inflexible whigs. They were advocates of strong and decisive measures. They believed that their rights had been invaded, and, 'with all brief and plain conveniency,' they would vindicate them. Sentiments of that temper did not accord with the lukewarm zeal of the committee; and, by a strict party vote, the motion of Captain Sears was lost. The committee then nominated

---

[1] Life and Works of John Adams, vol. ii., p. 348. 'He,' (Mr. Livingston), continues Mr. Adams, 'tells us that Dr. Chandler, Dr. Cooper, and other Episcopal clergymen were met together about the time of the news of the Boston Port Bill, and were employed night and day writing letters and sending despatches to the other colonies and to England. This, he thinks, was to form a union of the Episcopal party through the continent, in support of ministerial measures. He says they have never been able to obtain a charter for their burying-yard, or the ground on which their Presbyterian church now stands! They have solicited their Governors, and have solicited at home without success.' Again he says, *ibid*, p. 351, 'P. V. Livingston is a sensible man and a gentleman. He has been in trade, is rich, and now lives upon his income.'

The religious differences in New York may be distinctly traced in the formation of the political parties of that period. Between the Episcopalians and the Presbyterians there existed a strong feeling of mutual jealousy.

Philip Livingston, John Alsop, Isaac Low, James Duane, and John Jay; and directed that a publication be issued requesting the inhabitants of the city and county to meet on the 7th inst., to concur in the nomination of these gentlemen, or to choose others in their stead. Governor Colden, two days after the committee had made their nomination, writes to the Earl of Dartmouth to inform him of so important a proceeding. It would appear from the tenor of his letter, that the committee had not intended to make nominations, and were forced to that step against their wishes. 'In my letter of June 1st,' says Colden,[1] 'I informed your lordship that the people of this city had chosen a committee of fifty-one persons to correspond with the sister colonies on the present political affairs; that many of this committee were of the most considerable merchants, and men of cool tempers, who would endeavor to avoid all extravagant and dangerous measures. They have had a continual struggle with those of a different disposition, and having for several weeks succeeded in suspending any resolutions, I was in hopes they would have maintained the only conduct which can excuse them. But accounts repeatedly coming to hand, from different parts of the continent, of the appointment of deputies to meet in a general Congress, this measure was so strenuously pushed, that it was carried in the Committee of Fifty-one on Monday last, and five persons were named for the deputies from this province: the persons named are James Duane and John Jay, two eminent lawyers, Isaac Low, Philip Livingston, and John Alsop, merchants. I am told that a violent effort was made in the committee to have John Morin Scott, an eminent lawyer, and Alexander M'Dougall, named in the place of Jay and Alsop. It is said that the people are to be invited to meet on Thursday,

[1] Force's Am. Archives, 4th series, vol. i., p. 517. See also Gordon's History, vol. i., p. 238.

to approve of the deputies named by the committee. These transactions are dangerous, my lord, and illegal, but by what means shall Government prevent them? An attempt by the power of the civil magistrates would only show their weakness, and it is not easy to say upon what foundation a military aid should be called in; such a measure would involve us in trouble which it is thought much more prudent to avoid; and to shun all extremes, while it is yet possible things may take a favorable turn. The purpose of the Congress, it is said, is to petition for a redress of grievances, and to consider of a plan for settling the controversy with Great Britain. But no instructions for the deputies have yet appeared that I know of.'

In the appointment of the committee, the popular party had been defeated, and in the nominations by the committee they had again been defeated; a delegation supposed to be antagonistic to any decisive measures on the part of the Congress had been selected. It was feared that the common cause would suffer from the irresolute and lukewarm zeal which New York was likely to carry into the common councils. It was feared that the Congress might not adopt the only measure which, to the popular mind, seemed suited to the time and occasion. Under these discouraging circumstances, it was determined by the popular leaders to appeal to the people. Upon them rested the decision whether the nominations of the committee should be sanctioned, or a new ticket be substituted. Accordingly a meeting was convened on Wednesday, the 6th of July, long known as 'the great meeting in the fields.' The most enthusiastic spirit pervaded the assembled multitude. M'Dougall, whom neither danger nor persecution had been able to swerve from his principles, and who was endeared to his party by his sufferings in the cause, presided. Resolutions drawn by him were adopted. They denounced the Boston Port Act as unconstitutional in its principles, and dangerous to the liberties of all the colonies, and declared that the people of Boston were suffering in the common cause; that non-importation and non-exportation until the Port Act was repealed would prove the salvation of North America and her liberties; that importing and exporting, on the contrary, if continued, would be likely to fasten upon them the most odious oppression. The deputies, therefore, who should represent the colony in Congress, were instructed to engage with a majority of the principal colonies upon a non-importation from Great Britain of all goods, wares, and merchandizes, until the act for blocking up Boston Harbor was repealed. It was also recommended to the several counties to elect delegates to a colonial convention, for the purpose of choosing delegates to the Congress, or, if this was impracticable, to approve the delegates selected by the city and county of New York.[1]

It was on this occasion that the splendid orb of Alexander Hamilton first appeared above the horizon. He was but a youth of seventeen. The early display of his talents, the high hopes and aspiring wishes of the young West Indian, those conscious tokens of genius and often the precursors of coming greatness, had induced his friends to send him to New York for the advantages of an academic education. Five years before, while a merchant's clerk at St. Croix, writing to a school-fellow who had gone to New York, he said, with amusing artlessness, 'My ambition is prevalent, so that I contemn the grovelling condition of a clerk or the like, to which my fortune condemns me, and would willingly risk my life, though not my character, to exalt my station. I am confident, Ned, that my youth excludes me from any hopes of immediate preferment, nor do I desire it; but

[1] See these resolutions *in extenso,* in Force's Am. Archives, 4th series, vol. i., p. 312.

I mean to prepare the way for futurity. I'm no philosopher, you see, and may be justly said to build castles in the air. My folly makes me ashamed, and beg you'll conceal it; yet, Neddy, we have seen such schemes successful when the projector is constant. I shall conclude by saying, I wish there was a war.' He arrived in New York the latter part of the year 1772, and, at the time of the meeting in the fields, was a student in King's College. A natural fondness for politics had led him to investigate the grounds of the controversy between England and her colonies. At first he inclined to the ministerial side, but a visit to Boston just after the destruction of the tea, and while the city was in a blaze of patriotic ardor, kindled a kindred flame in his own bosom, and he returned to New York an enthusiastic advocate of the colonial claims. At the time when the approaching meeting in the fields was absorbing the public attention, he happened to be walking in the shade of some trees, in what is now Dey-street. Several persons residing in that neighborhood, who had frequently observed him in the same place, and been attracted by his thoughtful manner and a habit of soliloquy which lasted him through life, entered into conversation with him. Struck with the uncommon vigor of his thoughts, one of them urged him to address the popular meeting to which all eyes were now turned. At first he declined, but on going to the meeting, and listening to the several speakers, he found the various topics of discussion not yet exhausted. He determined to speak. When he presented himself before the anxious and excited multitude, his diminutive form and youthful aspect

> '—drew audience, still as night,
> Or summer's noontide air.'

At first he faltered, but recovering his confidence, and full of his theme, he stated with wonderful clearness the pretensions of Britain and the rights of the colonies. The enthusiasm that glowed in his manner and animated his speech, was communicated to the breasts of his hearers, and raised their minds 'to height of noblest temper.'

Alexander Hamilton was the most gifted and versatile genius that has yet appeared upon the theatre of American public affairs.

> 'Formed for all parts, in all alike he shined,
> Variously great; a genius unconfined!
> In converse bright, judicious in debate,
> In private amiable, in public great.'

Entering the army at the early age of nineteen, his career thenceforward was one of action. Engrossed with affairs, he had little time for abstract speculation. His thoughts were employed upon the pressing questions of the hour. And it was the peculiar characteristic of his versatile mind, that whatever subject it touched, it illuminated. Along those paths of investigation where ordinary mortals wandered darkling, he poured the radiance of unclouded day. His favorite profession was his earliest, and the fame of a successful soldier was one of the first and latest objects of his ambition. But his faculties were not confined to the circle of any one profession, or any one department of public life. He seemed born for every species of greatness. He was equally conversant with government in its principles, and administration in its details. He had a head to plan and a hand to execute. He wrote and spoke with equal power and equal distinction. He was a profound jurist, and, in some sort, one of the founders of the commercial law of this country. At a time when that branch of jurisprudence was *terra incognita* to the profession in New York, he had explored its foundations, and become familiar with its principles. He had studied Valin and Emerigon, and was among the first to introduce those authors to the notice of his legal brethren. On the organization of the Government which he had assisted as much as any one individual to create, he was made Secretary of the Treasury. He found the public credit at the lowest point of depression. He raised it to an unprecedented height, and established it on a sure foundation. 'He smote the rock of the national resources, and abundant streams of revenue gushed forth. He touched the dead corpse of the public credit, and it sprang upon its feet.'[1] Amid the various exhibitions of his pre-eminence, the admirer of Hamilton will recur, perhaps, with most pride, to his administration of the public finances as the field whereon he made the most signal display of his marvellous ability. Few men have ever been more loved by their friends, or dreaded by their enemies. The former were never content with his praise, nor the latter with his censure. Opinions were imputed to him which he never held, and purposes which he never entertained. Because in private he commended the British Constitution, he was charged with being an enemy to the institutions of his own country. The malevolence of party discovered in his admiration of the English Government an oblique censure of his own. But whether it will add or detract from his merit, it must be admitted that the political principles of Hamilton were high-toned. He lacked Jefferson's faith in democratic ideas—a faith which gave the latter such ascendency over the minds of his countrymen, and was the secret of his unbounded influence. Hamilton attached an undue importance to the hereditary principle of the English Government, and would have constructed ours upon such a basis as to render it, in a measure, independent of the surges of popular opinion.

[1] Daniel Webster. 'The fabled birth of Minerva,' continues Mr. Webster, 'from the brain of Jove, was hardly more sudden or more perfect than the financial system, as it burst forth from the conceptions of Alexander Hamilton.' Works, vol. i., p. 198.

In truth, he conceived, as men long conversant with affairs, and in stations of command, are apt to do, too high a notion of the regulating and controlling power of government. He over-estimated the value of that regulation and control. It is better understood now than in his day, that there is a law of things more potent than the law of the land; that anarchy is alien to the nature of civilized society, and 'the settled state of order, its normal condition. But when the constitution had received the sanction of the Convention, and was submitted to the people, he labored with untiring zeal and unmatched ability to procure its ratification. And all his subsequent acts evinced a determination, so far as any ability or influence of his could accomplish that result, to fortify and sustain it against all assaults from within or without.

It is idle, and worse than idle, to claim perfection for any human character; and it must be admitted of Hamilton, that the soundness of his judgment did not always correspond with the brilliancy of his talents. He had faults; but in the language of Mr. Burke, applied to a kindred genius, they were faults that, 'though they might in a small degree tarnish the lustre and sometimes impede the march of his abilities, had nothing in them to extinguish the fire of great virtues. In those faults there was no mixture of deceit, of hypocrisy, of pride, of ferocity, of complexional despotism, or want of feeling for the distresses of mankind.'

> 'False to their trusts, the mouldering busts decay,
> And soon effaced, inscriptions wear away,'

but the name of Hamilton will live in the annals of his country through all succeeding time. History and tradition are the eternal monuments of great deeds and illustrious men.

We now return to the proceedings of the Committee

of Fifty-one. The meeting which they had summoned for the 7th inst., to act upon their nominations, does not appear to have been numerously attended. The election was postponed. The committee of mechanics, in the meantime, had nominated another ticket. The meeting, therefore, recommended a mode and time to collect the popular voice upon the two nominations. On the evening of the same day, the committee came together, and, in a temper not very favorable to harmony. The proceedings of the meeting in the field were disavowed, as calculated to throw an odium on the committee, and to create groundless jealousies and suspicions of their conduct as well as disunion among the citizens. A sub-committee was appointed to draw and report resolutions to be submitted to the judgment of the city. The disavowal of the meeting in the fields at once caused a rupture in the committee. The next day, Francis Lewis, Joseph Hallett, Alexander M'Dougall, P. V. B. Livingston, Isaac Sears, Thomas Randall, Abraham P. Lott, Leonard Lispenard, John Broome, Abraham Brasher, and Jacobus Van Zandt, publicly withdrew from the committee. They assigned as the reason, that the course of the majority in condemning the meeting in the fields would prove injurious; that the people had a right to assemble, although not convened by the committee; that what they did was conformable to the general spirit of the other colonies; that the disavowal of their acts would induce the opinion in England that disunion prevailed among them, which would impede the public business and retard the redress of grievances; that therefore they could not act with the majority, and answer the end of their appointment.[1]

On the 13th day of July, the committee, shorn in a

[1] The committee had their proceedings published, in order that they might be sent to England in the same packet that carried the proceedings of the meeting in the fields.

measure of its strength by the withdrawal of so large a number of its members, met and agreed upon a set of resolutions, which were published and dispersed through the town. The citizens were summoned to consider them on the 19th, at the Coffee-house. It was also agreed to submit to their choice on that occasion, the gentlemen nominated by the committee as delegates to the proposed Congress. It is proper to observe in this place, that the attendance of Mr. Jay at the meetings of the committee had been very irregular. In the interval between the time of their appointment and the time of which we now speak, they had met on twelve different occasions. It does not appear that Mr. Jay had been present but on three of those occasions. After the rupture in the committee, his attendance was more constant. His position, however, was neither undecided nor misunderstood. He belonged to the party of the majority. He was not, however, an extremist. He was anxious to settle the dispute between the mother country and her colonies upon some permanent basis, and opposed to any measure that might jeopard that result.

The resolutions submitted to the citizens by the committee were received with great disfavor. They were unsuited to the time and occasion. The high and resolute spirit which had manifested itself in other colonies, the firm and decided tone which characterized their proceedings, had a visible effect upon the population of New York. Besides, the meeting in the fields had given an impetus to the popular cause, and awakened sentiments in the popular mind wholly averse to any temporizing expression of opinion, any resolutions 'half Trojan and half Greek,' as were deemed those of the committee. The first resolution declared that his most sacred majesty, George III., was their liege, lawful, and rightful sovereign; that it was their indispensable duty, to the utmost of their power, by all constitutional means, to maintain and support his crown and dignity; that it was their greatest happiness and glory to have been born British subjects, and that they wished nothing more ardently than to live and die as such; that they were one people, connected by the strongest ties of affection, duty, and interest, and that they lamented, as the greatest misfortune, every occurrence which had the least tendency to alienate or disturb that mutual harmony and confidence which, if properly cultivated, would not fail to render the British empire the admiration and envy of the world; that they therefore viewed, with inexpressible concern and grief, some late acts of the British Parliament, claiming rights and exercising powers which they humbly conceived were replete with destruction, and might be attended with the most fatal consequences to the colonies and their parent state.

The second resolution declared that vengeance separately directed was more dangerous in tendency, and more destructive to their liberty, than conjunctively, and hence it was the duty of all the colonies to render every reasonable assistance to a sister colony in distress. The remaining resolutions approved of the proposed Congress, but disapproved, as premature, any attempt on the part of any colony to anticipate their conduct by resolving what ought to be done. They expressed no opinion, except by implication, with respect to a non-importation agreement; but declared, that if adopted by the Congress, it ought to be very general, and faithfully adhered to, and not partially observed like the last, which would only be productive of further injuries. They declared that the delegates to the Congress ought to be so chosen or instructed, that they might be able, not only to speak the sentiments, but to pledge themselves for the good conduct of the people of the respective colonies. They expressed the most grateful thanks to the friends of the colonies in Great Britain, and particularly to those illustrious patriots in both houses of Parliament who had opposed the recent measures which, while subverting the liberties of America, manifestly tended to injure those of the mother country, and eventually overthrow their once excellent constitution.

On the day appointed, July 19th, the citizens assembled at the Coffee-House to express their judgment upon the resolutions, and to elect delegates to the Congress. They were addressed, among others, by John Morin Scott. He had long been eminent at the bar, and was accounted one of the readiest speakers upon the Continent. He was a man of decided ability, and in all the party contests of the province had shown himself the inflexible advocate of liberal principles. He was one of the most able and vigorous opponents of the pretensions put forward by Governor Colden in the case of Forsey *vs.* Cunningham. In religion, as in politics, he was on the liberal side, and could abide neither the arrogance of power nor the encroaching zeal of establishments. He was not fitted by nature or the habits of his life to play the part of either sycophant or courtier. He was a 'sensible man,' says John Adams, 'but not very polite,'[1] 'a character very much like that of old Mr.

[1] Adams' Works, vol. ii., p. 346. Mr. Adams, who was on his way to Philadelphia to attend the Congress, arrived in New York the latter part of August, 1774, and spent several days there. In his diary he makes frequent mention of Mr. Scott. 'This morning,' (August 22d, Monday,) he says, 'we took Mr. M'Dougall into our coach, and rode three miles out of town to Mr. Morin Scott's to breakfast — a very pleasant ride. Mr. Scott has an elegant seat there, with Hudson's river just behind his house, and a rural prospect all around him. Mr. Scott, his lady and daughter, and her husband, Mr. Litchfield, were dressed to receive us. We sat in a fine airy entry till called into a front room to breakfast. A more elegant breakfast I never saw — rich plate, a very large silver coffee-pot, a very large silver tea-pot, napkins of the very finest materials, toast and bread and butter in great perfection. After breakfast, a plate of beautiful peaches, another of pears, another of plums, and a musk-melon, were placed on the table.'

Auchmuty; sit up all night at his bottle, yet argue to admiration next day.'[1] With principles and ability such as we have described, Mr. Scott addressed the assembled electors. He denounced the resolutions as destitute of vigor, sense, and integrity. The citizens concurred in that opinion, and voted accordingly. The resolutions were rejected. Two of the candidates nominated by the committee were also defeated, viz., James Duane and Philip Livingston. A committee of fifteen was appointed to draw resolutions more conformable to the spirit of the times and the sentiments of the people. Mr. Jay was named one of this committee.

The Committee of Correspondence met on the evening of the day of election. They had suffered a sore defeat. The popular feeling had 'broke out like a wild overthrow.' But nothing daunted, the committee acted with a manly vigor. True, their resolutions had been rejected, and two of their candidates defeated. But they said only a small portion of the citizens had done this thing, and that the sentiments of the majority still remained uncertain. Therefore, 'to remove all doubts and uneasiness on that head,' they ordered certain amendments to be made to the resolves, and the whole to be immediately published. In a word, they determined to make another and more formal appeal to the public, not only

---

'Mr. Scott, Mr. William Smith, and Mr. William Livingston,' he says in another place, 'are the triumvirate who figured away in younger life against the church of England, who wrote the Independent Reflector, the Watch Tower, and other papers. They are all of them children of Yale College. Scott and Livingston are said to be lazy; Smith improves every moment of his time. . . . . . Mr. Scott is an eminent lawyer; he drew the answer of the Council to Governor Colden's reasons in favor of an appeal in the case of Forsey *vs.* Cunningham. He is said to be one of the readiest speakers on the Continent.' *Ibid*, p. 349.

[1] Adams' Works, vol. ii., p. 357. Mr. Adams here gives the impression he obtained of Mr. Scott from Mr. Sergeant, a young lawyer of Princeton, who afterwards rose to honorable distinction.

with respect to their resolutions, but with respect to the delegates nominated by the committee to attend the Congress.

Mr. Jay was present at this meeting of the committee, and concurred with its action. In accordance with it, himself, John Alsop, and Isaac Low published a card on the following day, declaring that notwithstanding the proceeding of the meeting convened at the Coffee-House, they could by no means consider themselves, or any others, duly chosen or authorized to act as delegates to the Congress. Mr. Jay also united with Isaac Low, John Moore, and Henry Remsen in another card to the public, declining to act as a member of the Committee of Fifteen. He refused to act with that committee, because it was appointed without any previous notice to the people, and was not a part of the business for which they were requested to assemble. Hence, his election, he thought, was too irregular to assume any authority, (in consequence of it,) to draw resolves for the town. He thought, too, that the appointment of this committee cast, or seemed to cast, an invidious reflection on the Committee of Correspondence, and tended to divide the citizens into factions and parties, at a time when they should be distinguished by concord and unanimity. Besides, the resolves of the Committee of Correspondence, with a few amendments, contained his sentiments.

The amendments which were made to the resolutions, by the committee, added to the vigor of their tone, and somewhat to the decisiveness of their views. To be sure, no opinion, except by implication, was expressed for or against the measure of non-importation, which was now the prominent issue and the obvious ground of difference between the parties that divided the town. But the implication was in favor of that measure. The ground, however, was trodden daintily, and with marked caution. The amendments declared that all acts of the

British Parliament imposing taxes on the colonies, were unjust and unconstitutional; that the Boston Port Act was in the highest degree arbitrary in its principles, oppressive in its operation, unparalleled in its rigor, indefinite in its exactions, subversive of every idea of British liberty, and hence, justly to be abhorred and detested by all good men; that the destruction of the tea was not the only motive for bringing such unexampled distress on the people of Boston, but the enforcement of the right of taxation over the colonies appeared to be the main design of that act of Parliament.

This was strong language, vigorous enough for the occasion, and agreeable even to the vehement sentiments of such men as Captain Sears. But what remedy did the committee propose for such mighty wrongs? What mode of redress did they recommend? Why, they declared that nothing less than dire necessity could justify, or ought to induce the colonies to unite in any measure that might materially injure their brethren the manufacturers, traders, and merchants in Great Britain; but that the preservation of their inestimable rights and liberties, as enjoyed and handed down to them by their ancestors, ought to supersede all other considerations; and hence, they did not doubt that the people of England, whose friendship on former occasions they had experienced, would, on mature consideration, not only applaud their motives, but co-operate with them in all constitutional measures for carrying their virtuous resolutions into execution, in order to obtain the just redress of their grievances.[1]

This was one step in advance. The measure of non-importation was looked in the face. But the amended resolution did not say in plain, unambiguous language, that a case of *dire necessity* had already arisen which would jus-

[1] These resolutions will be found *in extenso* in Force's Am. Archives, vol. i., pp. 315, 316. The 2nd, 3d, and 7th embrace the amendments.

tify that measure; that as a means to an end, and to compel a repeal of the obnoxious acts of Parliament, it should now be resorted to. It seemed to say that other means should first be employed before non-importation was admissible. Such was the interpretation put upon it by the popular party. The 28th day of July had been appointed by the committee to elect anew a delegation to the Congress. On the 26th, a committee of the citizens addressed a note to Mr. Jay and the other candidates, expressing a wish to avoid the inconveniences of a contested election, and therefore desiring to know whether they would use their utmost endeavors to procure the adoption of a non-importation agreement, until a redress of grievances was obtained. The candidates replied that they would use their utmost endeavors to carry every measure into execution at the proposed Congress that might then be thought conducive to the general interest of the colonies, and that at present they were of opinion that a general non-importation agreement faithfully observed, would prove the most efficacious means to procure a redress of their grievances. They added, that they were led to make this declaration of their sentiments because they thought it right, and not as an inducement to be favored with their votes, and that they had not the least objection to their electing any gentlemen as their delegates in whom they thought they could repose greater confidence than in their humble servants. This answer proved satisfactory, and the next day, July 28th, Philip Livingston, Isaac Low, John Alsop, and John Jay were unanimously elected as delegates to the Congress.

Thus the friends of a non-importation, by the most persistent, untiring efforts, had overcome a formidable opposition, and procured a delegation favorable to that measure. They might, indeed, have preferred a delegation differently composed, but as that delegation had embraced their views, all objections to it ceased. Governor Colden had written to the Earl of Dartmouth, on the first day of June, an account of the proceedings in New York in consequence of the Boston Port Act. Referring to the measure of non-importation, he said, 'I am informed that the new committee, in their answer to Boston, have given them no reason to expect that the merchants of this place will adopt so extravagant a measure; and people with whom I converse assure me that they think it cannot be brought about by the most zealous advocates of opposition.'[1] There are times and occasions when sudden changes of opinion do not involve inconsistency. A day or an hour may so alter the relation of things, that the opinion and purpose of yesterday are wholly unsuited to the exigencies of to-day. What appears to the remote spectator as inconsistent and strange, in the actual condition of affairs is wise and necessary conduct. Besides, the collision of feeling, opinion, and purpose, upon the eve of an important election, and on the hinge of great events, may well impart new and different views. In times of revolution, the conservative portion of society must either move with the current, or be ingulfed in the flood. That was a lesson which the late Sir Robert Peel endeavored to impress upon the reluctant understandings of the English aristocracy.

If the march of opinion had disappointed the wishes and hopes of Governor Colden, he found satisfaction in the circumstance that none of the zealots called the 'Sons of Liberty' had been elected to the Congress. He had submitted the opinion to the Earl of Dartmouth that the New York authorities could not prevent the frequent meetings of the people. A few days after the election, he wrote to his lordship that he was now convinced 'if Government had interfered, the most violent men would have gained great advantage, and would have prevented

[1] American Archives, vol. i., p. 372.

the acquiescence in the nomination of moderate men, which has now taken place, to meet at the general Congress of deputies from all the colonies, proposed to be held at Philadelphia next month.'[1]

On the 20th day of August, the delegates from Massachusetts arrived in New York on their way to attend the Congress. They remained in that city several days. Among their number was the future Colossus of Independence, John Adams. He had been accustomed to keep a diary. He did not intermit that practice on the present occasion. Its recent publication will throw some light on New York politics at that period. As we shall have frequent occasion to quote the statements and opinions of Mr. Adams, it may not be inappropriate, in the outset, to contemplate for a moment the character of that eminent person. Mr. Adams, at this time, had attained the mature age of thirty-nine. His active exertions in opposition to the ministerial measures had made his name familiar throughout the colonies. He was emphatically a man for the times. He had an erect, unconquerable spirit, an intrepidity that shrunk from no danger, and an integrity spotless as the sun. His nature was eager, daring, impetuous. He had deep conceptions, vigorous sense, and a power of expression, whether in speech or writing, strong, terse, and striking. His learning was extensive. Few of his contemporaries could boast acquirements so various and profound. His earnest, vehement spirit scorned all meanness, all low and grovelling arts. In spite of defects which we shall presently name, he possessed great amiability. To the last, there was a freshness and naturalness about him equally rare and attractive. His sympathies were strong and quick. His heart was stout and resolute, but tender as a woman's.

[1] American Archives, vol. i., p. 669. This letter of Governor Colden's breathes a conciliatory spirit which the state of public sentiment might well inspire.

At the recital of the 'oppressor's wrong, the proud man's contumely,' his indignation was instantly aroused. With him, liberty 'was the very stuff of the conscience.'

With great virtues, Mr. Adams had striking faults. His temper was inflammable, and vanity and jealousy were inherent in the 'substance and grain' of him. He lacked gentle manners. He knew books, but he was ignorant of the world and the motives that govern mankind. He wanted discretion and a spirit of conciliation. His passions not unfrequently betrayed his judgment. He was not versed in the arts of popularity. Indeed, he was too proud and self-reliant either to study or practise them. Besides, 'popularity is neither fame nor greatness.'

Mr. Adams acted a great part in the history of his country. His services during the Revolutionary period cannot be too highly estimated. The recent publication of his 'Life and Works' is an important contribution to historical science. They throw a strong light upon the events of the time in which he lived, and display his character in an advantageous point of view.

Two days after his arrival in New York, he took breakfast with John Morin Scott, at his 'elegant seat' upon the Hudson. Mr. M'Dougall was one of the guests. Both the host and M'Dougall seem to have given full expression to their opinions of men and things. 'Mr. M'Dougall,' says Mr. Adams,[1] 'gave a caution to avoid every expression here which looked like an allusion to the last appeal. He says there is a powerful party here who are intimidated by fears of a civil war, and they have been induced to acquiesce by assurances that there was no danger, and that a peaceful cessation of commerce would effect relief. Another party, he says, are intimidated lest the levelling spirit of the New England colo-

[1] Life and Works, vol. ii., p. 350.

nies should propagate itself into New York. Another party are prompted by Episcopalian prejudices against New England. Another party are merchants largely concerned in navigation, and therefore afraid of non-importation, non-consumption, and non-exportation agreements. Another party are those who are looking up to Government for favors.'

Of the delegates to the Congress, Mr. Adams did not obtain a very favorable impression, either from the information of others or his own observation. Mr. Jay he does not appear to have met, and only mentions him incidentally. 'Mr. Duane,' he says,[1] 'is an Episcopalian; so are all the delegates from New York excepting Mr. Livingston. Mr. Jay is a young gentleman of the law, of about twenty-six;[2] Mr. Scott says, a hard student and a good speaker. Mr. Alsop is a merchant, of a good heart, but unequal to the trust in point of abilities, as Mr. Scott thinks. Mr. Low, the chairman of the Committee of Fifty-one, they say will profess attachment to the cause of liberty, but his sincerity is doubted.'[3] In the course of the morning, 'about eleven o'clock,' says Mr. Adams, 'four of the delegates for the city and county of New York came to make their compliments to us — Mr. Duane, Mr. Livingston, Mr. Low, and Mr. Alsop.' He sketches their portraits with a bold hand. 'Mr. Livingston is a downright, straightforward man.' 'Mr. Alsop is a soft, sweet man.' 'Mr. Duane has a sly, surveying eye, a little squint-eyed; between forty and forty-

---

[1] Life and Works, vol. ii., p. 350.

[2] This is a mistake. Mr. Jay, at that time, was twenty-nine.

[3] The opinion at that time entertained of Mr. Low would seem to be confirmed by his subsequent course. A member of the Congress, and identified by his acts with the cause of his countrymen, he was not of force sufficient to persevere in the course he at first adopted. In that waning time of his country's fortunes, in the latter part of the year 1776, he sought British protection, and disappeared from the scene of affairs.

five I should guess; very sensible, I think, and very artful.' Brought into more familiar intercourse with his brother delegates of New York, Mr. Adams, in one or two instances, heightens the color upon the canvass, and presents their features in bolder relief. 'Phil. Livingston,' he says,[1] 'is a great, rough, rapid mortal. There is no holding any conversation with him. He blusters away; says if England should turn us adrift, we should instantly go to civil wars among ourselves, to determine which colony should govern all the rest; seems to dread New England, the levelling spirit, &c. Hints were thrown out of the Goths and Vandals; mention was made of our hanging the Quakers, &c. I told him the very existence of the colony was at that time at stake; surrounded with Indians at war, against whom they could not have defended the colony if the Quakers had been permitted to go on.' Again;[2] 'we afterwards dined in the Exchange Chamber, at the invitation of the Committee of Correspondence, with more than fifty gentlemen, at the most splendid dinner I ever saw; a profusion of rich dishes, &c. I had a great deal of conversation with Mr. Duane, who is a sensible, an artful, and an insinuating man.' At Princeton, he is told by 'Mr. Sergeant, a lawyer, a young gentleman of about twenty-five, perhaps, very sociable,' that 'Duane is a plodding body, but has a very effeminate, feeble voice.'

Although treated with marked respect by the leading characters of New York, and most hospitably entertained. Mr. Adams was not very favorably impressed with the manners of the place. 'With all the opulence and splendor of this city,' he says, 'there is very little good breeding to be found. We have been treated with an assiduous respect; but I have not seen one real gentleman, or well-bred man, since I came to town. At their

[1] Life and Works, vol. ii., p. 351. [2] Ibid., p. 354.

entertainments there is no conversation that is agreeable; there is no modesty, no attention to one another. They talk very loud, very fast, and all together. If they ask you a question, before you can utter three words of your answer, they will break out upon you again and talk away.'[1]

We have now stated the occasion on which Mr. Jay first appeared upon the theatre of affairs. We have endeavored to portray the position which he then held, and the sentiments of the community in which he lived. We have seen with what indignation and alarm the news of the Boston Port Act was received throughout the colonies. We have seen that that measure of coercion led to the appointment of the Committee of Fifty-one. We have traced the acts of that committee, and discovered in what manner they discharged their high and responsible trust. In another chapter we shall follow the course of Mr. Jay on that elevated theatre, where were collected for the maintenance of the public weal, the highest abilities of a continent.

---

[1] Life and Works, vol. ii., p. 353.

CHAPTER V.

THE CONGRESS OF 1774.

THE Congress of 1774 met on Monday the 5th of September, at the Carpenters' Hall, in Philadelphia. The members first assembled at the City Tavern, and walked in a body to the scene of their future deliberations.[1] Peyton Randolph of Virginia, who was familiar with parliamentary rules, from his experience as Speaker of the House of Burgesses of that colony, was chosen President, and Charles Thomson, 'a gentleman of family, fortune, and character,' was chosen Secretary.[2]

---

[1] 'At ten the delegates all met at the City Tavern, and walked to the Carpenters' Hall, where they took a view of the room and of the chamber where is an excellent library; there is also a long entry where gentlemen may walk, and a convenient chamber opposite to the library. The general cry was that this was a good room, and the question was put whether we were satisfied with this room, and it passed in the affirmative. A very few were for the negative, and they were chiefly from Pennsylvania and New York.' Life and Works of John Adams, vol. ii., p. 365.

The opposition of the delegates from those colonies proceeded from the fact that the Speaker of the Pennsylvania Assembly had offered the use of the State House, and they thought it but respectful to inquire whether it was not equally convenient as the Carpenters' Hall; and if it were, then it ought to be preferred, as it was a provincial, instead of a private house. Judge Jones, in his memoir of Mr. Duane, with an excusable *amour de lâ patrie*, says that 'this little incident displays the superiority, both in sagacity and habitual propriety of perception, of the New York gentleman of that day over the impulsive Southerner, and *even* over a well-bred Bostonian.' Documentary History of New York, p. 1070.

[2] 'Here,' (at Mr. Mifflin's,) 'we had much conversation with Mr. Charles Thomson, who is, it seems, about marrying a lady, a relation of Mr. Dickenson's, with five thousand pounds sterling. This Charles Thomson is the Sam. Adams of Philadelphia, the life of the cause of

With the exception of Edward Rutledge, it is believed that Mr. Jay was the youngest member of the Congress. He took a leading part in its proceedings. In debate and on committees, he was an able, active, and efficient member. He was open and explicit in the expression of his sentiments. He was anxious to adjust the present difficulties on terms safe and honorable to the colonies, and place their relations to the mother country on such a basis that future difficulties might not arise. We shall see as we proceed with our narrative, that he was in favor of Mr. Galloway's plan of adjustment. The idea of independence, at this time, was abhorrent to all his feelings. He allowed it no toleration until all hope of conciliation and harmony was cut off by the rapid succession of events and the steadfast policy of the English Cabinet. In this he was not singular. It was generally believed by the Congress of '74 that the result of its measures would be a restoration of the old order of things, as they stood anterior to the year 1764. This belief was clung to with fond tenacity, and even in the following year, when there appeared to be little or no ground upon which to build a hope of peaceful adjustment, John Adams made himself an object of scorn and detestation, by 'muttering in Congress and out of doors,' that they would be driven to the necessity of declaring independence. In his letter to Mr. Pickering with respect to the origin of that measure, Mr. Adams says,[1] 'It soon

liberty, they say.' — Life and Works of John Adams, vol. ii., p. 358. Mr. Adams says that Mr. Thomson was appointed Secretary without opposition, 'though Mr. Duane and Mr. Jay discovered at first an inclination to seek further.'

[1] Life and Works, vol. ii., p. 513, note. Doubtless the publication of Mr. Adams' intercepted letters to his wife and General Warren, which not only disclosed views tending directly to independence, but expressed a very contemptuous opinion of the leading man of Pennsylvania, John Dickenson, whom he characterized as 'a great fortune and

became rumored about the city that John Adams was for independence. The Quakers and proprietary gentlemen took the alarm; represented me as the worst of men; the true-blue sons of liberty pitied me; all put me under a kind of coventry. I was avoided, like a man infected with the leprosy. I walked the streets of Philadelphia in solitude, borne down by the weight of care and unpopularity.'

Mr. Jay, if he did not make such rapid strides as Mr. Adams and those who concurred with his views, nor always in the same direction, pursued the course which he deemed best suited to the interests of the colonies with unfaltering step; and when persuaded, by the turn of affairs, that independence had become a necessity, he embraced that measure with zeal, and employed the whole weight of his talents and influence to defend it.

At the era of the Revolution, sectarian jealousy and animosity, although not so bitter and intense as they formerly had been, were still full of life and activity. Personal and political considerations mingled with, and gave a tone to the religious feelings of the time. Differences of faith and worship at that day were inflamed by recollections of the past and apprehensions of the future. An ecclesiastical establishment was associated in the popular mind with tyranny and persecution. Propositions had been made at different times to introduce a hierarchy into the colonies, and were favorably entertained in England. This kept alive a vigilant and jealous watchfulness. Episcopacy was regarded as the

---

piddling genius,' contributed to the weight of unpopularity which at this time pressed upon him.

The social position of Mr. Dickenson was very high. He had many estimable qualities, and, as a man and citizen, was deservedly popular with the inhabitants of his adopted city. His friends would naturally manifest resentment at the blunt, irreverent style with which Mr. Adams spoke of him.

natural ally of power, and a covert enemy of the public weal. This feeling of dislike and apprehension was not likely to be less strong where, as in Virginia, the dissenters were in the majority, but compelled to pay taxes to support the pastors of the minority.[1] The Episcopalians, on the other hand, felt an equal aversion to sects whose very existence was a protest against the church; who had grown up in opposition to it, and in spite of its efforts to suppress them, and who still entertained an unaccountable and singular prejudice against tithes and bishops. The dissenting sects, too, united as they were in opposition to establishments, were separated upon other points by impassable barriers. A Baptist or Quaker whose ancestor had been hung, or mutilated, or driven forth into the wilderness simply for exercising the rights of conscience, as the descendant was taught to believe, could not be expected to regard with much favor the authors of such severity, nor those who were supposed to inherit their principles.[2] In New York, sectarian feelings, from a variety of causes, were peculiarly strong, and influenced more or less the political contests of the Province.

---

[1] 'This unrighteous compulsion,' says Mr. Jefferson, 'to maintain teachers of what they deemed religious errors, was grievously felt during *the regal government, and without a hope of relief. But the first* republican legislature, which met in '76, was crowded with petitions to abolish this spiritual tyranny. These brought on the severest contests in which I have ever been engaged.' Jefferson's Works, vol. i., pp. 31, 32.

[2] The uninformed reader will find the treatment of the Quakers by the Puritans fully discussed in the first volume of Grahame's History of the United States. Grahame was a rigid Calvinist; in some points resembling Jonathan Edwards, although by no means his compeer in dialectic ability. He admired the Puritans, and loved their principles. He was not, however, blind to their defects, nor insensible to their intolerance. He states all the facts, and the reader can judge of the correctness of his conclusions. See also his statement of the case of Roger Williams.

Aware of the religious differences in the colonies, and the hold they had upon the minds of men, Mr. Jay opposed the proposition to open the Congress with prayer. He thought the diversity of religious belief was so great, that the delegates could not unite in the same act of worship. In this opinion he was supported by Mr. Rutledge of South Carolina. Mr. Adams, in a letter to his wife, dated the 16th inst., gives a very interesting account of this transaction. 'When the Congress first met,' he says, 'Mr. Cushing made a motion that it should be opened with prayer. It was opposed by Mr. Jay of New York and Mr. Rutledge of South Carolina, because we were so divided in religious sentiments; some Episcopalians, some Quakers, some Anabaptists, some Presbyterians, and some Congregationalists, that we could not join in the same act of worship. Mr. Samuel Adams rose and said, 'he was no bigot, and could hear a prayer from a gentleman of piety and virtue, who was at the same time a friend to his country. He was a stranger in Philadelphia, but had heard that Mr. Duché (Dushay they pronounce it) deserved that character, and therefore he moved that Mr. Duché, an Episcopal clergyman, might be desired to read prayers to the Congress to-morrow morning.' The motion was seconded, and passed in the affirmative. Mr. Randolph, our President, waited on Mr. Duché, and received for answer that, if his health would permit, he certainly would. Accordingly, next morning he appeared with his clerks, in his pontificals, and read several prayers in the established form, and then read the collect for the seventh day of September, which was the thirty-fifth Psalm. You must remember, this was the next morning after we heard the horrible rumor of the cannonade of Boston. I never saw a greater effect upon an audience. It seemed as if heaven had ordained that psalm to be read on that morning. After this, Mr. Duché, unexpectedly to every body, struck out into an extempore prayer, which filled the bosom of every man present. I must confess I never heard a better prayer, or one so well pronounced. *Episcopalian as he is,* Dr. Cooper himself never prayed with such fervor, such ardor, such earnestness and pathos, and in language so elegant and sublime, for America, for the Congress, for the province of Massachusetts Bay, and especially the town of Boston. It has had an excellent effect upon every body here. I must beg you to read that psalm. If there was any faith in the *sortes virgilianæ,* or *sortes homericæ,* or especially the *sortes Biblicæ,* it would be thought providential. It will amuse your friends to read this letter and the thirty-fifth psalm to them. Read it to your father and Mr. Wibird. I wonder what our Braintree churchmen would think of this. Mr. Duché is one of the most ingenious men, and best characters, and greatest orators in the Episcopal order upon this Continent; yet a zealous friend of liberty and his country.'[1]

Mr. Adams, in the enthusiasm of the moment, bestowed undue praise upon Mr. Duché. A fair estimate of a man's abilities or character can hardly be made from a single observation of them. This is more especially true in times of excitement, when an unexpected sally of eloquence or a stirring appeal, suiting the already inflamed feelings of the auditor, is apt to be attributed to extraordinary powers. That Mr. Duché was a distinguished pulpit orator, there can be no doubt. He had in an eminent degree the physical attributes of an orator, a musical voice, graceful carriage, and flexibility of feature. He was a man, too, of cultivation, of earnest, and, at times, of enthusiastic piety. But he was unstable, and influenced in his conduct by the shows of things.

[1] See this letter in vol. ii. of his Life and Works, p. 368, note. It is stated on the authority of Peyton Randolph, that Washington was the only member of the Congress who knelt during the performance of this service.

He was born of the willow, and not of the oak. He reverenced wealth and social position. His feeble will succumbed to the prevailing tone of fashionable life. The sentiments and feelings of the circle with which for the time he mingled, gave color and direction to his own. A whig before the Declaration of Independence, and the chaplain of Congress for nearly three months after, he was supposed to be sincere in the opinions which his line of conduct indicated. But in the stormy and disastrous days of '77, when Philadelphia was in possession of the enemy, when society held a different language, and the cause of the colonies was considered vulgar as well as desperate, he changed his ground, and wrote his celebrated letter to Washington, advising him to negotiate for peace at the head of his army.[1]

Unanimity, in a deliberative assembly, upon all points, is not to be expected. Even if there is a common aim, there will be more or less diversity as to the means of attaining it. Difference of education, habit, and association, produces a corresponding difference of thought and action. Besides, a public body furnishes such a conspicuous theatre for the display of talent, that human vanity can hardly forego the tempting occasion.[2] All these reasons concurred to produce and prolong discussion in the Congress of 1774. The members, with few excep-

[1] In his letter to General Washington, he says that he acquiesced in the Declaration of Independence, as an expedient; but when he saw that separation from the mother country was the end actually aimed at, he resigned his chaplaincy, and no longer sympathized with the designs of his countrymen.

[2] We find Mr. Adams, a month after the Congress had convened, complaining of the 'immeasurable length' to which its deliberations were spun out. 'There is so much wit, sense, learning, acuteness, subtlety, eloquence, &c.,' he says, 'among fifty gentlemen, each of whom has been habituated to lead and guide in his own province, that an immensity of time is spent unnecessarily.' Life and Works vol. ii.. p. 395.

tions, were personally unacquainted. Many of them were wholly unknown out of their own provinces. There were but a few whose fame was extended over the Continent. Coming together from widely-separated communities, entertaining dissimilar views of the nature of their rights, of the modes of adjustment, and the means of resistance, it was natural that every proposition should be carefully canvassed. And discussion, on such an occasion, was pre-eminently serviceable. Its influence did not expire with the decision of the immediate question in debate. It disclosed the sentiments of the several speakers, and, by bringing them in contact with the sentiments of the body, served to familiarize and harmonize them.

Mr. Jay participated in most of the debates that arose, and, so far as we can judge from the meagre, but nevertheless interesting and valuable reports preserved by Mr. Adams, he spoke briefly and to the point. He had none of the fire and passion that animated the thought and gesture of a Henry, an Adams, a Lee, or a Hooper; but he had habits of reflection and solidity of judgment which, in the practical affairs of mankind, are admirable substitutes for more brilliant qualities. In an assembly convened on so grave an occasion, with such grave responsibility resting upon each of the members, with such momentous results depending upon their deliberations, mere declamation could only provoke contempt. In critical periods, when life and liberty are at stake, nothing less than good sense, direct, manly, and logical views, deep conceptions, noble and animating sentiments, are of force to fix attention and guide conduct.

The occasion upon which Mr. Jay first spoke was in relation to the method of voting by the Congress. It was a question of some difficulty. There were three modes proposed of collecting the voice of the body, and strong objections were urged to each. To vote by colonies was manifestly unequal, because five small colonies had it in their power to control the action of four large ones, containing treble their wealth and population. To vote by numbers, or by the poll, was open to a similar objection; for some of the colonies had sent more than their proportion of delegates, while others had sent less. To vote by interests was attended by difficulties that seemed insuperable. They had no standard by which to determine the relative importance of the colonies. But admitting that that could be supplied, and the population, trade, and resources of each colony were spread out before them; what then? Was the weight of a colony to be determined by the number of its inhabitants, or by the amount of its property, or by a combination of the two? Considering the difficulties attending these several modes, the Congress finally resolved that each colony should have one voice; but an entry was made upon the journals, to prevent it being deemed a precedent for the future.

In the debate upon this question, Patrick Henry made his celebrated speech, which confirmed the previous impression of his powers, and established his renown. His eloquence, 'deep, majestic, smooth, and strong,' if it did not always produce conviction, never failed to arouse in his auditors a blended feeling of awe, admiration, and delight. Before leaving Virginia, he had expressed the opinion that the contest would come to extremities, and, prophet-like, stated what in his judgment would be the course and issue of the strife. With that conviction deep rooted in his mind, with strong feelings and never-failing courage, he declared in this debate that Government was dissolved. The boldness of his propositions, and the unmistakable tendency of his views, must have struck most of the delegates with dismay and apprehension. He stood on an eminence to which they had not yet attained, and had a more comprehensive view of the condition of affairs. He penetrated beneath the letter, and clearly discerned the real significancy of the controversy.[1] 'Government,' he said, 'is dissolved. Fleets and armies, and the present state of things show that Government is dissolved. Where are your landmarks, your boundaries of colonies? We are in a state of nature, Sir. I did propose that a scale should be laid down; that part of North America which was once Massachusetts Bay, and that part which was once Virginia, ought to be considered as having a weight. Will not people complain? Ten thousand Virginians have not outweighed one thousand others. I will submit, however; I am determined to submit, if I am overruled. A worthy gentleman (Mr. Adams) near me seemed to admit the necessity of obtaining a more adequate representation. I hope future ages will quote our proceedings with applause. It is one of the great duties of the democratical part of the Constitution to keep itself pure. It is known in my province that some other colonies are not so numerous or rich as they are. I am for giving all the satisfaction in my power. The distinctions between Virginians, Pennsylvanians, New Yorkers, and New Englanders, are no more. I am not

[1] Although Mr. Henry was in advance of most of his countrymen at this time, yet in the spring of 1776, when the question of independence was agitating the public mind, and the particular friends of Mr. Henry, with whom he had been accustomed to act, were advocating that measure, he hesitated. He did not hesitate about prosecuting the war with the utmost vigor; but he thought a declaration of independence premature. The pulse of France and Spain, he said, should be first felt. Besides, he feared that France might be diverted from giving her aid and countenance to the colonies, by an offer of partition from Great Britain.

See a letter of General Charles Lee to Henry, dated May 7th, 1776, in Force's American Archives, vol. i., p. 95, fifth series. In this letter Lee refers to a conversation with Henry on a previous occasion, and endeavors to combat the views he then expressed with respect to declaring the colonies independent.

a Virginian, but an American. Slaves are to be thrown out of the question, and if the freemen can be represented according to their numbers, I am satisfied.' Mr. Henry was followed by several of the most eminent members of the body; by Lynch, Rutledge, and Gadsden of South Carolina, by Lee, Bland, and Pendleton of Virginia, and by Governor Ward of Rhode Island. When they had concluded, he again took the floor, and reiterated his former position, that Government was dissolved. 'I agree,' he said, 'that authentic accounts cannot be had, if by authenticity is meant attestations of officers of the Crown. I go upon the supposition that Government is at an end. All distinctions are thrown down. All America is thrown into one mass. We must aim at the minutiæ of rectitude.'

Mr. Jay could not concur with Mr. Henry's view of the condition of affairs. He had not accustomed his mind to contemplate the disruption of those bonds of law, habit, tradition, and affection, which had hitherto firmly bound the colonies to the British empire. He fondly hoped that all wrongs would be redressed, and old relations re-established and maintained. It is no wonder, therefore, that the declarations of Mr. Henry startled and surprised him. 'Could I suppose,' he said as he rose to reply, 'that we came to frame an American constitution instead of endeavoring to correct the faults in an old one? I can't think that all government is at an end. The measure of arbitrary power is not yet full, and I think it must run over before we undertake to frame a new constitution. To the virtue, spirit, and abilities of Virginia we owe much. I should always, therefore, from inclination as well as justice, be for giving Virginia its full weight. I am not clear that we ought not to be bound by a majority, though ever so small; but I only mentioned it as a matter of danger worthy of consideration.'

The brief abstracts of the debates, which Mr. Adams has preserved, necessarily contain only the salient points. The argument, the illustration, the tone and bearing of the several speakers, must be inferred from what we know of their respective characters and powers, their modes of expression, and habits of thought. In one or two instances, tradition has supplied the place of inference, and furnished the basis upon which genius and eloquence have built up a durable memorial of the illustrious characters whose career they have traced. If the eye of the historian or the critic should discover in that memorial embellishments which do not belong to it, which were suggested and supplied by the fancy of the architect, enough will still remain true to life and nature, to preserve for the admiration and gratitude of future generations, the memory of the great names and great services it was intended to commemorate.

Congress determined the method of voting in the manner we have stated, and on the same day, viz., the 6th of September, resolved to appoint a committee to state the rights of the colonies in general, the several instances in which they had been violated, and the proper mode of restoring them to their former basis. The next day it was agreed to place upon the committee two members from each colony. Mr. Jay and Mr. Duane were the members from New York. The committee at once entered upon the discharge of their duties. Of their proceedings, Mr. Adams, who was a member, has given us in his autobiography a very interesting account.[1] 'It would be endless,' he says, 'to attempt even an abridgment of the discussions in this committee, which met regularly every morning for many days successively, till it became an object of jealousy to all the other members of Congress. It was, indeed, very much against my

[1] Life and Works, vol. ii., pp. 373, 374.

judgment that the committee was so soon appointed, as I wished to hear all the great topics handled in Congress at large in the first place. They were very deliberately considered and debated in the committee, however. The two points which labored the most were, 1st, Whether we should recur to the law of nature as well as to the British Constitution, and our American charters and grants. Mr. Galloway and Mr. Duane were for excluding the law of nature. I was very strenuous for retaining and insisting on it, as a resource to which we might be driven by Parliament much sooner than we were aware.[1] 2d: The other great question was, what au-

[1] Life and Works, vol. ii., p. 373, 374. In Mr. Adams' diary, under date of the 8th inst., is the following entry: 'Attended my duty on the committee all day, and a most ingenious, entertaining debate we had.' Of this 'ingenious, entertaining debate,' Mr. Adams preserved a brief abstract. Richard Henry Lee, who had already made a great impression upon the Congress, by his graceful and effective eloquence, opened the discussion. He placed the rights of the colonies on a four-fold foundation; on nature, on the British Constitution, on charters, and on immemorial usage. He was followed by Mr. Jay, who contended that it was necessary to recur to the law of nature and the British Constitution, to ascertain their rights. The constitution of Great Britain would not apply, he said, to some of the charter rights. He then referred to the subject of emigration and allegiance. Here he took high ground. He maintained that the inhabitants of an over-populated country have a right to emigrate; that allegiance and protection are reciprocal; that the former does not exist independently of the latter; and hence, emigrants beyond the reach of that protection, and consequently divested of their allegiance, have a right to erect what government they please. He denied the position that the British Constitution inseparably attached to the person of every subject. On the contrary, it derived its authority from compact. Might not that authority, then, he asked, be given up by compact? He denied, too, the position that a subject discovering land does it for the state to which he belongs.

The abstract of Mr. Jay's observations on this occasion is so brief, that it is difficult to determine the exact tendency and character of his views. The logical result of his positions would lead to a total independency of Great Britain. Of course he qualified them. The rights of expatriation and allegiance, however, which he asserted, and to a much

thority we should concede to Parliament; whether we should deny the authority of Parliament in all cases; whether we should allow any authority to it in our internal affairs; or whether we should allow it to regulate the trade of the empire with or without any restrictions. These discussions spun into great length, and nothing was decided. After many fruitless essays, the committee determined to appoint a sub-committee to make a draught of a set of articles that might be laid in writing before the grand committee, and become the foundation of a more regular debate and final decision. I was appointed on the sub-committee, in which, after going over the ground again, a set of articles were drawn and debated one by one. After several days' deliberation, we agreed upon all the articles excepting one, and that was the authority of Parliament, which was indeed the essence of the whole controversy. Some were for a flat denial of all authority; others for denying the power of taxation only; some for denying internal, but admitting external taxation.'

Amid this multiplicity and collision of opinion, Mr.

greater extent than he asserted them, are founded on an eternal law of nature. While the benefits of a government are received, while the shield of its protection guards and protects the citizen, he is bound to obedience; but if he no longer asks the protection of the government, if he withdraws from the sphere of its operation, goes into a different country, and under a different jurisdiction, without the *animus* of returning, his allegiance, in reason and justice, ought to be deemed at an end. The citizens of a State are not the property of the Government; are not chained like serfs to the soil. 'The world is before them, where to choose their place of rest, and Providence their guide.' The English doctrine of allegiance is a monstrous absurdity. It is the offspring of the feudal system, and wholly repugnant to the more enlightened ideas of modern times. Wherever feudality is exploded, the notion of perpetual allegiance is obsolete. While thus asserting the abstract right of expatriation, we do not forget that cases may arise where the restraint of its exercise would be justifiable. But such restraint should only be imposed in a case of necessity, clear, obvious, and unmistakable.

Adams was fortunate enough to produce an article upon the delicate topic of Parliamentary power, which, if it did not fully satisfy the discordant views of his colleagues, harmonized their action.[1] This article is the fourth in the series of resolutions adopted by the Congress. It declared that the colonies were entitled to a free and exclusive power of legislation in their several provincial legislatures, where their right of representation could alone be preserved in all cases of taxation and internal polity, subject only to the negative of their sovereign, in such manner as had been theretofore used and accustomed. But, from the necessity of the case, and a regard to the mutual interest of both countries, they cheerfully consented to the operation of such acts of the British Parliament as were *bona fide* restrained to the regulation of their external commerce, for the purpose of securing the commercial advantages of the whole empire to the mother country, and the commercial benefits of its respective members; excluding every idea of taxation, internal or external, for raising a revenue on the subjects in America without their consent.[2] The opinion was gaining ground

[1] Vide Post Life of Rutledge.

[2] The same day on which the committee was appointed to state the rights of the colonies, &c., another committee, consisting of one member from each colony, was appointed to examine and report the several statutes which affected the trade and manufactures of the colonies. This committee made a report on Saturday, the 17th day of September. On Monday, the 19th inst., their report was read and referred to the committee appointed to state the rights of the colonies, &c. To this committee were then added three additional members; namely, Thomas Cushing, Patrick Henry, and Thomas Mifflin. As these gentlemen were members of the second committee, whose report was referred to the first one, they were doubtless added to this latter committee as representatives of the former one, to unfold and explain its report, and not, I apprehend, as a concession to Virginia, Massachusetts, and Pennsylvania, and 'thus framing a species of compromise between the two principles of federation and population presented in the first day's debate,' as is suggested by the Editor of Mr. Adams' Works. See vol. ii.,

that the Parliament had no power whatsoever of legislation for the colonies. This opinion was held and maintained by several of the leading minds in the Congress. This article, therefore, was admirably framed to suit the extremes of opinion. It neither directly asserted, nor denied, the authority of Parliament. Indirectly, however, and by implication, it denied it. It declared the consent of the colonies to the exercise of such authority in certain cases, not because of any inherent right in the Parliament, as derived from the Constitution, but *from the necessity of the case, and a regard to the mutual interest of both countries.* Those who maintained the legislative power of Parliament, since it was assented to in the accustomed mode of its exercise, might well yield their objections to the ground upon which that assent was placed; while those who denied it could not complain, since they were not called upon to surrender their position. They were called upon to consent to the operation of certain acts of Parliament, not because they were constitutionally bound by them, but because necessity and mutual advantage rendered it expedient. Legislation, however, which derives all its vigor and authority, not from any admitted power in the body whence it emanates, but from a supposed necessity and mutual advantage, rests on a very infirm and unreliable basis. At present it is submitted to, but times and opinions change, and it is soon discovered that the necessity and mutual advantage, which alone support it, no longer exist. Certainly, those members who denied that Par-

---

p. 376, note. The action of the committee was not final. Their report was to be passed upon by the Congress, where the method of voting was by colonies and not by numbers. True, in determining the character of the committee's report, the three colonies mentioned would have a preponderance; but this could hardly have been from design. The addition of Cushing, Henry, and Mifflin, if a concession at all, was doubtless a concession to their high standing and acknowledged talents.

liament possessed any power of legislation whatever for the colonies, could not object to the acts regulating trade, when they were asked to consent to them upon the grounds we have stated.

On the 13th inst., the sub-committee reported to the grand committee their draught of articles.[1] Here the ground was gone over again. After nine days of discussion and deliberation, the articles, as drawn up by the sub-committee, were reported to the Congress. Their report was but partial, and related only to the rights of the colonies. On the 24th, a second report was made, which was confined to the violations of those rights. The articles embodied in the first report constitute the first ten in the series of resolutions adopted by the Congress. They found the rights of the colonies on the laws of nature, on the principles of the English Constitution, and on their charters. The second report embraced the labors of the second committee, as modified after that committee was merged in the larger one, and constitutes that part of the resolutions adopted by the Congress which follow the tenth.[2] Before coming to a decision upon these reports, Congress proceeded to consider the most proper means to obtain a restoration of their rights.

On the 26th day of September, Richard Henry Lee made a motion for a non-importation. It was the occasion of a discussion which continued during that and the following day. Had it been foreseen that the contest with the mother country was to be decided by an appeal to arms, and not by a suspension of trade, obvious considerations would have induced Congress to encourage importations, and secure a supply of manufactures and munitions of war. The want of them was severely felt throughout the revolutionary struggle. But that tre-

[1] See the preceding note.

[2] They were adopted October 14th.

mendous issue, with a few exceptions, was not then contemplated. It was very generally believed that non-importation and non-exportation would prove an effectual mode of redress. The advocates of those measures entertained very exaggerated notions of the consequences likely to flow from them. They thought a total cessation of commerce would occasion such distress in Great Britain, such stagnation of trade and manufactures, such loss of revenue, that individual and national bankruptcy could only be averted by the Government acceding to the demands of the colonies.[1] This was a great error.

---

[1] Life and Works of John Adams, vol. ii., pp. 383–386. 'A total non-importation and non-exportation to Great Britain and to the West Indies,' said Mr. Chase of Maryland, 'must produce a national bankruptcy in a very short space of time.' Mr. Lynch, of South Carolina, was of the same opinion. 'I believe the Parliament would grant us immediate relief,' he said. 'Bankruptcy would be the consequence if they did not.' 'Great Britain cannot do without naval stores from North Carolina,' said the accomplished Hooper of that respectable province. Colonel Dyer of Connecticut was of the opinion that the withdrawal of all commerce with Great Britain at once, 'would come upon them like a thunder-clap.' 'By what I heard yesterday,' he continued, 'Great Britain is much more in our power than I expected—the masts from the northward, the naval stores from North Carolina.' John Sullivan had enumerated 'masts, boards, planks, fish, oil, and some potash,' as the exports of New Hampshire, while Mr. Hooper had specified 'tar, pitch, and turpentine,' as the exports of North Carolina. In addition to these means of coercion, Colonel Dyer thought that 'the stoppage of flax-seed to Ireland would greatly distress them.'

Mr. Adams, in his diary of the 3d of September, ibid. 362, mentions a breakfast at Dr. Shippen's, where he met Richard Henry Lee, whom he designates as 'a masterly man,' and records the opinions which he expressed. Mr. Adams has made a mistake as to the time, for Mr. Lee had not arrived in Philadelphia at the opening of Congress on the 5th. He made his appearance, however, the next day, as is mentioned in the Congressional Journal. See also his Life, by his grandson. Mr. Lee, he says, was absolutely certain that the same ship which carried home the resolution of non-consumption, would bring back the redress. The delegates from Virginia were at first divided upon the question of non-exportation, not on account of any doubt as to the expediency of the

The idea, however, was common in their day, and has not yet been wholly eradicated from the minds of men, that States producing staple commodities possess the power to coerce the action of a commercial and manufacturing people by a suspension of trade. But whenever attempted, it will be found that the blow which was to prostrate their enemies, rebounds upon themselves. They will inflict distress and impoverishment at home, without any corresponding effect abroad. Commerce is, in its nature, active, enterprising, continually seeking and finding new channels of trade. The diversified industry of a nation, if obstructed in one branch of its employment, will either overcome the obstruction, or exert its energies in a different pursuit. An agricultural people, conversant with but a single mode of life, which, however healthful and virtuous, makes no very great demands upon the intellectual faculties, do not possess that quickness, aptness, flexiblility, and invention that characterize a community where there is a variety of employment, where competition, collision, and necessity stimulate all those qualities to their highest point of development. Hence, such a people resorting to an interdiction of trade to accomplish their objects, engage in an unequal warfare. They must either remain passive sufferers, which soon 'relaxes and wears out the spring of their spirit,' or change and diversify their mode of industry, which, in their circumstances, will prove a slow, painful, and discouraging process. Their intended victims, on the contrary, with energies quickened by the necessities of the occasion, will soon find out other sources whence to supply their wants, or invent substitutes for the products which are withholden and cannot elsewhere be obtained.

measure, but upon the ground of insufficient powers. See Drayton's Memoirs of the American Revolution, vol. i., p. 168. They finally yielded this objection, and acted in harmony with the other colonies.

As the event proved, the Congress misconceived the efficacy of their measures. At the time, however, it was believed that they would prove effectual, and their support was, in some sort, made the test of patriotism. Their opponents were generally to be found among those who would either submit to the pretensions of Great Britain entirely, or purchase immunity from the whole, by conceding a part.

'Negotiation, suspension of commerce, and war,' said Mr. Jay in the discussion that ensued upon Mr. Lee's motion, 'are the only three things. War is, by general consent, to be waived at present. I am for negotiation and suspension of commerce.'[1]

On the 27th day of September, Congress adopted a non-importation and non-consumption resolution, to take effect from and after the 1st day of the following December. The next day Mr. Galloway introduced his celebrated plan of adjustment, which was favorably received and referred for further consideration. It failed of a final adoption only from the want of two votes; yet all trace of the plan itself and the proceedings pending its consideration, were carefully expunged from the journals of the Congress, and Mr. Galloway's history of the transaction attempted to be discredited. The odium excited by his subsequent conduct attached to his previous acts, and both were believed to proceed from the same corrupted source of treachery and dishonor. Since therefore the unpopularity of the man has fallen upon his work, it will not be an impertinent digression to notice some points of his history, and some traits of his character.

Mr. Galloway was a native of Maryland, where he was born in the year 1730. He sprung from a family of respectability and good fortune. With such advan-

[1] Adams' Works, vol. ii., p. 385.

tages of early education as his situation in life secured to him, he entered upon the study of the law. Admitted to the bar, he established himself at Philadelphia. Without any slow and painful steps, he seems to have attained at once and *per saltum* business and position. At twenty-seven, we find him a leading and influential member of the Assembly. The coadjutor of Dr. Franklin, he was a steady and inflexible opponent of the proprietary interest. By the exertions of that party, he lost his election in the year 1764; but the next year he was re-elected, and chosen Speaker. This position, by successive re-elections, he held until the year 1774. The Assembly in that year chose him a member of the Congress. In his examination at the bar of the House of Commons in January, 1779, he stated the conditions upon which he was elected. 'I went into Congress,' he said, 'at the earnest solicitation of the Assembly of Pennsylvania. I refused to go, unless they would send with me, as the rule of my conduct, instructions agreeable to my own mind. They suffered me to draw up those instructions; they were, briefly to state the rights and grievances of America, and to propose a plan of amicable accommodation of the differences between Great Britain and the colonies, and of a perpetual union; I speak now from the records of Pennsylvania, where these instructions are.[1] Upon

[1] On the same day (July 22d) that the Assembly of Pennsylvania elected delegates to the Congress, but previous to the election, they unanimously adopted the following resolution. It was drawn up by Mr. Galloway, and contains the instructions to which he referred in his examination at the bar of the House of Commons. Resolved, That there is an absolute necessity that a Congress of Deputies from the several colonies be held as soon as conveniently may be, to consult together upon the present unhappy state of the colonies, and to form and adopt a plan for the purposes of obtaining redress of American grievances, ascertaining American rights upon the most solid constitutional principles, and for establishing that union and harmony between Great Britain and the colonies, which is indispensably necessary for the welfare and happiness of both '

this ground, and with a heart full of loyalty to my sovereign, I went into Congress, and from that loyalty I never deviated in the least. I proposed a plan of accommodation in the Congress, agreeable to my instructions. Some of the best men, and men of the best fortunes, espoused the plan, and drew with me. It was proposed and debated a whole day, and carried upon the question, six colonies to five that it should be resumed and further considered. I have in my hand the introductory resolve of Congress, in my own writing, which identically was delivered by me in Congress.' The position of Mr. Galloway at the time of his election was by no means anomalous. It was occupied by many of his countrymen. He was opposed to the policy and acts of the ministry, and equally opposed to the mode of redress adopted by the colonies. Anxious to preserve the British connection, he brought forward his plan to secure that end. Under the expectation that that or some other mode of adjustment would be adopted, he was 'weakly led,' he says, 'to sign the non-importation agreement, although he had uniformly opposed it; but in this he was disappointed.'[1] In the discussion of his plan, he declared, according to Mr. Adams' abstract of his speech, that he

---

[1] Candid Examination of the Mutual Claims of Great Britain and the Colonies, by Joseph Galloway. In this performance he gives the following statement of the fate of his scheme. 'The plan read and warmly seconded by several gentlemen of the first abilities, after a long debate, was so far approved as to be thought worthy of further consideration, and referred, under a rule for that purpose, by a majority of the colonies. Under this promising aspect of things, and an expectation that the rule would have been regarded, or at least that something rational would take place to reconcile our unhappy differences, the member proposing it was weakly led to sign the non-importation agreement, although he had uniformly opposed it; but in this he was disappointed. The measures of independence and sedition were soon after preferred to those of harmony and liberty, and no argument, however reasonable and just, could prevail on a majority of the colonies to desert them.'

was as much a friend of liberty as existed; and 'no man,' he said, 'shall go further in point of fortune or in point of blood, than the man who now addresses you.' His plan, however, being rejected, and measures pursued which he disapproved, he got himself excused, in the following year, from further service in Congress, and retired to his country-seat in Bucks county. Here he remained until the year 1776, when he openly joined the British standard, at New York. Whether the image of thirteen disunited, jealous, and festering democracies, which played before the imaginations of some of his contemporaries, and made them willing to endure present ills rather than incur the supposed consequences of colonial success, equally disturbed and alarmed his judgment, or whether despair of success in a contest with 'an old and haughty nation, proud in arms,' supplied the motive of his conduct, we cannot now determine. Galloway was a man of cold and calculating nature. He was a good hater, a character Dr. Johnson is said to have admired. His acquirements were solid, and his talents admirably well adapted for affairs. Native greatness of soul, a noble spirit of self-sacrifice, the distinguishing mark and sustaining power of the patriot, he did not possess. The natural proclivity of such a man would be to the side of power. The immediate motive, however, of his seeking British protection, was apprehension of mob violence.

We think it must be admitted that, in the case of Galloway, there was no sudden and unexpected change of sides. Before the Congress of 1774, his position was well understood. He became a member of that body with a well-defined purpose. His object, avowed to the Assembly of Pennsylvania, and approved by them, was to establish the union between the mother country and her colonies upon a firm and lasting basis. His support of the measures adopted by the Congress cannot fairly be deemed inconsistent with the views he then entertained. He supported those measures as a means to an end, viz., to procure the adoption of his plan of union. *Per se*, and standing alone, he condemned them. He openly declared his sentiments to that effect, on the floor of Congress. But as an expedient, and in the state of public sentiment at the time, he might very properly waive his objections, and lend his name and voice to a line of policy which his judgment disapproved. 'I cannot stand forward, and give praise or blame to anything which relates to human actions and human concerns, on a simple view of the object, as it stands stripped of every relation, in all the nakedness and solitude of metaphysical abstraction. Circumstances (which with some gentlemen pass for nothing) give in reality to every political principle its distinguishing color and discriminating effect. The circumstances are what render every civil and political scheme beneficial or noxious to mankind.'[1] Galloway was not the only member of the Congress who supported its measures, and finally adhered to the royal side. Isaac Low, of New York, pursued the same course. In truth, the position of Galloway was occupied by numbers of pure and honorable men in every colony. They started back with horror from the abyss of revolution. If their motives are not to be distrusted, whatever may be our opinion of their sagacity, neither should Galloway's.

From the man we now turn to his work. And we are bound to say, that considering the aspect of affairs, and the plan itself, we can discover in the one nor the other neither feature nor complexion which should have forbid a patriot to propose such a mode of adjustment, or a patriot to support it. It did not, it is true, touch existing legislation. It was doubtless the hope of its

---

[1] Burke.

advocates that, in conjunction with the other measures adopted by Congress, it would procure a repeal of the obnoxious acts of Parliament. It would have tended to that result, by removing the impression from the English mind, that the colonies intended to throw off the British connection. Its supporters believed that the interests of the two countries would be subserved by preserving that connection. In that they erred. But such being their opinion, Mr. Galloway's plan seemed eminently fitted to attain the end they had in view. Whether a more intimate union of the two countries was desirable, upon the supposition that union on some terms was to continue, was a grave question, which Mr. Galloway's plan of adjustment and reconciliation directly involved.

It proposed a British and American legislature for the administration of the general affairs of the colonies, to be composed of a President-General, appointed by the king, and a Grand Council, to be chosen once in every three years by the representatives of the people of the several colonies in their respective assemblies. The Grand Council were to choose their Speaker, and hold and exercise all the like rights, liberties, and privileges as were vested in the House of Commons of Great Britain. The President-General was to hold his office during the pleasure of the king. His assent was requisite to all the acts of the Grand Council, and it was his special duty to cause them to be executed. He was also, by and with the advice and consent of the Grand Council, to hold and exercise all the legislative rights, powers, and authorities necessary for regulating and administering all the general police and affairs of the colonies in which Great Britain and the colonies, or any of them, the colonies in general, or more than one colony, should be in any manner concerned, whether of a civil, criminal, or commercial nature. The President-General, and the Grand Council, were to constitute an inferior and distinct branch of the British legislature, united and incorporated with it for the general purposes we have mentioned; and any measure having any one of those objects in view, could originate, be formed and digested either in the Parliament of Great Britain, or in the Grand Council of the colonies; but whether originated in the one or the other, the assent of both was requisite to its validity. In time of war, however, all bills for granting aids to the Crown, prepared by the Grand Council and approved by the President-General, were to be deemed valid without the assent of the British Parliament. Within and under this colonial Government, each colony was to retain its present constitution and powers of regulating and governing its own internal police in all cases whatever.

Mr. Galloway made a very elaborate speech in vindication of his plan. He was a 'sensible and learned, but cold speaker.'[1]

He commenced by adverting to the remedies which had been adopted, or were contemplated by the Congress, and condemned them as unsuited to the exigencies of affairs, and as likely to prove injurious to themselves. He thought non-importation would be too gradual in its operation for the relief of Boston. 'A general non-exportation,' he said, 'I have ever looked on as an undigested proposition. It is impossible America can exist under a total non-exportation. We, in this province, should have tens of thousands of people thrown upon the cold hand of charity. Our ships would lie by the walls, our seamen would be thrown out of bread, our shipwrights, &c., out of employ, and it would affect the landed interest. It would weaken us in another struggle which I fear is too near.' He referred to the history of the stamp-act, and the authority which Great Britain claimed over the

---

[1] Adams.

colonies. 'Without some supreme legislature, some common arbiter, you are not, say they, part of the state.' His plan supplied that common arbiter. He denied that the colonies were comprehended within the circle of the supreme jurisdiction of the Parliament; they were independent states. 'The law of Great Britain,' he said, 'does not bind us in any case whatever. We want the aid, and assistance, and protection of the arm of our mother country. Protection and allegiance are reciprocal duties. Can we lay claim to the money and protection of Great Britain upon any principle of honor and conscience? Can we wish to become aliens to the mother state? We must come upon terms with Great Britain.'[1]

Mr. Galloway was followed by Mr. Duane of New York, who supported his proposition. In desiring a Congress, New York had a two-fold object; namely, the relief of

---

[1] The following is Mr. Adams' summary of Mr. Galloway's closing effort, which appears to have ended the debate.

Mr. Galloway. In every Government, patriarchal, monarchal, aristocratical, or democratical, there must be a supreme legislature.

I know of no American constitution; a Virginia constitution, a Pennsylvania constitution, we have: we are totally independent of each other.

Every gentleman here thinks the Parliament ought to have the power over trade, because Britain protects it and us. Why then will we not declare it?

Because Parliament and Ministry is wicked and corrupt, and will take advantage of such declaration to tax us, and will also reason from this acknowledgment to further power over us.

Answer. We shall not be bound further than we acknowledge it. Is it not necessary that the trade of the empire should be regulated by some power or other? Can the empire hold together without it? No. Who shall regulate it? Shall the legislature of Nova Scotia or Georgia regulate it? Massachusetts, or Virginia? Pennsylvania, or New York? It can't be pretended. Our legislative powers extend no further than the limits of our Governments. Where, then, shall it be placed? There is a necessity that an American legislature should be set up, or else that we should give the power to Parliament or King.' Works, vol. ii., p. 390.

Boston, and the adoption of a plan which would secure a lasting accommodation with Great Britain. Congress had departed from the contemplated purpose of their assembling, and he was unhappy that they had done so. He thought justice required that the right of regulating trade should be expressly ceded to Parliament.

Richard Henry Lee was opposed to any change in the ancient relations of the two countries. Under the old mode, for a hundred and sixty years, the colonies had flourished and grown. Restore affairs to the ground on which they had stood anterior to the year 1763, and he was content. Mr. Galloway's plan would make such changes in the legislature of the colonies, that he could not agree to it without consulting his constituents.

Mr. Jay, we have already observed, was in favor of this plan. He could not contemplate, without solicitude, the possible dismemberment of that vast empire, beneath whose shade, in spite of restriction and monopoly, the colonies had attained to their present growth and importance. For the redress of existing wrongs, he had assented to such measures of reprisal as were thought to be effectual for that purpose. He had assented to a non-importation, non-consumption, and non-exportation agreement.[1] He would now lay the corner-stone of the temple of peace. He would bind the colonies to the mother country in an indissoluble union. Mr. Galloway's plan was propitious to that end: it did not give up any one

[1] On Friday, the 30th day of September, Congress adopted the following resolution. Resolved: That from and after the 10th day of September, 1775, the exportation of all merchandise and every commodity whatsoever to Great Britain, Ireland, and the West Indies, ought to cease, unless the grievances of America are redressed before that time. On the 6th of October, a clause was added to the non-importation resolution, including, from and after the 1st day of the following December, molasses, coffee, and pimento from the British plantations and Dominica, and wines from Madeira and the Western Islands, and foreign indigo.

liberty, or interfere with any one right, and he was therefore led to adopt it. Such was his position.

Among the most vehement opponents of any change in the original relations of the colonies to the mother country, was Virginia's great orator, Patrick Henry. He could discover nothing in the proposed plan of union that promised to ameliorate the condition of the colonies. 'We shall liberate our constituents,' he exclaimed, 'from a corrupt House of Commons, but throw them into the arms of an American legislature that may be bribed by that nation, which avows, in the face of the world, that bribery is a part of her system of government. Before we are obliged to pay taxes as they do, let us be as free as they; let us have our trade open with all the world. We are not to consent by the representatives of representatives.' The whole force of his ardent nature was aroused against Mr. Galloway's plan, and, as if its advocates were inseparable from the plan itself, he seems, for the moment, to have regarded both with equal and impartial aversion. Mr. Adams, in his diary of October the 11th, has recorded an interview with Mr. Henry, in the course of which the latter spoke with great freedom both of himself, and the prominent supporters of the important measure then pending. 'Spent the evening,' he says, 'with Mr. Henry, at his lodgings, consulting about a petition to the King. Henry said he had no public education; at fifteen he read Virgil and Livy, and has not looked into a Latin book since. His father left him at that age, and he has been struggling through life ever since. He has high notions, talks about exalted minds, &c. He has a horrid opinion of Galloway, Jay, and the Rutledges. Their system, he says, would ruin the cause of America. He is very impatient to see such fellows, and not be at liberty to describe them in their true colors.'[1] Insisting upon a restoration of the old order of

[1] Life and Works, vol. ii., p. 396.

things, and content with that original condition, it was natural that Mr. Henry, with his strong and fervid feelings, should have denounced a measure proposing a different object, and entertained a momentary resentment against its supporters. Mr. Galloway's plan, as we have already mentioned, was defeated but by a single vote.

On the 11th day of October, Mr. Lee, Mr. Jay, and Mr. Livingston, were appointed a committee to prepare the draught of a memorial to the people of British America, and an address to the people of Great Britain. 'It was agreed in the committee,' says Mr. Jay in a letter giving an account of this transaction,[1] 'that Mr. Lee should prepare a draught of the proposed memorial, which was the first both in order and importance; and that I should prepare a draught of the proposed address to the people of Great Britain; both of which were done accordingly.' If the task assigned to Mr. Jay was deemed less important than the other, the manner of its performance attracted to it greater attention, and, in the eyes of posterity, it has assumed the superior place. Mr. Jay brought the whole force of his mind to the composition of that celebrated paper; he gave to it his undivided thought and attention.[2] On the 18th day of October, it

[1] This extract is taken from a letter of Mr. Jay's to the grandson of Richard Henry Lee, and is published in the Appendix to the first volume of the life of the latter, pp. 270, 271. The unaffected modesty of Mr. Jay, and the utter inability of his nature to glorify his own acts, are conspicuous throughout the whole of it. In another letter upon this subject, written to Mr. Adams, Mr. Jay says, 'Mr Livingston, who was my superior both in age and reputation, was desired to prepare the *address*. He declined it, and urged me to take it. I finally consented, and did write it.' Life and Correspondence, vol. ii., p. 382. Mr. Jay here refers to what took place in the committee.

[2] His son mentions, that 'to secure himself from interruption, he left his lodgings, and shut himself up in a room in a tavern, and there composed that celebrated state paper; not less distinguished for its lofty sentiments than for the glowing language in which they are expressed.' Life of John Jay, vol. i., p. 30.

was reported to Congress. On the 19th it was discussed paragraph by paragraph, and sundry amendments made. It was then recommitted, in order that the amendments might be taken in. On the 21st it was returned to Congress, and the amendments directed being made, the whole was approved.

The authorship of this address made Mr. Jay universally known to his countrymen. It is one of his many titles to the grateful recollection of his country. In all respects, it is an admirable production. It is characterized throughout for its manly tone, its eloquent and forcible statement, its earnest and fearless expostulation. To insure the perusal of the whole, we have only to lay before the reader a single extract. It presents the question of taxation in the following manner: 'Are not the proprietors of the soil of Great Britain lords of their own property? Can it be taken from them without their own consent? Will they yield it to the arbitrary disposal of any man or number of men whatever. You know they will not. Why, then, are the proprietors of the soil of America less lords of their property than you are of yours? Or why should they submit it to the disposal of your Parliament or any other Parliament or Council in the world not of their election? Can the intervention of the sea that divides us cause disparity in rights? Or can any reason be given why *English* subjects, who live three thousand miles from the Royal Palace, should enjoy less liberty than those who are three hundred miles distant from it? Reason looks with indignation on such distinctions, and freemen can never perceive their propriety. And yet, however chimerical and unjust such discriminations are, the Parliament assert that they have a right to bind us in all cases, without exception, whether we consent or not; that they may take and use our property when and in what manner they please; that we are pensioners on their bounty for all that we possess, and can hold it no longer than they vouchsafe to permit. Such declarations we consider as heresies in *English* politics, and which can no more operate to deprive us of our property, than the interdicts of the Pope can divest kings of sceptres which the laws of the land and the voice of the people have placed in their hands. At the conclusion of the late war—a war rendered glorious by the abilities and integrity of a minister to whose efforts the *British* empire owes its safety and its fame — at the conclusion of this war, which was succeeded by an inglorious peace, formed under the auspices of a minister of principles, and of a family unfriendly to the Protestant cause and inimical to liberty; we say at this period, and under the influence of that man, a plan for enslaving your fellow-subjects in *America* was concerted, and has ever since been pertinaciously carrying into execution. Prior to this era, you were content with drawing from us the wealth produced by our commerce. You restrained our trade in every way that could conduce to your emolument. You exercised unbounded sovereignty over the sea. You named the ports and nations to which alone our merchandise should be carried, and with whom alone we should trade; and though some of these restrictions were grievous, we nevertheless did not complain. We looked up to you as to our parent state, to which we were bound by the strongest ties, and were happy in being instrumental to your prosperity and your grandeur. We call upon you yourselves to witness our loyalty and attachment to the common interest of the whole empire. Did we not, in the last war, add all the strength of this vast continent to the force which repelled the common enemy? Did we not leave our native shores, and meet disease and death, to promote the success of *British* arms in foreign climates? Did you not thank us for our zeal, and even reimburse us large sums of money which you confessed we had advanced beyond our proportion, and far beyond our abilities? You did. To what causes, then, are we to attribute the sudden change of treatment, and that system of slavery which was prepared for us at the restoration of peace?'

"The question, 'who was the draughtsman of the address to the people of England?'" says Mr. Adams, "however unimportant to the public it may appear at this day, certainly excited a sensation, a fermentation, and a schism in Congress at the time, and serious consequences afterward, which have lasted to this hour, and are not yet spended. I fear, but I do not know, that this animosity was occasioned by indiscretions of Richard Henry Lee, Mr. Samuel Adams, and some others of the Virginia delegates, by whom Adams was led into error."[1] In reply to the letter containing this extract, Mr. Jay says, 'The subsequent occurrences you mention, have not escaped my recollection. I was informed, and I believe correctly, that one person in particular of those you specify,[2] had endeavored, by oblique intimations, to insinuate a suspicion that the address to the people of Great Britain was not written by me, but by Governor Livingston. That gentleman repelled the insinuation. He knew and felt what was due to truth, and explicitly declared it. Those persons are dead and gone. Their design did not succeed, and I have no desire that the memory of it should survive them.'[3]

The schism which Mr. Adams refers to, must have occurred in the Congress of the next year. At that time a coolness, not to say an enmity, had sprung up between Mr. Jay and Mr. Lee. They did not accord in their

---

[1] See a letter of Mr. Adams to Mr. Jay, on the appearance of Wirt's Life of Patrick Henry, dated January 9th, 1818, in the second volume of the Life and Works of John Jay, p. 380.

[2] Richard Henry Lee is here doubtless referred to.

[3] Life and Works of John Jay, vol. ii., p. 383. The letter which we have quoted from is dated January 31st, 1818.

political views, and besides, Mr. Lee was prejudiced against Mr. Jay by his brother, the bold, sincere, and fearless patriot, but suspicious, meddlesome, and choleric Arthur Lee.[1] We do not mean to insinuate that any feeling of dislike on the part of Mr. Lee would have led him to do Mr. Jay intentional injustice. As the arrangement, however, was made in committee, that Mr. Jay should write the address to the people of Great Britain, Mr. Lee could not be ignorant of that fact. It is no wonder, therefore, that Mr. Jay was indignant when informed that Mr. Lee had intimated that he was not the author of that celebrated paper. It touched him in a sensitive point. It was indirectly calling in question his capacity as well as his honesty; because if Mr. Lee's supposition was correct, he was wearing laurels that belonged to another. We think Mr. Lee was wrong, for although it might not have seemed improbable that Mr. Jay and Mr. Livingston subsequently made a different arrangement from the one in committee, it would have been better if Mr. Lee had made proper inquiries as to the fact, before expressing an opinion. But unintentionally wrong as we deem him to have been in this matter, wrong and groundless as were the suspicions which his brother had instilled into his mind, we nevertheless do willing honor to his memory. His signal services in the cause of his country, services equally efficient in the result and graceful in the performance, challenge the homage of every true American heart.

Mr. Wirt, in his Life of Patrick Henry, either from the defective recollection of his informant, or some lapse in his own, has fallen into one or two errors respecting the address to the people of Great Britain. It is due alike to Mr. Jay and Mr. Lee that we should notice them. As an evidence of the inequality between the public

[1] See Life and Works of John Adams, vol. iii., p. 5. See the next chapter as to rumors in London respecting the New York delegates.

efforts of Henry and Lee, and their labors in committee, Mr. Wirt gives the following account of the petition to the King, and the address to the people of Great Britain:[1] 'A petition to the king, an address to the people of Great Britain, and a memorial to the people of British America, was agreed to be drawn. Mr. Lee, Mr. Henry, and others, were appointed for the first; Mr. Lee, Mr. Livingston, and Mr. Jay for the two last. The splendor of their *debut* occasioned Mr. Henry to be designated by his committee to draw the petition to the king, with which they were charged; and Mr. Lee was charged with the address to the people of England. The last was first reported. On reading it, great disappointment was expressed on every countenance, and a dead silence ensued for some minutes. At length it was laid on the table, for perusal and consideration, till the next day, when first one member, and then another arose, and paying some faint compliment to the composition, observed that there were still certain considerations not expressed which should properly find a place in it. The address was therefore committed for amendment; and one prepared by Mr. Jay, and offered by Governor Livingston, was reported and adopted with scarcely an alteration. These facts are stated by a gentleman to whom they were communicated by Mr. Pendleton, and Mr. Harrison of the Virginia delegation, (except that Mr. Harrison erroneously ascribed the draught to Governor Livingston,) and to whom they were afterwards confirmed by Governor Livingston himself.[2] Mr. Henry's draught of a petition to the king was equally unsuccessful, and was re-committed for amendments.'

The whole of the foregoing statement, so far as it connects Mr. Lee with the authorship of the address to the

---

[1] Life of Patrick Henry, p. 108, 109.

[2] The gentleman here referred to is probably Mr. Jefferson.

people of Great Britain, is unfounded. We have already given the true history of that transaction, as communicated by Mr. Jay himself. The memorial to the people of British America was drawn up by Mr. Lee, was reported to Congress on the 19th, was debated by paragraphs, and approved without re-commitment or amendment, on the 21st. The latter fact does not, perhaps, imply superior merit in the composition, but it does indicate a wise appreciation and selection of topics, leaving nothing to be suggested or supplied.

Mr. Wirt is equally mistaken with respect to the petition to the king. The original draught was not drawn by Mr. Henry, but by Mr. Lee. And here doubtless is the source of Mr. Wirt's erroneous statement. He probably confounds two distinct transactions. The circumstances which he relates might possibly have attended the report of the petition to the king, but they could not have arisen from the cause which he assigns. The surprise or disappointment on the countenances of the members, of which he speaks, was not occasioned by any want of vigor or pretension in the important paper to which they were listening, but from the excess of those qualities. Mr. Lee's draught 'was disapproved because it did not manifest sufficiently that spirit of conciliation which then animated Congress.'[1] The draught which was finally approved, was from the pen of Mr. Dickenson, who was added to the committee upon the re-commitment of their report. Whether Mr. Lee's draught was thrown wholly aside, which would have been an invidious proceeding, or whether Mr. Dickenson retained its substance and modified its tone to suit the tenor of his own views and the prevailing ones of Congress, is not known. The latter hypothesis would seem the most probable.

---

[1] Marshall's Life of Washington, vol. iv., p. 627.

That Mr. Lee was more eminent for oratory than authorship, is undoubtedly true. It is equally true of more celebrated names than his — of Chatham, Mirabeau, and Fox. This might have arisen partly from natural causes, and partly from neglecting composition as an art. His style, however, is not deficient either in grace or force. It is by no means universally nor necessarily true, that success as an orator implies talents incompatible with success as an author. Demosthenes, 'whose resistless eloquence, wielded at will that fierce democratie, shook the arsenal, and fulmined over Greece,' carefully elaborated his orations, in the solitude of his study. Cicero is a conspicuous example of genius triumphant equally in written and spoken eloquence. His pen was not less effective than his tongue. Burke is an example, not of the orator failing of success as an author, but an author discovering too much of his art in his oratory. His speeches were too refined, too much in the style of a professor's disquisition, although afar off and infinitely superior, to suit the coarser taste of eager and impatient partisans. Yet that he was an orator, as well as a profound, philosophic, and variously accomplished statesman, no one will doubt who is familiar with his career. During the early part of his service in the House of Commons, he was heard with signal applause. Even at a later period, when the contests and disappointments of an eventful public life had rendered him imperious and irascible, and faults of manner had grown upon him, he rose occasionally into the highest strains of oratory.

Madame D'Arblay, who was present at the trial of Warren Hastings, and shared the friendly feelings of the royal family towards the prisoner, confesses that the first part of Burke's speech interested, engaged, and at last overpowered her; 'not another wish in his favor remained.'[1] The testimony of Hastings himself is conclusive as to the power of that celebrated oration.

Excellence, however, in either written or spoken eloquence, is the result of training more or less severe, according to the writer's or speaker's natural capacity or aptitude. As between the two, the former must undergo longer vigils and severer discipline. The orator derives his stimulus from without, the author from within. The faculties of the one are aroused by the presence, attention, and expectation of his audience. The pressure of the occasion concentrates and calls them into activity. 'The orator feels the impulse of popular enthusiasm,

— Like proud seas under him.

The only Pegasus the writer has to boast is the hobby-horse of his own thoughts and fancies.' It is only by patient effort and long training that his mind becomes subject to his control, and moves in harmony with his powers of expression. His stimulus is in the 'difficulty of his subject, and the progressive nature of his task.' Whoever aspires to the double, but not conflicting honors of oratory and authorship, must submit to the discipline pre-requisite to success in either. There is no royal road to the temple of fame.

We have shown the errors of Mr. Wirt's statement with respect to Mr. Lee's connection with the address to the people of Great Britain, and from evidence of the highest authority — that of Mr. Jay himself. The gentleman to whom Mr. Wirt refers as his informant, was doubtless Mr. Jefferson, for the anecdote from the pen of the latter, which we are about to relate, gives substantially the same account of that transaction. Speaking of the Congress of 1775, Mr. Jefferson says, "I took my seat with them on the 21st of June. On the 24th, a

---

[1] Diary and Letters, vol. ii., pp. 58, 59.

committee which had been appointed to prepare a declaration of the causes of taking up arms, brought in their report, (drawn, I believe, by John Rutledge,) which, not being liked, the House re-committed it on the 26th, and added Mr. Dickenson and myself to the committee. On the rising of the House, the committee having not yet met, I happened to find myself near Governor W. Livingston, and proposed to him to draw the paper. He excused himself, and proposed that I should draw it. On my pressing him with urgency, 'we are as yet but new acquaintances, Sir,' said he, 'why are you so earnest for my doing it?' 'Because,' said I, 'I have been informed that you drew the address to the people of Great Britain, a production certainly of the finest pen in America.' 'On that,' said he, 'perhaps, Sir, you may not have been correctly informed.' I had received the information, in Virginia, from Colonel Harrison, on his return from that Congress. Lee, Livingston, and Jay had been the committee for that draught. The first, prepared by Lee, had been disapproved and re-committed. The second was drawn by Jay, but being presented by Governor Livingston, had led Colonel Harrison into the error. The next morning, walking in the hall of Congress, many members being assembled but the House not yet formed, I observed Mr. Jay speaking to R. H. Lee, and leading him by the button of his coat to me. 'I understand, Sir,' said he to me, 'that this gentleman informed you that Governor Livingston drew the address to the people of Great Britain.' I assured him at once that I had not received that information from Mr. Lee, and that not a word had ever passed on that subject between Mr. Lee and myself; and after some explanations, the subject was dropped. These gentlemen had had some sparrings in debate before, and continued ever very hostile to each other."[1]

[1] Jefferson's Works, vol. i., p. 8.

We need not notice that part of the foregoing anecdote which attributes the first draught of the address to the people of Great Britain to the pen of Mr. Lee. We have already shown that to be founded in error. As to the other part, which relates the scene between Mr. Jay and Mr. Lee, we were at first inclined to believe that, while it was substantially correct in the detail of facts, it was substantially wrong in the impression it left on the mind of the reader; that it gave the form and features of the transaction, but not its living expression. But Mr. Jefferson is indirectly confirmed by Mr. Adams. 'Mr. Lee,' says Mr. Adams, 'had expressed doubts whether Mr. Jay had composed the address to the people of Great Britain, and ascribed it to his father-in-law, Mr. Livingston, afterwards Governor of New Jersey. These things had occasioned some words and animosities, which, uniting with the great questions in Congress, had some disagreeable effects. Mr. Jay's great superiority to Mr. Livingston in the art of composition, would now be sufficient to decide the question if the latter had not expressly denied having any share in that address.'[1] The doubts expressed by Mr. Lee had reached the ears of Mr. Jay. He says himself, in the letter to Mr. Adams from which we have quoted, that he had been informed that Mr. Lee, 'by oblique intimations,' had insinuated that he was not the author of the address. He was naturally exasperated; and, attributing Mr. Jefferson's erroneous information to Mr. Lee, he might have used but little ceremony in the means he employed to contradict it.

On the 26th day of October, the Congress concluded their labors. They had adopted resolutions defining their rights and the foundation of them. They had declared the several instances in which, during the present reign,

---

[1] Life and Works, vol. iii., pp. 5, 6.

those rights had been violated. For the redress of their wrongs, they had entered into a non-importation, non-consumption, and non-exportation agreement or association. They had prepared an address to the people of Great Britain, a memorial to the inhabitants of British America, and a petition to the King. They hoped that these measures would prove successful, and 'restore them to that state in which both countries found happiness and prosperity.' But if 'intemperately, unwisely, fatally,' the mother country persevered in her course of measures, as wise men, looking before and after, the Congress had provided for that possible contingency. They had adopted a resolution declaring that, in their opinion, it would be necessary that a Congress should be held on the 10th day of the following May, unless the grievances of which they complained should be redressed before that time.[1]

[1] The following anecdote from the pen of Mr. Adams will show that the opinion was by no means unanimous that the measures of Congress would insure relief from the obnoxious legislation of the mother country. "When Congress," he says, "had finished their business, as they thought, in the autumn of 1774, I had, with Mr. Henry, before we took leave of each other, some familiar conversation, in which I expressed a full conviction that all our resolves, declarations of rights, enumerations of wrongs, petitions and remonstrances, addresses, associations, and non-importation agreements, though they might be expected by the people of America, and necessary to cement their union, would be but waste paper in England. He thought they might be of some use among the people of England, but would be totally lost upon the Government. I had just received a hasty letter, written to me by Major Joseph Hawley, of Northampton, containing 'a few broken hints,' as he called them, of what was proper to be done, and concluding with these words: 'After all, we must fight!' This letter I read to Mr. Henry, who listened to it with great attention, and as soon as I pronounced the words, 'After all, we must fight,' he erected his head, and with an energy and vehemence that I can never forget, broke out with, '*By G—, I am of that man's mind!*' I put the letter into his hand, and when he had read it, he returned it to me with an equally solemn asseveration that he agreed entirely in opinion with the writer. I considered this to be a sacred oath upon a very great occasion. I could have sworn it as religiously

The prudence and firmness which had been displayed by this body of patriots, under circumstances the most delicate and arduous, deserved and received the unanimous commendation of their friends in England. Referring to their proceedings, Lord Chatham, in the House of Lords, bestowed upon them an encomium, which, however it might run counter to the voice of a partial and exasperated majority, nevertheless bespoke the solemn judgment of history. 'When your lordships,' he said, 'look at the papers transmitted to us from America; when you consider their decency, firmness, and wisdom; you cannot but respect their cause, and wish to make it your own. For myself, I must declare and avow, that in all my reading and observation, and it has been my favorite study—I have read Thucydides, and have studied and admired the master states of the world — that for solidity of reasoning, force of sagacity, and wisdom of conclusion, under such complication of circumstances, no nation or body of men can stand in preference to the General Congress at Philadelphia.'

---

as he did. It was no contradiction to what you say in some part of your book, that he never took the name of God in vain." See Kennedy's Memoirs of William Wirt, vol. ii., p. 47.

CHAPTER VI.

1774—1776.

PROCEEDINGS IN NEW YORK, AND THE CONGRESS OF 1775 AND '76.

MR. Jay returned to his constituents from the Congress, with enlarged experience and enhanced reputation. Strong before in the confidence of the moderate party, he now received the thanks and approval of the more ultra.[1] The ministry had been led to believe that the delegates from New York would not lend their aid to what were termed rash and violent measures.[2] Indeed, in London it was 'confidently said, and universally believed,' that they had sent out large sums of money to bribe the continental delegates. 'It was openly avowed and vindicated, and great boast was made of ministerial success. It was said that they had effected a disunion which would be fatal to the cause of all America.'[3] How

---

[1] American Archives, 4th series, vol. i., p. 987. See letter from the Committee of Mechanics to the New York delegates, and their reply.

[2] The Earl of Dartmouth writes to Lieutenant-Governor Colden, under date of November 2d, 1774, and referring to the information which the former had communicated to him respecting the election in New York, he says, 'From the accounts you give of the characters and tempers of the five gentlemen appointed by the city of New York to be their delegates to the general Congress, I should suppose they would not be likely to support rash and violent measures; but there is too much reason to fear that the majority of delegates are of a different complexion.' Force's American Archives, vol. i., p. 953.

[3] Letters of Josiah Quincy, Jr., from London, to his wife and Joseph Reed, Esq., under the respective dates of December 16th and December 17th, 1774. Memoir of J. Quincy, pp. 272–275. In his letter to Reed, Quincy says, 'The information you give relative to the New York

fully the conduct of Mr. Jay and his colleagues vindicated their honor and integrity, the whole country beheld with delight; while those who counted on a different course of action, were filled with mortification. 'You cannot well imagine the chagrin,' says Quincy, 'with which the ministry received the result of that glorious body.'[1]

In New York, the address to the people of Great Britain was looked upon 'as one of the finest pieces of calm and cool reasoning which had appeared in America.'[2] Many gentlemen throughout the province had it, together with the resolves and other proceedings of the Congress, 'elegantly printed, framed, and glazed.'[3] It confirmed the previous impression of Mr. Jay's abilities in his own colony, and made them known throughout the others. But along with increased reputation comes increased responsibility. In the present chapter we shall see in what manner Mr. Jay performed the high and grave duties that devolved upon him, from the close of the Congress of '74, to his temporary withdrawal from that body in the year 1776.

Mr. Jay had affixed his name to the non-importation and non-consumption association. To organize the means of enforcing it, was the first business to be done. Congress had recommended the appointment of committees

---

defection, was the least we expected. The ministry, it is confidently said and universally believed, has been lavish of means in that quarter to foment discord. Nay, their setters and tools have made great vaunts of unexampled success with the great men of that city. Our coffee-houses were lately filled with scoffs at American virtue, and they boasted of success in creating a fatal disunion in our great Sanhedrim with a confidence that gained much credit. Did you but know the chagrin that took place on the arrival of the result of the Congress, it would gratify your keenest sensations'

[1] Ibid: Letter to his wife.

[2] American Archives, vol. i., p. 969. A letter from a gentleman in New York to his correspondent in London.

[3] Ibid.

in every county, city, and town, to observe the conduct of all persons with regard to it, to the end that all violators of it might be made known, and universally contemned as the enemies of American liberty. The Committee of Fifty-one at once notified a meeting of the freeholders and freemen of the city, to elect a committee of inspection, to consist of eight fit persons in each ward, to effect the contemplated object. This notification seems to have given great offence; for what reason, I have been unable to discover, but probably because it was considered that since the action of Congress, the proper occupation of the committee was at an end. Difficulties arose which led to a conference with the committee of mechanics. Upon consultation, it was mutually agreed that a committee of not less than sixty persons should be chosen, to continue in office until the 1st day of the following July. The election was held on the 22d day of November. A committee, previously nominated, and including among its numbers Mr. Jay and the other delegates to the Congress, were chosen, and without a dissenting voice. No record of the proceedings of this committee appears to have been preserved. There seems to have been little occasion for the summary employment of its authority. For while the measures of Congress interdicting trade were but little relished by the merchants of New York, and their utility 'flatly denied,'[1] they nevertheless very generally observed them. In the disorders of an opening revolution, when Government is tottering on its base, and power is returning to its original source, the very excesses into which a people thus situated are prone to fall, tend to hold in wholesome check the supporters of old abuses, and the contemners

[1] Life of Peter Van Schaack. Letter to John Jay, dated October 12th, 1774. See also letters of Governor Colden to the Earl of Dartmouth. American Archives, 4th series, vol. i., pp. 820, 957, 1030.

of the new order of things. Congress had no power to enforce its measures. It did not arrogate it. It only recommended. But the moral force of its recommendation was irresistible. The violators of the non-importation association were liable to no legal penalty. The only punishment that the Congress suggested, was the exposure of their names. That was sufficient. No man willingly incurs disgrace or popular vengeance.

The Parliament adhering to its measures, and the Colonial Assembly, which met on the 10th day of January, 1775, refusing to consider the proceedings of the last Congress or appoint delegates to the coming one, it became necessary for the committee to provide for that event. They accordingly requested the freemen and freeholders of the city and county of New York to assemble at the Exchange on the 6th day of March, at twelve o'clock, to signify their sense of the best method of choosing delegates to the next Congress, &c. On that day, it was determined by a vote of the citizens, but not until after a trial of physical strength between the opposing parties, that the general committee should nominate eleven persons to be proposed to the choice of the freemen and freeholders on the 15th inst., as deputies, to meet on the 20th day of April such deputies as the other counties might elect, for the single purpose of appointing from their own body delegates to the next general Congress.[1] Mr. Jay was one of the persons nominated by the committee.

---

[1] Gordon gives the following account of the 'battle royal' at New York. "The whig citizens," he says, "whose hearts were set upon having delegates for the new continental Congress, upon the Assembly declining to appoint them, contrived to collect their fellow-citizens together, in order to obtain their opinion. When assembled in a body, there was a confused cry of 'Congress, or no Congress?' After much altercation, the tories had a recourse to compulsive reasoning, and began dealing about their blows. The whigs were in the worst situation, not being provided with similar arguments, till two of their party repaired

The action of the committee in this matter was peculiarly obnoxious to the ministerial party. They were in favor of leaving the whole difficulty between the province and the mother country in the hands of the Colonial Assembly. They were therefore opposed to sending delegates to the Congress at all. Besides, they saw in the meeting of deputies from the several counties, the germ of a Provincial Congress, a measure which had been generally adopted by the other colonies, and which they beheld with alarm.

Another party, inclining to the ministerial side, but nevertheless in favor of sending delegates to the approaching Congress, feared that by transferring the election from the city and county of New York to an assembly of deputies from all the counties, their late delegation, in whose prudence and moderation they had confidence, might be defeated. Hence, every artifice was employed to prevent the election of the deputies nominated by the committee. Specious appeals were made to the citizens through the press; but they failed to accomplish their purpose. At the close of the poll on the 15th inst., it was found that the candidates nominated by the committee had received five-sixths of the entire vote.

The Provincial Convention assembled in the city of New York on the 20th day of April, 1775. It consisted of forty-three deputies from the different counties, and continued in session but three days. The late delegation,

---

to an adjoining cooper's yard, from whence they drew forth to the assistance of their friends a number of hoop-sticks, which they reduced to a proper length, and forwarded to the combatants. The whigs being thus supplied, soon carried the day by club-law, and beat their opponents off the ground. The tories, being worsted, and not a little terrified, lest the fury of Captain (whom they term, in a way of reproach, King,) Sears should lead him to head a mob and do them some capital injury, promoted a provincial convention, which otherwise would not have existed. The battle royal will prove the turning point in the colony." History, vol. i., p. 306.

with the exception of Mr. Low, who rendered himself ineligible by declining a seat in the convention, was unanimously re-elected. This was done as expressive of the approbation of the Convention of their conduct, and as a mark of the confidence reposed in them. The Convention also elected five additional delegates, and the next day was dissolved.[1]

On the following day, Sunday, April the 23d, about twelve o'clock, the news reached New York of the battle of Lexington. It occasioned a prodigious excitement. The moderate men were struck with consternation, and the more ardent in the cause were stung with resentment. The gravity of the occasion, the imminence of civil war, the very pressure of the time, served to produce a temporary harmony between the various parties in the city. In the presence of a great danger, minor differences are forgotten. But a harmony resulting from fugitive causes, and not based on common principles and common aims, is as unstable as the shifting sands of the desert.

Three days after, the committee met, and considering that their powers did not extend beyond the objects of the association, they recommended that a new committee be elected by the freeholders and freemen of the city and county, not only for that purpose, but for the present unhappy exigencies of affairs: that it consist of one

[1] American Archives, 4th series, vol. ii., p. 357. Mr. Adams, who had set out to attend the second Congress, on his arrival at Hartford heard of the proceedings in New York. He wrote to his wife from that place, under date of April 30th, 1775. 'New York,' he says, 'has appointed an ample representation in our Congress, and has appointed a Provincial Congress. The people of the city have seized the city arms and ammunition out of the hands of the Mayor, who is a creature of the Governor. Lord North will certainly be disappointed in his expectation of seducing New York. The tories there durst not show their heads. The Jerseys are aroused, and greatly assist the friends of liberty in New York.' Letters of John Adams, p. 36.

hundred members; that thirty-three be a quorum, and that they dissolve within a fortnight after the close of the next Congress. They also resolved that a Provincial Congress ought to be immediately summoned. The need of an authority extending over the province was at once perceived and provided for. The committee mentioned the names of one hundred persons as candidates for the new committee, and directed polls to be opened in each ward, to collect the voice of the citizens with respect to them. Many of the nominees were peculiarly obnoxious to the more zealous portion of the whigs. They were believed to be secret enemies of the cause, and it was deemed impolitic to place in a position of such power and delicacy, men who might betray the trust confided to them. A great excitement arose. Party spirit was evoked. Discord was in the ascendant. The city seemed on the verge of anarchy and interneciary strife. In this alarming crisis, the committee issued an address to the freeholders and freemen of the city and county. 'We regret, gentlemen,' they said, 'the necessity we are under of addressing you upon this occasion, and perceive with anxiety the disorder and confusion into which this city has been unfortunately involved.' To the objections urged against their nominations, the committee say, 'Many, no doubt, have become objects of distrust and suspicion, and, perhaps, not without reason: you have now an opportunity of trying them. It surely can never be good policy to put it out of their power to join us heartily. It is time enough to reject them when they refuse us their aid. In short, gentlemen, consider that our contest is for liberty; and therefore we should be extremely cautious how we permit our struggles to hurry us into acts of violence and extravagance inconsistent with freedom. Permit us to entreat you to consider these matters seriously, and act with temper as well as firmness, and by all means join in the appointment of some committee to whom you may resort for counsel, and who may rescue you from tumult, anarchy, and confusion.' They therefore recommended the appointment of a committee of one hundred, 'to consist of such persons as you, (the freemen and freeholders,) may think most worthy of confidence, and most capable of the arduous task.'

The election took place May 1st, 1775. A committee of one hundred was chosen. Mr. Jay was a member of this, as he had been of the two previous committees.

At the same time, twenty-one deputies to the Provincial Congress, to be holden at New York on Monday, the 22d of May, 1775, were chosen.[1] Mr. Jay's old master, Mr. Kissam, at this time appears upon the stage of affairs. He was elected a member of the committee, and one of the deputies to the Provincial Congress. His fellow-student, Lindley Murray, was also chosen a member of the committee. That portion of the whigs who had kept in the van of opinion, who were the exponents of the ultra sentiments of the party, were ably represented upon the committee by such men as John Morin Scott, M'Dougall, P. B. V. Livingston, Lamb, Sears, Mulligan the patriot tailor and friend of Hamilton, by Hallett, Lispenard, Randall, and others.

The new committee acted with vigor. They called upon the inhabitants to arm and perfect themselves in military discipline. They adopted measures to procure

---

[1] The day after the election, viz., May 2d, 1775, Mr. Adams, who had not yet left Hartford for Philadelphia, writes to his wife the following account of recent occurrences in New York. He could not have long received the news before writing. 'New York has shut up their port, seized the Custom House, arms, ammunition, &c., called a Provincial Congress, and entered into an association to stand by whatever shall be ordered by the Continental and their Provincial Congress. Dr. Cooper is fled on board a man-of-war, and the tories are humbled in the dust.' Letters of John Adams, p. 37.

arms, ammunition, and provisions. They prepared for the worst. At the same time they appointed a committee, of which Mr. Jay was a member, to present an address to the Lieutenant-Governor, assuring him that the committee would at all times 'exert their utmost endeavors to promote good order and support the civil magistrates as far as it should be compatible with the melancholy exigency of the public affairs.'[1] They also sent a circular letter to the several colonies, assuring them of the determination of the inhabitants of the city and county of New York to stand or fall with the freedom of the Continent. Sensible of the friendly sentiments which had hitherto animated the city of London upon the question of colonial rights, the committee addressed a very able and spirited letter to the Lord-Mayor and Corporation.[2] They expressed a confident hope that the cogent motives which they urged, 'a sincere regard to the public weal and the cause of humanity, a hearty desire to spare the further effusion of human blood,' &c., would, 'induce the most vigorous exertions of the city of London to restore union, mutual confidence, and peace to the whole empire.'[3]

After the first few meetings of the committee, Mr. Jay was prevented from further personal participation in their acts by the convening of the second Congress. He repaired to Philadelphia, and took his seat in that body May the 13th. The failure of the measures of the last Congress, the recent effusion of blood at Lexington, the

---

[1] This address was reported to the committee by John Morin Scott, and is probably from his pen. It is a singularly felicitous document, both in point of style and choice of topics.

[2] Wilkes was the Lord-Mayor at this time, and a professed admirer of the conduct of the Americans.

[3] This address was signed by the whole committee. It was probably drawn up by Mr. Kissam. It was reported by him from the sub-committee, which was appointed to prepare it.

spontaneous preparations that were making throughout the colonies for war, the universal resentment that had been awakened by the employment of force on the part of the English, placed the Congress in a situation of infinite difficulty and vast responsibility. The magnitude of the events that had occurred since the adjournment of the last Congress, the measures that had been adopted by the colonies, and the present perilous posture of affairs, all conspired to demand prompt and decisive action. But it was soon discovered that there was a discordance of opinion with respect to the mode of action. The more decided characters of the body would proceed to extremities at once. They would seize the Crown officers throughout the colonies, and hold them as hostages for the security of the people of Boston. They would recommend to the people of all the states to institute Governments for themselves, under their own authority, and that without loss of time; and finally, they would declare the colonies free, sovereign, and independent states. When these capital steps were taken, they would then inform Great Britain that they were ready to enter into negotiations for the redress of grievances.[1]

These measures at first appeared to be agreeable to the general sense of the Congress. It was found, however, that it would be impolitic, if not impossible, to adopt them. New York and Pennsylvania, the central links in the chain of colonies, were not yet prepared, even as an expedient, much less as a final and irrevocable step, to sunder the British connection. The sagacity of their leading men had not yet discovered that remonstrances and petitions would prove wholly vain and ineffectual to change the fixed and steadfast policy of the English Cabinet. Other colonies shared their sentiments and seconded their views. Private and social influences,

[1] Life and Works of John Adams, vol. ii., pp. 406, 407.

employed with 'art and assiduity,' moderated the tone of many of the members.[1] So that whatever might have been the prevailing sense of the Congress when it first convened, it soon became apparent that a declaration of independence and a recommendation to the colonies to form independent Governments, were measures of too vigorous a strain for that body, in its present temper, to adopt. Nevertheless, they proceeded with vigor, and evinced a firm purpose to defend their essential rights.

On the application of the New York delegation for advice and direction as to what conduct the people of New York should observe on the expected arrival of troops at that place, Congress recommended that they should act on the defensive, so long as might be consistent with their safety and security; that the troops should be permitted to remain in the barracks so long as they behaved peaceably and quietly, but that they should not be suffered to erect fortifications, or take any steps for cutting off the communication between the town and country; that if they committed hostilities, or invaded private property, then force should be repelled by force; that the warlike stores should be removed from the town; that places of retreat, in case of necessity, should be provided for the women and children of the city; and a sufficient number of men should be embodied and kept in constant readiness for protecting the inhabitants from insult and injury.

On the 26th day of May, after an animated discussion which had continued several days, it was resolved that, for the purpose of securing and defending the colonies, and preserving them in safety against all attempts to carry the obnoxious acts of Parliament into execution by force of arms, the colonies be immediately put into a state of defence. It was at the same time resolved that an humble and dutiful petition

---

[1] Life and Works of John Adams, vol. ii., pp. 406, 407.

be presented to the King, and that measures be entered into for opening a negotiation to accommodate the unhappy disputes between Great Britain and the colonies; and that this be made a part of the petition to his Majesty. The day previous, Congress had adopted several resolutions for the occupation of military posts in New York, and for the arming and training of her militia. On the 26th, it was recommended to the Provincial Congress of New York to persevere the more vigorously in preparing for their defence, as it was very uncertain whether the earnest endeavors of the Continental Congress to accommodate the differences between the mother country and the colonies by conciliatory measures would prove successful. Committees were appointed to devise ways and means of procuring ammunition and military stores, to estimate the amount of money necessary to be raised, and to prepare rules and regulations for the government of the army. It was voted to raise ten companies of riflemen in Pennsylvania, Maryland, and Virginia, to join the army in Boston. And on the 15th day of June Washington was appointed Commander-in-chief of the forces raised and to be raised in defence of American liberty.[1]

---

[1] The wisdom of this appointment was abundantly justified by the result. But it was not made without opposition. The secret motive of Washington's appointment is disclosed by Mr. Adams. After saying that there was a Southern party against a Northern, and a jealousy against a New England army under the command of a New England General, he proceeds as follows: "Whether this jealousy was sincere, or whether it was mere pride and a haughty ambition of furnishing a Southern General to command a Northern army, I cannot say; but the intention was very visible to me that Colonel Washington was their object, and so many of our staunchest men were in the plan, that we could carry nothing without conceding to it. Another embarrassment which was never publicly known, and which was carefully concealed by those who knew it, the Massachusetts and other New England delegates were divided. Mr. Hancock and Mr. Cushing hung back; Mr. Paine did not come forward, and even Mr. Samuel Adams was irresolute. Mr.

From this brief survey of the general acts of Congress, we recur to the particular services of Mr. Jay. Anxious to secure the co-operation of Canada in the approaching

---

Hancock himself had an ambition to be appointed Commander-in-Chief. Whether he thought an election a compliment due to him, and intended to have the honor of declining it, or whether he would have accepted it, I know not. To the compliment he had some pretensions, for, at that time, his exertions, sacrifices, and general merits in the cause of his country, had been incomparably greater than those of Colonel Washington. But the delicacy of his health, and his entire want of experience in actual service, though an excellent militia officer, were decisive objections to him in my mind. In canvassing this subject out of doors, I found, too, that even among the delegates of Virginia there were difficulties. The apostolical reasonings among themselves which should be greatest, were not less energetic among the saints of the ancient dominion than they were among us of New England. In several conversations, I found more than one very cool about the appointment of Washington, and particularly Mr. Pendleton was very clear and full against it."

The Gordian knot was cut by Mr. Adams making a motion that Congress adopt the army at Cambridge, and appoint a General. He declared his preference for Washington, as 'a gentleman whose skill and experience as an officer, whose independent fortune, great talents, and excellent universal character, would command the approbation of all America, and unite the cordial exertions of all the colonies better than any other person in the Union. Mr. Washington, who happened to sit near the door, as soon as he heard me allude to him, from his usual modesty darted into the Library room. Mr. Hancock, who was our President—which gave me an opportunity to observe his countenance while I was speaking on the state of the colonies, the army at Cambridge, and the enemy — heard me with visible pleasure; but when I came to describe Washington for the Commander, I never remarked a more sudden and striking change of countenance. Mortification and resentment were expressed as forcibly as his face could exhibit them. Mr. Samuel Adams seconded the motion, and that did not soften the President's physiognomy at all. The subject came under debate, and several gentlemen declared themselves against the appointment of Mr. Washington, not on account of any personal objection against him, but because the army were all from New England, had a General of their own, appeared to be satisfied with him, and had proved themselves able to imprison the British army in Boston, which was all they expected or desired at that time. Mr. Pendleton of Virginia, Mr. Sherman of Connecticut, were

contest, Mr. Jay, Mr. Samuel Adams, and Mr. Duane were appointed a committee to prepare a letter to its inhabitants. It was drawn by Mr. Jay, and in a style not unworthy the pen that wrote the address to the people of Great Britain. It represented the ties which bound them to the other colonies, the common ruin which threatened them, and called upon them to join with their sister colonies 'in resolving to be free, and in rejecting with disdain the fetters of slavery, however artfully polished.' It portrayed, in eloquent and forcible language, the condition of that colony under its present form of Government. In a strain of earnest, but rather hyperbolical statement, themselves, their wives, and children, were declared to have been made slaves. After a rapid and striking enumeration of the evils they were exposed to under their existing institutions, the address thus proceeds: 'It cannot be presumed that these considerations will have no weight with you, or that you are so lost to all sense of honor. We can never believe that the present race of Canadians are so degenerated as to possess neither the spirit, the gallantry, nor the courage of their ancestors. You certainly will not permit the infamy and disgrace of such pusillanimity to rest on your own heads, and the consequences of it on your children forever. We, for our parts, are determined to

---

very explicit in declaring this opinion; Mr. Cushing and several others more faintly expressed their opposition and their fears of discontents in the army and in New England. Mr. Paine expressed a great opinion of General Ward and strong friendship for him, having been his classmate at College, or at least his cotemporary; but gave no opinion upon the question. The subject was postponed to a future day. In the meantime, pains were taken out of doors to obtain unanimity, and the voices were generally so clearly in favor of Washington that the dissentient members were persuaded to withdraw their opposition, and Mr. Washington was nominated, I believe by Mr. Thomas Johnson of Maryland, unanimously elected, and the army adopted." Life and Works, vol. ii. pp. 415–419.

live free, or not at all; and are resolved that posterity shall never reproach us with having brought slaves into the world. . . . . As our concern for your welfare entitles us to your friendship, we presume you will not, by doing us injury, reduce us to the disagreeable necessity of treating you as enemies.'[1]

We have seen that Congress, on the 26th of May, resolved to send a petition to the King. This step was not taken without encountering strong opposition. The majority of the body were undoubtedly averse to it. Their last petition had been treated with neglect. Why then sacrifice their self-respect and send another? Besides, it would excite a delusive hope of reconciliation, and delay preparations for the impending struggle. On the other hand, it was contended that it would prove to the world that no proper efforts had been left untried to avert hostilities, and that it would serve to justify the consciences of their own countrymen, in taking up arms against their sovereign.

Foremost among the advocates for the petition were John Dickenson and Mr. Jay. Mr. Dickenson was a native of Maryland, where he was born in the year 1732. He received his academic education in that province; and his professional at Philadelphia, and at the Temple in London. Upon the completion of his legal studies, he established himself in the former city. Both in professional and political life, he took a prominent part. His 'Farmer's Letters' had an extensive circulation, and did immense service. They exposed the fallacy of the distinction between internal and external taxes. They gave Mr. Dickenson a wide reputation. His great wealth, his influential family connections, his pure life, his unsullied integrity, the general opinion of his abilities and services, made him at this time perhaps the most im-

[1] See the address in 'American Archives,' 4th series, vol. ii., p. 1838.

portant character in Pennsylvania. But he was not formed for a crisis. He had no firm, tenacious will, no original, manly, direct, and comprehensive views. He had no deep conceptions. He did not seize upon a subject with a firm grasp, and penetrate to its inmost depth and meaning. He was sensitive to the voice of coteries, and his conduct and opinions responded to that beguiling influence. In peaceful times he was eminently respectable. He was a man of cultivation,

——"Fair spoken and persuading;
Lofty and sour to them that loved him not,
But to those men that sought him, sweet as summer."

He was a good lawyer, and an honest politician. But placed in a different and unaccustomed scene, 'in the confusion of mighty troubles, and on the hinge of great revolutions,' he became timid and irresolute.

Mr. Adams, in describing the state of opinion at the opening of the second Congress, and the means employed by the moderate party to obtain their ends, relates the following anecdote of Mr. Dickenson. "When the party," he says,[1] "had prepared the members of Congress for their purpose, and indeed had made no small impression on three of my own colleagues, Mr. Dickenson made or procured to be made, a motion for a second petition to the King, to be sent by Mr. Richard Penn, who was then bound on a voyage to England. The motion was introduced and supported by long speeches. I was opposed to it of course, and made an opposition to it in as long a speech as I commonly made, not having ever been remarkable for very long harangues, in answer to all the arguments which had been urged. When I sat down, Mr. John Sullivan arose, and began to argue on the same side with me, in a strain of wit, reasoning, and fluency which, although he was always fluent, exceeded every

[1] Life and Works, vol. ii., p. 409.

thing I had ever heard from him before. I was much delighted, and Mr. Dickenson, very much terrified at what he said, began to tremble for his cause. At this moment, I was called out to the State House yard, very much to my regret, to some one who had business with me. I took my hat, and went out of the door of Congress Hall. Mr. Dickenson observed me, and darted out after me. He broke out upon me in a most abrupt and extraordinary manner, in as violent a passion as he was capable of feeling, and with an air, countenance, and gestures as rough and haughty as if I had been a schoolboy, and he the master. He vociferated, 'What is the reason, Mr. Adams, that you New Englandmen oppose our measures of reconciliation? There now is Sullivan, in a long harangue, following you in a determined opposition to our petition to the King. Look ye! if you don't concur with us in our pacific system, I and a number of us will break off from you in New England, and we will carry on the opposition by ourselves in our own way.' I own I was shocked with his magisterial salutation. I knew of no pretensions Mr. Dickenson had to dictate to me, more than I had to catechize him. I was, however, as it happened, at that moment in a very happy temper, and I answered him very coolly: 'Mr. Dickenson, there are many things that I can very cheerfully sacrifice to harmony, and even to unanimity; but I am not to be threatened into an express adoption or approbation of measures which my judgment reprobates. Congress must judge, and if they pronounce against me, I must submit, as, if they determine against you, you ought to acquiesce.' These were the last words which ever passed between Mr. Dickenson and me in private. We continued to debate in Congress upon all questions publicly, with all our usual candor and good humor. But the friendship and acquaintance was lost forever, by an unfortunate accident which must now be explained."

The unfortunate accident to which Mr. Adams here refers, was the interception of his letters by the English. One of them was addressed to General Warren, and contained the following not very flattering allusion to Mr. Dickenson: 'A certain great fortune and piddling genius, whose fame has been trumpeted so loudly, has given a silly cast to our whole doings.'

On the 3d day of June, Mr. Dickenson, Mr. Johnson, Mr. John Rutledge, Mr. Jay, and Dr. Franklin, were appointed a committee to report a petition to the King, in accordance with the previous determination of Congress. It was drawn by Mr. Dickenson, and on the 8th day of July engrossed and signed by all the delegates. Mr. Jefferson gives the following account of it. 'Congress,' he says, 'gave a signal proof of their indulgence to Mr. Dickenson, and of their great desire not to go too fast for any respectable part of our body, in permitting him to draw their second petition to the King according to his own ideas, and passing it with scarcely any amendment. The disgust against its humility was general, and Mr. Dickenson's delight at its passage was the only circumstance which reconciled them to it. The vote being passed, although further observation on it was out of order, he could not refrain from rising and expressing his satisfaction, and concluded by saying, 'There is but one word, Mr. President, in the paper, which I disapprove, and that is the word Congress;' on which Ben. Harrison rose and said, 'There is but one word in the paper, Mr. President, of which I approve, and that is the word Congress.''[1]

Mr. Jay defended the propriety of the petition at the time, and always maintained that it was productive of benefit. It realized the advantages which he had anticipated from it. Its rejection reconciled the people to the

[1] Jefferson's Works, vol. i., p. 9.

declaration of independence, and gave the timid a sufficient argument for taking up arms. Such was Mr. Jay's opinion. Mr. Adams, on the contrary, thought it was an impolitic measure, and followed by very injurious consequences. 'This measure of imbecility,' he says,[1] 'the second petition to the King, embarrassed every exertion of Congress; it occasioned motions and debates without end for appointing committees to draw up a declaration of the causes, motives, and objects of taking arms, with a view to obtain decisive declarations against independence,' &c. Again he says,[2] 'I have always imputed the loss of Charlestown, and of the brave officers and men who fell there, and the loss of a hero of more worth than all the town, I mean General Warren, to Mr. Dickenson's petition to the King, and the loss of Quebec and Montgomery to his subsequent unceasing, though finally unavailing efforts against independence. These impeded and paralyzed all our enterprises. Had our army been acknowledged in season, which acknowledgment ought to have been our first step, and the measures taken to comfort and encourage it, which ought to have been taken by Congress, we should not have lost Charlestown,' &c.

If the petition to the King produced harmony where otherwise would have been discord, if it quieted the consciences of any considerable number of the inhabitants of the colonies, and thereby removed obstacles to the future vigorous prosecution of the war, then the positive mischiefs of that proceeding were in some sort compensated. Mr. Jay always maintained that it exercised an auspicious influence upon the revolution.

The same day on which Mr. Jay was appointed upon the committee to draught a petition to the King, he was placed upon another committee, to whom was referred a letter from the Convention of Massachusetts, asking

[1] Life and Works, vol. ii., p. 415. [2] Ibid.

'explicit advice respecting the taking up and exercising the powers of civil government,' and suggesting the propriety of Congress taking the regulation and general direction of the army into their own hands. His colleagues upon the committee were John Rutledge, Thomas Johnson of Maryland, and James Wilson of Pennsylvania. They were instructed to report to Congress what, in their opinion, was the proper advice to be given to the Massachusetts Convention. On the 7th day of June the committee brought in their report. It was laid on the table for further consideration. On the 9th day of June, it was resolved that, inasmuch as no obedience was due to the act of Parliament for altering the charter of the Massachusetts colony, nor to a Governor and Lieutenant-Governor who would not observe its directions, those offices were to be considered as vacant; and, in order to conform as near as possible to the spirit and substance of the charter, it was recommended to the Provincial Convention to provide for the election of an Assembly, according to the old mode, who should proceed to the election of Counsellors; and that the Assembly or Council should exercise the powers of government, until a Governor of his Majesty's appointment would consent to govern the colony according to its charter. The committee had several conferences with the delegates from Massachusetts, in the course of which, Mr. Adams supposes, the hint was suggested that they adopted in their report. He says, too, that although the recommendation of Congress was in a great degree conformable to the New York and Pennsylvania system, or, in other words, to the system of Mr. Dickenson and Mr. Duane, he thought it an acquisition, for it was a precedent of advice to the separate states to institute governments, and he doubted not they would soon have more occasion to follow that example.[1]

[1] Life and Works, vol. iii, pp. 16, 17.

A few days after the election of Washington as Commander-in-Chief of the army, Mr. Jay was appointed one of a committee of five, to draw up a declaration, to be published by the General upon his arrival at the camp before Boston.[1] The address to the people of Ireland was from the pen of Mr. Jay. He was not a member of the committee for that draught, but wrote it at the request of his father-in-law, Governor Livingston, who was.[2]

Congress took a recess during the month of August, fatigued 'with the incessant labors, debates, intrigues, and heats of the summer.'[3] But such was the agitation of the times, that the delegates, we may well suppose, obtained but little repose from the adjournment. It gave them an opportunity, however, to visit their families, to mingle with, and learn the sentiments of their constituents. They came together again on the 5th day of September, but not in sufficient numbers to enter upon business. On the 13th, they resumed their labors. The petition to the King, from which many of the delegates anticipated relief, and the consequent hesitancy to adopt any measure that was calculated to delay or thwart reconciliation, undoubtedly embarrassed the proceedings of Congress. 'Every important step,' says Mr. Adams, 'was opposed and carried by bare majorities, which obliged me to be almost constantly engaged in debate; but I was not content with all that was done, and almost every day I had something to say about advising the states to institute governments, to express my total des-

---

[1] This committee was appointed June 23d.

[2] Mr. Sedgwick, in his Life of Governor Livingston, says he was informed by the Governor's son, that the address to the people of Ireland was written by his father. This is a mistake. See Life of John Jay, vol. i., p. 37

[3] Life and Works of John Adams, vol. ii., p. 419.

pair of any good from the petition, or any of those things which were called conciliatory measures.'[1]

The services performed by Mr. Jay during the autumn and winter, judging from the number of committees upon which he was placed, were important and various. To give a list of these committees, would only encumber our pages without throwing additional light upon the history of the times or the character of Mr. Jay. It is only the more important points of his Congressional career that invite and will reward a more attentive examination. On the 22d day of September, Dr. Franklin, John Rutledge, Mr. Jay, Mr. Randolph, Mr. Johnson, Mr. Duane, and Mr. Willing, were appointed a committee to take into consideration the state of the trade of America. On the 30th inst., the committee brought in their report. On the 4th day of October, it became the subject of an animated debate, which was continued on several subsequent days. The point immediately involved in the discussion was, whether the colonies excepted from the operation of Lord North's restraining act should also be excepted from the association agreement of the previous year, and permitted to carry on their accustomed trade. The restraining act, as originally passed, cut off the trade of New England elsewhere than to Great Britain, Ireland, and the British West Indies, and suspended their prosecution of the Newfoundland fishery. About a month later, the provisions of the restraining bill were extended to all the colonies except New York, North Carolina, the lower counties upon the Delaware, and Georgia. The assemblies of New York and Georgia had refused to adopt the American association, which placed those provinces within the pale of ministerial favor. Why so patriotic a province as North Carolina was selected as the object of such invidious privilege, was

[1] Life and Works, vol. ii., p. 503.

not owing to any compliances on her part, but to the delusive hopes of her loyalty, held out by Martin, the royal Governor. He counted upon the fidelity of the Scotch, who were more numerous and ignorant, perhaps, in that province than in any other.

The wants of the army, the limited supply of manufactured articles in the country, their enhanced price notwithstanding the association agreement, and the immediate prospect of distress, from the absence of supplies, suggested a very obvious reason why trade should be permitted. But it was contended that if they opened their ports, and invited trade with all the world, England, by means of her naval force, would either deter or destroy it. Why, then, it was asked, should not the excepted colonies be permitted to obtain from Great Britain and her dependencies, without risk or uncertainty, such supplies as the situation of the country required. The most earnest and able advocates of these views were Robert R. Livingston and Mr. Jay of New York, Stone and Johnson of Maryland, and Dr. Zubly of Georgia. This latter gentleman was a Swiss minister, of the Independent persuasion, a linguist, and distinguished for his learning. His temper was warm and zealous; his abilities of a very high order, as is abundantly shown by the part he took in the debates of this Congress. His views were striking, if not always sound, and his style, nervous and singularly adapted to the *tone* of his sentiments. The incidental opinions he expressed in this particular debate, foreshadowed his subsequent defection from the cause.[1]

---

[1] Works of John Adams, vol. ii., pp. 421, 469. 'A republican government,' he said, 'is little better than government of devils. I have been acquainted with it from six years old. We must regulate our trade so as that a reconciliation be obtained, or we enabled to carry on the war. Can't say, but I do hope for a reconciliation, and that this winter

To permit the excepted colonies to have the privilege of carrying on commerce with the mother country, with Ireland, and the West Indies, was very obnoxious to the sentiments of the major part of Congress. It was opposed upon the ground that it would be unjust, impolitic, and fatal to their union. 'The ministry will answer their end,' said Mr. Gadsden of South Carolina, 'if we let the custom-houses be open in New York, North Carolina, the lower counties and Georgia; they will divide us. One colony will envy another, and be jealous. Mankind act by their feelings. Rice sold for three pounds; it won't sell now for thirty shillings. We have rich and poor there as well as in other colonies; we know that the excepted colonies do n't want to take advantage of the others.' 'I will follow Mr. Gadsden and simplify the proposition,' said Mr. Lee, 'and confine it to the question whether the custom-houses shall be shut. If they are open, the excepted colonies may trade, others not, which will be unequal; the consequences, jealousy, division, and ruin. I would have all suffer equally. But we should have some offices set up, where bonds should be given that supplies shall not go to our enemies.' [1]

At a subsequent day, Mr. Lee made a formal motion that the custom-houses be shut and the officers discharged. This, he contended, would remove jealousies and divisions, and put New York, North Carolina, the lower counties, and Georgia upon the same footing with the other colonies. Mr. Gadsden seconded Mr. Lee's motion, and affirmed that they could carry on trade from one end of the continent to the other. This proposition called up Mr. Jay. 'This should be the last business we undertake,' he said. 'It is like cutting the foot to the shoe,

---

may bring it. I may enjoy my hopes for reconciliation; others may enjoy theirs, that none will take place. A vessel will not go without sails or oars. Wisdom is better than weapons of war.'

[1] Life and Works, vol. ii., pp. 456, 457.

not making a shoe to the foot. Let us establish a system first. I think we ought to consider the whole, before we come to any resolutions. Now gentlemen have their doubts whether the non-exportation was a good measure. I was, last year, clear against it. Because the enemy have burned Charlestown, would gentlemen have us burn New York? Let us lay every burden as equal on all the shoulders as we can. If Providence or ministry inflict misfortunes on one, shall we inflict the same on all? I have one arm sore; why should not the other arm be made sore too? But jealousies will arise; are these reasonable? is it politic? We are to consult the general good of all America. Are we to do hurt to remove unreasonable jealousies? Because ministry have imposed hardships on one, shall we impose the same on all? It is not from affection to New York that I speak. If a man has lost his teeth on one side of his jaws, shall he pull out the teeth from the other, that both sides may be upon a footing? Is it not realizing the quarrel of the belly and the members? The other colonies may avail themselves of the custom-houses in the exempted colonies.'

On a subsequent day, Mr. Jay again opposed the proposition to shut up the custom-houses. 'It would introduce,' he said, 'a most destructive scheme; a scheme which will drive away all your sailors, and lay up all your ships to rot at the wharves.' He contended that they had more to expect from the enterprise, activity, and industry of private adventurers than from the lukewarm zeal of assemblies; for public virtue, he said, is not so active as private love of gain. These views did not meet with favor. Congress, as was said by R. R. Livingston, were between hawk and buzzard, puzzling themselves between a commercial and warlike opposition. Accordingly, it was resolved that New York, the lower counties on the Delaware, North Carolina, and Georgia, ought not to avail themselves of the benefit allowed to them by the Restraining Act.

Upon the question which arose in Congress respecting the appointment of field officers for the two battalions recommended to be raised in New Jersey, Mr. Jay was earnestly in favor of retaining the appointment in the hands of Congress. He went further, and would have Congress appoint every officer, even an ensign. The union, he said, depended much upon breaking down Provincial Conventions.[1] The Congress of New Jersey addressed a spirited but respectful letter to Congress upon the subject. It would facilitate the expeditious raising of men, they said, if it was first ascertained that they were invested with the nomination of the field officers. 'We also humbly conceive,' they observe, 'that as other provinces have been indulged with this privilege, we cannot, in justice to our constituents, nor consistent with the honor of our Province, give up this claim.'[2] The Congress disregarded the pretensions of New Jersey; but their future system did not correspond with the rule they adopted on the present occasion. Had they adhered to a settled policy upon this subject, the service would have been benefited, and complaint and dissatisfaction rendered less frequent. But they made discriminations highly offensive to the states affected by them. In the next chapter we shall see that the convention of New York, in the following year, was placed in a similar position to the Congress of New Jersey on the present occasion, and that they deeply resented it. Mr. Jay, who was a member of the convention at that time, was among the most earnest in denouncing the partial and exceptional course pursued by the Congress in that instance.[3]

---

[1] Life and Works of John Adams, vol. ii., p. 468.

[2] American Archives, 4th series, vol. iii., p. 1050.

[3] Congress proceeded to the election of field officers for the two New Jersey battalions on Tuesday, November 7th. Lord Stirling was chosen Colonel of the first battalion.

The New Jersey Assembly began a sitting at Burlington on the 15th day of November. On the 28th inst., the House appointed a committee to draught a petition to the King, 'humbly beseeching him to use his interposition to prevent the effusion of blood; and to express the great desire this House hath to a restoration of peace and harmony with the parent state, on constitutional principles.'

Three days after, the committee reported. On the 4th day of December their draught of the petition was read a second time, and referred to a committee of the whole House. Information of this proceeding was communicated to the continental Congress. They at once, and unanimously, resolved, that it would be very dangerous to the liberties and welfare of America for any colony separately to petition the King or either house of Parliament. They also resolved that a committee of three be appointed to confer with the Assembly of New Jersey. Mr. Dickenson, Mr. Wythe, and Mr. Jay were the members chosen. The next day, December 5th, they proceeded to Burlington. The petition had already been amended and engrossed. The steps that were then taken are described by Franklin, the Royal Governor, (an illegitimate son of Dr. Franklin, whose maxims of economy and morality are universally and deservedly applauded,) in a secret and confidential letter to the Earl of Dartmouth, dated at Perth Amboy, January 5th, 1776. 'By the minutes of December 5th,' he says, 'your lordship will perceive that the Assembly had it in their intentions to petition his Majesty again on the subject of the present unhappy disputes; but after the draught of an address was prepared, which would probably have passed the House, a committee of the General Congress at Philadelphia came in great haste to Burlington, desired admittance into the Assembly, which being granted, they harangued the House for about an hour on the subject, and persuaded them to drop the design. That your lordship may have some idea of the arguments they used on this occasion, I have obtained a copy of the notes taken by a gentleman present, which contain the substance of the speech of Mr. Dickenson of Philadelphia. The other members of the committee were Mr. Jay of New York and Mr. Wythe of Virginia. I have not seen the draught of the address, but I am told that it contained some plan or proposals for an accommodation, and that it was this part which alarmed the Congress and occasioned them to take so extraordinary a step to prevent its being sent; they being of opinion that no colony ought to presume to make separate proposals, or to take separate measures on the present occasion, but to leave the whole to their management.'[1]

From the notes of the gentleman who was present and heard the arguments of the Congressional committee, it appears that Mr. Jay spoke about twelve minutes. He said, 'We had nothing to expect from the *mercy* or *justice of Britain*. That *petitions* were now not the means; vigor and unanimity the only means. That the petition of united America, presented by Congress, ought to be relied on; others unnecessary, and hoped the House would not think otherwise.'[2]

It was early perceived by the leading whigs in the country, that if the controversy between Britain and the colonies resulted in an appeal to the sword, France and Spain would not permit so favorable an opportunity to wound their ancient enemy to pass away unimproved. The successive stages of the dispute had been watched with eager and sleepless interest by the French Court. The mercurial Parisians were as vehement patriots as the people of Boston or Virginia. Their cafés resounded with animated discussions on American affairs. The Government had sent over emissaries at different times,

[1] American Archives, 4th series, vol. iii., p. 1871.

[2] Ibid. pp. 1874, 1875.

to ascertain the condition of public sentiment, to animate resistance, and drop hints of the friendly disposition of the French Court. In the autumn of '75, it became apparent that the whole power of the British empire would be put forth to coerce the colonies into submission. Congress was compelled, therefore, to look steadily in the face that menacing danger, and provide for the impending struggle. On the 29th day of November, they took the first steps to ascertain from what quarter aid could be obtained in the rugged contest upon which they had adventured. On that day, Harrison, Franklin, Johnson, Dickenson, and Jay were appointed a committee for the sole purpose of corresponding with the friends of the colonies in Great Britain, Ireland, and other parts of the world. The committee were to lay their correspondence before Congress when directed, and were empowered to send agents on this service.

It would appear that in consequence of jealousy and division among the delegates, there was a good deal of address employed in the election of this committee. 'Within a day or two after its appointment,' says Mr. Adams, 'Mr. Jay came to my chamber to spend an evening with me. I was alone, and Mr. Jay opened himself to me with great frankness. His object seemed to be an apology for my being omitted in the choice of the two great secret committees of commerce and correspondence. He said in express terms, that my character stood very high with the members, and he knew there was but one thing which prevented me from being universally acknowledged to be the first man in Congress, and that was this; there was a great division in the House, and two men had effected it, Samuel Adams and Richard Henry Lee, and as I was known to be very intimate with those two gentlemen, many others were jealous of me. My answer to all this was, that I had thought it very strange, and had imputed it to some intrigue out of doors, that no member from Massachusetts had been elected on either of those committees; that I had no pretensions to the distinction of the first man in Congress, and that if I had a clear title to it, I should be very far from assuming it or wishing for it. It was a station of too much responsibility and danger, in the times and circumstances in which we lived and were destined to live. That I was a friend very much attached to Mr. Lee and Mr. Adams, because I knew them to be able men and inflexible in the cause of their country. I could not, therefore, become cool in my friendship for them for the sake of any distinctions that Congress could bestow. That I believed too many commercial projects and private speculations were in contemplation by the composition of those committees, but even these had not contributed so much to it as the great division in the House on the subject of independence, and the mode of carrying on the war. Mr. Jay and I, however, parted good friends, and have continued such without interruption to this day.'[1]

The immediate motive for the appointment of the committee of correspondence is probably disclosed in the following anecdote from the Life of Mr. Jay, by his son.[2] "Some time in the course of this year, probably about the month of November, Congress was informed that a foreigner was then in Philadelphia, who was desirous of making to them an important and confidential communication. This intimation having been several times repeated, a committee, consisting of Mr. Jay, Dr. Franklin, and Mr. Jefferson, was appointed to hear what the foreigner had to say. These gentlemen agreed to meet him in one of the committee-rooms in Carpenters' Hall. At the time appointed, they went there, and found already arrived an elderly lame gentleman, having the

[1] Life and Works, vol. iii., p. 45; 8th of March, 1805.

[2] Life and Writings of John Jay, vol. i., pp. 39, 40.

appearance of an old wounded French officer. They told him they were authorized to receive his communication; upon which he said that his Most Christian Majesty had heard with pleasure of the exertions made by the American colonies in defence of their rights and privileges; that his Majesty wished them success, and would, whenever it should be necessary, manifest more openly his friendly sentiments towards them. The committee requested to know his authority for giving these assurances. He answered only by drawing his hand across his throat, and saying, 'Gentlemen, I shall take care of my head.' They then asked what demonstrations of friendship they might expect from the King of France. 'Gentlemen,' answered the foreigner, 'if you want arms, you shall have them; if you want ammunition, you shall have it; if you want money, you shall have it.' The committee observed that these assurances were indeed important, but again desired to know by what authority they were made. 'Gentlemen,' said he, repeating his former gesture, 'I shall take care of my head;' and this was the only answer they could obtain from him. He was seen in Philadelphia no more. It was the opinion of the committee that he was a secret agent of the French Court, directed to give these indirect assurances, but in such a manner that he might be disavowed if necessary. Mr. Jay stated that his communications were not without their effect on the proceedings of this Congress."

The committee immediately opened a correspondence with Franklin's friend, M. Dumas, a Frenchman residing at the Hague, with Arthur Lee in London, and other friends of the American cause in France and Holland. Beaumarchais was soon after sent to England as a secret agent of the French Court, to watch the course of events. He knew Lord Rochford, the then Minister of Foreign Affairs under Lord North, and was intimate with Wilkes, then the Lord-Mayor of London. Having access to such sources of information, he soon came to the conclusion, as he wrote to the King, that America was slipping through the fingers of the English.[1] The committee had

---

[1] Beaumarchais had been long known for his literary abilities as well as for expertness in negotiations requiring delicacy and tact. In the previous reign he was not in favor at Court. He was disliked by the King, and had quarrelled with the King's mistress, Madame Du Barri. Through her intrigues, the Barber of Seville was not acted during the reign of her royal lover. However, when the profligate Chevalier De Morande threatened to bring out, in London, the memoirs of the *Comtesse*, she became reconciled to Beaumarchais, and employed him to procure the suppression of the work. He accomplished her wishes, by paying the infamous Morande twenty thousand livres, with a pension of four thousand more.

Beaumarchais was the son of a watchmaker of Paris. He was born in the year 1732. He began his career in the business of his father, and, while young, invented a new kind of escapement. Turning his attention to music, he was fortunate enough to make some improvements on the harp, which procured him an introduction to the daughters of Louis XV. He was engaged to teach them the harp and guitar, and was admitted on the most friendly footing to their private concerts and parties. Here he became acquainted with Paris Duverney, a rich financier, with whose assistance he embarked in various speculations, from which he realized an ample fortune. With an inventive genius, and talents for affairs, Beaumarchais combined a love of literature which he cultivated with great success. At the age of thirty-five he produced the drama of Eugenia—three years later, the Two Friends. Becoming involved in a lawsuit, he acquired more reputation from the exquisite wit, humor, satire, and argument he displayed in drawing up the pleadings and memorials, than from his professed literary labors. The year previous to his appointment as secret agent of the French Court at London, he brought out with immense applause the Barber of Seville.

The history of Beaumarchais' connection with our early negotiations with France, is well known. He became the principal medium through whom the French Government secretly supplied the Americans with arms, military stores, &c. When he ceased to be employed in those transactions, he again resumed his pen. In 1784 he produced the Marriage of Figaro. The opera of Tarare he brought out amid the throes and convulsions that preceded the horrors of the French revolution. Its mischievous tendency was happily neutralized by the folly and extravagance that pervade and characterize it. During the Reign of Terror, he was arrested and thrown into prison. He escaped the

not to create and stimulate an interest in the resistance of the colonies, but to avail themselves of a zeal already existing, and anxious to serve them. So favorable were the results of their negotiations, that in the following spring they secretly despatched Silas Deane as a political agent of America at the Court of France. From the appointment of Deane, Mr. Jay appears to have been the medium of his communication with the committee. To prevent exposure, in the event of Deane's letters being intercepted by the English, they were written with invisible ink, which Mr. Jay rendered legible by means of some chemical preparation. But as mere blank sheets would provoke suspicion, Mr. Deane prefaced his secret communications with a short letter in common ink, under a feigned name, and referring to some fictitious person or business.[1] The particulars of Mr. Deane's mission are

---

guillotine, however, and lived until the year 1799. His latter years were embittered by the loss of the greater part of his fortune. As he had acquired it by speculations, so he lost it in the same way. An expensive edition of Voltaire was one of the projects that caused him great loss.

[1] Robert Morris, who was subsequently appointed a member of the secret committee, in acknowledging the receipt of one of Deane's letters, which had been transmitted to him by Mr. Jay, to whom it was addressed, thus playfully alludes to the device which was employed to elude detection. 'Your favor of the 7th ult.,' he says, 'came safely to hand. Timothy Jones is certainly a very entertaining, agreeable man; one would not judge so by anything contained in his cold, insipid letter of the 17th of September, unless you take pains to find the concealed beauties therein : the cursory observations of a sea-captain would never *discover* them; but transferred from his hand to the penetrating eye of a *Jay*, the diamonds stand confessed at once. It puts me in mind of a search after the philosopher's stone; but I believe not one of the followers of that phantom have come so near the mark as you, my good friend. I handed a copy of your discoveries to the committee, which now consists of Harrison, R. H. Lee, Hooper, Dr. Witherspoon, Johnson, you, and myself, and honestly told them who it was from, because measures are necessary in consequence of it; but I have not received any directions yet.' This letter was dated February 4th, 1777. Mr. Jay, at that

too well known to need repetition. His letters, or the greater part of them, are published in the American Diplomatic Correspondence.

In addition to his labors in Congress, Mr. Jay was much occupied with the progress of affairs in New York. Important subjects, demanding immediate attention, were constantly referred to him and his brother delegates by the Committee of Safety and the Provincial Congress. The condition of things in that colony was not favorable. The tories were numerous. The Provincial Congress was very generally suspected of being lukewarm in the cause. Rivington's Gazette, which was ably and artfully conducted, did various mischief. It confirmed the doubtful tories in their loyalty, and excited suspicions and distrust among the whigs. It was an object of very general detestation throughout the colonies. Of the virulence of this latter sentiment, Rivington had disagreeable proof, in the destruction of his press. On the 23d day of November, Captain Sears, with a troop of seventy-five horse from Connecticut, entered New York at noon-day, marched down the main street, and drew up in close order before Rivington's printing-office. A small detachment entered it, and in about three-quarters of an hour brought off the principal part of his types, for which they offered to give an order on Lord Dunmore. They then marched out of the city to the tune of *Yankee Doodle*, and amid the cheers of the vast concourse of people assembled at the Coffee-House bridge.

Mr. Jay, who could not tolerate acts of lawless vengeance, and on one occasion, as we shall hereafter see, nearly lost his life in opposing a popular tumult, would not allow himself to sanction this summary mode of silencing a press of antagonistic views. 'I don't approve

time, was absent from his seat in the Continental Congress. The situation of affairs in New York rendered his services more important at home than at Philadelphia.

of the feat,' he wrote to the New York Congress, 'and I think it neither argues much wisdom or much bravery: at any rate, if it was to have been done, I wish our own people, and not strangers, had taken the liberty of doing it. I confess I am not a little jealous of the honor of the province, and am persuaded that its reputation cannot be maintained without some little spirit being mingled with its prudence.'[1]

Such was the state of public sentiment in New York in the latter part of the autumn of '75, that it was difficult to persuade persons of suitable character to accept military commissions in the militia of the province. 'The tories are cheerful,' wrote M'Dougall to Jay, 'and too many of the whigs make long faces. Men of rank and influence refuse to accept of commissions as field officers of the militia, so that these commissions have gone a-begging for six or seven weeks.'[2] Under these discouraging circumstances, Mr. Jay soon after accepted the commission of 'Colonel of the Second Regiment of Militia of Foot of the city of New York.' The acceptance of this commission was important only as an example, for such was the pressing nature of his civil duties, that his presence was more needed in Congress than in the field.

As it was naturally supposed that the enemy would endeavor to take possession of New York, the division

---

[1] American Archives, vol. iii., p. 1675, 4th series. The New York Congress addressed a letter to Governor Trumbull of Connecticut, complaining of the insult offered to New York by the conduct of the Connecticut troops, and requesting the return of all the types carried off. 'We believe you will not consider this requisition,' they say, 'as an attempt to justify the man from whom the types were taken. We are fully sensible of his demerits; but we earnestly wish that the glory of the present contest for liberty may not be sullied by an attempt to restrain the freedom of the Press.'

[2] This letter was dated October 30th, '75. See Life and Writings of John Jay, vol. i., p. 39.

of opinion in that province was the occasion of very general solicitude. On the 27th day of December, Congress appointed a committee, consisting of Mr. Lynch, Mr. Deane, Mr. Wythe, Mr. W. Livingston, and Mr. Jay, to take into consideration the state of New York, and report thereon. The committee confined their report to the situation of Queen's county. It is not certainly known who drew the draught of it. The style bears a resemblance to Mr. Jay's. After declaring in the preamble that it is reasonable that those who refuse to defend their country should be excluded from its protection, and prevented from doing it injury, the report proceeded to recommend that all the inhabitants who had voted against sending deputies to the Provincial Convention of New York should be put out of the protection of the united colonies, and not be permitted to travel or abide beyond the limits of their county; that any lawyer who should bring or defend any action for them should be deemed and treated as an enemy to the American cause; and that six hundred men from New Jersey, and as many from Connecticut, should be marched into the county to disarm the disaffected, and to arrest and keep in custody till further orders certain specified individuals. The report was adopted.

In the early part of the year 1776, Mr. Jay was absent from Congress for several weeks. The Provincial Congress, in the preceding December, had resolved, that the delegates of the colony in the Continental Congress make such an arrangement among themselves, as that five of them only continue their attendance and represent the colony at any one time. In case either one or two of the five should be absent, then three or four of them were to constitute a quorum, and authorized to represent the colony during such absence. It was doubtless in conformity with an arrangement of this kind, that Mr. Jay was enabled to leave Philadelphia. His presence and influence in New

York could not fail to be of service. Notwithstanding the scheme of disarming the tories, they were a source of constant apprehension. They might at any moment, it was argued, be supplied with fresh arms by the enemy. 'They are so riveted in their opinions,' wrote General Lee to the President of Congress, 'that I am persuaded, should an angel descend from heaven with his golden trumpet, and ring in their ears that their conduct was criminal, he would be disregarded.'[1]

At what precise time Mr. Jay resumed his seat in Congress, does not appear. It was probably about the 1st day of March. On the 9th day of that month, he was appointed on a committee to take into consideration the state of the colonies in the southern department. In a letter to his friend Robert R. Livingston, dated at Philadelphia, March 4th, he mentions that he wrote him from Elizabethtown the previous week. He was then doubtless on his return to Congress. The failing health of his parents at this time, was a source of anxious solicitude. 'The prospect of being soon deprived of a father, and probably a mother, whom you know I tenderly love, the unhappy situation of some of my family, added to the distress I feel for the late misfortunes and sickness of my friend, have occasioned more gloomy ideas in my mind than it has ever before been the subject of; despondency, however, ill becomes a man. I hope I shall meet every severe stroke of fate with firmness and resignation, though not with sullen indifference. It gives me consolation to reflect that the human race are immortal, that my parents and friends will be divided from me only by a curtain which will soon be drawn up, and that our great and benevolent Creator will, if I please, be my guide through this vale of tears to our eternal and blessed habitation.'

[1] American Archives, vol. iv., p. 805. This letter is dated January 22d, 1776.

In this letter to his friend Livingston, Mr. Jay exhibits that religious feeling which was one of his marked characteristics. Mankind are variously distinguished by their different faculties, tastes, and feelings. Some have a nice sense of the beautiful or sublime, an eye for painting, and an ear for music; while others, destitute of these fair and radiant gifts, may find compensation in force and vigor of will. But in nothing, perhaps, is their diversity more strikingly manifested, than in their religious aptitudes. Sentiments of devotion and reverence exist everywhere. They are confined to no color, and restricted to no climate. 'The shuddering tenant of the frigid zone,' or 'the negro panting at the line,' may be endued with a love and adoration for their gods to which many a Christian, born under far happier influences, and professing a far happier faith, can make no pretensions. With some, religion is a thing of the heart; with others, a thing of the head, a dogma, a ceremonial. We fear the Pharisees of every religion greatly outnumber the genuine disciples. Mr. Jay's religion entered into the very texture of his feelings, and he could not have been otherwise than a religious man had he been born beneath the crescent instead of the cross, amid the palm-trees and golden sands of India, or within the palace walls of the Grand Lama. In the pagoda as in the church, he would have been a humble and devout worshipper.

On the 19th day of March, Congress took a step which evinced that they were fast approaching the position, which, for their own fame and the good of their country, they assumed on the 4th day of the ensuing July. The idea had been entertained, and clung to with tenacious grasp by the Americans, that the English people sympathized with them in their struggle. But that delusion was no longer to impede the vigor of the public councils. Their friends in England had condemned with indignant but ineffectual emphasis, the ministerial policy. It was evident that in the contest now waging, the ministry had the support of the nation. On the day we have mentioned, Congress resolved to stand no longer on the defensive, but to assail their enemy in his most vulnerable point; to let loose upon his commerce the marine energies of the continent; to send forth upon the sea, which was whitened with his canvass, that roving and destructive warfare which, under the name of privateering, adds the stimulus of irregular gain to those higher considerations which arm the citizen to defend the liberties of his country.

This step was taken with due deliberation, and was accompanied with an appropriate declaration of the causes that suggested and justified it. Wythe, Jay, and Wilson were the committee to draw up this declaration. On the 23d day of March they reported a declaration which was adopted. After setting forth that the petitions of the united colonies to the King had been treated with scorn and contempt; that an unjust war had been commenced against them, which was conducted with the utmost vigor, and in a cruel manner; that a late act of Parliament had declared the colonies to be in open rebellion, and their property, wherever found upon the water, liable to seizure and confiscation, the declaration proceeded as follows: 'It being therefore necessary to provide for their defence and security, and justifiable to make reprisals upon their enemies, and otherwise to annoy them, according to the laws and usages of nations, the Congress, trusting that such of their friends in Great Britain (of whom, it is confessed, there are many entitled to applause and gratitude for their patriotism and benevolence, and in whose favor a discrimination of property cannot be made) as shall suffer by captures, will impute it to the authors of our common calamities, do declare and resolve as followeth,' &c.[1]

[1] It is supposed that the public sentiment of the world is favorable to

It is curious to observe what a change the rapid succession of events within the last few months had wrought in the sentiments of Congress. On the 5th day of the

---

a general renunciation of privateering as an element of legitimate warfare. The modern principle undoubtedly is, that war is to be waged against those only who are engaged in actual hostilities; that private persons and property are exempt from its ravages, unless the stern necessities of the occasion demand that the exemption should not be allowed. This is the rule of warfare on land. But maritime captures have heretofore been upheld, not by any formal vindication, but by universal practice. The facility with which property at sea is secured when captured, the withdrawal of such sources of supply from the revenue of the enemy, and the fact that the loss does not ordinarily fall wholly upon the merchant, but upon the insurer, who takes such risks for a commensurate premium, may be among the reasons which have hitherto operated to continue a mode of warfare which is supposed to be irreconcilable with the more humane principles of modern times. Whether these principles, however generous and exalted the source from whence they spring, are calculated to produce all the benefit that is anticipated from their enlarged application, may be questioned. They may and will mitigate the harsher features of war, but is there not danger, in diminishing its horrors, of multiplying its repetition? If war is to be considered the concern of Governments and not of individuals, and to be waged only by its accredited agents, if private property and persons are to remain unmolested, while its stern realities fall only upon the actual combatants, then a state of war becomes a state of prosperity to large classes of the citizens of the belligerent powers, and a public opinion is thus created in favor of war, which otherwise would prove a conservator of the public peace.

If this state of prosperity, therefore, is to remain untouched and uninterrupted; if the principle is to have universal application on the sea and on the land, that only public property and public agents are to feel the force and severity of war, then as strong a motive as animates human conduct will be forever operating to disturb the peace of nations. Mankind do not trace effects to their causes with the precision of science. They compare and balance results. And they have a far livelier remembrance of the impulsive energy that is imparted by war, and of its glories and excitements, than of the languor and stagnation which, at a certain stage of its progress, are apt to succeed.

It may be said that public opinion, in its present enlightened state, with religion and morality for its basis, would not tolerate unjust and unnecessary war. But it is at all times an unsafe experiment to place the inte-

preceding October, it was moved that a committee of three be appointed to prepare a plan for intercepting two vessels which were on their way to Canada, laden with arms and powder, and that the committee proceed on that business immediately. This motion was carried, but not without strong and earnest opposition. 'The opposition to it,' says Mr. Adams, 'was very loud and vehement. Some of my own colleagues appeared greatly alarmed at it, and Mr. Edward Rutledge never displayed so much eloquence as against it. He never appeared to me to discover so much information and sagacity, which convinced me that he had been instructed out of doors by some of the most knowing merchants and statesmen in Philadelphia. It would require too much time and space to give this debate at large, if any memory could attempt it. Mine cannot. It was, however, represented as the most wild, visionary, and mad project that ever had been imagined. It was an infant taking a mad bull by the horns; and, what was more profound and remote, it was said it would ruin the character and corrupt the morals of all our seamen. It would make them selfish, piratical, mercenary, bent wholly upon plunder, &c. These formidable arguments and this terrible rhetoric were answered by us by the best reasons we could allege, and the great advantages of distressing

---

rests of mankind and their morals in an antagonistic relation. The danger and the practical consequence ordinarily is, that the tone of the latter is gradually and unconsciously, perhaps, so modified, that no effectual bar interposes to the vigorous prosecution of the former.

The more vigorously war is waged, the sooner it will end. The more directly you place the interests of individuals in jeopardy, the more jealously will they scrutinize the acts and policy of their Government. They become conservators of peace, rather than fomenters of discord. If this benefit is derived from enlarging the sphere of hostile operations, and from the extended, but temporary suffering and distress that are thereby occasioned, is not the end attained an abundant compensation for the means which are employed?

the enemy, supplying ourselves, and beginning a system of maritime and naval operations, were represented in colors as glowing and animated. The vote was carried,' &c.[1] This was the state of feeling in October. But in the following March it was proposed and adopted without opposition, so far as appears, to assail the entire commerce of the enemy.

On the 6th day of April, Congress resolved to throw open the ports of the country and set their commerce at liberty, except so far as concerned the goods, wares, and merchandise of the growth, production, and manufacture of Great Britain, or such as were brought from any country under the dominion of Great Britain. East India tea was also excluded from importation. But a considerable quantity of tea was already in the colonies. By the third article of the association entered into by the Congress of '74, it was agreed that from that day, (the 24th of October,) the inhabitants of the colonies 'would not purchase nor use any tea imported on account of the East India Company, nor any on which a duty had been or should be paid; and from and after the 1st day of March the next following, they would not purchase nor use any East India tea whatever.' This limitation of time for the consumption of the tea then on hand was designed to enable the holders to dispose of it. To have prohibited the sale at once, would have been manifestly unjust to the merchant. But before the limitation expired, considerable quantities of tea had been brought into the country surreptitiously. Indeed, it was said at the time, that the effect of this article of the association was to encourage smuggling. The fair trader could not import without calling down upon himself the vengeance of his countrymen; but even if he escaped that danger, nobody would buy his tea, because it had

[1] Life and Works, vol. iii., pp. 7, 8.

paid a duty. Whereas the smuggler, if he escaped his Majesty's revenue cutters, was none the less a good patriot for having bilked his Majesty's customs. Within the specified time, his tea was a purchasable commodity. But this time proved too short for the consumption of the tea, and when the limitation expired, great quantities remained unsold.

As Congress, by the resolutions of the 6th day of April, prohibited the future importation of East India tea, it became a question what was to be done with that already on hand. Robert Morris, Mr. Jay, and Mr. M'Kean were appointed a committee to bring in a resolution for disposing of and using it. On the 13th day of April, the committee brought in their report. The preamble set forth that many zealous friends to the American cause, who had imported large quantities of tea, with design not merely to advance their fortunes, but to counteract the plan then pursued by the ministry and India Company, to introduce and sell in the colonies tea subject to duty, were likely to become great sufferers — the greater part of the estates of many of them being vested in that article, and they, by that means, rendered incapable not only of paying their debts and maintaining their families, but also of vigorously exerting themselves in the service of their country, and that it was originally the design of Congress that all India tea which had been imported agreeably to the tenor of the association, might be sold and consumed; but the time limited for that purpose had proved too short.

Such being the premises, it followed naturally enough that Congress should permit the tea thus imported and remaining on hand, to be sold and used. As future importation, however, was prohibited, and a scarcity would be thus occasioned, of which the tea-holders might be tempted to avail themselves and exact exorbitant prices for an article which the report of the committee declared to be of little real value in itself, and which owed its worth to a habit in many respects pernicious to the inhabitants of the colonies, Congress resolved that Bohea tea ought not to be sold in any colony at retail, for more than three-fourths of a dollar per pound, nor other teas at a price greater than should be fixed by the committees of the town or county where it was sold. And it was further resolved, that any person who should either give or take more than the specified prices, ought to be considered an enemy to the American cause, and treated accordingly.

We have now put the reader in possession of the salient facts of Mr. Jay's career in the Congress of '75 and '76. In the following chapter we shall contemplate his services on a different theatre. In the month of April, he was chosen a member of the Provincial Congress of New York. As the delegation in the Continental Congress from that province were not elected by the people, but by the former Provincial Congress, the new Congress, which assembled at New York May 14th, 1776, claimed and exercised a control over them. It was by the express direction of this latter body that Mr. Jay returned home to assist in their deliberations.

CHAPTER VII.

1776.

SERVICES IN THE NEW YORK CONGRESS.

Mr. Jay took his seat in the Provincial Congress on the 25th day of May. The day before, he had been appointed on a committee to consider whether the Congress had sufficient authority to establish a new form of Government, or whether the question should be submitted to the people, and explicit authority be obtained. Gouverneur Morris maintained that the Congress had no power whatever to institute an independent Government. John Morin Scott, on the contrary, was of opinion that they had, or, at least, the question was doubtful whether the Congress had not the power, and therefore he contended that the point should be reserved, and a committee be appointed to consider and report upon it. It was in accordance with Mr. Scott's views that the committee was appointed. They were instructed to report with all convenient speed.

This subject had been presented to the attention of the New York Congress by a resolution of the Continental Congress of the 10th inst., recommending to the assemblies and conventions of the united colonies, where no government sufficient to the exigencies of affairs had been hitherto established, to adopt such government as should, in the opinion of the representatives of the people, best conduce to the happiness and safety of their constituents in particular and America in general. This proceeding of the Continental Congress was considered at the time as one of the most decisive steps yet taken towards independence.[1] By many it was deemed premature. In colonies where the tories were numerous, as in New York, it was calculated to arouse them at once into activity. It was changing, *in invitum*, their allegiance, and putting them in a state of infinite embarrassment. Besides, many whigs in that colony were not yet prepared to renounce all hope of reconciliation and take a step that would probably render reconciliation impossible.

Mr. Duane represented the views of this portion of his constituents with boldness and ability. He opposed the original resolution, and equally opposed the preamble which was adopted on the 15th inst. 'Congress,' he said, 'ought not to determine a point of this sort about instituting government. What is it to Congress how justice is administered? You have no right to pass the resolution any more than Parliament has. How does it appear that no favorable answer is likely to be given to our petitions? Every account of foreign aid is accompanied with an account of commissioners. Why all this haste? why this urging? why this driving? Disputes about independence are in all the colonies. What is this owing to but our indiscretion? I shall take the liberty of informing my constituents that I have not been guilty of a breach of trust. I do protest against this piece of mechanism, this preamble.'[2]

---

[1] 'Mr. Duane called it to me, a machine for the fabrication of independence. I said, smiling, I thought it was independence itself, but we must have it with more formality yet.' Life and Works of John Adams, vol. iii., p. 46.

[2] Adams' Works, vol. ii., pp. 489, 490. The preamble referred to by Mr. Duane, declared that it appeared absolutely irreconcilable to reason and good conscience for the people of the colonies now to take the oaths and affirmations necessary for the support of any Government under the Crown of Great Britain; and it was necessary that the exercise of every kind of authority under the said Crown should be totally suppressed, and all the powers of Government exerted under the authority of the people of the colonies, &c.

It was with reference to the interesting question of instituting a new form of government, that Mr. Jay took his seat in the New York Congress. The committee upon which he had been placed made their report on the 27th day of May. It declared that the right of framing, creating, or remodelling civil government is, and ought to be, in the people; that doubts having arisen whether the present Congress was invested with sufficient authority to frame and institute a new form of internal government and police, those doubts could, and ought to be, removed by the good people of the colony alone; that an opportunity ought to be given to each several and respective county in the colony to remove said doubts, either by declaring their respective representatives in the present Congress, in conjunction with the representatives of the other counties respectively competent to establish such new form of internal police and government, or else to elect another body, clothed with the same powers as were vested in this Congress, and with superadded authority to institute and establish a new and regular form of Government.

This report was embodied in resolutions and published. One of the resolutions declared that the elections in the several counties for the foregoing purpose, ought to be held at such time and place as should be designated by their respective committees. At the same time, it was recommended to the committees to fix such early days for the election, as to enable the deputies to meet in the city of New York by the second Monday of July.

Having thus provided for the establishment of a better form of government than the present, which, in the opinion of Mr. Jay, could no longer work anything but mischief,[1] the Congress meanwhile continued in session,

---

[1] In a letter to his friend R. R. Livingston, dated at New York, May 29th, 1776, he says: 'Our Convention will, I believe, institute a better Government than the present, which, in my opinion, will no longer

exercising the powers originally delegated to them. But the question of independence was now absorbing the attention of the whole country, and was presented to the New York Congress in a manner so pressing that they were obliged to consider it. On the 5th day of June, they received from the General Convention of Virginia their unanimous resolves in favor of independence; and on the 10th, a letter from the New York delegates in Congress, saying that that question would soon be agitated, and requesting their sentiments upon it.

Mr. Jay and Mr. Morris were appointed a committee to reply to the letter and resolves of the Virginia Convention, and Mr. Jay and Mr. Remsen a committee to answer the letter of the New York delegates in Congress. Mr. Jay was clearly of opinion that the New York Congress were not vested with a power to deliberate and determine on the question of independence. The opinion of the majority of that body coincided with his. He also thought that it would be imprudent, while measures were pursuing to obtain the consent and authority of the people, to establish a new form of government, to require their sentiments upon the question of independence. He thought it might create division, and have an unhappy influence on the other and pending question. The letter, therefore, to the Virginia Convention, without expressing any direct opinion upon the subject matter of their resolves, merely assured them that the New York Congress would invariably adopt and pursue every measure which might tend to promote the union and secure the rights and happiness of the united colonies. The letter, however, to the New York delegates, expressed the unanimous opinion of the Congress that they were not author-

work anything but mischief; and although the measure of obtaining authority by instructions may have its advocates, I have reason to think that such a resolution will be taken as will open the door to the election of new or additional members.' Life and Writings, vol. ii., p. 6.

ized to give the sense of the colony upon the question of independence, and that the Congress had no authority to instruct them upon that point. But they were assured, that when the question of establishing a new form of government was determined, the earliest opportunity would be embraced to ascertain the sentiments of the people upon the question of independence, and to obtain their consent to vest the Congress of the colony, for the time being, with authority to deliberate and determine on that and every other matter of general concern, and to instruct their delegates in Continental Congress thereupon.

This letter was dated June 11th, and on the same day Mr. Jay presented several resolutions, which embodied the sentiments of it, and were unanimously adopted. The substance of them was, that, as the people of the colony had not authorized their representatives to declare the colony independent of Great Britain, and yet, as recent events required some determination on that, as well as many other important points, it was necessary for the powers of the representatives to be enlarged, and it was therefore resolved that it should be earnestly recommended to the freeholders and other electors, not only to invest the deputies with the authority heretofore required for instituting a new form of government, but also 'with full power to deliberate and determine on every question whatever that may concern or affect the interests of this colony, and to conclude upon, ordain, and execute every act and measure which to them shall appear conducive to the happiness, security, and welfare of this colony; and that they hold and exercise the said powers until the second Tuesday in May next, or until a regular form of government shall be established.' The electors were further recommended 'to instruct or otherwise to inform the said deputies of their sentiments relative to the great question of independency and such other points as they may think proper.' To prevent any unfavorable influence upon the important subject that was now engaging the attention of the people, viz., the institution of a Government, the publication of Mr. Jay's resolutions was postponed until after the election of deputies with powers for that purpose.

While the question of a new form of government, and the question of independence, were agitating the public mind, the presence of a military force in New York, the anticipated arrival of the enemy, and the machinations of the tories, conspired to raise the popular excitement to an unexampled pitch. Amid the surges of this angry ocean, the Provincial Congress displayed a becoming firmness. They employed the most vigorous measures to discover and defeat the plots of the tories. Their committees for this purpose were armed with almost dictatorial powers.

Mr. Jay was constantly employed. He was chairman of a committee appointed to inquire into the conduct and sentiments of certain specified persons, and to summon or apprehend others not specified, whom they might be informed were dangerous. Upon proof of their enmity to the cause, the committee were empowered to imprison or assign them another place of residence, either in New York, or one of the neighboring colonies, as the public safety might dictate. Such persons as were not adjudged to be friends of the cause, yet against whom did not appear any decisive acts of enmity, the committee were required to discharge; not unconditionally, however, but upon their parole, or other security as should appear to be most prudent. The committee held their first meeting on Sunday, the 15th inst., at the City Hall. They were occupied with these examinations until June 30th, when the Provincial Congress adjourned to White Plains.

On the 17th inst., Philip Livingston, Gouverneur Morris, and Mr. Jay were appointed a secret committee to confer with General Washington relative to certain secret intelligence communicated to the Congress, with authority to make such examinations as they might deem proper.

On the 20th, the committee informed Congress that they had discovered certain dangerous persons who ought to be arrested. This information related to a plot; not, however, regularly digested or well defined, but having, or supposed to have, among its objects, to arm the tories, blow up the magazine, murder or carry off Washington and the principal officers, and secure the passes of the town. Authority to make the arrests was immediately granted to the committee, and, for that purpose, to employ the militia of the colony, or obtain detachments of Continental troops from the Commander-in-Chief. Sundry arrests were made. Among others was Matthews, the Mayor of the city.

The situation of the colony was critical. The arrival of the British army under Lord Howe was daily anticipated. The purposes of the tories, from what had already been discovered, were known to be of the most dangerous character. A general feeling of insecurity and apprehension prevailed in the city. To be prepared for any emergency, the Congress authorized their President to call to his assistance during their daily adjournments, any five or more of the members, and take such measures as they might judge necessary for the safety and preservation of the colony. This dictatorial power was placed in his hands only for five days.[1]

On the 25th day of June, Sir William Howe arrived at Sandy Hook, and three days after was joined by the

[1] This resolution of the Congress was adopted the 20th day of June, the same day on which the committee made their disclosures.

entire British force from Halifax. An immediate attack on the city was apprehended. It was apparent, that in the confusion of such an occasion, Congress could not with safety conduct the public business. Hence, after investing General Washington with supreme authority over the military strength of the colony, to be employed within its limits, the Congress adjourned on the 30th to White Plains.[1] They were to assemble again on the 2d day of July. A quorum, however, did not meet at that time. Indeed, no further business was transacted by this Congress. This was doubtless owing to the fact that the new Congress, with enlarged powers, was to convene on Tuesday, the 9th inst.

On that day, the members of the new Congress assembled at White Plains and organized. Mr. Jay, together with nineteen others, had been chosen to represent the city and county of New York for the ensuing year, clothed with the additional power of framing a new form of government for the colony.

Since the adjournment of the previous Congress on the 30th ult., interesting events had taken place. The Declaration of Independence was reported to the Continental Congress on the 28th day of June. On the 2d day of July the New York delegates wrote a pressing letter, asking instructions how to vote on the question of independence, which was hastening to a decision. They were placed in a situation of peculiar embarrassment. Having no authority by their present instructions

---

[1] In a letter to Edward Rutledge, written a week later than the time mentioned in the text, Mr. Jay says, 'Your friendly letter found me so much engaged by plots, conspiracies, and chimeras dire, that, though I thanked you for it in my heart, I had no time to tell you so either in person or by letter. Your ideas of men and things, (to speak mathematically,) run for the most part parallel with my own; and I wish Governor Tryon and the devil had not prevented my joining you on the occasion you mentioned.' The date of this letter is July 6th, 1776.

to vote on such a question, they demanded to know what course they should pursue. Should they retire from Congress? Because if independence was declared without the vote and co-operation of New York, they could no longer remain in Congress. They could not take part in an independent Government. At any rate, they had no such authority from their constituents. They therefore asked the Provincial Congress whether they should consider New York bound by the vote of the majority in favor of independency, and vote at large on such questions as might arise in consequence thereof, or only concur in such measures as might be absolutely necessary for the common safety and defence of America, exclusive of the idea of independency. This letter was not answered. Indeed, the question was decided before it was received. The New York delegates, therefore, being without instructions, said they were for the declaration themselves, and were assured their constituents were for it; but as they had no authority to act upon a question of that nature, they did not think themselves justified in voting on either side, and asked leave to withdraw from the question, which was granted.[1]

The New York delegates enclosed a draught of the declaration to the Provincial Congress. It was received and read on the very day the Congress assembled. It was immediately referred to a committee consisting of Mr. Jay, Mr. Yates, Mr. Hobart, Mr. Brasher, and Mr. William Smith. When the convention came together in the afternoon, their committee reported several resolutions in the handwriting of Mr. Jay, which were unanimously adopted. The first declared that the reasons assigned by the Continental Congress for declaring the united colonies free and independent states, were cogent and conclusive; and that while they lamented the cruel

[1] Jefferson's Memoirs, &c., vol. i., p. 15.

necessity which had rendered that measure unavoidable, they approved the same, and would, at the risk of their lives and fortunes, join with the other colonies in supporting it. Copies of the declaration, together with this resolution, were directed to be transmitted to the various county committees within the state, with instructions to have them published in the several districts of their respective counties. Another resolution authorized their delegates to consult and adopt all such measures as they might deem conducive to the happiness and welfare of the United States of America.

If Mr. Jay had not the honor of affixing his name to the Declaration of Independence, he gave it his instant sanction, and ever after earnestly and steadily supported it.

It will be recollected that Mr. Jay, while in the Continental Congress during the previous year, had expressed the opinion that the appointment of all officers in regiments raised for the Continental service, should be made by that body.[1] But while his views prevailed in that particular case, a different policy had since been very generally observed. The provincial authorities nominated the officers of the regiments raised in their respective states, and returned their names to the Continental Congress for approval. Such had hitherto been the common usage. A discrimination was now made, in the case we are about to mention, highly invidious to New York. It occasioned much ill-feeling, and called forth a spirited protest from the New York Convention. These were the circumstances. On the 21st day of June, it was resolved that the Convention of New York be requested to set on foot the raising another regiment, on Continental establishment, to serve for three years, or during the war, unless sooner discharged by Congress;

---

[1] See Ante, p. 148.

and that, in forming the said regiment, they commission such officers as served in the last campaign in Canada, and had not yet been provided for. At the same time, it was recommended to the Convention to make suitable provision for Major Dubois, with whose conduct they were well satisfied, and return his name, with the names of the other field-officers, for the approbation of that body.

The action of the Congress had thus far been regular, except that the recommendation of Mr. Dubois tended to impair, in some measure, the liberty of nomination. But four days later, Congress resolved that a Colonel's commission be immediately issued to Major Dubois, with instructions forthwith to raise a regiment to serve for three years, or during the war, and that the corps of officers be composed of such as had served with credit in Canada. The next day, viz., June 26th, they resolved that certain gentlemen be appointed officers of the battalion to be raised under Colonel Dubois, and that the President write to the Convention of New York, and explain to them the reasons that induced the Congress to enter into the foregoing resolve, and to request the Convention to appoint the other officers, &c.

Mr. Jay was very indignant at the action of the Congress in this affair. His feelings were shared by his fellow-members of the Convention. The officers, too, who had been either wholly omitted in the arrangements made by Congress, or superseded in rank, were highly disgusted. The very day the Convention assembled at White Plains, Mr. Miller, Mr. Jay, and Colonel Rensselaer were appointed to take into consideration and report on all the letters received from Congress on this subject. The next day Mr. Jay brought in a report. It was considered, recommitted, and Mr. Hobart and Mr. Morris were added to the committee. On the following day, viz., July 11th, Mr. Morris, on behalf of the committee, reported the draft of a letter to be written to the Continental Congress. It contained the substance of the report as draughted by Mr. Jay, but his language in several instances was modified.

One of the reasons assigned by that body for depriving the Convention in this instance of the right of nomination was, the good of the service and the danger of delay.

It may not be uninteresting to the reader to see the reply to this, as originally drawn by Mr. Jay, and the reply, as modified by Mr. Morris' report, and actually adopted by the Convention.

'The necessity of the case,' says the report as drawn by Mr. Jay, 'has in all ages and nations of the world been a fruitful, though dangerous, source of power. It has often sown tares in the fair fields of liberty, and, like a malignant blast, destroyed the fruits of patriotism and public spirit. The whole history of mankind bears testimony against the propriety of considering this principle as the parent of civil rights; and a people jealous of their liberties will ever reprobate it. We believe Congress went into this measure with pure intentions and with no other wish than that of serving their country; and we entertain too high an opinion of their virtue and integrity to apologize for a plainness of speech becoming freemen, and which we know can give offence only to that counterfeit and adulterated dignity which swells the pride of those who, instead of lending, borrow consequence from their offices. And, Sir, we beg leave to assure Congress, that though we shall always complain of and oppose their resolutions when they injure our rights, we shall ever be ready to risk our lives and fortunes in supporting the American cause.'

In the reply, as drawn by Mr. Morris and approved by the Convention, the language of Mr. Jay is changed as follows: 'We are deeply impressed with the idea that your respectable body were actuated by the purest intentions of serving their country, and we entertain so well-founded an opinion of their wisdom and integrity, that we shall not presume to apologize for that plainness of speech which distinguishes freemen, and which can never give offence to those who, from the dignity of their private characters, impart lustre to the offices they hold. We shall observe, therefore, that though the necessity of the case has in all nations and ages been the fruitful source of extraordinary power, yet it has but too frequently sown with tares the fertile fields of liberty, and blasted the fair fruits of patriotism and public spirit. The whole history of mankind bears testimony against the propriety of considering this principle as the parent of civil rights, and therefore a people jealous of their liberties must forever reprobate it. At the same time, we take leave to assure you, Sir, that, however we may be calumniated by individuals whose censure we consider as praise, we shall ever continue ready, with our lives and fortunes, to support the cause and rights of America.'

The critical condition of affairs in the State, the sudden emergencies that arose and claimed immediate action, rendered it necessary for the Convention, as we have already seen, to confer on committees of their body very extraordinary powers. The confidence evinced by the Convention on these occasions in the character, in the ability, and integrity of Mr. Jay, speaks his praise in forcible and unmistakable language. It is stated in their journals of the 12th inst., that Mr. Sampson Duyckinck came from the city of New York, and informed the Congress that three ships of war had passed the Fort and Battery at New York, and sailed up Hudson's River;[1]

[1] There were but two ships, viz., the Phœnix and the Rose, accompanied by two tenders. "When the men-of-war passed up the river," said General Washington in a letter to the New York Convention, dated August 17th, (advising the removal of 'the great number of women and children and infirm persons' remaining in the city of New York,

that they were fired upon from all the batteries along the banks of the river; that he believes they have already passed King's Bridge. Upon this, it was ordered that Mr. Jay, Major Lockwood, Mr. Mills, Colonel Drake, and Mr. Schenck be a committee to take such measures on this occasion as to calling out such parts of the militia, sending expresses to the forts in the Highlands, and all such other measures as they shall think necessary.

The most active efforts were made by the committee, with the co-operation of the Convention, to defeat the designs of the enemy, who were supposed to have for their object the seizure of certain defiles in the Highlands upon which the communication with Albany depended, and thus cut off all intercourse, both by land and water, between the American forces in New York and those on the northern frontier. Detachments of the militia were called out, expresses sent in various directions, to give warning and enable the whigs to secure whatever stores or provisions might be exposed to the enemy.

The two British ships sailed twenty-five miles up the river, and took their station opposite Tarrytown. On the 16th, the Convention received information from Colonel Hammond, who commanded there, that the ships had weighed anchor, and were then sailing up the river with a fair wind. Suitable orders were immediately issued to put the Highlands in a state of defence, and reinforce, if expedient, the garrisons of forts Montgomery and Constitution.[1] Mr. Jay and five others were appointed a secret committee to devise and carry into execution such

---

which was soon to be 'the scene of a bloody conflict,') "the shrieks and cries of those poor creatures running every way with their children, was truly distressing, and, I fear, will have an unhappy effect on the ears and minds of our young and inexperienced soldiery."

[1] The ships anchored on the same day about ten or twelve miles below the first-named fort.

measures as to them should appear most effectual for obstructing the channel of Hudson's River, or annoying the enemy's ships in their navigation of the said river; and the Convention pledged themselves for the charges incident thereto. The next day they were empowered to impress boats, vessels, teams, wagons, horses, and drivers, when they should find it necessary for the public service, and call out the militia if occasion should require. In order that they might expedite 'the important business with which they were intrusted,' the Treasurer of the State was directed to advance them £5000.

The duties and exertions of this committee were constant and arduous. Their time was fully and variously occupied. Mr. Jay did not again resume his seat in the Convention until after the ships returned down the river, on the 18th day of August. Soon after the appointment of the committee, he was despatched to Salisbury, in Connecticut, to procure a supply of cannon and shot for the forts in the Highlands, which were sadly deficient in *materiel*. Upon his arrival there, he found that the proprietors of the foundry would not part with the cannon without an order from Governor Turnbull.[1] As the summary powers

---

[1] From this place he writes to his wife, under date of July 29th, 1776. He says: 'I am now returning to Poughkeepsie, where I am to meet some members of the Convention on the 7th of August. How long I may stay there is entirely uncertain. Unless some unforeseen business should intervene, I purpose returning to the White Plains by the way of Elizabethtown. The journey will be long and fatiguing, but as all the inconveniences of it will be amply compensated by the pleasure of spending a day or two with you, I consider it with satisfaction, and shall pursue it with cheerfulness. Don't, however, depend on it, lest you be disappointed. In these days of uncertainty, we can be certain only of the present; the future must be the object rather of hope than expectation. My dear Sally, are you yet provided with a secure retreat in case Elizabethtown should cease to be a place of safety? I shall not be at ease till this be done. You know my happiness depends on your welfare; and therefore I flatter myself your affection for me has, before this will reach you, induced you to attend to that necessary object,' &c.

with which he was invested could not be exercised in another jurisdiction, he was obliged to post off to Lebanon, the residence of the Governor, for the requisite order, which, after some delay, was granted. Hastening back to Salisbury, he engaged teams, and in a short time delivered at West Point ten 12 and ten 6 pounders, with fifty rounds of shot to each cannon. The head-quarters of the committee were, for the most part, at Poughkeepsie. They had obstructions sunk in the river, booms constructed, a vigilant watch kept upon the tories, and the exposed points along the river strictly guarded. Finally, in conjunction with General Clinton, who commanded at Fort Montgomery, they determined to burn the enemy's ships. For this purpose they had fire-rafts prepared and charged with the necessary combustible materials. Fire-ships were at the same time constructing at New York, and on the 16th day of August two were despatched up the North River after the British shipping, which was now laying in Haverstraw Bay. The night was dark, and they passed without seeing them. However, they fell in with one of the tenders, and burnt it. The light discovered the position of the ships. One of them, the Phœnix, was immediately grappled, but by the dexterity of her crew she got clear of the fire-ship and sunk her. The enemy, however, alarmed at this mode of attack, quitted their station two days after, and, with the aid of a fine wind, the tide, and a heavy rain, descended the river through a continual fire from the American batteries, without receiving material injury. They had accomplished their purpose, however, which was nothing more, it would seem, than to reconnoitre, and take soundings.

On the same day that the secret committee, clothed with such plenary powers, was appointed, the Convention resolved to postpone the consideration of their future form of government until the 1st day of the ensuing

August. They were too variously and earnestly occupied with the pressing business of the hour, to bestow immediate attention upon that interesting subject. In the meantime, however, all magistrates and other officers of justice throughout the State, who were friendly to the American cause, were requested to perform the duties of their respective offices; but whatever they did, in their several capacities, was to be in the name, and under the authority, of the State of New York.

The Declaration of Independence had wholly changed the relation of things. The Convention had become the representative of a sovereign and independent community. They claimed that the members of that community owed allegiance to their laws alone, and none whatever to those of Great Britain. As the State was now invaded, and the tories might take advantage of that condition of affairs and join the invader, the Convention thought proper to define the position which the inhabitants of the State would hereafter be held to occupy. It was unanimously resolved that all persons abiding in the State of New York, and deriving protection from the laws of the same, owed allegiance to the said laws, and were members of the State; and that all persons passing through, visiting, or making a temporary stay in the said State, being entitled to the protection of the laws during the time of such passage, visitation, or temporary stay, owed, during such time, allegiance thereto. That all such persons, either members of the community, or temporarily owing allegiance to its laws, who should levy war against the State within its limits, or adhere to the King of Great Britain or others, the enemies of the State within the same, giving to him or them aid and comfort, were guilty of treason against the State; and being convicted thereof, should suffer the pains and penalties of death.

This was severe, but necessary legislation. Self-preservation is an instinct of States as well as of individuals.

Upon those who adhered to the royal cause from principle, it bore with peculiar hardship. Their allegiance, by no consent of theirs, had been changed, and a line of conduct prescribed to them inconsistent with their original allegiance, which neither their honor nor conscience would permit them to renounce. But there were large classes who adhered to the royal cause from interest; who entertained so high an opinion of British power, that they did not doubt, when it should be put forth, that the colonies would infallibly be subjected. The most effectual means to restrain the active exertions of those classes, was to give them an adequate motive to remain quiet, to make loss of life or property the penalty for co-operation with the enemy. 'A treason law is, in politics, like the article for shooting upon the spot a soldier who shall turn his back. It turns a man's cowardice and timidity into heroism, because it places greater danger behind his back than before his face.'[1]

The movements of the enemy's fleet and army, the uncertainty of their operations as to time and place, and finally the disastrous defeat on Long Island, a defeat mainly attributable to the inexperience and negligence of our commanding officers, kept the Convention incessantly employed. It was constantly in session, either in its ordinary capacity, or by its representative, a committee of safety, who were meanwhile authorized to take such measures and exercise such powers as should appear to them necessary for the safety of the State.[2]

[1] John Adams to J. D. Sergeant, under date of July 21, 1776. Works, vol. ix., p. 435. Mr. Adams says, in this letter, that nine-tenths of the toryism in America had arisen from mere cowardice and avarice, and that when the tories came to see that there was greater danger to their persons and property from toryism than whiggism, the same avarice and pusillanimity would make them whigs. Few persons at the present day will doubt that Mr. Adams' theory of the cause of toryism was an exaggerated one.

[2] The Committee of Safety acted until there were members enough

Exposed to the incursions of the enemy, they successively adjourned from White Plains to Haerlem, Fishkill, Philip's Manor, Croton River, and again to Fishkill. 'Here, by a vote of the Convention, the members supplied themselves with arms and ammunition to prevent a surprise, in case any hostile bands should intrude upon their retirement; thus prepared to reverse the first part of Pliny's maxim, *cedant arma togæ*, whatever might be the fate of the other part, *concedat laurea linguæ*.'[1]

The present gloomy aspect of American affairs, a large and well-appointed army of the enemy in possession of New York city, while, at the same time, the State was threatened with a formidable invasion on its northern frontier, emboldened the tories, despite the penalties of treason which we have seen had been denounced against them, to take up arms, and, in a variety of instances, to seize and carry into New York influential whigs. Their machinations were a constant source of apprehension. More active and decisive measures were deemed necessary to hold them in check. Mr. Jay, in particular, thought the time had arrived when the laws of self-preservation forbade them to stand on ceremony. His whole conduct in this critical condition of affairs, was an illustration of that fine observation of Mr. Burke, that the heart of the citizen is a perennial spring of vigor to the State. Calm, inflexible, he stood unmoved amid all the violence of the storm, and discharged his duties to the Commonwealth with unsurpassed fidelity. So high a sense did he entertain of the requirements of patriotism, that his public conduct, at this portentous hour of his country's fortunes, evinced somewhat of severity. His

---

present to form a convention. All members of the Convention who were present at the meetings of the committee, acted with them, and were equally entitled to a voice in their proceedings, as if especially named.

[1] Sparks. Life of Morris, vol. i., p. 114.

virtue was of the Roman school. His fortitude would have done no discredit to Cato himself.

On the 10th day of September, he was appointed on a committee to devise ways and means to prevent the dangers which might arise from the disaffected inhabitants of the State. The committee brought in their report on the same day. Debates grew out of it, and it was postponed until the following day. It was then moved and seconded that the report be rejected. This gave rise to further discussion and another postponement. But on the 21st day of September, the report was adopted. The preamble set forth that the measures hitherto pursued to detect and suppress the iniquitous practices and conspiracies to subjugate the United States of America, had not been effectual; that from the situation of affairs, they found themselves reduced, by the great laws of self-preservation and the duties they owed to their constituents, to provide that no means in their power be left unessayed to defeat the barbarous machinations of their domestic as well as external enemies. It was therefore resolved, that a committee be appointed for the express purpose of inquiring into, and detecting and defeating all conspiracies which may be formed in this State against the liberties of America; that they be empowered to send for persons and papers; to call out such detachments of the militia or troops in the different counties as they might from time to time deem necessary for suppressing insurrections; to apprehend, secure, or remove such persons as they should judge dangerous to the safety of the State; to make drafts on the treasury for a sum not exeeeding five hundred pounds; to enjoin secrecy on their own members or whoever they might employ, whenever they should judge the same necessary; and, in general, to do every act and thing whatsoever which might be necessary to enable them to execute the trust reposed in them. They were authorized, if they should think it necessary, to raise officers, and put under pay any number of men not exceeding two hundred and twenty, officers included, and to station them in such places, and employ them in such services, as they should judge expedient for the public safety.

The minutes of this committee, which are still extant, and many of them in Mr. Jay's handwriting, bear ample testimony to the energy with which they exercised their power. Their influence was felt throughout the State; the arrests, imprisonments, and banishments made by them were almost numberless. Many tories, with their families, were sent into New York, and some banished to other States.[1] Many were compelled to give security to reside within certain limits; occasionally the jails, and even the churches, were crowded with prisoners. Emissaries were employed to discover and counteract the plans of the tories; and, in short, a vigilant and vigorous system of police was exercised by this committee in every part of the State, which in no small degree contributed to keep it faithful to the common cause.[2]

But while the committee exerted their powers with the utmost vigor and energy to counteract the designs of their internal enemies, and while their efforts were seconded by the zeal of the Convention, who voted them at different times liberal supplies of money for their pur-

---

[1] About two hundred were sent to New Hampshire. Mr. Jay wrote to the General Court of that State, respecting the treatment of such prisoners as might be sent there. 'The committee desire,' he said, 'that all such of the prisoners as are not directed to be confined, and not in circumstances to maintain themselves, be put to labor and compelled to earn their subsistence. And they have directed the bearer, Egbert Benson, Esq., chairman of the committee of this county, to pay you two hundred dollars on account of the expenses you may be put to by complying with their request.'

[2] William Jay. Life of John Jay, vol. i., p. 50. The minutes of this committee are published in the 3d volume of the 5th series of Force's American Archives.

poses, gloom and misfortune gathered rapidly around the fortunes of the State. A fatality seemed to attend all our military movements. The operations of General Howe had been crowned with success. Washington was compelled to withdraw from New York, which left that State, for the most part, in the hands of the enemy. Despondency seized upon the public mind, and 'the British General, availing himself of the panic occasioned by his successes, scattered abroad his proclamations, offering pardon and protection to repenting rebels.'[1] And he did not do this in vain. Great numbers in New York, New Jersey, and other colonies, considering any effectual resistance to the British arms as now hopeless, took advantage of the proffered pardon, and submitted to the royal authority. 'Between you and me,' wrote Washington on the 18th day of December, 'I think our affairs are in a very bad condition; not so much from General Howe's army, as from the defection of New York, the Jerseys, and Pennsylvania. In short, the conduct of the Jerseys has been most infamous. Instead of turning out to defend their country, and affording aid to our army, they are making submissions as fast as they can.'[2]

To arouse the inhabitants from the gloom into which they had sunk, and raise their minds to a proper sense of their duties, the Convention of New York, on the 23d day of December, published an address to their constituents. It was drawn by Mr. Jay, and is one of the most admirable papers that ever proceeded from his pen. So high an opinion was entertained of its merits and its fitness to the present state of affairs, that Congress earnestly recommended it to the serious perusal and attention of the inhabitants of the United States, and ordered it to be translated and printed in the German language,

---

[1] Life of John Jay, p. 51.

[2] Letter to John A. Washington, written from the Camp, near the Falls of Trenton. Force's American Archives, vol. iii., p. 1275.

at the expense of the Continent. One or two extracts must suffice to gratify the reader's curiosity.

'At this most important period,' says the address, 'when the freedom and happiness, or the slavery and misery of the present and future generations of Americans is to be determined on a solemn appeal to the Supreme Ruler of all events, to whom every individual must one day answer for the part he now acts, it becomes the duty of the representatives of a free people to call their attention to this most serious subject, and the more so at a time when their enemies are industriously endeavoring to delude, intimidate, and seduce them by false suggestions, artful misrepresentations, and insidious promises of protection.

'You and all men were created free, and authorized to establish civil government for the preservation of your rights against oppression, and the security of that freedom which God hath given you, against the rapacious hand of tyranny and lawless power. It is, therefore, not only necessary to the well-being of society, but the duty of every man, to oppose and repel all those, by whatever name or title distinguished, who prostitute the powers of government to destroy the happiness and freedom of the people over whom they may be appointed to rule. Under the auspices and direction of Divine Providence, your forefathers removed to the wilds and wildernesses of America. By their industry they made it a fruitful, and by their virtue, a happy country. And we should still have enjoyed the blessings of peace and plenty, if we had not forgotten the source from which those blessings flowed, and permitted our country to be contaminated by the many shameful vices which have prevailed among us.

'It is unnecessary to remind you that during the space of between one and two hundred years, every man sat under his own vine and under his own fig-tree, and there was none to make him afraid. That the people of Britain never claimed a right to dispose of us and every thing belonging to us, according to their will and pleasure, until the reign of the present King of that Island. And that to enforce this abominable claim, they have invaded our country by sea and by land. From this extravagant and iniquitous claim, and from the unreasonable as well as cruel manner in which they would gain our submission, it seems as though Providence were determined to use them as instruments to punish the guilt of this country, and bring us back to a sense of duty to our Creator. . . . . . . By our vigorous efforts, and by the goodness of Divine Providence, those cruel invaders were driven from our country in the last campaign. We then flattered ourselves that the signal success of our arms, and the unanimity and spirit of our people, would have induced our foes to desist from the prosecution of their wicked designs, and disposed their hearts to peace. But peace we had not yet deserved. Exultation took the place of thanksgiving, and we ascribed that to our own prowess which was only to be attributed to the great Guardian of the innocent.

'The enemy, with greater strength, again invade us—invade us not less by their arts than their arms. They tell you, that if you submit, you shall have protection; that their King breathes nothing but peace; that he will revise (not repeal) all his cruel acts and instructions, and will receive you into favor. But what are the terms on which you are promised peace? Have you heard of any, except absolute, unconditional obedience and servile submission? If his professions are honest — if he means not to cajole and deceive you — why are you not explicitly informed of the terms, and whether the Parliament mean to tax you hereafter at their will and pleasure? Upon this and other like points, these military commissioners of peace are silent; and, indeed, were not authorized to say a word, unless a power to grant pardons implies a power to adjust claims and secure privileges, or unless the bare possession of life is the only privilege which Americans are to enjoy. For a power to grant pardons is the only one which their Parliament or Prince have thought proper to give them. And yet they speak of peace. But they hold daggers in their hands. They invite you to accept of blessings, and stain your habitations with blood. Their voice resembles the voice of Jacob, but their hands are like the hands of Esau.

'If their sovereign intends to repeal any of the acts we complain of, why are they not especially named? If he designs you shall be free, why does he not promise that the claim of his Parliament to bind you in all cases whatsoever, shall be given up and relinquished? If a reasonable peace was intended, why did he not empower his commissioners to treat with the Congress, or with the deputies from all the assemblies? or why was not some other mode devised, in which America might be heard? Is it not highly ridiculous for them to pretend that they are authorized to treat of a peace between Britain and America with every man they meet? Was such a treaty ever heard of before? Is such an instance to be met with in the history of mankind? No! The truth is, peace is not meant; and their specious pretences and proclamations are calculated only to disunite and deceive.

'If the King of Britain really desires peace, why did he order all your vessels to be seized and confiscated? Why did he most cruelly command that the men found on board such vessels should be added to the crews of his ships of war, and compelled to fight against their own countrymen; to spill the blood of their neighbors and friends, nay, of their fathers, their brothers, and children? And all this before his pretended ambassadors of peace had arrived on our shores. Does any history, sacred or profane, record anything more impious, more horribly, more execrably wicked, tyrannical, or devilish? If there be one single idea of peace in his mind, why does he order your cities to be burnt, your country desolated, your brethren to starve, and languish, and die in prisons? If anything was intended besides destruction, devastation, and bloodshed, why are the mercenaries of Germany transported near four thousand miles, to plunder your houses, to ravish your wives and daughters, to strip your infant children, to expose whole families naked, miserable, and forlorn, to want, to hunger, to inclement skies, and wretched deaths? If peace were not totally reprobated by him, why are those pusillanimous, deluded, servile wretches among you, who, for present ease or impious bribes, would sell their liberty, their children, and their souls — who, like savages, worship every devil who promises not to hurt them, or obey any mandate, however cruel, for which they are paid — how is it that these sordid, degenerate creatures, who bow their knee to this King, and daily offer incense at his shrine, should be denied the peace so repeatedly promised them? Why are they indiscriminately abused, robbed, and plundered, with their more deserving neighbors? But in this world, as in the other, it is right and just that the wicked should be punished by their seducers.'

Treating the idea of peace as delusive, the address enumerates the advantages the Americans possess over their enemies, notwithstanding the present gloom. Their prospects are rapidly and strikingly contrasted with those of the British. Even if Philadelphia should be taken or abandoned, the conquest of America would still be at a great distance. 'Millions, determined to be free, still remain to be subdued—millions who disdain to part with their liberties, their consciences, and the happiness of their posterity in future ages, for infamous protections and dishonorable pardons.' Shown to be possessed of the means of defence, the citizens of the State were called on to employ them. 'Rouse, therefore, brave citizens! do your duty like men! and be persuaded that Divine Providence will not permit this western world to be involved in the horrors of slavery. Consider that, from the earliest ages of the world, religion, liberty, and empire have been bending their course towards the setting sun. The holy gospels are yet to be preached to these western regions, and we have the highest reason to believe that the Almighty will not suffer slavery and the gospel to go hand in hand. It cannot, it will not be.'[1]

While denouncing the enemy in language thus severe, and at the same time pursuing the most stringent measures against the disaffected, making humanity to individuals subordinate to public considerations, when they were irreconcilable, no spirit of vindictiveness or cruelty governed any part of Mr. Jay's conduct. His heart remained the seat of all kindly charities and warm, sympathetic feelings. Even towards England, a country which had inflicted so much distress upon his own, he could cherish no resentment. In a letter, written fifteen months later than the period of which we now speak, he says, 'I view a return to the domination of Britain with horror, and would risk all for independence; but that point ceded, I would give them advantageous commercial terms. The destruction of Old England would hurt me; I wish it well: it afforded my ancestors an asylum from persecution.'[2] About the same time he wrote to his old friend Peter Van Schaack, who had assumed a position of neutrality in the pending controversy which the whigs could not consistently, perhaps, respect: 'Any services in my power, command; I mean never to forget my friends, however different our noses or sentiments may be.'[3] He would not countenance in others, any more than he

[1] American Archives, vol. iii., 5th series, pp. 1382–1388.

[2] Life and Writings, vol. ii., p. 24.

[3] Life of Peter Van Schaack, p. 99. The life of this gentleman, by

would practise himself, unnecessary rigor towards either internal or external enemies. When the demands of the public safety and welfare were satisfied, he was the advo-

---

his descendant, Henry C. Van Schaack, is a work of decided merit and interest. It is written in a spirit of impartiality and candor, and gives the reader a very pleasing impression of its subject. Peter Van Schaack was a man of ability, of high character, and honorable sentiments. Those who live amid the hatred, enmity, and strife of civil war, and preserve the spring of gentle affections pure and clear, evince a charity equally 'hard and rare.' And this praise belongs to Mr. Van Schaack. Amid all the severe trials of his life, he never forgot what was due to his opponents nor what belonged to himself. He united moderation with firmness, and while his old friends might regret his politics, they never doubted his integrity, his candor, or his sincerity. He and Mr. Jay early contracted a friendship for each other, which no subsequent circumstances served to impair.

The following extracts from a letter, written by the latter to the former, dated at Paris, September 17th, 1782, disclose the governing motives of the writer's public conduct: 'In the course of the present troubles I have adhered to certain fixed principles, and faithfully obeyed their dictates, without regarding the consequences of such conduct to my friends, my family, or myself; all of whom, however dreadful the thought, I have ever been ready to sacrifice, if necessary, to the public objects in contest. Believe me, my heart has nevertheless been, on more than one occasion, afflicted by the execution of what I thought, and still think, was my duty. I felt very sensibly for you and for others; but as society can regard only the political propriety of men's conduct, and not the moral propriety of their motives to it, I could only lament your unavoidably becoming classed with many whose morality was convenience, and whose politics changed with the aspect of public affairs. My regard for you, as a good old friend, continued notwithstanding. God knows, that inclination never had a share in any proceedings of mine against you; from such 'thorns no man could expect to gather grapes;' and the only consolation that can grow in their unkindly shade is a consciousness of doing one's duty, and the reflection that as, on the one hand, I have uniformly preferred the public weal to my friends and connections, so, on the other, I have never been urged by private resentment to injure a single individual. Your judgment, and consequently your conscience, differed from mine on a very important question; but though, as an independent American, I considered all who were not for us, and you among the rest, as against us, yet, be assured, that John Jay did not cease to be a friend to Peter Van Schaack. No

cate of lenity. On one occasion, having been led to believe that a committee-man in Westchester County had exercised his power with unjustifiable severity, he procured a vote of the Convention, censuring his conduct. As the man was not summoned before the Convention to defend the charges preferred against him, but was condemned unheard, he certainly had just cause of complaint. Meeting Mr. Jay some time after, he assured him of his innocence, and complained of the *ex parte* proceedings against him. 'You are right, and I was wrong,' said Mr. Jay, 'and I ask your pardon.' Grasping his hand, the committee-man exclaimed, 'I have often heard that John Jay was a great man, and now I know it.'

On the 15th day of October, it was ordered by the Convention 'that Mr. Jay have leave of absence, to assist in removing his aged parents, with their effects, out of danger of the enemy.' He repaired to Rye, and succeeded in removing them to Fishkill, where his excellent mother died in the early part of the following year. The family estate at Rye soon after fell into the hands of the enemy, and was not regained until after the war. If Mr. Jay's views had prevailed, the whole southern

---

one can serve two masters: either Britain was right and America wrong, or America was right and Britain wrong. They who thought Britain right, were bound to support her; and America had a just claim to the services of those who approved her cause. Hence, it became our duty to take one side or the other; and no man is to be blamed for preferring the one which his reason recommended as the most just and virtuous. Several of our countrymen indeed left and took arms against us, not from any such principles, but from the most dishonorable of human motives. Their conduct has been of a piece with their inducements, for they have far out-stripped savages in perfidy and cruelty. Against these men, every American must set his face and steel his heart. There are others of them, though not many, who, I believe, opposed us because they thought they could not conscientiously go with us. To such of these as have behaved with humanity, I wish every species of prosperity that may consist with the good of my country."

portion of the State would, before this, have first been desolated, and then abandoned to the enemy. He explained the mode of defence he would have adopted, in a letter to his friend Gouverneur Morris, dated at Fishkill, October 6th. The following extract will disclose his plan.

'Had I been vested with absolute power in this State, I have often said, and still think, that I would, last Spring, have desolated all Long Island, Staten Island, the city and county of New York, and all that part of the county of Westchester which lies below the mountains. I would then have stationed the main body of the army in the mountains on the east, and eight or ten thousand men in the Highlands, on the west side of the river. I would have directed the river at Fort Montgomery, which is nearly at the southern extremity of the mountains, to be so shallowed as to afford only depth sufficient for an Albany sloop, and all the southern passes and defiles in the mountains to be strongly fortified. Nor *do I think the shallowing of the river* a romantic scheme. Rocky mountains rise immediately from the shores. The breadth is not very great, though the depth is. But what cannot eight or ten thousand men well worked effect? According to this plan of defence, the State would be absolutely impregnable against all the world on the sea side, and would have nothing to fear except from the way of the lake. Should the enemy gain the river, even below the mountains, I think I foresee that a retreat would become necessary, and I can't forbear wishing that a desire of saving a few more acres may not lead us into difficulty.'[1]

[1] Force's American Archives, 5th series, vol. ii. He wrote to the same effect, a few days after, to his friend Edward Rutledge. 'I wish,' he said, 'our army well stationed in the Highlands, and all the lower country desolated; we might then bid defiance to all the further efforts of the enemy on that quarter.' This letter was dated October 11th, 1776. Life of John Jay, vol. ii., p. 7.

When Mr. Jay returned to New York at the time and for the purpose we have described, he had no expectation of being absent from his seat in the Continental Congress more than a few weeks. The arduous circumstances of the State, however, rendered his presence at home more important than at Philadelphia. 'How long I may be detained here,' he writes to his friend Edward Rutledge, on the 6th day of July, 'is uncertain; but I see no prospect of returning to you for a month or two yet to come.'[1] He did not then foresee the cheerless gloom that was soon to darken the fortunes of the State, and postpone his return to Congress for more than two years. Three months later, viz., on the 11th day of October, he writes again to the same gentleman: 'Although extremely anxious to be with you, the circumstances of this State will not admit of my leaving it. Governor Tryon has been very mischievous; and we find our hands full in counteracting and suppressing the conspiracies formed by him and his adherents.'[2]

One or two extracts from the letters of his particular friends, Edward Rutledge, whose ideas of men and things ran, for the most part, parallel with his own, and Robert Morris, whose various services to his country, especially in the administration of the finances, were of the most important character, will evince, in some measure, how highly Mr. Jay's abilities and character were estimated by his contemporaries. 'I wish you had done with your Convention,' writes Morris on the 23d day of September, 'you are really wanted exceedingly in Congress; they are very thin.'[3] 'Why,' he again writes on the 4th day of the following February, 'are we so long deprived of your abilities in Congress? Perhaps they are more usefully exerted where you are; that may be the case: but

---

[1] Life of John Jay, vol. i., p. 62. [2] Ibid, vol. ii., p. 7.
[3] Ibid, vol. i., p. 66.

such men as you, in times like these, should be everywhere.'[1] 'As several of the reasons which operated against your or Livingston's leaving the State,' says Rutledge, in a letter dated November 24th, 1776, 'are now removed, I think you would be of vast service in Congress. You know that body possesses its share of human weakness, and that it is not impossible for the members of that House to have their attention engrossed by subjects which might as well be postponed for the present, while such as require despatch have been—I had almost said — neglected. This may be the case with the measures which should be taken for the defence of your State. It is, therefore, your interest and your duty, if you are not prevented by some superior public concern, to attend the House, and that soon; you have a right to demand their attention, and I trust they will give you early assistance.'[2]

Mr. Rutledge, at this time, was on the point of leaving Congress and returning home. He thought, from various circumstances, that General Howe intended to make South Carolina the scene of military operations, and, consequently, that his services would be more valuable in the field than in the Cabinet. 'I could not, however, think of quitting this part of the Continent,' he says in the letter to Jay from which we have quoted, 'without writing you what appeared to me of consequence; especially when I consider that it is probable, at least possible, that this may be the last time I may have it in my power to give you any evidence of my affection. I shall add no more than that you have my best wishes for your happiness, and that if I fall in the defence of my country, it will alleviate my misfortune to think that it is in support of the best of causes, and that I am esteemed by one of the best of men.'[3]

---

[1] Life of John Jay, vol. i., p. 65. [2] Ibid, vol. ii., p. 9.
[3] Force's American Archives, 5th series, vol. iii., p. 825.

We have now seen how various and important had been Mr. Jay's services in the New York Congress and Convention. We have yet to describe the part he performed in framing the constitution and organizing the government of that State. Constitution-making, in our day, is not regarded as a very serious business. Frequent experiments have made all the steps of the process familiar, and the modern politician goes to this task with an assured confidence in his skill as an architect, and the fitness of his materials for the governmental edifice. But at the era of the Revolution, the construction of a government was considered as a very solemn concern; it was a novel enterprise, and the architect had to rely upon his invention rather than upon his memory. In New York there was great diversity of opinion as to the leading principles which should be incorporated into the framework of the Constitution. 'We have a government, you know, to form,' wrote Jay to Rutledge, 'and God only knows what it will resemble. Our politicians, like some guests at a feast, are perplexed and undetermined which dish to prefer.' [1] In the next chapter we shall see what success attended the labors of Mr. Jay to temper their various tastes.

[1] Life of John Jay, vol. i., p. 62.

CHAPTER VIII.

1776—1777.

FORMATION OF THE NEW YORK CONSTITUTION.

THE great writer or painter, it has been observed, represents man in situations possible to the individual, but not common to mankind. The great lawgiver, on the contrary, regards slightly, or not at all, exceptional cases, and adapts his legislation to the actual circumstances of his time and country. He contemplates the community 'in the whole body of its solidity and compound mass,' and on a just apprehension of its collective condition depends all the efficacy of his measures. The merit of the framers of the several American constitutions consists in this; that they comprehended the actual necessities of the time, and the actual sentiments of the people. They saw clearly, that along with the change in the political condition of the country, other changes, not less radical, had taken place. The revolution was both political and moral. It severed the bond that united the colonies to England, and, at the same time, disinthralled the minds of the people. The superstitious reverence that 'doth hedge' and support ancient institutions, was dissipated. The unpopularity of the monarch had equally involved monarchy, and rendered any scheme of government founded on that basis wholly impracticable. Aristocracy, created by law, sustained by privilege, and made hereditary, was out of the question. The proposition would not for a moment have been entertained. The time and occasion had arrived when republican institutions were again to be inaugurated, and under more favorable circumstances than had hitherto attended the existence of that description of government.

But while there was a very general concurrence of opinion among the leading minds of the country as to the fundamental principles that should distinguish their future governments, there was no little diversity as to the precise forms in which those principles should be embodied. The important considerations were, as to the constitution of the several departments of state—whether the executive should be clothed with more or less power; whether the legislature should consist of a single assembly, or of two houses, whose concurrence should be necessary to the passage of any law, and whether the tenure of office should be limited to a definite period, or be held *quam diu se bene gesserit.*

The views of Mr. Jay upon these interesting topics will appear as we proceed to state the part he took in framing the Constitution of New York. He and his coadjutors, happily succeeded in satisfying the demands of the time, and reconciling the discordant sentiments of individuals. Mr. Adams pronounced it the best constitution that had yet been adopted. It was conformable to his ideas, as set forth in his celebrated letter to Mr. Wythe, which was published in the spring of 1776.[1] He had apprehended, however, from the supposed politics of Mr. Jay, a different result. In a letter to Hugh Hughes, who had recently been appointed General Schuyler's Assistant Quarter-Master-General, and dated at Philadelphia, June 4th, 1776, he thus refers to Mr. Jay's presence at New York: 'I am very glad that Mr. J. is with you, and hope he will be of great service there; but will he not be for making your Governor and Counsellors for life, or during good behavior? I should dread

[1] Life and Works, vol. iii., p. 59.

such a Constitution in these perilous times, because however wise and brave and virtuous these rulers may be at their first appointment, their tempers and designs will be very apt to change, and then they may have it in their power to betray the people, who will have no means of redress. The people ought to have frequently the opportunity, especially in these dangerous times, of considering the conduct of their leaders, and of approving or disapproving. You will have no safety without it.'[1]

It may not be amiss to notice, in this place, the suggestions of another distinguished gentleman of that period, as to the future government of New York. Edward Rutledge wrote to Mr. Jay on the 24th day of November, 1776, and after recommending certain plans for the defence of the State, he makes the following observations: 'If these things be done, and that soon, your country, I think, will be safe; provided you establish a good government, with a strong executive. A pure democracy may possibly do, when patriotism is the ruling passion; but when the State abounds with rascals, as is the case with too many at this day, you must suppress a little of that popular spirit. Vest the executive powers of government in an individual, that they may have vigor, and let them be as ample as is consistent with the great outlines of freedom.'[2]

We have seen in the preceding chapter that the Convention postponed the consideration of their future form of government until the 1st day of August. When that time arrived, the whole energy of the representative body was needed to provide for the common defence. A committee, however, was appointed to frame a constitution and bill of rights. It consisted of Mr. Jay, John Sloss Hobart, William Smith, William Duer, Gouverneur Mor-

[1] Life and Works, vol. ix., p. 388.

[2] Life and Writings of John Jay, vol. ii., p. 8.

ris, Robert R. Livingston, John Broome, John Morin Scott, Abraham Yates, Henry Wisner, Sen., Samuel Townshend, Charles De Witt, and Robert Yates. Subsequently Mr. Duane was added to the committee.

Mr. Jay was opposed to hastening deliberations upon so grave a subject. He thought, in the present arduous circumstances of the State, it would prove injurious; and that so serious an undertaking should await a more tranquil period. He thought they should first secure a State to govern, before they proceeded to organize a government. "He adopted the poet's motto, '*festinare nocet*,' and considered caution as the garland of wisdom, in a movement of so high a bearing on the destinies of the republic —

'Tempora quæque suo qui facit, ille sapit.'"[1]

But different views prevailed in the Convention. It was thought that a regularly-organized government would command more respect and act with more efficiency than authority as at present constituted. Accordingly, the committee were directed to make their report on the 26th day of August; a time surely too short for digesting a system of government, unless indeed it was supposed that a constitution would burst forth, Minerva-like, from the happy conceptions of the gentleman charged with that important duty. Mr. Jay, at this time, was absent on business connected with the Secret Committee. On the 12th day of August the Convention addressed a letter to him and R. R. Livingston, directing their attendance upon the committee to form a new government, if their present engagements would permit. In the meantime, however, the Convention were informed by General Clinton of the nature of their service elsewhere, and they resolved that it would be improper to call them from it.

---

[1] Sparks. Life of Morris, vol. i., p. 120.

The demands upon the members of the committee were too various and urgent to admit of their making a report at the time designated. The subject did not again engage the attention of the Convention until the 28th day of September. On that day the committee were instructed to report a form of government on or before the 12th day of the ensuing October; and it was ordered that they should sit every afternoon until they were ready to report. That the absence of members on other duties might not interrupt the deliberations of the committee, the chairman and any four of them were hereafter to be considered as a quorum. But pressed as the committee were for a report, it was delayed from time to time, until the 12th day of the following March. It was drawn up by Mr. Jay. The Constitution, as finally adopted, was chiefly the work of his hands. The long time that intervened between the appointment of the committee and their report was not without benefit. The sentiments of the members were matured and harmonized. Their report was made the order of the day, and when the urgent business of the Convention would admit of it, was called up and discussed by paragraphs.[1] Con-

---

[1] While these discussions were proceeding, the British undertook an expedition to Peekskill, to destroy a quantity of stores which the Americans had collected at that place. In a letter to his wife, dated at Kingston, March 25th, 1777, Mr. Jay thus refers to it: —

'We have lately received an uncertain, though unpleasant, account of the enemy's landing at Peekskill. How did your nerves bear the shock? My father and mother, I apprehend, were very uneasy. I should be happy, were it in my power, to bear all their, as well as your misfortunes. The infirmities of age, added to the terrors and calamities of war, conspire in depriving them of ease and enjoyment. I most sensibly feel for, and pity them. God grant them the only remedy against the evils inseparable from humanity — fortitude founded on resignation. The moment I may suspect you to be exposed to danger, I shall set out for Fishkill. As yet, I think you very safe; for, if the reports we have heard be true, the enemy's force is not sufficient to penetrate the country. I congratulate Peter on his recovery and return.

sidering the character of the Convention, Mr. Jay had thought it prudent that certain provisions should be omitted in the body of the instrument, and submitted as amendatory of it. They were, for the most part, introduced and supported by himself, Mr. Duane, Gouverneur Morris, R. R. Livingston, and a few others. On Sunday, the 20th of April, 1777, the frame of government, under which the people of New York lived and prospered for nearly half a century, received its finishing stroke. All the members of the Convention present on that occasion, with but a single exception, gave it their approval. Mr. Jay was absent. He had been called to Fishkill, to attend at the bedside of his dying mother.

The whole proceeding, in its last stages, was conducted with a good deal of precipitancy. The President of the Convention, General Ten Broeck, was necessarily absent. The Vice-President, Pierre Van Cortlandt, was on the opposite side of the river, detained by adverse weather. The Secretaries requested a delay in the vote, that they might have an opportunity to engross a proper copy for the signatures of members. But the Convention were not to be dissuaded from immediate and final action. The question was put and carried, and, as we have already observed, with but a single dissentient voice. The draft of the Constitution, as adopted, is now in existence, but in a very shattered condition, with many interlineations and erasures. It was signed by the President *pro tem.*, Leonard Gansevoort, but not countersigned by the Secretaries. The Convention had disregarded their request for delay, and they took that method to express their dissatisfaction.

Remind him of sending to Captain Platt's for the barley. Let not the fear of the enemy deter him from pursuing the business of the farm. The same Providence which enables us to sow may enable us to reap.

I am, my dear wife,

Your very affectionate

JOHN JAY.'

The Constitution being adopted, the Convention directed one of their secretaries to proceed to Fishkill, and have five hundred copies printed without the preamble, and twenty-five hundred with it. He was instructed to give gratuities to the printers, to have the work executed with despatch. Its formal promulgation was celebrated on the following Tuesday, at the Court-House in Kingston. The occasion was not distinguished for its splendor or solemnity. The whole proceeding was conducted in a very primitive style. A platform was erected on the end of a hogshead, and, from this simple rostrum, one of the secretaries, Robert Benson, read this important document.

And thus, amid the din of arms and in circumstances of confusion and peril, was framed and inaugurated the future government of New York. The political fathers of that great and flourishing commonwealth, unappalled by the dangers that menaced them, 'even in the depths of their calamity, and on the very ruins of their country, laid the foundations of a towering and durable greatness.'[1]

---

[1] The difficulties and dangers that environed New York during this period of her history, and the zeal and resolution with which they were encountered, are described by Chancellor Kent in the following passage from his Discourse before the New York Historical Society. 'The Congress of this colony, during the years 1775 and 1776, had to meet difficulties and dangers almost sufficient to subdue the firmest resolution. The population of the colony was short of 200,000 souls. It had a vast body of disaffected inhabitants within its own bosom. It had numerous tribes of hostile savages on its extended frontier. The bonds of society seemed to have been broken up, and society itself resolved into its primitive elements. There was no civil government but such as had been introduced by the Provincial Congress and county committees as temporary expedients. It had an enemy's province in the rear, strengthened by large and well-appointed forces. It had an open and exposed seaport, without any adequate means to defend it. In the summer of 1776, the State was actually invaded, not only upon our Canadian, but upon our Atlantic frontier, by a formidable fleet and army, calculated by the power that sent them, to be sufficient to annihilate at once all our infant

The general outlines and peculiar characteristics of their work will necessarily arrest our attention.

The supreme legislative power of the State was lodged in two separate and distinct bodies, the one called the Assembly, and the other the Senate. The members of the Assembly were elected annually; the members of the Senate, every four years.

The supreme executive authority was lodged in a Governor, whose term of office was three years.

The judicial power was vested in a Chancellor, Judges of the Supreme Court, and the first Judges of County Courts. They were to hold their offices during good behavior, or until they attained the age of sixty years.

Every male inhabitant of full age, who had personally resided within one of the counties of the State for six months immediately preceding the day of election, was entitled to vote for representatives of such county in the Assembly, if during the said time, he had been a freeholder within the county of the value of twenty pounds, or had rented a tenement therein of the yearly value of forty shillings, and had been rated and actually paid taxes to the State.

To vote for Senators required the possession, on the part of the elector, of a freehold of the value of one hundred pounds over and above all debts charged thereon.

The common law, the Statute law of Great Britain and of the Colonial Legislature, which together formed the law of the colony on the 19th day of April, 1775, were declared to be the law of the State, subject to such alterations as the Legislature might subsequently make.

---

republics. In the midst of this appalling storm, the virtue of our people, animated by a host of intrepid patriots, the mention of whose names is enough to kindle enthusiasm in the breasts of the present generation, remained glowing, unmoved, and invincible. It would be difficult to find any other people who have been put to a severer test, or, on trial, gave higher proofs of courage and capacity.'

But every part of the said statute or common law that might be construed 'to establish or maintain any particular denomination of Christians or their ministers,' or that was repugnant to the constitution, was abrogated and rejected. The free exercise and enjoyment of religion was secured to all without discrimination or preference. But ministers and priests were declared to be ineligible to, and incapable of holding any civil or military office within the State.[1]

One or two features of the Constitution, distinguished for their singularity and the conflicts and embarrassments that attended their practical operation, deserve particular mention. The *Council of Appointment* was an anomaly in politics. It owed its origin to the antagonistic views of leading members of the committee and Convention, and the necessity of some plan which should harmonize action. Mr. Jay was its author. In the original draft of the Constitution, the appointing power was vested in the Governor and Legislature; the former nominating, and the latter confirming or rejecting his nominations. This clause was not satisfactory to Mr. Jay, but was approved by the majority of voices in the committee. The Convention, however, concurred with Mr. Jay, and rejected it. Various expedients were proposed as a substi-

[1] Soon after the Convention came together, one of the members, Mr. Kettletas, who was a clergyman, asked leave of absence for a short time, in order to visit his parish. The resolution introduced on the occasion by Mr. Jay, and adopted by the House, indirectly exhibits the opinion he entertained of ministers leaving the pulpit to serve in public bodies. It ran thus: 'Whereas, the Rev. Mr. Kettletas, one of the deputies from Queen's County, having been solemnly devoted to the service of God and the cure of souls, has good right to expect and claim an exemption from all such employments as would divert his attention from the affairs of that kingdom which is not of this world — Resolved, that the said Mr. Kettletas be at liberty to attend this House at such times only as he may think proper, and that his absence be not considered by this House as a neglect of duty.'

tute. Some were for investing the Legislature with the power; some for reversing the recommendation of the committee, and giving the Legislature the power of nomination, and the Governor the power of appointment. Others proposed to vest the power in the Governor and Judges of the Supreme Court. This latter proposition provoked a long and fruitless discussion. In the evening of the day it occurred, Mr. Jay and Mr. Morris met at the rooms of R. R. Livingston. Here the subject was again considered. Mr Jay finally proposed to constitute a council of appointment, in the mode we shall presently describe. His project was acceded to by Morris and Livingston, who agreed to support it in the Convention. That body approved it, and thus was created what subsequently became the most unpopular element of the Constitution. The clause in which it was embodied required the Assembly, once in every year, to nominate and appoint one of the Senators from each of the four great districts into which the State was divided, who should form a council for the appointment of all officers whose appointment was not otherwise provided for by the Constitution. The Governor was made the President of this Council, and had a casting vote, but none other. With the advice and consent of the Council, constituted as we have described, he was to appoint all officers except those we have mentioned. To avoid the casting vote of the Governor, Mr. Jay would have made the Speaker of the Assembly a sixth member of the Council. And he would have restrained the Council from granting offices to themselves.[1]

[1] It does not clearly appear that the danger of this practice suggested itself to Mr. Jay before the adoption of the Constitution. But in a letter to Mr. Morris, dated nearly a year after that event, viz., on the 14th day of April, 1778, he condemns it, and thinks the Constitution defective in not having guarded against it. Vide Sparks' Life of Morris, vol. i., p. 123, a work to which I am materially indebted for the seeret history of the New York Constitution.

But in this, as in some other particulars, his views were not followed. The appointment of the registers, clerks, and marshals of the respective courts, was conferred on the Chancellor and Judges. This he thought a defect. He objected, too, to the clause requiring attorneys, solicitors, and counsellors-at-law to be licensed by the first judge of every court in which they should respectively practise. He thought this power should be wholly vested in the Supreme Court.

The *Council of Revision* was another peculiar feature of the Constitution. It was composed of the Governor, the Chancellor, and the Judges of the Supreme Court, or any two of them. All bills, before they became laws, were to be presented to the Council for their revisal and consideration. In a word, the veto power, as lodged by the Constitution of the United States in the executive, was lodged, by the Constitution of New York, in the *Council of Revision.* This branch of the government, from collision with the Legislature in times of high party excitement, became exceedingly unpopular. But with obvious defects in its arrangement, it is impossible to deny that on the whole it operated beneficially. It did good, and it prevented mischief. The result of the experiment, however, will not be likely to invite a repetition of it. It brought the officers of the judiciary in conflict with the Legislature, and tended to weaken the hold they had upon the respect and confidence of the people. The system was directly calculated to induce partisanship on the part of the judges, and a combination with the executive to carry out his political views. Besides, it can rarely be advisable to enable the members of the judiciary, holding their offices upon such a tenure as the Judiciary of New York, and not likely, from their situation, their habits of life and thought, to keep pace with the rising and progressive energies of the State, to check and repress the process of growth and development. Judges seldom make good legislators. Their views are apt to be timid and absurdly conservative. Their scheme of politics is usually merely defensive of property and old institutions. But existing law, so far as it is the exponent of whatever is eternal in the nature of society, will assert itself. So far as it is the exponent of present civilization, it is mutable, and ought not, and will not, long survive the condition of things whence it originated. Government should never be constructed in such mode that it may impede the onward career of mankind.

It was a favorite maxim with Mr. Jay 'that those who own the country ought to govern it.'[1] His views were embodied in the Constitution, which, we have already seen, restricted the right of suffrage in several instances to freeholders. If the only concern of government was the protection of property, there could be no doubt of the propriety of Mr. Jay's dogma. It would be merely repeating, in different language, the old formula that property should make the law for property. But if that proposition is admitted, the corollary is obvious and undeniable, that persons should make the law for persons. But property and persons cannot be kept totally distinct, and the principle which we have mentioned can never be practically applied. Authority finds its natural source in the people. Property is one of their incidental rights; but it is confounding all just distinctions to give to the incident the place of the principle. Or, in other words, to give property privileges which are denied to persons. It is impolitic and injurious to disfranchise any portion of the commonwealth. An element of discontent is thereby created which will forever foment disorder and embarrass the State. Conditions of society may readily be conceived, where necessity would justify a different rule. When the people are sunk in vice and ignorance,

[1] William Jay. Life of John Jay, vol. i., p. 70.

and not habituated to liberty and subordination to law, it would ill consist with the security and happiness of the community, to endow them with privileges which are the guerdon of virtue and intelligence. But in that state of things, it would be the absence of something very different from property that operated to exclude them from a voice in the government. In our country, and in our age, with a free press and free schools, nobody need be alarmed at the most ample extension of the right of suffrage. The collected voice of such a people may confound the calculations of politicians, but experience will generally demonstrate that their action proceeds from a large and sagacious view of their wants and interests.

To that clause of the Constitution, allowing the free exercise of religion within the State, Mr. Jay proposed to add, 'except the professors of the religion of the Church of Rome, who ought not to hold lands in, or be admitted to a participation of the civil rights enjoyed by the members of this State, until such time as the said professors shall appear in the Supreme Court of the State, and there most solemnly swear that they verily believe in their consciences that no pope, priest, or foreign authority on earth has power to absolve the subjects of this State from their allegiance to the same. And farther, that they renounce, and believe to be false and wicked, the dangerous and damnable doctrine that the pope, or any other earthly authority, has power to absolve men from sins described in, and prohibited by, the Holy Gospel of Jesus Christ; and, particularly, that no pope, priest, or foreign authority on earth has power to absolve them from the obligation of this oath.' This proposition was rejected.

The next day Mr. Jay introduced the clause which, as subsequently amended, was incorporated into the Constitution. It reads thus: 'Provided that the liberty of conscience hereby granted shall not be construed to encourage licentiousness, nor be used in such manner as to disturb or endanger the safety of the State.' The latter part of this clause, on the motion of Gouverneur Morris, was amended so as to read — 'or justify practices inconsistent with the peace and safety of this State.'

The curious exception to religious freedom introduced and supported by Mr. Jay in the Convention, would no doubt be deemed by numbers, even at the present day, as wise and salutary. The idea is not wholly exploded that the professors of the Romish faith acknowledge a paramount authority in the Pope in all matters, civil as well as religious, and that conjunctures may arise when that authority will be exerted. Undoubtedly every State may guard itself, as far as possible, against the danger, if danger there be, of foreign interference, whether by pope or king, with the primary obligations of its citizens. And if the head of the Catholic Church did arrogate to himself the right to absolve members of that communion from allegiance to the Government under which they live, and they admitted the pretension, then surely it would be proper for such Government to defend itself, in some adequate mode, from the consequences of such an assumption. But in our day, and among the enlightened portion of mankind, any apprehension of danger to Government from that source is laughed to scorn.

Mr. Jay, however, thought differently. He believed there was a very real and sensible danger. He was not singular in that belief. Many members of the Convention agreed with him. It was a common notion both in England and this country. He would guard against it. Solicitude for the welfare of the Commonwealth, and not 'odd, perverse antipathies,' suggests the motive that swayed him in introducing the clause we have mentioned. Had he gone no further than to make the holding of lands, and the enjoyment of civil rights dependent on a condition purely civil in its nature, viz., that Catholics should consider their allegiance binding, and beyond the power of the Pope to absolve them, however much we might question its expediency, we could not doubt the abstract right of the Convention to impose it. But when he proceeded to annex another condition, as the *sine qua non* of their participation in the privileges of citizenship, viz., that they should 'renounce, and believe to be false and wicked, the dangerous and damnable doctrine that the Pope or any other earthly authority has power to absolve men from sins described in, and prohibited by, the Holy Gospel of Jesus Christ,' he proposed what was obviously violative of the first principles of religious liberty. To give civil rights to a man who believes that God will absolve him from sin upon prayer and repentance, and deny them to another who believes that, upon the same condition, the Pope possesses such power of absolution, is certainly neither toleration nor charity.

Before the Revolution, the propriety and rectitude of slavery were scarcely doubted. With that event came a marked change in the public sentiment. The idea, now professed, that the condition of slavery is right in principle — a benefit to the slave and a blessing to the State — was entertained but by few. Nor, on the other hand, had the dogmas of the Abolitionists been received and admitted as obvious truths. Slavery was very generally regarded by the leading minds of the country as indefensible in theory and injurious in practice, but nevertheless so inwrought into the very texture of society in many of the colonies, that no rude hand should be laid upon it.[1] Their only hope of its final extinction was in

[1] In the course of his speech to the young men of Albany, Mr. Webster, referring to the change of opinion that had taken place upon this vexed and perplexing subject of slavery, said: 'I allude to this only to show that the introduction of slavery into the Southern States is not to be visited upon the generation that achieved the independence of this

some scheme founded on a comprehensive forecast, and on a large and liberal view of all the varied circumstances of a case full of difficulty and full of danger. They saw clearly, that an institution 'which was combined with the interest of the great and the many; which was moulded into the laws, the manners, and civil institutions' of extensive communities, could not suddenly be brought to the ground, 'without a fearful struggle,' nor 'without a violent concussion of itself and all about it.'

Mr. Jay was among the first who saw in the existence of slavery a singularly inconsistent commentary on the principles of the Declaration of Independence. He would have liberty as broad and general as the air, but he

---

country. On the contrary, all the eminent men of that day regretted its existence. And you, my young friends of Albany, if you will take the pains to go back to the debates of that period, from the meeting of the first Congress in 1774, I mean the Congress of the Confederation, to the adoption of the present Constitution and the enactment of the first laws under it — you, or any body who will make that necessary research, will find that Southern men and Southern States, as represented in Congress, lamented the existence of slavery in far more earnest and emphatic terms than the Northern; for, though it did exist in the Northern States, it was a feeble taper just going out, soon to end, and nothing was feared from it; while leading men of the South, and especially of Virginia, felt and acknowledged that it was a moral and political evil; that it weakened the arm of the freeman, and kept back the progress and success of free labor; and they said with truth, and all history verifies the observation, 'that if the shores of the Chesapeake had been made as free to free labor as the shores of the North River, New York might have been great, but Virginia would have been great also.' That was the sentiment." The Works of Daniel Webster, vol. ii., p. 573.

In further corroboration of what is stated in the text, we may cite the sentiments of Washington. 'To set the slaves afloat at once,' he wrote to Lafayette, 'would, I really believe, be productive of much inconvenience and mischief; but, by degrees, it certainly might, and assuredly ought, to be effected; and that, too, by legislative authority.' Writings of Washington, vol. ix., p. 163.

See also Writings of Jefferson. Hildreth's History of the U. S., vol. iii.

would not follow the counsels of folly and fanaticism. Hence, he strenuously urged the insertion of an article in the Constitution, recommending the future Legislature of the State to take effectual measures for abolishing domestic slavery, as soon as it could be done consistently with public safety and the rights of private property, 'so that in future ages every human being who breathes the air of this State shall enjoy the privileges of a freeman.' But this proposition, although supported by some of the most eminent characters of the Convention, was not adopted.

Since we have had occasion to refer to this subject, we shall violate the order of time and arrangement, and bring together in this place the general opinions and practice of Mr. Jay with regard to it. In a letter, written in the year 1780, while in Spain, to his friend Egbert Benson,[1] who, at that time, was the Attorney-General of New York, he says: 'An excellent law might be made out of the Pennsylvania one for the gradual abolition of slavery. Till America comes into this measure, her prayers to Heaven for liberty will be impious. This is a strong expression, but it is just. Were I in your legislature, I would prepare a bill for the purpose with great care, and I would never cease moving it till it became a law, or I ceased to be a member. I believe God governs the world, and I believe it to be a maxim in his

[1] 'Egbert Benson rendered eminent service to this State throughout the whole period of the American war. He was zealous, firm, active, and extensively useful, from the very beginning of the contest. In 1777 he was appointed Attorney-General, and in that office, in the Legislature, and in Congress, his devotion to the public interest was unremitted. The value of his services as a member of the Legislature throughout the war, was beyond all price; and in the able, constant, accurate, and faithful discharge of the duties of that station, he has scarcely had an equal in the legislative annals of this State.' Chancellor Kent: Discourse before the New York Historical Society: New York Hist. Col. (N. S.), vol. i., p. 31.

as in our court, that those who ask for equity, ought to do it.' In another letter, written at a later period, he observes: 'It is much to be wished that slavery may be abolished. The honor of the States, as well as justice and humanity, in my opinion, loudly call upon them to emancipate these unhappy people. To contend for our own liberty, and to deny that blessing to others, involves an inconsistency not to be excused.'

In 1788, three years from the date of this last letter, he wrote, on behalf of a society which we shall presently describe, to a society in England, formed for promoting the abolition of slavery. In that letter he says: 'That they who know the value of liberty, and are blessed with the enjoyment of it, ought not to subject others to slavery, is, like most other moral precepts, more generally admitted in theory than observed in practice. . . . . The United States are far from being irreproachable in this respect. It undoubtedly is very inconsistent with their declarations on the subject of human rights to permit a single slave to be found within their jurisdiction, and we confess the justice of your strictures on that head. Permit us, however, to observe, that although consequences ought not to deter us from doing what is right, yet that it is not easy to persuade men in general to act on that magnanimous and disinterested principle. It is well known that errors, either in opinion or practice, long entertained or indulged, are difficult to eradicate, and particularly so when they have become, as it were, incorporated in the civil institutions and domestic economy of a whole people.'

After referring to the progression of opinion upon this subject, he says: 'We have good reason to hope and believe that if the natural operations of truth are constantly watched and assisted, but not forced and precipitated, that end we all aim at will finally be attained in this country.'[1]

---

[1] Life of John Jay, vol. i., pp. 229–235.

These extracts from the letters of Mr. Jay indicate his opinions with regard to slavery, and are illustrated by his practice. Viewed in that connection, it is evident that while he was an advocate of abolition, he discountenanced all violent and impracticable schemes to promote that object. He considered the temper of the times and the situation of affairs. He respected the laws. He consulted the opinions of others as well as his own. He trusted to the gradual amelioration of public sentiment. His conscience did not tell him that an institution which he deemed wrong in principle must therefore, without regard to any other consideration, be instantly abolished. He contemplated the interests of the owner as well as the freedom of the slave. He never proposed any other than a gradual plan of emancipation. In this he had the concurrence of Washington.

Mr. Jay was in the habit of purchasing slaves, and manumitting them at proper ages, and when their faithful services afforded a reasonable retribution.[1] 'As free

[1] As illustrative of this practice, the following instrument may not be without interest. 'To all to whom these presents shall come or may concern: I, John Jay, of the city of New York, in America, Esq., but now residing at Chaillot, near Paris, in France, send greeting. WHEREAS, in the month of December, in the year 1779, I purchased at Martinico, a negro boy, named Benoit, who has ever since been with me: And WHEREAS, the children of men are, by nature, equally free, and cannot, without injustice, be either reduced to, or held in, slavery; And WHEREAS, it is therefore right that after the said Benoit shall have served me until the value of his services amount to a moderate compensation for the money expended for him, he should be manumitted: and whereas, his services for three years more would, in my opinion, be sufficient for that purpose. NOW, KNOW YE, that if the said Benoit shall continue to serve me with a common and reasonable degree of fidelity for three years from the date hereof, he shall ever afterward be a free man. And I do, for myself, my heirs, executors, and administrators, consent, agree, and declare, that all my right and title to the said Benoit shall then cease, determine, and become absolutely null and void, and that he shall thenceforth

servants,' says his son, 'became more common, he was gradually relieved from the necessity of purchasing slaves.' Such being his practice, he would hardly prescribe a different rule for others. He would hardly say, that whilst he might reimburse himself for the purchase of these people, others were under an obligation to manumit them, without any regard to their own interests whatever.

In 1785, Mr. Jay was chosen the President of a society formed in New York, 'for promoting the manumission of slaves, and protecting such of them as have been, or may be, liberated.' This society, Mr. William Jay tells us, neither expected nor attempted to effect any sudden alteration in the laws relating to slavery, but its exertions were chiefly directed to the protection of manumitted

---

be as free to all intents and purposes as if he had never been a slave. In witness whereof, I have hereunto set my hand and seal, at Chaillot, the 21st day of March, in the year of our Lord, 1784.'

'JOHN JAY. [L. S.]'

We may insert here, as evidence of the humanity of Mr. Jay, one or two additional extracts from his letters. While in Spain in 1781, he is informed that a number of armed robbers had taken from his father's family their money, plate, &c. He wrote to his brother on the occasion, and referring to the condition of the family, he says: 'On considering the state of the family, I am really at a loss to see how the number of it can be considerably reduced. As to the old servants, who have expended their strength and youth for the family, they ought and must be taken good care of, while we have the means of doing it; common justice, and, I may say, gratitude, demands it.'

In reply to a letter from his friend Robert R. Livingston, dated May 22d, 1782, informing him of the death of his father, Mr. Jay, who was then at Paris, writes, under date of August 13th, as follows: 'I hear my father has given some of the servants freedom, and that some other of the older ones have been put out. Old servants are sometimes neglected. Desire Mr. Benson to keep an eye over them, and not let any of them want; and, for that purpose, place fifty pounds in his hands, which he will apply at his discretion, as necessity may, from time to time, require. He must also reimburse himself for any expenses he may be at on this account.'

slaves, and to the education of colored children. Mr. Jay continued at the head of this society until he became Chief Justice of the United States, when, thinking it possible that questions might be brought before him in which the society was interested, he deemed it proper to dissolve his official connection with it.[1]

It will be recollected that Mr. Jay was absent when the Constitution was adopted. Omissions were made which he regretted, and additions which he disapproved. In a letter to his friends R. R. Livingston and Gouverneur Morris, dated April the 29th, he thus indicates his opinions: 'The difficulty of getting any government at all,' he says, 'you know has long been an apprehension of little influence on my mind, and always appeared to be founded less in fact than in a design of quickening the pace of the House. The other parts of the Constitution I approve, and only regret that, like a harvest cut before it was ripe, the grain has shrunk. Exclusive of the clauses which I have mentioned, and which I wish had been added, another material one has been omitted, viz., a direction that all persons holding offices under Government should take an oath of allegiance to it, and renounce all allegiance and subjection to foreign kings, princes, and states, in all matters ecclesiastical as well as civil. I should also have been for a clause against the continuation of domestic slavery, and for the support and encouragement of literature, as well as some other matters, though perhaps of less consequence. Though the birth of the Constitution was, in my judgment, premature, I shall, nevertheless, do all in my power to nurse and keep it alive, being far from approving the Spartan law, which encouraged parents to destroy such of their children as, perhaps by some cross accident, might come into the world defective or misshapen.'[2]

[1] Life of John Jay, vol. i., p. 235.

[2] Ibid, p. 69. Sparks' Life of Morris, vol. i.

But whatever the real or supposed defects of the Constitution, it was received with very general favor. 'Our Constitution is universally approved,' wrote Jay to Gansevoort on the 5th of June, 1777, 'even in New England, where few New York productions have credit.'[1] As we have already mentioned, it continued in existence nearly half a century. Meanwhile, a new condition of things had arisen, obvious changes had taken place, new ideas prevailed, the schoolmaster had been abroad, and the Convention which assembled at Albany in the summer of 1821, scarcely left untouched a single tile or stone of the venerable fabric erected by the patriots of the revolution.[2]

[1] Life and Writings of John Jay, p. 12.

[2] The debates in this Convention were conducted with great ability. Several of the most eminent men who have done honor to their times and country were members. Among the number were Rufus King, Henry Wheaton, Chancellor Kent, Chief Justice Spencer, Martin Van Buren, Stephen Van Rensselaer, Peter R. Livingston, and Daniel D. Tompkins. There is scarcely one of the doctrines advocated by Mr. Calhoun in the latter part of his life, and supposed to be peculiar to him, that was not held by one or other of the speakers in the course of these discussions.

CHAPTER IX.

1777—1778.

A MEMBER OF THE COUNCIL OF SAFETY, AND CHIEF JUSTICE OF NEW YORK.

It will be recollected that the Constitution was adopted on Sunday, the 20th of April. The same day, Livingston, Scott, Morris, Yates, Jay, and Hobart were appointed a committee to report a plan for organizing the new Government. Their report provided for holding elections, and the provisional appointment of officers necessary for the distribution of justice. They also recommended a *Council of Safety*, clothed with all the powers requisite for the safety and preservation of the State, until a Governor and Legislature should be duly chosen and in a condition to act. The Convention, by their resolution of the 8th day of May, adopted the recommendations of their committee, and on the 13th dissolved.

The Council of Safety, thus clothed for a season with absolute power, consisted of only fifteen men; but they were not sunshine patriots. Their souls were formed of nobler materials. They had every claim to public confidence, and they did not abuse it. Their names, in the order in which they stand in the resolution of the Convention, were John Morin Scott, Robert R. Livingston, Christopher Tappen, Abraham Yates, Jr., Gouverneur Morris, Zephaniah Platt, John Jay, Charles De Witt, Robert Harper, Jacob Cuyler, Thomas Tredwell, Pierre

Van Cortlandt, Matthew Cantine, John Sloss Hobart, and Jonathan D. Tompkins.[1]

Such was the authority the Convention had provided to guide the ship of state amid the appalling dangers that threatened her. We have now arrived at the period when the fortunes of New York touched their lowest point of depression. Great as had hitherto been her distresses, she was now threatened with overwhelming calamities. The campaign of the present year had in view, on the part of Great Britain, her utter prostration. The design was, to penetrate the State with two separate armies from the North and South, and thus cut off the communication between New England and the Middle and Southern States. The means provided to accomplish this object were on a grand scale. The whole southern district of the State was already in possession of the enemy. Burgoyne, with a well-appointed army of ten thousand men, advanced through the Lakes towards the Hudson. Ticonderoga was abandoned at the approach of the invader. Colonel St. Leger, with a large force of regulars, Indians, and tories, attacked the State on her western frontier, filling the settlers along the banks of the Mohawk with terror and dismay. The disaffected were everywhere aroused into activity. Even the well-disposed, in many instances, were disheartened at the gloomy prospect of affairs. 'There was never, perhaps, in the history of a free people struggling for their liberties, a more portentous crisis. We were driven in on every side. The extremities of the State were destroyed. There was no pulsation but at the heart. Every thing seemed to be lost but hope, virtue, and trust in the Providence of God.'[2]

---

[1] Chancellor Kent: Discourse before the New York Historical Society.

[2] Ibid. In the course of this campaign there was not a county in the State, as it then existed, which escaped a visit from the arms of the enemy.

In this conjuncture, the Council of Safety acted with vigor. Their resolution was equal to the pressure of the occasion:—

> —'No thought of flight,
> None of retreat; no unbecoming deed
> That argued fear,'

marked any part of their conduct. But they had a difficult task to perform. They had to arouse and animate the spirit of the inhabitants along the exposed frontier, whose fears for the moment paralyzed their energies, and disposed them to passive and inglorious submission to what they considered inevitable calamities. Mr. Jay had no sympathy or patience with such despondency. He denounced it in warm and indignant language. He did not, perhaps, make due allowance for that first misgiving of the heart which is apt to accompany the approach of a great peril. 'The nature of courage is, without a question, to be conversant with danger; but in the palpable night of their terrors, men under consternation suppose, not that it is the danger, which, by a sure instinct, calls out the courage to resist it, but that it is the courage which produces the danger. They therefore seek for refuge from their fears in the fears themselves, and consider a temporizing meanness as the only source of safety.'[1] Such was the effect upon the inhabitants on Tryon county of the approach of St. Leger with his tory and Indian allies.[2] They were on the frontier. They were directly exposed to the tomahawk of the savage and the equally-dreaded cruelties of the tory. Hell itself could not vomit forth more obdurate wretches than were many of this latter description of persons.

---

[1] Burke.

[2] Tryon county embraced all that part of the State lying west of a line running north and south, nearly through the centre of what is now Schoharie county. It was named after Tryon the royal Governor.

They were deaf to the supplicating voice of mercy, and dead to every feeling of humanity. In many instances they were more merciless than their savage allies. They wreaked their vengeance on smiling infancy and hoary age. They were monsters, whose crimes made 'the face of Heaven to glow with horror and indignation.' [1]

Many of the people saw no safety but in submission. They had no confidence in their ability to make a successful defence. It was doubtful whether the Council of Safety, who directed the military operations of the State, would be able to induce them to take the field. Gouverneur Morris, whom the Council had sent to Fort Edward, the head-quarters of General Schuyler, to confer with him in what manner best to employ the military resources of the State, wrote on the 16th of July that he had just mentioned to the General the calling out of the militia of Tryon county. 'He says we may *call*, but we shall not get them. This is by no means a comfortable idea.' Five days later, Jay writes to Morris that the situation of Tryon county is both shameful and alarming. 'Such abject dejection and despondency as mark the letters we have received from thence, disgrace human nature. God

[1] What is said in the text is confined, and properly confined, to a part only of the tories. Many of them took up arms and defended their principles and consistency without, at the same time, sacrificing their humanity. They feared God as well as honored the King. But others, by their perfidious and cruel conduct, disgraced their cause, and dishonored human nature itself. No one who has not carefully studied the annals of the Revolution, would believe the one-half that could be told him, and told upon authority that cannot be impeached, of the murderous and fiendish acts of that class of people. 'Europe neither knows nor can be made to believe what inhuman, barbarous wretches the greater part of them have been, and therefore is disposed to pity them more than they deserve.' Thus wrote Mr. Jay, while at Paris negotiating the peace that closed the war. It must be admitted, while thus characterizing the conduct of the tories, that the whigs, in many instances, were guilty of acts deserving the severest condemnation, and which stand unrelieved by a single palliating circumstance.

knows what to do with or for them. Were they alone interested in their fate, I should be for leaving their cart in the slough till they would put their shoulders to the wheel.'

On the following day, July 22d, on behalf of the Council of Safety, he wrote an inspiriting letter to the General Committee of that county. 'It is with the utmost concern,' say the committee, 'that we hear of the universal panic, despair, and despondency which prevail throughout your county. We flattered ourselves that the approach of the enemy would have animated and not depressed their spirits. What reason is there to expect that Heaven will help those who refuse to help themselves, or that Providence will grant liberty to those who want courage to defend it. Are the great duties they owe to themselves, their country, and posterity so soon forgotten? Let not the history of the present glorious contest declare to future generations that the people of your county, after making the highest professions of zeal for the American cause, fled at the first appearance of danger, and behaved like women!'

After showing the folly of accepting *protections* from the enemy, and their ability to defend themselves, the letter proceeds: 'Let all differences among you cease. Let the only contest be who shall be foremost in defending his country. Banish unmanly fear, acquit yourself like men, and with firm confidence trust the event with that Almighty and benevolent Being who hath commanded you to hold fast the liberty with which he has made you free; and who is able as well as willing to support you in performing his orders. If you can prevail on your people to exert their own strength, all will be well. Let us again beseech and entreat you, for the honor and reputation, as well as the safety, of the State, to behave like men.'

In the meantime, General Herkimer had issued a proclamation, calling upon the inhabitants between the ages of sixteen and sixty to repair to the place appointed by his orders, then march 'to oppose the enemy with vigor, as true patriots.' These appeals were not unheeded. The panic had subsided. With the arrival of the invader, all fear seemed to have vanished. By the 30th of July, Herkimer found himself at the head of between eight hundred and a thousand militia, eagerly demanding to be led against the enemy.

With this force, he advanced to the relief of Fort Schuyler, now beleagured by St. Leger, with four hundred regulars, six hundred tories, and seven hundred Indians.[1] On the 6th day of August, when within eight miles of the Fort, he fell into an ambuscade prepared for him by the Indians and tories, under the command of Brant and Butler. Herkimer, who was equally brave and, if possible, more illiterate than General Putnam, but inferior to him in military capacity, had advanced on the morning of the action contrary to his judgment, provoked thereto by the taunts of his officers, who imputed his prudence and caution to cowardice and toryism. He advanced, too, without due precaution, without adequate flanking parties, or any sufficient *reconnoissance* of the ground over which he was to pass. The road which he traversed was crossed by a deep ravine, about two miles west of Oriskany, and six from Whitesborough. This ravine was of a semi-circular form, bending away towards the Fort. 'The bottom of it was marshy, and the road crossed it by means of a causeway. The ground, thus partly enclosed by the ravine, was elevated and level. The ambuscade was laid upon the high ground west of the ravine.'[2]

As Herkimer, with his undisciplined militia, advanced across the causeway, and began to ascend the elevated

---

[1] The Fort was invested August 3d.

[2] Campbell's Annals of Tryon County. Life of Brant.

ground beyond, a terrific yell, followed by a destructive fire, disclosed the dangers that encompassed him. His rear-guard, separated from the main body by the suddenness and completeness of the surprise, 'instantly and ingloriously fled.'[1] But their companions fought with a heroism unsurpassed. After a long, desperate, and bloody conflict, victory declared itself in their favor. But it was purchased at a dreadful cost of life. Besides the wounded, the killed numbered two hundred. Among the former, but who subsequently died, was the gallant Herkimer.[2] The field of this sanguinary engagement, for days after

---

[1] Campbell's Annals of Tryon County. Life of Brant, p. 236.

[2] "The veteran Herkimer fell wounded in the early part of the action — a musket-ball having passed through and killed his horse, and shattered his own leg just below the knee. The General was placed upon his saddle, however, against the trunk of a tree for his support, and thus continued to order the battle. . . . . . But even in this deplorable situation, the wounded General — his men dropping like leaves around him, and the forest resounding with the horrid yells of the savages, ringing high and wild over the din of battle — behaved with the most perfect firmness and composure. . . . . . The brave old man, notwithstanding the imprudence of the morning—imprudence in allowing a premature movement at the dictation of his subordinates — had nobly vindicated his character for courage during the day. Though wounded, as we have seen, in the onset, he had borne himself during the six hours of conflict, under the most trying circumstances, with a degree of fortitude and composure worthy of all admiration. Nor was his example without effect in sustaining his troops amid the perils by which they were environed. At one time during the battle, while sitting upon his saddle raised upon a little hillock, being advised to select a less exposed situation, he replied, 'I will face the enemy!' Thus, 'surrounded by a few men, he continued to issue his orders with firmness. In this situation, and in the heat of the onslaught, he deliberately took his tinder-box from his pocket, lit his pipe, and smoked with great composure.' At the moment the soldiers were placing him in the litter, while adjusting the blankets to the poles, three Indians approached, and were instantly shot down by the unerring rifles of three of the militia. These were the last shots fired in that battle." Life of Brant.

General Herkimer died soon after the battle, in consequence of the unskilful amputation of his wounded limb.

showed the desperation with which it had been contested. 'There was found the Indian and the white man, born on the banks of the Mohawk, their left hand clinched in each other's hair, the right grasping, in a gripe of death, the knife plunged in each other's bosom: thus they lay frowning.' [1]

Although the victory remained with the militia, they were not in a situation to cut their way through to the relief of the Fort. But their success inflicted a severe blow upon the enemy. The Indians were dispirited, and rendered morose and discontented. At the same time they redeemed the character of their county, and covered themselves with imperishable honor. The action at Oriskany, if less known than others in the Revolutionary contest, is surpassed by none in the patriotism that contested, and in the courage that achieved it.

The Council of Safety, who had so recently, speaking through Mr. Jay, characterized the dejection and despondency of the people of Tryon County in language severe and unmeasured, now had the more grateful task of recording their praise. In a letter to the New York delegates in Congress, written a few days after the action we have described, they say: 'By the papers enclosed you will find that our troops and militia have behaved with becoming spirit in Tryon County; but as it is out of our power to support them, we fear that that county must fall into the hands of the enemy.' After reviewing the general state of the colony, the Council add: 'We are resolved if we do fall, to fall as becomes brave men.' But the clouds that had lowered upon the fortunes of the State, began to break. Hope and confidence revived.

[1] Gouverneur Morris. Address before the New York Historical Society. The valor and heroism displayed by the New York militia in this action is in striking contrast with the conduct of the regulars under Braddock, at the battle of the Monongahela. Vide Sargent's History of Braddock's Expedition.

All the efforts of St. Leger to reduce Fort Schuyler proved unavailing. Gansevoort and Willett defended that post with a courage and determination which nothing could shake. At length, on the 22d day of August, when those qualities could not much longer have availed them, the siege was suddenly raised. St. Leger's Indian allies, by a *ruse-de-guerre* of General Arnold, who was advancing to the relief of the Fort, were panic-struck, and refused to remain any longer.[1] The result was a sudden and precipitate flight.[2]

On the very day that the Fort bearing his name and illustrated by a gallant and glorious defence, was relieved of danger by the hasty and unexpected withdrawal of the besiegers, General Schuyler, whose prudence, steadiness, and vigilance had frustrated the plans of Burgoyne, and laid the foundation of his final and complete overthrow, was subjected to that mortification, than which, a brave and sensitive nature can hardly know a sharper or more difficult to be borne — he was deprived of his command.[3]

We shall pause a moment over this transaction. Jay was a warm and attached friend of Schuyler. He knew and appreciated his merits. He was indignant at the injustice done him, and with 'zeal and anxious affection

---

[1] Arnold had in his hands a tory, Hon-Yost Schuyler, who had been captured and condemned as a spy. He gave him his life upon the condition that he would hasten to Fort Schuyler, and so alarm the camp of St. Leger, as to induce him to raise the siege. Hon-Yost's brother remained with Arnold as a hostage for the performance of the condition. The convicted spy was well known to the Indians, and upon his arrival at the camp, so alarmed them by exaggerated accounts of the number and proximity of Arnold's forces, that St. Leger was compelled to a sudden retreat.

[2] Life of Brant, p. 260.

[3] And this, at the very moment, as he himself said, 'when our affairs were at the worst, and when no change could happen but what must be for the better.' Life of Morris, vol. i., p. 143.

attended him through that his agony of glory.' Schuyler was his senior by twelve years. His family was Dutch. He had served as a captain in the French and Indian War. In civil life, he had won distinction as a member of the Colonial Assembly, where uniformly, and with admitted ability, he opposed the ministerial pretensions. He was a member of the second Continental Congress, and on the 19th day of June, 1775, was appointed by that body the third Major-General in the armies of the United Colonies. In character he was somewhat stern, determined in purpose, sagacious, and penetrating. With his friends he was urbane and conciliatory, but his general bearing was not calculated to win the regards of the people. He was something high. Chancellor Kent, who knew and loved him, and has done honor to his memory, assigns 'the dignity of his deportment' as one of the causes of the popular jealousy and ill-will of which he was a victim. He was 'little blessed with the set phrase of speech,' and his communications to Congress and other public bodies gave great offence by the bluntness of their tone. He spoke right on, with small regard to 'taffeta phrases, or silken terms precise.' 'You know Congress,' wrote a member of that body to him, 'like a hysteric woman, wants cordials. Write truths, without making any reflections of your own.' In speech, as in action, 'prudent, cautious self-control is wisdom's root.' Schuyler had a clear well-balanced intellect, and great energy of character. For no officer in the service had the enemy greater respect, and they evinced it by ungraciously fostering the suspicions and prejudices that prevailed against him. 'His versatile talents, equally adapted to investigation and action, rendered his merits as an officer of transcendant value.' [1]

We shall now briefly state the causes of his removal,

---

[1] Chancellor Kent.

a removal which 'intercepted from his brow' 'the laurels he was in preparation to win by his judicious and distinguished efforts, and which he would very shortly have attained.'[1] On the 2d day of July, Burgoyne appeared before Ticonderoga. Neither the condition of the Fort nor the strength of the garrison justified its defence. St. Clair, who had the command, wisely determined to abandon it. A great clamor ensued. The country had been taught to believe that the post was impregnable. Even Washington shared that opinion, and while he would not condemn St. Clair unheard, he could not withhold the expression of his astonishment. 'We shall never be able to defend a post till we shoot a General,' wrote John Adams on this occasion. Ticonderoga, being within the military department of General Schuyler, he was held responsible for its evacuation. He was charged with treachery. The most absurd rumors were circulated; and nothing was too absurd for an excited public to believe. It was said, and, what is more strange, credited, that Burgoyne fired *silver* balls into St. Clair's camp, who picked them up, and transmitted them to Schuyler at Fort George. It was not only in New England, where Schuyler, from the commencement of the war, had been thoroughly unpopular, that suspicions of his integrity were entertained, but in New York, and even in the Council of Safety. 'The evacuation of Ticonderoga,' wrote Jay to Schuyler, the 21st of July,[2] 'continues to be the subject, not only of general speculation, but also of general censure and reproach. The public, not being furnished with the reasons for that measure, are left to form their own conjectures, and seem very universally to impute it to treachery and practice with the enemy; nor are the four Generals alone the object of suspicion; it reaches

[1] Chancellor Kent.

[2] Life, vol. i., p. 74. The fort was abandoned the night of the 6th instant.

you. It is unnecessary to observe that, like many other worthy characters, you have your enemies; and it is also true that countenance is indirectly given to the popular suspicion by persons from whom I should have expected more candor, or I may say, more honesty. It is said, but I know not with what truth, that St. Clair, on being asked by some of his officers why the Fort was evacuated, replied generally, that he knew what he did; that on his own account he was very easy about the matter, and that he had it in his power to justify himself. From hence, some inferred that he must have alluded to orders from you.[1] Another report prevails, that some short time before the Fort was left, a number of heavy cannon were by your order dismounted and laid aside, and small ones placed in their room. This is urged as circumstantial proof against you. The ship-carpenters have come down, much dissatisfied and clamorous. In short, Sir, that jealousy which ever prevails in civil wars, added to the disappointment and indignation which the people feel on this occasion, together with the malice of your enemies, require that the integrity and propriety of your conduct be rendered so evident, as that there may not be a hook or loop whereon to hang a doubt. I forgot to mention that stress is also laid on your distance from the Fort at the time of the enemy's approach, and from this circumstance unfavorable conclusions are drawn.'

After mentioning the arguments which the General's friends had employed to allay the suspicions of the public, and suggesting the propriety of his writing a letter to the Council of Safety, which 'should not look like a defence, though it should amount to it,' and which they could publish, Jay observes: "In one of your late letters to the Council was this sentiment — 'You wished the

---

[1] St. Clair wrote to Mr. Jay respecting this report, and took the responsibility of the evacuation upon himself. See vol. i. of Wilkinson's Memoirs, where St. Clair's letter is inserted.

evacuation might not be too much depreciated;' and your reasons for this caution may have weight; but, Sir, a certain gentleman at that board, whom I need not name, and from whom I do *not* desire this information should be concealed, is, in my opinion, your secret enemy. He professes much respect, &c., for you; he can't see through the business; he wishes you had been nearer to the Fort, though he does not doubt your spirit; he thinks we ought to suspend our judgment, and not censure you rashly; he hopes you will be able to justify yourself, &c. Observe so much caution, therefore, in your letters, as to let them contain nothing which your enemies may wrest to their own purposes.'

The Council of Safety appointed Mr. Jay and Gouverneur Morris a committee to repair to head-quarters to confer with Washington on the state of Schuyler's army, the means of reinforcing it, &c. They left Kingston on this mission the 27th day of July. Unfortunately, they did not arrive at Philadelphia until the very day (August 1st) Congress had determined to send Gates to take command of the Northern department. That body succumbed to the public clamor and a supposed necessity. The New England members declared that their militia would not turn out in defence of New York while Schuyler had the command. Indeed, it was agreed that the Eastern prejudices against him, were the only motives for his recall.[1]

In this connection, the following extract from the works of Mr. Adams cannot fail to interest the reader. Acccording to him, the competition between Gates and Schuyler was not less fraught with important political than personal consequences.[2] Recording the appointment

[1] Sparks' Life of Morris, vol. i., p. 147.

[2] Gates was Schuyler's evil genius. He entered the army originally as Adjutant-General, with the rank of Brigadier. The following year, viz., May 16th, 1776, he was appointed a Major-General. On the 17th

of Gates as Major-General, he observes: 'I take notice of this appointment of Gates, because it had great influence on my future fortunes. It soon occasioned a competition between him and Schuyler, in which I always

day of June, Congress directed Washington to send Gates into Canada, to take command of all the forces in that province. But before he reached Albany on his way thither, the army had evacuated Canada, and retired within the military department of General Schuyler. As Gates had been appointed to the command *in Canada*, it was obvious, that in the present position of the army, the command belonged to Schuyler; but Gates claimed it. The two Generals, however, amicably referred the affair to Congress. The decision was in favor of Schuyler. But notwithstanding, on the 25th day of March of the following year, Gates was directed to take command at Ticonderoga. As this fortress was within the military department of Schuyler, he was thus, *pro tanto*, superseded. Disgusted at this implied censure of his conduct, or want of confidence in his capacity, he repaired to Philadelphia with the general purpose of settling his accounts, obtaining an inquiry into his conduct, and withdrawing from the service. But Congress, upon investigation, finding his services had been far beyond any estimate that had been formed of them, repealed the resolution that fixed his head-quarters at Albany, and directed him to proceed forthwith to the Northern department, and take the command. This action of Congress occurred May 22d. On the 3d of June, Schuyler resumed his original authority, thus superseding Gates. The latter was very indignant. He went to Philadelphia, and, by a *ruse* of Mr. Sherman, was admitted to the floor of Congress, where he complained in warm terms of the treatment he had received from that body. See an account of this curious scene in Sparks' Life of Morris, vol. i., pp. 139, 140.

Although Gates had the manners of a gentleman, he had very little nobleness of spirit. His conduct was often mean and contemptible. Notwithstanding the injustice done Schuyler by his removal, he told Gates he would stay in the department, and afford him every assistance in his power, and entreated he would call upon him whenever he thought proper. 'He has, however,' wrote Schuyler on the 7th day of September, 'not done it. He sent for General Ten Broeck from town, to a council of war, but not for me. After that, I could not with propriety give him my opinion of what ground he ought to possess, if Burgoyne should retreat. What I intended to have done, had I remained in the command and been reinforced, I fully communicated to him, and showed the orders I had given Generals Lincoln and Arnold.' Ibid, p. 149.

contended for Gates; and the rivalry occasioned great animosities among the friends of the two Generals, the consequences of which are not yet spent. Indeed, they have affected the essential interests of the United States, and will influence their ultimate destiny. They effected an enmity between Gates and Mr. Jay, who always supported Schuyler, and a dislike in Gates of Hamilton, who married Schuyler's daughter, with which Mr. Burr wrought so skilfully, as, in 1800, to turn the elections in New York not only against Hamilton, but against the Federalists. Gates' resentment against Jay, Schuyler, and Hamilton, made him turn, in 1799, against me, who had been the best friend and the most efficacious supporter he ever had in America. I had never in my life any personal prejudice or dislike against General Schuyler; on the contrary, I knew him to be industrious, studious, and intelligent. But the New England officers, soldiers, and inhabitants knew Gates in the camp at Cambridge. Schuyler was not known to many, and the few who had heard of him were prejudiced against him from the former French war. The New England soldiers would not enlist to serve under him, and the militia would not turn out. I was, therefore, under a necessity of supporting Gates. Mr. Duane, Mr. Jay, Colonel Harrison, &c., supported Schuyler.'[1]

The issue of Burgoyne's vaunted expedition is too well known to need repetition. His surrender diffused universal joy throughout the whole country. In New York, whose very existence had been menaced, the exultation was unbounded. 'I can speak of the events of that year,' says Chancellor Kent,[2] 'with some of the impressions of a cotemporary witness. I heard the noise and fury of the assault upon the fortresses on the Hudson; and I

---

[1] Life and Works, vol. iii., p. 47.

[2] Address before the New York Historical Society.

perfectly recollect the general distress, terror, and bitterness of grief that were visible in the earlier part of the campaign, as well as the tones of joy, admiration, and gratitude at our final and triumphant deliverance.'

But before this latter event had occurred, and while Burgoyne was yet unconquered, and another army was preparing in New York to march to his relief and effect the junction originally contemplated, that promised 'crown and consummation' of the campaign; in this condition of affairs, the temple of justice was again opened in New York. Before the Convention dissolved, they appointed Mr. Jay Chief Justice until the Legislature should meet and the Constitutional power of appointment be organized. Robert R. Livingston was, at the same time, and upon the same tenure, appointed Chancellor, and Egbert Benson, Attorney General. On the 9th day of September, the Supreme Court held its first term at Kingston. The Chief Justice presided. His charge to the Grand Jury could hardly fail to allude to the situation and prospects of the country. 'The late disasters on the frontiers, the invasion of the State, and the approach of the enemy, threw no shades over the bright prospect of his country's glory and happiness, which, in prophetic vision, he saw rising before him.' [1]

'It affords me, gentlemen,' he said, 'very sensible pleasure to congratulate you on the dawn of that free, mild, and equal Government which now begins to rise and break from amid those clouds of anarchy, confusion, and licentiousness which the arbitrary and violent domination of Great Britain had spread in greater or less degrees throughout this and the other American states. This is one of those signal instances in which Divine Providence has made the tyranny of princes instrumental in breaking the chains of their subjects, and rendered the most

---

[1] William Jay.

inhuman designs productive of the best consequences to those against whom they were intended. The infatuated sovereign of Britain, forgetful that kings were the servants, not the proprietors, and ought to be the fathers, not the incendiaries of their people, hath, by destroying our former constitutions, enabled us to erect more eligible systems of government on their ruins; and, by unwarrantable attempts to *bind us in all cases whatever*, has reduced us to the happy necessity of being *free from his control in any*.

'Whoever compares our present with our former Constitution, will find abundant reason to rejoice in the exchange, and readily admit that all the calamities incident to this war will be amply compensated by the many blessings flowing from this glorious revolution — a revolution which, in the whole course of its rise and progress, is distinguished by so many marks of the Divine favor and interposition, that no doubt can remain of its being finally accomplished.'

After referring to the extraordinary character of the contest that was now waging, extraordinary in its origin, and extraordinary for the events that had distinguished its progress, extraordinary that thirteen colonies, 'divided by variety of government and manners, should immediately become one people, and, though without funds, without magazines, without disciplined troops, in the face of their enemies unanimously determine to be free,' and notwithstanding these difficulties, 'raise armies, establish funds, carry on commerce, grow rich by the spoils of their enemies, and bid defiance to the armies of Britain, the mercenaries of Germany, and the savages of the wilderness,' after referring to these things, the Chief Justice proceeds: —

'Blessed be God, the time will now never arrive when the prince of a country in another quarter of the globe will command your obedience, and hold you in vassalage.

His consent has ceased to be necessary to enable you to enact laws essential to your welfare; nor will you in future be subject to the imperious sway of rulers instructed to sacrifice your happiness whenever it might be inconsistent with the ambitious views of their royal master. . . . . . But let it be remembered, that whatever marks of wisdom, experience, and patriotism there may be in your Constitution, yet like the beautiful symmetry, the just proportion, and elegant forms of our first parents before their Maker breathed into them the breath of life, it is yet to be animated, and till then may indeed excite admiration, but will be of no use: from the people it must receive its spirit, and by them be quickened. Let virtue, honor, the love of liberty and of science be and remain the soul of this Constitution, and it will become the source of great and extensive happiness to this and future generations. Vice, ignorance, and want of vigilance will be the only enemies able to destroy it. Against these be for ever jealous.

'This, gentlemen, is the first court held under the authority of our Constitution, and I hope its proceedings will be such as to merit the approbation of the friends, and avoid giving cause of censure to the enemies of the present establishment.'

The day after the delivery of this charge, the Legislature met, and soon after the organization of the Council of Appointment, he was duly re-appointed Chief Justice of the State, under the Constitution.[1] For want of a

---

[1] The Legislature met on the 1st of September, but a quorum was not present until the 10th. 'Our Senate is doing I know not what,' wrote Gouverneur Morris to General Schuyler, September 18th. 'In Assembly we wrangle long to little purpose. You will think so, when I tell you that from nine in the morning till dusk in the evening, we were employed in appointing Scott, Pawling, Yates, and Webster to be the Council of Appointment. I tremble for the consequences, but I smile, and shall continue to do so, if possible.' Life of Morris, vol. i., p. 145.

'*vates sacer*,' we have no account of the nature of the causes that came before his court, nor of the character of his decisions. The only notice I find among his correspondence of his labors in this department, is in a letter to his friend Morris, written at Albany in the spring of the following year. 'I am now engaged,' he says, 'in the most disagreeable part of my duty, trying criminals. They multiply exceedingly. Robberies become frequent; the woods afford them shelter, and the tories food. Punnishments must of course become certain, and mercy dormant—a harsh system, repugnant to my feelings, but nevertheless necessary. In such circumstances lenity would be cruelty, and severity is found on the side of humanity.'[1] From the language of this letter, it is quite evident that while Mr. Jay was ready to perform his duty, and with that degree of rigor which circumstances might demand, he cannot properly be numbered in the category of 'hanging judges.'

In the autumn of 1778, Washington visited Mr. Jay at Fishkill, to confer with him in regard to the plan, at that time engaging the attention of Congress, for an invasion of Canada. They concurred in disapproving it. They were both apprehensive that, if an expedition into that province was undertaken by the aid of a French fleet and army, and should prove successful, the French Government, upon one pretext or other, would appropriate the conquest to themselves. But they wholly misconceived the views of France. That power was opposed to the expedition, and opposed to wresting Canada from the possession of England.[2] The project was nevertheless wisely abandoned.

[1] Life and Writings, vol. ii. This letter is dated April 29th, 1778.

[2] Sparks' Life of Washington. Writings of Washington, vol. vi., pp. 112–149. Life of Morris, vol. i., p. 189. Life of John Jay, vol. i., p. 83. Mr. William Jay erroneously fixes the date of Washington's visit to Fishkill in the autumn of 1777.

Mr. Jay continued to hold his office of Chief Justice until September, 1779; but for a good part of the time he did not discharge its duties. The Constitution restrained the Judges of the Supreme Court from holding any other office, except that of delegate to Congress, on a *special occasion*. It is well known that Vermont, taking advantage of the Revolutionary contest, withdrew from the jurisdiction of New Hampshire and New York, and set up an independent government. This proceeding occasioned great indignation in the latter State. The newly-elected Governor, General George Clinton, shared that feeling, and did not fail to urge the claims of New York with earnestness and zeal. The subject early engaged the attention of the Legislature, and on the 21st day of October they declared that a special occasion existed, in which the Chancellor and Judges of the Supreme Court might be elected delegates to the General Congress; and on the 4th day of November, they proceeded to elect Mr. Jay to represent the State in that body, until the 1st day of the following March. His powers, as delegate, were subsequently continued, and he remained in Congress until the month of September of that year.[1] At that time, and in view of another field of service which was shortly opened to him, he resigned his office of Chief Justice.

In the next chapter we shall accompany Mr. Jay back to the scene whereon he won his earliest laurels, and then contemplate his career on the wider theatre of diplomacy.

---

[1] He was appointed Minister to Spain, September 27th, 1779.

CHAPTER X.

1778—1779.

PRESIDENT OF CONGRESS.

After an absence of more than two years, Mr. Jay again took his seat in Congress on the 7th day of December, 1778. He found a great change in the character of that assembly. The men who stood 'proudly eminent' in the Congress of 1774, when 'the great consult began,' and who had guided by their counsels, and illustrated by their eloquence, the politics of the two following years, were now for the most part employed in other departments of the public service. Their successors were generally men of far inferior note. 'The public believe,' wrote Washington to Benjamin Harrison, the Speaker of the House of Delegates of Virginia, on the 18th day of December, '(and if they do believe it, the fact might almost as well be so,) that the States at this time are badly represented, and that the great and important concerns of the nation are horribly conducted, for want either of abilities or application in the members, or through the discord and party views of some individuals.'[1] He wrote again to the same individual, on the 30th inst.,

[1] Writings, vol. vi., p. 142. See also vol. v., pp. 326, 508. 'The mighty Senate of America is not what you have known it,' wrote Morris to Jay in the previous February. 'The Continental Congress and currency have both depreciated, but in the hands of the Almighty Architect of empires, the stone which the builders have rejected may easily become head of the corner.' Life of Morris, vol. i., p. 153.

having, in the meantime, visited Philadelphia, and personally observed the state of affairs there. 'If I were to be called upon,' he said, 'to draw a picture of the times and of men from what I have seen, heard, and in part know, I should in one word say that idleness, dissipation, and extravagance seem to have laid fast hold of most of them; that speculation, peculation, and an insatiable thirst for riches seem to have got the better of every other consideration, and almost of every order of men; that party disputes and personal quarrels are the great business of the day, whilst the momentous concerns of an empire, a great and accumulating debt, ruined finances, depreciated money, and want of credit, which, in its consequences, is the want of every thing, are but secondary considerations, and postponed from day to day, from week to week, as if our affairs wore the most promising aspect. After drawing this picture, which from my soul I believe to be a true one, I need not repeat to you that I am alarmed, and wish to see my countrymen roused. I have no resentments, nor do I mean to point at any particular characters. This I can declare upon my honor; for I have every attention paid to me by Congress that I can possibly expect, and I have reason to think that I stand well in their estimation. But, in the present situation of things, I cannot help asking where are Mason, Wythe, Jefferson, Nicholas, Pendleton, Nelson, and another I could name? And why, if you are sufficiently impressed with your danger, do you not, as New York has done in the case of Mr. Jay, send one extra member or two, for at least a certain limited time, till the great business of the nation is put upon a more respectable and happy establishment?'[1]

When Mr. Jay arrived at Philadelphia, the public councils were distracted in regard to the conduct of our

[1] Writings, vol. vi., p. 151.

diplomatic agents abroad. Silas Deane had returned home, and two days before had published his address to the 'Free and Virtuous Citizens of America,' which threw the public mind into a convulsion, and occasioned great heats in Congress.[1] Deane was a native of Connecticut, and a graduate of Yale College. He first kept a school, then studied law, then married a rich widow, and then engaged in trade.[2] He was a member of the Congress of 1774 and 1775. In January, 1776, he was appointed by the Secret Committee in the twofold capacity of commercial and political agent to France.[3] In March he sailed on his mission, and arrived at Paris in July. 'He was active, diligent, subtle, and successful; having accomplished the great purpose of his mission to advantage.'[4] In September, 1776, Congress associated Dr. Franklin

---

[1] Gordon's History, vol. ii., p. 406.

[2] Adams' Works, vol. ii., p. 341.

[3] Ante, p. 155.

[4] Adams' Works, vol. iii., p. 139. In his letter to the President of Congress, dated October 12th, 1778, Mr. Deane gives the following striking account of his services: 'I desire it may be remembered, that when I went abroad, charged with the transaction of political and commercial business for Congress in the year 1776, I arrived at Paris as late in the season as the month of July, without funds, uncertain of remittances, without credit, ignorant of the language and manners of France, and an utter stranger to the persons in power and influence at Court; that I had not the patronage of any person of importance, and had no correspondence or connexions established in any part of Europe. The news of our misfortunes in Canada arrived in France with me, and that of our subsequent misfortunes immediately after, and was, as usual, exaggerated by the British ambassador and his emissaries. In a word, without remittances or even intelligence from Congress, and under all these disagreeable circumstances, I had to oppose the artifice, the influence, and the power of Great Britain; yet I have the pleasing reflection that before the 1st of December following, I procured thirty thousand stand of arms, thirty thousand suits of clothes, more than two hundred and fifty pieces of brass artillery, tents, and other stores to a large amount, provided the ships to transport them, and shipped a great part of them for America.' Sparks' Diplomatic Correspondence, vol. i., p. 131.

and Arthur Lee with Deane in the commission to the French Court.[1] They joined him at Paris in the following December. In the course of the following year, divisions and personal antipathies arose, which, in the end, were productive of very interesting personal and political results. The commercial business of the mission was intrusted very much to Deane. Both before and after the arrival of Franklin and Lee, he kept his accounts in a very loose and immethodical manner. It is admitted, too, that he lived extravagantly. He had two establishments, one at Paris, and another in the country, at Passy, with two sets of horses, carriages, and servants. His personal expenses in the course of fifteen months amounted to nearly ten thousand dollars more than the expenses of either of his colleagues.[2] Here, then, so far as we can discover, is the head and front of Deane's offending. He kept no proper system of accounts, and lived more expensively than the other commissioners. That he embezzled or misapplied the public funds, though insinuated and surmised, was never proved, and we believe to be insusceptible of proof. He fully enjoyed the confidence of the French Court; and the Comte De Vergennes, at the time of his recall, placed in his hands his unsolicited testimony 'to the zeal, activity, and intelligence with which he conducted the interests of the United States.' Dr. Franklin, on the same occasion,

[1] Franklin, Deane, and Jefferson were appointed the commissioners September 26th, 1776; but the state of Mr. Jefferson's family not permitting him to go, Mr. Lee was elected in his stead, October 22d.

[2] During the period from December 1776 to March 1778, Deane expended between $22,000 and $23,000, and Franklin and Lee, between $12,000 and $13,000 each. See Sparks' Diplomatic Correspondence, vol. ii., p. 159. The 3d vol. of Adams' Works, pp. 123–165 *passim*, contains frequent allusions to the difficulties and quarrels of the commissioners, and is very curious.

The commissioners were directed to live in a style 'to support the dignity of their public character.' Their expenses were to be paid, and they were to receive 'a handsome allowance for their time, trouble, risk, and services.'

wrote to the President of Congress that he esteemed him a faithful, active, and able minister, who, to his knowledge, had done in various ways great and important services to his country.[1] However, it was not long be-

[1] Mr. Sparks has inserted the letters of Vergennes and Franklin in the first volume of The Diplomatic Correspondence of the Revolution, pp. 119, 120.

We make no mention of Deane's contracts with Mons. Du Coudray and other officers, for though they may not give us a favorable opinion of his firmness and discretion, involve no want of integrity.

Those contracts were disowned by Congress. But Franklin wrote to a member of the Committee of Foreign Affairs (James Lovell) the following exculpation of Deane, with regard to them. 'I, who am upon the spot, and know the infinite difficulty of resisting the powerful solicitations of great men, who, if disobliged, might have it in their power to obstruct the supplies he was then obtaining, do not wonder that, being then a stranger to the people, and unacquainted with the language, he was at first prevailed on to make some such agreements, when all were recommended, as they always are, as *officers expérimentés, braves comme leurs épées, pleins de courage, de talents, et de zéle pour notre cause, &c.;* in short, mere Cæsars, each of whom would have been an invaluable acquisition to America.' Franklin's Works, vol. viii., p. 228. Nor should it be forgotten, as Mr. Sparks observes in his Life of Morris, vol. i., p. 197, that among the officers who came over under those contracts, were such men as Lafayette, De Kalb, and others who did honor to themselves and the cause and country they served.

The foreign officers, in many instances, were a source of great trouble and vexation. In a letter to Gouverneur Morris, dated July 24th, 1778, Washington says: 'They may be divided into three classes, viz., mere adventurers without recommendation, or recommended by persons who do not know how else to dispose of or provide for them, and men of great ambition, who would sacrifice every thing to promote their own personal glory; or mere spies, who are sent here to obtain a thorough knowledge of our situation and circumstances, in the execution of which, I am persuaded some of them are faithful emissaries, as I do not believe a single matter escapes unnoticed or unadvised at a foreign Court.' And he concludes by saying that with the exception of Lafayette, he 'devoutly wishes there was not a single foreigner among us. Writings of Washington, vol. vi., pp. 14–18.

Resentment at the attempt of 'Conway's Cabal' to supplant him in the army, and in the affections of his countrymen, the principal actors being officers of foreign birth, doubtless had an influence upon Wash-

fore Mr. Lee began to indulge suspicions and jealousies of Deane, and indeed of Dr. Franklin, and so freely expressed them in his letters to members of Congress, that Deane was finally recalled.

We have before had occasion to allude to Mr. Lee.[1] We have no wish to derogate from his fair fame. 'I invoke no Acheron to overwhelm him in the whirlpools of its muddy gulph.' He was an ardent and inflexible patriot. He was always absolutely in earnest. His abilities were fair, his reading extensive, his industry unwearied. In every part of his varied career, so far as loyalty to the public was concerned, he could enjoy the dignified consciousness of pure and independent conduct. And yet, in almost every instance where he attacked his rivals, he was evidently as much impelled by personal considerations as zeal for the public interests.[2] He was ambitious to supplant Franklin and Deane at the French Court, and to attain his object he employed unworthy means. The misfortune of Lee's life, a bar to all the usefulness of which he was otherwise capable, and, we believe, solicitous, was a jealous, suspicious, and restless disposition. Dr. Franklin described him as a man 'of an anxious, uneasy temper, which made it disagreeable to do business with him; that he seemed to be one of those men of whom he had known many in his day, who went on through life quarrelling with one person or another till they commonly ended with the loss of their reason.'[3]

Mr. Adams, who was on a friendly footing with Lee, and whose dislike of Franklin is everywhere apparent,

---

ington in this summary description of their general character. Certainly, not to mention such names as Steuben, De Kalb, Pulaski, and Kosciusko, the benefit to the service, of the foreign officers in the artillery and engineer departments, was great and obvious.

[1] Ante, p. 114. [2] Sparks' Life of Franklin, pp. 447–451.

[3] Works of John Adams, vol. iii., p. 123.

relates a conversation with Mr. Grand, the American banker at Paris, in which the character of Lee was discussed. 'Called,' he says, 'at M. Garnier's; he not at home. At Mr. Grand's; he and his son began about the address[1]—*bien faché*, &c. I said, coolly, that I was astonished at the publication of it, without sending it to Congress; that I believed Mr. Lee a man of integrity, and that all suggestions of improper correspondence in England were groundless;[2] that my brother Lee was not of the sweetest disposition, perhaps, but he was honest; that virtue was not always amiable. Mr. Grand replied, *Il est soupçonneux, il n'a du confiance en personne, il croit*

[1] Mr. Deane's Address, which had now arrived in Paris. It was published in Philadelphia the 5th day of December. The entry in Mr. Adams' Diary quoted in the text, is dated February 9th, 1779.

[2] Lee's known intimacy with Lord Shelburne and other important characters in England, together with his undisguised contempt and dislike of the French, made him very obnoxious to the French Court. His secretary, too, proved faithless, and for stock-jobbing purposes, revealed the secrets of the mission. As soon as his treachery was discovered, Lee promptly dismissed him. But Vergennes, having suspected the channel through which the English Court became informed of the secret negotiations at Paris, kept Lee, in several instances, ignorant of what was going on. Lord Stormont, the English Ambassador at Paris, mentions this circumstance in a letter to Lord Weymouth, dated December 28, 1777. 'But to leave the future intentions,' he says, 'and speak of the actual conduct of this Court. *That* is certainly as unfriendly as possible, notwithstanding all their professions. My repeated representations have had no other effect than to put them more upon their guard in their manner of assisting and treating with the rebels. They do not now convey any thing material through M. Chaumont or Beaumarchais. Monsieur Gérard treats directly with Franklin and Deane. *Lee is little trusted, and has not the real secret.* M. Gérard goes to Passy in the night, and Franklin and Deane make him nightly visits at Versailles. These visits have been very frequent of late, and must no doubt have some material object.' Mahon's History of England, vol. vi., p. 51 of Appendix.

The closing sentence of this letter is explained by the treaties of commerce and alliance, which were signed a few weeks after, viz., on the 6th of February, 1778, the negotiation of which was then going on.

que tout le monde est—I can't remember the precise word. I believe this is a just observation. He has confidence in nobody; he believes all men selfish, and no man honest or sincere. This, I fear, is his creed, from what I have heard him say. I have often, in conversation, disputed with him on this point; however, I never was so nearly in his situation before. There is no man here that I dare trust at present. They are all too much heated with passions, and prejudices, and party disputes. Some are too violent, others too jealous, others too cool and too reserved at all times, and, at the same time, every day betraying symptoms of a rancor quite as deep. The wisdom of Solomon, the meekness of Moses, and the patience of Job, all united in one character, would not be sufficient to qualify a man to act in the situation in which I am at present; and I have scarcely a spice of either of these virtues. On Dr. Franklin the eyes of all Europe are fixed, as the most important character in American affairs in Europe: neither Lee nor myself are looked upon of much consequence. The attention of the Court seems most to Franklin, and no wonder; his long and great reputation, to which Lee's and mine are in their infancy, are enough to account for this; his age and real character render it impossible for him to search every thing to the bottom, and Lee, with his Privy Council, is evermore contriving: the results of their contrivances render many measures more difficult.'[1]

The chief spirit of this 'Privy Council' was Ralph Izard of South Carolina. He was educated at the university of Cambridge, and married a daughter of Chief Justice De Lancey of New York. His fortune was large and his character fair. When Congress resolved to send a minister to the Grand Duke of Tuscany, for no reason in the world that I can discover, except that the

[1] Works, vol. iii., pp. 188, 189.

Grand Duke was a brother of Marie Antoinette, and the consequent supposition that the mission would have an indirect influence upon the French Court, Mr. Izard was nominated for that post, and recommended by the delegation from South Carolina 'for his integrity, good sense, and information.'[1] He was appointed on the 7th day of May, 1777. He never entered on his mission, but remained at Paris, and contributed very much to those suspicions and animosities which Congress, by their resolution of April 20th, 1779, declared to be 'highly prejudicial to the honor and interest of these United States.' Dr. Franklin gave Mr. Adams the following account of him: 'He said Mr. Izard was there, too, and joined in close friendship with Mr. Lee; that Mr. Izard was a man of violent and ungoverned passions; that each of these had a number of Americans about him, who were always exciting disputes and propagating stories that made the service very disagreeable; that Mr. Izard, who, as I knew, had been appointed a minister to the Grand Duke of Tuscany, instead of going to Italy, remained with his lady and children at Paris; and instead of minding his own business, and having nothing else to do, he spent his time in consultations with Mr. Lee, and in interfering with the business of the commission to this Court; that they had made strong objections to the treaty, and opposed several articles of it; that neither Mr. Lee nor Mr. Izard was liked by the French,' &c.[2]

[1] Works of John Adams, vol. iii., p. 141. His commission was dated July 1st, 1777.

[2] Ibid, p. 123. Mr. Izard was indignant that he was not consulted respecting the treaty, considered himself slighted, and vented his complaints in very violent language. The celebrated article with regard to molasses was an especial object of his denunciation. His quarrel with Dr. Franklin was very much aggravated by the latter refusing to pay his salary. Franklin reminded him that he had never entered upon his mission, never performed any services, and expressed the hope that he would refund what he had already received, and not increase the distresses of his country by asking for more. Franklin's Works, vol. viii., p. 309.

In consequence of the representations of Deane's enemies at Paris, Congress determined on his recall.[1] He arrived at Philadelphia on the 13th day of July. On the 17th and 21st days of August, he gave Congress a general account of his transactions since his absence in their service. Finding that charges had been preferred against him of misapplying the public funds, Deane was very solicitous that an examination should be made of those charges, and at Paris, where were the papers and vouchers. But Congress, coming to no conclusion upon his case, neither approving nor disapproving his conduct, nor appointing any person to audit his accounts, nor determining upon his further employment in the public service, he imprudently and improperly appealed to the public. His address, as we have before mentioned, was published on the 5th day of December. It occasioned a prodigious excitement, not only in Congress but throughout the country. It exposed to the world the dissensions that had taken place abroad, and reflected upon the integrity not only of members of the American *corps diplomatique*, but of leading members of Congress.[2]

---

[1] He was recalled by a resolution of Congress of November 21st, 1777. By another resolution of December 8th, he was directed to embrace the first opportunity of returning to the United States, to give Congress information of their foreign affairs.

[2] Deane was finally discharged from further attendance on Congress, in August, 1779. No disposition was made of the charges preferred or insinuated against him, and he was not *in capacity* to show what his accounts were. Congress voted him $10,000 for his attendance upon them since the 4th day of June, 1778. This sum he declined to receive. He went to Paris in August, 1780, for the purpose of adjusting his accounts. But Mr. Johnson (the father of the late Mrs. John Quincy Adams) whom Congress had appointed to audit the accounts of our agents abroad, declining to act, and Deane refusing the services of Mr. Searle, whom Dr. Franklin had suggested to him, on the ground that Searle was his enemy, his accounts were left unclosed, and he without means of support. He claimed £12,000 as the sum due him from Congress, but which, in the absence of an auditor, (for Congress ne-

It was at this moment of excitement, of individual and party resentment, that Mr. Jay resumed his seat in Congress. We have elsewhere seen that he was not on very friendly terms with Richard Henry Lee, the brother of Arthur, and Chairman of the Committee of Foreign Affairs.[1] He could not be unaware of Arthur Lee's injurious sus-

---

glected to appoint a successor to Mr. Johnson,) remained unadjusted and unsettled. He fell into pecuniary straits, became alienated from his country's cause, and wrote home letters favoring an accommodation with England. They were intercepted by the enemy and published. It is needless to add that the public character of Deane, in the estimation of his countrymen, was instantly destroyed. Mr. Jay, who had hitherto been his sincere friend, and so late as December, 1780, declared that he knew he had been hardly treated, that he believed him honest, and thought him injured, upon receiving from Dr. Franklin a copy of one of his intercepted letters, representing the American cause as desperate, and recommending an immediate reconciliation with Great Britain, renounced his friendship at once. He had suspended Deane's portrait in his parlor at Madrid, but upon this evidence of his apostasy, he took it down and burnt it. He ever after showed great reluctance to speak of the original. Life, vol. i., pp. 115–119, 132. When he was in France in 1783 and 1784, Deane sought an interview with him, but he declined it. He would have gladly seen him, but an insurmountable obstacle intervened to prevent it. 'I was told by more than one on whose information I thought I could rely,' he thus wrote Deane, 'that you received visits from, and was on terms of familiarity with, General Arnold. Every American who gives his hand to that man pollutes it.' Writings, vol. ii., p. 144. Deane entered Congress with the reputation of great wealth, but he died in a state of extreme poverty, at Deal, in England, August 23d, 1789. He certainly rendered his country great service, but he was not of force to love and serve her, despite her ingratitude, real or supposed. He retired, he said in one of his last communications to Congress, 'loaded with the most outrageous and unmerited reproaches, into obscurity, poverty, and exile.' Diplomatic Correspondence, vol. i., p. 212.

[1] Ante, p. 114. In the previous August (1778) Gouverneur Morris wrote Jay as follows: 'I wish you were here. Many persons whom you know are very liberal of illiberality. Your friend Deane, who has rendered most essential services, stands as one accused. The storm increases, and I think some of the tall trees must be torn up by the roots.' Life of Morris, vol. i., p. 198.

picions of his own political integrity, and might, on that account, give less heed to his suspicions and representations as to the conduct of others. Be that as it may, he supported Deane with earnestness and zeal. Mr. Laurens, the President of Congress, a man of honor, pure life, and solid abilities, with equal earnestness and zeal opposed him. He thought, as Deane had appealed to the public and arraigned before that tribunal the conduct of the foreign agents of Congress, it concerned the honor of that body to leave him to the tribunal he had selected, and pay no attention to charges contained in a paper not addressed to themselves.[1] But different counsels prevailed, and it was resolved to give Mr. Deane an opportunity to lay before them such intelligence respecting the foreign affairs of the country as he might deem proper. In consequence of this action of Congress, Mr. Laurens resigned the chair on the 9th inst.

In the selection of his successor, there was an obvious propriety in choosing him from some one of the Middle States. Three presiding officers of the Congress had already been taken from the Southern and Eastern States, and it would have been an invidious proceeding to have overlooked, on the present occasion, the claims to that compliment of the remaining division of states. Accordingly, we find that upon the resignation of Mr. Laurens, it was determined that one of the New York delegates should succeed him. The next question was, upon whom should the honor be bestowed? The friends of General Schuyler, doubtless thinking it would be some requital for the mortifications he had experienced in the military department, proposed his name. But as he was not present, Mr. Jay was chosen. Mr. Duane, in a letter to Governor Clinton, written on the 10th inst., the day of

[1] Gordon's History, vol. ii., p. 406.

the election, gave him the following account of this transaction. 'We held up General Schuyler,' he says, 'which seemed to be very agreeable. On account of his absence, Mr. Jay was prevailed on to take the chair, with a resolution on his part to resign in favor of General Schuyler as soon as he attends.'[1] As General Schuyler did not attend Congress until late in the autumn of the following year, Mr. Jay continued in the chair until he vacated it for a foreign mission. A few days after his election, Washington wrote to congratulate him on the honorable and important post he had been chosen to fill. 'The opinion I entertain of your public character,' he said, 'concurs with every personal consideration to make the choice pleasing to me.'

Hitherto Congress had made no provision for the salary or expenses of their presiding officer. But now they resolved to provide him with 'a convenient furnished dwelling-house, and a table, carriage, and servants.' The committee on the Treasury were, at the same time, directed to employ a steward who should have the superintendence of the President's household, together with the necessary expenditures, and be accountable for such moneys as should from time to time be advanced for the purposes of his appointment.[2] Doubtless the recent alliance with France, and the consequent residence of a

---

[1] Writings of Washington, vol. vi., p. 378, note by Mr. Sparks. Lord Mahon alludes to the election of Mr. Jay as follows: 'It was a mere transitory appointment,' he says, 'since the decision of the majority was not, it seems, that Mr. Jay or any one else was the fittest man, but only that some member from the great state of New York should now be chosen.' History of England, vol. vi., p. 276.

His lordship is evidently ignorant of the considerations that induced Congress to make this election. But why he should deem it a merely transitory appointment, simply because it was made from the great state of New York, is difficult to perceive.

[2] Provision was made at the same time for payment to the representa-

French Minister at Philadelphia, suggested to Congress the propriety of providing for the great additional expense their presiding officer would naturally be subjected to. He was in some sort the representative of his country, and compelled to live in a style becoming that character.

The alliance with France was an important event in the history of the Revolution; but it was not nearly so important and decisive as the popular mind, in the height of its joy and enthusiasm, was disposed to regard it. Great and exaggerated expectations were formed of the extent and efficiency of French aid. It was supposed that their powerful ally would be able, in a very short time, to drive the British out of the country, and both people and Congress made less vigorous exertions than the crisis demanded. The army was ill-fed, ill-clothed, and ill-paid. The paper money had been multiplied to a fearful extent, and had depreciated in a ratio still more fearful and disproportionate. The measures adopted by Congress to arrest the evil, such as embargoes, commercial restrictions, and limitation of prices, were mere expedients, founded on an erroneous idea of the deep-seated cause of mischief, and directly calculated to inflame and aggravate the wound they sought to cure. The pay of those engaged in the public service, with a currency thus depreciated, was of course wholly inadequate to their support. 'A rat, in the shape of a horse,' wrote Washington to a friend, 'is not to be bought at this time for less than two hundred pounds, nor a saddle under thirty or forty; boots twenty, and shoes and other articles in like proportion. How is it possible, therefore, for officers to stand this without an increase of pay? And how is

---

tives of Mr. Randolph, deceased, to Mr. Middleton, Mr. Hancock, and Mr. Laurens, for the expenditures in support of their households during the time they held the office of President of Congress.

it possible to advance their pay when flour is selling at different places from five to fifteen pounds per hundred weight, hay from ten to thirty pounds, and beef and other essentials in this proportion?'[1] This letter was written in October, 1778, but the condition of things constantly grew worse, and in the following April Washington, in a letter to Mr. Jay, declares that 'a waggon-load of money will now scarcely purchase a waggon-load of provisions.'[2]

To maintain their credit, and arrest the alarming depreciation of their money, Congress now resolved to fix a limit to their future emission of bills.[3] They placed that limit at two hundred millions. One hundred and sixty millions had already been issued, and of the remaining forty millions, they resolved that only such part should be emitted as might be absolutely necessary for public exigencies before adequate supplies could be obtained from the exertions of the several States. These resolutions of Congress were communicated to the States, accompanied by a circular letter prepared at their request by Mr. Jay. It bears throughout the impress of his peculiar ability and eloquence. It is a clear and

---

[1] Letter to Gouverneur Morris, October 4th, 1778. Writings of Washington, vol. vi. p. 80.

[2] Letter to Mr. Jay, then President of Congress, April 23d, 1779. Ibid, p. 228. Writings of John Jay, p. 47. The reader will find in Washington's letters of this period, constant mention of the deplorable state of the public credit.

In December of this year, an English officer, one of the Convention troops, while in Maryland, received an inn-keeper's bill, which amounted in paper money to £732 and some shillings, and he paid it in gold with four guineas and a half. Aubury's Travels, vol. ii., p. 492. See also Writings of Jay, vol. ii., p. 19.

[3] Upon the question of limiting the emission of bills of credit to the sum of two hundred millions, there were but five votes in the negative, Mr. Jay's being of the number. Virginia voted in the negative, and South Carolina was divided. Mr. Laurens voted with Mr. Jay.

forcible statement of the financial condition of the country, and was well calculated to rouse the States from the dormant condition into which they had sunk, and impel them to vigorous exertions. It exhibits evidences, however, that Mr. Jay had not profoundly studied the interesting question of currency. Indeed, with the exception of Dr. Witherspoon, we doubt if any of the leading men of that day had made themselves masters of this subject. The *proton pseudos*, the radical error into which Mr. Jay fell, was in supposing that the excess of emission beyond the purposes of a circulating medium, (provided the credit of the money could be supported,) would only produce a natural depreciation proportioned to such excess. Now all experience proves that the depreciation of money on account of quantity, is like the depreciation of every other commodity, irregular, rapid, increasing, and out of all proportion to the excess. Take the grain of a country, for example. If the supply exceeds the demand by a fifth, the depreciation of price will not be limited exactly and in arithmetical progression to that proportion, but it will probably be one-half. Let the supply of any article exceed the demand by one-half, and it usually becomes a drug in the market. It is precisely so with money. It was exemplified during the progress of the war. In the years 1776 and 1777, when the fortunes of the country seemed desperate, the Continental money was universally circulated, and its depreciation was slow. But in the two following years, when the gloom began to disappear, when the French alliance inspired hope and promised certain success, the depreciation was in a fearfully rapid ratio. The reason is obvious. Congress multiplied their money to such an extent, that it became a drug; nobody wanted it. The result had been foreseen. Dr. Witherspoon, who had studied the subject with care, and brought to its investigation a mind, less comprehensive and philosophical, perhaps, than Dr. Franklin's, but not inferior to his in acuteness, in culture, and a certain practical sagacity, after the first or second issue, urged the propriety of making loans and establishing funds for the payment of interest.[1] He knew full well, that after the emissions exceeded what was necessary as a medium for the purposes of commerce, the extent of the depreciation would be out of all proportion to the amount of the excess, notwithstanding the confidence of the people in the capacity of the Government to ultimately redeem their credit, might be fully preserved.

With these preliminary observations, we shall now lay before the reader a few extracts from Mr. Jay's draught of the letter of Congress to their constituents. The first will exhibit the necessity that impelled Congress to make emissions at all: 'The ungrateful despotism and inordinate lust of domination,' says the letter, 'which marked the unnatural designs of the British King and his venal Parliament to enslave the people of America, reduced you to the necessity of either asserting your rights by arms, or ingloriously passing under the yoke. You nobly preferred war. Armies were then to be raised, paid, and supplied; money became necessary for these purposes. Of your own there was but little; and of no nation in the world could you then borrow. The little that was spread among you could be collected only by taxes, and, to this end, regular Governments were essential; of these you were also destitute. So circumstanced, you had no other resource but the natural value and wealth of your fertile country. Bills were issued on the credit of this bank, and your faith was pledged for their redemption. After a considerable number of these had

[1] In the fourth volume of Dr. Witherspoon's Works are inserted one or two of his speeches in Congress upon the finances of the country, and an 'Essay upon Money,' which the student will find well worth studying, even though he may be familiar with the more recent labors in the same department of Mills and Ricardo.

circulated, loans were solicited, and offices for the purpose established. Thus a national debt was unavoidably created, and the amount of it is as follows: bills emitted and circulating, $159,948,880; moneys borrowed before the 1st of March, 1778, the interest of which is payable in France $7,545, 196$\frac{67}{90}$; moneys borrowed since the 1st of March, 1778, the interest of which is payable here, $26,188,909; money due abroad, not exactly known, the balances not having been transmitted, supposed to be about $4,000,000. . . . The taxes have as yet brought into the treasury no more than $3,027,560, so that all the moneys supplied to Congress by the people of America, amount to no more than $33,761,665$\frac{67}{90}$, that being the sum of the loans and taxes received. Judge, then, of the necessity of emissions, and learn from whom and from whence that necessity arose.'

Having given a short and plain state of the debt, and pointed out the necessity of punctuality in furnishing the supplies already required, the letter proceeds to remark on the depreciation of the currency as follows: 'The depreciation of bills of credit is always either natural or artificial, or both. The latter is our case. The moment the sum in circulation exceeded what was necessary as a medium of commerce, it began and continued to depreciate in proportion as the amount of the surplus increased; and that proportion would hold good until the sum emitted should become so great as nearly to equal the value of the capital or stock on the credit of which the bills were issued. . . . . . The natural depreciation is to be removed only by lessening the quantity of money in circulation. It will regain its primitive value whenever it shall be reduced to the sum necessary for a medium of commerce. This is only to be effected by loans and taxes.'

Here it will be observed that Mr. Jay supposes the natural depreciation of money will be in proportion to the excess of emissions beyond what is necessary as a medium in commerce. We have shown, and all experience proves it, that instead of the depreciation being definite and proportioned to any fixed standard, it is indefinite, unreliable, and totally disproportioned to the amount of the excess.

After stating that a distrust, entertained by the mass of the people, either in the ability or inclination of the United States to redeem their bills, was the cause of their artificial depreciation, he inquires how far reason will justify that distrust. 'The ability of the United States,' he says, 'must depend on two things; first, the success of the present revolution, and secondly, on the sufficiency of the natural wealth, value, and resources of the country. That the time has been when honest men might, without being chargeable with timidity, have doubted the success of the present revolution, we admit; but that period has passed. The independence of America is now as fixed as fate, and the petulant efforts of Britain to break it down are as vain and fruitless as the raging of the waves that beat against their cliffs. Let those who are still afflicted with these doubts consider the character and condition of our enemies. Let them remember that we are contending against a kingdom crumbling into pieces; a nation without public virtue, and a people sold to, and betrayed by, their own representatives; against a prince governed by his passions, and a ministry without confidence or wisdom; against armies half paid, and generals half trusted; against a Government equal only to plans of plunder, conflagration, and murder; a Government, by the most impious violations of the rights of religion, justice, humanity, and mankind, courting the vengeance of Heaven, and revolting from the protection of Providence. Against the fury of these enemies you made successful resistance when single, alone, and friendless, in the days of weakness and infancy, before your hands had been taught to war or your fingers to fight. And can there be any reason to apprehend that the Divine Disposer of human events, after having separated us from the house of bondage, and led us safe through a sea of blood towards the land of liberty and promise, will leave the work of our political redemption unfinished, and either permit us to perish in a wilderness of difficulties, or suffer us to be carried back in chains to that country of oppression, from whose tyranny he hath mercifully delivered us with a stretched-out arm? In close alliance with one of the most powerful nations in Europe, which has generously made our cause her own, in amity with many others, and enjoying the good will of all, what danger have we to fear from Britain? Instead of acquiring accessions of territory by conquest, the limits of her empire daily contract. Her fleets no longer rule the ocean, nor are her armies invincible by land. How many of her standards, wrested from the hands of her champions, are among your trophies, and have graced the triumphs of your troops? and how great is the number of those, who, sent to bind you in fetters, have become your captives, and received their lives from your hands? In short, whoever considers that these States are daily increasing in power; that their armies have become veteran; that their governments, founded in freedom, are established; that their fertile country and their affectionate ally furnish them with ample supplies; that the Spanish monarch, well prepared for war, with fleets and armies ready for combat, and a treasury overflowing with wealth, has entered the lists against Britain; that the other European nations, often insulted by her pride, and alarmed by the strides of her ambition, have left her to her fate; that Ireland, wearied with her oppressions, is panting for liberty, and even Scotland displeased and uneasy at her edicts: whoever considers these things, instead of doubting the issue of the war, will rejoice in the the glorious, the sure and certain prospect of success.'

Having established this point, he next considers whether the natural wealth, value, and resources of the country will be equal to the payment of their debt. Anticipating the future growth and grandeur of his country, and contemplating her vast domain, yet to be filled up by an increasing and happy population, he prophetically sketches what the eyes of the present generation have already beheld: —

'Extensive wildernesses, now scarcely known or explored, remain yet to be cultivated, and vast lakes and rivers, whose waters have for ages rolled in silence and obscurity to the ocean, are yet to hear the din of industry, become subservient to commerce, and boast delightful villas, gilded spires, and spacious cities rising on their banks.'

Observing upon the future commerce of the country, and deriving from that additional source of national income the ability of the United States to redeem their bills, he next, and by what Gordon terms 'inverse, romantic reasoning,' 'represents the paper currency as a blessing, at the expense of Scripture language.'[1] He says: "Let it also be remembered that paper money is the only kind of money which cannot 'make unto itself wings, and fly away.' It remains with us, it will not forsake us, it is always ready and at hand for the purposes of commerce or taxes, and every industrious man can find it."

Having shown that there was no reason to doubt the ability of the United States to pay their debt, he proceeds to consider whether as much can be predicated of their inclination to pay it. He does not tolerate for a moment the suggestion of the possible violation of the

---

[1] Gordon's History, vol. iii., p. 29.

public faith. 'We should pay an ill compliment,' he says, 'to the understanding and honor of every true American, were we to adduce many arguments to show the baseness or bad policy of violating our national faith, or omitting to pursue the measures necessary to preserve it. A bankrupt, faithless republic would be a novelty in the political world, and appear among reputable nations like a common prostitute among chaste and respectable matrons. The pride of America revolts from the idea; her citizens know for what purposes these emissions were made, and have repeatedly plighted their faith for the redemption of them; they are to be found in every man's possession, and every man is interested in their being redeemed; they must therefore entertain a high opinion of American credulity who suppose the people capable of believing, on due reflection, that all America will, against the faith, the honor, and the interest of all America, be ever prevailed upon to countenance, support, or permit so ruinous, so disgraceful a measure. . . . . Rouse, therefore: strive who shall do most for his country; rekindle that flame of patriotism which, at the mention of disgrace and slavery, blazed throughout America and animated all her citizens. Determine to finish the contest as you began it, honestly and gloriously. Let it never be said that America had no sooner become independent than she became insolvent, or that her infant glories and growing fame were obscured and tarnished by broken contracts and violated faith, in the very hour when all the nations of the earth were admiring and almost adoring the splendor of her rising.'

These noble and animating sentiments, clothed in language so eloquent and appropriate, should be imprinted on every American heart, and find a responsive echo in every American State. Then, our 'infant glories, and growing fame' assuredly never would be 'obscured and tarnished by broken contracts and violated faith.' There would be no stain of repudiation on our escutcheon, nor self-inflicted wound upon our honor.

It will be recollected that the 'special occasion' which justified the appointment of Mr. Jay as a delegate to Congress, while holding the office of Chief Justice of New York, was the Vermont controversy. When he received his special commission, he did not apprehend that this matter was in a more particular manner confided to him than to his colleagues, though some of them considered it in that light. 'The commission vested me,' he wrote to Governor Clinton, 'with no further power than what any other of your delegates possessed; nor was any matter given more particularly in charge to me than to the others by the Legislature. Their late instructions, however, speak a different language. I am satisfied to be viewed in that light, that is, to be the responsible man; and, provided the measures I adopt are not thwarted, I am confident that I shall be able to bring all these matters to a happy conclusion. I hope, however, that this will not be considered as a hint for my being continued in the delegation; I assure you, nothing but an adherence to the resolutions and principles of action I adopted and professed at the commencement of the war would induce me to remain here at the expense of health as well as property; for though I shall always be ready to serve my country when called upon, I shall always be happy to find it consistent with my duty to remain a private citizen.'[1]

Mr. Jay's first object was to prevail upon Congress to interpose, though in the smallest degree; well knowing, that if they once interfered ever so little, they might with more ease be led to a further and more effectual interposition. But it was a very delicate and difficult subject. The opinion generally prevailed in Congress,

[1] Life, vol. i., p. 94. This letter was dated September 25th, 1779.

that they had no authority to interfere in the quarrels of the States; that they were instituted for the sole purpose of opposing the tyranny of Britain, and afterward of establishing the independence of the country; and that their proper power was confined to those important objects. But admitting that they had the power, which we think they clearly had not, independently of the confederation which was not yet completed, it was contended that a business of this nature should be postponed until all the States had acceded to the confederation, an event then daily expected. Other objections to any interference by Congress were urged. They were chiefly objections of expediency. It was feared that harsh measures against Vermont might induce them to join the enemy, and increase their force. Certainly there was no ground to suspect the patriotism of the Green Mountain Boys, who were as loyal as they were brave; but nevertheless, if Congress should make a decision adverse to their claims, it was apprehended that the same spirit which led them to take up arms against British aggression, might impel them to resist the determinations of Congress. It was argued that they possessed a strong country, were numerous, warlike, and determined; and that more force would be required to reduce them than could be spared from the general defence.[1]

Aware of these objections, and others of a more private character, such as the secret wishes of New England in favor of Vermont, Mr. Jay delayed pressing the subject upon the attention of Congress till he had prepared the way for it by acquiring a knowledge of the members of that body. Besides, they were so heated by divisions for the greater part of the winter, on points of great general importance, that it would have been improper and imprudent to have called upon them to decide

[1] Life, vol. i., p. 94. Sparks' Life of Morris, vol. i., pp. 208–215.

on this delicate business till more temper and calmness had taken place. At length, on the 22d of May, certain resolutions were proposed on the part of New York, declaring, among other things, that none of the States ought to be, or should be, divested of any land or territories over which they respectively exercised jurisdiction at the time when they were subject to the Crown of Great Britain, unless by judgment of Congress in favor of certain other of the States claiming the same, or any part thereof, and prosecuting that claim in the way prescribed by the articles of confederation; and that no part or district of one or more of the said States should be permitted to separate therefrom and become independent thereon, without the express consent and approbation of such State or States respectively. At the same time, it was recommended to the inhabitants of the 'pretended State of Vermont' to return peaceably to their former jurisdictions, viz., to the jurisdictions of New York and New Hampshire.

With the views which Mr. Jay found prevailing in Congress upon this subject when he took his seat among them, it is a little singular that so complete a revolution of opinion should have taken place in so short a time. We must look for its explanation in the prudence, moderation, and high character of Mr. Jay. But he was not the man to endanger greater interests by pertinaciously pursuing those of less consequence. It was urged that it would be highly unjust and impolitic to determine against Vermont without previous inquiry into the merits of her pretensions, and giving her an opportunity of being heard. This objection, so far as it respected her claim to independence, Mr. Jay thought absurd though plausible; but inasmuch as a resolution against it could be carried only by a small majority, he wisely promoted the measure of appointing a committee of inquiry.

Accordingly, a committee was appointed to repair to

the inhabitants of Vermont, and inquire into the reasons why they refused to continue citizens of the respective States which had heretofore exercised jurisdiction over them. The committee were instructed to take every prudent measure to promote an amicable settlement of all differences, and prevent divisions and animosities so prejudicial to the United States.

Oliver Ellsworth, a future Chief Justice of the United States, was chairman of this committee. It so happened, but from what cause does not appear, that they never had a formal meeting, never executed the business committed to them, or made a regular report to Congress.[1] The individual reports of the members, however, were favorable to the pretensions of New York. Meantime, the Legislature of that State adopted resolutions respecting those pretensions which were characterized by moderation and by a liberal, but at the same time, a very spirited tone. They added strength to their cause, while, on the other hand, the proceedings of the Vermont Government, especially a law for whipping, cropping, and branding New York magistrates, made an impression greatly to their disadvantage. Mr. Jay availed himself of this state of feeling in Congress, and pressed them to adopt such measures as the public exigencies called for, and thereby prevent the flames of civil war from raging. 'It would not, I believe,' so he wrote to Governor Clinton, 'have been difficult to have obtained what some among you would call very spirited and pointed resolutions, but which, in my opinion, would have been very imprudent ones; because, among other reasons, they would not have been unanimous.'

The resolutions which his judgment approved, and the

[1] The committee consisted of five, any three of whom were empowered to act. The requisite number never met in the disputed territory, and, of course, no action could be taken. Mr. Ellsworth, Mr. Edwards, Mr. Witherspoon, Mr. Atlee, and Mr. Root, composed the committee.

Congress adopted, recommended the States interested in the controversy, to authorize Congress to hear and determine upon it in the mode prescribed by the articles of confederation, by the 1st day of the following February; in which event, Congress pledged their faith to carry into execution the decision which they might adopt. In the meantime, they declared it the duty of the people of the disputed territory to abstain from exercising any power over such of the inhabitants therein as professed themselves citizens of the States claiming the jurisdiction; and that such States ought not to execute their laws over any of the inhabitants, except those who confessed allegiance to them.[1]

Three days after the adoption of these resolutions, Mr. Jay ceased to be a member of Congress. The good effects he anticipated from them were not realized. The people of Vermont disregarded the recommendations of Congress, and proceeded, as a separate Government, to make grants of land and sales of estates which they had confiscated, and exercised civil and military authority over the inhabitants who professed themselves to be citizens of New York. Congress declared their conduct highly unwarrantable, and subversive of the peace and welfare of the United States; but from one cause or other, the consideration of the disputed jurisdiction was postponed from time to time, and nothing decisive was effected. It was not until after the Constitution of the United States was adopted that the controversy was adjusted, and then by an amicable arrangement between the parties themselves; New York conceding the claims of Vermont in consideration of the payment of thirty thousand dollars as indemnity to her citizens for lands lying within the limits of the revolted State.[2]

---

[1] These resolutions were adopted on the 24th of September, 1779.

[2] Sparks' Life of Morris, vol. i., p. 215. Mr. Morris was of the number of those who foresaw the futility of the attempt to reduce

Very little of Mr. Jay's private correspondence during the time he was President of Congress has been preserved. Owing to the danger of letters being intercepted, he seldom wrote without adverting to the consequences of mis-

---

Vermont under the jurisdiction of New York. 'Strange that men,' thus he wrote to Jay, whose views on this subject ran counter to his, in the very act of revolting should so little consider the temper of revolters. But this is eternally the case. We can reason well in our closets about past events; we come out into the world, and act blindly; we look towards the future, and are bewildered.' His heretical opinions upon this subject were a principal cause of his not being re-elected to Congress at the expiration of his term in the autumn of 1779. Time, however, which sets all things even, proved him to have been in the right. After his retirement from Congress, but while the controversy was still pending, he thus wrote to Governor Clinton: 'If I differ with you in sentiment on any occasion, it must be because we have a different view of the subject. Neither of us can be influenced by improper motives, especially on the present occasion. You speak of submitting cheerfully to the decision of Congress. Two questions arise here. Will Congress decide? Will the disaffected submit? I doubt, both as to the one and the other. . . . . . Again, the revolt has daily less in it of novelty, and mankind have a reluctance to shake what looks like establishment. We contemplate effects, and seldom concern ourselves about causes. In a hundred years, not above one American in a hundred will care about the Tea Act or Stamp Act, or examine whether the Declaration of Independence was justifiable or unjustifiable. Further, the Congress have daily less weight and more embarrassments. It is needless to ask why, supposing the fact. The Congress, therefore, will not, I believe, make any decision. Indeed, if all other obstacles were removed, still a great question will remain. Can Congress interfere between a State and its subjects? Admitting, however, their *decision* in all its force; would it be obeyed? No more nor sooner than the pope's bull. What then remains? Just what is now before us; either compulsion or neglect. Either let these people alone, or conquer them. I prefer the latter, but I doubt the means. If *we* have the means, let them be used, and let Congress deliberate and decide, or deliberate without deciding; it is of no consequence. Success will sanctify every operation. Forty victims to public *justice* or *wrath*, and submission from the rest of the people, will convince every body. These are arguments which are perfectly irresistible. If we have not the means of conquering these people, we must let them quite alone. We must

carriage; and hence the reserve and caution that is observable whenever he alludes to political topics, which, however, is seldom. His letters to his friend Robert R. Livingston, whose wealth, freeing him from the necessity of vigorous exertion, together with the imaginative cast of his mind, dwelling on visions not to be realized, disposed him to querulousness and despondency, have a peculiar charm, from the kindly and genial spirit that pervades them. 'The complexions of resignation, of soft complaint, and joyless sensibility,' he writes, a few weeks after his return to Congress, 'are so blended in your letter, that if anonymous, one would suppose it written by a wayworn traveller through this vale of tears, who, journeying towards his distant haven through sultry and dreary paths, at length lays his languid limbs under some friendly shade, and permits the effusions of his soul to escape in words. My friend, a mind unbraced and nerves relaxed are not fit company for each other. It was not a *man* whom the poet tells us

> —Pined in thought,
> And sat, like Patience on a monument,
> Smiling at Grief.

In such rugged times as these, other sensations are to be cherished. Rural scenes, domestic bliss, and the charming group of pleasures found in the train of peace, fly at the approach of war, and are seldom to be found

continue our impotent threats, or we must make a treaty. If we let them alone, they become independent *de facto* at least. Hundreds will resort to them for different reasons. They will receive lands from them, and cultivate them under the powers which are. When the dispute is again renewed, these cultivators will, I believe, be better soldiers than logicians, and more inclined to defend their possessions than examine their titles. . . . . . On the whole, then, my conclusion is here, as on most other human affairs, act decisively, fight or submit, conquer or treat.' Sparks' Life of Morris, vol. i., pp. 212–214.

in fields stained with blood, or habitations polluted by outrage and desolation. I admire your sensibility, nor would I wish to see less milk in your veins; you would be less amiable. In my opinion, however, your reasoning is not quite just. I think a man's happiness requires that he should condescend to keep himself free from fleas and wasps as well as from thieves and robbers.'[1]

Again he writes, and in the following extract from his letter he frankly discloses to his friend a prevailing fault of his character: 'That you have deserved well of your country is confessed, and that you became latterly a little relaxed is not disputable. You have never been thrown out or distanced in the pursuit of virtue; but, like some game horses, you sometimes want the whip. This is a coarse simile—friendship will pardon it. . . . . . The state of your politics is much as I expected. I fear some of your measures are more severe than wisdom or humanity will justify. Posterity will think dispassionately, and probably condemn, especially when informed that they were hastened, lest the influence of resentment should be lost.'[2]

We have seen in the preceding chapter with what suspicion and alarm the abandonment of Ticonderoga was received throughout the country, and the influence that event had upon the fortunes of General Schuyler. His reputation demanded that his conduct should be investigated by a court-martial. That investigation was made, and he was acquitted with the highest honor, of the charges exhibited against him. The proceedings of the court-martial were confirmed by Congress. With his honor thus vindicated, General Schuyler determined to withdraw from the service. Accordingly, he sent his resignation to Congress, but they declined to receive it.

---

[1] Letter to R. R. Livingston, February 16th, 1779. Writings of John Jay, p. 28.

[2] Letter to same. March 14th, 1779. Ibid, p. 30.

Mr. Jay wrote him on the occasion, and in a spirit of true and manly friendship. 'Congress,' he said, 'has refused to accept your resignation. Twelve States were represented. New England and Pennsylvania against you. The delegates of the latter are new men, and not free from the influence of the former. From New York south you have fast friends. Mr. ——'s disposition is at least questionable. Delaware was unrepresented. What is now to be done? You best can answer this question. Were I in your situation, I should not hesitate a moment to continue in the service. I have the best authority to assure you that the Commander-in-Chief wishes you to retain your commission. The propriety of your resignation is now out of the question. Those laws of honor which might have required it, are satisfied: are you certain they do not demand a contrary conduct? You have talents to render you conspicuous in the field, and address to conciliate the affections of those who may now wish you ill. Both these circumstances are of worth to your family, and, independent of public considerations, argue forcibly for your joining the army. Gather laurels for the sake of your country and your children — you can leave them a sufficient share of property — leave them also the reputation of being descended from an incontestably great man—a man who, uninfluenced by the ingratitude of his country, was unremitted in his exertions to promote her happiness. You have hitherto been no stranger to these sentiments, and therefore I forbear to enlarge. Would it not do you honor to inform Congress that, while in their opinion your services ought not to be withheld from your country, neither the derangement of your private affairs, the severities you have experienced, nor regard to your health, already impaired in their service, shall restrain you from devoting yourself to the execution of their commands; but that whenever the situation of our affairs may cease to call you to the field, you hope they will permit you to retire and attend to the duties you owe your family.'[1]

Mr. Jay's correspondence with Washington during the period he presided over Congress was of a confidential and interesting character, and served to confirm those sentiments of respect and esteem which they already entertained for each other. In a letter to the President of Congress, dated March 15th, 1779, General Gates made an indirect attack upon General Washington. Mr. Jay enclosed the obnoxious passages of that letter to Washington, who replied in a very long communication, explaining the state of his relations with Gates. A single extract from Mr. Jay's answer may not be uninteresting. 'I have perused,' he says, 'the several papers with which you favored me. The delicacy, candor, and temper diffused through your letters form a strong contrast to the evasions and design observable in some others. Gratitude ought to have attached a certain gentleman to the friend who raised him; a spurious ambition, however, has, it seems, made him your enemy. This is not uncommon. To the dishonor of human nature, the history of mankind has many pages filled with similar instances; and we have little reason to expect that the annals of the present and future times will present us with fewer characters of this class. On the contrary, there is reason to expect that they will multiply in the course of this revolution. Seasons of general heat, tumult, and fermentation favor the production of some great virtues, and of many great and little vices. Which will predominate, is a question events not yet produced, nor now to be discerned, can alone determine. What parties and factions will arise, to what objects be directed, what sacrifices

[1] Letter to General Schuyler, March 21st, 1779. Writings of John Jay, p. 33.

they will require, and who will be the victims, are matters beyond the sphere of human prescience. New modes of government, not generally understood, nor, in certain instances, approved; want of moderation and information in the people; want of abilities and rectitude in some of their rulers; a wide field open for the operations of ambition; men raised from low degrees to high stations, and rendered giddy by elevation and the extent of their views; a revolution in private property and in national attachments; laws dictated by the spirit of the times, not the spirit of justice and liberal policy; latitude in principles as well as commerce; suspension of education; fluctuations in manners, public counsels, and moral obligations; indifference to religion, &c., are circumstances that portend evils which much prudence, vigor, and circumspection are necessary to prevent or control. To me, there appears reason to expect a long storm and difficult navigation. Calm repose and the sweets of undisturbed retirement appear more distant than a peace with Britain. It gives me pleasure, however, to reflect that the period is approaching when we shall become citizens of a better-ordered State; and the spending a few troublesome years of our eternity in doing good to this and future generations, is not to be avoided nor regretted. Things will come right, and these States will be great and flourishing. The dissolution of our Government threw us into a political chaos. Time, wisdom, and perseverance will reduce it into form, and give it strength, order, and harmony. In this work you are, to speak in the style of one of your professions, a master-builder; and God grant that you may long continue a *free* and *accepted* mason.'[1]

---

[1] Letter to Washington, April 21st, 1779. Writings of John Jay, p. 43.

On the 27th day of September, 1779, Mr. Jay was appointed to represent the American States at the Court of Madrid. He had presided over Congress not quite a year; but during that time, by his moderation, prudence, and impartiality, he had conciliated universal esteem, and allayed the spirit of party. 'May health, success, and every felicity accompany you,' wrote Edmund Pendleton in a letter congratulating him upon his recent appointment, 'but while I am sensible of the advantages we shall reap from your eminent services there, I have my fears that they will be missed importantly where you now are; and that the spirit of party, almost laid to sleep, will revive upon your absence.' [1]

In the next chapter we shall contemplate Mr. Jay's services on a new and unaccustomed scene, and trace his course amid the tortuosities of European diplomacy.

---

[1] Writings of John Jay, p. 52. October 11th, 1779.

CHAPTER XI.

MINISTER TO SPAIN.

1779—1782.

THERE was a difference of opinion among the statesmen of the Revolution, as to the propriety of seeking foreign alliances. Dr. Franklin thought a 'virgin State should preserve the virgin character, and not go about suitoring for alliances, but wait with decent dignity for the application of others.'[1] John Adams, on the contrary, thought it the better policy to solicit alliances, and make themselves known at foreign Courts. 'The more they know us,' he said, 'the better they will like us.' Franklin was overruled, and the views of Mr. Adams prevailed. In accordance with that policy, ministers were sent to various Courts in Europe, without any assurances that they would be received in character, or, in fact, that they would be received at all. The history of our earlier missions to the Courts of Vienna, Madrid, Berlin, and Florence, would seem to confirm the wisdom of Dr. Franklin's opinion, and serve for all future 'virgin states,' not as a 'pattern to imitate, but as an example to deter.'

The first attempt to open a negotiation with Spain was early in the year 1777, when the commissioners to France deputed Arthur Lee one of their number to that country. After Lee's departure, a commission from Congress to Franklin, as minister to Madrid, was received by the Doctor, together with instructions to propose to the

[1] Franklin's Works, vol. viii., p. 209.

Court of Spain a treaty of commerce and alliance, similar to the one proposed to France, with the additional clause that if his Catholic Majesty would join with the United States in war against Great Britain, they would assist in reducing to the possession of Spain the town and harbor of Pensacola; provided that the citizens of the United States should have the use of that harbor, as well as the free and uninterrupted navigation of the Mississippi; and would, provided it was true that Portugal had insultingly expelled the vessels of the United States from her ports, or had confiscated any of them, declare war against that power, if that measure should be agreeable to, and supported by, the Courts of France and Spain. And for this purpose, he was authorized to offer the assistance of six frigates, manned, of not less than twenty-four guns, and provisions equal to two millions of dollars.

Dr. Franklin declined this commission, and sent the instructions to Lee, who was then at Burgos. King Charles, though very bitter against the English, was not prepared to wage war against them. To avoid giving umbrage to the British embassy at Madrid, he stopped Lee at Burgos, whither he sent to meet him his leading minister, the Marquis de Grimaldi, and M. Gardoqui, an eminent merchant of Bilboa, who had been long engaged in the American trade. They had several interviews; but, for greater secresy and dispatch, Lee returned to Vittoria, where he was again met by Grimaldi and Gardoqui. These secret negotiations had no other result than the grant of a small sum of money on the part of Spain, which was subsequently transmitted to Lee at Paris, and considerable military stores, which were shipped to the United States from Bilboa.[1] No pledges

[1] Life of Arthur Lee, vol. i., pp. 79–81. Diplomatic Correspondence, vol. ii. North American Review for 1830, vol. xxi, (N. S.), p. 470.

were given, nor much encouragement held out of future support.

Such was the result of the first attempt on the part of the United States to effect an alliance with Spain. The conduct of that power towards this country during the period embraced by the Revolution, was in striking contrast with the open and liberal policy of France. She was willing to be an instrument in humbling Great Britain, but without going so far as to insure independence to the United States. With a keen appreciation of their own interests, and a sagacious view of the future, the Spanish nation, in general, were of opinion that the Revolution was of bad example to the Spanish colonies and dangerous to Spain, as the United States, if they should become ambitious, and be seized with the spirit of conquest, might aim at Mexico and Peru.[1] But when Spain saw that independence was inevitable, that it must soon be accomplished, she endeavored to take advantage of the present condition of affairs, the darkness that precedes the dawn, and make important concessions to her, the *conditio sine qua non* of her rendering any efficient aid. This insight into the views and policy of the Spanish Court will explain the conduct that was observed

---

Franklin's Works, vol. viii., p. 205, note, 207. Mahon's History of England, vol. vi., p. 149. Secret History of Congress, vol. ii., p. 40. For the first grants, no return was stipulated, but in the course of a few months Lee was informed by Gardoqui that for all aids the Colonies might hereafter receive from his House, remittances of American produce would be expected. The money received by Lee does not appear to have exceeded the sum of 187,500 livres. Mr. Jay, in writing to Franklin from Madrid, October 30th, 1780, says that he had often been told of the former supplies, (i. e., the supplies furnished by Spain,) and asked how they were to be reimbursed. 'My answer has uniformly been, that I knew neither their amount nor terms, and that I wished to be furnished with an account of both, &c. As yet I have not been able to obtain it.' Writings of Jay, p. 65.

[1] Adams' Works, vol. iii., p. 234.

towards Mr. Jay during the whole period of his residence at Madrid.

M. Gérard, the French Minister, who arrived at Philadelphia in the summer of 1778, early intimated to Congress the propriety of adopting measures to enlist Spain in the common cause. He often enlarged on the policy and objects of that Court, one of which was to regain the Floridas, and to become possessed of the exclusive navigation of the Gulf of Mexico, and, of course, the Mississippi. He said he was confident that if these were ceded to her, it would not be difficult to induce her to join us; and especially as the Family Compact, and the refusal of Britain to accept her mediation, would afford a good pretext. He further insinuated, that the United States might reasonably expect to obtain from that Court a considerable sum of money, which, considering the state of our finances, was a desirable object.[1]

Congress were desirous of an alliance with Spain, but were embarrassed as to whom they should employ on this service. The friends of Arthur Lee insisted that he ought to be the man; but his appointment was strenuously opposed, and upon the ground that the difficulties in which he had been involved at Paris, together with the known fact that he was disliked by the French Court, and, consequently, in a certain degree, by the Spanish Court, rendered it inexpedient. 'By these unfortunate circumstances, nearly a year was wasted in fruitless altercation, and the opportunity of obtaining loans from Spain lost, by her having entered into the war, and having occasion for all her money to defray the expense of it.'[2]

The particulars of Mr. Jay's election to the Spanish

---

[1] From the history of his mission, which Mr. Jay began while in Spain but never completed. Only a few of the first pages were found among his papers. Mr. William Jay has inserted several extracts from these in his Life of John Jay, pp. 95–101.

[2] Ibid.

mission are best known from a manuscript letter written by M. Gérard to the Comte de Vergennes.[1] 'There is as much intrigue in this State House as in the Vatican, but as little secresy as in a boarding school.'[2] Thus wrote Jay to Washington a few months previous to the transaction of which we now speak, and the fact which he discloses will explain the means by which the French Minister became possessed of the interesting narrative which follows.

'September 25th. — Congress proceeded to the choice of a minister to Spain. The friends of Arthur Lee made strong efforts to have his commission renewed.[3] The motion was put in a direct form, and lost by so large a majority as to destroy all hope of his succeeding. A motion was then put that they should proceed to the choice of a person or persons who should be charged with the powers of making peace. This was carried. A member then proposed that Franklin and John Adams should be appointed jointly. Many members were opposed to a junction of any sort. The party from the East then proposed Mr. Adams, and the party from the South, Mr. Jay. The decision of the question was deferred till the next day. The event of the election would seem to be problematical. Four States have declared for Adams, and the same number for Jay. The accidental presence or absence of any of the deputies of the other States would decide the question. Your letter to Mr. Adams has produced an impression highly favorable to him.

---

[1] Writings of Washington, vol. vi., p. 385, note by Mr. Sparks.

[2] Writings of Jay, vol. ii., p. 48. This letter is dated April 26th, 1779. Nearly two months later, viz., June 12th, 1779, Lafayette wrote Washington in a similar strain. 'For God's sake prevent the Congress from disputing loudly together. Nothing so much hurts the interests and reputation of America as these intestine quarrels.'

[3] Upon Dr. Franklin declining the mission to Spain in 1777, Lee was appointed in his stead. His commission was dated June 5th, 1777.

'September 26th.—The election of ministers plenipotentiary occurred to-day. The first ballot gave five States for Adams and four for Jay. The act of confederation requires seven votes for a valid election. The second ballot gave six votes for Jay, and five for Adams. The friends of the former, perceiving that Arthur Lee was perpetually the cause of division on this subject, as on all others, put the motion, 'Shall a minister plenipotentiary to Spain be nominated?' The affirmative was sustained by seven States against two. Only seven individuals of thirty-eight were for the negative. By this vote the commission of Arthur Lee was virtually revoked. One of his partisans then named him as minister plenipotentiary. There are now three candidates, and the election is deferred till to-morrow. It is hoped by some, that Mr. Adams will be named for Spain, and Mr. Jay for the peace. This arrangement promises to conciliate the parties, and M. de la Luzerne thinks with me that we shall have reason to be satisfied.

'September 27th.—At length the plenipotentiaries are chosen. Mr. Jay is destined for Spain, and the full powers for peace are confided to Mr. Adams. One vote only was found in favor of Arthur Lee. The choice of Mr. Jay leaves nothing to desire. To much intelligence and the best intentions, he joins a conciliating spirit. As to Mr. Adams, I am not acquainted with him, nor is he known to but a few of the present members of Congress. He has the reputation of an honest man; and the presumption that he would be agreeable to you, has influenced their opinions.'

The day succeeding Mr. Jay's election, William Carmichael, a member of Congress from Maryland, was elected his secretary. He was a Scotchman by birth, a man of considerable talents, but of an intriguing spirit, and regarded by those who knew him best, as something of an adventurer. Mr. Jay selected for his private secretary his brother-in-law, Brockholst Livingston, afterwards Judge Livingston of the Supreme Court of the United States. Congress fixed his salary, which was to be in full for his services and expenses, at £2,500. But a few days before his departure, upon Mr. Jay desiring to be informed in what manner he was to be supplied with money for his expenses on his arrival in Europe, and whether he would be allowed any money for secret services, or should advance money to distressed Americans who might apply to him,[1] it plainly appeared that Congress had no funds for any of these purposes. However, they resolved that a letter be written to Dr. Franklin at Paris, desiring him to take the most effectual means for supplying Mr. Adams and Mr. Jay, and their secretaries, with two thousand louis d'or, in distributions proportioned to their respective salaries; and assuring him, on the faith of Congress, that speedy and proper measures would be adopted, both for repaying that sum and for establishing a fund for the future support of all the embassies of the United States in Europe.[2]

At the time of Mr. Jay's appointment, the Confederacy, a Continental frigate, was lying in the Delaware, nearly ready to convey M. Gérard, the late French Minister, to France. Immediate preparations were made for all necessary accommodations on board the frigate for Mr. Jay and his family. The lateness of the season and the importance of an early arrival in Europe, rendered his departure at the earliest moment of great consequence. Accordingly, neither himself nor Mrs. Jay, who happened to be at Philadelphia when he was appointed, had an opportunity to take leave of but few of their friends and relatives. He received his instructions on the 16th day of October, and on the 26th, the Confederacy sailed on her voyage.

---

[1] Secret Journals of Congress, vol. ii., p. 274.

[2] Ibid, pp. 279–281. The letter to Franklin was dated October 16th, 1779.

M. Gérard had been on very intimate and friendly terms with Mr. Jay. 'On my coming to Congress in the fall of 1778,' says the latter, 'and constantly after, both M. Gérard and M. Mirales, the Spanish agent, had shown me every mark of civility and attention, though I have reason to think that both of them entertained higher opinions of my docility than were well founded.'[1] M. Gérard, too, had made himself very acceptable to the members of Congress. 'You carry with you the affections of a whole people,' was the language of Washington's valedictory letter to him, 'and leave behind you a reputation which will have the peculiar fortune to be everywhere admired by good men.'[2] He had been secretary to the King's Council, and was the principal person concerned in negotiating the treaties of alliance and commerce with the American commissioners. During his residence at Philadelphia, he acquired an extensive knowledge of American affairs. 'He seems better acquainted with republics,' wrote Mr. Jay to Governor Clinton, 'than almost any man I have ever known.'[3]

The friendship which had grown up between Mr. Jay and M. Gérard was now lost by several unfortunate events, which, as they fall naturally within the line of our narrative, we shall briefly notice.

On the 7th of November, when the Confederacy was off the Banks of Newfoundland, going nine knots an hour, in a brisk breeze and rough sea, her bowsprit and all her masts gave way in less than three minutes. During the following night, the shank of the rudder was so much wrenched and split, that the Captain thought it a greater misfortune than the loss of the masts. So great was the swell off the Banks, and so high the winds, that nearly a fortnight was required to put the ship in

[1] Mr. Jay's account of the Spanish mission. Life of John Jay, p. 99.
[2] Writings of Washington, vol. vi., p. 348. [3] Ibid.

sailing condition. On the 23d of November, a council of officers was held, to consider the propriety of continuing their course towards Europe. The decision of the council was, that they ought not to attempt to go to Europe, but to sail for Martinique. The Captain gave Mr. Jay their report, but at the same time assured him of his readiness to proceed to any port whatever that M. Gérard and himself should direct. M. Gérard thought they had better sail for Cadiz. He used many arguments to persuade Mr. Jay to adopt his opinion. 'Every consideration,' wrote Mr. Jay to Congress,[1] 'called me to Spain; private as well as public good forbade a difference with Mr. Gérard. I had reason to believe him well disposed towards me; I perceived clearly that he could not, with any patience, admit the idea of being absent from Europe at so important a season; and that he could scarcely treat with common decency the reasons urged for going to Martinique.' Nevertheless, after careful deliberation, Mr. Jay determined to adhere to the opinion of the officers, and proceed to that island.

A middle course, viz., to order the Captain to land his passengers on one of the Western Islands, and then leave the ship to shift for herself, would have extricated him from his unpleasant situation. 'This,' he said, 'would have satisfied M. Gérard, and we should have been as good friends as ever.'[2] But he considered this a desperate proposition, which he could not reconcile to his principles of action, and hence he rejected it. The ship proceeded towards Martinique, having all the way fair breezes, and, except in the latitude of Bermuda, smooth seas and scarce any calms. M. Gérard, disappointed in his expectations of being seasonably in France, and perhaps mortified that Mr. Jay should prefer his own sentiments to his, ceased to observe that cordiality and frankness which

---

[1] Diplomatic Correspondence, vol. vii., p. 181. [2] Ibid.

had before attended his conduct towards him. 'Nay, he once went so far,' says Mr. Jay, 'as to tell me I had my reasons for coming here. I appeared not to understand him, and continued to endeavor to render the conversation as light and general as possible. This was a tax imposed on my feelings by regard to public good; as a private man, I should have acted differently.'[1]

The breach between them was further increased by another difference of opinion. About ten or twelve days before their arrival at Martinique, M. Gérard observed to Mr. Jay, in the presence of the Captain, that it was time to think which side of the island it would be most prudent for the ship to go, the north or south side, and proceeded to state the reasons which ought to induce them to prefer the north. But Mr. Jay concurred with the Captain in thinking that it was impossible to determine on which side of the island it would be best to go, until they were at or near the parting point, for that circumstances at present unforeseen might render that way rash, which they might now think prudent; for instance, an unexpected change in the wind or the appearance of an enemy. M. Gérard was very much offended at this decision, and, on a subsequent day, when the party were assembled in the cabin, he recapitulated his reasons for the northern passage. He grew very warm, and addressing himself to the Captain, expressed his surprise that so little attention was paid to his facts and observations; 'that he owed it to his conscience and personal safety to mention and enforce them, and that he should represent the whole matter to his Court,' &c. As the subject was so serious, Mr. Jay desired the Captain to send for the master, who had been at the taking of Martinique the last war, and was well acquainted with its bays, harbors, and coasts. He wished to be informed

---

[1] Diplomatic Correspondence, vol. vii., p. 186.

upon certain points which he thought needed explanation. On this, M. Gérard, after saying that he was satisfied with the opinion he had given, &c., and repeating what he had before said about his conscience, &c., "was opening the door to go on deck, when I asked him," says Mr. Jay, "if he would not stay and hear what the master had to say. He said, no, he did not want to hear anything further about it; he had done his duty in delivering what he had to us, and we might do as we pleased about the matter."[1]

Mr. Jay's examination of the master confirmed him in the opinion that it would be invidious to give the Captain any positive orders on the subject, and he gave none. When the time came for a decision, the opinion of the Captain coincided with M. Gérard's, and the northern passage was taken. This happened very fortunately, for had they taken the southern passage, they would in all probability have been captured. On the very day the Confederacy arrived at St. Pierre, a fleet of twenty-five French merchantmen, under the convoy of a frigate, were attacked on the southern side of the island, near Port Royal, by a number of English ships of war from St. Lucia. Fourteen merchantmen were captured, and two driven on shore. The rest escaped during a very severe action between three line-of-battle ships under M. le Motte Piquet, (who went from Port Royal to their relief,) and double the number of the enemy.[2]

Notwithstanding the decision of the Captain conformed to M. Gérard's opinion, he was not at all mollified. He and Mr. Jay ceased to be friendly. 'We observed, and still observe, great politeness towards each other,' said the latter in the letter to the President of Congress from which we have derived this account, 'but it proceeds more from the head than the heart.'[3]

---

[1] Diplomatic Correspondence, vol. vii., p. 189.

[2] Ibid, p. 172.

[3] Ibid, p. 189.

Another cause that aggravated the ill-feeling between Mr. Jay and M. Gérard, was the indelicate attempt of the latter to find out his instructions. John Adams, in commenting upon a letter of the Comte de Vergennes, which he thought was designed to draw from him his instructions, says: 'Mr. Jay, with whom M. Gérard went to Europe in the same ship, can tell the world if he will, as he has told me, the arts and importunities, even to rudeness and ill-manners, which he employed with him to obtain his instructions.' [1]

These difficulties with M. Gérard, together with the conduct of the Count de Montmorin, the French ambassador at Madrid, which Mr. Jay thought not very civil to the objects of his mission, may account, perhaps, in some sort, for that dislike of the French character, and that distrust of the French Court, which he subsequently professed. 'Mr. Jay,' says Mr. Adams, 'likes Frenchmen as little as Mr. Lee and Mr. Izard did. He says they are not a moral people; they know not what it is: he don't like any Frenchman; the Marquis de Lafayette is clever, but he is a Frenchman.' [2]

The Confederacy arrived at St. Pierre the 18th of December. This unexpected termination of the voyage placed her officers in a very disagreeable situation. They were without money or the means of getting any. 'The idea,' wrote Mr. Jay to the President of Congress, 'of our officers being obliged to sneak, as they phrase it, from the company of French officers, for fear of running in debt with them for a bottle of wine, or a bowl of punch, because not able to pay for their share of the reckoning, was too humiliating to be tolerable, and too destructive to that pride and opinion of independent equality, which I wish to see influence all our officers. Besides, some of

[1] Adams' Works, vol. iii., pp. 262, 301. [2] Ibid, p. 303.

them wanted necessaries too much to be comfortable, or, in this country, decent.'[1]

The feelings of Mr. Jay at once prompted him to draw on Dr. Franklin for a hundred guineas of the scanty sum pointed out for the payment of part of his salary, to be divided among the officers according to their respective ranks.[2]

After further differences of opinion with M. Gérard as to the proper measures to be taken to refit the Confederacy, it was finally agreed by the commanding officer of the French fleet and the Governor of Martinique, that the French frigate Aurora, of thirty guns, should convey the passengers of the Confederacy to France. They left Martinique on the 28th day of December, bound for Toulon, but with orders to touch at Cadiz for intelligence. They arrived at that port on the 22d day of January, where they were informed that the English had acquired a decided superiority in the Mediterranean, and that the coast was infested by their cruisers, all of whom the Aurora had fortunately escaped. It was of course deemed imprudent to proceed to Toulon.

Mr. Jay found himself very disagreeably circumstanced. He was without bills of credit or letters of introduction. The Chevalier Roche, however, a passenger with him from America, kindly procured him a credit for about two hundred pounds sterling, with a relation of his, to whom Mr. Jay gave a bill on Dr. Franklin. He afterwards became acquainted with the house of Le Couteulx and Company, who offered him what money he might want; an offer of which he availed himself.[3] He was

---

[1] Diplomatic Correspondence, vol. vii., p. 191.

[2] Mr. Bingham, the American agent at Martinique, perceiving, when Mr. Jay came to close his accounts, that this money for the officers was to come out of Mr. Jay's salary, kindly advanced it on the credit of Congress, and thereby saved Mr. Jay the necessity of drawing.

[3] Diplomatic Correspondence, vol. vii., p. 221.

treated by many of the gentlemen of Cadiz with true Spanish hospitality and politeness. His public character doubtless recommended him to their friendly offices. Count O'Reilly, the Governor-General of Andalusia, was particularly cordial in his attentions to him. He invited Mr. Jay to his house, described to him the politics of the Court, and the personal characters of those who composed it, not excepting the King himself; but he knew the jealous temper of the power he served, and when he took leave of Mr. Jay, he said: 'You feel, I perceive, grateful for the civilities I have had the pleasure to show you, and upon your arrival at Madrid, you will perhaps think it proper to write and thank me for them. Be pleased to do no such thing. Let there be no correspondence between us. Should you wish to make any communication to me, mention it verbally to my friend the Count D'Yranda. I shall hear it from him.'[1]

On the 27th of January, Mr. Jay sent forward his secretary, Mr. Carmichael, to Madrid, with a letter to M. Galvez, the Spanish Minister, communicating to him his appointment and arrival. He remained himself at Cadiz, until the pleasure of the Spanish Court should be signified to him. He adopted this course, he said, because it would compel a decisive answer, and because, if present at Madrid, he would probably be amused with verbal answers capable of being explained away, if necessary, until the two Courts of France and Spain should have time to consult and decide on their measures.[2]

About the 1st of March, Mr. Jay received from the Count de Florida Blanca an answer to his letter to M. Galvez. Divested of the gloss of politeness, it amounted to this, that Spain would acknowledge the independence of the United States for a consideration. Mr. Jay was

---

[1] Life of John Jay, p. 106.

[2] Diplomatic Correspondence, vol. vii., p. 217.

invited to Madrid, but, at the same time, informed that it would not be proper for him to assume a formal character, which must depend on a public acknowledgment and a future treaty. He suspected France was determined to manage between Spain and the United States, squeeze 'a little reputation out of the business,' and make both seem indebted to her for their mutual concessions.[1] He determined, however, to concede nothing. 'There was a time,' he wrote the President of Congress, at the moment of receiving the Count de Florida Blanca's letter, 'when it might have been proper to have given that country something for their making common cause with us, but that day is now past. Spain is at war with Britain.'[2]

Soon after receiving the Count de Florida Blanca's letter, Mr. Jay proceeded to Madrid, where he arrived on the 4th day of April. He applied to the Count de Montmorin, the French ambassador, to countenance and support him in his negotiation. He showed him a resolution of Congress, by which the King of France was requested to aid him. Montmorin said he could not do it without instructions from his Court; that he would write for instructions. Mr. Jay heard no more of it until three years after, when he was informed at Paris by Lafayette that Montmorin told him no such instructions had ever been sent him. This, says Mr. Adams, Mr. Jay considered as a 'fresh proof and example of their vile schemes.'[3]

Mr. Jay's mission had a twofold object; first, to form treaties with Spain, the same or analogous to those with France, with one or two additional particulars, and secondly, to obtain a loan of five millions of dollars. 'The

[1] Diplomatic Correspondence, vol. vii., p. 218. Life of John Jay, p 107.

[2] Diplomatic Correspondence, vol. vii., p. 218.

[3] Adams' Works, vol. iii., p. 366.

Spaniards will not easily give their dollars,' Lafayette had written Washington,[1] and Mr. Jay found them as little disposed to form a treaty. The Count de Florida Blanca, in one of their earlier interviews, plainly intimated to him that the pretensions of America to the navigation of the Mississippi constituted an insuperable obstacle; that the King was immovable on that point, &c.[2]

Mr. Jay, at one time, and while in Congress, was in favor of complying with the views of Spain. He was of opinion that the United States should quit all claim to the Floridas, and grant Spain the navigation of the Mississippi below their territories, provided she would give them a convenient, free port on it, under regulations to be specified in a treaty, acknowledge their independence, defend it with their arms, and grant them either a proper sum of money, or an annual subsidy for a certain number of years. 'But when Spain afterwards,' he says, 'declared war for objects that did not include ours, and in a manner not very civil to our independence, I became persuaded that we ought not to cede to her any of our rights, and of course that we should retain and insist upon our right to the navigation of the Mississippi.'[3]

There were great fluctuations of opinion in Congress respecting the propriety of yielding the navigation of that river. Few had a proper sense of its value. None anticipated the vast extension and growth of the country which was beheld by the succeeding generation. But there were not wanting those who clearly saw that population would gradually extend westward, and that the free navigation of the Mississippi, if not important to their generation, would be indispensable to the coming ones. 'Poor as we are,' thus Franklin wrote Jay, 'yet

---

[1] Writings of Washington, vol. vi., p. 551, June 12th, 1779.

[2] Diplomatic Correspondence, vol. vii., p. 260, 261.

[3] Life of John Jay, p. 100.

as I know we shall be rich, I would rather agree with them to buy, at a great price, the whole of their right on the Mississippi, than sell a drop of its waters. A neighbor might as well ask me to sell my street door.'[1] Gouverneur Morris, on the other hand, whose anticipations of the future growth and grandeur of his country might well have been deemed wild and chimerical, was in favor of yielding to Spain on this point. 'We stand in need of assistance, and you must procure it,' he wrote Jay. 'As to the navigation of the Mississippi,' he said, 'everybody knows that the rapidity of the current will forever prevent ships from sailing up, however easily they may float down. Now, unless some new dragon shall be found whose teeth, sown on the banks of the Ohio, will produce seamen, I know not where else they will be obtained to navigate ships abroad, which can never return home.'[2] The wonders of steam were then undreamt of.

Not less unlike were the characters of Franklin and Morris, than the opinions which, on the subject of the Mississippi, they communicated to Mr. Jay. The fame of Franklin is co-extensive with the civilized world. His great and luminous mind, his wisdom, sagacity, large views, and comprehensive benevolence, shone conspicuously forth throughout his varied career, and attracted, and will continue to attract, the admiration and regards of mankind. If the figure of Gouverneur Morris is eclipsed by the superior proportions of Franklin's, he was, nevertheless, no common man. He had extensive information, and vigorous faculties. He had quick and clear perceptions, and admirable talents for affairs. He was sagacious, reflective, acute, and versatile. He had employed his mind chiefly upon law, politics, and the practical concerns of life, though he was by no means insensible to the attractions of literature. His imagination

---

[1] Writings of Franklin, vol. viii., pp. 449, 450.

[2] Life of Morris, p. 225.

was lively, but his genius was eminently practical. He was voracious of facts, and was conversant with the details of finance, trade, manufactures, and agriculture. The character of his mind disposed him to subjects of immediate interest, rather than remote inquiries. He reverenced order, had high respect for the advantages of fortune, and was uncompromisingly opposed to every scheme of politics that might endanger either. He had great powers of eloquence. His illustrations were apt and pointed; his elocution flowing and graceful. Unlike duller mortals, he never spun 'the thread of his verbosity finer than the staple of his argument.' He was a great talker, and fitted to enlighten, instruct, and adorn society. His conversation was lively and various, but frequently offended by a tone of dogmatism which he never could correct. He did not bear his faculties meekly. He had not the grace of conciliation. With undoubting confidence in his own convictions, he had small respect for those of other people. He had a brave, outspoken nature, scorned to conceal his sentiments, and was not veered from his course,

> 'By every little breath that under Heaven is blown.'

He stood firmly on the earth, and his feelings never soared beyond it. He walked by sight and not by faith. The spiritual had small dominion over him.

With his free, unrestrained wit, he would have put to flight a whole troop of transcendentalists, with their water-gruel, aspirations, and yearnings after imaginary good. He had high animal spirits, and voluptuous tastes. 'He is fond of his ease,' said Madame de Damas, a French lady, who knew him intimately and admired him much, 'does his best to procure it, and enjoys it as much as possible. He loves good cheer, good wine, good company. His senses, as well as his mind, have a high relish of perfection, and strive to attain it. He never eats a bad dinner without a severe censure upon the cook, as he never listens to folly without a keen rebuke.'[1]

The views of Mr. Jay, as we have already seen, had changed, and now fully coincided with those of Franklin. He was inflexibly opposed to the surrender of his country's pretensions to the navigation of the Mississippi, and in that particular his feelings and instructions concurred. But Congress, soon after he left the United States, pressed by their necessities, adopted a measure which placed him in a very embarrassing and disadvantageous situation. On the 23d of November, 1779, they resolved to draw bills upon him for £100,000 sterling. This they thought they might risk, considering the importance of the object. But as the time of his arrival in Europe was uncertain, and as the negotiation might not be immediately practicable, the bills were drawn at six months sight. On the 27th day of the following April, Mr. Jay received information of this action of Congress, and at once communicated it to the Spanish minister. He represented to him that the Congress were well persuaded, in adopting this measure, 'that they could avail themselves of his Majesty's friendship on no occasion more agreeable to him and advantageous to them, than on one so interesting to the United States and important to the common cause.'[2] His Catholic Majesty doubtless had a proper sense of this uncommon mark of confidence in his royal beneficence.

On the 11th of May, Mr. Jay had a conference with the Count de Florida Blanca. The bills of exchange drawn on him were one of the topics of discussion. The Count very frankly stated the pecuniary condition of Spain. She had money, he said, but was in the situation of Tantalus, who, with water in view, could not make

[1] Life of Morris, vol. i., p. 507.

[2] Diplomatic Correspondence, vol. vii., p. 254.

use of it; alluding to their inability to draw their revenues from America. He spoke of the great expenses of the war, and the great losses they had sustained in their marine and commerce; but at the same time he assured Mr. Jay that it was his Majesty's intention to give America all the assistance in his power. He pointed out the means by which Spain could be reimbursed. He said they wanted light frigates, cutters, or swift-sailing vessels of that size. He also mentioned timber for vessels, but said that was an article not so immediately necessary. With respect to the bills of exchange which might be presented, he said that at the end of the present year, or in the beginning of the next, he would have it in his power to advance twenty-five, thirty, or forty thousand pounds sterling, and in the meantime, should these bills be presented for payment, he would take such measures as would satisfy the owners of them, viz., by engaging, in the name of his Majesty, to pay them, observing that the King's good faith and credit were so well known, that he did not imagine this would be a difficult matter.

The last of May, two of the bills drawn on Mr. Jay by Congress arrived. He mentioned the circumstance to Count Florida de Blanca. The Count asked the amount, and being told between six and seven hundred dollars, he said, smiling, that Mr. Jay might accept them, and he hoped so to arrange matters, as, in a short time, to make him easy on that head.[1] This occurred on the 2d of June. On the 7th, the minister addressed a note to Mr. Jay on the subject of pecuniary aids. He informed him that the demands of the war, and the difficulty of transporting to Spain the treasures of the King in America, rendered it impracticable to furnish there, in specie, the sum which Congress had drawn on him. He suggested, however, that some expedient might be found to remedy this inconvenience. For example: if the owners

[1] Diplomatic Correspondence, vol. vii., p. 310.

of the bills of exchange would be content with the security or responsibility of his Catholic Majesty to pay them in the term of two years. The King, he said, would readily agree to such an arrangement, even if it should be found necessary to add a moderate interest. If Mr. Jay should adopt this expedient, the Count proposed, as a means of payment, that Congress should engage to build, without delay, some handsome frigates and other smaller vessels of war, fixing the price of each, and the time when they would be finished.[1]

Mr. Jay replied to this note on the 9th inst. He frankly told the minister, that inasmuch as bills of exchange, immediately on being drawn and sold, became a medium in commerce, and passed through various hands in satisfaction of various mercantile contracts; that the drawer and every endorser became responsible for their credit at every transfer; and that the object of the merchants last holding the bills, as well as of all other merchants, is money in hand or actively employed in trade, and not money lying still, at an interest greatly inferior to the usual profits to be gained in commerce; he said, on considering these things, it appeared to him that, although no objection could be made to the good faith of his Majesty, which all the world acknowledged, yet that the last holders of the bills would prefer recovering the amount of them, with the usual damages on protests, to delay of payment for two years.

With respect to the plan proposed for the repayment of such sums as Spain might lend to the United States, viz., by furnishing her with frigates, Mr. Jay clearly showed that it was impracticable. The materials for the frigates Congress could not procure without money. If, therefore, the money which Congress obtained from Spain should be turned into frigates, the obvious ends of the

---

[1] Diplomatic Correspondence, vol. vii., p. 312.

loan would be defeated. Congress required funds to prosecute the war, not to build ships for the Spanish marine.

There was no further official communication between Mr. Jay and the Count Florida Blanca until the 19th inst., when Mr. Jay, having received notice of another bill drawn upon him for three hundred and thirty-three dollars, communicated that fact to the minister. The next day he was informed that the bill would be paid, but the language of the minister was ominous. 'We cannot forbear observing to Mr. Jay,' he said, 'that it will be impossible to show the same complaisance for other bills without consulting the pleasure of the King. The means hitherto proposed not having been considered as agreeable to Congress, it has become necessary to seek for others, and Mr. Jay will do well to think seriously on this subject, and communicate to the Count de Florida Blanca whatever his wisdom and information may suggest to him.' 'This,' as Mr. Jay wrote to the President of Congress, 'looked dry, and indicated a degree of irritation, though it held up the idea of further means.'

At this stage of the negotiation, it is necessary, in order fully to understand the influences operating on the Spanish Court, to notice the introduction of another person on the scene. The day before Mr. Jay wrote the Count de Florida Blanca respecting the bill of three hundred and thirty-three dollars, Cumberland the dramatist, whom Goldsmith, in his poem called 'Retaliation,' describes as

> 'The Terence of England, the mender of hearts,'

arrived at Aranjuez, where the Court then were, with his wife and two daughters. They appeared publicly, and were openly visited and received by persons of distinction. Cumberland had been sent out by the British Ministry to sound the Spanish Court, and, if circumstances favored, to open a negotiation with the minister Florida Blanca. It was given out, and Mr. Jay was officially informed, that Cumberland and his family were desirous of passing through Spain to Italy; that the journey was undertaken on account of the ill health of a daughter, to whom the Duke of Dorset was much attached; that the opposition made by his friends to the marriage had affected her health, &c. The minister assured Mr. Jay that whatever proposals Mr. Cumberland might make should be candidly communicated to him. It is needless, perhaps, to add that no such communication was made. Cumberland had not been long at Madrid before the arrival of Count D'Estaing, who was specially commissioned to traverse his negotiation, and detach the Spanish Court from their projected treaty with Great Britain. The people, said Mr. Jay, supposed Cumberland's errand to be secret overtures for peace, and, as far as he could judge, were very glad of it. In truth, the war with England was very unpopular with the Spaniards. 'They appear to me,' wrote Mr. Jay, 'to like the English, hate the French, and to have prejudices against us.'[1] 'Many of them have even serious doubts of our being civilized, and mention a strange story of a ship driven into Virginia by distress, about thirty years ago, that was plundered by the inhabitants, and some of the crew killed in a manner and under circumstances which, if true, certainly indicate barbarity.'[2]

The evening of the day following his arrival, Cumberland had his first interview with the Count de Florida Blanca. He was cordially received. 'I had,' he says, 'repeated interviews with the minister, whom I visited by night, ushered by his confidential valet through a suite of five rooms, the door of every one of which was constantly locked as soon as I had passed it.'[3] Everything

---

[1] Diplomatic Correspondence, vol. vii., p. 281. [2] Ibid.

[3] Cumberland's Memoirs, p. 193.

seemed in a happy train, and the honors of successful diplomacy were ripening fast for Cumberland, when news arrived at Madrid of Lord George Gordon's riots. 'How this intelligence operated on the mind of his Catholic Majesty,' says the unlucky diplomatist, 'can only be conceived by such as were acquainted with his character, and know to what degree he remained affected by the insurrection, then not long passed, in his own capital of Madrid. I will only say that my treaty was in shape, and such as my instructions would have warranted me to transmit and recommend. . . . . . The crisis was decidedly in my favor; my reception flattering in the extreme; the Spanish nation was anxious for peace, and both Court, ecclesiastics, and military, professedly anti-Gallican. . . . I never had any reason, upon reflection, to doubt the sincerity of Count Florida Blanca at this moment, and verily believe we should have advanced the business of the preliminaries if the fatal news of the riots had not most critically come to hand that very day on which, by the minister's own appointment, we were to meet for fair discussion of the terms, while nothing seemed to threaten serious difficulty or disagreement between us.'[1] Cumberland went to the minister, according to appointment, perfectly ignorant of what had happened in his own country, and confident that the interview would crown his mission with success. He did not wait more than two minutes in the minister's inner chamber before he came out of his closet, 'and in a lamentable tone,' says Cumberland, 'sang out the downfall of London; King, Ministers, and Government whelmed in ruin; the rebellion of America transplanted to England, and heartily as he condoled with me, how could he, under such circumstances, commit his Court to treat with me?'[2] In the course of a very few days news arrived that the rioters were quelled,

[1] Cumberland's Memoirs, p. 194. [2] Ibid.

Lord George Gordon committed to the Tower, and indemnification ordered to the sufferers in the tumult; but the favorable moment had passed. 'The minds and understandings of those with whom I had to deal,' says Cumberland, 'were not easy to be cured of alarms once given, or prejudices once received.'[1]

The arrival of Count D'Estaing, following close upon the news of the riots, completed the ill-fortune of the English negotiator. D'Estaing was received with high favor, and much caressed. Cumberland returned to England in the spring of 1781, with the objects of his mission unaccomplished.

The observations of Cumberland with regard to the characters of those with whom it was his lot to treat, are interesting and pertinent to our inquiries respecting the mission of Mr. Jay. 'Great men are the guide-posts and land-marks in the State. The credit of such men at court or in the nation, is the sole cause of all the public measures.'[2] 'There was a gloomy being,' says Cumberland, 'out of sight and inaccessible, whose command, as confessor, over the royal mind, was absolute, and whose bigotry was disposed to represent everything in the darkest colors against a nation of heretics, whose late enormities afforded too good a subject for his spleen to descant upon; and in the mind where no illumination, no elasticity resides, impressions will strike strongly and sink deep.'[3]

Of the two principal ministers of King Charles, he gives us the following description. 'A mind so fluctuating and feeble as that of the Spanish minister,' he says, 'was not formed to preserve equanimity in success, or to persist in its resolutions against the counteraction of opinions. He was at this period[4] absolutely intoxicated, not only by

---

[1] Cumberland's Memoirs, p. 195.

[2] Burke.

[3] Memoirs, p. 195.

[4] The summer of 1780.

the capture of our trading ships, but by the alluring promises of D'Estaing, and surrendered himself to the self-interested counsels of Galvez, minister of the Indies, for the continuance of the war. That minister, (the creature of France to all intents and purposes,) had, like himself, been raised to high office from the humble occupation of a petty advocate, and by early habits of intimacy, as likewise by superiority of intellect, acquired a power over his understanding little short of absolute ascendancy.'[1]

Having seen the issue of Cumberland's negotiation, we now return to trace the progress of Mr. Jay's. The reader will recollect that the last note of the Spanish minister to Mr. Jay was dated the 20th of June, two days subsequent to Cumberland's arrival, and that it 'looked dry, and indicated a degree of irritation.' Mr. Jay replied to it on the 22d. He assured the minister that the United States would not be able to pay their debts during the war, and that any plan calculated on a contrary position would be fruitless. 'I am ready,' he said, 'to pledge their faith for repaying to his Majesty, within a reasonable term after the war, and with a reasonable interest, 'any sums he may be so kind as to lend them. What more can I offer? What more can they do? If there be any services they can do to his Majesty, consistent with their safety and defence, they are ready and will be happy to render them.'[2] This letter was not answered. On the 28th, Mr. Jay addressed another note to the minister, and enclosed certain resolutions of Congress, adopted on the 18th of March, 1780, and designed to put the American finances on a permanent footing. 'Finding,' he says, 'the minister's heart and imagination much attached to his favorite idea of getting

[1] Memoirs, p. 197.

[2] Diplomatic Correspondence, vol. vii.,.p. 325.

American frigates at the expense of the United States, he hinted to him that when the plan of Congress should be fully executed, it would furnish them with resources equal to all the exigencies of the war, and probably enable them to supply his Catholic Majesty with vessels, &c.[1]

This note was accompanied with another, informing the Count de Florida Blanca that Mr. Jay had been called upon to accept bills to the amount of between ten and eleven thousand dollars; that the greater part of them belonged to Messrs. Joyce of Madrid, who had agreed to wait for an answer until the following Monday. 'The Count can give no positive answer hereon,' was the reply Mr. Jay received the next day, 'without first taking the orders of the King, his master, and having a meeting with the other ministers; and some of these having already gone to Madrid, a determination cannot be immediately had, which renders it necessary for Mr. Jay to require Messrs. Joyce to wait some days longer for the answer in question.'[2] Mr. Jay's hopes were encouraged. The idea of an interference in favor of the bills was kept up. On the 3d of July, the Count having in the meantime removed to Madrid, wrote to inquire when the bills in the hands of Messrs. Joyce would become payable. 'Thus things were apparently in good train,' wrote Mr. Jay to the President of Congress; but the next day the news of the loss of Charleston became credible, and, like the news of the London riots, it changed the aspect of affairs. 'The effect of it,' says Mr. Jay, 'was as visible as that of a hard night's frost on young leaves.'[3] He requested a conference with the minister, and had one on the evening of the 5th. After the usual compliments, the surrender of Charleston became the topic of conver-

[1] Diplomatic Correspondence, vol. vii., p. 328.
[2] Ibid, p. 330. The Court at this time was at Aranjues.
[3] Ibid, p. 331.

sation. The Count seemed to think it strange that the place had not been better defended, and that more vigorous measures had not been taken to impede the enemy's progress, and observed that if the town was not in a condition to stand a siege, it would have been better to have withdrawn the troops and stores, and reserved them for the defence of the country. Mr. Jay replied, that probably when all the circumstances relative to this affair were known, there might be reasons which would account for the conduct of the Americans; to the truth of which remark the Count appeared to assent. He then mentioned the death of M. Mirales,[1] and regretted his loss at this time. He said he had recommended to his Majesty a person to succeed him whom they knew, who spoke English, whom he expected soon, and to whom he would explain his ideas on the subject of the bills, and on other matters touching which Mr. Jay had written to him, and who would confer with Mr. Jay respecting them. He spoke of the bills of exchange in the possession of the Messrs. Joyce, and seemed to be surprised that that house should be possessed of so many of them. He advised Mr. Jay to be cautious of those gentlemen, saying that they were as much English in their hearts as the ministry of that country; that he had known them long, that he thought their conduct extraordinary in being so urgent for the acceptance of the bills.[2] 'In this conference,' says Mr. Jay, 'not a single nail would drive. Everything was to be postponed till the arrival of the person intended to succeed M. Mirales.'[3] The minister indeed told Mr. Jay, that if the Messrs. Joyce were pressing, he might accept their bills, payable at Bilboa, and throughout the whole conference gave him warm and repeated

---

[1] Mirales was the Spanish agent residing at Philadelphia. Ante, p. 283.

[2] Diplomatic Correspondence, vol. vii., pp. 331–333.

[3] Ibid, p. 336.

assurances, not only of the King's good faith and friendly disposition towards America, but of his own personal attachment to her interest, on both of which, as well as in his candor and promises he desired him to place the greatest reliance.

The minister did not mention the name of the person intended to succeed M. Mirales. 'I supposed,' says Mr. Jay, 'that he alluded to one of the Gardoquis, three of whom speak English, and I was well acquainted with one of them. But as another of them had been heretofore employed by the Court, it appeared most probable that he was the person meant. They are brothers, and have a strong family likeness.'[1] Early in August, the Court removed to St. Ildefonso. The illness of Mrs. Jay and the death of a child detained Mr. Jay at Madrid. Mr. Carmichael, however, went to St. Ildefonso; and on the 12th, he wrote Mr. Jay that a person had arrived at the same inn where he lodged, whom he supposed to be the one so long expected. By the 20th of August, bills to the amount of $21,600 had been presented to Mr. Jay for acceptance, exclusive of the bills in the hands of the Messrs. Joyce. The holders were impatient. He applied to the minister, but no other answer could be obtained than that he awaited the arrival of the person whom he had mentioned. Pressed by the holders of the bills, he was compelled, however disagreeable to his feelings, again and again to appeal to the minister. He wrote him on the 16th, the 18th, and the 25th of August; but no answer was returned to his notes. He went to St. Ildefonso on the 25th, having first visited the holders of the bills and obtained a further extension of time. The Messrs Joyce would not be put off, and he accepted their bills, payable at Bilboa, as directed by the minister at their conference on the 5th of July. The

[1] Diplomatic Correspondence, vol. vii., p. 339.

morning after his arrival at St. Ildefonso, he went to pay his respects to the minister, but being told he was sick, he left a card. Mr. Jay was not deceived by this excuse, for he knew that the French ambassador and others had been with him in the morning, and he rode out as usual in the afternoon. He was convinced, too, that the person so often mentioned, and for whose arrival everything was postponed, had already come. Mr. Carmichael informed him, that in passing by a wicket-gate of the King's private gardens, he had observed the person whom he had before seen at the inn, walking in them, and that his servant had learned from a barber of his acquaintance that he dressed a gentleman who spoke English and lodged at M. Del Campo's, a confidential secretary of the Count de Florida Blanca.

At length, on the 3d of September, this important personage made his appearance, and presented a note to Mr. Jay from the minister. It was Don Diego Gardoqui of Bilboa, whom Mr. Carmichael took to be the same person whom he first saw at the inn, and afterwards walking in the private gardens. 'Hence it appears,' says Mr. Jay, 'that these strange delays were not unavoidable. Probably the desire of further intelligence of the enemy's operations in America, and the undecided state of Mr. Cumberland's negotiation, might have given occasion to them. To these may perhaps be added an expectation that our distresses would render us more pliant, and less attached to the Mississippi.'[1]

M. Gardoqui entered into a long conversation with Mr. Jay. The point upon which he chiefly dwelt was, that Mr. Jay offered no *consideration* for the money he solicited. He mentioned ship-timber, and inquired if there was nothing on the side of the Mississippi that Mr. Jay could offer. 'In the evening,' says Mr. Jay, 'M.

[1] Diplomatic Correspondence, vol. vii., p. 353.

Gardoqui again paid me a visit, and pointedly proposed my offering the navigation of the Mississippi, as a consideration for aids. I told him that object could not come in question in a treaty for a loan of one hundred thousand pounds, and Spain should consider that to render alliances permanent, they should be so formed as to render it the interest of both parties to observe them; that the Americans, almost to a man, believed that God Almighty had made that river a highway for the people of the upper country to go to the sea by; that this country was extensive and fertile; that the General, many officers, and others of distinction and influence in America were deeply interested in it; that it would rapidly settle; and that the inhabitants would not readily be convinced of the justice of being obliged either to live without foreign commodities, and lose the surplus of their productions, or be obliged to transport both over rugged mountains and through an immense wilderness, to and from the sea, when they daily saw a fine river flowing before their doors, and offering to save them all that trouble and expense, and that without injury to Spain.'[1]

The next day Mr. Jay again met M. Gardoqui at M. Del Campo's. The conversation was with this latter person. He held very high language, whether 'from natural arrogance,' or 'to affect my temper, I cannot say,' observes Mr. Jay. The bills and the proposal of a treaty were the topics of discussion. Del Campo said America, while seeking aid, did not seem inclined to gratify Spain in the only point in which she was deeply interested. The conference resulted in nothing positive. 'I gave M. Del Campo credit for his frankness,' says Mr. Jay in a letter to the Comte de Vergennes, 'and wish I could with propriety have extended it to his delicacy.'

On the 6th of September, M. Gardoqui told Mr. Jay

[1] Diplomatic Correspondence, pp. 355, 356.

he might accept certain bills, amounting to $1,110; but on the 13th, he brought this message from the minister: 'That the exigencies of the State would not permit his Majesty to provide for the payment of more of the bills drawn upon Mr. Jay than had been already accepted.' If this was the final determination of Spain, Mr. Jay thought it important that it should be communicated in writing. Accordingly, the next day he wrote the minister Florida Blanca, requesting to be told frankly whether the United States might expect any, and what aids from Spain.

The same day 'some glorious reports from America arrived,' says Mr. Jay. 'It seemed as if she had risen like a giant refreshed with sleep, and was doing wonders. . . . . . . I began again to be seen, and, in a few instances, to be known.' On the 15th, a paper was delivered to him by M. Gardoqui, containing the minister's sentiments. He said it was not his Majesty's intention to stop assisting the United States, whenever means could be found to do it, but that it would be impossible to supply them with money in Europe, there being none to spare; but if Mr. Jay or his constituents should find money upon credit, to the amount of $100,000 or $150,000, payable in three years, his Majesty would be answerable for it; that he would, besides, do all that was possible to assist them with clothing and other things. This was the substance of the communication. Many things were repeated which had been urged upon Mr. Jay's attention before, such as the impropriety of drawing bills without giving previous notice, and asking loans without giving any tokens of a recompense, &c. Count Montmorin imputed the conduct of Spain to resentment against M. Necker, for opposing a certain scheme of Spanish finance which he thought interfered with his plan. Indeed, a hint to that effect was given by the minister, Florida Blanca, in the paper delivered to Mr.

Jay by M. Gardoqui. Mr. Jay appears to have thought that partial resentments had been permitted to have an undue influence, and that the minister forgot, in his zeal for a certain scheme of finance, that it was unjust to wound opponents through the sides of their friends.[1] He knew, notwithstanding the expenses of the war and the detention of her treasure in America, that Spain, if cordial in her friendship, could have made the loan he asked.

The bills already accepted, and for which Spain undertook to provide, amounted to about $14,000. Others to the amount of nearly $50,000 remained unaccepted. Spain declined to interfere in their favor, and Mr. Jay was reduced to the necessity either of promising to accept them, and thus make himself personally liable for their payment, or permit the credit of Congress to perish with them. 'I could not long hesitate,' he said, 'I promised to accept them.'[2] 'I determined to continue accepting the bills, to attempt the loan, and, by a representation of my situation to the French Court, endeavor to save the necessity of protesting them for non-payment.' He immediately wrote to Congress by several conveyances, to stop drawing on him.[3]

Mr. Jay's conduct in thus accepting the bills has elicited, and properly elicited, much praise. It was an act of disinterested public virtue. Its performance evinced his patriotism, and proved him equal to his position. We say proved him equal to his position, for we think he was bound to preserve the credit of his country. He was not without resources. Six months would intervene before the bills became due. He could offer the responsibility of Spain for a loan of $150,000. It is true, he

[1] Letter to Vergennes, September 22d, 1780. Diplomatic Correspondence, vol. vii., p. 357. [2] Ibid, p. 369.

[3] Congress received his letter on the 4th day of December, and stopped drawing.

was unable to effect the loan; but he could not foresee that. He could, too, apply to France, as he did. Even Congress, informed of the necessity of providing means to pay their bills, might succeed in supplying him with the funds. 'Almost anything will be better than a protest,' said Mr. Jay in a letter to Franklin, 'for, exclusive of the disgrace, which is intolerable, the consequences of it would cost Congress more than the expense of saving their credit, be it almost what it will.'[1] Even strangers, upon whom Congress had no claims whatever, who were bound by no ties of interest or birth, but sympathized in the struggles of a distant people, felt as Mr. Jay felt, and did what Mr. Jay did. Mr. Laurens, who had been appointed minister to Holland, and upon whom Congress had also drawn bills, did not sail for that country as soon as was intended, and was finally captured by the enemy on his passage. When the bills began to arrive at Amsterdam, Mr. Laurens not being present, and the cause of his absence unknown, great surprise was manifested. The house of De Neufville and Son was applied to. 'We said at the first,' wrote those gentlemen to Mr. Jay, 'that we expected Mr. Laurens would be in town very soon, begging them to keep those bills a fortnight, and that, at all events, we would accept them.'[2] Mr. Laurens not arriving, they did accept them. If, therefore, Mr. Jay had not risen superior to private considerations; if he had not confided in the honor of Congress, and done what even strangers did, he would have failed on a great occasion, and marred the symmetry of his life.

On the 22d of September, Mr. Jay wrote to the Comte de Vergennes, requesting him to interpose the amity of

[1] Diplomatic Correspondence, vol. vii., p. 370.

[2] Ibid, p. 286. They wrote to Dr. Franklin, offering to accept all the bills that should precede the arrival of Mr. Laurens, provided he would give them permission to re-draw directly on him at seven or eight months.

France, and enable him to preserve American credit unimpaired. He endeavored also, but without success, to effect a loan, on the security of the King, in Spain, France, and Holland. He wrote, too, to Dr. Franklin, urging him to exert his abilities and influence to promote the success of his application to the French Court. Vergennes wrote to Montmorin, and expressed doubts whether he would be able to render Mr. Jay the services he requested of him. 'I shall do my best in this exigency,' he said, 'but am not sure of success; beyond this, it would be impossible for me to go.'[1] In October, he received from Dr. Franklin $25,000, which was kindly and generously advanced by France. 'If you find any inclination to hug me for the good news of this letter,' wrote Franklin on this occasion, 'I constitute and appoint Mrs. Jay my attorney, to receive in my behalf your embraces.'[2] Not only did Franklin aid Mr. Jay, but he undertook for all the bills drawn on Mr. Laurens that had yet appeared.

By the 30th of October, Mr. Jay's acceptances amounted to $100,000. In December he had a long and interesting conference with Count de Florida Blanca. He expressly promised him $150,000. As the bills afterwards became due, Mr. Jay applied for money to pay them, and received $34,880 dollars. On the 15th of March, 1781, he sent the minister a list of the bills payable in April, which amounted to $89,083. On the 25th he was informed that the payment of this sum could not possibly be made at that time, but that the balance of the $150,000 should be paid in the course of six months. This last instance of inconsistency between the promises of the minister and his conduct 'appeared to me,' says Mr. Jay, 'to be really cruel; for if he had intended to withhold the necessary supplies, he ought to have given

[1] Diplomatic Correspondence, vol. vii., p. 385, 410.
[2] Writings of Franklin, vol. viii., p. 449.

me notice of it, and not, by keeping up my expectations to within a few days before the holders of the bills were to call upon me for their money, reduce me to such imminent danger of being obliged to protest them.'[1] Count Montmorin intimated to him that the Spanish Court expected that he would make some further overtures respecting the Mississippi. Mr. Jay told him he had no authority to make any other than what he had already made. He replied, that the minister Florida Blanca believed he had. It was not until nearly two months after, that Mr. Jay could understand the reason of the minister's belief. On the 18th of May, he received a letter from James Lovell, on behalf of the Committee of Foreign Affairs, enclosing a copy of a resolution of Congress adopted on the 15th of the preceding February, instructing him no longer to insist on the free navigation of the Mississippi below the southern boundary of the United States, nor on a free port or ports below the same. Mr. Jay immediately suspected that the official letter, communicating the action of Congress, had fallen into the minister's hands, and that he critically withheld the pecuniary aids promised, in order to extort overtures from him, which the minister, though mistaken, had reason to believe he was in a capacity to make. The Spanish Court were, at all times, well informed of the situation of American affairs, and had minute information of what was passing in Philadelphia. Almost every letter that Mr. Jay received bore evident marks of inspection, so that the contents of his despatches from Congress were known to the minister before they were delivered to him.

It was not until after the defeat of General Gates at Camden that a disposition to yield the navigation of the Mississippi began to manifest itself in Congress. It was

[1] Diplomatic Correspondence, vol. vii., p. 456.

then apprehended by many of the Southern delegates that Congress might accede to a peace on the principle of *uti possidetis*, and to avoid that possible result, they were anxious to secure the aid of Spain.

Among the Virginia delegates, Colonel Bland was foremost in urging the relinquishment of the navigation of the Mississippi as the *quid pro quo* of a Spanish subsidy and alliance. His colleague, James Madison, was opposed to the proposition. The subject was referred to the Virginia Assembly. Unfortunately, it was brought forward during Arnold's invasion of the State, and it was determined according to the complexion of affairs rather than the merits of the case.

The resolution instructing Mr. Jay to yield the navigation of the Mississippi, provided it should be unalterably insisted upon by Spain, was moved by the delegates of Virginia, in pursuance of instructions from their constituents. It was adopted, as we have already observed, the 15th of February, 1781. There were but three dissentient votes, viz., the votes of Massachusetts, Connecticut, and North Carolina.

Uninformed of this action of Congress, it only remained for Mr. Jay to use his utmost endeavors to provide funds to pay the bills that would be due in April. He applied to Count Montmorin. 'I must do him the justice to say,' wrote Mr. Jay to the President of Congress, 'that his conduct on this occasion merits our thanks.'[1] Montmorin saw the minister Florida Blanca, but the only arrangement that he could effect was, that the amount of the April bills should be paid to Mr. Jay in six equal monthly payments. This still left him unprovided with the means of paying the approaching demands; but the Count engaged the Marquis d'Yranda to advance the sums necessary to pay them.

---

[1] Diplomatic Correspondence, vol. vii., p. 410.

'Thus, my dear Sir,' wrote Jay to Franklin, 'I have been as it were reprieved by the kind offices of the French ambassador from protesting any of the bills due this month; but every ensuing month will bring with it new dangers and solicitudes, and particularly the month of May, in the course of which I shall be called upon for no less than $96,288. I am in a cruel situation, and without the least expectation of succor, except from France.'[1]

That nothing in his power might be left undone, Mr. Jay sent on the 1st of April an express to Dr. Franklin, representing to him his true situation, and the injury American credit would sustain from the protest of a single bill drawn by order of Congress. The express returned on the 19th inst., with the cheering intelligence that he might draw on Franklin for $142,220, that being the amount of the bills, (exclusive of those that might yet arrive,) that would be payable between May and September. 'You will not wonder at my loving this good Prince; he will win the hearts of all America.'[2] Thus wrote Franklin to Jay, when communicating to him a fresh instance of the noble and liberal conduct of the French Court, a conduct to which the United States owed much, and for which they should never cease to be grateful.

As Mr. Jay, by the action of Congress, was now enabled to remove what had been hitherto interposed as the chief obstacle to a treaty, he thought it expedient to wait on the minister Florida Blanca, and again renew that subject. The letter from the President of Congress, communicating the instructions of the 15th of February, had not yet been received. Mr. Jay was in doubt whether

---

[1] Writings of Jay, p. 77. This loan was obtained on the personal credit of Montmorin and Mr. Jay's consenting that the six monthly payments from the Spanish Government should be applied to the repayment.

[2] Writings of Franklin, vol. viii., p. 499.

the letter had actually miscarried, or Congress had reconsidered the subject, and altered or repealed their resolutions. He deemed it imprudent, therefore, to hazard overtures on the ground of instructions which had not been officially communicated to him. He had a conference with the minister on the 19th of May. 'He received me,' says Mr. Jay, 'with more than usual cordiality.' The subject of a treaty was introduced. The minister said that the views of Congress were such as would not permit his Majesty to form a treaty with the States; that he wished Congress had been more disposed to oblige the King. He told Mr. Jay that he ought to preach to them forcibly, 'for that he thought a good preacher (*un bon prédicateur*,) would do much good,' 'thereby intimating, as I understood it,' observes Mr. Jay, 'that Congress were not sufficiently apprised of the importance of Spain and the policy of complying with her demands.'[1] To all this, Mr. Jay briefly replied, that even if Congress should be inclined to yield the navigation of the Mississippi, it was doubtful whether new delays and obstacles to a treaty would not arise to postpone it. 'The Count smiled, said he always spoke frankly, and that whenever I should announce to him my having authority to yield that point, I might depend on his being explicit and candid, but as matters stood at present, he could say nothing on that head.'[2] Other topics were introduced, and the conference ended. 'I flatter myself that Congress will never again attempt to form an alliance on principles of equality in *forma pauperis*,'[3] wrote Mr. Jay to Charles Thomson, the Secretary of Congress, a few weeks previous to this interview with the minister. Indeed, his position was a very embarrassing one. Spain considered America in the light of a petitioner, and

[1] Diplomatic Correspondence, vol. vii., p. 460. [2] Ibid, p. 462.
[3] Writings of Jay, p. 79: April 23d, 1781.

treated her accordingly. Mr. Jay was uniformly of opinion that had Congress drawn no bills on him, and shown themselves inflexible with regard to the navigation of the Mississippi, Spain would have endeavored to purchase their claims by money or a free port. 'I have not the least doubt,' he said, 'but that almost any spirit will prosper more here than that of humility and compliance.'[1]

On the 23d of May, Mr. Jay had another interview with the Spanish minister. 'He seemed a little hurried in his spirits, and behaved as if he wished I had not come.' 'He asked me rather abruptly,' continues Mr. Jay, 'if I had anything particular to communicate to him, and whether I had received any further letters.'[2] Mr. Jay told him that Congress viewed the speedy accomplishment of the union between Spain and the United States as very important to the common cause, and if Spain would forthwith consent to come into it, they would gratify his Majesty by ceding to him the navigation of the Mississippi below their territories, on reasonable terms.[3] Considering the previous language of the minister, we might naturally suppose that the point being yielded which he had all along urged as the only obstacle to a treaty, nothing would now interpose to prevent the accomplishment of that object. But strange to say, he now intimated that a treaty could with more facility be adjusted at a general peace than at present. 'Throughout the whole of this conversation,' says Mr. Jay, 'the Count appeared much less cordial than in the preceding one; he seemed to want self-possession, and to that cause I ascribe his incautiously mentioning the general peace as the most proper season for completing our political connexions.'[4]

On the 2d of July, Mr. Jay addressed a letter to Count

---

[1] Diplomatic Correspondence, vol. vii., p. 465. [2] Ibid, p. 466.
[3] Ibid, p. 468. [4] Ibid, p. 469.

Florida Blanca, making a formal overture for a treaty, on the ground of his instructions. He also solicited the favorable interposition of the Count Montmorin, to facilitate the negotiation. Mr. Jay, however, even at that time, doubted whether the French Ambassador had received any instructions from his Court other than generally to favor the treaty and manage his interference in such a delicate manner as, without alarming the pride of Spain, to give both parties reason to think themselves obliged.[1] Notwithstanding Mr. Jay had thus offered to remove the only obstacle which the Spanish minister had repeatedly assured him interposed to prevent a treaty, his overtures were received with 'silent inattention.' The minister repeatedly promised to name a time when he would confer with Mr. Jay on this important subject, but, upon one pretext or other, the interview was constantly postponed.

At length he wrote Mr. Jay that, notwithstanding his pressing engagements and continued indisposition, he would, 'nevertheless, be charmed to converse a moment' with him 'one of those leisure evenings, when there is no business with the King.'[2] He named Saturday evening, the 8th of September. The conference was brief. The subject of the treaty was hastily referred to, and instantly dismissed. The minister said he hoped in the course of the following week to enter upon it seriously, and would give Mr. Jay notice of the day. The week passed, and witnessed no notice or conference. But on the evening of the 19th, he had a long interview at St. Ildefonso with the Count Florida Blanca. He assigned ill-health and multiplicity of business as the causes of the delays to which Mr. Jay had been so long subjected, and observed, that, as these causes still existed, he con-

---

[1] Diplomatic Correspondence, vol. vii., p. 472. See Ante, p. 290.
[2] Ibid, p. 481.

ceived it necessary that some person, duly authorized to confer with Mr. Jay, should be appointed by his Majesty; that he intended, on the following Sunday, to recommend this measure to the King, &c.

Notwithstanding Congress had expressly authorized Mr. Jay to surrender the navigation of the Mississippi, and notwithstanding he had already offered to treat on that basis, yet the Spanish minister had the effrontery to tell him that his Court 'had as yet received from Congress nothing but good words and fair assurances, and that though his Majesty had given them some little aids, yet they had discovered no disposition, by acts, to acknowledge them.'[1]

He pressed Mr. Jay to commit to paper his ideas of the outlines of the proposed treaties of commer e and alliance, and furnish him with a copy before Sunday, adding, that he sincerely wished nothing might be wanting to put the business in a proper train. On Saturday, Mr. Jay sent him sundry propositions as the basis of a treaty of amity and alliance. In offering the relinquishment of the navigation of the Mississippi, he took occasion to state the circumstances and expectations which dictated the offer, and declared if the acceptance of it, together with the proposed alliance, should be postponed to a general peace, the United States would cease to consider themselves bound by any propositions or offers which he might now make in their behalf.

This condition as to the time of accepting his propositions was reasonable, and demanded by the procrastinating policy of the Spanish Court. 'To me they appear,' wrote Mr. Jay, 'desirous of avoiding the expense that the aids which a treaty we should expect would render unavoidable, and which at present would not be very convenient for them. . . . . . . I think it is their de-

[1] Diplomatic Correspondence, vol. vii., p. 493.

sign, therefore, to draw from us all such concessions as our present distress and the hopes of aid may extort, and by protracting negotiations about the treaty, endeavor to avail themselves of these concessions at a future day, when our inducements to offer them shall have ceased.'[1] In forming his propositions, Mr. Jay endeavored to make them so clear, 'so free from disputed or disputable points, as that no plausible pretexts for delay should arise from the face of them.'[2] He knew well, however, that the minister would procrastinate to suit his convenience. In the good intentions of the King, he had confidence. 'From everything I can hear,' he said, 'the King is honestly disposed to do us good, and were he alone consulted in this business, I believe it would soon be concluded.'[3]

Mr. Jay's propositions were laid before the King on Sunday, the 23d of September. A few days after, he was promised that a person should be appointed to confer with him, and that his instructions should be completed before the Court removed from St. Ildefonso to the Escurial, which was soon to take place. But this was not done. In December, Mr. Jay was told that M. Del Campo had been appointed nearly three months before to confer with him, but the state of his health had prevented his entering upon the business. 'The minister is too sick, or too busy to attend to American affairs,' wrote Jay to Franklin on the 11th of January, 1782. 'He refers me to M. Del Campo, who has been named for the purpose, and when I apply to him, he tells me that his instructions are not yet completed, and that he cannot tell when they will be.'[4] And thus he was kept suspended between Count Florida Blanca's incapacity to

---

[1] Diplomatic Correspondence, vol. vii., p. 502.

[2] Ibid, p. 503.

[3] Ibid.

[4] Ibid, vol. viii., p. 49.

do business, and M. Del Campo's want of instructions. 'The conduct of this Court bears few marks of wisdom,' again wrote Jay to Franklin. 'The fact is, they have little money, less credit, and very moderate talents.'[1]

Mr. Jay remained at Madrid until the middle of May, 1782, subjected to the same delays, evasions, and subterfuges that characterized and disgraced the conduct of the Spanish Court from the moment of his arrival until that of his departure. No treaty was formed or even seriously contemplated. The instructions which were to be prepared for M. Del Campo Mr. Jay was told should be sent to the Count d'Aranda, the Spanish ambassador at Paris. Count Montmorin, who was sincerely attached to the American cause, and, at critical moments, was of material service to Mr. Jay, told him 'that he believed Spain wished to modify our independence, and to keep herself in a situation to mediate between us and England at the general peace.'[2]

Having seen the issue of Mr. Jay's attempts to negotiate an alliance with Spain, we now return to trace his efforts to preserve the credit of his country.

By the aid of Dr. Franklin, he was enabled to pay all the bills that became due during the autumn and winter of 1781 and 1782. The amount of those payable in the spring, was about $120,000. He had very little hope of receiving additional aid from France. The only fund upon which he could certainly rely, was the balance due on the $150,000 furnished by Spain. This sum, however, was but $26,000. In this emergency, he determined to wait on the minister Florida Blanca, state the reasons why he expected aid from the Spanish Court, and the impolicy of withholding it. He went to the Pardo on the 9th of March, and was received by the

[1] Diplomatic Correspondence, vol. viii., p. 64: February 11th, 1782.
[2] Ibid, p. 87.

minister with great cordiality. 'He was in uncommon good spirits,' says Mr. Jay.[1] The subject of Mr. Jay's embarrassments was introduced. 'After a few hesitations, he told me cheerfully and smilingly that when I found myself very hard pressed, I should desire M. Cabarrus to wait upon him.'[2] M. Cabarrus was Mr. Jay's banker, and was extensively employed by the Court. As bills to a considerable amount would be payable on the 14th of March, Mr. Jay sent M. Cabarrus to the Pardo, to confer with the minister on the subject. He saw the minister, and mentioned the purpose of his visit. The minister said Mr. Jay must have misunderstood him; that it was not until the last extremity that M. Cabarrus was to be sent to him. We should here observe that M. Cabarrus had offered to supply Mr. Jay with the amount he needed, on the promise of either France or Spain to repay him in ten or twelve months.

The 14th of March arrived, and the bills then due were presented. Mr. Jay prevailed on the holders to wait till the next day at noon for his answer. 'As the last extremity, in the most literal sense, had now arrived,' he says, 'I presumed the minister would not think me too hasty in requesting his determination.'[3] Accordingly, he wrote and informed him of his critical situation, and desired an explicit answer whether he might expect any relief. He also solicited the interposition of the French ambassador. Count Montmorin went to the Pardo on the morning of the 15th. The Count Florida Blanca told him, and probably falsely told him, that he had not received Mr. Jay's letter of the day before. It was sent by the Court courier, and could hardly have miscarried. He also told him, that if M. Cabarrus was still willing to wait on the Court the length of time he had mentioned

---

[1] Diplomatic Correspondence, vol. viii., p. 74. [2] Ibid, p. 74.
[3] Ibid, p. 78.

to Mr. Jay, for repayment, he might advance him to the amount of $50,000. On the previous day, M. Del Campo unexpectedly dined with M. Cabarrus, who kept an open table every Thursday. Mr. Carmichael was also present. 'Some earnest and private conversation passed between M. Del Campo and M. Cabarrus.'[1] Mark the sequel. Immediately on being informed by the Count Montmorin of the result of his interview with the Count Florida Blanca, Mr. Jay gave the Count's letter to Mr. Carmichael, with instructions to show it to M. Cabarrus, and bring back his answer without delay, for he was then expecting the notary and others with bills. 'Mr. Carmichael returned and informed me,' says Mr. Jay, 'that he had communicated the letter to M. Cabarrus, and that instead of abiding by his former offer, to be content with the minister's engaging to see him repaid in ten or twelve months, he insisted on being repaid in four months, in four equal monthly payments, and those payments secured by orders on the rents of the general post-office, and that M. Cabarrus promised either to write or speak to the minister about it.'[2]

It was obvious that this conduct of the banker was the result of an understanding with the minister. For, exclusive of other circumstances, it was not probable, as Mr. Jay justly reasoned, that, considering the lucrative connexions of M. Cabarrus with the Government, he would risk treating the promise of the minister, made in consequence of his own offer, with so little respect as to demand such formal and unusual securities for the performance of it, unless there had been some previous concert or indirect management in the case.[3]

When the banker's new proposition, as to the time of repayment, was communicated to the Court, the repre-

---

[1] Diplomatic Correspondence, vol. viii., p. 79.

[2] Ibid, p. 81.

[3] Ibid, p. 83.

sentative and impersonation of their treachery, M. Del Campo, was, of course, perfectly ready to communicate their answer. It was, 'That they could not possibly comply with M. Cabarrus' terms.'[1] Mr. Jay had no resource left, and the bills were protested. Not many days elapsed, however, before he received a letter from Dr. Franklin, authorizing him to draw upon him for the sums necessary to pay them. 'It made me very happy,' says Mr. Jay, 'and enabled me to retrieve the credit we had lost here by those protests.'[2]

Having now seen the issue of Mr. Jay's mission, the objects for which it was undertaken, and the causes that defeated its success, we have only to contemplate for a moment the more personal incidents of his residence in Spain. He was most disagreeably situated. Between the suppression of his letters by the Spanish post-office, and their interception by the enemy, his communication with his friends was very infrequent. More than a year elapsed after his departure from America before he received a letter from any member of his family. 'You can easily conceive how painful it is to be so long in ignorance and suspense,' he wrote his friend Egbert Benson, 'about the situation and welfare of persons so near and dear to me, as many of those are to whom I allude.'[3] Mr. Jay was very tenacious in his friendships. 'There are some hearts,' thus he wrote Robert Morris, 'which, like feathers, stick to everything they touch, and quit each with equal ease. Mine is not of this kind; it adheres to few, but it takes strong hold. You must, therefore, write to me; and if you would make your letter very agreeable, dwell on the objects you will find at or near the hills, and within your own walls.'[4]

---

[1] Diplomatic Correspondence, vol. viii., p. 83. [2] Ibid, p. 89.

[3] Writings of Jay, p. 68: November, 1780.

[4] Ibid, p. 67: November 19th, 1780.

With all this eagerness to hear from his friends, he had not, so late as March, 1781, received a single letter from any friend or relative in his native State. He mentions this circumstance in a letter to Egbert Benson. 'I never loved or admired America so much as since I left it,' he writes in the same letter, 'and my attachment to my friends in it seems to have increased in proportion as distance of time and place separated me from them.'[1]

His salary was not only inadequate in amount, but he suffered great inconvenience from the irregularity of its payment. The credit given him by Congress on Dr. Franklin was expended as early as May, 1780, and he was without other means of obtaining supplies than by incurring debts which he was at a loss to satisfy. 'To apply to, and be maintained by the Court,' thus he wrote the President of Congress, 'is, in my opinion, too humiliating to be for the public good; and as yet I have neither received nor heard of remittances from America.'[2] Congress, either from neglect or inability, provided no funds for the payment of the salary they had assigned him, and he was compelled to rely wholly on Dr. Franklin. In April, 1781, when asking the aid of Franklin to relieve him from the necessity of protesting the bills drawn upon him, he says: 'I am also constrained to add, that our situation here is daily becoming more disagreeable, from the want of our salaries. To be obliged to contract debts and live on credit is terrible. I have not, to this day, received a shilling from America; and we should indeed have been greatly distressed had it not been for your good offices. Endeavor, I beseech you, to provide us with supplies on this account, and deliver me, if possible, from the many disagreeable sensations which such a variety of unpleasant circumstances naturally creates.'[3]

---

[1] Writings of Jay, p. 74: March, 1781.

[2] Diplomatic Correspondence, vol. vii., p. 273: May 26th, 1780.

[3] Writings of Jay, p. 78.

In January, 1782, a few months before he left Spain, he is again compelled to call the attention of Franklin, not only to the necessity of providing funds for the bills, then becoming due, but to his own personal affairs. 'I also begin,' he says, 'severely to feel the want of my back salary. It is in vain for me to expect it from America, and unless you can supply it, it will be necessary for me immediately to disencumber myself of most of my expenses, and confine myself to mere necessaries until a change may take place for the better.'[1]

He was at the most expensive Court in Europe. The King and his ministers were never stationary, passing part of the year in no less than five different places, viz., Madrid, Pardo, Aranjuez, St. Ildefonso, and the Escurial. Mr. Jay was compelled to follow the Court, and this involved a considerable expenditure. He was unable, from the narrowness of his salary, to take Mrs. Jay with him, and, in consequence, he was frequently separated from her. 'I shall always live agreeably to my circumstances,' he wrote the President of Congress. . . . . . 'So far as I am personally interested, I am content.'[2] His salary was inadequate to the expense of private couriers, and all his letters by the public post, both in Spain and France, were opened. Hence, he brought the subject to the attention of Congress.

His social position was unpleasant. He was not received in a public character, and, representing a country whose independence was not yet acknowledged, the foreign ministers at Madrid were very reserved in their intercourse with him. 'They are cold,' he wrote the President of Congress, 'and I have received nothing more than common civility from any of them, except the ministers of Holland and Sweden, and indeed not much

---

[1] Diplomatic Correspondence, vol. viii., p. 49.

[2] Ibid, vol. vii., p. 279.

more from them.'[1] He was not even invited to dine with the Count Florida Blanca on the days appointed for entertaining the foreign ministers. Official etiquette prevented it. But in the latter part of March, the Spanish Court were informed that the British Parliament had resolved to advise the King to cease all offensive operations against the United States. The influence of that news was obvious. Mr. Jay and the country he represented began to be deemed of importance. Their friendship was worth conciliating. On the 30th of March he was much surprised to receive a note from the Spanish minister, saying, 'he hopes to have the honor of the company of V. S.[2] at his table, every Saturday after the 11th of May next ensuing.'[3] Mr. Jay had not called to pay his respects to the minister since the protest of the bills. 'My judgment,' he says, 'as well as my feelings approved of this omission.'[4] He mentioned to Count Montmorin his invitation to the table of Count Florida Blanca, and, to remove any doubt as to whether it was intended for him, he requested Montmorin to speak to the minister with regard to it. Montmorin was told, when he called the minister's attention to the matter, that it must have happened by mistake, but that he was glad it had occurred, for it would give him an opportunity to obtain the King's permission to invite Mr. Jay. Accordingly, he mentioned the subject to the King, 'who, with many expressions of regard for our country,' permitted his minister 'to invite me as a private gentleman of distinction belonging to it.'[5]

This invitation Mr. Jay refused, and for this, among other reasons, that no minister or representative of an independent sovereign could, with propriety, accept any

---

[1] Diplomatic Correspondence, vol. vii., p. 280.

[2] Vuestra Senoria. '*Your Lordship*,' or '*Your Excellency*.'

[3] Diplomatic Correspondence, vol. viii., p. 97. [4] Ibid, p. 96.

[5] Ibid, pp, 100, 101.

invitation which, in the terms of it, impeached his title to that character. He considered the United States an independent power, and this rule applicable to their ministers.

It was not only in his public and social relations that Mr. Jay's position was an unpleasant one. 'There were great divisions in Spain among the Americans,' says John Adams,' and Mr. Jay had as much trouble with his own family, Mr. Carmichael, Mr. Brockholst Livingston, and Mr. Littlepage, as I had at Paris.'[1] In a brief sketch of Mr. Carmichael, Mr. Adams says, 'What was his moral character, and what his conduct in Spain, I shall leave to Mr. Jay.' Mr. Jay, however, has left no memorials to enable us to judge either of his character or conduct; but he told Mr. Adams that he 'aimed at founding himself upon a French interest, and was more supple to the French ambassador at Madrid, and to M. Gérard, than was approved by him.'[2] The differences between Mr. Jay and Mr. Carmichael were fomented and aggravated by the duplicity of young Littlepage, 'a plant which, with a friendly hand,' Mr. Jay had undertaken to water and protect. He was a native of Virginia, and, at the request of his friends, Mr. Jay received him into his family, where he 'lived free from cost.' His guardian, Ben. Lewis, sent no funds to provide for his expenses, and he was wholly indebted to Mr. Jay for all the money he received. His advances to and for him in Spain amounted to more than a thousand dollars. Afterwards, and while Secretary of Foreign Affairs, having, in the meantime, become familiar with his character and conduct, Mr. Jay sued Littlepage for that sum. Upon this, Littlepage published in the New York Daily Advertiser,[3] an abusive attack upon him. Mr. Jay thought proper to reply. He

[1] Life and Works of John Adams, vol. iii., p. 143.

[2] Ibid, p. 301.

[3] For December 6th, 1785.

said it was the first time in his life he had been arraigned before the public, and 'it is a little mortifying,' he added, 'that it should now be by a young man, every part of whom, except his soul, had increased and grown while enjoying hospitality under my roof and at my table.' He stated all the circumstances of the case necessary to his complete vindication from 'the scurrilous reflections of an impudent and thankless boy.'[1] He mentioned the fact, that while Littlepage lived in his family, a coolness subsisted and continued between Mr. Carmichael and himself; that Littlepage often communicated to him anecdotes of that gentleman's conduct and language with which it was impossible that he could be pleased; and that subsequently, at Paris, he and Mr. Carmichael had a free and friendly explanation. The latter intimated that he had good reason to believe that Littlepage had played a double game between them; that after Mr. Jay left Madrid, he had taken him into his house and lent him money; and that Littlepage told him many things to the disadvantage of Mr. Jay. Among others, that he had left him at Madrid expressly to be a spy upon Mr. Carmichael, and had given him a cipher to enable him to send his communications more safely. This Mr. Jay declared 'a most impudent and most execrable falsehood.' 'Had he been tempted to it,' said Mr. Jay, 'by great provocation, it might have been some little palliation; but after having parted with me in a friendly manner, to go with my money in his pocket, and my meat still sticking in his teeth, to traduce and abuse me by such an atrocious falsehood, and to a man whom he himself had, under his hand, represented as one of the most vile; and then enter into the doors of that very man, and there smilingly enjoy his munificence and hospitality, is, to be sure, a stretch, a degree, a sublimation of corruption and depravity of which

[1] From a letter of Edward Rutledge to John Jay, March 27th, 1787. Life of Jay, p. 228.

I have never known another instance, (except, perhaps, in the character of Iago,) and I pray God I never may.'[1]

Mr. Jay bade adieu to Madrid, which, during the whole period of his residence, had been a scene of trouble, vexation, and anxiety, about the 20th of May, 1782. He was summoned to Paris by a letter from Dr. Franklin, to assist in the negotiation of a treaty which was to place his country among the independent powers of the earth. 'I have undertaken to pay all the bills of your acceptance that have come to my knowledge,' wrote Franklin, 'and I hope in God no more will be drawn upon us, but when funds are first provided. In that case, your constant residence at Madrid is no longer so necessary. . . . Here you are greatly wanted. . . . . I wish, therefore, that you would resolve upon the journey, and render yourself here as soon as possible. You would be of infinite service. Spain has taken four years to consider whether she would treat with us or not. Give her forty, and let us, in the meantime, mind our own business.'[2]

We cannot more appropriately close this chapter than with a single extract from an official letter of Congress to Mr. Jay. It was written by Mr. Madison. 'It is with pleasure, Sir, that I obey the direction of Congress to inform you that throughout the whole course of your negotiations and transactions, in which the utmost address and discernment were often necessary to reconcile the respect due to the dignity of the United States with the urgency of their wants and the complaisance expected by the Spanish Court, your conduct is entirely approved by them.'[3]

---

[1] Mr. Jay's answer to Littlepage appeared in the paper that contained the attack, on the following day. Afterwards he published a pamphlet, containing the correspondence between himself and his assailant, copies of which are still extant.

[2] Writings of Franklin, vol. ix., p. 211.

[3] Diplomatic Correspondence, vol. vii., p. 415.

CHAPTER XII.

COMMISSIONER TO NEGOTIATE PEACE.

1782—1784.

Before M. Gérard left America, he suggested to Congress the propriety of appointing a minister plenipotentiary to reside in Europe, ready to negotiate a peace whenever he might be invited to it. The Chevalier de la Luzerne, upon his arrival in Philadelphia, renewed the suggestion. 'In both cases, it was the expectation of the French ministry,' says Mr. Adams, 'that Dr. Franklin would be elected.'[1] If this expectation was entertained, it was disappointed. In 1779, Mr. Adams was appointed as sole minister plenipotentiary for peace, and also to make a treaty of commerce with Great Britain.[2] In 1781, Congress associated with Mr. Adams in the commission for peace, Mr. Jay, Mr. Franklin, Mr. Laurens, and Mr. Jefferson. Mr. Adams' commission to negotiate a treaty of commerce was annulled, and not renewed to the five commissioners who were appointed in his stead.

Mr. Jay arrived at Paris the 23d of June, 1782. After placing his family in a hotel, he went immediately out to Passy to pay his respects to Dr. Franklin. 'He certainly is a valuable minister,' he wrote to the Secretary for Foreign Affairs, 'and an agreeable companion.'[3] Mr. Adams was still at Amsterdam, Mr. Jefferson in America, and the health of Mr. Laurens so much impaired from his confinement in the Tower, that he thought of

[1] Adams' Works, vol. iii., p. 259.

[2] Ante, p. 281.

[3] Diplomatic Correspondence, vol. viii., p. 115.

going to the United States rather than to Paris. The skirmishing business of the negotiation, therefore, devolved upon Mr. Jay and Dr. Franklin. How this was conducted, the sequel will disclose.

In the meantime it is proper to observe that Congress, through the influence and address of the Chevalier de la Luzerne, expressly instructed their commissioners 'to make the most candid and confidential communications upon all subjects to the ministers of our generous ally, the King of France, and to undertake nothing in the negotiations for peace or truce without their knowledge and concurrence.' This action of Congress was highly distasteful to Mr. Jay. It was equally so to Mr. Adams. 'Congress,' he says, 'surrendered their own sovereignty into the hands of a French minister. Blush! blush, ye guilty records! blush and perish! It is glory to have broken such infamous orders. Infamous, I say, for so they will be to all posterity. How can such a stain be washed out? Can we cast a veil over it and forget it?'[1] Mr. Jay requested Congress to take an early opportunity of relieving him from a station 'where, in character of their minister,' he said, 'I must necessarily receive and obey (under the name of opinions) the directions of those on whom I really think no American minister ought to be dependent, and to whom, in love for our country and zeal for her service, I am sure my colleagues and myself are at least equal.'[2] But, however unpalatable the instructions of Congress might have been to their servants, they were, nevertheless, bound to obey them, unless very cogent reasons required a different line of conduct. It must be recollected, too, that it was stipulated in the treaty of alliance, 'that neither of the two parties should

[1] Adams' Works, vol. iii., p. 359. Mr. Adams was very indignant that his commission was annulled, and others associated with him in the negotiation.

[2] Diplomatic Correspondence, vol. vii.; Letter to the President of Congress, September 20th, 1781.

conclude either truce or peace with Great Britain without the formal consent of the other first obtained.'

When Mr. Jay arrived at Paris, he found there Mr. Richard Oswald, a London merchant who had lived in America, was familiar with the country, its people, circumstances, commerce, &c. He had the reputation of being a man of candor and integrity. Dr. Franklin described him as an old man, who seemed 'to have no desire but that of being useful in doing good,'[1] and Lord Shelburne as 'a pacifical man, conversant in those negotiations which are most interesting to mankind.'[2] He had been at Paris since April, with authority to consult Dr. Franklin on the mode of beginning and pursuing a negotiation. Mr. Thomas Grenville was also there, with instructions to treat with M. de Vergennes. He was a son of the celebrated George Grenville, who, as Chancellor of the Exchequer, brought into form the Stamp Act, and established it by act of Parliament. He was the friend of Fox, who described him as a man of 'excellent qualities of heart and head.'[3] 'I sometimes a little doubt Mr. Grenville,' said Dr. Franklin. He 'is clever, and seems to feel reason as readily as Mr. Oswald, though not so ready to own it. . . . . . A young man, naturally desirous of acquiring reputation, seems to aim at that of being an able negotiator.'[4]

On the 7th of August, Mr. Oswald communicated to Dr. Franklin and Mr. Jay a copy of the King's order to the Attorney-General to prepare a commission to pass the great seal, empowering him to negotiate a peace or truce 'with any commissioner or commissioners named, or to be named, by the thirteen colonies or plantations in North America, or any body or bodies, corporate or politic, or any assembly or assemblies, or description of

---

[1] Franklin's Works, vol. ix., p. 336. [2] Ibid, p. 240.
[3] Ibid, p. 271. [4] Ibid, p. 336.

men, or any person or persons whatsoever.' The commission itself was to be sent in eight or ten days.

Mr. Oswald first called on Dr. Franklin at Passy, then returned to Paris, and called on Mr. Jay. 'He is a man of good sense,' he wrote Mr. Secretary Townsend, 'of frank, easy, and polite manners; he read over the copy of the commission, and Mr. Townsend's letter accounting for its not being under seal, and then said, by the quotation from the act of Parliament on the commission, he supposed it was meant that independence was to be treated upon, and was to be granted perhaps as the price of peace; that it ought to be no part of a treaty; it ought to have been expressly granted by act of Parliament, and an order for all troops to be withdrawn previous to any proposal for treaty. As that was not done, the King, he said, ought to do it now by proclamation, and order all garrisons to be evacuated, and then close the American war with a treaty. . . He said many things of a retrospective kind. . . He returned to the subject of independence, as not being satisfied with its being left as a matter of treaty. . . He said peace was very desirable, and the sooner the better. But the great point was, to make such a peace as should be lasting. . . The peace he meant was such, or so to be settled, that it should not be to the *interest* of either party to violate it. This, he said, was the only security that could be proposed to prevent those frequent returns of war, by which the world was kept in continual disturbance.'[1]

On the 10th of August, Dr. Franklin and Mr. Jay had a conference with M. de Vergennes on the subject of Oswald's commission. Vergennes said names signified

[1] Mr. Oswald to Mr. Secretary Townsend, August 7th 1782. Franklin's Works, vol. ix., p. 377. The valuable letters of Mr. Oswald were furnished to Mr. Sparks by the Marquis of Lansdowne, and he has printed extracts from them as notes to illustrate Franklin's correspondence of this period.

little; that the King of Great Britain styling himself the King of France was no obstacle to the King of France treating with him; that an acknowledgment of the independence of the United States, instead of preceding, must, in the natural course of things, be the effect of the treaty, and that it would not be reasonable to expect the effect before the cause. This opinion of M. de Vergennes we cannot help thinking was well founded. It coincided with Franklin's. He thought the commission would do. But Mr. Jay insisted that it would be descending from the ground of independence to treat under the denomination of colonies. 'I told the minister,' he says, 'that we neither could nor would treat with any nation in the world on any other than an equal footing.'[1] He suspected that the French Court wished to postpone an acknowledgment of American independence by England for sinister purposes.

After Mr. Oswald's interview with Mr. Jay, he took 'a quiet and convenient opportunity' to bring to the attention of Dr. Franklin some of the topics which had been discussed in the course of it. The Doctor asked Mr. Oswald if he had instructions. He said he had, and that they were under his Majesty's hand and seal, and authorized him to grant independence unconditionally in every sense, and he saw no reason why it should not make the first article of the treaty. He was sure, he said, that all pretensions would be as properly, expeditiously, and effectually settled under his present commission as in the way proposed by Mr. Jay. 'The Doctor replied,' says Mr. Oswald, 'that Mr. Jay was a lawyer, and might think of things that did not occur to those who were not lawyers. And he at last spoke as if he did not see much or any difference; but still used such a mode of expression as I could not positively say would preclude him from

[1] Letter to Gouverneur Morris, October 13th, 1782. Writings of Jay, p. 105.

insisting on Mr. Jay's proposition, or some previous or separate acknowledgment.'[1]

In a subsequent conversation with Mr. Jay, Oswald found him willing to yield his former proposal that the King should cede independence by proclamation, as liable to sundry objections. The truth is, the King had no authority to issue such a proclamation. Mr. Jay 'then proposed that it should be done by a particular and separate deed or patent, under the great seal,' in which Mr. Oswald's commission for a treaty might also be narrated. This proposal was favorably received by Mr. Oswald, and upon Mr. Jay bringing him a draft of the patent, he agreed to send it over to the Secretary of State by a courier. But subsequently he suggested that a preliminary article in the treaty, not depending on the event of other and succeeding articles, would answer the same purpose, and he showed Mr. Jay his instructions on this point. 'Upon the perusal, Mr. Jay said that was enough, and he was fully satisfied; and there was no occasion for any other writing on the subject; that resting upon this would save time, and he was happy also that this discovery of his mistake[2] prevented their asking of his Majesty any further proof of his good intentions towards them than what were actually meant and conveyed in those my instructions.'[3] But on communicating to the English ministry the result of his conference with Mr. Jay, Mr. Oswald was informed that the Enabling Act, which empowered the King to make peace,

[1] Richard Oswald to Thomas Townsend, August 13th, 1782. Franklin's Works, vol. ix., p. 386.

[2] Mr. Jay had the impression, and expressed it in the preamble to his draft of a patent, that Sir Guy Carleton had orders to propose a treaty of peace to the Congress. He was convinced of his mistake by reading a copy of Sir Guy's instructions.

[3] Franklin's Works, vol. ix., p. 389. Oswald to Townsend, August 15th.

did not authorize him to cede independence as a single, separate article, to be ratified by itself; but it might be the first article of the treaty, unconditionally of any compensation or equivalent. Mr. Jay objected to this, but finally said that 'if Dr. Franklin would consent, he was willing, instead of an express and previous acknowledgment of independence, to accept of a constructive denomination of character, to be introduced in the preamble of the treaty by only describing their constituents as the Thirteen United States of America.'[1] Dr. Franklin agreed to this proposal. Mr. Oswald then asked Mr. Jay if the alteration in his commission was made, and he empowered to treat with the commissioners of the Thirteen United States of America, whether, in that case, he and Dr. Franklin would go on with the treaty, and without any other declaration of independence than as an article in the treaty. Mr. Jay replied, 'that with this they would be satisfied, and that immediately upon such commission coming over, they would proceed in the treaty. And more than that,' he said, 'they would not be long about it; and perhaps would not be over hard upon us in the conditions.'[2]

The commission, together with Oswald's dispatches, was accordingly sent back to London. 'A meeting of the King's confidential servants,' says Mr. Townsend, 'was held as soon as possible, to consider the contents of them; and it was at once agreed to make the alteration' proposed by Mr. Jay.[3] The new commission was received by Mr. Oswald the 27th of September, and the more solid parts of the negotiation commenced.

---

[1] Franklin's Works, vol. ix., p. 407. Lord Camden was of opinion that the Enabling Act did not authorize the King to acknowledge the independence of America.

[2] Oswald to Townsend, September 10th. Franklin's Works, vol. ix., pp. 406. 407.

[3] Ibid, p. 408. Townsend to Oswald, September 20th.

It will be remarked that Mr. Jay did not accomplish his original purpose of obtaining a previous acknowledgment of independence, and only succeeded in having a change in the description of the parties to be treated with. This was not an object of material importance. It was, as Mr. Sparks justly observes, 'a thing of form and not of substance.'[1] Mr. Jay, however, thought differently. 'Had I not violated the instructions of Congress,' thus he wrote Gouverneur Morris, 'their dignity would have been in the dust; for the French minister even took pains, not only to persuade us to treat under that commission, but to prevent the second by telling Fitzherbert that the first was sufficient.'[2]

Changes in the British ministry, in consequence of the death of Lord Rockingham and the resignation of Fox, occasioned a change at Paris. In place of Mr. Grenville, Lord Shelburne sent over, the latter part of July, Alleyne Fitzherbert, afterwards known as Lord St. Helen's. 'Mr. Jenings,'[3] says Mr. Adams, 'let me into the character of Mr. Fitzherbert. His father was prevailed on by Lord North to vote with him, but he was never easy in his mind about it, and finally cut his own throat. The gentleman at Paris is about thirty-three, wholly dependent on Lord Shelburne, has parts, but very conceited and assuming; not liked by the English while at Brussels, because he did not keep a table. He was only resident, and his appointment small, not more than fifteen hundred pounds. He writes from Paris that the Count de Vergennes has a great character, but that he sees nothing in him. This is evidence of vanity; for that minister has at least a vast experience, and too much reserve to give proofs of great or little qualities so

[1] Life of Frankin, p. 484.

[2] Writings of Jay, p. 105: October 13th, 1782.

[3] Mr. Edmund Jenings of Maryland, an intimate friend of Mr. Adams, and at this time in Europe.

soon to this young gentleman. His parts are quick, and his education has been good. He has sometimes treated the English with cool contempt, and sometimes with hot pride.'[1]

Fitzherbert, whatever the real or supposed defects of his character, conducted the business with which he was intrusted with marked ability. He and Oswald acted in concert with each other, although, as we have seen, negotiation with the American commissioners was confided to Oswald, and negotiation with the European powers to Fitzherbert. It was not long before the British agents thought they discovered an indisposition in the French and Spanish Courts to bring the war to a speedy close. Hence, it was an object of great importance to negotiate a separate pacification with the United States. The American envoys had already manifested a disposition to conclude a treaty in that mode. We find Oswald writing Lord Shelburne, as early as July 11th, that they 'have shown a desire to treat, and to end with us on a separate footing from the other powers.'[2] It is not apparent that Oswald intended to convey the idea that they desired to do this without the previous knowledge and consent of their ally. But with a predisposition of this kind, it is not singular that certain doubtful and unexplained circumstances which afterwards appeared should have awakened in the breast of Mr. Jay a distrust, a suspicion of the French Court, which induced him to persist in the purpose of negotiating a separate treaty, not only without their concurrence, but concluding it without their knowledge. The truth is, during the last two years he had lived in an atmo-

[1] Adams' Works, vol. iii., p. 296. Afterwards, upon seeing Mr. Fitzherbert, Mr. Adams says that he seemed 'pretty discreet and judicious, and did not discover those airs of vanity which are imputed to him.' Ibid, p. 330.

[2] Oswald to Shelburne, July 11th: Franklin's Works, vol. ix., p. 363.

sphere of duplicity and falsehood. He had become doubtful of professions and jealously alive to every indication of insincerity. Whether his suspicions of the good faith of the French Court were well founded, or

> —'Little else but dreams,
> Conjectures, fancies, built on nothing firm,'

we shall now proceed to inquire.

The ground of his distrust of the intentions of France was fourfold:

First: he thought the opinion of M. de Vergennes as to Oswald's commission, proceeded from interested views. He surmised that the French minister wished to postpone the acknowledgment of American independence until France and Spain had accomplished their objects. We cannot concur in the propriety of this inference. The mode of securing independence suggested by M. de Vergennes, was the natural and obvious one. It was proper that this concession should be an article of the treaty. It is worthy of observation, that the difference between Fox and Lord Shelburne on this very point was a principal cause assigned by the former for his withdrawal from the Cabinet. Fox contended that the independence of the colonies should be acknowledged by a previous declaration, and Shelburne, that it should be done by an article of the treaty. 'So far as the two courses are compared,' says Lord Mahon, 'Lord Shelburne's appears the more natural and just in theory, and certainly in practice bore no evil fruit.' [1]

Secondly: Jay inferred, from a letter addressed to him by M. de Rayneval, the principal secretary of M. de Vergennes, that the French Court would oppose the extension of the United States to the Mississippi, and their free navigation of that river. He also thought they

[1] Mahon's History of England, vol. vii., p. 199: Boston ed., 1854

would support the pretensions of England to all the country north of the Ohio, if not to all above the 31st degree of latitude. The views disclosed by M. de Rayneval were calculated to alarm. Jay could not believe that the confidential secretary of M. de Vergennes would declare such sentiments and offer such propositions without his knowledge and consent.[1] France was the ally of Spain as well as of the United States, and there were obvious reasons why she should favor the views of a branch of the house of Bourbon in preference to those of a new and distant people.

Thirdly: Mr. Jay received M. de Rayneval's letter on the 6th of September. On the following day, Count d'Aranda, contrary to his usual practice, went with post-horses to Versailles, and was closeted with M. de Vergennes and M. de Rayneval between two and three hours. On the same day, M. de Rayneval set out for England. It was pretended he had gone into the country, and several precautions were taken to keep his real destination a secret. These facts came to the knowledge of Jay on the 9th. On the 10th, M. Marbois' celebrated letter to M. de Vergennes, which we shall presently describe, was put into his hands by the English negotiators. He immediately conjectured that the object of M. de Rayneval's journey was, to prevent an acknowledgment of American independence by England except as an article of treaty, to exclude the United States from the fisheries, and obtain such curtailment of the boundaries they asserted as would satisfy Spain and leave to Britain all the country north of the Ohio. The inferences of Mr. Jay in this instance, it would seem, were not well founded.

[1] 'M. de Rayneval is a *chef-de-bureau*. But we must be very ignorant of all Courts not to know that an under-secretary of State does not carry on such a correspondence without the knowledge, consent, and orders of his principal.' Diplomatic Correspondence, vol. vii., p. 68: Mr. Adams' letter to the Secretary for Foreign Affairs.

M. de Rayneval's instructions, his correspondence with M. de Vergennes while he was in London, and notes of his conversations with Lord Shelburne, have been perused by Mr. Sparks; and he declares that M. de Rayneval was instructed to insist on the independence of the United States as a preliminary measure. In reporting the result of his conversations with the British minister, M. de Rayneval states the points discussed in their order: first, 'independence; this article is agreed upon; it shall be without restriction;' *il sera sans restriction.* It was the main object of M. de Rayneval's mission, says Mr. Sparks, to settle the difficulties in the Spanish treaty, and the affairs of America formed no part of his mission except to insist on unconditional independence. 'As it is possible,' said his instructions, 'that the English ministers may speak to M. de Rayneval concerning the affairs of America and of the United Provinces, he will declare that he has no authority to treat on these topics.'[1] It should be mentioned that two days after hearing of M. de Rayneval's departure, Jay, unknown to Dr. Franklin, who did not participate his suspicions of the French Court, sent over Mr. Vaughan, an English gentleman then residing at Paris, and professing friendly sentiments to the American cause, to counteract M. de Rayneval's mission. It does not appear, however, that Mr. Vaughan's journey was productive of any material result.

Fourthly: A letter of M. Marbois to M. de Vergennes, written the 13th of March, was intercepted by a British cruiser, and communicated to the American commissioners. M. Marbois was the secretary of the French Legation at Philadelphia. He had previously been *Chargé d'Affaires* at Munich. After the peace he was appointed Consul-General of the United States, and subsequently

[1] Sparks' Life of Franklin, p. 493. Diplomatic Correspondence, vol. viii., p. 210. Mr. Sparks has appended a very able note to Mr Jay's despatch, (ibid, p. 120,) which should be read in this connection.

Intendant of St. Domingo. He survived the French Revolution, and was employed by Napoleon in 1803 to negotiate the sale of Louisiana to this country. He was a man of studious habits, and had acquired an extensive knowledge of public affairs. When he came to the United States in 1779, Mr. Adams was a passenger in the same ship. 'M. Marbois, the secretary,' he says, 'is a tall, genteel man, and has a countenance extremely pleasant; he has the appearance of delicacy in his constitution.'[1] 'This M. Marbois is one of the best-informed and most reflecting men I have known in France.'[2]

From the man, we now turn to his work. The letter which he wrote to M. de Vergennes not only disparaged the claims of the United States to the fisheries, but pointed out the means by which he supposed they could be most effectually defeated. One of these means was, to have the King intimate to Congress or their ministers 'his surprise that the Newfoundland fisheries have been included in the additional instructions;[3] that the United States set forth therein pretensions without paying regard to the King's rights, and without considering the impossibility they are under of making conquests and keeping what belongs to Great Britain.' He mentioned the suggestion that England, to conciliate the affections of the Americans, might endeavor to admit them to a participation of the fisheries of the Great Bank, and says: 'But it does not seem likely that she will act so contrary to her true interest, and were she to do so, it will be for the better to have declared at an early period to the Americans, that their pretension is not founded, and that his Majesty does not mean to support it.'[4]

---

[1] Adams' Works, vol. iii., p. 211. [2] Ibid, p. 216.

[3] M. Marbois doubtless refers to instructions then being considered in Congress, directing the commissioners in France to represent to that Court that the United States claimed the right of taking fish in the North American seas, and particularly on the banks of Newfoundland.

[4] See this letter in Pitkin's History of the United States, vol. ii., p.

Mr. Jay inferred from the letter of M. Marbois, what he inferred from the letter of M. de Rayneval, viz., that it spoke the sentiments of M. de Vergennes. Dr. Franklin, on the other hand, was of opinion, even admitting the letter to be genuine, that 'the forward, mistaken zeal of a Secretary of Legation should not be imputed to the King, who has in so many ways proved himself our faithful and firm friend and ally.'[1] M. de Vergennes, in a letter to M. de la Luzerne, employs the same argument. 'An intercepted letter from M. de Marbois,' he says, 'was communicated to the American commissioners by the British ministry, which, by a forced interpretation, was designed to render us suspected in regard to the fisheries. In the first place, the opinion of M. de Marbois is not necessarily that of the King; and, in the next place, the views indicated in that despatch have not been followed.'[2] It is not, to be sure, absolutely and necessarily true that the sentiments of M. Marbois were the sentiments of M. de Vergennes, although the tone of his letter certainly indicates a previous understanding and an entire harmony of views and wishes. But what was the fact? Here we are enabled to speak with confidence. We have evidence of the sentiments and designs of the French Court, clear and explicit. In a note addressed by M. de Rayneval to Lord Shelburne, occurs this passage: 'An arrangement for the fisheries of Newfoundland. This matter has been treated discursively with Mr. Fitzherbert.

---

528. Mr. William Jay has also inserted it in the Appendix to his Life of John Jay.

[1] Franklin to Samuel Cooper, December 26th, 1782. Franklin's Works, vol. ix., p. 462. With regard to the genuineness of this letter, we have the testimony of M. Marbois himself. He acknowledged afterwards that he wrote it, and admitted that the translation, although not in all respects entirely accurate, had yet done him no injustice. See Life of John Jay, p. 146, note.

[2] Franklin's Works, vol. ix., p. 463, note. Vergennes to Luzerne, September 7th, 1783.

If the ideas which have been proposed to him are judged impracticable, I am persuaded they will be weighed with equity at Versailles.' The nature of the propositions submitted by M. de Vergennes to the English negotiators is disclosed by Mr. Fitzherbert. They related, he says, 'entirely to a certain enlargement of the limits of the French fisheries, as defined by former treaties. But in the course of these discussions, M. de Vergennes never failed to insist on the expediency of a concert of measures between France and England, for the purpose of excluding the American States from these fisheries, *lest they should become a nursery for seamen*.'[1]

This statement of Fitzherbert is of historical importance. It comes from an actor on the scene, and abundantly confirms the suspicions entertained by Mr. Jay of the objects contemplated by the French Court. The letter of M. Marbois spoke his sentiments as to the fisheries, and we may safely conclude from thence that M. de Rayneval, in his letters and conversations,[2] equally spoke his

[1] As this statement by Mr. Fitzherbert is now for the first time printed, it is important to mention one or two facts as to its origin and authenticity. The Life of John Jay, by his son, Mr. William Jay, was sent to Fitzherbert, then Lord St. Helen's, in 1838. He returned it to the person from whom he received it, with a letter and a few marginal notes. The letter and notes were transmitted to Mr. William Jay, who has politely submitted a transcript of them to my use. The statement printed in the text is contained in one of the notes. An extract from the letter will be found on a subsequent page.

[2] Mr. Jay, in his private memoranda, mentions having dined on one occasion in company with M. de Rayneval. 'We retired,' he says, 'with Rayneval. He asked how matters stood between us and Oswald. We told him that we could not agree about all our boundaries. We mentioned the one between us and Nova Scotia. He asked what we demanded to the North. We answered that Canada should be reduced to the ancient bounds. He then contested our right to those back lands, &c. He asked what we expected as to the fisheries. We said, the same right we had formerly enjoyed. He contested the propriety of that demand; adding some strictures on the ambition and restless views of Mr.

sentiments as to the Western lands and the navigation of the Mississippi. The legal maxim, *falsus in uno, falsus in omnibus*, is applicable here.

To the suggestion of M. de Vergennes that the views of M. Marbois were not followed, we reply that it was impossible they should be. The English Ministry did not choose to prolong the war for the objects proposed to them. Had the American commissioners governed their conduct by their instructions, and submitted to the advice of Vergennes, we think it apparent that the United States would have been deprived of the fisheries, of the Western lands, and the navigation of the Mississippi. But in spite of the conviction thus forced upon us, we cannot forget the generous aid France afforded this country in her struggle to secure a national existence. She sent a fleet and army to fight our battles, she loaned us eighteen millions of livres, and gave us twelve millions. That she should propose to herself some equivalent gain for the expenses of the war is not surprising. We do not look for wholly disinterested conduct in the dealings of nations. But when it is obvious that one ally is endeavoring, by indirection, by concert with the enemy and another ally, to deprive a third one of advantages justly belonging to him, it is well that the intrigue should be counteracted and its profligacy exposed. Previous good conduct may soften the severity of our condemnation, but it cannot justify guilt.

Oswald's new commission, as we have seen, arrived on the 27th of September, and the negotiators at once entered upon the serious business of their mission. Several preliminary propositions were made by Jay and Franklin, which Oswald approved and sent to his Court. They

---

Adams, and intimated that we might be contented with the coast fishery.' Life of John Jay. p. 151.

Viewing this language of the confidential secretary of Vergennes in connection with the positive statement of Fitzherbert, on what ground can it be pretended that the suspicions of Mr. Jay were not justified?

were drawn up by Jay. The first article determined the question of independence in the manner we have mentioned. The boundaries were described in accordance with a previous instruction of Congress, except that the line between Nova Scotia and New England was to be settled by commissioners after the peace. The fishery in the American seas was left *in statu quo;* each party being entitled to the same rights as before the war.

On the 23d of October, the English Cabinet sent over Mr. Strachey, under-Secretary of State, to procure better terms. Strachey arrived at Paris about the same time as Mr. Adams, who came from the Hague to assist in the negotiation. The latter thus describes him: 'Strachey,' he says, 'is as artful and insinuating a man as they could send; he pushes and presses every point as far as it can possibly go; he is the most eager, earnest, pointed spirit.'[1] But Adams evidently thought his own colleagues a full match for him. 'Between two as subtle spirits as any in this world,' he says, 'I shall have a delicate, a nice, a critical part to act. Franklin's cunning will be to divide us; to this end he will provoke, he will insinuate, he will intrigue, he will manœuvre. My curiosity will at least be employed in observing his invention and his artifice. Jay declares roundly that he will never set his hand to a bad peace. Congress may appoint another, but he will make a good peace or none.'[2] Adams had no ground of complaint against Franklin, but he could never forgive him his superior reputation and influence. His rancor towards him breaks out on all occasions. 'Dr. Franklin,' said Mr. Laurens, 'knows very well how to manage a cunning man; but, when the Doctor converses or treats with a man of candor, there is no man more candid than himself.'[3]

---

[1] Adams' Works, vol. iii., p. 303. [2] Ibid, p. 300.

[3] Franklin's Works, vol. ix., p. 241.

Jay soon disclosed to Adams his conjectures of the views of France and Spain, and the part he thought they ought to act. 'Our allies don't play fair, he told me,' says Adams, 'they were endeavoring to deprive us of the fisheries, the Western lands, and the navigation of the Mississippi; they would even bargain with the English to deprive us of them; they want to play the Western lands, Mississippi, and whole Gulf of Mexico into the hands of Spain.'[1]

Adams fully concurred with Jay on all these points, and Dr. Franklin, who was slow to suspect the good faith of an ally from whom his country had derived such efficient aid, nevertheless agreed to proceed in the negotiation without the privity of the French Court.[2]

There was much contestation about the boundaries, but the real points of difficulty in the treaty, were the fisheries and the tories. 'The British minister struggled hard for two points,' says Franklin, 'that the favors

[1] Adams' Works, vol. iii., p. 303.

[2] 'As soon as I arrived in Paris,' says Mr. Adams, 'I waited on Mr. Jay, and learned from him the rise and progress of the negotiations. Nothing that has happened since the beginning of the controversy in 1761, has ever struck me more forcibly, or affected me more intimately, than that entire coincidence of principles and opinions between him and me. In about three days I went out to Passy, and spent the evening with Dr. Franklin, and entered largely into conversation with him upon the course and present state of our foreign affairs. I told him, without reserve, my opinion of the policy of this Court, and of the principles, wisdom, and firmness with which Mr. Jay had conducted the negotiation in his sickness and my absence, and that I was determined to support Mr. Jay to the utmost of my power in the pursuit of the same system. The Doctor heard me patiently, but said nothing. The first conference we had afterwards with Mr. Oswald, in considering one point or another, Dr. Franklin turned to Mr. Jay, and said, I am of your opinion, and will go on with these gentlemen in the business without consulting this Court. He has, accordingly, met us in most of our conferences, and has gone on with us in entire harmony and unanimity throughout, and has been able and useful, both by his sagacity and his reputation, in the whole negotiation.' Ibid, p. 336.

granted to the loyalists should be extended, and all our fishery contracted.'[1]

After a good deal of discussion, certain changes were agreed upon in the first set of articles, and on the 5th of November, Strachey set out for London with the amended ones. 'Mr. Oswald wanted Mr. Jay to go to England; thought he could convince the ministry. Mr. Jay said he must go with or without the knowledge and advice of this Court, and, in either case, it would give rise to jealousies; he would not go.'[2] This was in consequence of a letter from Lord Townsend to Fitzherbert that compensation to the loyalists would be insisted on.

Strachey returned to Paris on the 23d of November. He had waited personally on every one of the King's Cabinet Council, and communicated the last propositions to them. 'Every one of them,' he told the assembled negotiators, 'unanimously condemned that respecting the tories, so that that unhappy affair stuck, as he foresaw and foretold that it would. The affair of the fishery, too, was somewhat altered. They could not admit us to dry on the shores of Nova Scotia, nor to fish within three leagues of the coast, nor within fifteen leagues of the coast of Cape Breton. The boundary they did not approve; they thought it too extended, too vast a country, but they would not make a difficulty.'[3]

Mr. Adams combated the new proposals as to the fisheries with great energy and force. Dr. Franklin was immovable on the subject of the tories; 'more decided a great deal on this point than Mr. Jay or myself,' says Adams.[4] 'Jay desired to know,' we quote again

---

[1] Franklin's Works, vol. ix., p. 440.

[2] Adams' Works, vol. iii., p. 312.

[3] Ibid, p. 327. Mr. Adams says, 'I could not help observing, that the ideas respecting the fishery appeared to me to come piping hot from Versailles.'

[4] Adams' Works, vol. iii., p. 332.

from Adams, 'if the propositions now delivered us were their ultimatum. Strachey seemed loath to answer, but at last said, No. We agreed these were good signs of sincerity.'[1]

Mr. Laurens arrived at Paris on the 29th, and notwithstanding 'his deplorable affliction under the recent loss of so excellent a son,' his apprehension, Adams tells us, was as quick, his judgment as sound, and his heart as firm as ever.[2] Thus reinforced, the American commissioners met Oswald, assisted by Strachey and Fitzherbert, at Jay's, *Hotel d' Orleans*. The whole day was spent in discussions about the fisheries and the tories. Adams said he never could put his hand to any treaty without satisfaction as to the first point. Laurens, 'with great firmness,' said the same. 'Mr. Jay spoke up and said, it could not be a peace, it would only be an insidious truce without it.'[3] When it was proposed to refer the subject once more to the ministry in London, Dr. Franklin, 'ever ingenious and fertile of resources,' said, 'if another messenger was to be sent to London, he ought to carry something more respecting a compensation to the sufferers in America.'[4]

It should be observed that the Doctor had already silenced the British negotiators on their original demand of restitution to the loyalists for the losses they had suffered, by threatening to produce an account of the mischief done by those people. He now proposed a new article, with a note of facts to support it, which he desired might be referred to the ministry along with the

[1] Adams' Works, vol. iii., p. 330.

[2] Ibid, p. 337. Colonel John Laurens, universally beloved and admired for his qualities of head and heart, after surviving the dangers of Brandywine, Germantown, Monmouth, Savannah, and Charleston, had recently fallen in a trifling skirmish.

[3] Ibid, p. 335.

[4] Mahon's History of England, vol. vii., p. 200. Adams' Works, vol. iii., p. 334. Franklin's Works, vol. ix., p. 440.

objectionable article respecting the fishery. The substance of it was, that his Britannic Majesty should earnestly recommend to Parliament to make compensation for all the injuries inflicted by his troops or adherents in the United States. Upon this, Adams recounted the losses of the people of Boston. 'Dr. Franklin mentioned the case of Philadelphia, and the carrying off of effects there, even his own library. Mr. Jay mentioned several other things; and Mr. Laurens added the plunders in Carolina of negroes, plate, &c.' [1]

After hearing all this, the English negotiators retired for consultation. Upon returning, they said they had concluded to accept the ultimatum proposed to them respecting the fisheries and the loyalists. Accordingly, the next day, November 30th, 1782, the provisional articles thus agreed upon were signed by the four American commissioners on the one side, and by Oswald on the other. These articles were to be binding and effective, but in order to keep within the letter of the alliance with France, they were not to be concluded until the terms of a peace should be agreed upon between Great Britain and that country.[2]

---

[1] Adams' Works, *supra*, p. 335.

[2] M. de Vergennes was naturally enough surprised and indignant when informed by Franklin that the provisional articles had been concluded. 'You have concluded your preliminary articles without any communication between us,' thus he wrote the Doctor, 'although the instructions from Congress prescribe that nothing shall be done without the participation of the King. . . . . You are wise and discreet, Sir; you perfectly understand what is due to propriety; you have all your life performed your duties. I pray you to consider how you propose to fulfil those which are due to the King. I am not desirous of enlarging these reflections; I commit them to your own integrity.' This letter was dated December 15th, 1782. Four days later, he wrote to the French minister at Philadelphia, and if the suspicion did not interpose that his letter was intended to have an effect on Congress, we should be free to confess that it conveys an impression of sincerity. 'You will surely be gratified,' he says, 'as well as myself, with the very extensive advantages which

Of the value of Jay's services in this important negotiation, we have abundant testimony. Adams says all his colleagues, throughout the whole business, when they attended, were very attentive and very able; 'especially

---

our allies the Americans are to receive from the peace; but you certainly will not be less surprised than I have been, at the conduct of the commissioners. . . . The American commissioners will not say that I have interfered, and much less that I have wearied them with my curiosity. They have cautiously kept themselves at a distance from me. Whenever I have had occasion to see any one of them, and inquire of them briefly respecting the progress of the negotiation, they have constantly clothed their speech in generalities, giving me to understand that it did not go forward, and that they had no confidence in the sincerity of the British ministry. Judge of my surprise when, on the 29th of November, Dr. Franklin informed me that the articles were signed. The reservation retained on our account does not save the infraction of the promise which we have mutually made not to sign except conjointly. I owe Dr. Franklin the justice to state, however, that on the next day he sent me a copy of the articles. He will hardly complain that I received them without demonstrations of sensibility. . . . This negotiation is not yet so far advanced in regard to ourselves as that of the United States; not that the King, if he had shown as little delicacy in his proceedings as the American commissioners, might not have signed articles with England long before them.' See the two letters from which we have quoted in Franklin's Works, vol. ix., pp. 449–452.

Lord Mahon has given a convenient summary of the articles which constituted the Treaty of Paris, in the last volume of his History of England, p. 201. The articles themselves may be seen *in extenso* in the Diplomatic Correspondence, vol. x., pp. 109, 115. We may do the reader a service by re-producing the substance of them, and in the language of his lordship.

'The first Article acknowledged in the fullest terms the independence of the United States. The second fixed their boundaries advantageously for them. The third gave their people the right to take fish on all the banks of Newfoundland, but not to dry or cure them on any of the King's settled dominions in America. By the fourth, fifth, and sixth articles, it was agreed that the Congress should earnestly recommend to the several Legislatures to provide for the restitution of all estates belonging to real British subjects who had not borne arms against them. All other persons were to be at liberty to go to any of the provinces, and remain there for twelve months, to wind up their affairs, the Congress

Mr. Jay, to whom the French, if they knew as much of his negotiations as they do of mine, would very justly give the title with which they have inconsiderately decorated me, that of '*Le Washington de la négociacion;*' a very flattering compliment indeed, to which I have not a right, but sincerely think it belongs to Mr. Jay.'[1] 'I can safely add my testimony,' says Lord St. Helen's, 'to the numerous proofs afforded by these Memoirs, that it was not only chiefly, but solely through his means, that the negotiations of that period between England and the United States were brought to a successful conclusion.'[2]

After signing the provisional articles, the commissioners appear to have passed a very agreeable time in Paris. Jay, however, was a sufferer from ill-health. The climate of Spain, and his recent close application to business, had impaired his constitution. In hope of restoring

---

also recommending the restitution of their confiscated property, on their repayment of the sums for which it had been sold. No impediment was to be put in the way of recovering *bonâ fide* debts; no further prosecutions were to be commenced, no further confiscations made. It was likewise stipulated in the seventh and eighth articles, that the English should at once withdraw their fleets and armies from every port or place which they still possessed within the limits of the United States; and that the navigation of the Mississippi, from its source to the ocean, should be for ever free and open to both parties. To these provisions was added a secret article respecting the limits of West Florida, if, at the close of the war, it should be, or be put, in the possession of England.

[1] Adams' Works, vol. iii., p. 339.

[2] As to the letter from which this extract is taken, see ante, p. 343, note 1. Lord St. Helen's doubtless attributed the favorable conclusion of the treaty to Jay's inflexible determination to proceed separately in the negotiation, and not conjointly with the French. He must be a very ignorant or stolid man who does not acknowledge the great, the efficient services of Franklin in bringing to a satisfactory result the negotiations of that period. See Mr. Jay's testimony upon this point, Diplomatic Correspondence, vol. viii., p. 214: Sparks' Life of Franklin, p. 498: Writings of Jay, pp. 125, 127.

it, he left Paris early in January, on an excursion into Normandy. But he does not seem to have derived much benefit from this change of air and scene. On his return to Paris the latter part of the month, it would appear that the resentment he entertained against M. de Vergennes induced him to omit a point of *bienséance.* The French minister desired Lafayette to ask Jay why he did not come and see him. "Mr. Jay says he answered, 'How can he expect it, when he knows he has endeavored to play us out of the fisheries and vacant lands?' Mr. Jay added that he thought it would be best to let out by degrees, and to communicate to some French gentlemen the truth, and show them Marbois' letter: he particularly mentioned the Count Sarsfield.'[1] Jay's temper was quite as inflexible as his will. 'I have never broken the bands of friendship in my life,' he has said, 'nor, when once broken, have I ever been anxious to mend them.'[2] We think, nevertheless, he owed M. de Vergennes the usual mark of attention observed by persons in his station, and should have called and paid his respects to him.

When Jay left Madrid, he was told that the instructions intended for M. Del Campo should be sent to Count d'Aranda, the Spanish ambassador at Paris. D'Aranda was one of the most distinguished Spaniards of his time. He was possessed of immense wealth, lived in the finest situation in Paris, and in great splendor. He was ostentatious, but able, firm, and sagacious. 'Aranda,' said the King on one occasion, 'you are the most obstinate man of all Arragon.' 'No, Sire,' replied the Count, 'there is one still more obstinate than I am.' 'And who is that?'

---

[1] Adams' Works, vol. iii., p. 366. This entry in Adams' Diary is under date of May 2d, 1783. I infer that Jay had kept away from M. de Vergennes all this time.

[2] Letter to Robert Morris, February 25th, 1784. Writings of Jay, p. 151.

said the King. 'The King of Arragon,' answered the Count. D'Aranda was opposed to the Inquisition, and employed the most effectual method to overthrow it, by advising the King to have its proceedings public, like those of other Courts. The King was pleased with the suggestion, 'but his confessor,' the Count told Mr. Jay, 'was too cunning: he became acquainted with the plan, perceived its consequences, and persuaded the King to reject it.' [1]

A few days after Jay's arrival at Paris, M. de Rayneval suggested to him and Franklin that it would be well for them to wait on d'Aranda;[2] and said he had authority to assure them they would be well received. Accordingly, the next morning they went, and were received with great civility and politeness. D'Aranda introduced the subject of the treaty, 'and mentioned in general, as a principle, that the two powers should consider each other's conveniency, and accommodate and compensate each other as well as they could. . . . On our going out, he took pains himself to open the folding doors for us, which is a high compliment here, and told us he would return our visit, (*rendre son devoir,*) and then fix a day with us for dining with him.' [3] Accordingly, he returned their visit on the following day, and gave them an invitation to dine with him a few days afterwards. On that day Jay was taken sick, and was unable, from

[1] See Life of John Jay, p. 140, 141.

[2] The rule of etiquette at Paris prescribed that the last comer should make the first visit. Jay had already written d'Aranda, informing him of his arrival, and readiness to commence the necessary conferences. He did this, because he was doubtful whether if he made the Count a visit he would return it; and to avoid that risk, he wrote him. The Count answered his letter, and said he would receive him at whatever hour was most convenient to him. Diplomatic Correspondence, vol. viii., p. 149.

[3] Franklin's Works, vol. ix., p. 350, 351. Franklin's Journal, June 29th.

that cause, to meet the Count on business till a month afterwards. Then a serious difficulty interposed, which proved an effectual bar to their negotiation. Jay utterly refused to treat with D'Aranda without exchanging powers. M. de Vergennes endeavored to persuade him to proceed without that formality. D'Aranda assured him he had full authority to confer with him, but could not exchange copies of their commissions, because Spain had not yet acknowledged the independence of the United States. Jay replied that neither the terms of his commission nor the dignity of his country would permit his treating on any other than an equal footing. This put an end to the negotiation. After the provisional articles had been settled and ratified, D'Aranda informed him that the Spanish Court was ready to receive him, not only in form, but *très honnêtement.* Jay determined to go to Madrid, and, if possible, conclude a treaty with Spain, but the delays attending the conclusion of the definitive treaties, and the delicate state of his health, induced him to resign his commission.

The preliminaries of peace between France, Spain, and England were signed at Versailles on the 20th of January, 1783. On the 27th inst., copies of all three preliminary treaties were submitted to Parliament. Fox and Lord North leagued together against them. The motive of their attack was rather opposition to the minister than to the treaties. Lord Shelburne's administration was overthrown, and, 'from a new and strange coalition, an ill-formed and rickety Government struggled into life.'[1]

The latter part of April, David Hartley and the Duke of Manchester were sent to Paris to settle the definitive treaties. Hartley was 'a member of Parliament, a per-

[1] Lord Mahon's History of England, vol. vii., p. 207. 'They have at last settled a ministry,' wrote Franklin to Livingston, April 15th, 1783, 'but of such a composition as does not promise to be lasting.' Franklin's Works, vol. ix., p. 513.

sonal friend of Franklin, a constant advocate, to a measured extent, of the Americans, and a sort of self-offered, clandestine, but tacitly recognized medium for a kind of understanding, at some critical periods, between the English Government and Dr. Franklin, without costing the ministers the condescension of official intercourse and inquiry.'[1]

Commercial articles were discussed between him and the American commissioners, but without result. It was finally agreed to lay aside, for the present, all the new propositions that had been made, and adopt the provisional articles as the definitive treaty. On the 3d of September, 1783, the ceremony of signing was performed at Paris, and thus closed the drama of the Revolution.[2]

Jay's letters of this period all breathe an anxious desire to return to his native country. He had strong family and local attachments. 'My affections are deeply rooted in America,' he wrote his friend Morris, 'and are of too long standing to admit of transplantation. . . . I have, as yet, met with neither men nor things on this side of the water which abates my predilection, or, if you please, my prejudices in favor of those on the other. I have but few attachments in Europe much stronger

[1] Foster's Contributions, vol. i., p. 481.

[2] The definitive treaties with France and Spain were signed on the same day at Versailles. The Duke of Manchester had been unable to effect any material change in the preliminary articles. The following anecdote, however, would indicate that Fox was very well satisfied with the changes that were made. "Soon after the celebrated coalition between Fox and Lord North, the former was boasting at Brookes's of the advantageous peace he had ratified with France, adding, that he had at length prevailed on the Court of Versailles to relinquish all pretensions to the gum trade in favor of Great Britain. Selwyn, who was present, and, to all appearance, asleep in his chair, immediately exclaimed, 'That, Charles, I am not at all surprised at, for, having permitted the French to draw your *teeth*, they would be indeed d——d fools to quarrel with you about your *gums*.'" George Selwyn and his Contemporaries, vol. i., p. 21.

than those we sometimes feel for an accidental fellow-traveller, or for a good inn and a civil landlord. . . . . Your account of my son pleases me. I expect and wish to see him next summer; for it is time to lay the foundation of those habits and principles by which I am desirous that his conduct through life should be influenced. Nature has not given to children any instinctive affections for their parents; and youth, that fair season of virtue and ingenuousness, presents the only opportunity for our perfectly gaining their hearts. . . . My little girls are well, and their mother is not much otherwise.'[1]

'From the day I left him,' he wrote on hearing of his father's death, 'I never ceased to regret that it was not in my power to soften his troubles by those soothing attentions and returns of gratitude which he had a right to expect, and which always make the most pleasing impressions on those by whom we have been the most highly obliged. His affection for me was unbounded, and he knew how sensible I was of it. He has had severe trials, but they are over. . . . Thank God, there is another world in which we may meet and be happy. His being there is a new motive to my following in his

[1] Letter to Gouverneur Morris, September 24th, 1783. Writings of Jay, p. 130. He closes his letter to Morris with a few lines on politics. Considering the present posture of affairs in Europe, the following extract will not be uninteresting. After observing that there will be wars as long as there are knaves and fools in the world, and that uninterrupted peace and harmony would be more surprising than the absence of hostilities, he says: 'You have heard that the Ottoman and Russian empires are on the point of unsheathing the sword. The objects of the contest are more easy to discern than the issue; *but if Russia should extend her navigation to Constantinople, we may be the better for it. That circumstance is an additional motive to our forming a treaty of commerce with her.* . . . But whatever we have to do abroad, it is of little consequence when compared to what we have to do at home. I am perfectly convinced that no time is to be lost in raising and maintaining a national spirit in America. Power to govern the Confederacy, as to all general purposes, should be granted and exercised.'

footsteps.'[1] His solicitude for the comfort and welfare of his family was constant. He sent them money and various articles of convenience which they could not procure, in consequence of the war. 'Assure Peter,' he wrote on one occasion to his friend Livingston, the Secretary for Foreign Affairs, 'that it would distress me greatly were he, or indeed any of the family, to experience embarrassments in my power to obviate. He may share with me to the last shilling; and so may Nancy, about whom, until within a day or two, I had been very uneasy. . . . I write to Frederick by this opportunity, and authorize him to draw upon me for £150, York money, to be divided between the three.'[2]

An English historian, and one of the most agreeable writers of his country, has not thought it beneath the dignity of his subject to record, as an evidence of the kindly nature of the conqueror of De Grasse, the affection he entertained even for his dog.[3] Under the sanction of that authority, and as disclosing a trait of Jay's character, we may venture to quote the following extract from a letter to Egbert Benson: 'If my old mare is alive,' thus he wrote from Bath, whither he had gone in the autumn of 1783 in search of health, 'I must beg of you and my brother to take very good care of her. I mean that she should be well fed and live idle, unless my brother Peter should choose to use her. If it should be necessary to advance money to recover her, I am content you should do so, even to the amount of double her value. Draw upon me for what may be necessary for this purpose.'[4]

He returned to Paris in January, 1784. He had 'passed

[1] Letter to Mrs. Livingston, August 26th, 1782: Life of John Jay, p. 166.

[2] Letter to R. R. Livingston, July 19th, 1783: Ibid, p. 174.

[3] Mahon's History of England, vol. vii., p. 176.

[4] Life of John Jay, p. 181.

between three and four sad months in England. Bad weather and bad health almost the whole time. . . . 'Bath has done me good,' he wrote, notwithstanding, 'for it removed the pain in my breast, which has been almost constant for eighteen months.' [1]

On the 27th of March, Carmichael arrived at Paris with the public accounts, which Jay insisted should be settled before he returned to America. Barclay, however, the agent whom Congress had appointed to audit the accounts of their ministers abroad, was absent in England. 'Nothing but the settlement of these accounts now detains me here,' thus he wrote on the 7th of April, 'and a mortifying detention it is, considering that the best season for being at sea is passing away.' [2] 'After having passed so many years in scenes of trouble and difficulty of various kinds,' he wrote Miss Kitty Livingston on the same day, 'I look forward with emotion not to be described to that peaceful circle of my friends and family where I again expect to meet the enjoyments which have so long deserted me.' [3] Having at length effected a settlement of his accounts, he left Paris on the 16th of May for Dover, whence he sailed for New York.

---

[1] Letter to Gouverneur Morris, February 10th, 1784: Writings of Jay, p. 146.

[2] Letter to Charles Thomson, April 7th, 1784: Ibid, p. 156.

[3] Ibid, p. 155.

CHAPTER XIII.

SECRETARY FOR FOREIGN AFFAIRS.

1784—1789.

THE vessel in which Jay embarked, arrived at New York on the 24th of July, 1784. He had now been absent from his native city for a period of eight years. And what momentous changes had taken place in that time! When the Provincial Congress of New York adjourned to White Plains in the summer of 1776, the war had yet hardly begun. The career of Jay, through all the intervening time, at home and abroad, had justified and confirmed the confidence of his fellow-citizens. They received him on his return with sentiments of admiration and esteem. He was presented with the freedom of the city in a gold box, 'as a pledge of our affection;' such was the language of the accompanying address by the Corporation, 'and of our sincere wishes for your happiness.'

When Jay resigned his appointments in Europe, he intended to resume the practice of his profession. 'I know how to live within the limits of any income, however narrow,' he wrote his friend Morris from Paris, 'and my pride is not of a nature to be hurt by returning to the business which I formerly followed.'[1] But on his arrival at New York, he learned that Congress had appointed him Secretary for Foreign Affairs. This office was established in 1781. It was filled by R. R. Livings-

[1] Letter to Gouverneur Morris, February 10th, 1784. Writings of Jay, p. 147.

ton until the 4th of June, 1783.[1] Since his retirement it had remained vacant. The election of his successor was postponed from time to time, until May 7th, 1784, when Congress, being informed by a letter from Dr. Franklin that Jay proposed to embark for America in April, chose him to the vacant post. He remained undecided whether to accept it for several months. 'I am told Mr. Jay is not determined upon accepting,' wrote Lafayette to Hamilton on the 8th of October.[2] The day before, he had written Jay himself. 'With my usual frankness,' he said, 'I assure you that your refusal could not but be attended with very bad circumstances.'[3] Jay flattered himself that he was insensible to the ordinary objects of ambition, and served his country in stations of honor solely from a sense of duty. On this point public men are very apt to deceive themselves. 'You mistake your own heart when you say you are unambitious,' wrote Livingston to him when he was yet at Madrid; and in his letter, congratulating him on his return to his native shore, he says, 'If you are not cured of your ambition, you have every thing to hope for both in the State and Continental line.'[4] Jay was evidently hurt at the suggestion that he could act from such a motive, and thus replied: 'How far either of us have been, or may be, under the influence of am-

---

[1] 'He would have remained, if such augmentation of his salary had been made as would have secured him against future expense. But besides the disinclination of several members to augment salaries, there was no prospect of a competent number of States for an appropriation of money, until he must have lost the option of Chancellorship of New York.' Madison to Jefferson, June 10th, 1783: Madison Papers, vol. i., p. 546.

[2] Works of Hamilton, vol. i., p. 421.

[3] Writings of Jay, p. 159.

[4] Letters from R. R. Livingston, August 26th, 1780 and July 30th, 1784. Writings of Jay, p. 59: Life, p. 185.

bition, are questions which, however clear to ourselves, must necessarily be less so to others.' [1]

After remaining in New York two or three weeks, Jay with his family went into the country. The contrast between the condition of things at home and abroad did not tend to diminish his affection for his native land. 'I am more contented than I expected,' he wrote. 'Some things, it is true, are wrong, but more are right. Justice is well administered, offences are rare, and I have never known more public tranquillity or private security. . . . The spirit of industry throughout the country was never greater. The productions of the earth abound.' [2] When the State Legislature met in the autumn, they appointed Jay one of their delegates to Congress. Another honor, of a different description, was tendered him, which he at once declined, viz., an honorary membership of the Cincinnati. 'The institution of the order of Cincinnatus,' thus he had written from Paris, 'does not, in the opinion of the wisest men whom I have heard speak on the subject, either do credit to those who formed and patronised, or to those who suffered it.' [3]

Jay took his seat in Congress, which was convened at Trenton, on the 6th of December. On the 21st, he accepted the Secretaryship for Foreign Affairs. On the 24th, Congress adjourned to meet in New York. We shall not dwell long upon this portion of Jay's career. It possesses little of historical or personal interest. Its prominent feature was the renewal of negotiations with Spain. Don Diego Gardoqui was sent as Spanish minister to this country in the spring of 1785. He was publicly received by Congress on the 2d of July.[4] 'Our negotiations with

[1] Life of Jay, p. 186. Letter to R. R. Livingston, August 18th, 1784.

[2] Writings of Jay, p. 158. Letter to Benjamin Vaughan.

[3] Letter to Gouverneur Morris, February 10th, 1784. Writings of Jay, p. 146.

[4] On the 21st of June, Jay had written Gardoqui, and informed him of

him will soon commence,' wrote Jay to Lafayette on the 15th, 'and I sincerely wish that the issue of them may be satisfactory to both countries. To prepare for war, and yet be tenacious of peace with all the world, is, I think, our true interest.'[1] On the 20th, Congress invested Jay with full power 'to treat, adjust, conclude, and sign with Don Diego de Gardoqui, *encargado de negocios* of his Catholic Majesty, whatever articles, compacts, and conventions may be necessary for establishing and fixing the boundaries between the territories of the United States and those of his Catholic Majesty, and for promoting the general harmony and mutual interest of the two nations.'[2] He was, nevertheless, instructed previous to his making propositions to the Spanish minister, or assenting to those offered by him, to communicate them to Congress.[3] But on the 20th of August this extensive grant of authority was repealed, and Jay was instructed 'to stipulate the right of the United States to their territorial bounds and the free navigation of the

---

the etiquette that would be observed on his reception. 'At such time,' he said, 'as may be appointed by Congress for a public reception, the Secretary for Foreign Affairs will conduct you to the Congress chamber, to a seat to be placed for you, and announce you to Congress, the members keeping their seats and remaining covered. Your commission and letters of credence are then to be delivered to the Secretary of Congress, who will read a translation of them, to be prepared by the Secretary for Foreign Affairs from the copies to be left with the President. You will then be at liberty to speak, (and, if you please, deliver to the Secretary of Congress in writing,) what you may think proper to Congress, who will take what you may say into consideration, and, through the Secretary of Foreign Affairs, will communicate whatever answer they may resolve upon. When you retire, you will be reconducted by the Secretary for Foreign Affairs. A visit will be expected by every member of Congress, as well those who may then be in town as others who may afterwards arrive during your residence here.'

[1] Writings of Jay, p. 167.

[2] Secret Journals of Congress. vol. iii., p. 563.

[3] Ibid, p. 570.

Mississippi from the source to the ocean, as established in their treaties with Great Britain.' And he was further instructed not to conclude or sign 'any treaty, compact, or convention with the said *encargado de negocios*, until he hath previously communicated it to Congress, and received their approbation.' [1]

The Spanish minister was immovable in respect to the navigation of the Mississippi. Jay became convinced that the pretensions of his country in that regard must either be asserted by arms, or be permitted for the present to lie dormant. He was in favor of the latter alternative. Spain was ready to conclude a liberal commercial treaty, which promised great advantages to the United States. There was scarcely a single production of this country that could not be advantageously exchanged in the Spanish European ports for gold and silver. The influence of Spain with European powers and the States of Barbary, her ability to promote or oppose our political interests with those countries, was an additional and powerful motive to cultivate her friendship. These views were ably enforced by Jay in a written speech which he delivered before Congress August 3d, 1786. 'My letters written from Spain,' he said, 'when our affairs were the least promising, evince my opinion respecting the Mississippi, and oppose every idea of our relinquishing our right to navigate it. I entertain the same sentiments of that right, and of the importance of retaining it, which I then did. . . . Circumstanced as we are, I think it would be expedient to agree that the treaty should be limited to twenty-five or thirty years, and that one of the articles should stipulate that the United States would forbear to use the navigation of that river below their territories to the ocean.'

He thought it expedient to make that concession for

[1] Secret Journals of Congress, vol. iii., p. 586.

several reasons: First, 'because unless that matter can in some way or other be settled, the treaty, however advantageous, will not be concluded. Secondly, as that navigation is not at present important, nor will probably become much so in less than twenty-five or thirty years, a forbearance to use it while we do not want it is no great sacrifice. Thirdly, Spain now excludes us from that navigation, and with a strong hand holds it against us. She will not yield it peaceably, and therefore we can only acquire it by war. Now as we are not prepared for a war with any power; as many of the States would be little inclined to a war with Spain for that object at this day; and as such a war would, for those and a variety of obvious reasons, be inexpedient, it follows that Spain will, for a long space of time yet to come, exclude us from that navigation. Why, therefore, should we not (for a valuable consideration, too,) consent to forbear to use what we know is not in our power to use?'[1]

These sentiments of Jay were striking, and 'controverted,' to use the language of Washington, 'by only one consideration of weight, and that is, the operation which occlusion of the river may have on the minds of the Western settlers, who will not consider the subject in a relative point of view, or on a comprehensive scale, and may be influenced by the demagogues of the country to acts of extravagance and desperation, under the popular declamation that their interests are sacrificed.'[2]

The Western country was rapidly populating. A rage for emigrating thither had prevailed since the peace. 'The Continental Land-Office is opened,' Jay had written the previous year, 'and the seeds of a great people are daily planting beyond the mountains.'[3] These people

[1] Secret Journals of Congress, vol. iv., pp. 45, 53.

[2] See Writings of Washington, vol. ix., pp. 172, 180, 205, 261.

[3] Letter to William Bingham, May 31st, 1785: Writings of Jay, p. 166.

would not submit to see a fine river flowing before their doors without using it as a highway to the sea for the transportation of their productions. 'I have the utmost confidence,' wrote Jefferson, 'in the honest intentions of those who concur in this measure; but I lament their want of acquaintance with the character and physical advantages of the people, who, right or wrong, will suppose their interests sacrificed on this occasion to the contrary interests of that part of the Confederacy in possession of present power. . . . I will venture to say, that the act which abandons the navigation of the Mississippi, is an act of separation between the Eastern and Western country.'[1]

The sentiments avowed by Jay were highly displeasing to that section of the Confederacy at whose earnest instigation, but little more than five years before, Congress had expressly instructed him, while minister at the Court of Spain, to relinquish forever the navigation of the Mississippi as the price of a Spanish subsidy and alliance.[2] A motion was now made by Pinckney of South Carolina,[3] and seconded by Carrington of Virginia, to revoke his commission to conduct the negotiation. The vote on this motion was the result of sectional views and feelings. Every Southern delegate, with the exception of Few of Georgia, supported it, while the entire Northern delegation opposed it.[4] Unquestionably, the surrender of the navigation of the Mississippi for a term of years, with such violent opposition arrayed against it at the West, would have been an impolitic measure. But Jay had only recommended it. By his present instructions he could not conclude a treaty on that basis. The attempt, therefore,

---

[1] Letter to James Madison, January 30th, 1787: Jefferson's Works, vol. ii., p. 87.

[2] Ante, Chap. xi., tit. Minister to Spain.

[3] Charles Pinckney, a cousin of Charles Cotesworth.

[4] Secret Journals of Congress, vol. iv., p. 85.

to revoke his powers, could only discredit his opinions, without affecting his action.

On the day following the defeat of Pinckney's motion, viz., on the 29th of August, 1786, seven States against five voted to rescind the instructions of the previous year, which bound Jay to insist on the right of navigation, and left him at liberty to conclude a treaty with Gardoqui according to his own views, without even communicating it to Congress before signing.[1] We think it clear that this was an unconstitutional delegation of authority. The Articles of Confederation expressly declared that the United States should not enter into any treaty or alliance, unless nine States in Congress assented to the same.[2] Surely, then, Congress, by a vote of seven States, could not do that by another which they were restrained from doing themselves, except by a vote of nine States. Or, in other words, if Congress could not conclude a treaty with Gardoqui without the assent of nine States, they could not authorize Jay to do it by a vote of seven States. It does not appear, however, that Jay considered his authority defective. Nevertheless, he made no treaty with Gardoqui. He *adjusted*, but did not *conclude* with the Spanish negotiator, an article ceding the Mississippi for a term of years.

'The negotiations with Spain are carried on,' wrote Madison to Randolph the 11th of March, 1787, 'if they go on at all, entirely behind the curtain. The business has been put into such a form, that it rests wholly with Jay how far he will proceed with Gardoqui, and how far he will communicate with Congress.'[3] A few days later he thus alludes to the same subject, in a letter to Jefferson: 'The Spanish project sleeps. A perusal of the attempt of seven States to make a new treaty by repealing

---

[1] See ante, p. 362. Secret Journals of Congress, vol. iv., pp. 109, 110.

[2] Art. ix.

[3] Madison Papers, vol. ii., p. 620–622.

an essential condition of the old, satisfied me that Mr. Jay's caution would revolt at so irregular a sanction. A late accidental conversation with Gardoqui proved to me that the negotiation is arrested. . . . But although it appears that the intended sacrifice of the Mississippi will not be made, the consequences of the intention and the attempt are likely to be very serious. . . . Mr. Henry's disgust exceeds all measure, and I am not singular in ascribing his refusal to attend the Convention, to the policy of keeping himself free to combat or espouse the result of it, according to the result of the Mississippi business among other circumstances.' [1]

On the 4th of April, 1787, Jay was directed by Congress to report the state of his negotiation with Gardoqui. This he did on the 11th.[2] 'The report,' wrote Madison on the occasion, 'shows that Jay viewed the act of seven States as valid, and has even adjusted with Gardoqui an article for suspending our use of the Mississippi during the term of the treaty.[3] A subsequent report[4] on a re-

---

[1] Letter to Jefferson, March 19th, 1787. Secret Journals of Congress, vol. iii., p. 623. The Convention referred to by Madison was the Convention for revising the federal system of Government, which assembled in the following May. [2] Secret Journals of Congress, vol. iv., p. 296.

[3] Jay, in his report, after describing the difficulties he encountered respecting this article, says, 'It was, however, finally so adjusted as in my opinion, to save the *right*, and only suspend the *use* during the term of the treaty; and at the expiration of which, this, and every other article in it, would become null and void.' This was but one article of the treaty, and it does not appear from Jay's report whether Gardoqui had authority to assent to it without instructions from his Court. At any rate, it was dependent on the contingency of a treaty being made, which was not effected. Jay thus concluded his report: 'A variety of circumstances and considerations which I need not mention, *render this negotiation dilatory, unpleasant, and unpromising;* and it is much to be wished that the United States could jointly and unanimously adopt and pursue some fixed and stable plan of policy in regard to Spain, especially during the residence of M. Gardoqui,' &c. Ibid, pp. 596–300.

[4] This report was made on the 12th of April, 1787. Secret Journals, vol. iv., p. 301.

ference of Western information from Virginia and North Carolina denotes little confidence in the event of the negotiation, and considerable perplexity as to the steps proper to be taken by Congress. . . . We mean to propose that Jefferson be sent, under a special commission, to plead the cause of the Mississippi at Madrid.'[1]

In accordance with this plan, Madison made a formal motion on the 20th to send Jefferson to Madrid for the purpose stated. 'This motion was referred to Mr. Jay,' wrote Madison to Jefferson on the 23d, 'whose report disapproves of it. In this state the matter lies. Eight States only being present, no effective vote is to be expected. . . . . Maryland and South Carolina have hitherto been on the right side. Their future conduct is somewhat problematical. The opinion of New Hampshire is only conjectured. The conversion of Rhode Island countenances a hope that she too may, in this instance, desert the New England standard.'[2]

Congress did not choose 'to chicane with their situation, rather than be instructed by it.' All reflecting men perceived that with the existing Confederation tottering to its base, with the Western country in a state of extreme exasperation, and ready to resist, with the strong hand, any prohibition of the navigation of the Mississippi, a postponement of the negotiation with Spain was the only wise and practicable course. Accordingly, when, on the 11th of May, a motion was made by Few, of Georgia, to the effect, that the proceedings of Congress did not authorize the Secretary of the United States to enter into any stipulation with Spain, whereby the right of the United States to the free navigation of the Mississippi should be relinquished or impaired, an amendment was moved by

---

[1] Letter to Edmund Randolph, April 15th, 1787. Madison Papers, vol. ii., pp. 634, 637.

[2] Madison Papers, vol. ii., pp. 639, 642.

Rufus King, by which it was declared that the proceedings of Congress did not authorize the Secretary of the United States to enter into *any* stipulation with the minister of his Catholic Majesty. Ten States were present, and the amendment was carried by a vote of seven States against three.[1]

The influence of Spain with the Barbary States, it will be recollected, was one of the motives assigned by Jay for concluding a treaty with that power. In the autumn of 1785 the news arrived in this country that the Algerines had declared war against it. Jay communicated this intelligence to Congress. 'This war,' he said, 'does not strike me as a great evil. The more we are ill-treated abroad, the more we shall unite and consolidate at home. Besides, as it may become a nursery for seamen, and lay the foundation for a respectable navy, it may eventually prove more beneficial than otherwise. . . . For my own part, I think it may be demonstrated that, while we bend our attention to the sea, every naval war, however long, which does not do us essential injury, will do us essential good.'[2]

Congress referring the subject to him, he recommended the arming of all American ships trading in the Mediterranean, at the public expense, and the building of five forty-gun ships, and the organization of the board of admiralty and a requisition on the States for the necessary supplies. These recommendations, wisely conceived as they were, could not be carried into effect, from the inherent weakness of the existing Government.

On the 1st of June, 1785, John Adams, the first minister of the United States at the Court of St. James, was

---

[1] Secret Journals of Congress, vol. iv., pp. 345, 346.

[2] Letter to the President of Congress, October 13th, 1785. See also letter to John Adams of the following day. Writings of Jay, pp. 175, 177.

presented to the King. The war being ended, it was obviously the interest of both parties to cultivate friendly sentiments. 'Mutual civility and respect,' wrote Jay to Adams on the 6th of September, 'must, in the nature of things, precede mutual benevolence and kindness. The manner of your reception and treatment indicates their attention to this consideration, and yet the detention of the posts, the strengthening their garrisons in our neighborhood, the encouragement said to be given to settlers in those parts, and various other sentiments, speak a language very different from that of kindness and good will.'[1]

William Pitt was now Prime Minister. The following extract from Jay's letter will not be uninteresting. 'As to their present minister,' he says, 'he has neither been long enough in administration, nor perhaps in the world,[2] for a decided judgment to be formed, either of his private or public character. He seems to possess firmness as well as abilities; and, if to these be added information and comprehensive, as well as patriotic views, he may be worthy of his father. England will probably be either much the better or much the worse for him.'[3]

---

[1] Writings of Jay, p. 171.

[2] Pitt was now in his twenty-seventh year.

[3] Pitt had great abilities and extraordinary powers of eloquence. What he lacked, says Horace Walpole, was 'originality, philosophy, and genius.' He might have added, also, information. George III. said his Prime Minister had never read Vattel. He had but a limited knowledge of foreign affairs. In that particular he was incontestably inferior to Fox. His whole foreign policy, his defence of that miserable delusion, legitimacy, all proceeded from false principles and limited views. 'There is divinity in speech,' it has been said; nevertheless there is nothing, perhaps, so fallacious as political oratory. It is, of all things, the most unsafe criterion of intellectual *power*, of those qualities that test the absolute worth of a man. Who does not more respect the *will* of a Jackson, than the *eloquence* of a Webster. The oratory of Pitt was undoubtedly great. It secured the triumph of a policy unjust in principle and injurious in effect.

It is curious to observe the impression made on such a man as John

By the seventh article of the treaty, the posts held by the British within the United States were to be evacuated. By the fourth article, every facility was to be allowed to British subjects to collect the debts due to them in the several States. It cannot be said that the fulfilment of this latter article was strictly a precedent condition to the performance of the former; yet it must be admitted, if the one party violated the treaty, the other could not be held to a rigid observance of it. When, therefore, the American minister formally complained of the detention of the

---

Adams by the youthful minister. He certainly misconceived his position and influence. 'Pitt,' wrote Adams to Jay, '*is but a tool, and an ostensible pageant, a nose of tender virgin wax:* he could not carry in Parliament nor in the cabinet, any honest system with America, if he meant to do it; but he is himself very far from being steady in his American politics, any more than Camden or Richmond; and Sidney and Carmarthen are cyphers.' November 24th, 1785. Diplomatic Correspondence, (N. S.,) vol. iv., pp. 443, 444.

A few days later, Adams wrote again, and sketched another portrait of Pitt, which, if it does not do full justice to the original, is certainly more truthful and lifelike than the fulsome performances of his indiscreet admirers. 'Mr. Pitt is very young, Sir,' he says, 'he has discovered abilities and firmness upon some occasions; but I have never seen in him any evidence of greater talents than I have seen in members of Congress, and in other scenes of life in America, at his age. I have not yet seen any decided proofs of principle, or patriotism, or virtue; on the contrary, there are many symptoms of the want of these qualities, without which, no statesman ever yet appeared uniformly great, or wrought out any memorable salvation for any country. In American affairs, he has vibrated credit as a pendulum, and no one can yet guess when he will have fixed. His attention appears to have been chiefly given to two objects, preserving tranquillity and raising the stocks. His attention to these would have been laudable if he had not neglected others equally essential in the end, though not so urgent for the present period. . . . The stocks he has raised, and if he can keep them up they will support him, and intoxicate the nation to such a degree, that I presume it will be impossible for him to pursue that system towards America and Ireland which is indispensable for the complete preservation of the remainder of the empire.' December 1785: Ibid, pp. 467, 468.

posts, he was told that British creditors, in direct contravention of the treaty, were obstructed in the collection of their just debts by legislative enactments. This answer of the British ministry was transmitted to Congress, by whom it was referred to the Secretary for Foreign Affairs. 'The result of my inquiries into the conduct of the States relative to the treaty,' thus he wrote Adams, and substantially reported to Congress, 'is, that there has not been a single day since it took effect on which it has not been violated in America, by one or other of the States; and this observation is just, whether the treaty be supposed to have taken effect either at the date or exchange of the provisional articles, or on the day of the date of the definitive treaty, or of the ratifications of it.' [1]

Jay presented his report to Congress on the 13th of October, 1786. 'The amount of the report, which is an able one,' wrote Madison to Jefferson, 'is, that the treaty should be put in force as a law, and the exposition of it, left, like that of other laws, to the ordinary tribunals.' [2] In pursuance of Jay's recommendation, Congress resolved that the treaty, having been constitutionally formed, was the law of the land, and urged a repeal of all laws contravening it.[3] These resolutions were transmitted to

---

[1] Jay to Adams, November 1st, 1786. Writings of Jay, p. 191. See Writings of Washington, vol. ix., p. 179, for opinion of Washington respecting the infractions of the treaty. Adams' complaints of the violation of the treaty on the part of Great Britain were embodied in a memorial dated November 30th, 1785, and presented to the British Government on the 8th of December. He received a reply in February, 1786. See Diplomatic Correspondence, (N. S.,) vol. iv., p. 454

[2] Madison Papers, vol. ii., p. 622.

[3] These resolutions were adopted March 21st, 1787. Secret Journals of Congress, vol. iv., p. 294. See also Jay's report, *in extenso:* Ibid, pp. 185, 287.

This report is, as Madison pronounced it, a very able one. It is worthy of observation for its fearless, manly tone, its direct and truthful avowal of opinions. He showed conclusively, that if Great Britain had

the several States, accompanied by a circular letter prepared by Jay.[1]

But it is useless to resolve and recommend, where no power exists to enforce. And so it proved in this case. Indeed, the affairs of the country were rapidly approaching a crisis. The utter inefficiency of the existing Government was felt and seen by all men. It neither inspired confidence nor afforded security. It was manifest that some step must be taken, some scheme devised, to check the downward tendency of things, or the glory and utility of the Revolution would prove a delusion and a jest to all mankind. 'As the knaves and fools of this world are forever in alliance,' wrote Jay to Jefferson, 'it is easy to perceive how much vigor and wisdom a Government, from its construction and administration, should possess, in order to repress the evils which naturally flow from such copious sources of injustice and evil. . . . Changes are necessary; but what they ought

violated the treaty, the United States had antecedently violated it. With respect to the negroes carried away by the British, he divided them into three classes: 1st, Such as had been captured and disposed of as booty. 2d, Such as belonged to American inhabitants within the British lines. 3d, Such as fled to the British, confiding in proclamations and promises of freedom and protection. The first class, he contended, were not comprehended in the stipulation 'not to carry away any negroes or other property of the American inhabitants.' The remaining classes, he agreed, came within its meaning and design. But with regard to the last class, he contended that the British ought to stand excused for carrying away the negroes embraced by it, provided they paid their full value. Whether this was the correct interpretation of the treaty, is considered in a subsequent chapter. Vide Post., chap. 15, tit. Jay's Treaty.

[1] Madison Papers, vol. ii., p. 639. The utter feebleness of the National Government under the Confederation, was shown in its inability to enforce, on the part of the States, the provisions of a solemn treaty into which it had entered. The historian of the United States finds but little to awaken his pride in contemplating the condition of his country during the period that intervened between the close of the Revolutionary War, and the formation of the existing Government.

to be, what they will be, and how and when to be produced, are arduous questions. I feel for the cause of liberty, and for the honor of my countrymen who have so nobly asserted it, and who, at present, so abuse its blessings. If it should not take root in this soil, little pains will be taken to cultivate it in any other.' [1]

It is well known that the Convention which assembled at Annapolis in the autumn of 1786, to devise a uniform system of commercial regulations, in consequence of an inadequate representation, wisely forbore to consider that subject, but recommended a convention of delegates from the several States, to revise the articles of confederation. 'To me, the policy of such a convention appears questionable,' wrote Jay to Washington. 'Their authority is to be derived from acts of the State Legislatures. Are the State Legislatures authorized, either by themselves or others, to alter Constitutions? I think not. They who hold commissions can, by virtue of them, neither retrench nor extend the powers conveyed by them. Perhaps it is intended that this Convention shall not ordain, but only recommend. If so, there is danger that their recommendations will produce endless discussions, and perhaps jealousies and party heats.' [2] He thought the better mode would be for Congress to advise the States to assemble Conventions, 'with the sole and express power of appointing deputies to a general Convention, who, or the majority of whom, should take into consideration the articles of confederation, and make such alterations, amendments, and additions thereto, as to them should appear necessary and proper; and which being by them ordained and published, should have the same force and obligation which all, or any of the present articles, now have.' [3]

[1] October 27th, 1786: Writings of Jay, p. 190.

[2] January 7th, 1787: Life of Jay, p. 255.

[3] Ibid.

This letter was written in January, 1787. Jay, it will be observed, while approving a Convention, objected to the proposed one on the ground of its insufficient authority. Entertaining that opinion, and doubting the issue of a convention thus constituted, he did not favor the appointment of delegates to it by New York. 'Hamilton,' wrote Rufus King to Gerry, 'who is a member of the assembly of this State, will exert himself to induce them to send members; Jay and others are opposed to the measure, not alone because it is unauthorized, but from an opinion that the result will prove inefficacious.'[1] On the 21st of the following February, Congress recommended a Convention of delegates from the several States, for the sole and express purpose of revising the articles of Confederation. Such alterations and additions as might be made were to be reported to Congress, and when approved by that body and confirmed by the States, to be binding and effective. This action of Congress conformed in a measure to Jay's views. It does not appear, however, that he was very sanguine of a favorable result.

The Convention thus recommended assembled at Philadelphia on the 14th day of May, in the year 1787. Jay was not a member. It has been said that his official situation, and the necessity of his attendance on Congress, then in session, prevented his being included in the delegation from the State of New York. This was not the only, and, we suspect, not the strongest reason for his being omitted. On the 8th of March, Yates, Hamilton, and Lansing were appointed the delegates from that State. As Yates and Lansing were anti-Federal in their views, and as the rule of the Confederation of voting by

[1] Life of Elbridge Gerry, vol. ii., p. 4. King's letter to Gerry was written on the very day that Jay wrote to Washington, viz., January 7th, 1787. King's opinion as to the legality of the Convention coincided with Jay's.

States might be adopted by the Convention, Hamilton proposed to the Assembly to add two additional members to the delegation. 'I think it proper to apprise the House,' said Hamilton on the occasion, 'of the gentlemen on some of whom I wish their choice to fall, and with a view to which, I bring forward the present motion. . . I mean Mr. Chancellor Livingston, Mr. Duane, Mr. Benson, and Mr. Jay; the particular situation of the latter may require an observation. His being a servant of Congress might seem an objection to his appointment; but surely this objection, if it had any weight, would apply with equal force to a member of that body.[1] . . . His knowledge, abilities, tried integrity, and abundant experience in the affairs of the country, foreign and domestic, will not permit us to allow any weight to any objection which would imply a want of confidence in a character that has every title to the fullest confidence.'[2] Hamilton's motion succeeded in the Assembly, but was defeated in the Senate. We may well suppose, that the motive to the Senate's dissent, was apprehension of having a majority of the delegation, who would advocate a stricter union, and a more energetic National Government.

Although not a member of the Convention, Jay had formed and expressed opinions as to what should be the leading features of the future government of his country. 'Let Congress legislate,' thus he wrote Washington; 'let others execute; let others judge. Shall we have a king? not, in my opinion, while other expedients remain untried. Might we not have a Governor-General, limited in his prerogatives and duration? Might not Congress be divided into an upper and lower house; the former

[1] Lansing, whom the Legislature had already elected a delegate, is here referred to.

[2] Life of Hamilton, vol. ii., pp. 453, 454.

appointed for life, the latter annually; and let the Governor-General, (to preserve the balance,) with the advice of a Council, formed for that only purpose, of the great judicial officers, have a negative on their acts? Our Government should, in some degree, be suited to our manners and circumstances, and they, you know, are not strictly democratical. What powers should be granted to the Government so constituted is a question which deserves much thought. I think the more the better; the States retaining only so much as may be necessary for domestic purposes, and all their principal officers, civil and military, being commissioned and removable by the National Government.'[1]

Jay deemed a consolidated, high-toned, republican Government essential to the best interests of his country. In that he may have erred; but the liberality of the age in which we live, will seek some other test by which to try the men of the Revolution, than their speculative opinions upon politics. It is enough for us, that when the Convention assembled at Philadelphia, after mature deliberation, agreed to a Constitution, Jay urged its adoption with undoubted earnestness and ability. It was not in all respects conformable to his sentiments, but he sacrificed his individual preferences and partialities to the general good.[2]

When the labors of the Philadelphia Convention were submitted to the people, a strong, a determined, a violent opposition was immediately excited. In New York especially, the new Constitution was assailed with undisguised hostility. Four-sevenths of the inhabitants, it was estimated, were opposed to it.

In this condition of the popular mind, Jay undertook,

---

[1] Life of Jay, p. 255. See also letter to John Adams, May 4th, 1786. Ibid, p. 249. Letters to Jefferson of August 18th and December 14th, 1786. Ibid, pp. 250, 251.

[2] See letter to Washington, September 21st, 1788. Writings of Jay, p. 195.

in conjuction with Hamilton and Madison, to explain and vindicate the proposed instrument of Government through the press. The Federalist, 'equally admirable for the depth of its wisdom, the comprehensiveness of its views, the sagacity of its reflections, and the fearlessness, patriotism, candor, simplicity, and elegance with which its truths are uttered and recommended,'[1] is the joint production of these three personages. It appeared originally in a series of numbers, published in the New York daily papers, between October, 1787, and June, 1788. 'They were read with admiration and enthusiasm as they successively appeared,' says Chancellor Kent, who attempted to abridge them for the benefit of a country village print. 'No constitution of Government,' we quote again from the same high authority, 'ever received a more masterly and successful vindication.'[2] The second, third, fourth, fifth, and sixty-fourth numbers were written by Jay. The particular subjects which he discussed were the dangers to be apprehended from foreign force and influence, and the power of the Senate in making treaties.

In April, 1788, there was a serious riot in New York, known, in the annals of the city, as 'The Doctors' Mob.' The grave had been violated in several instances by members of the medical profession, and the popular indignation vented itself against the whole fraternity. Several of the most obnoxious were confined in the city prison as a protection from the popular fury. This the mob attempted to force. Under the lead of Hamilton, Jay and other citizens hastened to the prison to prevent so great an outrage. They were attacked by the mob, and Jay received a deep and dangerous wound in his temple.[3] On his recovery, he published an anonymous

[1] Chancellor Kent. Commentaries, vol. i., p. 241.

[2] Ibid.

[3] Watson's Annals of New York, p. 298. Life of Jay, p. 261.

address to the people of New York, written with 'good sense, forcible observations, temper, and moderation.'[1] Admitting that the proposed Constitution was not perfect in all its features, he submitted whether it was probable a better plan could be obtained. Whether, if attainable, it was likely to be in season. What would be their situation, if, after rejecting this, all their efforts to obtain a better should prove fruitless? The discussion of the two first questions induces a negative response. In reply to the third, he says: 'Then every State would be a little nation, jealous of its neighbors and anxious to strengthen itself by foreign alliances against its former friends. Then farewell to fraternal affection, unsuspecting intercourse, and mutual participation in commerce, navigation, and citizenship. Then would arise mutual restrictions and fears, mutual garrisons and standing armies.'

The Legislature of New York, on the 1st day of February, 1788, passed a resolution, providing for the election of delegates to a Convention expressly authorized to adopt or reject the proposed Constitution. The election was held on the last Tuesday of April. In New York city the Federalists were completely triumphant. Jay was elected a delegate by nearly a unanimous vote. The Convention assembled at the Court-House in Poughkeepsie on the 17th of June. It was composed of fifty-seven delegates, forty-six of whom were opposed to the Constitution.

Nevertheless, there were sources of hope. There had been a gradual change of sentiment in the people auspicious to the Constitution, and it was probable that it would be ratified by nine States before the Convention finally decided. In that event, New York would only have the alternative of following their example, or remaining an insulated State in the midst of a powerful

[1] Washington.

nation. Besides, it was apprehended that if the Constitution was rejected, it would result in a division of the State — New York city and the adjacent district joining the Confederacy. Before the meeting of the Convention, Governor Clinton had, in private conversations, declared the Union unnecessary; but in the Convention itself, he held very different language, though still opposing the ratification of the instrument that was to insure it.[1]

The first three weeks were spent in committee of the whole on the general merits of the question. These discussions, the personal influence of the leading Federal members, but more than all, the intervening accession of New Hampshire and Virginia to the Confederation, changed the sentiments of the Convention, and secured New York to the Union.

Jay did not often nor elaborately address the Convention. But who does not know that action is more influenced and ideas more effectually changed by private persuasion than by public speech. Jay's important services, his high character, the general opinion of his integrity and abilities, themselves not indifferent arguments in favor of his views, would naturally give great weight to his opinions, uttered in the freedom of private conversation. On the 11th of July he moved that the Constitution ought to be ratified, and whatever amendments might be deemed useful or expedient recommended. This motion gave rise to debates which continued during the next four days. On the 19th, a motion was made by Lansing, and carried, to take into consideration the draft of a conditional ratification, with a bill of rights prefixed, and amendments subjoined. On the 23d, the ground of a conditional ratification was abandoned, the Convention

---

[1] Hamilton's Works, vol. i., p. 452. Elliott's Debates, vol. ii., p. 359. Letters of Jay to Washington, May 29th and June, 1788. Life of Jay, pp. 265–268.

ratifying, not on condition, but in full confidence that their proposed amendments would be adopted.

On the 26th, the bill of rights, amendments, and form of ratification were finally submitted to the Convention, and agreed to by a vote of thirty to twenty-seven.[1]

We have now traced the career of Jay through the scenes of Revolutionary strife, and endeavored to portray the extent and variety of his services, at home and abroad, during the war and since the peace. In the next chapter we shall behold him in a new situation, and discover in what manner he performed the high duties of Chief Justice of the United States.

---

[1] Elliott's Debates, vol. ii., pp. 411, 412. The amendments were submitted to the several States, accompanied by a circular letter written by Jay, recommending a general Convention to consider them.

CHAPTER XIV.

CHIEF JUSTICE OF THE UNITED STATES.

1789—1794.

The 4th of March, 1789, was the day assigned for the assembling of the new Congress, but a quorum of the House was not formed until the 1st of April, and of the Senate until the 6th. 'The public will forget the Government before it is born,' wrote Fisher Ames on the 25th of March. 'The resurrection of the infant will come before its birth. . . . The old Congress still continues to meet, and it seems to be doubtful whether the old Government is dead, or the new one alive.'[1] General Washington arrived at New York on the 23d of April.[2] He was received at Elizabethtown Point by a deputation from Congress in a barge 'splendidly fitted up for the occasion, and rowed by thirteen pilots in white uniforms. This barge was accompanied by several others, in one of which were the members of the Treasury Board, the Secretary for Foreign Affairs, and the Secretary of War.'[3] On the 30th, the President was formally received by both Houses of Congress in the Senate-chamber. The oath of office was administered to him by

[1] Ames to Minot, March 25th, 1789. Life and Works of Fisher Ames, vol. i., p. 30, 31.

[2] The votes of the electors were opened and counted on the 6th of April. Washington was officially informed of his election on the 14th, and commenced his journey on the 16th. Writings of Washington, vol. x., p. 460–464.

[3] Ibid, p. 462.

Chancellor Livingston.[1] 'He addressed the two Houses in the Senate-chamber; it was a very touching scene,' thus wrote Fisher Ames, 'and quite of the solemn kind. His aspect grave, almost to sadness; his modesty actually shaking; his voice deep, a little tremulous, and so low as to call for close attention; added to the series of objects presented to the mind, and overwhelming it, produced emotions of the most affecting kind upon the members. I, Pilgarlic, sat entranced. It seemed to me an allegory, in which virtue was personified, and addressing those whom she would make her votaries. Her power over the heart was never greater, and the illustration of her doctrine by her own example was never more perfect.'[2]

Several months elapsed before Congress passed the laws instituting the several executive departments under the new Government. Consequently, the chief officers were not appointed until September. The department of State was assigned to Jefferson, but he did not enter upon its duties before the following March. Meanwhile, Jay continued to fill the office.

The Judiciary bill, approved the 24th of September, provided for the appointment of a Chief Justice and five Associate-Justices, who should constitute the Supreme Court of the United States. Washington had manifested the opinion he entertained of Jay's character and abilities, by giving him a choice of the offices under the Government. He preferred the Chief-Justiceship, as according with his turn of mind, his education, and habits. He was therefore nominated to that post, and confirmed by the Senate the 26th of September, 1789. 'In nominating

[1] The oath was administered in the outer gallery or balcony of the Senate-chamber, in order that a larger number of persons might witness the ceremony. Upon returning into the Senate-chamber, Washington delivered his address.

[2] Life and Works of Ames, vol. i., p. 34. Ames to Minot, May 3d, 1789.

you for the important station which you now fill,' wrote the President, 'I not only acted in conformity with my best judgment, but I trust I did a grateful thing to the good citizens of these United States.'[1]

The first term of the Supreme Court was held at New York in February, 1790. Several rules were established, and the Court adjourned. It does not appear that any business was brought before them until the August term of the following year. In the meantime, however, Circuit Courts were held twice a year, agreeably to the provisions of the Judiciary bill.[2] Jay's district embraced New York and New England. His first Circuit was held in the city of New York on the 4th of April, 1790. A single extract from his charge to the Grand Jury may not be uninteresting. The sentiments were eminently proper to the occasion. 'It cannot be too strongly impressed on the minds of all,' he said, 'how greatly our individual prosperity depends on our National prosperity, and how greatly our National prosperity depends on a well-organized, vigorous Government, ruling by wise and equal laws faithfully executed. Nor is such a Government unfriendly to liberty — to that liberty which is really estimable. On the contrary, nothing but a strong government of laws, irresistibly bearing down arbitrary power and licentiousness, can defend it against those two formidable enemies. Let it be remembered that civil liberty consists, not in a right to every man to do just as he pleases, but it consists in an equal right to all the citizens to have, enjoy, and do, in peace, security, and without molestation, whatever the equal and constitutional laws of the country admit to be consistent with the public good.'

---

[1] Washington to Jay, enclosing the latter's commission, October 5th, 1789. Writings of Washington, vol. x., p. 35.

[2] The Circuits were held by two Justices of the Supreme Court and a District Judge.

Upon the adjournment of this Court; the Chief Justice commenced his first circuit through New England. He had received various invitations from his friends to reside with them while holding his Courts. 'As a man, and your friend,' thus he wrote on one of these occasions, 'I should be happy in accepting it; but, as a Judge, I have my doubts — they will occur to you without details.' On considering the subject, he thought there was a propriety in declining all invitations of this character, and lodging only at public houses.[1]

Jay's services in negotiating the treaty of peace, his recent efforts to conclude a commercial arrangement with Spain, an object greatly desired by New England, together with his pure and unsullied character, made him a favorite in that quarter. 'The New-England people talk of making you an annual *fish-offering*,' Hamilton wrote him after the signing of the Provisional Articles, 'as an acknowledgment of your exertions for the participation of the fisheries.'[2] Everywhere on the circuit he was honored with public and private civilities. Harvard University conferred on him the degree of Doctor of Laws.

It does not appear that his first circuits were attended with much business. Few of his decisions, while he remained on the Bench, were of a character to amuse or instruct the reader. Nor do they enable us to judge of the extent of his juridical acquirements; nevertheless, they evince a juridical faculty, a power of analysis, an aptitude for logical processes, and a ready apprehension of principles. The case of *Chisholm, Ex'r*, v. *Georgia*,[3] attracted great and unusual interest at the time, and as connected with the history of the Constitution, is worthy of observation, even at the present day. It involved the question,

---

[1] Life of Jay, p. 277.

[2] Writings of Jay, p. 122. July 25th, 1783.

[3] 2 Dall. R., p. 419.

whether a State is suable by individual citizens of another State? The case was argued at the February term of the Court, 1793. The decision was in the affirmative. The Judges delivered their opinions *seriatim*. 'As this opinion,' said the Chief Justice, 'though deliberately formed, has been hastily reduced to writing between the intervals of the daily adjournments, and while my mind was occupied and wearied by the business of the day, I fear it is less concise and connected than it might otherwise have been.'

He inquires, 1st: In what sense Georgia is a sovereign State? 2d: whether suability is incompatible with such sovereignty. 3d: Whether the Constitution (to which Georgia is a party) authorizes such an action against her. In answer to the first inquiry, he considers the political situation of the country prior to the Revolution, and the political rights that emerged from it. 'From the Crown of Great Britain,' he said, 'the sovereignty of their country passed to the people of it; and it was not then an uncommon opinion, that the unappropriated lands which belonged to that Crown, passed, not to the people of the colony or State within whose limits they were situated, but to the whole people. . . Experience disappointed the expectations they had formed from it,' (i. e., the Confederation,) 'and then the people, in their collective and national capacity, established the present Constitution. It is remarkable that, in establishing it, the people exercised their own rights and their own proper sovereignty, and, conscious of the plenitude of it, they declared with becoming dignity, 'We, the people of the United States, do ordain and establish this Constitution.' Here we see the people acting as sovereigns of the whole country; and in the language of sovereignty, establishing a Constitution by which it was their will that the State Governments should be bound, and to which the State Constitutions should be made to conform. Every State Constitution is a compact made by and between the citizens of a State to govern themselves in a certain manner; and the Constitution of the United States is likewise a compact made by the people of the United States to govern themselves as to general objects in a certain manner. By this great compact, however, many prerogatives were transferred to the National Government, such as those of making war or peace, contracting alliances, coining money, &c.'

In reply to the second inquiry, whether suability is compatible with State sovereignty, he concedes no difference between the right to sue a Corporation and the right to sue a State. 'In this city, (viz., Philadelphia,) there are forty odd thousand free citizens, all of whom may be collectively sued by any individual citizen. In the State of Delaware, there are fifty odd thousand free citizens, and what reason can be assigned why a free citizen, who has demands against them, should not prosecute them? Can the difference between forty odd thousand and fifty odd thousand make any distinction as to right? Will it be said that the fifty odd thousand citizens in Delaware, being associated under a State Government, stand in a rank so superior to the forty odd thousand of Philadelphia, associated under their charter, that although it may become the latter to meet an individual on an equal footing in a Court of Justice, yet that such a procedure would not comport with the dignity of the former? In this land of equal liberty, shall forty odd thousand in one place be compelled to do justice, and yet fifty odd thousand in another place be privileged to do justice only as they may think proper?'

To the third inquiry, whether the Constitution authorizes the present action, he finds no difficulty, either in the design of the Constitution, or the letter and express declarations of it.

This decision of the Supreme Court caused great alarm.

It was regarded as touching, in a fundamental point, the rights of the States. At the very next session of Congress, an amendment of the Constitution was proposed, and subsequently ratified, declaring that the judicial power of the United States should not extend to suits against a State by a citizen of another or a foreign State.

In May of this year, the Chief Justice held a Circuit at Richmond, in Virginia. He went thither, it would seem, for a special purpose. The convulsions of Europe could not fail to agitate this country. France had been our ally; England, our unnatural enemy. Friendship was retained for the former, and enmity for the latter. War was now raging. England, Austria, Prussia, the United Netherlands, and Sardinia were arrayed on the one side, and France, drunk with blood, and ruled by Terror, on the other. With what sentiments Jay viewed the awful drama now enacting, and how far he sympathised with the promoters and actors of the French Revolution, is worthy of observation. In the Revolution which overthrew the despotic Government of France, he cordially rejoiced. He approved the Constitution f 1791. He equally disapproved and reprobated the acts of the National Convention. That subsequent Revolution, which, on unhappy France,

'Treble confusion, wrath, and vengeance poured,'

which abolished the newly-established Constitution, and brought the King to the scaffold, excited his utmost abhorrence. 'This revolution had, in my eye,' he says, 'more the appearance of a woe than a blessing. It has caused torrents of blood and of tears, and been marked in its progress by atrocities very injurious to the cause of liberty, and offensive to morality and humanity.' [1]

[1] Jay to Robert Goodloe Harper, January 19th, 1796. Writings of Jay, p. 261.

Nevertheless, the 'magic force' of Burke's book [1] did not cheat his reason, nor was his mind 'in sweet madness robbed of itself.' The dictation of a Government to France, by the combined powers of Europe, was 'an interference,' he said, 'not to be submitted to. I wished success to the Revolution, so far as it had for its object not the disorganizing and managing of other States, which neither ought to be attempted nor permitted, but the exclusive ordering of all internal affairs, and the establishment of any constitution which the nation should prefer.' [2]

On the execution of the King, it was perceived that a Regency would arise and claim to represent France. It is well known that Washington desired the advice of his Cabinet whether, should the future Regent send a minister to the United States, he ought to be received.[3] Hamilton proposed the same question to Jay. 'If we receive one from the Republic and refuse the other,' he inquired, 'shall we stand on ground perfectly neutral?' [4] 'Mere locality,' said Burke, in arguing this very question as to the real representative of France, 'does not constitute a body politic. . . . . Nation is a moral essence, not a geographical arrangement or a denomination of the nomenclator. France, though out of her territorial possessions, exists; because the sole possible claimant, I mean the proprietary and the government to which the proprietary adheres, exists and claims. . . . The regicides in France are not France. France is out of her bounds, but the kingdom is the same.' [5] On this ground, Pitt refused to treat with Bonaparte, when, as first Consul,

[1] Reflections on the Revolution in France.

[2] Ibid: Writings of Jay, p. 261.

[3] Writings of Washington, vol. x., pp. 533, 534.

[4] Hamilton to Jay, April 9th, 1793. Writings of Jay, p. 298.

[5] Letters on a Regicide Peace: Burke's Works, vol. ii., pp. 243, 244. Harper's edition, 1849.

he proffered peace. 'Restore the Bourbons,' was his arrogant reply to the pacific overtures he then received. Jay's judgment on the question proposed to him by Hamilton was in accordance with what is now deemed the true doctrine of international law. 'I would not receive any minister from a Regent,' he said, 'until he was Regent *de facto*.' [1]

Genet, the minister plenipotentiary to the United States from the French Republic, arrived in this country in the spring of 1793, and was received. On the 22d of April, Washington issued his proclamation, declaring it the duty and interest of the United States, with sincerity and good faith, to 'adopt and pursue a conduct friendly and impartial towards the belligerent powers.' 'I have given instructions to those officers to whom it belongs,' said the President, 'to cause prosecutions to be instituted against all persons who shall within the cognizance of the Courts of the United States violate the law of nations with respect to the powers at war, or any of them.' This proclamation gave great dissatisfaction. There was a strong sympathy felt in this country for France. Genet contended that the treaty of alliance bound the United States to join in the war. His instructions authorized a course of conduct on his part which was directly calculated to involve them in it, *nolens volens*. He issued naval and military commissions, and gave orders for fitting out and arming privateers. Gideon Henfield, a citizen of the United States, sailed, in quality of an officer, in one of these privateers, which brought into Philadelphia a British vessel, taken as prize.

It was with reference to this case, and the class of cases to which it belonged, that the Chief Justice prepared the charge which he delivered to the Grand Jury, impannelled for the Court of the United States, holden

---

[1] Jay to Hamilton, April 11th, 1793. Writings of Jay, p. 300.

at the Capitol, in the city of Richmond, on the 22d of May, 1793. It was printed by the Government for the purpose of explaining abroad the position of the United States. Its leading doctrine, that the federal judiciary, independently of any act of Congress, 'defining and punishing offences against the laws of nations,' have jurisdiction of an offence against those laws, and may proceed to punish the offender according to the forms of the common law, has since been abandoned as untenable. After various observations on the rights and duties of neutral and belligerent nations, the Chief Justice thus stated to the Grand Jury the result of his inquiries: 'That the United States are in a state of neutrality relative to all the powers at war, and that it is their duty, their interest, and their disposition to maintain it; that, therefore, they who commit, aid, or abet hostilities against these powers, or either of them, offended against the laws of the United States, and ought to be punished; and consequently it is your duty, gentlemen, to inquire into and present all such offences as you shall find to have been committed within this district.'[1]

---

[1] The prosecution of Henfield, in accordance with the doctrines laid down by the Chief Justice, raised a great clamor. 'It was universally asked' (viz. by the Democratic papers,) says C. J. Marshall, 'what law had been offended, and under what statute was the indictment supported? Were the American people already prepared to give to a proclamation the force of a legislative act, and to subject themselves to the will of the Executive? But if they were already sunk to such a state of degradation, were they to be punished for violating a proclamation which had not been published when the offence was committed, if indeed it could be termed an offence to engage with France, combating for liberty against the combined despots of Europe?' Life of Washington, vol. ii., pp. 273, 274.

Mr. Wharton, after referring to the opinions, upon this subject, of Judges Wilson and Iredell, Edmund Randolph, Mr. Jefferson, and Chief Justice Marshall, makes the following well-considered remarks: 'By none of these is there the least intimation of a doubt as to the jurisdiction of the Court; and when the character of the men themselves is

At the April session of the Circuit Court in 1794, for the Pennsylvania district, the Chief Justice again applied the doctrine that the Federal Courts have a common-law jurisdiction in criminal cases. Ravara, a consul of Genoa, had been indicted for a misdemeanor in sending anonymous and threatening letters to Hammond the British minister, Holland a citizen of Philadelphia, and several other persons, with a view to extort money. It was argued that the offence committed was not an offence at common law, nor made so by any positive law of the United States; but the Court found the defendant guilty, the offence being held indictable at common law.[1]

The last session of the Supreme Court at which Jay presided was held in February, 1794. The case of *Georgia* v. *Brailsford*,[2] which had been pending for several years, was now finally disposed of. The question involved was, whether the property of a certain bond belonged to Brailsford or Georgia. Brailsford was a British subject, residing in Great Britain. The bond was executed to him by Kensall and Spalding, citizens of Georgia. Georgia claimed the property of the bond by virtue of her confiscation act, which sequestered to the

---

recollected—the sound, wary, experienced judgment of Chief Justice Jay—the singular sagacity of Mr. Jefferson in every branch of our system, and his peculiar sensitiveness to judicial encroachments, and the excellent capacity and long experience of Judge Iredell, Judge Wilson, and Judge Peters—it cannot now be said that the jurisdiction was assumed inconsiderately or acquiesced in blindly. It undoubtedly was exercised because the united opinion of the day required its exercise.[1] It was exercised in conformity with the opinion announced by Washington in his proclamation of neutrality, a paper unanimously adopted by the Cabinet as a correct exposition to foreign States of the Federal Government, that the Federal Government, in such cases, could, through its Courts, punish the offender.' Wharton's State Trials, p. 88, note.

[1] U. S. *v.* Ravara, 2 Dallas, p. 297.

[2] 2 Dallas, pp. 403, 415. 3 Dallas, 1.

[1] Mr. Wharton doubtless means the united opinion of the *leading men* of the day.

State all debts, dues, and demands, due or owing to merchants or others residing in Great Britain. To determine this question, an amicable action was entered and tried at the bar of the Supreme Court at this term. The verdict was in favor of Brailsford. The charge of the Chief Justice to the jury is curious, from the opinions he expressed as to the extent of their powers. His statement of the law on that point was clearly erroneous. 'This cause,' he said, 'has been regarded as of great importance; and doubtless it is so. It has accordingly been treated by the Counsel with great learning, diligence, and ability; and on your part it has been heard with particular attention. It is, therefore, unnecessary for me to follow the investigation over the extensive field into which it has been carried: you are now, if ever you can be, completely possessed of the merits of the cause. . . . We are of opinion that the debts due to Brailsford, a British subject residing in Great Britain, were, by the statute of Georgia, subjected, not to confiscation, but only to sequestration; and, therefore, that his right to recover them revived at the peace, both by the law of nations and the treaty of peace. . . It may not be amiss here, gentlemen, to remind you of the good old rule, that on questions of fact it is the province of the jury, on questions of law, it is the province of the Court, to decide. But it must be observed, that, by the same law which recognizes this reasonable distribution of jurisdiction, you have, nevertheless, a right to take upon yourselves to judge of both, and to determine the law as well as the fact in controversy. On this, and on every other occasion, however, we have no doubt you will pay that respect which is due to the opinion of the Court; for, as on the one hand it is presumed that juries are the best judges of facts, it is, on the other hand, presumable that the Court are the best judges of law. But still both objects are lawfully within your power of decision.

While the Chief Justice was at Philadelphia holding the April session of the Circuit Court, he was nominated and confirmed as envoy extraordinary to England. The circumstances attending this appointment will be considered in the following chapter. Without vacating his seat on the bench, Jay went to England, negotiated the treaty which has since borne his name, and returned to this country in the spring of the following year. Having in the meantime been elected Governor of New York, he resigned the Chief-Justiceship, and thus closed his judicial career.

We omitted to mention, in the order of time, an interesting event in the life of Jay, to which we shall now briefly recur. At the April election, in the year 1792, he was a candidate for Governor of New York. His competitor was George Clinton, who had held the office, under successive re-elections, since the year 1777. Clinton's conspicuous position in the politics of New York during a long and interesting period, will justify a moment's survey of his character and career. He was Jay's senior by six years. He was bred to the bar, but it was not in the walks of his profession that he rose to distinction. He was made, as Burke says of his son, 'a public creature.' He served as a subaltern in the French and Indian war, and, at the age of twenty-nine, was elected a member of the Colonial Assembly. With Philip Schuyler for his coadjutor, he uniformly opposed every attempt of the Royal party to infringe the real or supposed rights of the colony. He was a member of the Congress of '75, and, though not particularly distinguished in that body, he was known as the advocate of vigorous measures. He was appointed a Brigadier-General in the Continental service, and approved himself a valuable officer. In June, 1777, he was elected Governor of New York, and continued in that office for the long period of eighteen years. He was unanimously chosen President of the Convention which assembled at Poughkeepsie in 1788, to deliberate on the Federal Constitution. It is well known that he was one of the most earnest and inflexible opponents of that instrument. In 1801 he was again elected Governor of New York. He continued in that office three years, and was then elevated to the Vice-Presidency of the United States. This position he retained until his death, which occurred at Washington, in 1812. Such are the outlines of his public life.

Clinton had clear, distinct views, and plain, good sense. His intellectual qualities were of a solid, rather than of a shining order. He had great energy and decision of character, a firm, intrepid spirit, and patriotic views. He was frank in his manners, amiable in disposition, but withal a good hater. He possessed the spirit of popularity, a power over the popular will and affections surpassed by no man who has ever lived in the State of which he was so eminent a citizen. He sprung from the people, and was of them. He rose to distinction without the adventitious aids of wealth or family. His sympathies were quick and strong. His heart was open 'to the genial impulses of nature and truth.' Though distinguished for directness and simplicity of character, he had great tact. Cautious and circumspect, he seldom was betrayed by irritation. Clinton was a democrat, not merely professedly and theoretically, but radically, in substance and grain. He preferred 'the convulsive struggles of anarchy' to 'the slow poison of despotism.' To the Republican party he was a tower of strength.

It was deemed of great importance, at this time, by the friends 'to national and good government,' as they styled themselves, or in other words, by the Federalists, to defeat his election. To accomplish that object, it was essential to select a candidate who possessed the requisites of fitness and popularity. The judicial position of Jay seemed to preclude the general wish of his friends that he would accept the nomination. He was nevertheless applied to, and declined. But on further consideration, he yielded to the earnest and pressing solicitations of his friends, and consented to be a candidate.[1] It was unfortunate thus to bring the judiciary into the arena of politics, and weaken its hold upon the confidence and homage of the people. But at that day it was not deemed improper for a judge to engage in the conflicts of party, nor to hold, at the same time, a civil and judicial office.

The election was conducted with equal zeal and bitterness. The private character of the chief-justice afforded no mark for the shafts of malice, and escaped assault. But his political opinions were unsparingly assailed. His views respecting slavery were exaggerated and misrepresented. It was said that he desired to rob every Dutchman of the property most dear to his heart, viz. his slaves. Not only that, but he wished further to compel them to educate the children of those slaves, although they might be unable to educate their own. In reply to a friend, who informed him of this election tale, he acknowledged himself an advocate of manumission, but in such mode as should be consistent with the actual state of society, and with the justice due both to the slave and master. 'These considerations,' he added, 'unite in convincing me that the abolition of slavery must necessarily be gradual.[2]

Jay's early friend and law-partner, Chancellor Livingston, was now found among his most influential opponents. The Chancellor changed his politics in 1790. It has been said, that chagrin at not receiving the appointment conferred upon Jay, was the real cause of this

---

[1] He was nominated on the 13th Feb., 1792, at a meeting of his friends in New York. Stephen Van Rensselaer was at the same time nominated for Lieutenant-Governor.

[2] Life of J. Jay, p. 285. Ante, pp. 215–220.

abandonment of his party.[1] Livingston had great powers of eloquence, brilliant talents, and fascinating manners:

> ———— 'he seem'd
> For dignity composed and high exploit.'

What he lacked was sincere, intellectual culture, the 'soul supreme,' the firm mind, that abides, unchanged, the neglect of friends, and the injustice of enemies. He had acute sensibilities, and an exaggeration of morbid feeling. Adhering to the republican party, he defended its principles and policy, with an energy, and to an extent, that affixed to him, and the aspiring and influential family of which he was the head, the sinister motto:

> ———— Rem, facias rem,
> Si possis recte, si non, quoque modo, rem.[2]

Jay left the State before the election commenced, to hold the Eastern Circuit, and did not return until several weeks after it was determined. He received a majority of the votes, but his competitor was declared the successful candidate. This needs explanation. In the first place, the body who counted the votes, and declared the result of an election in New York, for Governor, Lieutenant-Governor, and Senators, was composed of a joint committee of the two houses of the Legislature. Their decision was final and conclusive. Secondly, the law required the votes of the electors in each town to be delivered to the sheriffs of their respective counties, whose duty it was to transmit them, in a sealed box, to the Secretary of State. Upon examining the votes in this

---

[1] Hammond's Political History of New York, vol. i., p. 107.

[2] Wharton's State Trials, p. 47. Notwithstanding Livingston's withdrawal from the Federal party, Washington tendered him the mission to France upon the recall of Gouverneur Morris, in 1794. Writings of Washington, vol. x., p. 406.

instance, the committee differed in opinion as to whether they could canvass and allow those returned from the counties of Otsego, Clinton, and Tioga. If allowed, Jay must be declared the successful candidate. But there were informalities in the mode of returning the votes, and a supposed defect of authority in the persons making the return, which induced the canvassers to reject them. The majority for Jay in the county of Otsego was nearly four hundred. But the commission of the person returning the votes from that county, as sheriff, had expired several weeks previously. His successor, however, had not taken possession of the office. The question was, whether he was qualified to act as sheriff. The canvassers requested the opinion of Rufus King and Aaron Burr upon this and other points. King was of opinion that he was legally sheriff of the county at the time the votes were forwarded. If not sheriff *de jure*, he was at all events sheriff *de facto;* and whatever acts he performed in that capacity, which tended to the public utility, were valid. Burr, on the contrary, was of opinion that the Otsego votes ought to be rejected, because the right of a sheriff to hold over was in England created by statute, which was evidence that at common law the right did not exist. In New York there was no such statute, and the common law must govern. The committee of canvassers acted upon the opinion of Burr, rejected the votes of Otsego, as well as the votes of the two other counties, but on other grounds, and declared George Clinton governor.[1]

[1] Memoirs of Aaron Burr, vol. i., p. 366. Hammond's Political History of New York, vol. i., pp. 62–67. 'To my mind,' says Mr. Hammond, 'the reasons assigned by Mr. King and by the minority of the committee in their protest, are strong and convincing. I think Richard R. Smith, if not *de jure*, was *de facto* sheriff, and that his acts as such in this case were valid. It would be preposterous to assume that the law of this state, as it then existed, could have been fairly construed; that whenever from insanity, sudden death, or any other cause, the new

This decision was announced on the 12th of June. The Chief Justice was still on his circuit. 'A Hartford paper which I have just read,' thus he wrote Mrs. Jay, 'mentions the result of the canvass; after hearing how the Otsego votes were circumstanced, I perceived clearly what the event would be. The reflection that the majority of the electors were for me, is a pleasing one; that injustice has taken place does not surprise me, and I hope will not affect you very sensibly. The intelligence found me perfectly prepared for it. Having nothing to reproach myself with in relation to this event, it shall neither discompose my temper nor postpone my sleep.'[1]

Completing his circuit, the Chief Justice returned to New York the latter part of June. He found great exasperation on the part of the citizens, at the decision of the canvassing committee. At many public meetings he was declared to be the rightful governor of the State. He received, at different points on his journey home, strong and flattering proofs of the affection felt for him. His arrival and departure from Albany and Hudson was announced by salvos of artillery. The citizens and military turned out to do him honor. But instead of adding fuel to the flame, instead of still further exciting the exasperated and indignant feelings of his friends, he poured oil on the troubled waters. He counselled moderation and forbearance. The decision of the canvassing

sheriff, after he received his commission, did not qualify himself to discharge the duties of his office by the very day the term of office of the old sheriff expired, that in such case the county was without a sheriff. That no such construction had been recognized, is proved by the fact that the settled usage and practice had long been that the old sheriff held until the new one actually took possession of the office.' See to the same effect, Life of J. Jay, p. 287, 288.

[1] Life of J. Jay, p. 289. 'A few years,' he adds, 'will put us all in the dust, and it will then be of more importance to me to have governed myself than to have governed the State.'

committee might be unjust, but the law declared it to be final, and they were bound to submit. In reply to an address presented to him by a committee of the citizens of New York, he used this commendable language: 'They who do what they have a right to do, give no just cause of offence; and, therefore, every consideration of propriety forbids that difference of opinion respecting candidates should suspend or interrupt the mutual good-humor and benevolence which harmonize society, and soften the asperities of human life and human affairs.' The result was, that Clinton was sworn into office, and the government proceeded without interruption.[1]

At this period of his life, Jay enjoyed an enviable popularity. He was an object of affection and confidence to a great portion of his countrymen. His character was universally esteemed. But in this 'high and palmy state' of his greatness, he negotiated a treaty, 'which excited the insolent rage of France, without a color of justice,'[2] and prostrated at a blow his well-earned popularity. But when the passions of the hour had passed away, when living feelings and living griefs were extinguished in the grave, resentful and cotemporary judgment was reversed; and, however men differed as to the wisdom of his negotiation, none doubted the purity of his intentions. 'The test of greatness is the page of history.'

---

[1] Life of J. Jay, p. 293, 294.

[2] Adams's Works, vol. iii., p. 265, 266.

CHAPTER XV.

JAY'S TREATY.

1794—1795.

THE year 1794 opened with the imminent prospect of another war with England. The resentment engendered against that country by the revolutionary struggle, and the enthusiasm for France, notwithstanding the excesses of her revolution, still possessed the minds of the great body of the people. The former spirit was fostered and inflamed by the inexecution of the treaty respecting the posts and negroes, and more recently by violations of our neutral rights and commercial interests. 'I do not believe that Great Britain intends to force us into a war,' wrote Fisher Ames, the 25th of February; 'but she intends to make our neutrality unpleasant to our feelings and unprofitable to our navigation, &c.; and in doing this, she probably cares little whether it is war or peace. Our gallicism hurts her pride, and she is heated enough to punish all the friends of her foes.' [1]

The posture of affairs seemed to offer but a single alternative, either to declare war for existing causes, which certainly were many and cogent, or first seek to

[1] Ames to Christopher Gore. Works of Ames, vol. i., p. 135. Several weeks later, John Adams thus wrote to Mrs. Adams: 'We are ill-treated by Britain, and you and I know it is owing to a national insolence against us. If they force us into a war, it is my firm faith that they will be chastised for it a second time, worse than the first.' Letters of John Adams, vol. ii., p. 157. April 19th, 1794.

remove them by negotiation. Washington determined on the latter course. 'Peace,' he said, 'ought to be pursued with unremitted zeal, before the last resource which has so often been the scourge of nations, and cannot fail to check the advanced prosperity of the United States, is contemplated.'[1] He also determined to send to London a special minister, as corresponding with the solemnity of the occasion, and evincing to the world a solicitude for a friendly adjustment, and a reluctance to hostility. Our resident minister at London was Mr. Thomas Pinckney of South Carolina. He was a courteous, unaffected gentleman, slight of person, reserved in manner, and inclined to taciturnity. His character was excellent, and his understanding good. He was supposed to entertain prejudices against England and partialities for France, which gave him less weight at the Court of St. James than he might otherwise have had. This circumstance was doubtless an additional motive with the administration for entrusting the negotiation to a special envoy. 'Mr. Pinckney,' thus wrote Fisher Ames, the intimate friend of Hamilton, and familiar with the views and wishes of the government, 'is evidently sour, and also gallican. Here the man is void of moderation and prudence.[2] The cross-fire of their accounts is enough to raise a quarrel. Our man has the most coolness, undoubtedly. But it is lamentable that the true history of events should be given by men under such prejudices. . . . On looking over the page, I see that I use too strong expressions respecting Mr. Pinckney; he is a sober, calm man, and will not irritate; but he has prejudices, and unless a man has a mind above them, he can do little service there.'[3]

---

[1] Writings of Washington, vol. x., p. 404.

[2] Hammond, the English minister, 'of all petulant, imprudent men, the most so.'

[3] Ames to Christopher Gore, March 5, 1794. Works of Fisher Ames, vol. i., p. 137.

The party hostile to the administration were strongly opposed to the mission, and still more averse to its being entrusted to Hamilton, the President's favorite counsellor. Undoubtedly the first choice of Washington fell on that gentleman. He had the utmost confidence in his abilities, information, prudence, and discretion. The supporters of his administration shared that preference. 'Who but Hamilton,' wrote Ames, 'would perfectly satisfy all our wishes?'[1] Hamilton himself recommended Jay. 'Of the persons whom you would deem free from any constitutional objections,' he wrote the President, 'Mr. Jay is the only man in whose qualifications for success there would be thorough confidence, and him whom alone it would be advisable to send.'[2] Acting on this advice, which the clamor against Hamilton rendered eminently judicious, Washington nominated Jay to the Senate on the 16th of April. 'Senate has been three days in debate,' wrote the Vice-President on the 19th, 'upon the appointment of Mr. Jay to go to London. It has this day been determined in his favor, eighteen versus eight. You cannot imagine what horror some persons are in, lest peace should continue. The prospect of peace throws them into distress. . . . The opposition to Mr. Jay has been quickened by motives which always influence everything in an elective government. Pretexts are never wanting to ingenious men, but the views of all the principal parties are always directed to the election of the first magistrate. If Jay should succeed, it will recommend him to the choice of the people for President, as soon as a vacancy shall happen. This will weaken the hopes of the Southern

[1] Ames to Christopher Gore, March 26th. Works of Fisher Ames, vol. i., p. 139, 140.

[2] Works of Hamilton, vol. iv., p. 519, 531. April 14th, 1794. As to the clamors against Hamilton, vide Writings of Washington, vol. x., p. 399, 557.

States for Jefferson. This I believe to be the secret motive of the opposition to him, though other things were alleged as ostensible reasons; such as, his monarchical principles, his indifference about the navigation of the Mississippi, his attachment to England, his aversion to France, none of which are well founded, and his holding the office of Chief Justice, &c.'[1]

Adams, Jay, and Jefferson, were at this time prominent in the public eye, as successor to Washington. If Jay should negotiate a treaty that commended itself to the sober part of the community, it would be a new title to the public confidence. But everybody foresaw, that, no matter how favorable might be the issue of his negotiation, it would not escape assault; while, if it should prove liable to serious objection in any of its features, the popular denunciation would be unmeasured. Jay accepted the commission with reluctance, and from a sense of duty. 'Nothing can be much more distant,' he wrote Mrs. Jay, the day before his nomination to the Senate, 'from every wish on my own account. . . . This is not of my seeking; on the contrary, I regard it as a measure, not to be desired, but to be submitted to.' 'No appointment,' he again wrote, 'ever operated more unpleasantly upon me; but the public considerations which were urged, and the manner in which it was pressed, strongly impressed me with a conviction that to refuse it would be to desert my duty for the sake of my ease and domestic concerns and comforts.'[2]

The French government, having requested the recall of Gouverneur Morris, it occurred to Washington that this would be a good opportunity to make a change in the Legation at London. Accordingly, he wrote Jay on

---

[1] Letter to Mrs. Adams, April 19th, 1795. Letters of John Adams, vol. ii., p. 156.

[2] Letters to Mrs. Jay, of April 15th and 19th. Life of Jay, p. 310, 311.

the 29th inst., and after stating the necessity of recalling Morris, and the difficulties that occurred in finding a successor, he says: 'These considerations have induced me to ask you, if it could be made to comport with your inclination, after you shall have finished your business as Envoy, and not before, to become the resident Minister Plenipotentiary at London, that Mr. Pinckney, by that means, might be sent to Paris.'[1] In his reply of the next day, Jay said: 'There is nothing I more ardently wish for than retirement, and leisure to attend to my books and papers; but, parental duties not permitting it, I must acquiesce and thank God for the many blessings I enjoy. If the judiciary was on its proper footing, there is no public station that I should prefer to the one in which you have placed me. It accords with my turn of mind, my education, and my habits. I expect to sail in the course of a fortnight, and if my prayers and endeavors avail, my absence will not be of long duration.'[2]

Jay embarked at New York on the 12th of May, in presence of a large concourse of the citizens. He arrived at London on the 15th of June. The business of his mission was at once entered upon. Lord Grenville was the negotiator on the part of England.[3] The negotiation

---

[1] Writings of Washington, vol. x., p. 404. [2] Ibid., p. 405.

[3] He was a son of the celebrated George Grenville, and a brother of Thomas Grenville, whom Fox sent to Paris in 1782, with instructions to treat with M. de Vergennes. Ante, p. 331. 'The endowments of his mind,' observes Lord Brougham, 'were all of a useful and commanding sort—sound sense, steady memory, vast industry. His acquirements were in the same proportion valuable and lasting—a thorough acquaintance with business in its principles and in its details; a complete mastery of the science of politics, as well theoretical as practical; of late years a perfect familiarity with political economy, and a just appreciation of its importance; an early and most extensive knowledge of classical literature, which he improved, instead of abandoning, down to the close of his life; a taste formed upon those chaste models, and of which his lighter compositions, his Greek and Latin verses, bore testi-

was conducted in an informal manner, chiefly by personal discussions, nothing being deemed binding that might be suggested or proposed on these occasions. Thus their respective views were elicited, and each could perceive what concessions and propositions would be admitted. 'Formal discussions of disputed points,' wrote Jay to the Secretary of State, 'should, in my judgment, be postponed, until the case becomes desperate; my present object is to accommodate, rather than to convert or convince. Men who sign their names to arguments seldom retract.'

So favorable were the results of this mode of conducting the negotiation, that he was enabled to write Washington on the 5th of August, as follows: 'Our prospects become more and more promising as we advance in the business. . . . A treaty of commerce is on the carpet. . . . The King observed to me the other day, 'Well, Sir, I imagine you begin to see that your mission will probably be successful.'—'I am happy, may it please your Majesty, to find that you entertain that idea.'—'Well, but don't you perceive that it is like to be so?' 'There are some recent circumstances (the answer to my representation, &c.) which induce me to flatter myself that it will be so.' He nodded with a smile, signifying that it was to those circumstances that he alluded.[1]

mony to the last. . . . He was in this greatest quality of a statesman pre-eminently distinguished, that, as he neither would yield up his judgment to the clamor of the people, nor suffer himself to be seduced by the influence of the court, so would he never submit his reason to the empire of prejudice, or own the supremacy of authority or tradition.' Statesmen of the Reign of George III.

It is a little singular, that in the published correspondence of Lord Grenville, during the pendency of his negotiation with Jay, no mention whatever is made of it. Even in writing to his brother Thomas, then British Minister at Vienna, not an allusion to American affairs escapes him. See Court and Cabinets of George III., by the Duke of Buckingham and Chandos.

[1] Jay to Washington, Aug. 5th, 1794. Writings of Jay, p. 220.

On the 19th of November the negotiation was terminated by a treaty. 'The minister flatters himself,' wrote Jay to Oliver Ellsworth, a future Chief Justice of the United States, 'that this treaty will be very acceptable to our country, and that some of the articles in it will be received as unequivocal proofs of good-will. We have industriously united our efforts to remove difficulties, and few men would have persevered in such a dry, perplexing business, with so much patience and temper as he has done.' [1]

The three grand objects contemplated by Jay's mission were—1st, Compensation for negroes carried away. 2d, Surrender of the Western posts. 3d, Compensation for recent spoliations. Peace depended on the adjustment of these three points. That secured, a commercial treaty was important, and contemplated by his instructions. It was stipulated by the treaty of Paris, that his British Majesty should, with all convenient speed, withdraw his armies, garrisons, and fleets from the United States, without 'carrying away any negroes or other property of the American inhabitants.' Negroes captured during the war were not included within the meaning and design of this stipulation. The difficult point was, whether those negroes who had fled to the British on the faith of their proclamations, were in the same predicament. Jay, when Secretary for Foreign Affairs under the Confederation, contended that they were not, but came within the meaning of the stipulation. He was of opinion, however, that the British ought to stand excused for not giving them up, provided they made compensation for them.[2] In this we think he erred; for it would seem obvious that when the enemy obtained possession of the

---

[1] Jay to Ellsworth. Writings of Jay, p. 235.

[2] Secret Journals of Congress, vol. iv., pp. 185–287. Ante, p. 373, note.

negroes, either by capture or by means of their proclamations, they were free to set them at liberty. Having done that, the grant was irrevocable. For, by the law of nations, which in this respect but repeats the law of nature, liberty once granted to a human being cannot be resumed. 'Negroes or other property' is the language of the stipulation; thus putting negroes on the footing of property. Hence, whatever had lost that designation was not included in the stipulation. This was the construction adopted by England. She insisted that the object of this article of the treaty was to secure the American inhabitants from depredation, not to entitle them to the restitution of property lost by the fortune of war. Lord Grenville utterly refused to make any compensation, and Jay waived the claim.[1]

It was agreed that the Western posts should be surrendered on or before the 1st of June, 1796. The federal courts were now open to British creditors, and no impediments existed to the prosecution of their claims. But in consequence of those which had been interposed prior to the establishment of the present government, many debts had been altogether lost from the intervening death, insolvency, &c., of the debtors. In these cases the British government claimed reparation, and it was

---

[1] The number of negroes carried away was about 3000.

'It is a fact,' said Hamilton, writing as Camillus, 'which I assert on the best authority, that our Envoy made every effort in his power to establish our construction of the article relating to this subject, and to obtain compensation; and that he did not relinquish it till he became convinced that to insist upon it would defeat the purpose of his mission, and leave the controversy between the two countries unsettled.' Hamilton's Works, vol. vii., p. 208.

'It cannot admit of a serious doubt, that the affair of the negroes was too questionable in point of right, too insignificant in point of interest, to have been suffered to be an impediment to the immense objects which were to be promoted by an accommodation of differences acceptable in other respects.' Ibid.

agreed that commissioners should be appointed to award compensation for such losses as could not be repaired in the ordinary course of justice. Jay urged, but could not procure, indemnification for the detention of the posts. This was made a serious objection to the treaty. But the English view of the question, and the ministry would adopt none other, was this, viz., that the posts were detained because the United States had not fulfilled the treaty respecting British debts, and hence they could not, with any pretence of right, demand indemnification for damages sustained, in consequence of their own acts. It was not a case, they said, of mutual injury, where there should be mutual compensation, but a case where the first injury caused and justified the second.

In violation of our neutral rights, in contempt of justice, and the opinion of the civilized world, Great Britain had made numerous seizures of American vessels and cargoes, not because they were amenable to capture by the law of nations, which, however, she pretended, but in consequence of a series of British Orders in Council.[1] To obtain compensation for these spoliations was a principal object of Jay's mission. It was anticipated that this would prove a difficult point in the negotiation. For

---

[1] By one of these orders, issued the 8th of June, 1793, all vessels carrying grain or flour to France, or to ports occupied by French troops, were directed to be captured, and sent into a British port, the cargoes being purchased for the government, unless security was given that they should be landed in a country at peace with England. By another, issued the 6th of November following, all vessels carrying supplies to any French colony, or laden with its produce, were directed to be captured. How far provisions are contraband of war, see Kent's Comm., vol. i., pp. 136, 137, 140. By Jay's Treaty, it was admitted that provisions were not generally contraband, but might become so according to the existing law of nations, in certain cases, and those cases were not defined. Whenever deemed contraband, the captors were to pay the owner the full value of the articles, with freight, and a reasonable profit.

if compensation was allowed, it was an admission on the part of Great Britain, that she had knowingly violated the law of nations. The result was attained, but in a manner not to arouse her pride. Commissioners were to be appointed, to decide, according to equity, justice, and the law of nations, upon claims relating to captures of American vessels and property, under color of authority and commissions derived from the King, and for which redress could not be obtained in the English courts.[1]

The commercial branch of the treaty was open to serious objections. They occurred to Jay; but as he conceived that no better terms could be procured, and as those proposed offered advantages of which, in the absence of a treaty, the United States could not avail themselves, he concluded to accept them. It was undoubtedly within the competency of Great Britain to admit or exclude the United States from a participation in her colonial trade. If she admitted them, she had an unquestionable right to prescribe the conditions of such admission.

Jay was precluded from signing any treaty of commerce that did secure to the United States the West India trade. He finally agreed to an article which admitted into the West India ports American vessels of seventy tons burden, on condition that the cargoes taken should be landed in the United States, and that no molasses, sugar, coffee, cocoa, or cotton, should be shipped from the United States to any other part of the world. The duration of this article was limited to two years after the termination of the existing war. The *quid pro quo*, in this instance, was out of all proportion to the privilege granted. A fact, unknown to Jay, raised an insuperable objection to this article. Cotton, hitherto only produced in quantities barely sufficient for domestic consumption, was fast be-

[1] The amount recovered in consequence of this provision of the treaty was ten millions, three hundred and forty-five thousand dollars.

coming one of the most valuable staples of the Southern States. To inhibit its exportation, not only during the present war, which might be prolonged indefinitely, but two years after, was wholly inadmissible. The Senate, it is well known, consented to the ratification of the treaty on condition that the part relating to the intercourse with the West Indies should be suspended.[1]

Jay remained in England until the following spring. He was treated with marked consideration. We suspect the personal attentions that were lavished upon him, deceived him as to the friendly feelings really entertained in that country towards this. 'The best disposition towards us prevails here,' he wrote, 'and the indications and proofs of it daily increase. . . . It may seem strange, and yet I am convinced, that next to the King, our President is more popular in this country than any man in it.'[2] 'I would not have my son go so far as Mr. Jay,' said John Adams, 'and affirm the friendly disposition of that country to this. I know better. I know their jealousy, envy, hatred, and revenge, covered under pretended contempt.'[3]

On the 28th of May, 1795, Jay arrived at New York. As on his departure, so on his return, the citizens turned

---

[1] Jay thus wrote Washington respecting this article of the treaty: 'It breaks the ice, that is, it breaks in upon the navigation act. The least stream from a mass of water passing through a bank will enlarge its passage. The very article stipulates that the arrangements to succeed it shall have in view the further extension of commerce. — March 6th, 1795. Writings of Jay, p. 245, 252. Objections were not only made to the terms of the commercial articles, but it was said that no treaty whatever should have been made. 'The difficulty is not to overcome the objections to the terms,' said Fisher Ames in his celebrated speech; 'it is to restrain the repugnance to any stipulations of amity with the party.' Works of Fisher Ames, vol. ii., p. 37.

[2] Jay to Tench Coxe, Dec. 18th, 1794. Writings of Jay, p. 240.

[3] Letter to Mrs. Adams, April 9th, 1796. Adams's Letters, vol. ii., p. 216.

out in large numbers, to testify their attachment and respect. He was attended to his dwelling by a numerous concourse, amid the ringing of bells and firing of cannon. Having been elected governor of New York, as we have mentioned in the preceding chapter, he resigned his seat on the bench. Although he anticipated that his treaty would be the object of attack, and give occasion to much declamation, he could not foresee the storm of opposition that it encountered. Washington resolved to ratify it, if approved by the Senate. It was submitted to that body on the 8th of June. 'Mr. Jay is in fine spirits,' wrote John Adams on the 14th, 'and his health improves.'[1] On the 24th, the Senate advised the President to ratify the treaty, with the exception of the article relating to the West India trade. As yet its contents were unknown to the public. But on the 24th of June, one of the Virginia Senators sent a copy of it to a printer in Philadelphia, who published it on the 2d of July.[2] The tocsin was immediately sounded. There was a universal tumult, alarm, and uproar. 'The fury of litigious war blew her horn on the mountains.' 'Everything above ground, and everything under ground, was in arms.' The treaty and its negotiator were denounced in terms of unmeasured bitterness. The fires of popular fury were enkindled and inflamed by every appeal that could arouse the pride, the prejudice, or the interests of the people. Even sober men, and supporters of the administration, were carried away by the ferment and excitement. 'Jefferson's party,' wrote Fisher Ames, 'seize the moment to discredit their most dreaded rival, Jay.'[3] The President's delay in the ratification doubtless increased the violence and extravagance of the opposition.

[1] Letter to Mrs. Adams. Letters of Adams, vol. ii., p. 182.

[2] James S. Mason was the Senator, and the Aurora the newspaper.

[3] Ames to Dwight, Aug. 24th, 1794. Works of Fisher Ames, vol. i., p. 171.

The treaty certainly, in several of its features, was objectionable. Nobody pretended to give to it unqualified approbation. But it was the best that could be obtained. That, we think, is demonstrated by the result of all subsequent negotiations with Great Britain during a period of nearly fifty years. And the alternative was, the treaty or war. Who can doubt that Washington decided judiciously in ratifying it? Jay could not fail to perceive that the unmeasured attacks on himself and his treaty, would, naturally enough, impair, with the contemporary age, his well-earned reputation. Nevertheless, he reposed with unshaken confidence upon the rectitude of his intentions, and the ultimate judgment of his countrymen. He preserved his equanimity. 'The approbation of one judicious and virtuous man,' he said, 'relative to the conduct of the negotiations in which I was lately engaged, affords me more satisfaction, than all the clamors raised on that subject, by intrigue and passion, have given me concern.'[1]

If Jay's treaty was attacked with uncommon zeal and bitterness, it was defended with unsurpassed eloquence and ability. The series of papers published by Hamilton, under the signature of Camillus, extorted even the admiration of his foes. They are remarkable for force of argument, precision, and felicity of style, and judicious arrangement of topics.[2] The speech of Fisher Ames in the House of Representatives, urging the passage of the laws necessary to give effect to the treaty, has seldom, if ever, been equalled, in the impression made upon an audience. It appealed to the judgment, and it commanded the homage of the heart. Few of his auditors

---

[1] Letter to Rev. Dr. Thatcher, May 26th, 1796. Writings of Jay, p. 270.

[2] They are included in the Works of Hamilton, vol. vii., pp. 172-528.

could restrain their tears. 'He was attended to with a silence and interest never before known,' wrote the Vice-President, 'and he made an impression that terrified the hardiest, and will never be forgotten. Judge Iredell and I happened to sit together. Our feelings beat in unison. 'My God! how great he is,' says Iredell, 'how great he has been!' 'He has been noble,' said I. After some time Iredell breaks out, 'Bless my stars, I never heard anything so great since I was born!' 'It is divine,' said I; and thus we went on with our interjections, not to say tears, till the end. Tears enough were shed. Not a dry eye, I believe, in the House, except some of the jackasses who had occasioned the necessity of the oratory. These attempted to laugh, but their visages 'grinned horribly ghastly smiles.'[1]

A single extract from that justly-admired speech will close this chapter. 'The honor of the United States was saved, not forfeited by treating. The treaty itself, by its stipulations for the posts, for indemnity, and for a due observation of our neutral rights, has justly raised the character of the nation.'

---

[1] Letters of John Adams, April 30th, 1796, vol. ii., p. 225, 226. The speech was delivered on the 28th. Mr. Ames was very feeble, and scarcely able to stand, but his health from this time improved.

CHAPTER XVI.

GOVERNOR OF NEW YORK.

1795—1801.

THE result of the last State election, one candidate receiving a majority of the votes for governor, and the other, nevertheless, filling the post, produced, as we have seen, great excitement and exasperation.[1] A very natural desire was entertained to repair the injustice Jay was supposed to have suffered on that occasion. As the time for the next election approached, meetings were held in various parts of the State, at which he was again brought forward as a candidate. He was in England, and it appears that his friends put him in nomination without his knowledge or consent. However, as he yielded to their wishes at the previous election, they were warranted in supposing that he would do no less at the ensuing one.

His former competitor, governor Clinton, declined a re-election. His present one was Chief Justice Yates. Jay was elected by a large majority. The result was officially declared on the 26th of May. On the 28th, Jay arrived at New York. We have seen how cordially he was received.[2] Scarce one 'little month' elapsed, before from among the same population that had vied with each other to do him honor, were found those who heaped upon him the most unmerited abuse. He was burnt in effigy, his character traduced, and his motives impeached The outcry that followed on the publication of his treaty

[1] Ante, p. 399, 400. [2] Ante, p. 412.

was not a favorable omen for the tranquillity of his administration.

One of the first of his official acts was, to recommend a day of public thanksgiving, in consequence of the recent cessation of the yellow fever in the city of New York. His proclamation, containing this recommendation, did not escape the shafts of malevolence, and distempered party zeal. Wit, ridicule, and even more serious weapons, were employed to assail it. It was invading the province of the clergy, and assuming an authority unwarranted by the Constitution. 'Am I mistaken,' inquired Judge Hobart, in a playful letter to the governor, in which he parodied several of the objections urged against the proclamation, 'or do my glasses magnify too much when I fancy I see the cloven foot of monarchy in this business? Alas! where are the direful effects of this extraordinary envoyship to end? — the benefits of our commerce transferred to Britain — the usurpations of its monarchy transferred to us.' [1]

We do not propose to review all the acts of Governor Jay's administration. The detail would rather fatigue and disgust the reader, than amuse or instruct him. The prominent features of his gubernatorial term alone invite our attention. The Legislature met on the 6th of January, 1796. 'To regard my fellow-citizens with an equal eye,' said the governor in his opening speech, 'to cherish and advance merit wherever found, to consider the National and State governments as being equally established by the will of the people, to respect and support the constituted authorities under each of them; and, in general, to exercise the power vested in me with energy, impartiality, and freedom, are obligations of which I perceive and acknowledge the full force.'

The practice of removing subordinate officers, on a change of administration, had not yet been introduced.

---

[1] Hobart to Jay, Nov. 18th, 1795. Life of Jay, p. 386.

Governor Jay dismissed no officer during the six years of his administration on account of his political opinions. On one occasion he was urged to remove a member of his own party, who had little or no influence, to make room for one of the opposite party, who possessed a great deal, and would, if appointed, use it in favor of his new connections. 'And do you, Sir,' replied the governor to this unusual application, 'advise me to sell a friend that I may buy an enemy?'[1]

He recommended to the Legislature the passage of laws providing for the defence of the State, for the amelioration of the penal code, for the reformation and employment of criminals, and for a retiring pension to the Chancellor and Judges of the Supreme Court. Though Jay was an opponent of a sanguinary code, and successfully urged its abolition, yet when the law affixed a penalty to an offence, he was not disposed to shield an offender from its operation by means of the pardoning power. This branch of his authority he considered as a trust to be executed, 'not according to my will and inclination,' he said, 'but with sound discretion, and on principles which reconcile mercy to offenders with the interests of the public.' No solicitation, however pressing or affecting, or however high the source whence it came, could move him from this line of conduct.

In April, 1798, another election of governor was held. It occurred in the midst of the excitement growing out

[1] Life of Jay, p. 392. Mr. Hammond, in his Political History of New York, (vol. i., p. 127,) a work, so far as I have observed, written with candor, supposes that changes were made, in one or two instances, on political grounds, during Jay's administration. As this supposition, however, is founded on inferences, and not on facts, I can perceive no reason for doubting the accuracy of the statement contained in the text. In filling offices that became vacant, the Governor was quite content with the merit he found in his own party, without making any particular search for it in other directions. At all events, none but Federalists, except, I believe, in one instance, were appointed to office during his term.

of the publication of the despatches from our commissioners to France. The indignities heaped on this country by the Directory, the degrading demand of a sum of money for themselves, and another for the Republic, as the preliminary conditions to a treaty, created universal disgust and indignation among all classes of our people. 'Millions for defence, not a cent for tribute,' was the universal cry. The Federal party added much to its strength in consequence of this feeling. This effect, however, was not very perceptible in New York; for although Jay was elected over Chancellor Livingston, the Republican candidate, and by an increased majority, the opposition succeeded in choosing six out of the ten members of Congress.

Apprehension of war with France, which seemed imminent, induced the Governor to convene the Legislature, in order that measures might be adopted for the defence of the State. The session was opened at Albany on the 2d of August. 'We may be involved in a severe contest,' was the language of the Governor's speech, 'but we have no reason to despair of success. The United States cannot be conquered but by civil discord under foreign dictation; and it is useful to recollect, that to this cause all fallen republics have owed their destruction. History will declare to future ages that the United States were as kind as a neutral nation could with justice be to the republic of France, in the day when her destiny was doubtful: it is to be hoped that history will also declare, that when, in the day of her power, France became tyrannical as well as triumphant, and had indecently required us to descend and take a place among her tributaries, the United States spurned her requisition, and maintained their dignity.'

The Legislature voted an address to the President, pledging the support of New York in his endeavors to maintain the rights and honor of the nation, and made an appropriation, to be expended at the discretion of the Governor, for the defence and fortification of the State.

At the regular session of the Legislature in the following January, the Governor laid before them certain amendments to the Constitution of the United States, which had been proposed by the Legislature of Massachusetts, increasing the disabilities of aliens. Jay was desirous of accomplishing the same object, but, it would appear, in a different mode. 'In my opinion it would be wise to declare explicitly,' thus he wrote Timothy Pickering, 'that the right and privilege of being elected or appointed to, or of holding and exercising any office or place of trust or power under the United States, or under any of them, shall not hereafter be granted to any foreigner; but that the President of the United States, with the consent of the Senate, be nevertheless at liberty to appoint a foreigner to a military office.'[1] At this session, a bill for the gradual abolition of slavery was introduced, and passed into a law. This was the fourth and successful attempt to effect that object.

The third embassy to France, a measure exceedingly distasteful to the leading Federalists, and undertaken by President Adams, against the earnest wishes of the majority of his Cabinet, together with the recent death of Washington, were severe blows to the ascendency of the Federal party. The wisdom of the mission to France was justified by the event; but whether the conduct of the President, in sending it, proceeded from purely disinterested and patriotic views, has elicited much discussion. We have considered the subject in another place.

The decline of the Federal party, and the growth of the Republican, was demonstrated by the result of the election in New York, in April, 1800. Since the com-

[1] Letter to Timothy Pickering, May 13th, 1798. Life of Jay, p. 407.

mencement of his administration, Jay was happy in having a majority of his party friends, in both branches of the Legislature. But, at the recent election, a great change was effected, and the opposition returned a majority of their members to the assembly. As the political year, however, did not expire until the first of July, Hamilton, in order to prevent Jefferson, whom he characterized as 'an atheist in religion, and a fanatic in politics,' from getting possession of the helm of State, advised Jay to convene the existing Legislature, the object being to refer the choice of electors to the people distributed into districts, which would be likely to ensure a majority of votes in the United States for a Federal candidate. Hamilton maintained that this course was justified by unequivocal reasons of public safety, and that there was a very solemn obligation to adopt it. Jay, on the other hand, deemed it a party measure, which he did not think it would become him to sanction. Had the advice of Hamilton been pursued, and the choice of electors referred to the people, instead of being appointed by the Legislature, the defeat of Jefferson would probably have been the result.[1]

On the 4th of November, the new Legislature assembled at Albany. A committee of the Federal members solicited Jay's consent to be a candidate for re-election.

---

[1] In a letter to a Federal committee, who had enclosed to him the copy of a resolution, adopted by the Federal freeholders of New York city, expressive of the sense they entertained of his public services, he thus referred to the recent elections for President in the several States: 'They place us in a new situation,' he said, 'and render it proper for us to consider what our conduct under it should be. I take the liberty, therefore, of suggesting whether the patriotic principles on which we profess to act, do not call upon us to give (as far as may depend upon us) fair and full effect to the known sense and intention of a majority of the people, in every constitutional exercise of their will; and to support every administration of the government of our country which may prove to be intelligent and upright, of whatever party the persons composing it may be.' Jan. 27th, 1801. Life of Jay, p. 422.

But he had determined to renounce public employments, and pass the evening of his day in retirement. 'The period is now nearly arrived,' thus he wrote the committee, 'at which I have for many years intended to retire from the cares of public life, and for which I have been for more than two years preparing; not perceiving, after mature consideration, that any duties require me to postpone it, I shall retire accordingly. But I retain and cherish the warmest affection for my country, as well as the esteem which I entertain for many, and the good-will which I bear to all my fellow-citizens.'[1]

In a little more than a month after thus declaring his intention to withdraw himself from public employments, he was again nominated, and confirmed as Chief Justice of the United States. 'You have now,' wrote the President, communicating to him his appointment, 'a great opportunity to render a most signal service to your country. I therefore pray you most earnestly to consider of it seriously, and accept it.'[2] But the honor thus tendered he at once declined.

His administration, hitherto, had been attended with no disagreeable personal incidents; but the last year of his official term gave rise to a contest with the council of appointment, which was well calculated to disturb and annoy him. The Governor was the President of the Council, and had a casting vote. From the commencement of the government, until the last term of Governor Clinton, the practice had been uniform for the Governor to nominate, and the Council to approve or reject the nomination. But, at that time, the Council claimed and exercised, (in a single instance,) a concurrent right with the Governor to the nomination of officers. Governor Clinton protested against this proceeding, and insisted

[1] To Richard Hatfield, Chairman of Federal Meeting, Nov. 8th, 1800. Life of Jay, p. 419.

[2] Adams to Jay, Dec. 19th, 1800. Ibid., p. 421.

that the Constitution vested in him the exclusive right of nomination. As the question had thus been agitated, Jay, in his first speech to the Legislature, recommended the removal of all doubt and difficulty on the subject, by a declaratory act. Unfortunately, this recommendation was not heeded.

If the Governor possessed the exclusive right of nomination, it was obvious, that notwithstanding the recent triumph of the Republican party, they would not secure the fruits of victory. His nominations would be made from the ranks of his political friends, rather than from those of his political enemies. The new Council met for the first time on the 11th of February. The Governor made eight successive nominations for the office of Sheriff of Duchess county. They were rejected. The Council, after approving several other nominations, adjourned to the 18th instant. On that occasion, Williams, a Republican, was appointed Sheriff of Duchess. On the 24th, the Council again met. An unsuccessful attempt was made to appoint Sheriffs for the counties of Orange and Schoharie. The Governor made several nominations for the former, but they were rejected. De Witt Clinton, who was a member of the Council, then made a nomination. The Governor, without regarding it, nominated another person. The majority of the Council now refused to vote. In this predicament, the Governor desired time for consideration. He addressed a message to the Legislature, stating the difficulties of the case, and asking their directions. They declined to act. He requested the opinion of the Chancellor and Judges of the Supreme Court, but they declined giving it, upon the ground that the subject did not come within the scope of their official duties. Sincerely believing that he was vested by the Constitution with the exclusive right of nomination, and that he could not share it with the Council without violating his oath, he determined not to convene them again.

Accordingly no appointments were made during the remainder of his term.[1]

In May, about six weeks before the expiration of his official period, Jay finally bade adieu to public life, and at the age of fifty-six, 'descended joyfully and serenely into the shades of retirement.' 'He retired from public life, and almost from the world, and passed the remainder of his days at the family estate at West Chester. He took no part in political affairs, and was not publicly heard of, except in two or three instances, when he answered inquiries concerning facts within his knowledge.'[2]

---

[1] Hammond's Political History of New York, vol. i., p. 155–158. Life of Jay, p. 423–425. A convention was subsequently assembled, and it was declared that the right of nomination was equally vested in the Governor and each member of the Council.

[2] Sullivan's Familiar Letters on Public Characters, p. 59.

CHAPTER XVII.

CONCLUSION.

1801—1829.

It will be recollected, that Jay, in his letter to Washington, declining the post of Resident Minister at the Court of St. James, expressed a strong desire to retire from public employments. Parental duties, however, at that time, forbade it.[1] No considerations of that nature now interposed to prevent the fulfilment of his wishes.

His estate at Bedford, which he had inherited from his ancestors, and comprising about eight hundred acres, was situated in a secluded part of West Chester county, fifty miles distant from New York. It had been long neglected, and was hastening to decay. In view of his retirement, he had recently commenced a house, but several months elapsed before it was in a suitable condition to admit of being occupied by his family. Mrs. Jay was in a feeble state of health, and meanwhile remained at Albany. In making repairs and improvements, Jay aimed at durability, rather than ornament. His tastes were simple, and he instinctively shrunk from ostentation. Expensive rural decorations he regarded 'as inconsistent with the state of American society and fortunes, and too often leading to the alienation of the estate itself.' A friend, observing the substantial nature of his buildings, &c., and aware of his religious views and feelings, remarked, that Governor Jay, 'in all his conduct,

[1] Ante, p. 405.

seemed to have reference to perpetuity in this world, and eternity in the next.'

In a few months he was again surrounded by his family. The health of Mrs. Jay was much improved. From the *salons* of European capitals, and the fashionable society of her own country, to the seclusion of Bedford, was indeed a great change. It nevertheless occasioned no regret. 'I can truly say,' she wrote, 'I have never enjoyed so much comfort as I do here.' But this comfort was destined to be of short duration. She had been at Bedford less than a year, when a severe illness, lasting but a few days, terminated in her death. Her sudden and unexpected dissolution was a sad interruption to those pleasing anticipations of 'domestic life in rural leisure passed,' which Mr. Jay had so fondly indulged. Nevertheless, he met this severe stroke with the calmness and fortitude of a Christian. Leading his children from the bedside of their departed mother into an adjoining room, 'with a firm voice but glistening eye,' he read to them the fifteenth chapter of First Corinthians; 'thus leading their thoughts to that day when the lifeless but beloved form they had just left would rise to glory and immortality.'

The death of Mrs. Jay, necessary separation from his children, and vicissitudes in his own health, were calculated to disturb the serenity of his mind; but these interruptions to his happiness were borne with patience and resignation. 'My expectations from retirement have not been disappointed,' thus he wrote at this period; 'and had Mrs. Jay continued with me, I should deem this the most agreeable part of my life. The post, once a week, brings me our newspapers, which furnish a history of the times. By this history, as well as by those of former times, we are taught the vanity of expecting, that from the perfectibility of human nature and the lights of philosophy, the multitude will become virtuous and wise, or their demagogues candid and honest.' 'The burden of time,' he again wrote, 'I have not experienced. Attention to little improvements, occasional visits, the history which my recollections furnish, and frequent conversations with the 'mighty dead,' who, in a certain sense, live in their works, together with the succession of ordinary occurrences, preserve me from *ennui*. . . . Party feuds give me concern; but they seldom obtrude upon me.'

There was but little to vary the uniformity of his life. He was very regular and exact in all his habits. He rose with the sun, had his meals served with punctuality, and passed most of the day in the open air, and on horseback. Family worship was regularly observed, morning and evening, and was neither postponed nor suspended from the presence of company. He usually retired to rest before ten, unless courtesy to his guests induced him to keep later hours. 'I attend every election,' thus he wrote to a friend, 'even for town officers, and having delivered my ballot, return home without having mingled in the crowd or participated in their altercations. . . . The fact is, that I live very much as I have long wished to do. I have a pleasant situation, and very good neighbours. I enjoy peace, and a competency proportionate to my comforts and moderate desires; with such a residue of health as, while it constantly whispers '*memento mori*,' still permits me to see my friends with cheerfulness and pleasure.'

Jay took great interest in the religious movements of his day, was President of several religious societies, and frequently presided at their anniversary meetings. He was a member of the Episcopal church, and sincerely attached to it, both from conviction and habit. He was at the same time catholic towards other sects, and when applied to, as was frequently the case, cheerfully contributed to the expense of erecting their churches. He was without bigotry, either in his head or heart. To the doctrines of the high-church he was thoroughly opposed. 'There never was a time,' he said, 'when those doctrines promoted peace on earth or good-will among men. Originating under the auspices, and in the days of darkness and despotism, they patronized darkness and despotism down to the Reformation.' He was of opinion that these doctrines were not accommodated to the state of society, nor to the tolerant principles, nor to the ardent love of liberty which prevail in our country.

As time advanced, Jay's health wore gradually away; but calm and serene, he glided placidly on towards that ocean, whither most of his contemporaries had already been borne. In 1827, a severe illness prostrated his strength, and gave sure indication that his life had well-nigh reached its period. He survived, however, nearly two years. They were years of debility and suffering. 'For many months before his death, he was unable to walk without assistance. During the day, he passed much of his time in his own room; the evenings were spent with his children and guests, partly in conversation, and partly in listening to books which were read aloud by one of the family. Unable to attend church, he occasionally had the Lord's Supper administered to him in his chamber.'[1]

In the night of the 14th May, 1829, he was seized with palsy. He lingered until the 17th, when his long and distinguished life was closed. His funeral, according to the directions contained in his will, was decent, but not ostentatious. 'No scarfs — no rings,' was the language of that solemn instrument. 'Instead thereof, I give two hundred dollars to any one poor deserving widow or orphan of this town, whom my children shall select.' On the conclusion of the funeral services, his remains were conveyed to the family cemetery at Rye.

Mr. Sullivan, in his agreeable Letters on Public Cha-

---

[1] Life of Jay, p. 418.

racters, thus states his recollection of the personal appearance of Mr. Jay: 'His height,' he says, 'was a little less than six feet; his person rather thin, but well formed. His complexion was without color, his eyes black and penetrating, his nose aquiline, and his chin pointed. His hair came over his forehead, was tied behind, and lightly powdered. His dress black. The expression of his face was exceedingly amiable. When standing, he was a little inclined forward, as is not uncommon with students long accustomed to bend over a table. His manner was very gentle, and unassuming.[1] This impression of him was renewed in 1795, in New York. He had returned from his mission to England in that year, and had been chosen Governor of New York, which office he assumed in July. He was then about fifty, (December, 1795.) His deportment was tranquil and unassuming; and one who had met him, not knowing who he was, would not have been led to suppose that he was in the presence of one eminently gifted by nature with intellectual power, and who had sustained so many offices of high trust and honor.' Except as to the color of his eyes, which were blue, Mr. Sullivan's description is said to be accurate.

Mr. Jay's character is disclosed in the record of his life. His moral and intellectual qualities were in harmony. His public principle commanded the respect of the world. His private virtues attracted the affection and homage of his friends. He was modest, claimed no merit, assumed no importance, and seldom alluded to the great events of his life. He was charitable, not impulsively bestowing his means without discrimination, like Goldsmith's village preacher, whose 'pity gave ere charity began,' but with a judicious selection, and from a sense of duty. His economy was exact, but liberal. 'A wise

[1] Mr. Sullivan speaks of him as he appeared on his first circuit at Boston. His age at that time was forty-four.

man,' he said, 'has money in his head, but not in his heart.' The recipients of his bounty were numerous. He had an elevated sense of justice, and the claims of humanity. His religion was a part of his being, and displayed itself in the uniform tenor of his life. He acted under the habitual conviction of accountability. 'All his serious thoughts had rest in heaven.'[1] His feelings were always under the control of his will, and hence he was never guilty of those extravagances of conduct which too often mar the career of genius. He was tenacious in his friendships, and equally so, we suspect, in his enmities. 'Having once had good cause to doubt a man's sincerity or integrity, he never after trusted him.' His disposition was cheerful, — his conversation equally instructive and entertaining.

The intellectual endowments of Jay are easily described. His mind was vigorous, exact, logical. To genius he could make no pretensions. Judgment, discriminative, penetrating, was the characteristic of his understanding. If over the other faculties of his intellect imagination had presided, the compass of his thought would have been enlarged, and grace and flexibility been imparted to his mind. Jay was not a variously learned man. Modern genius did not delight him. Of the ancients, Cicero was his favorite. The Bible was his constant study. Observing steadily throughout his life, the great principles of justice and rectitude, he 'ascended to the temple of honor through the temple of virtue.'

---

[1] On one occasion Mr. Jay was visited, in his retreat, by a Quaker. On his return home, the disciple of Fox thus wrote to his host: 'I thought while sitting by thee, and about to take my leave, I could with propriety give thee the right hand of fellowship, as one whose attainments in the vitality of religion entitled thee to pre-eminence.' Life of Jay, p. 451.

THE LIFE

OF

JOHN RUTLEDGE.

THE

LIFE OF JOHN RUTLEDGE.

CHAPTER I.

HIS ANCESTRY.

THE Revolution of 1719, which substituted Royal for Proprietary Government in South Carolina, was an important and salutary event in the history of that colony. The feeble control, and ineffectual aid of the Proprietaries, were exchanged for the vigorous encouragement and protection of the Crown. A great change took place. The pirates who had hitherto infested the coasts, and made captures even off the bar of Charleston, were effectually repressed by the ships of war, now sent out, for the protection of trade.[1] The harassing hostility of

[1] For the existence of piracy the Proprietaries were not responsible. They denounced it, and continually urged the authorities in Carolina to use their utmost endeavors to suppress it. In 1687, when the expedition was sent out under the command of Sir Robert Holmes, the Governor and Council of Charleston were required to co-operate with and assist him in his enterprise. But the pirates were by no means considered as enemies of the human race, and acting *animo furandi*, by the early population of South Carolina. In this they were not without historical justification. They could plead the example of the Heroic Ages, when piracy was universally practised, and esteemed honorable. *Latrocinium maris gloriæ habebatur.* Besides, the wild and lawless depredations of the pirates fell chiefly upon the rich commerce of the

the Spaniards, if not wholly subdued, was held in wholesome check. The mildness and general salubrity of the climate, the fertility of the soil, and the liberal terms upon which lands were obtained, allured thither numerous emigrants. Settlements began to extend along the line of all the great rivers. Hitherto, from dread of the Indians, they had been kept within convenient proximity to the coast. The habitations of the country people, from increasing means, and a sense of security, began to exhibit evidences of taste and comfort. Charleston, with its five or six hundred ill-constructed houses, (mostly built of timber,) was gradually improved by the introduction of a better style of architecture.

Ireland contributed largely to the population of the now flourishing colony. Great numbers came over in the years 1734 and '35. Williamsburg was founded by them in the former year. Among the natives of that country who sought their fortunes in the fresher clime

---

Spaniards, between whom and the colonists existed mutual suspicion and animosity. By trafficking with them too, the obnoxious restrictions, imposed by the acts of navigation, were successfully evaded. Commercial restrictions, framed upon an unjust and oppressive basis, will be more or less counteracted by smuggling. But latterly a change had been wrought in the sentiments of the people. The pirates no longer confined their operations to the Spanish commerce. No vessel whatever was safe in those seas. Their numbers multiplied, and their ferocity increased. Bonnet and Worley, from their station at the mouth of Cape Fear river, kept the adjacent coast in continual alarm. Robert Johnson, a son of Sir Nicholas, and the last of the Proprietary Governors, made vigorous exertions to extirpate these bold marauders. The success that attended his efforts added materially to his popularity in the colony. The expeditions under Johnson and Rhett broke up the haunts of the pirates. The ships of war sent out by the government were therefore mainly useful, as they served to deter or repress their occasional incursions. To the honor of the Proprietaries, it must be said, that if they did not effectually suppress piracy within the limits of their government, it was neither owing to want of inclination nor the employment of such means as they could command.

of the new world, were two brothers, John and Andrew Rutledge, who arrived in Charleston about the year 1735.

John was a physician, and established himself in that city. Of his history we know little. He practised his profession with considerable success for several years; but shortly after his marriage, which occurred in December, 1738, he abandoned the service of Esculapius, and resigned himself to the superior charms of uninterrupted domestic life. He died in the year 1749.

The maiden name of his wife was Sarah Hext. All accounts concur in speaking her praise. Nature bestowed upon her liberal endowments, and her gifts were improved and cultivated by education. She was distinguished for fortitude and wisdom. Her manners were good and her temper amiable. We often meet with persons of religious feelings, but devoid of religious principles. Their piety, such as it is, does not animate their conduct, and sway their actions. The religion of Mrs. Rutledge was of a higher strain, and more pervasive character. It was a part of her being. It shone conspicuously forth in the habitual performance of all her duties. She was a woman, too, of spirit, and devoted patriotism. In the Revolution, when Charleston was in possession of the enemy, the commandant ordered her to be removed from her country residence, and confined within the limits of the town. The reason assigned for this apparent harshness was, that from such a woman much was to be apprehended. The indirect praise of an enemy speaks a more forcible language than the partial eulogy of a friend. It neither proceeds from the suggestions of interest nor the blindness of affection. It is extorted by the virtues of its object.

A mother at fifteen, and a widow at twenty-six, with seven small children to protect and educate, Mrs. Rutledge atoned for the want of experience by a sound and discriminating judgment. She had brought her husband what, in those days, was considered a large estate; but prudence was not his characteristic virtue, and at his death his means were found to be much impaired and wasted. Mrs. Rutledge, however, appears to have been endowed with a happy administrative talent, which enabled her to encounter, successfully, the various difficulties of her situation. She knew and appreciated too well the rich advantages of education, 'to choke up the days' of her children 'with barbarous ignorance.' She practised uncommon self-denial and economy to place those advantages within their reach. And if they afterwards rendered important and honorable service to their country, her self-sacrificing spirit, and judicious training, must share the praise and distinction. For next in order and value to a happy constitution of mind, is a proper discipline, and direction of its powers. And for the latter, the children of Mrs. Rutledge were indebted to their mother.

This excellent woman, whose character we have thus briefly delineated, died at Charleston in 1792.

CHAPTER II.

HIS BIRTH AND EDUCATION.

1739—1761.

John Rutledge, the second Chief Justice of the Supreme Court of the United States, and a distinguished character of our Revolutionary History, was the eldest child of John and Sarah Rutledge, of whom we have given a brief sketch in the preceding chapter. He was born at Charleston in September, 1739. Of his early years we have been able to collect but few particulars. 'The childhood shows the man, as morning shows the day.' But it is only an observant and discriminating eye that discovers a child's genuine traits and characteristics. The thousand and one anecdotes of the childhood of distinguished men which we find gravely related in books of biography, as certain indications of future eminence, are more frequently evidence of the puerility of the author, than the genius of the child. To the 'wonder-waiting eyes' of parents, the most trifling acts of their children assume an air of importance. They witness all the steps of the process, and at each advance in the rapid unfolding of the infantile mind, they are apt to discover, or think they discover, something extraordinary. A few years rectifies their judgment. Their prognostics are seldom justified by the event; and the prodigy of childhood, who was to shine the boast and wonder of mankind, sinks to the common level, and is heard of no more.

His early education was conducted by his father. After his death, and at the age of eleven, he was placed under the charge of the Rev. Mr. Andrews, an English clergyman, who lived in Christ Church Parish. He was a man of superior attainments. Doubtless, to supply the deficiencies of a scanty salary, he received a small number of boys into his family, and thus exercised a superintending control over their morals, as well as education.

Young Rutledge remained with Mr. Andrews, pursuing his classical and other studies, several years. He was a favorite pupil of his teacher. Tradition says that Mr. Andrews was greatly pleased with him, for he was not only an apt and studious scholar, but in all his conduct upright and conscientious. On leaving Mr. Andrews, he attended, for a short time, the school of David Rhind, whom Dr. Ramsay describes, as an excellent classical scholar;[1] but the family of Rutledge, I am informed, never spoke of Rhind's instructions, as among his advantages.

In the summer of 1755, and a few months before arriving at the age of seventeen, he left school, and entered upon the study of his future profession.[2] 'Although much culture is indispensable to the development of the intellectual powers, and to the refinement of taste, this culture may be applied, without the knowledge of a great variety of languages, and without any deep insight into science. No Greek knew any language but that which he learned from his nurse; and Shakspeare could not have gone through an examination as hard as that of many modern parish schools. Far be it from me to discourage the acquisition of classical and scientific lore: this is delightful in itself, and it gives the best chance of success in every liberal pursuit; but where true genius

[1] Ramsay's History of South Carolina, vol. ii., p. 510.

[2] It has been erroneously stated that he was sent to England to pursue his preliminary studies.

exists, it may be brought into full operation and efficiency, by suitable discipline within very narrow limits; and a man may be superior to all others in his art, and be ignorant of many things which it is disgraceful to the common herd of mortals not to know.'[1] Those who suppose that a great character can only be formed but by means of a prescribed formula of education, should reflect, that mere acquisition is not education. Power is vastly more important than knowledge. It is the *conditio sine qua non* of any great success, and is only to be attained by self-education, by 'the introversion of the faculties upon themselves.' If the discipline of young Rutledge was within narrow limits, his genius 'supplied every deficiency and cymmetrized every disproportion.'

The gentleman under whose direction he entered upon the study of the law, was James Parsons, a barrister of distinction at the colonial bar of South Carolina, and a devoted patriot of the Revolution. He was an Irishman by birth, but an American in principle, and uniformly firm in the cause of his adopted country. He held several important offices during the revolutionary period; and at the time of his death, which occurred in 1779, was Vice-President of South Carolina.

When Rutledge began the study of the law, the path to the temple of Themis, as we have elsewhere observed,[2] was both laborious and repulsive. Blackstone had not yet shown the possibility of explaining the difficult problems of a difficult science, in language at once elegant and exact, of disencumbering that science of the scholastic refinements and subtle niceties with which it had hitherto been hedged, and displaying its fundamental principles to the student, in a manner at once systematic and luminous. Under the old system of study, the student usually began with Coke-Littleton, and 'broke through.' If nature had

[1] Lord Campbell. Lives of the Lord Chancellors, vol. vi., p. 551.—Am. Ed.

[2] Ante, pp. 34–38.

not given him a mind of peculiar aptitude for abstruse and apparently barren speculations, or if perseverance and indomitable plodding did not supply the place of that natural aptitude, he was likely to abandon at the outset a discouraging pursuit, or continue on in confusion, and 'ever-during dark.' And even where he mastered the harsh and crabbed learning of his future profession, the effect of the study upon the mind, unless balanced by studies of an opposite tendency and more liberal character, was to restrain and confine its action, to sharpen its faculties, at the expense of their enlargement, to render them more acute, but less comprehensive. Undoubtedly, that is the tendency of the study of so artificial a system as the common law, however happily simplified; but the tendency was ten-fold more operative, before the rude elements had been shaped by the plastic hand of a master.[1]

---

[1] Mr. Burke, himself the son of a lawyer, and intended for that profession, from which he was allured by the irresistible attractions of philosophy, literature and politics, thus speaks of the law, in connection with the celebrated George Grenville: 'He was bred in a profession. He was bred to the law, which is, in my opinion, one of the first and noblest of human sciences; a science which does more to quicken and invigorate the understanding, than all the other kinds of learning put together; but it is not apt, except in persons very happily born, to open and liberalize the mind exactly in the same proportion.' Speech on American Taxation.

Again: in speaking of the disproportion of lawyers in the composition of the *Tiers Etat* in France, he observes:—'God forbid I should insinuate anything derogatory to that profession, which is another priesthood, administering the rites of sacred justice. But whilst I revere men in the functions which belong to them, and would do, as much as any man can do, to prevent their exclusion from any, I cannot, to flatter them, give the lie to nature. They are good and useful in the composition; they must be mischievous if they preponderate so as virtually to become the whole. Their very excellence in their peculiar functions may be far from a qualification for others. It cannot escape observation, that when men are too much confined to professional and faculty habits, and, as it were, inveterate in the recurrent employment of that narrow

Rutledge continued in the office of Mr. Parsons for two years, and then proceeded to London, and entered as a student in the Temple. This was in 1758, in his nineteenth year. It was a period of unusual interest in British politics, and remarkable for the number of eminent men, who adorned almost every department of life. It was at the close of the reign of George II. The star of Pitt was in the ascendant. The year before he had been placed at the head of affairs, and opened that career of British success which raised the empire to the highest pitch of grandeur. Mansfield was presiding in the King's Bench. He had but recently escaped to this more congenial sphere, from the contests of the House of Commons, where, notwithstanding his great talents and persuasive eloquence, he was eclipsed and overawed by the

---

circle, they are rather disabled than qualified for whatever depends on the knowledge of mankind, on experience in mixed affairs, on a comprehensive connected view of the various complicated external and internal interests which go to the formation of that multifarious thing called a state.' Reflections on the Revolution in France.

In the heat of passion, and when under a high state of exasperation, Mr. Burke did not speak of the legal profession with the same candor and philosophic discrimination, as in the above extracts. When Erskine, the most eminent of British advocates, and, despite his vanity, one of the most genial and agreeable of men, contended in the House of Commons, that a dissolution of Parliament having taken place since the grand impeachment of Warren Hastings, the proceeding was thereby ended, he naturally aroused Mr. Burke, whose speech on the occasion was full of bitterness and personality. In the course of his remarks, Erskine observed that the country should be governed by law. Burke, in reply, said, 'that he should be glad to see the country governed by law, but not by lawyers.' Erskine complained of the length of the trial. Burke asked in reply, 'whether the learned gentleman remembered, that if the trial had continued three years, the oppressions had continued twenty? whether, after all, there were hour-glasses for measuring the grievances of mankind? or whether they, whose ideas never travelled beyond a nisi prius case, were better qualified to judge what ought to be the length of an impeachment, than a rabbit who breeds six times a year was able to judge of the time proper for the gestation of an elephant.'

superior genius of Pitt. The jovial and boisterous Henley, afterwards Lord Northington, was now Lord Keeper. If there was but little in his talents or character to inspire respect, he has nevertheless a claim upon the grateful recollection of posterity, for having raised the sinking spirits, and successfully introduced into practice, the celebrated Charles Pratt, afterwards Lord Chancellor, and Earl Camden, who, after waiting eight or nine years in vain for business, was about to abandon the bar for the church. Henley himself had felt the stings of poverty, as well as ambition; but in his subsequent elevation retained a pleasant recollection of his early troubles, and often recurred to the humble residence in Bedford Row, the scene of his earlier married life, 'where a leg of mutton lasted them three days—the first day hot—the second day cold—and the third day hashed.' Pratt was now Attorney-General. Burke was just rising into fame. Johnson was in the vigor of his faculties, and the autocrat of literature. Him, 'whose death eclipsed the gaiety of nations,' the inimitable Garrick, was in the zenith of his fame, and the undisputed monarch of the mimic world.[1] Thurlow, the burly Chancellor, who filled so

---

[1] I am sure the reader will not be disposed to quarrel with me for transcribing from Boswell's Life of Johnson, vol. iii., p. 336, the following anecdote of Garrick:—'I told him' (Johnson) says Boswell, 'that one morning when I went to breakfast with Garrick, who was very vain of his intimacy with Lord Camden, he accosted me thus: 'Pray now did you—did you meet a little lawyer turning the corner, eh?' 'No Sir,' said I; 'pray what do you mean by the question?' 'Why,' replied Garrick, with an affected indifference, yet as standing on tip-toe, 'Lord Camden has this moment left me. We have had a long walk together.' Johnson—'Well, Sir, Garrick talked very properly—Lord Camden was a *little lawyer* to be associating so familiarly with a player.'

Whether Johnson expressed his deliberate opinion, or only gave vent to his spleen, which, it must be confessed, Garrick's ridiculous vanity was well calculated to inspire, the intelligent and cultivated portion of mankind will hardly agree that Lord Camden demeaned himself by associating on familiar terms with a man equally distinguished as himself,

large a space in the public eye, 'when George III. was King,' had just begun to emerge from the obscurity and dissipation of the coffee-houses to position at the bar.

We account it not among the least of Rutledge's advantages of education, that he had an opportunity, at so plastic a period of his life, to listen to the commanding eloquence of Pitt, the luminous judgments of Mansfield, the lucid oratory of Pratt, and to witness Garrick's 'powers of acting, vast and unconfined.' No man comes in contact with a superior mind, without deriving benefit therefrom; nor, if of a liberal strain, contemplates the displays of an illustrious character, without feeling 'the ennobling stir' of a generous ambition. To live at a period of great intellectual activity, and when the heroic virtues are in the ascendant, is a high and exalted privilege. By his residence in London, Rutledge was brought into contact with new and various minds. He studied life as well as law. He got rid of local prejudices. His horizon was enlarged. He who is bred up in a small community is apt to imbibe the confined ideas that prevail there. Hence the value of National Universities. They draw together the youths of all sections of a country. They bring with them a great variety of ideas and opinions. They have been accustomed to diversified modes of thought. A new world is opened before them. New views are imparted; and in this interchange of

---

although in a different walk, and esteemed for his varied information, his kind heart, and

> 'For all the gentler morals, such as play,
> Through life's more cultur'd walks, and charm the way.'

It is for vulgar breasts, who live in seclusion from the world, and from communion with its more liberal views, to compensate for their obscurity by the assumption of consequence, and seek a retreat for their dulness within their own confined and kindred circle. But those on whom nature has bestowed more liberal endowments, and more conspicuous advantages, dishonor the generous source from whence their distinction flows, when they hold a language such as we have quoted above, of Johnson's.

mind, this giving and receiving, consists the chief advantage.

While Rutledge was still a student at the Temple, great expectations were formed of him. The letters of his fellow-students to their friends at home, spoke of his talents in terms of admiration. He remained three years at the Temple, *in statu pupillari*, was then called to the bar, and returned home. This was in the year 1761. Even before his arrival at Charleston, he received flattering proof of the reputation that had preceded him. For while the vessel in which he was returning was eight or ten miles below the town, a gentleman, who was defendant in a suit for breach of promise, which was coming on for trial, went down in a pilot-boat to meet him, and engage him for his advocate. I have been unable to ascertain the precise date of his enrolment as an attorney in the Provincial Courts of South Carolina. 'I have searched in the clerk's office,' writes a venerable gentleman of Charleston, to whose courtesy I am much indebted, 'for the date of his admission to the Bar, but without success, although it is stated to have been in 1761. I have heard, however, a little family anecdote connected with that occasion which ought not to be lost, as it shows the confidence of genius in its own powers. On returning home the day he was enrolled, he threw what money he had about him into his mother's lap, that it might be said, 'he had begun life without a guinea in his pocket.'

Having thus brought him to the vestibule, as it were, of his profession, we shall reserve for the next chapter the few particulars we have been able to collect, of his services and success, within the temple itself.

CHAPTER III.

HIS EARLY CAREER AT THE BAR.

1761—1764.

WHEN Rutledge came to the bar, Charleston 'was the source and centre of all judicial proceedings.'[1] It was the seat of justice for the Province. The colonial judicatures were a Court of King's Bench and Common Pleas, a Court of Chancery and Vice-Admiralty. A Chief Justice appointed by the King, and certain associate justices appointed by the general assembly, with the concurrence of the home government, composed the two first courts. The Court of Chancery was held by the Governor and Council; the Court of Vice-Admiralty by a judge appointed by the Crown. There was but one Ordinary for the Province, who resided at Charleston. This centralization of judicial proceedings became so burdensome and inconvenient to the people of the country districts, to 'parties, witnesses, and jurors, who were obliged to attend the court, and especially to suitors and prosecutors, who were often worn out by 'the law's delay,' insulted by 'the insolence of office,' and ruined by costs and expenses most unreasonably incurred, and cruelly exacted,'[2] that they formed themselves into associations, under the designation of Regulators, to redress their grievances,

[1] Ramsay's History of South Carolina, vol. ii., p. 125. Justices of the peace, however, throughout the Province, held courts which had civil jurisdiction, as high as twenty pounds current money. Brevard's Digest, Intro., p. 14.

[2] Ibid.

without resorting to the law. This condition of affairs led to the passage of the Circuit Court Act of 1769, which created upon the basis of the English system, six districts or circuits, wherein were to be held, twice a year, courts of general sessions and common pleas.

The bar was not numerous. We have not been able to ascertain the precise number, but have reason to suppose that it did not exceed twenty. The rules of court interposed obstacles to a rapid increase. None but natives of the Province, or regularly-bred European lawyers, except in rare cases, were admitted to practice in the colonial courts of South Carolina. The lawyer of the present day, accustomed to Revised Statutes, with carefully prepared indexes, will appreciate his advantages, when he learns that the lawyers of South Carolina, before the Revolution, were obliged for the most part to resort to the public records, to obtain a knowledge of the Provincial laws. The compilation by Chief Justice Trott embraced only the acts of the assembly to the year 1734, while Simpson's related exclusively to the acts pertaining to the powers and duties of justices of the peace. After the Revolution Judge Grimké compiled all the material laws of the Province, from its settlement to the year 1789; and also a work similar to Simpson's, and another relating to the powers and duties of Executors and Administrators. But, until these labors of Judge Grimké, the only resource of the lawyer was the compilation of Trott, and the public records.[1]

If the lawyers of that day were few, the legal business of the Province was by no means in disproportion to their number. The great expense attending legal proceedings contributed to repress litigation. The average number of judgments entered up in Charleston for the seven years preceding the Revolution was two hundred

---

[1] Ramsay's History of South Carolina, vol. ii., p. 152.

and thirty-six each year. This included all the judgments obtained in the Province, for the new circuit courts were not courts of record, all writs and other civil process issuing from, and being returnable to the court of Common Pleas in Charleston.[1]

Judicial proceedings, at that period, were conducted with a good deal of state. The lawyers wore wigs and gowns as in England. 'Amongst the old customs of the Bar, now abolished,' says the venerable Mr. Fraser, who is known and honored in his native State as an accomplished gentleman and artist, 'was the preaching of session sermons, for which the minister was allowed, by law, a sum of three pounds, to be paid by the sheriff, out of fines and forfeitures. . . . Looking over an old State Gazette of January, 1799, I found the notice of a sessions sermon to be preached in St. Michael's church, by the Rev. Dr. Purcell; and this recalled to my mind an incident connected with that very occasion. Mr. John Rutledge, of Revolutionary celebrity, chanced to meet me near the church, whilst the judge and sheriff, and a few officers of the court, were crossing over from the court-house. Seeing this scant and motley procession, he asked what it meant. I told him they were going to hear a sessions sermon, when he observed how differently it had been conducted formerly, when the judges in their scarlet robes, and the lawyers also robed, and all the attendants of the court, proceeded in great form to the church. This meeting is further impressed upon my recollection, by his offering to walk up with me to General C. C. Pinckney's house, to show me Stuart's portrait of Washington, then recently sent here, which he accordingly did.'[2]

---

[1] Ramsay's History of South Carolina, vol. ii., p. 157, note.

[2] Reminiscences of Charleston, by Charles Fraser, p. 86, 87. This work, from which we shall have occasion to quote again, contains a good deal of curious information, and abounds with just and appropriate re-

Rutledge's first effort at the bar was in the breach-of-promise case, which we have before mentioned.[1] 'I have heard,' says the venerable correspondent, whom we have quoted in a preceding page,[2] 'that his success in the first cause he was engaged in, gave him at once a prominent standing at our bar. From some accidental cause he was unexpectedly called to manage it, and in doing so, displayed so much readiness and ability, that he acquired a practice which he always after retained until summoned into judicial and political life.'[3] 'His eloquence,' says Ramsay, in speaking of the same occasion, 'astonished all who heard him.'[4] He obtained a verdict for his client, and received a hundred guineas for his fee — in those

---

flections. One feels instinctively that it is the production of a mind possessed of both liberal sentiments and liberal accomplishments.

In respect to the customs of the bar, in 'the olden time,' the following extract, from a well-known letter of John Adams, will serve to illustrate the text. He is speaking of the celebrated trial, in the case of Writs of Assistance, in 1761. 'In this chamber,'* he says, 'near the fire, were seated five judges, with Lieutenant-Governor Hutchinson at their head, as Chief Justice; all in their new fresh robes of scarlet English cloth, in their broad bands, and immense judicial wigs. In this chamber was seated, at a long table, all the Barristers of Boston, and its neighboring county of Middlesex, in their gowns, bands, and tye-wigs. They were not seated on ivory chairs; but their dress was more solemn and more pompous than that of the Roman Senate, when the Gauls broke in upon them. In a corner of the room must be placed Wit, Sense, Imagination, Genius, Pathos, Reason, Prudence, Eloquence, Learning, Science, and immense Reading, hung by the shoulders on two crutches, covered with a cloth great-coat, in the person of Mr. Pratt, who had been solicited on both sides, but would engage on neither, being about to leave Boston forever, as Chief Justice of New York.' Adams to Judge Tudor, March 29th, 1818. Tudor's Life of Otis.

[1] Ante, p. 442.

[2] Ante, p. 442.

[3] The accidental cause, referred to by my correspondent, I presume, was nothing more than Rutledge's accidental arrival, at the time the case was coming on for trial.

[4] History of South Carolina, vol. ii., p. 511.

---

* The Council-Chamber of the old Town-House in Boston.

days considered a large sum. To the praise of his filial piety, it should be mentioned, that he gave the whole purse to his mother, whose self-denial and economy, cheerfully practised for the well-being of her children, commanded and received their unfailing love and gratitude.

The legal profession furnishes numerous examples of distinguished lawyers, who, after years of poverty and obscurity, were indebted to some unexpected opportunity for displaying their talents, and then at once rose into fame and fortune. It has been said of Lord Mansfield, that he never knew the difference between total destitution and £3000 a year. This is exaggeration; but it is known that he was two years at the bar before getting a brief. Erskine suffered the stings of poverty, while preparing for the bar; but, by a lucky accident, got a brief in a few months after being called to it. He used to say that, before his success, he lived on 'cow-heel and tripe.' When Admiral Keppel sent him two notes of £500 each for his splendid services on the Admiral's memorable trial, he hastened with boyish delight to his friends the Reynolds's, (Reynolds the comic writer,) and exhibiting his wealth, exclaimed, 'Voila!' the nonsuit of *cow*-beef, my good friends.' Lord Eldon has related that during the year following his admission to the bar, he received but half a guinea.[1] He remained several years without business, and not until after the case of Ackroyd *v.* Smithson, and the Clitheroe Election Petition, was his success insured. He had then attained the ripe age of thirty.

Rutledge is an example of immediate success attending the ambitious hopes of the legal aspirant. When he came to the bar, he was only twenty-two; but he was armed with precocious faculties, and ready for the contests of his profession. 'Instead of rising by degrees,' says Ram-

[1] Twiss's Life of Lord Eldon, vol. i., p. 72.

say, 'to the head of his profession, he burst forth at once the able lawyer and accomplished orator. Business flowed in upon him. He was employed in the most difficult causes, and retained with the largest fees that were usually given. The client in whose service he engaged was supposed to be in a fair way of gaining his cause.'[1] Rutledge's qualities, as a lawyer and advocate, were of a character to insure success. He had a penetrating judgment, and great quickness of perception. He intuitively seized upon the strong points of a case, and presented them to the court and jury with remarkable earnestness and energy. His professional learning was based on a systematic course of five years' study. The lawyers of his day were uncommonly well-grounded in the common law. If their studies were confined within a narrower circle, than the studies of their successors, they were, perhaps, for that very reason, more thoroughly mastered.

As an advocate, if we may rely on tradition, and contemporary testimony, Rutledge stood in the very first line. 'His ideas,' says Ramsay, 'were clear and strong—his utterance rapid but distinct—his voice, action, and energetic manner of speaking, forcibly impressed his sentiments on the minds and hearts of all who heard him. At reply he was quick—instantly comprehended the force of an objection—and saw at once the best mode of weakening or repelling it. He successfully used both argument and wit for invalidating the observations of his adversary: by the former he destroyed or weakened their force; by the latter he placed them in so ludicrous a point of light that it often convinced, and scarcely ever failed of conciliating and pleasing his hearers. Many were the triumphs of his eloquence at the bar and in the Legislature; and in the former case probably more

[1] Ramsay's History of South Carolina, vol. ii., p. 511.

than strict impartial justice would sanction; for judges and jurors, counsel and audience, hung on his accents.'[1] 'I asked General Pinckney,' says Mr. Fraser,[2] 'about Mr. John Rutledge's style of speaking. He told me that it was strong and argumentative, and remarkable for close reasoning; and said that it resembled Mr. Dunning's (the celebrated Lord Ashburton) more than that of any speaker he had ever heard. Now, in General Pinckney's day, Mr. Dunning was the most celebrated advocate in England.'

The limits of professional morality, beyond which the advocate is not at liberty to go, have never been very accurately defined. The subject has often employed the wits of casuists, without any sufficiently comprehensive rule being discovered, to govern the practice of the bar, or satisfy the scruples of the conscientious. Dr. Johnson is reported to have said, 'that as it was the duty of counsel to give information to the court, he ought to state facts correctly, to quote cases accurately, to misrepresent nothing with respect either to facts or cases; and having accurately stated facts and quoted cases, he was at liberty in conscience to reason upon them to the very best of his powers and abilities; and as the law supposed the judge to be an abler man, and an abler lawyer than the counsel, the judge was to reason better upon the facts and the cases, than the counsel; and, proceeding in this way, the counsel did nothing wrong in thus gaining the cause for his client.'

If the law supposes the judge to be an abler man and lawyer than the counsel, the law supposes what is by no means generally the case. If, therefore, Dr. Johnson's rule would justify an inferior advocate in employing his ineffectual powers to mystify and mislead the court and

[1] Ramsay's History of South Carolina, vol. ii., p. 513.

[2] Reminiscences of Charleston, p. 71.

jury, because the law supposes them incapable of being misled by such an advocate, it certainly would not justify an advocate of superior character, who employs that superiority in framing arguments above the grasp of the judge, and thereby gains his cause. In determining a case of conscience, we must take facts as they exist, not as they may be supposed to exist. But, however we may refine upon the subject, it is not probable that the bar will aspire to a morality above that prescribed by Dr. Johnson.

The extraordinary facility which leading advocates acquire, in framing arguments of the most opposite character, to sustain the side upon which they may chance to be employed, was never perhaps more forcibly illustrated than in the case of Dunning, to whom Rutledge, in the general style of his argumentation, has been compared. 'I had, very early after I was called to the bar,' says Lord Eldon,[1] 'a brief in business in the King's Bench, as junior to Mr. Dunning. He began the argument, and appeared to me to be reasoning very powerfully against our client. Waiting till I was quite convinced that he had mistaken for what party he was retained, I then touched his arm, and, upon his turning his head towards me, I whispered to him that he must have misunderstood for whom he was employed, as he was reasoning against our client. He gave me a very rough and rude reprimand for not having sooner set him right, and then proceeded to state, that what he had addressed to the court was all that could be stated against his client, and that he had put the case as unfavorably as possible against him, in order that the court might see how very satisfactorily the case against him could be answered; and, accordingly, very powerfully answered what he had before stated.'

[1] Twiss's Life of Lord Eldon, vol. i., p. 75.

Two years after being called to the bar, Rutledge was married to Miss Elizabeth Grimké, a union from which he derived unalloyed happiness. He was passionately attached to his wife; and her death, which occurred in 1792, was the source of the most poignant grief; and, as we shall see hereafter, one of the concurring causes of the malady which clouded the evening of his day. The year following his marriage, viz., on the 17th September, 1764, Rutledge was appointed, *pro tempore*, Attorney-General of the Province, and performed the duties of that position until the 5th of June, 1765.

In the next chapter, we shall survey him on a different and more conspicuous theatre, and witness the first steps of that political career, which has honorably identified his name with the history of his country.

CHAPTER IV.

HIS POLITICAL CAREER.

1764—1774.

THE seeds of opposition to the future pretensions of Great Britain had been planted in several of the colonies, before even the Stamp Act had yet engaged the attention of Parliament. John Adams has said that the argument of Otis in the case of Writs of Assistance in 1761, was the origin of our Independence. 'American Independence,' he says, 'was then and there born. The seeds of patriots and heroes, to defend the *Non sine Diis animosus infans*—to defend the vigorous youth—were then and there sown. Every man, of an immense crowded audience, appeared to me to go away as I did, ready to take arms against writs of assistance. Then, and there, was the first scene of the first act of opposition to the arbitrary claims of Great Britain — then and there the child Independence was born. In fifteen years, viz., in 1776, he grew up to manhood, and declared himself free.'[1] Others might discover in Patrick Henry's argument in the Parson's cause, the original of his famous resolutions on the Stamp Act, which produced an electrical effect throughout the colonies, and raised the spirit of resistance to parliamentary encroachments 'to height of noblest temper.'

In South Carolina, the unwise and unwarrantable interference of Boone, the Royal Governor, with the privi-

[1] Adams to Judge Tudor, March 29th, 1818. Tudor's Life of Otis.

leges of the Commons House of Assembly, had produced an irritation of feeling, and a jealousy of their rights, which prepared the people to take a resolute stand against a measure of so obnoxious a character as the Stamp Act.

Boone, as early as March, 1762, had called the attention of the Assembly to the election law of 1721, which he considered defective, and recommended a new law as absolutely necessary. The Assembly did not concur with the Governor in his objections to the law, which chiefly related to the mode of issuing and executing the election writs. They sent him a message to that effect. Subsequent to this action of the House, Christopher Gadsden was elected a member of the Assembly from St. Paul's Parish. The election was sanctioned by the House, and the proper qualification-oath administered to Gadsden. It was necessary, however, before he could take his seat, that the Governor should administer to him what were termed the State oaths, viz., the oath of allegiance to Great Britain, and the oath disclaiming the right of the Pretender's family to the throne. These oaths the Governor refused to administer, upon the ground that the church-wardens, to whom the election writs were issued, had not been sworn previous to Gadsden's election. To this it was replied, that it was a part of the general duty of the church-wardens to hold these elections, and when appointed to that office, they had duly sworn to execute its duties. But the Governor maintained that they must be sworn previous to each particular election, and 'not only refused to admit the election of Mr. Gadsden, but dissolved the House of Assembly for their late contumacy.'[1]

Without inquiring whether the Governor's technical

[1] Johnson's Traditions of the Revolution. Mr. Johnson has given a full and circumstantial account of the transactions referred to in the text.

objection to the validity of the election was not well-founded, it must be obvious to the commonest understanding, that the question was not for him to decide. It was the province of the House to judge of the qualifications of their members. When they decided that a member was duly elected, the Governor was bound to administer the requisite oaths. His duty in the premises was ministerial, not judicial; to act, not decide.

Upon the convocation of the Assembly the next winter, it was found that Gadsden had again been elected. The members at once remonstrated against the dissolution of the last Assembly, and adopted sundry resolutions censuring the course pursued by the Governor, and asserting in strong terms their right to examine and determine the legality and validity of all elections to the Commons House of Assembly. That was a right (they declared) solely and absolutely vested in the representatives of the people met in General Assembly.

The Governor still adhering to his position, the Assembly, on the 16th day of December, 1762, resolved that they would enter into no further business with him, until he should concede the just claims of the House, solely to examine and determine the validity of the election of their own members. They paid no attention to his messages and recommendations, except to lay them upon the table, and refused to make the ordinary appropriations, even for the payment of officers' salaries. Two years after the dispute commenced, the Governor exhibited a better temper, and seemed no longer disposed to interfere with the rights of the House; but as he gave no security for the future by any public renunciation of his former pretensions, the House refused to renew their intercourse with him.

It was in the midst of these difficulties, the Governor and Assembly in relations of hostility, the business of legislation suspended, and the feelings of the people highly exasperated, that John Rutledge made his appearance upon the field of politics. He was elected a member of the Assembly, and, as at the bar, so on this new and untried theatre, he at once asserted and maintained a position of pre-eminence. 'In rousing the Assembly and the people,' says Ramsay, 'to resist all interferences of the Royal Governors, in deciding who should, or who should not be members of the Commons House of Assembly, John Rutledge kindled a spark which has never since been extinguished.' [1]

The Assembly refused to recede from the position they had taken. Governor Boone's presence in the colony, therefore, was both unnecessary and unprofitable. Accordingly, in May, 1764, he went to England to justify his conduct. The Assembly had preferred charges against him, and the ministry had sent him leave of absence. On his departure, harmony was immediately restored in the colony, in consequence of the temperate course pursued by Boone's successor, Lieutenant-Governor Bull. The public attention was now directed to England, whither the controversy had been transferred. A hearing was had before the Board of Trade and Plantations. A report was made censuring the conduct of both Governor and Assembly. The latter appealed, but while the appeal was still pending, and the Province irritated and indignant at the censure put upon them, a new element of discord was intermingled, by the project now brought forward, to impose a tax upon the colonies.

The history of the Stamp-Act is too well known to be repeated. Its most efficient promoter, George Grenville, was a man of narrow principles, but intrepid resolution. He saw clearly, but he did not see far. This defect in his mental vision was partly natural, and partly acquired. The habits of office, to which he was early addicted, were not likely to ameliorate the original constitution of his

[1] Ramsay's History of South Carolina, vol. ii., p. 511.

mind. In many particulars, the character of Grenville bore a strong resemblance to the character of George III. He had the same inflexible will, the same tenacity of purpose, the same obstinate adherence both to his prejudices and principles. But he had more. He had an open nature, which scorned concealment, and disdained everything like finesse. He went straight to his objects, and defended his measures with a fearless, manly logic. His faculties, within their orbit, were of the most vigorous strain. He could not have been otherwise than an important character in the politics of his time and country.

Whether the idea of American taxation was original with Grenville, or suggested from some other quarter, 'certain it is, that with the best intentions in the world, he first brought this fatal scheme into form, and established it by act of parliament.'[1] On the twenty-second day of March, 1765, it received the Royal assent.[2] This measure, big with future mischief, the beginning of a line of policy, which issued in war and the dismemberment of an Empire, scarcely attracted more attention in England than any ordinary and unimportant act of legislation. The colony-agents did what they could to oppose it, (with the exception of Mauduit and Knox, the agents of Massachusetts and Georgia, who favored the tax,) but they had no idea of the storm of opposition it was destined to encounter on the other side of the water. In the colonies, it was regarded as an unconstitutional and dangerous innovation upon ancient usage — as 'a fair foundation laid whereon to build their ruin.'

When the news of its passage reached Charleston, no little excitement prevailed. The consequent proceedings

---

[1] Burke's Speech on American Taxation. This plan of taxation was conceived by Jenkinson, favored by Lord Bute, and adopted and brought into form by Grenville.

[2] The assent was given by a commission. George III., at this time, was the unhappy victim of mental alienation.

to the northward inflamed it. As the discussion proceeded, and the minds of men awakened to the dangerous tendency of the measure, the people, and especially the tradesmen and mechanics, resolved that it should not be enforced. Their determined sentiments confirmed and supported the resolutions of the Assembly. When that body came together, without assuming a position which would commit them to resist an act of Parliament, they sought how they might best prevent its execution. Ascertaining upon inquiry of Lieutenant-Governor Bull, that the Stamp-Act had been transmitted to him by Governor Boone, the Assembly declared that it had not been received from an authentic source, and informed him that he was under no obligation to enforce it. But as other acts had been transmitted to the Lieutenant-Governor through the same channel, and as the Assembly were well aware of that circumstance, yet never interposed so novel an objection, it appeared to the unsophisticated understanding of his Excellency that they were estopped from urging it now. This obvious conclusion could not fail to have struck Rutledge and the lawyers of the Assembly; but, as the object was to elude the enforcement of the act, they adhered to their position.

The next step taken by the Assembly was the passage of a series of resolutions, very ably drawn, and declaring their rights in very comprehensive and emphatic language. They insisted upon their exclusive right of taxation, a right inseparable from representation; and representation of the colony in the House of Commons of Great Britain, they declared to be impracticable. They objected, too, in strong terms, to the late extension of the Admiralty jurisdiction, a jurisdiction peculiarly obnoxious to the people of the colonies in general, and regarded as subversive of their rights and liberties. Referring to the good old mode of requisition and supply, they expressed their readiness, whenever called upon in a constitutional way, 'to grant to his Majesty their proportion, according to their ability, of men and money, for the defence, security, and other public services, of the British American colonies.'

Massachusetts, as early as the 6th of June, at the suggestion of Otis, had proposed a meeting of committees from the colonial assemblies, to be held at New York on the first Tuesday of October, 'to consult together,' in this arduous crisis of affairs, and 'consider of a united representation to implore relief.'—A circular was accordingly sent to the Assemblies of the several colonies, inviting their co-operation in the proposed Congress.

When this letter reached Charleston, it produced instant opposition. The proposed measure was a novel one. It was unknown to the Constitution, and unsanctioned by practice. Its propriety was doubted, and its legality questioned. No colony south of New England had yet agreed to it. To produce union, where there was such diversity of opinion, was no easy task. To the abilities and influence of John Rutledge and Christopher Gadsden, chiefly belongs the honor of accomplishing it. The former put forth his best exertions on this important occasion. 'Objections vanished — prejudices gave way before his eloquence. The public mind was illuminated, and a more correct mode of thinking took place.'[1] The Assembly, in harmony with the sentiments of their constituents, resolved to send deputies to the Congress.[2] Thomas Lynch, the father of the Thomas Lynch whose name is affixed to the Declaration of Independence, a gentleman of large estate, and highly honorable character; Christopher Gadsden, of whom we shall have occasion hereafter more particularly to speak; and John Rutledge, were appointed to that responsible position.

---

[1] Ramsay, vol. ii., p. 512.

[2] Had they decided adversely, it is doubtful if the Congress would have taken place. See Bancroft, vol. v., p. 294.

They sailed from Charleston on the 4th of September, and arrived at New York on the 15th. But little is known of the individual action of the Stamp-Act Congress. No report was made of the discussions that took place; and neither tradition nor private letters have brought down to us any minute account of the part enacted by the several members. There were but twenty-seven delegates present. Four colonies were unrepresented. The first question that arrested the attention of the Congress, which met and organized on the 7th day of October, was, upon what foundation the rights of the colonies should be asserted. It provoked warm and earnest discussion. One party relied on charters, on royal grants, and on usage; another, on a law higher than any charter, paramount to any grant of the crown, and superior to usage, viz., the law of justice, of eternal and universal right. The delegates from New England would found their rights on the exemptions and privileges conferred by their charters; but the delegates of South Carolina disdained that ground. 'We should stand,' said Gadsden, 'upon the broad common ground of those natural rights that we all feel and know as men, and as descendants of Englishmen.'[1] Charters might be relied on, to confirm their essential and common rights as Englishmen, but any further dependence on them, he thought, might be fatal.[2]

These views were sanctioned by the Congress, and embodied in their Declaration of Rights and Grievances. They did not deduce, nor attempt to deduce their essential rights and liberties from Royal grants, but from the nature of things. 'It is inseparably essential to the freedom of a people, and the undoubted right of Englishmen,' they said, 'that no taxes be imposed on them but with

[1] MS. Letter of Christopher Gadsden, quoted in Bancroft, vol. v., p. 335.

[2] Ibid.

their own consent, given personally, or by their representatives.'

This declaration of the Congress was the result of serious deliberation. The discussion upon it lasted two weeks. Otis took a leading part. One of the questions was, whether Parliament could lay duties on trade. Robert R. Livingston, of New York, was in favor of making an explicit acknowledgment of the power. If it were denied, Britain, he said, would never give up the point of internal taxation. But it was vehemently insisted that there was no valid distinction between internal and external taxes; that the power of Parliament no more extended to the one than to the other. Otis, in his book, On the Rights of the Colonies, had already declared, that the imposition of taxes by Parliament, 'whether on trade or on land, on houses or ships, on real or personal, fixed or floating property, in the colonies, is absolutely irreconcilable with the rights of the colonists as British subjects and as men.' Rutledge agreed with him, and the Congress, by his hand, 'erased from the declaration of rights the unguarded concession.'[1] But while the power of Parliament to impose external duties was not admitted, neither was it explicitly denied. The Congress was not prepared to take either ground. They forbore to touch the question of right, but complained of the late restrictions on the trade of the colonies, as grievances.

Having agreed upon a statement of grievances, the Congress, after listening to objections from Gadsden and Lynch, to approaching Parliament with a petition at all, determined on that course, and appointed committees to prepare an address to the King, a memorial and petition to the House of Lords, and a petition to the House of Commons. Rutledge, although the youngest member of the Congress, was appointed chairman of the committee

---

[1] MS. Letter of Christopher Gadsden, quoted in Bancroft, vol. v., p. 335.

to prepare the memorial and petition to the House of Lords. His colleagues on the committee were Edward Tilghman of Maryland, and Philip Livingston of New York. They were appointed on Saturday, October 19th, and directed to bring in their report on the following Monday. Accordingly, on that day, 'they laid on the table, and humbly submitted to the correction of the Congress,' the draught of a memorial and petition to the Lords in Parliament. It was read, and, after sundry amendments, was approved and ordered to be engrossed. It dwelt chiefly on the inherent right of the colonies to trial by jury, exemption from all taxes but such as might be imposed on the people by their several Legislatures, and complained of the Stamp-Act, as it tended to deprive them of those two fundamental and invaluable rights and liberties; and also of several other late acts of Parliament, which extended the jurisdiction and powers of Courts of Admiralty in the colonies, beyond their limits in Great Britain, thereby making an unnecessary and unhappy distinction as to the modes of trial between them and their fellow-subjects at home, who never had excelled them in duty and loyalty to their common Sovereign.

The important and leading part taken by the South Carolina delegates, in the deliberations of the Congress, appears to have given that colony a consideration that had not hitherto been accorded to it. 'In the means of education,' says Ramsay, 'that Province was far behind those to the northward. Of it, little more was known or believed, than that it produced rice and indigo, and contained a large proportion of slaves, and a handful of freemen, and that most of the latter were strangers to vigorous health—all self-indulgent, and none accustomed to active exertions, either of mind or body. From such a province nothing great was expected. A respectable committee of its Assembly, and the distinguished abilities of one of them who was among the youngest members of the Congress, produced, at this first general meeting of the colonies, more favorable ideas of South Carolina, than had hitherto prevailed.'[1]

Several of the delegates to this Congress were afterwards fellow-laborers with Rutledge in more important scenes. But the chief spirit of the Congress, the man whom Rodney of Delaware, said, was the completest master of every subject, and threw most light on every question, viz., Otis,[2] he now met, for the first and last time. Between Otis and Rutledge there were many points of resemblance. They possessed the same fiery, aspiring qualities, and were distinguished for the same rapid, glowing eloquence. Otis was a son of Harvard, and a ripe and various scholar. Literature, however, had not restrained his faculties, nor confined their activity within formal limits. It served, not as weights to impede, but as wings to sustain the flights of his genius. Rutledge, without the specific training of Otis, displayed the intellectual qualities which many suppose only such training can bestow. Otis, we should say, had the deepest insight, and Rutledge the more rapid intuition. Otis traced far back to their native, original source, the rights of mankind, and the sanctions of government; while Rutledge, confining his view to the immediate question before him, formed his judgment upon a reference to its practical relations, rather than to theoretical principles. If we regard them as popular leaders, Rutledge was incomparably the superior. 'Otis was a prophet, not the leader of a party; full of sagacity in his inspirations, but wanting steadfast consistency of conduct.'[3] The

---

[1] History of South Carolina, vol. ii., p. 512.

[2] See Letter of John Adams to Dr. Morse, Nov. 29th, 1815, published in Morse's Revolution, pp. 195, 197. See Adams's opinion to the same effect, in the same letter.

[3] Bancroft, vol. v., p. 205.

administrative talents of Rutledge were of a distinguished order. He shone as conspicuously in action and council as in the forum. The same rapid, prompt, and decisive judgment, was evinced at the bar, on the bench, and at the head of civil affairs. As Otis and Rutledge resembled each other in certain points of character, so too there were certain points of resemblance in their history. Both, after long, ardent, and important public service, were deprived of the sunlight of reason, and descended to the grave amid the shades of mental alienation.

When the delegates from South Carolina arrived at Charleston on their return from the Congress, they found public affairs wearing a very serious aspect. The civil authority, here as elsewhere, had been set at defiance. Fort Johnson had been surprised and taken by a party of one hundred and fifty citizens; a portion of the stamped paper which had been deposited there for safety, was secured, and sent back in the same sloop of war which brought it out. The houses of several respectable but suspected citizens had been broken open, and searched for the obnoxious stamps. Chief Justice Skinner had been compelled to drink 'Damnation to the Stamp-Act;' and Colonel Laurens, who was equally averse to the obnoxious tax, and all irregular opposition to it, had barely escaped personal violence, by the exhibition of the utmost coolness and courage.[1] The bar had evinced a disposition to comply with the provisions of the act; but the excitement at home, and the tumults which had occurred to the northward, warned them of the danger of braving the popular will. Besides, when the first day of November arrived, the time fixed for the stamp-act to go into

[1] Drayton's Memoirs, vol. i., pp. 43–48. Johnson's Traditions of the Revolution, p. 14. Mr. Johnson has published in a note several letters of Mr. Laurens, describing the visit he received from the party in pursuit of stamped paper. They are curious, as showing the temper of the times.

operation, no stamps could be procured in the colony; and the clerk of the Court of Common Pleas, Dougal Campbell, refused to issue any process without them. The result was, that all judicial business was suspended in South Carolina, until news of the repeal of the stamp-act reached Charleston, early in the following May.[1]

'After the repeal of the Stamp-Act,' says Ramsay, 'John Rutledge was for some years no further engaged in politics than as a lawyer, and a member of the Provincial Legislature.'[2] Although he could not fail to regard the policy of the mother country with apprehension, yet there was nothing in the state of public affairs, for the next six or eight years, to interrupt his professional business. The ample means he now acquired were swallowed up during the Revolution, by liberal contributions to the public service, and by the destruction and depreciation that befell all private property during the distresses of that period.

In 1769, as we have already mentioned, the Circuit Court system was established in South Carolina.[3] Beaufort, Georgetown, Cheraw, Camden, Orangeburg, and Ninety-Six, were appointed the shire-towns of the districts, created by that act. The courts held in Charleston were not, strictly speaking, Circuit Courts. They were regarded, as are the courts of Westminster Hall, in England. All writs, and other civil process, issued from, and were returnable to the Court of Common Pleas in Charleston; and the practice was similar to that of the Courts of Assize and Nisi Prius.[4] The new system, undoubtedly, added much to the emoluments of the bar; for the people of the country districts, now having the means of legal redress at their own doors, appealed to

---

[1] Drayton's Memoirs, *supra*, pp. 49–59.

[2] History of South Carolina, vol. ii., p. 513. [3] Ante, p. 443.

[4] Brevard's Digest, Intro., vol. i., p. xiv.

the law, instead of administering justice in the wild and irregular manner that had hitherto been the vogue.

Referring to a conversation with General Pinckney, as to Rutledge's style of speaking, Mr. Fraser proceeds to say: 'Both of those gentlemen informed me, that when the circuits were first established, they rode them on horseback. General P. said that the most profitable part of the day to him was the morning, before the meeting of the court, in giving opinions to clients; and, when required to give them in writing, he took care to endorse on them, 'given on circuit,' not having the aid of books. He mentioned that he had once received fifty guineas before breakfast.'[1] Now, at the period referred to by Mr. Fraser, General Pinckney had not been long at the bar, and of course his practice was very unequal to Rutledge's. From this statement, therefore, of the professional receipts of the former, we may conceive the income of the latter.

On the 16th of August, 1771, occurred the fatal duel between Dr. John Haley, of Charleston, a man of distinction in his profession, and a son of Chief Justice De Lancey, of New York, 'an elegant, accomplished royalist,' and 'a brother of Mrs. Ralph Izard.' It arose out of a political discussion, 'at a genteel house of entertainment in St. Michael's alley. . . . De Lancey being irritated, probably from being foiled in argument, insulted Dr. Haley, by giving him the 'lie.' Haley immediately challenged De Lancey to fight with pistols at that house, and proposed that they should go together to an upper room, alone, and without seconds. De Lancey accepted the challenge, and the proposed arrangement. He took one of the pistols offered to him by Haley; they fought across a table, fired at the same moment, and De Lancey was killed. . . . De Lancey being a very distinguished

[1] Reminiscences of Charleston, p. 71.

man among the royalists, much irritation was exhibited among them at his death, and the circumstances attending it. The whigs, on the other hand, defended Dr. Haley, and concealed him until his trial came on.'[1] Rutledge was one of his counsel. It was proved that De Lancey was the aggressor; that he not only accepted the challenge, but the terms also; that he took Haley's offered pistol, and voluntarily followed him up stairs into a private room, as had been proposed; that he fired with intent to kill Haley with his own pistol; for the two balls with which it was loaded were taken out of the wall just back of his adversary, one on each side of where he stood. Haley was acquitted, and his acquittal was considered a great triumph by the whigs and popular party, situated as they were under the royal government. It was also considered by the royalists a proportionate source of chagrin.'[2]

In the early part of the year 1773, there arrived at Charleston a young man who had not yet attained the age of thirty, but whose genius, learning, and patriotism, had already inscribed his name on the rolls of fame. This was Josiah Quincy, Jun., of Boston. His journal mentions Rutledge but in a single instance. In other respects, however, it is quite curious. The following extract, as exhibiting the legislative manners of the period, is not without interest. Under the date of March 19th, he says: 'Spent all the morning in hearing the debates of the house; had an opportunity of hearing the best speakers in the province. The first thing done at the meeting of the house is to bring the mace, a very superb and elegant one, which cost ninety guineas, and lay it on the table before the Speaker. The next thing is for the clerk to read over, in a very audible voice, the doings of the preceding day. The Speaker is robed in

[1] Johnson's Traditions of the Revolution, pp. 45–47. [2] Ibid.

black, and has a very large wig of State, when he goes to attend the chair, (with the mace borne before him,) on delivery of speeches, &c. T. Lynch, Esq., spoke like a man of sense, and a patriot; with dignity, fire, and laconism. Mr. Gadsden was plain, blunt, hot, and incorrect, though very sensible. In the course of the debate, he used these very singular expressions, for a member of parliament:—'And, Mr. Speaker, if the Governor and Council don't see fit to fall in with us, I say, let the general duty-law, and all, go to the devil, Sir, and we go about our business.' Parsons, J. Rutledge, and Charles Pinckney, Sen., (the three first lawyers in the province,) spoke on the occasion; the two last very good speakers. The members conversed, lolled, and chatted, much like a friendly, jovial society, when nothing of importance was before the House; nay, once or twice, while the Speaker and clerk were busy in writing, the members spoke quite loud across the room to one another—a very unparliamentary appearance. The Speaker put the question sitting; the members gave their votes by rising from their seats; the dissentients did not rise.'[1]

The year following Quincy's visit to Charleston, a new scene opened upon the colonies; and, in the succeeding chapters, we shall trace the course of Rutledge, amid events of the most interesting character, in stations of grave responsibility, and high command, and see upon what foundation rests the distinguished reputation he enjoyed among his contemporaries, and which history and tradition have transmitted to posterity.

---

[1] Memoirs of J. Quincy, p. 112.

CHAPTER V.

ELECTED A DELEGATE TO CONGRESS.

1774.

A FEW months after the repeal of the Stamp-Act, the Rockingham administration was dismissed. It was succeeded by that heterogeneous cabinet so inimitably described by Burke, in a well-known passage of his speech on American Taxation. At its head was Pitt, now created Earl of Chatham; but his guiding hand was withdrawn by that mysterious sickness that confined him at Hayes nearly the whole period that he held the seals of office. The Chancellor of the Exchequer was the witty, genial, and versatile Charles Townshend. 'He had almost every great talent, and every little quality. His vanity excelled even his abilities; and his suspicions seemed to make him doubt whether he had any. With such a capacity he must have been the greatest man of his age, and perhaps inferior to no man in any age, had his faults been only in a moderate proportion — in short, if he had had but common truth, common sincerity, common honesty, common modesty, common steadiness, common courage, and common sense.'[1]

Townshend had advocated and voted for the Stamp-Act. With that versatility of opinion and conduct which gave him the title of the weather-cock, he voted for its repeal. Soon after coming into office, he discovered a

[1] Lord Orford's Memoirs, vol. ii., p. 59. Compare Burke's Sketch of Townshend, in his speech on American Taxation.

total change in the sentiments of Parliament with respect to the repeal. In a giddy moment, without any concert with his colleagues, and to their great astonishment and chagrin, he threw out an intimation that he should bring forward some measure to derive a revenue from America.[1] The project of American taxation had again become popular. The land-tax had been reduced, and the country gentlemen were glad to impose the burden from which they had been relieved, upon the distant colonies, while the partizans of authority were eager to atone for what they deemed the disgrace of the repeal-bill. Townshend was continually urged to perform what was treated as a deliberate engagement. He was forced to act. Accordingly, in May, 1767, a little more than a year after the repeal of the Stamp-Act, he introduced the memorable bill, imposing duties on all glass, lead, painters' colors, tea, and paper, imported into the American provinces.

Townshend's bill was framed on the idea that the Americans would not object to external or port-duties. They were understood to admit the constitutional right of parliament to impose them. That had been the public declaration of Franklin only the year before. Many Americans, who happened to be in London, and were attached to the British connexion, assured the Chancellor of the Exchequer, that if the tax only bore the appearance of port-duties, it would not be objected to.[2] The result showed how widely they mistook the sentiments of their countrymen. The discussions of the time had provoked reflection and inquiry.[3] The very foundations of parliamentary power had been fearlessly explored. Thinking minds began to doubt the competence of parliament to legislate for the colonies in any case whatsoever. The

[1] Grafton's MS. Memoirs. Orford's Memoirs, vol. ii., p. 36.

[2] Lord Orford's Memoirs, vol. ii., p. 25, note. Cavendish's Debates, vol. i., p. 213.

[3] Adams's Works, vol. ii., p. 154.

Tea-Act led to an immediate scrutiny of the question whether there was any difference between external and internal taxes. The conclusion was, that while external or port-duties, as a regulation of trade, were admissible, parliament had no power to impose them, as a source of supply. The preamble to the bill stated the latter to be the object of the import; and it became, as might have been foreseen, 'a tax of disputation, a tax of war and rebellion, a tax for anything but benefit to the imposers, or satisfaction to the subject.'[1]

Its fruit was the Boston Port-Bill, which brought the dispute between the colonies and the mother country to a crisis. The intelligence of that act reached Charleston, May 31st, 1774. Here, as elsewhere, it was received with sentiments of indignation and alarm. If New England was subjugated, the evil genius of tyranny, it was said, would soon triumph over the liberties of the whole continent. 'Where gay fields now smile,' was the language of one of the publications, issued on this occasion, 'bedecked in the yellow robe of full-eared harvest, soon would desolation frown over the uncultivated earth. Suns would in vain arise, and in vain would showers descend; for who would be industrious when others would reap the fruit of his labor? After the subjugation of Boston, New York, and Philadelphia, our turn would be next.'[2]

On the 13th of June, the General Committee met, and unanimously agreed to call a meeting of the inhabitants of the colony on the 6th of July, 'to consider of the papers, letters, and resolutions, transmitted to the committee from the Northern colonies; and also of such steps as are necessary to be pursued, in union with the inhabitants of all our sister colonies on this continent, in order to avert the dangers impending over American liberties

---

[1] Burke. [2] Force's Archives, (4th series,) vol. i., p. 382, 383.

in general, by the late hostile Act of Parliament against Boston, and other arbitrary measures of the British ministry.'[1]

Public notice was immediately given of this action of the committee in the Gazettes; and circular letters were despatched by express to all the leading men throughout the colony, 'to engage their union, assistance, and influence, in their several districts, to attend, either personally, or by deputies authorized to declare their sentiments,'[2] at the general meeting, convened at Charleston.

On that occasion, 'the largest body of the most respectable inhabitants'[3] that had ever been brought together in the colony, assembled at the Exchange in Charleston. 'Gentlemen of the greatest property and character, ... notwithstanding the extreme inconvenience of the season, from even the remotest parts of the country, attended.'[4] One hundred and four delegates appeared; but it was determined that whoever came to the meeting, 'and a crowded meeting it was,' might give his vote.[5] 'The 6th, 7th, and 8th instant,' wrote Miles Brewton to Josiah Quincy, Jun., on the 12th of July, 'we had the greatest assembly of the inhabitants of this colony I ever

---

[1] This meeting of the committee of the colony appears to have been an informal one, at which were present the inhabitants of Charleston. Indeed, Drayton speaks of it as 'a meeting of the inhabitants of Charleston.' Memoirs, vol. i., p. 112. (See also Ramsay's Revolution of S. C.) But the minute of the proceedings on that occasion shows, that they were conducted by the committee. Vide Force's Archives, (4th series,) vol. i., p. 408.

[2] Letter from a gentleman in Charleston to his correspondent in New York, June 13th, 1774. Ibid.

[3] Letter from a gentleman in Charleston to a gentleman in Boston, July 11th, 1774. Force's Archives, vol. i., p. 531. [4] Ibid.

[5] Drayton's Memoirs, vol. i., p. 120. 'It was proposed, and agreed to unanimously, that the deputies should be chosen by ballot, and that every free white person residing in the province should be entitled to vote.' Force's Archives, vol. i., p. 532.

saw.'[1] There was a general concurrence of opinion as to the propriety of sending deputies to the proposed Congress; but the merchants, and the inhabitants of the interior, were opposed to a non-importation and non-exportation agreement. Indeed, that was the prevailing sentiment of the colony. It was urged that prior to any suspension of commerce with Great Britain, the general Congress should send a petition and remonstrance to the Throne. If these were ineffectual, it would then be proper to test the efficacy of non-importation and non-exportation. These views were supported by Rutledge. The subject was warmly discussed at the meeting. On the second day the vote was taken, and the measure of non-exportation and non-importation was rejected.

This was a triumph for the moderate party, to which Rutledge, notwithstanding the impetuosity and vehemence of his character, at this time belonged. It was next resolved, that five deputies should be chosen by ballot, to represent the colony in the general Congress at Philadelphia. As that body, however, might contain a majority of delegates in favor of non-importation and non-exportation, it was an object of great importance with the opponents of that measure, to define and limit the powers of the South Carolina delegates. Rawlins Lowndes, the Speaker of the Commons House of Assembly, contended, that unless their powers were limited, being outnumbered by the Northern deputies, they and their constituents would be bound by measures, whose propriety and legality they absolutely denied.[2] 'In this crisis, John Rutledge, in a most eloquent speech, advocated a motion which he brought forward, to give no instructions whatever, but to invest the men of their choice, with full authority to concur in any measure they thought

---

[1] Force's Archives, *supra*, p. 534. See also, Quincy's Quincy.

[2] Drayton's Memoirs, vol. i., pp. 126–131. Force's Archives, vol. i., pp. 531–534.

best; and to pledge the people of South Carolina to abide by whatever they would agree to. He demonstrated that anything less than plenary discretion to this extent would be unequal to the crisis. To those who, after stating the dangers of such extensive powers, begged to be informed what must be done in case the delegates made a bad use of their unlimited authority to pledge the State to any extent, a laconic answer was returned: 'HANG THEM.' An impression was made on the multitude. Their minds were subdued by the decision of the proposed measure, and the energy with which it was supported.' [1]

The motion advocated by Rutledge, and adopted by the meeting, did not pledge the support of the colony to the measures of the general Congress, but only to such measures as might be agreeable to the opinions of their deputies. It was, nevertheless, regarded by the advocates of vigorous action, of non-importation, and non-exportation, as some compensation for the rejection of that line of policy. 'Do not be surprised at not seeing any non-importation or exportation resolves,' wrote a gentleman in Charleston, to his friend in New York. 'We had such, but gave them up, to succeed in the allowing full powers to our deputies, which was gaining a grand point.' [2]

Having determined to send deputies to the Congress, and with such powers as we have described, the important question now was, who those deputies should be. The merchants dreaded nothing so much as a non-importation and non-exportation agreement. 'Hence they aimed that such men should be elected deputies as were against the adoption of that measure.' [3] The candidates they supported were Henry Middleton, Rawlins Lowndes, Charles Pinckney, Miles Brewton, and John Rutledge. The poll

---

[1] Ramsay's History of South Carolina, vol. ii., p. 514.

[2] Force's Archives, vol. i., p. 525. July 8th, 1774.

[3] Drayton, vol. i., p. 131.

was opened at two o'clock, and closed at six. The merchants appeared there in a body. They also sent for their clerks to come and vote. The opposite party took the alarm; 'many of them ran to all parts of the town to collect people, and bring them to the poll; in consequence of which the merchants were defeated, and, except two gentlemen, other deputies than those they supported were chosen.'[1] 'At midnight, in presence of several hundred spectators, the election was declared in favor of'[2] Henry Middleton, John Rutledge, Thomas Lynch, Christopher Gadsden, and Edward Rutledge.[3]

Aware of the temper that prevailed in the General Assembly, Lieutenant-Governor Bull had effectually prevented their adopting any resolutions respecting public affairs, by repeatedly proroguing them. He had pursued this course since March. It was now deemed very desirable, that the proceedings of the general meeting of the colony, should be recognized and sanctioned, by the Legislative authority of the Province. The Assembly stood prorogued to the 2d of August. The members privately agreed to convene early in the morning of that day, and, if possible, adopt resolutions suitable to the occasion, before the Lieutenant-Governor should have an opportunity to prorogue them.[4] The result is disclosed in the follow-

[1] Drayton, vol. i., p. 131.

[2] Letter from Charleston, received in Boston, July 11th, 1774. Force's Archives, vol. i., p. 532.

[3] 'Their powers are unlimited,' wrote Miles Brewton to Josiah Quincy, Jun., 'and I hope the other colonies will do the same, and place entire confidence in their deputies; they can do nothing effectual without such powers. I should suppose the first step taken by Congress would be to remonstrate, and petition King, Lords, and Commons. Our grievances should be all stated in the way of a bill of rights; and some of the deputies should go to England with the petition. If redress does not come, then all to enter into a non-import and non-export agreement. I think this seems to be the sense of almost all the colonies.' Ibid., p. 534. July 12th, 1774. See also Quincy's Quincy, p. 174.

[4] Drayton, vol. i., p. 137. Force's Archives, vol. i., p. 671, 672.

ing extract from a letter of that functionary to the Earl of Dartmouth, written the 3d of August: 'It having been expected,' he says, 'that I should prorogue the General Assembly yesterday, at the usual time, about ten or eleven o'clock, the Assembly privately and punctually met at eight o'clock in the morning, and made a house which was very uncommon. They had not been assembled five minutes before I was apprized of it. I immediately went to the Council Chamber, in order to prorogue them, and waited a few minutes for one or two of the Council to be present. As soon as I sent for the Assembly they attended, and I prorogued them to the 6th of September. But their business having been ready prepared, in which they were all previously agreed, it required only a few minutes to pass through the forms of the House. They came to two resolutions, one approving and confirming the election of the five persons, chosen on the 6th of last month, to assist at the Congress of the several Provinces; and the other, that they would provide for the expense of their voyage.[1] I returned to my own house again in less than twenty minutes past eight. Your Lordship will see by this instance, with what perseverance, secrecy, and unanimity, they form and conduct their designs.'[2]

Of the delegates, whom we have thus seen elected to the Congress, John Rutledge and Christopher Gadsden stood, as the representatives of opinions, totally distinct and opposed. Their characters were unlike, and the line of policy they respectively advocated, equally so. Gadsden was in favor of immediate non-importation and non-exportation. Rutledge was opposed to it. Gadsden believed the discordant views of the two countries to be

---

[1] They voted £1500 sterling for defraying the expenses of the five delegates.

[2] Force's Archives, vol. i., p. 672.

irreconcilable, and was even now an advocate of independence. Rutledge clung to the British connection, as essential to the welfare of both England and the colonies, and was among the warmest, as well as ablest, who desired an accommodation of their differences.

Gadsden was a pure, unselfish patriot, with clear views, sagacious mind, and undoubted honor. He was a sincere and ardent republican. He had true courage, not merely the courage that belongs to the animal creation, but courage of a nobler strain, that which maintains the convictions of the judgment, and the dictates of the conscience, unappalled by danger, and unswerved by obloquy or clamor. His aims were single, and he pursued them with undiverted attention. His political consistency was like 'one entire and perfect chrysolite.' He was not so remarkable for intellectual elevation as for the thorough sincerity with which he held his opinions, the unfaltering steadiness with which he maintained them, and the clear, unclouded apprehension he had of the results of political events. He was no orator, but abrupt, blunt, and direct.

> ——'He poured out all as plain,
> As downright Shippen, or as old Montaigne.'

It has been said that he was obstinate, and did not yield proper respect to the opinions and wishes of his coadjutors. To be sure, he was inflexible, and had 'damnable iteration in him;' but it must be remembered that he was in advance of most of those with whom he acted. He contemplated different results, and supported measures that had in view, what he foresaw, must be the inevitable future condition of affairs. We never hear complaints of his obstinacy from such men as John and Samuel Adams, Samuel Chase, Patrick Henry, and the Lees. Their system of politics was in harmony, and their action accordant.

The reputation of Gadsden, for talents and oratory, was

inferior to Rutledge's. The life of the latter, from the commencement of his career, had been crowned with uninterrupted success. At an age when most young men are determining the choice of a profession, he had won the honors of his; and then passing from the triumphs of the bar to the deliberations of the Senate, he rose at once, without delay or laborious gradation, to a lead in the politics of the Province. He was distinguished now, as ever after, for his penetrating judgment and decisive will. His powers of eloquence did not constitute his chief excellence as a public man. They were, nevertheless, undoubtedly great. His distinction as a public speaker, was mainly owing to the force and earnestness of his own convictions, the luminous manner with which he displayed his views, and the impression conveyed by his high and dauntless character. His illustrations were drawn from natural and familiar sources, and forced home his meaning to the commonest understanding. He was too intent on his objects, too resolute in the assertion of his sentiments, to be deluded himself, or attempt to delude others, by the tinsel of rhetoric. His speeches were more calculated to arouse and animate, than to touch the heart, and 'ope the sacred source of sympathetic tears.' Patrick Henry enchained and subdued the feelings of his auditors by the depth of his emotion, by his wonderful powers of expression, his voice, look, gesture, and his entire harmony with nature. The vehemence of Rutledge frequently hurried him beyond the 'golden mean,' and in his action, there was 'wasteful and superfluous excess.' He was particularly effective in retort, and rose to his full power, when provoked by frivolous objections to his views.

'I have heard from his contemporaries, the Generals Pinckney, Judge Bay, and Mr. Pringle,' writes one of his descendants, to whose kind and generous aid, I owe much, 'that though his manner was imperious when the occasion required, it was marked, under ordinary circumstances, by the calmness that always accompanies mental strength. When there was anything to be done, he saw at once, instinctively, as it were, the best, often, the only course to be pursued. For this, he would state his reasons with wonderful force and clearness; then, if his coadjutors wavered, or refused to see what he had thrown a strong light on, he would turn on them a Jupiter Tonans look, and break forth, with a power and eloquence, that carried the timid and doubting, along with the convinced.'[1]

> 'So looks the chafed lion
> Upon the daring huntsman that has galled him,
> Then, makes him nothing.'

With character and powers such as we have described, Rutledge took his seat in the Congress of 1774; and in the next chapter we shall contemplate his services in that distinguished Assembly.

---

[1] Vide Post, Chap. VII., as to the conflicting opinions of John Adams and Patrick Henry, respecting Rutledge's merits as an orator.

CHAPTER VI.

SERVICES IN THE CONGRESS OF 1774.

RUTLEDGE came to the Congress of 1774, prepared to take a leading part in its deliberations, not less from his personal and intellectual qualities, than his legislative experience. He was 'native and endued unto that element.' The members of this Congress, though, as a body, men of high character, the first, in abilities and estimation, of their respective colonies, were, for the most part, strangers to each other. Of those who had been delegates to the Stamp-Act Congress, there now reappeared on this more important scene, Rutledge, Gadsden, and Lynch of South Carolina, M'Kean and Rodney of Delaware, Dickinson[1] and Morton of Pennsylvania, Philip Livingston of New York, and Dyer of Connecticut.

Philadelphia, at this period, enjoyed a high reputation for the hospitality and refinement of its society. The delegates to the Congress were shown every mark of attention and respect. In the polished intercourse of social life attachments were formed, opinions interchanged, and sympathies and feelings created, which were at once the bond of personal harmony, and the surest and most durable support of political union. The diary of John Adams makes frequent mention of the agreeable parties at which he was present, while Congress was in session; and his impressions, which he has not failed to record, of the several persons with whom he was brought in contact, on these occasions, are very curious.

---

[1] Mr. Dickinson took his seat in Congress October 17, 1774.

The Congress assembled and organized, on the 5th of September. Many of the delegates, however, had arrived at Philadelphia several days before. Adams appears to have met Rutledge, for the first time, on the 1st instant. 'In the evening,' he says, 'all the gentlemen of the Congress who were arrived in town met at Smith's the new city tavern, and spent the evening together. Twenty-five members were come; Virginia, North Carolina, Maryland, and the city of New York, were not arrived. Mr. William Livingston, from the Jerseys, lately of New York, was there. He is a plain man, tall, black, wears his hair; nothing elegant or genteel about him. They say he is no public speaker, but very sensible and learned, and a ready writer. Mr. Rutledge, the elder, was there; but his appearance is not very promising. There is no keenness in his eye, no depth in his countenance—nothing of the profound, sagacious, brilliant, or sparkling, in his first appearance.'[1] We shall see, hereafter, that when Adams was brought into more intimate relations with Rutledge, and observed the powers of his mind, and the force and energy of his character, he recorded a very different estimate of him than in the above extract. 'Dined at Mr. Thomas Mifflin's,' says Adams' diary of the 2d instant, 'with Mr. Lynch, Mr. Middleton, and the two Rutledges with their ladies. The two Rutledges are good lawyers. . . . . We were very sociable and happy.' The following evening, Adams, the Rutledges, and several others, were again at Mr. Mifflin's. 'Spent the evening at Mr. Mifflin's, with Lee and Harrison from Virginia, the two Rutledges, Dr. Witherspoon, Dr. Shippen, Dr. Steptoe, and another gentleman. An elegant supper; and we drank sentiments till eleven o'clock. Lee and Harrison were very high; Lee had dined with Mr. Dickinson, and drank Burgundy the whole afternoon.'

---

[1] Adams' Works, vol. ii., p. 361.

After mentioning Edward Rutledge, and in terms not the most flattering, Adams thus speaks of John Rutledge: 'His brother,' he says, 'still maintains the air of reserve, design, and cunning, like Duane, and Galloway, and Bob Auchmuty. Cæsar Rodney is the oddest-looking man in the world; he is tall, thin, and slender as a reed; pale. His face is not bigger than a large apple, yet there is sense and fire, spirit, wit, and humor in his countenance.'[1] These personal impressions, made by so distinguished a character as Rutledge upon an able contemporary, when tested by subsequent observation and the lights of history, are interesting and worthy of notice. What Adams describes as an 'air of reserve, design, and cunning,' was doubtless nothing more than a disinclination, on the part of Rutledge, to be drawn into a discussion of points that would engage the attention of the Congress, and with regard to which, opinions were not altogether in harmony. His manner, however, at times, and especially in the latter part of his life, was high, remote, and 'prouder than when blue iris bends.'

On the 5th of September, the delegates to the Congress, as we have elsewhere seen, met and organized.[2] The President, Peyton Randolph, and the Secretary, Charles Thomson, were both proposed by Mr. Lynch, whom Adams describes as 'a solid, firm, judicious man,' and unanimously chosen. The first question that engaged the attention of the Congress was, the method of voting, whether it should be by Colonies, or by poll, or by interests. In Adams' notes of the discussion that ensued, he does not distinguish between the Rutledges, and we are left to conjecture whether it was John or Edward who participated in the debate.[3] Lynch was of

---

[1] Adams, vol. ii., p. 364.

[2] Ante, p. 81.

[3] He leaves us in the same uncertainty as to which of the brothers opposed the proposition to open Congress with prayer. See Ante, p. 85.

opinion that the weight of a colony should be determined by a compound of numbers and property. Gadsden said, he could see no way of voting, but by colonies; and Rutledge observed that they had no legal authority; and obedience to their determinations would only follow the reasonableness, the apparent utility and necessity of the measures they adopted. They had no coercive or legislative authority; their constituents were bound only in honor to observe their determinations. Congress finally resolved that each colony should have one vote; but an entry was made upon the journals, to prevent this determination being considered a precedent for the future.

On the 6th instant, it was unanimously resolved, that a committee be appointed to state the rights of the colonies in general, the several instances in which those rights had been violated or infringed, and the means most proper to be pursued for obtaining a restoration of them. The next day it was determined that the committee should consist of two delegates from each colony. Lynch and Rutledge were appointed on the part of South Carolina. On the 8th instant, the committee assembled, 'and a most ingenious, entertaining debate we had,' says Adams.[1] The great points of discussion were, whether they should recur to the law of nature, as well as to the British constitution, and to their American charters and grants; and secondly, whether they should deny the authority of Parliament in all cases; whether they should allow any authority to it in their internal affairs; or whether they should allow it to regulate the trade of the empire, with or without any restrictions.[2]

We have seen that Jay contended for the right of emigration, where a mother country was surcharged with inhabitants; and that in such a case the emigrants were

---

[1] Adams, vol. ii., p. 370.

[2] Ante, pp. 92–97. Adams, vol. ii., p. 374.

no longer bound to allegiance, and might erect what government they pleased.[2] Rutledge combated his positions, and denied that emigrants would have a right to set up what constitution they pleased. A subject, he said, could not alienate his allegiance. That was the prevailing doctrine of his day; but it is repugnant to the principles and practice of that government which he assisted to create, as well as to the more enlightened ideas of modern times.

The discussions of the committee, says Adams, 'spun into great length, and nothing was decided. After many fruitless essays, the committee determined to appoint a sub-committee to make a draught of a set of articles that might be laid in writing before the grand committee, and become the foundation of a more regular debate and final decision. I was appointed on the sub-committee, in which, after going over the ground again, a set of articles were drawn and debated one by one. After several days' deliberation, we agreed upon all the articles excepting one, and that was the authority of Parliament, which was indeed the essence of the whole controversy; some were for a flat denial of all authority;[2] others for denying the power of taxation only; some for denying internal, but admitting external, taxation. After a multitude of motions had been made, discussed, and negatived, it seemed as if we should never agree upon anything. Mr. John Rutledge of South Carolina, one of the committee, addressing himself to me, was pleased to say, "Adams, we

[1] Adams, vol. ii., p. 93.

[2] 'Visited Mr. Gadsden,' says Adams, in his Diary of September 14th, 'Mr. Deane, Colonel Dyer, &c., at their lodgings. Gadsden is violent against allowing to Parliament any power of regulating trade, or allowing that they have anything to do with us. 'Power of regulating trade,' he says, 'is power of ruining us; as bad as acknowledging them a supreme legislative in all cases whatsoever; a right of regulating trade is a right of legislation; and a right of legislation in one case is a right in all; this I deny.' Adams' Works, vol. ii., p. 379.

must agree upon something; you appear to be as familiar with the subject as any of us, and I like your expressions,—'*the necessity of the case*,' and '*excluding all ideas of taxation, external and internal*;' I have a great opinion of that same idea of the necessity of the case, and I am determined against all taxation for revenue. Come, take the pen and see if you can't produce something that will unite us." Some others of the committee seconding Mr. Rutledge, I took a sheet of paper and drew up an article. When it was read, I believe not one of the committee was fully satisfied with it; but they all soon acknowledged that there was no hope of hitting on anything in which we could all agree with more satisfaction. All therefore agreed to this, and upon this depended the union of the colonies. The sub-committee reported their draught to the grand committee, and another long debate ensued, especially on this article, and various changes and modifications of it were attempted, but none adopted.'[1]

While this discussion was occupying the attention of the committee, the other committee which had been appointed

---

[1] This article is the 4th in the series of resolutions adopted by the Congress, and is as follows: Resolved, That the foundation of English liberty, and of all free government, is a right in the people to participate in their legislative council: and as the English colonists are not represented, and from their local and other circumstances cannot be properly represented in the British Parliament, they are entitled to a free and exclusive power of legislation in their several Provincial legislatures, where their right of representation can alone be preserved, in all cases of taxation and internal polity, subject only to the negative of their Sovereign, in such manner as has been heretofore used and accustomed. But, from the necessity of the case, and a regard to the mutual interest of both countries, we cheerfully consent to the operation of such Acts of the British Parliament, as are, *bona fide*, restrained to the regulation of our external commerce, for the purpose of securing the commercial advantages of the whole empire to the mother country, and the commercial benefits of its respective members; excluding every idea of taxation, internal or external, for raising a revenue on the subjects in America, without their consent.' See Ante, p. 97.

to examine and report the several statutes which affect the Trade and Manufactures of the Colonies, brought in their report. This was on the 17th of September. On the 19th, it was referred to the committee appointed to state the Rights of the Colonies. This latter committee made their report on the 22d. On the 24th, it was resolved, that the Congress do confine themselves, at present, to the consideration of such rights only as have been infringed, since the year 1763. The committee now brought in a second report, which related to the violations of such rights.

When the South Carolina delegates returned home, 'many questions were proposed to them,' by the Assembly, 'relative to various parts of the proceedings. . . . One of the most important of these was, why, at a time when a number of gentlemen were sent to Congress, from all parts of America, for the express purpose of considering and stating the American grievances, and for devising the proper means of redressing them, why did they limit their researches to the year 1763, and not trace back, as could easily have been done, the many aggressions which had been committed by Great Britain upon her infant colonies; in the jealousies, monopolies, and prohibitions, with which she was so prodigal towards them; for the express purpose of depressing their population—confining their trade — and crippling their attempts, at even the most domestic and necessary manufactures?'[1] To this it was answered, that while the delegates of South Carolina, as well as the greater part of the other delegates, were willing to have fully displayed all their grievances, the Virginia delegates were limited in their powers, and could not go further back than the year 1763. Besides, they declared in conversation, that it had been agreed upon at home, not to go beyond that year, as they would thereby throw greater odium on the reign of George III.[2]

[1] Drayton's Memoirs, vol. i., p. 158. [2] Ibid., p. 159.

The reports of the committee were ultimately adopted by Congress; but meanwhile that body proceeded to consider the most proper means to obtain a restoration of their rights. We have elsewhere stated[1] that the merchants of Charleston voted for delegates who were opposed, or supposed to be so, to non-importation and non-exportation, and that among the number was Rutledge. But when he came to the Congress, he was prepared to support that measure. His views upon this subject, like those of Jay, yielded to the necessity of the occasion, and the wishes of the people. But to make the measure, as he contended, equal and effective, he was for its immediate adoption, and for the total detention of all American commodities, in the colonies. Undoubtedly, it would have been the better policy to have followed this advice. 'You would have saved a civil war, if you had,' said Chase of Maryland, when discussing this subject, in the Congress of 1775; 'but it could not be carried; the gentlemen from South Carolina could not prevail to stop our exports to Britain, Ireland, and West Indies.'[2] The Virginia delegates were restrained by their instructions, from assenting to a non-exportation agreement, before the 10th of August, 1775.[3] 'Though the Virginians are tied up,' said Gadsden, 'I would be for doing it without them. Boston and New England can't hold out. The country will be deluged in blood, if we don't act with spirit. Don't let America look at this mountain and let it bring forth a mouse.' 'I am both for non-importation and non-exportation, to take place immediately,' said Edward Rutledge. But the North Carolina and Mary-

[1] Ante, p. 473.

[2] Adams' Works, vol. ii., p. 477. Rutledge's proposition was, that trade should be stopped to all the world; and that all remittances should cease.

[3] See these instructions, *in extenso*, in Force's Archives, vol. i., p. 689.

land delegates said their exports were similar to those of Virginia, and if they acted independently of her, their commodities would be carried to her ports, and shipped as usual. 'We can't come into a non-exportation immediately, without Virginia,' observed Chase of Maryland. Richard Henry Lee said, that 'all considerations of interest, and of equality of sacrifice, should be laid aside. Produce of the other colonies is carried to market in the same year when it is raised, even rice. Tobacco is not until the next year.'

As immediate non-exportation could not be carried, Rutledge and his colleagues, with the exception of Gadsden, insisted that rice and indigo should not be included within the operation of the article. This proposition was very unfavorably received, and well-nigh occasioned a division in Congress. Business was suspended for several days, in order to give the South Carolina delegation time for reflection.[1] When the non-importation, non-consumption, and non-exportation association was being perfected, and the members were affixing their signatures to that instrument, Middleton, the two Rutledges, and Lynch, withdrew. Gadsden offered to sign alone. 'Carolina was on the point of being excluded the association, when our deputies,' we are quoting Gadsden's explanation to the Provincial Congress,[2] 'being again summoned

[1] We follow Gadsden's statement to the Provincial Congress, as reported by Drayton, vol. i., p. 164, though it is impossible to determine, from the journals of Congress, when the suspension of business, he speaks of, could have occurred.

[2] Drayton's Memoirs, vol. i., p. 164. This exception, in favor of the rice-planters, gave very general offence to the Whigs throughout the colonies; whilst the ministerial party made it the subject of taunt and ridicule. In a very able pamphlet, printed by Rivington of New York, entitled, 'What think ye of the Congress now? or An Inquiry, How Far the Americans are bound to abide by, and execute the Decisions of the late Congress?' the obnoxious article of the association is thus referred to: 'The reason of this partiality is known in part. The dele-

by the Secretary, they returned into Congress, yielding up the article of indigo; and Congress, only for the sake of preserving the union of America, allowed the article rice to be added to the association.'[1] The language of this agreement, as finally adopted, was, that if the obnoxious acts of Parliament were not repealed before the 10th of September, 1775, the colonies would not, directly or indirectly, export any merchandise, or commodity whatsoever, to Great Britain, Ireland, or the West Indies, *except rice to Europe.*[2] The reason assigned by Congress for this suspension of non-exportation, was an earnest desire not to injure their fellow-subjects upon whom it was to operate.

---

gates from Carolina were firmly attached to the interests of their constituents, and would not consent to their immediate ruin. They opposed and remonstrated with spirit; and, rather than they should be suffered to withdraw themselves from the Congress, as they threatened, their requisition was granted. Had the delegates from this province, who are not suspected of wanting as firm an attachment to our interests, been possessed of as intrepid a resolution as their brethren from Carolina, and followed their spirited example, we might have come in too for some share of indulgence. But they always suffered themselves to be borne down by a majority of votes, from the republicans of the East, and the aristocracies of the South; and the consequence is, that we have received no more benefit from an actual representation in the Congress, than from a virtual one in Parliament." This pamphlet is in the Philadelphia Library, No. 1594, O.

[1] 'This phraseology,' says the writer of the pamphlet above mentioned, 'is original, and hardly intelligible. In exactly the same style the Provincial Congress of the Massachusetts Bay might resolve: "We will export nothing to Pennsylvania, the three Lower counties, or Long Island, *except codfish to the North American colonies.*" But, to let this pass — By the *artful* construction of the sentence, it seems to have been the design of the Congress to delude the Americans, with an insinuation that rice might be exported from Carolina to Europe in general, without sending any part of it to Great Britain.' On a subsequent page we have considered the effect of this article of the association, in connection with the Acts of Parliament respecting the exportation of rice.

[2] South Carolina, at this time, exported about twelve thousand weight of indigo, one hundred and fifty thousand tierces of rice, and employed about three hundred ships.

We shall see hereafter, that the discrimination in favor of the rice-planters was very odious to the people of South Carolina, and a subject of violent discussion in the provincial legislature.

In the debate that ensued in Congress, when the motion was first made for a non-importation, Rutledge said, he thought all the ways and means of redress should be proposed. He was anxious, at this serious and portentous crisis, to adopt some comprehensive scheme, that should harmonize the discordant elements, and establish the connection between the mother country and her colonies on a firm and durable basis. Accordingly, when Galloway, on the 28th of September, presented to the Congress his 'plan of a proposed union between Great Britain and the Colonies,' Rutledge was among those who supported it. 'I came with an idea,' said Edward Rutledge in the discussion that ensued, 'of getting a bill of rights and a plan of permanent relief. I think the plan may be freed from almost every objection. I think it almost a perfect plan.' Its leading features we have described elsewhere.[1] It was favorably received, and, after a long debate, was referred for further consideration. It was finally defeated by the close vote of six colonies to five. Foremost among its opponents, as would appear from Adams' brief notes of the discussion, were Patrick Henry and Richard Henry Lee. 'The original constitution of the colonies,' said the former, 'was founded on the broadest and most generous base. The regulation of our trade was compensation enough for all the protection we ever experienced from her.' 'How did we go on,' inquired Lee, 'for one hundred and sixty years before the year 1763? We flourished and grew. This plan would make such

[1] Ante, p. 105, 106. See the plan *in extenso*, in Force's Archives, vol. i., p. 905. See a letter from Franklin, then in London, to Galloway, respecting his plan. Works of Franklin, vol. viii., p. 144, Feb. 26, 1775.

changes in the legislature of the colonies, that I could not agree to it without consulting my constituents.' The feelings of Henry were strongly enlisted against this plan of reconciliation and adjustment; and he appears to have regarded its supporters with even less complacency than the plan itself. 'He has a horrid opinion of Galloway, Jay, and the Rutledges,' says Adams, in recording an interview with him, on the 11th of October. 'Their system, he says, would ruin the cause of America. He is very impatient to see such fellows, and not be at liberty to describe them in their true colors.'[1]

On the first of October, Richard Henry Lee, John Adams, Thomas Johnson, Patrick Henry, and John Rutledge, were appointed a committee to prepare a loyal address to the King, stating the grievances of the colonies, and requesting his majesty's interposition for their removal. The first draft of this address was from the pen of Mr. Lee. When reported to the Congress, it was found to be too high-toned for the prevailing sentiments of that body. It was re-committed, and John Dickinson, at the same time, added to the committee. The draft, as adopted by the Congress, was his production.[2]

The Congress adjourned on the 26th of October. Notwithstanding the apparent harmony that is indicated by their published proceedings, there is reason to suppose that many of the delegates were opposed to several of the measures that were adopted. They were bound, however, to lend to them the sanction of their names, by a previous agreement, that whatever was carried by a ma-

---

[1] Ante, p. 109. Adams' Works, vol. ii., p. 396. The Address to the King was now under consideration, and doubtless the sentiments of conciliation that Rutledge proposed, in addition to his support of Galloway's plan, led to Henry's harsh censure of his system of politics.

[2] See Ante, p. 116, as to conflicting statements respecting the authorship of this Address.

jority of votes, should be subscribed by all the members, and that no protest or dissent should appear on the journals.[1] But the great mass of the people of the colonies hailed the result of their labors with unaffected satisfaction, and yielded to their recommendations a cheerful obedience.

The opponents of the ministry in Great Britain,

---

[1] In a contemporaneous publication, (What think ye of the Congress now? See Ante, p. 487,) the author, who criticises, with great vigor and ability, the proceedings of that body, gives the following history of the agreement mentioned in the text: 'The Congress being met together,' he says, 'and having inspected and compared their various commissions, were next to proceed upon business. With a view of facilitating the proceedings, a very worthy and respectable member, eminent both for his knowledge of the law and his love of constitutional liberty, presented a plan, which he carefully drew up in the cool hours of leisure and retirement, and in which he endeavored to point out such claims of the colonies as might be prudently asserted, and the particular modes of address that would be most likely to secure them. This paper of proposals at first met with all the respect that was due to the author's abilities; and nothing appeared that was inconsistent with the genuine spirit of candor and moderation on one side, and a due regard to the dignity and honor of Great Britain on the other. During this state of flattering tranquillity, the artful leaders of the Congress found no great difficulty in persuading those members who were patriots in reality, moderate and pacific, honest and unsuspicious, to bind themselves in an agreement, that their names should be subscribed to whatever should be carried by a majority of votes, and that no protest or dissent should appear in the minutes. After this great point was secured, it was not long before those same leaders took occasion to throw off their mask, and to discover their own natural features. This new appearance was no more expected by some that were present, than the springing of a mine, or the bursting of a bomb, in Carpenter's Hall; nor was it less astonishing to them than such an explosion would have been. The moderate party soon found that they had been circumvented and ensnared; that they were allowed to have no influence in the debates; that their remonstrances were slighted; and that everything was borne down by the impetuosity of their managers. Then it was that duty and honor required them, as I conceive, to leave the Hall. This account of the unpublished transactions within doors is not a fiction of the writer's imagination, but what he has collected from credible report.'

both in Parliament and out of it, applauded the measures of the Congress in firm and manly language. We have elsewhere quoted the eloquent tribute of Lord Chatham to the merits of their proceedings, in his great and admired speech on American affairs, wherein he urged the recall of the troops from Boston, and a repeal of the obnoxious legislation.[1] It was a question of the greatest magnitude, involving the fate of empire, and appealing powerfully to the feelings of that illustrious character, whose attachment to the glory and welfare of his country was the strongest passion of his breast. 'Lord Chatham,' says Quincy, who was present on this memorable occasion, 'rose like Marcellus,—*viros supereminet omnes.* He seemed to feel himself superior to those around him. His language, voice, and gesture, were more pathetic than I ever saw or heard before, at the bar or senate. He seemed like an old Roman senator, rising with the dignity of age, yet speaking with the fire of youth. The illustrious sage stretched forth his hand with the decent solemnity of a Paul, and, rising with his subject, he smote his breast with the energy and grace of a Demosthenes.'[2] 'As an Englishman, by birth and principle,' said the great orator, 'I recognize to the Americans their supreme, unalienable right in their property; a right which they are fortified in the defence of, to the last extremity. To maintain this principle is the common cause of the Whigs on the other side of the Atlantic and on this. "'Tis liberty to liberty engaged," that they will defend themselves, their families, and their country. In this great cause they are immovably allied. It is the alliance of God and nature—immutable, eternal, fixed as the firmament of heaven.'

---

[1] Ante, p. 122.

[2] Quincy's Quincy, p. 318, 319. The date of this speech was Jan. 20, 1775.

CHAPTER VII.

1774—1775.

PROCEEDINGS IN SOUTH CAROLINA.

'CONGRESS,' says Wirt, in his Life of Patrick Henry, 'rose in October, and Mr. Henry returned to his native county. Here, as was natural, he was surrounded by his neighbors, who were eager to hear not only what had been done, but what kind of men had composed that illustrious body. He answered their inquiries with all his wonted kindness and candor; and having been asked by one of them, 'whom he thought the greatest man in Congress,' he replied — 'If you speak of eloquence, Mr. Rutledge of South Carolina, is by far the greatest orator; but if you speak of solid information, and sound judgment, Colonel Washington is, unquestionably, the greatest man on that floor.' [1]

John Adams has recorded a very different estimate of Rutledge's oratorical abilities. He thus describes several of the eminent speakers of the Congress, and Rutledge among the number. 'Johnson of Maryland,' he says, 'has a clear and a cool head, an extensive knowledge of trade as well as law. He is a deliberating man, but not a shining orator; his passions and imagination don't appear enough for an orator; his reason and penetration appear, but not his rhetoric. Galloway, Duane, and Johnson, are sensible and learned, but cold speakers. Lee, Henry, and Hooper, are the orators; Paca is a deli-

[1] Life of Patrick Henry, p. 113. See to the same effect Garden's Anecdotes, p. 174, 176.

berator too; Chase speaks warmly; Mifflin is a sprightly and spirited speaker; John Rutledge don't exceed in learning or oratory, though he is a rapid speaker; young Edward Rutledge is young and zealous, a little unsteady and injudicious, but very unnatural and affected as a speaker; Dyer and Sherman speak often and long, but very heavily and clumsily.'[1]

From the 'marked opposition' of Adams' opinion, to that ascribed by Wirt to Henry, as well as from the fact that the latter 'betrays anything but enthusiasm for, or admiration of the Rutledges,' in the paragraph from Adams' Diary, which we have quoted in a preceding page,[2] the Editor of Adams' Works, doubts, whether Henry ever expressed the opinion, that Wirt attributes to him.[3] But the attentive reader will not fail to observe, that Henry, in the paragraph to which allusion is made, speaks of the political system of Galloway, Jay, and the Rutledges, not of their oratory or talents. He might condemn, as he did, their line of policy, and yet applaud the ability and eloquence with which they defended it. That Rutledge was a distinguished orator, we must believe, or discredit all contemporary testimony. At the same time, his oratory was by no means his principal merit. He had faults of style. He did not 'use all gently,' and in the torrent of passion observe the temperance that may give it smoothness. These defects Adams observed, and recorded. Doubtless, between his opinion, and the opinion attributed to Henry, is 'the golden mean,' whence we may deduce Rutledge's real merits, as a public speaker.[4]

---

[1] Adams' Works, vol. ii., p. 395, 396. Adams elsewhere speaks of the Rutledges' style of oratory in very unfavorable terms. 'John,' he says, 'dodges his head rather disagreeably, and both of them spout out their language in a rough and rapid torrent, but without much force or effect.' Ibid., p. 422.

[2] Ante, p. 490. [3] Adams' Works, vol. ii., p. 396, note. [4] Ante, p. 477.

'I long to tell you what we have done,' wrote Edward Rutledge to Judge Bee, while Congress was still sitting, 'but am prevented from silence having been imposed upon us all by consent, the first week in Congress; this, however, I may say, that the province will not be able to account for our conduct until we explain it, though it is justifiable upon the strictest principles of honor and policy.'[1] We shall see presently, that Rutledge and his colleagues were soon called upon by their constituents, to explain their conduct respecting the non-importation agreement, which had occasioned very great dissatisfaction.

The South Carolina delegates arrived at Charleston on the 6th of November, 'and were respectfully received.'[2] On the 9th, the general committee honored them 'with an elegant entertainment.'[3] To strengthen the public union, the committee now issued resolutions for a meeting of the colony, (by representation,) to receive an account of the proceedings of the late Continental Congress, to elect delegates for the next Congress, as well as a new General Committee, and to establish such regulations as the urgency of the times might render necessary.[4] The time fixed for this important meeting, was the 11th of January, 1775. Accordingly, on that day, one hundred and eighty-four representatives, elected by districts and parishes, as previously described by the committee, assembled at the Exchange in Charleston, and having

---

[1] Sanderson's Biography, vol. iii., p. 16. Mr. Rutledge, in the letter from which the extract in the text is taken, speaks of Gadsden as, 'if possible, worse than ever; more violent, more wrong-headed.' But no member of the Congress had a deeper insight into the real merits of the controversy than Christopher Gadsden. His prescience discovered that war was inevitable; that the future union of the two countries was impossible; and, as the struggle must come, he urged upon Congress to attack and overcome General Gage, in Boston, before he could receive reinforcements. We may well believe, that this proposition was received, by many members of that body, with sentiments, akin to horror.

[2] Drayton, vol. i., p. 154. [3] Ibid. [4] Ibid., p. 155.

organized, adjourned to the chamber of the Commons House of Assembly.[1]

Rutledge was elected a member of the Provincial Congress, as that body styled itself, for the Parish of Christ-Church. His colleagues to the Continental Congress were also returned as members, from other districts of the colony. The province 'will not be able to account for our conduct until we explain it,'[2] Edward Rutledge had written from Philadelphia. He had not misconceived the necessity for justification and defence. The exception in favor of rice, in the non-exportation agreement, 'had created an alarming disunion throughout the whole colony; in consequence of which, the representatives had met with jealous feelings on the subject.'[3] By that agreement, it was stipulated, that after the 10th of September, 1775, the colonies would neither directly nor indirectly export any merchandize or commodity whatsoever to Great Britain, Ireland, or the West Indies, *except rice to Europe.* This vagueness of expression was calculated to mislead, and was doubtless employed with the intent to mislead the public, as to the real import and effect of the exception. One would naturally suppose, from the language of the article, that rice might be exported to any part of Europe, except to Great Britain and Ireland. That, however, was not its meaning. The design of the

---

[1] On the 19th of December, 1774, Lieutenant-Governor Bull had written to the Earl of Dartmouth that he did not expect anything new in the colony, relative to American discontents, would occur until this meeting in January, 'when something may, perhaps, be produced, either from some bold dissentient or daring demagogue, with which I shall not fail to acquaint your Lordship, if anything is of consequence enough to deserve your Lordship's notice.' Force's Archives, vol. i., p. 1050. The Lieutenant-Governor, as well as the other crown-officers, must have discerned in this meeting of the representatives, in the chamber of the Assembly, an omen of the speedy overthrow, or attempted overthrow, of all royal authority in the colony.

[2] Ante.

[3] Drayton, vol. i., p. 168.

exception was, to enable the planters to send their rice to Great Britain, as usual.

In truth, by various acts of Parliament, they were restrained from sending it to any other part of Europe, except upon conditions that were calculated to render the privilege nugatory. By an act in the reign of Queen Anne, all rice produced in America that should be sent abroad, was required to be imported into England, Wales, or Berwick-upon-Tweed, or to some other of the English plantations, under certain securities and penalties, prescribed by an act of the 12th Charles II. But by an act of 3d George II., rice was permitted to be carried from Carolina directly to any part of Europe, south of Cape Finisterre, without landing it in England, on these conditions, viz.:—that the vessels in which it was exported should be built in Great Britain, owned by persons residing in Great Britain, navigated chiefly by British sailors, and cleared outwards from some port in Great Britain, for Carolina; that the masters of such vessels, before entitled to a clearance, should obtain a license from the commissioners of the customs, for loading in Carolina with rice, for ports south of Cape Finisterre; but, to obtain such license, they were to produce a certificate from the collector and comptroller of the port where the license was applied for, stating that they had given bond, with sufficient security, for not less than £1000 sterling, without reference to the capacity of the vessel; that no tobacco, sugar, &c., should be taken on board, except for the necessary use of the ship. This was not all. Every such vessel, after landing its rice in the southern European ports, was bound to proceed to Great Britain *before* returning to America, when the captain was to produce, within a limited time, a certificate from the British consul, or, in his absence, from some principal merchants of the foreign port, whither the rice had been carried, that it had been landed in the manner prescribed, or incur a forfeiture of his bond. There were various other formalities and limitations to be observed in the ports of Carolina, all designed to restrain the exportation of rice elsewhere than to Great Britain.

It was not the exportation of rice to Europe, under the restrictions we have mentioned, that the Congress intended to sanction. That would have been superfluous. There was nothing in their agreement that prevented any of the colonies from exporting to Europe exclusively of Great Britain, &c., to the extent allowed them, by the acts of navigation. The obnoxious exception, under an ambiguity of expression, was intended to permit the accustomed exportation of rice to Great Britain. It was so understood in Carolina. 'This exception,' says Drayton, 'had given so general a disgust, that the whole interior of the province considered their interests as sacrificed to the emolument of the rice-planters.' [1]

The subject immediately engaged the attention of the Provincial Congress. It was moved and seconded that the delegates to the ensuing Continental Congress use their endeavors to have the obnoxious exception expunged. A 'long and violent debate' succeeded.[2] Gadsden narrated the circumstances which led to the adoption of this feature of the association,[3] and concluded by expressing the opinion that, for the common good, as well as the honor of the province, the words 'except rice to Europe,' ought to be struck out of the fourth article of the association. Rutledge 'now undertook his own defence, and that of his three associates.' [4] He stated the fact, that early in the session they had warmly pressed immediate non-importation, and total non-exportation. 'Such measures, however, could not be effected; the northern colonies resolving to remit to England, as usual, to pay their debts by the circuitous mode of their flour and fish-trade to the rest of Europe. In short, the com-

[1] Drayton, vol. i. p. 168.
[2] Ibid.
[3] Ante, p. 487.
[4] Drayton, vol. i. p. 169

modities they usually sent to the mother-country were but trifling; and their real trade would be but little affected by the association. For instance, Philadelphia carried on a trade of export, to the amount of £700,000 sterling; whereas scarce £50,000 value of it went to the market of the mother-country. That, as it was evident, those colonies were less intent to annoy the mother-country in the article of trade, than to preserve their own trade; so he thought it was but justice to his constituents, to preserve to them their trade as entire as possible. That, as the northern trade would be but little affected by the association, he saw no reason why ours should be almost ruined; for nearly all our indigo, and two-thirds of our rice, went to the ports of the mother-country. That, if we must bear burdens in the cause of America, they ought to be as equally laid as possible. Upon the whole, he said, the affair seemed rather like a commercial scheme, among the flour colonies, to find a better vent for their flour through the British channel; by preventing, if possible, any rice from being sent to those markets: and that, for his part, he could never consent to our becoming dupes to the people of the North, or, in the least, to yield to their unreasonable expectations. That, as by the association the rice-planters preserved their property, so it had been the idea of the delegates at the Congress, that they should make compensation to the indigo-planters, who could not send their crops to the mother-country. Such a plan was just and practicable; and it ought to be the subject of our debate, rather than expunging the means of exporting a great part of our annual crop, and therewith supplying ourselves with those necessaries we might require.'[1]

We are bound to say, that this defence by Rutledge, of himself, and his three colleagues, rests on errors of fact,

[1] Drayton, vol. i., p. 169, 170.

and appeals exclusively to considerations of interest. We have stated, in the preceding chapter,[1] that the Virginia delegates were restrained, by their instructions, from assenting to a non-exportation before the 10th of August, 1775. 'The earnest desire we have to make as quick and full payment as possible of our debts to Great Britain, and to avoid the heavy injury that would arise to this country from an earlier adoption of the non-exportation plan, after the people have already applied so much of their labor to the perfecting of the present crop, by which means they have been prevented from pursuing other methods of clothing and supporting their families, have rendered it necessary to restrain you in this article of non-exportation.'[2] Such was the reason assigned by the Virginia Convention for imposing this restriction upon their delegates. To act independently of Virginia, joined as she would be by Maryland and North Carolina, was obviously impolitic.

Rutledge's statement, that the exports of the northern colonies were but trifling, and that their trade would be but little affected by non-exportation, was erroneous. The export of grain, including rice, from the thirteen colonies, to Great Britain, Ireland, and the West Indies, exceeded a million sterling; their entire export trade amounted to nearly five millions; and to this Carolina only contributed twelve thousand weight of indigo, and one hundred and fifty thousand tierces of rice. The whole of this trade, by the non-exportation agreement, was to be lost to twelve of the colonies, while Carolina was permitted to send her rice to market, as usual. That

[1] Ante, p. 486.

[2] Force's Archives, vol. i., p. 689. The efficacy of non-exportation doubtless depended, as Rutledge asserted, upon its immediate adoption, and withholding all remittances. His error, as we conceive, consisted in claiming special privileges for his own province, which were calculated to disaffect the other provinces, and produce division among his own constituents.

this distinction should have been odious, except to those who enjoyed the benefit of it, is not surprising.[1]

The compensation scheme, proposed by Rutledge, elicited a warm discussion. It continued throughout the day. At its close, a committee was appointed, to arrange a plan of compensation. The next morning they made their report; but 'so intricate, and so little satisfactory,' was their *projet*, that it was rejected. The original question, whether the words 'except rice to Europe,' should be struck out of the non-exportation agreement, now engaged the attention of the Congress. The debate was prolonged until dark. 'Great heats prevailed—and the members were on the point of falling into downright uproar and confusion. At length, all parties being wearied out, the question was put by candle-light; and by mere accident, at the desire of one among the indigo party, it was put in a manner that lost it. For, instead of voting as usual, by acclamation, to save time and mistakes in counting, each man's name was called; and he declared himself yea, or nay, which was minuted down. By this mode, some were overawed, either by their diffidence, circumstances, or connexions; and, to the surprise of the nays, they themselves carried the point, by a majority of twelve voices—eighty-seven to seventy-five.'[2]

The scheme of compensation, being thus adopted, a committee was appointed to adjust a mode of carrying it into effect. 'For, as rice was to be exported, the indigo-planters chose to have some mode of compensation, however little satisfactory the same might be; and the other

[1] In the following year, viz. Nov. 1, 1775, the Continental Congress repealed the invidious exception, by the following resolution: Resolved, That no rice be exported, under the exception contained in the 4th article of the association, from any of the United Colonies, to Great Britain, Ireland, or the islands of Jersey, Guernsey, Sark, Alderney, or Man, or any other European island or settlement within the British dominions.

[2] Drayton, vol. i., p. 173.

party, sensible the same would never be executed, as either there would not be any occasion for it, or the hostile situation of affairs would render the compensation a dead letter, very readily agreed to indulge them in the most feasible manner.'[1] Accordingly, the committee reported, and the Congress adopted resolutions, ascertaining the mode of compensation, 'by those who raise articles which may be exported, to those who cannot raise such articles, for the losses which they may sustain by not exporting the commodities which they raise.'[2]

Having approved the American association, after the heats and opposition we have described, the Provincial Congress now ordered their President[3] to 'return the most cordial and grateful thanks of this Congress to each of the late delegates from this colony to the late Continental Congress, for their able and faithful discharge, in the said Congress, of the high trust reposed in them by their country.'[4] They were also appointed to represent the colony in the next Congress, 'with full power to concert, agree upon, direct and order such further measures as, in the opinion of the said deputies and the delegates of the other American colonies to be assembled, shall appear to be necessary for the recovery and establishment of American rights and liberties, and for restoring harmony between Great Britain and her colonies.'[5] 'They were elected,' says Drayton, 'without any opposition; for, as their late proceedings had been confirmed in the whole, it was deemed a service to the common cause, that a confidence should be evinced in their abilities and future proceedings. But, had the late warmly-contested question, respecting the exception of rice, been carried the other way, there was no doubt but that no

[1] Ibid. p. 173. [2] Force's Archives, vol. i., p. 1114.

[3] Charles Pinckney.

[4] See the Proceedings of this Congress, in Force's Archives, supra, pp. 1109–1118. [5] Ibid.

more than three of them at most would have been re-elected.'[1]

The Provincial Congress adjourned on the 17th of January; but not without having, in effect, established a revolutionary government.[2] Their body was to continue in being until the next general meeting of the inhabitants of the colony, and was to be summoned for the despatch of business, upon any emergency, by the Charleston committee. Of this committee every delegate to the Congress, who might happen to be in Charleston, was to be considered a member. Its general duty was of an executive character, to enforce the resolutions of both the Continental and the Provincial Congress. An opportunity soon occurred to test the force of its authority. A family who had been residing in England, on

[1] Drayton, vol. i., p. 176.

[2] The General Assembly met on the 24th of January, 1775, and, on the proceedings of the Continental Congress being laid before them, resolutions were adopted approving those proceedings, and expressing a grateful sense of the obligation all America were under to the several members of that Congress, for the wise measures they had concerted and pursued for the relief of the colonies. Lynch, Gadsden, and John Rutledge, being present, Rawlins Lowndes, the Speaker, delivered them the public thanks of the Assembly for their late services. 'You stood high in the esteem of your country before,' he said, 'and possessed a large share of her confidence, the reward of repeated services. The present instance of your zeal, attachment, and love for her; the sacrifice you made of your ease, your convenience, and your private concerns, when the public called you to attend her interests in a distant country, have still endeared you more to her, and established your reputation upon the firmest foundation. . . . . You have the particular happiness, gentlemen, of standing foremost in the rank of patriots; posterity will pay a just tribute to your memories, and will revere the names of the members of the Continental Congress.'

The Assembly, again, nominated and appointed them 'to meet the deputies of the other colonies, in General Congress, at Philadelphia, or elsewhere;' and resolved to provide £1500, to pay the expenses of said deputies, in going to, attending upon, and returning from, the said Congress.'

their return to Carolina, in the month of March, brought with them their household furniture and horses. Application was made to the committee for liberty to land them. It was not without great opposition, and until after a long contest, that it was granted. This determination of the committee gave great offence, and occasioned a great excitement among the citizens. It was considered a violation of the non-importation agreement. A representation upon the subject, numerously signed, was presented to the chairman of the committee, requesting a reconsideration of the obnoxious vote. A meeting of the committee was convened; great numbers of the people came to it; passion, rather than reason, ruled the hour, and a final decision was postponed. Three days after, the committee again convened; 'and great was the press of people who attended.'[1] Charleston was in a state of prodigious excitement. It was publicly declared, that if the horses were landed, they should be killed. The majority of the military refused to act for their protection. 'Under these unpleasant aspects, the debates began.'[2]

Gadsden contended, that the horses ought not to be landed; that the determination of the committee was contrary to the non-importation agreement; that not only were the people dissatisfied with it, but it would cause dissatisfaction and alarm at the North. The Rev. Mr. Tennent urged the same arguments. On the other hand, and in favor of adhering to the determination of the committee, Edward Rutledge, Rawlins Lowndes, Thomas Bee, and Thomas Lynch, insisted that they ought to be governed by the spirit, and not by the letter of the association agreement; that if the latter was to be observed, they could import from England neither

---

[1] Drayton, vol. i., p. 183.

[2] Ibid. See also Force's Archives, vol. ii., p. 162.

arms or ammunition, an idea which the Congress never entertained.

William Henry Drayton, who acted a conspicuous part in the politics of South Carolina during the succeeding five years, and by his ardor, activity, decision, and patriotism, achieved an honorable fame, replied to these arguments. He was a vigorous writer, and an effective speaker. His talents and eloquence were of a popular character, and calculated to win applause. Drayton owed much to nature, but was little indebted to grace. His distinction, as a public man, is attributable, rather to the native force and energy of his physical temperament, than to his purely intellectual qualities. His speech on the present occasion was a very able one. It was always safer, he said, to follow the letter, than to explore the spirit of a law; that the letter of the association was clearly in support of the motion, to reverse the vote of the committee; and, in the present situation of affairs, the spirit of that instrument was equally in favor of it. 'Union,' he said, 'was the rock upon which the American political edifice was founded; and whatever hazards its existence, is to militate against the ground-work of the association. Hence, it was evident, landing the horses hazarded our union; for the people were in commotion against it. Upon all public and general questions, the people ever are in the right; so said Lord Mansfield, in the House of Commons; and the people now think the late vote was wrong. Can it be prudent to oppose our constituents? In civil commotions, the common people ever struck those blows which were of any effect. If you retract, there can be no just cause of fearing contempt; as it is not reasonable those should contemn you who have ever honored you; and whose opinions would be in favor of your retraction.'[1]

---

[1] Drayton, vol. i., p. 186.

'John Rutledge now arose, and endeavored to take off the force of the arguments which had been urged; but, failing in his endeavors, he only added to the many instances he had previously given, of his ability as a good speaker.' [1]

There can be no doubt, we conceive, as to the propriety of Rutledge's construction of the association agreement. It could not have been designed to apply to a case like the one we have described; but, in view of the prevailing excitement, the committee doubtless acted judiciously in reversing their former vote.[2] 'However,' says Drayton, from whom we have derived the history of this transaction, 'it is worthy of remark, that this is the first instance of a point of importance and controversy, being carried against those by whose opinions the people had been long governed. And, such was the powerful effect of habit, that this important question was carried only by a majority of one vote.' [3]

The advices from England, which were received at Charleston about the middle of April, indicated a deter-

---

[1] Drayton, vol. i., p. 186.

[2] The people were apprehensive 'lest, from the admission of the horses, it should be suggested that there was an inclination in this colony to depart from the association; they feared that the conduct of the people, which had always been consistent, and who continued remarkably strict in their adherence to the resolves and recommendations of the Congress, might, in this instance, be misrepresented abroad. Their zeal for the reputation of their country threw them into great agitation; none meant the least reflection on the conduct of their committee, but all wished that the horses might not be landed.' See an account of this transaction in Force's Archives, vol. ii., p. 162. Rutledge's construction of the association agreement was subsequently adopted by the Continental Congress, in the case of the books, papers, and household furniture of Dr. Franklin, which were in his use when he lived in London. 'Such importation,' said the resolution of Congress, 'is not to be comprehended within the meaning of the said first article of the association.' See Journal of Congress for Sept. 13th, 1775.

[3] Drayton, vol. i., p. 186.

mination on the part of the ministry, to enforce their measures with the strong hand. 'It was now that the poor looked for consolation to the rich, and the few animated the efforts of the many; while, in a steady reliance on Divine Providence, they all moved forward in a firm and determined opposition to arbitrary sway.'[1] Military companies were formed, the spirit of resistance animated the inhabitants of Charleston, and was diffused among the people of the country districts.

The delegates to the Continental Congress sailed for Philadelphia on the 3d of May.[2] They went from a community, anxious, excited, but determined in purpose, and resolved to put to hazard everything most dear to man, in defence of their rights and liberties. When they returned, the war had already begun; and having, in the mean time, witnessed the services of Rutledge in the Continental Congress, we shall then see how conspicuously were his energy, high spirit, and decisive will, displayed in the affairs of his native Commonwealth.

---

[1] Drayton, vol. i., p. 218.

[2] News of the battle of Lexington reached Charleston five days after, on the 8th of May.

CHAPTER VIII.

SERVICES IN THE CONGRESS OF 1775.

'THE Congress met at a time when all minds were so exasperated by the perfidy of General Gage, and his attack on the country-people, that propositions for attempting an accommodation were not much relished.'[1] Thus wrote Franklin to his friend Priestley; and his statement is confirmed by Adams.[2] But when measures leading directly to independence were urged upon the attention of Congress; when they were even confronted with a formal proposition to sunder the British connection, a more moderate spirit began to manifest itself. It became evident, that they wished to keep the door open for an accommodation.[3]

---

[1] Franklin's Works, vol. viii., p 155; July 7, 1775.

[2] Adams' Works, vol. ii., pp. 406, 407. See Ante, p. 132; also Force's Archives (4th series), vol. 4, p. 1874.

[3] See Gordon's History of the Revolution, vol. i., p. 336. 'Parson Gordon, of Roxbury,' says Adams, in his Diary of September 16th, 'spent the evening here. I fear his indiscreet prate will do harm in this city. He is an eternal talker, and somewhat vain, and not accurate nor judicious; very zealous in the cause, and a well-meaning man, but incautious, and not sufficiently tender of the character of our province, upon which, at this time, much depends; fond of being thought a man of influence at head-quarters, and with our council and House, and with the general officers of the army, and also with gentlemen in the city and other colonies. He is a good man, but wants a guide.' Adams' Works, vol. ii., pp. 423, 424. This, we suspect, is a pretty faithful portrait of the historian. His history, however, is valuable, and contains information not elsewhere to be obtained. He did not deem it the part of a good historian to conceal the faults, nor habitually to magnify the merits of the actors on the revolutionary scene. This is no slight tribute to his honor and fidelity.

Adams ascribes the change of tone, in Congress, to private and social influences. 'In some of the earlier deliberations in May,' he says, 'after I had reasoned at length on my own plan, Mr. John Rutledge, in more than one public speech, approved of my sentiments; and the other delegates from that state, Mr. Lynch, Mr. Gadsden, and Mr. Edward Rutledge, appeared to me to be of the same mind. Mr. Dickinson himself told me, afterwards, that when we first came together the balance lay with South Carolina. Accordingly, all their efforts were employed to convert the delegates from that state. . . . . The proprietary gentlemen, Israel Pemberton, and other principal Quakers, now united with Mr. Dickinson, addressed themselves, with great art and assiduity, to all the members of Congress whom they could influence, even to some of the delegates of Massachusetts; but most of all to the delegates from South Carolina. Mr. Lynch had been an old acquaintance of the Penn family, particularly of the Governor. Mr. Edward Rutledge had brought his lady with him, a daughter of our former President, Middleton. Mr. Arthur Middleton, her brother, was now a delegate in place of his father. The lady and the gentlemen were invited to all parties, and were visited perpetually by the party; and we soon began to find that Mr. Lynch, Mr. Arthur Middleton, and even the two Rutledges, began to waver, and to clamor about independence. Mr. Gadsden was either, from despair of success, never attempted, or, if he was, received no impression from them.'[1]

Adams, in this statement, has obviously mingled and confounded two distinct periods. In the first place, Arthur Middleton was not a member of the Congress of 1775 at all. He did not take his seat in that body until the following year.[2] In the second place, Rutledge's

[1] Adams' Works, vol. ii., p. 408.

[2] Henry Middleton, on the 16th of February, 1776, while attending the Provincial Congress of South Carolina, then in session, requested

approval of the sentiments, at this time, avowed and defended by Adams, would not accord with the system of politics which he had all along professed. If, however, the news of the action at Lexington, which met him on his arrival at Philadelphia, together with the multiplying evidences of the ministry's intention to enforce their measures with the sword, exasperated his mind, as it did the minds of others, and led him to approve the measures recommended by Adams, he very soon reverted to his original sentiments. He cherished the hope of reconciliation, clung to it with tenacity, and, so far as we can discover, was not an advocate of independence prior to its declaration.[1] But, while thus anxious for a restoration of harmony, he would prepare for the worst; and it will appear, as we proceed with our narrative, that he supported many of the most vigorous propositions brought forward in this Congress, for the defence of the colonies.

The time of the Congress, for the first two weeks after it assembled, was spent in committee of the whole, on the state of America. No report of the discussions that took place has been handed down to us. The result, however, is on record. On the 26th of May, Congress resolved, that the colonies be immediately put into a state of defence; but, to restore the harmony formerly subsisting between them and the mother-country, they resolved, at the same time, that an humble and dutiful petition be presented to his majesty. The petition was conceded to the earnest wishes of the more moderate portion of Congress. It encountered, however, strong

that body not again to appoint him a delegate to the Continental Congress, 'as the infirmities of age, which were creeping on, deprived him of the ability of rendering so much service to the public as in his earlier days he might have done.' His request was complied with, and on the same day his son, Arthur Middleton, was chosen in his stead. He did not take his seat in Congress, however, until several weeks after

[1] Vide post, chap. ix.

opposition at the time, and its propriety has been much questioned since.[1] Rutledge was among the number of its supporters, and appointed on the committee to prepare it. The chairman of the committee was John Dickinson; and the petition, as reported and adopted by Congress, with scarcely any amendment, was his production.

On the 2d of June, a letter from the Provincial Convention of Massachusetts was laid before Congress, stating the condition of that State, and expressing the hope that the representative body of the continent would favor them with their 'most explicit advice respecting the taking up and exercising the power of civil government.' This was a subject of grave importance. It 'lay with great weight upon my mind,' says Adams, 'as the most difficult and dangerous business that we had to do. . . And when this letter was read, I embraced the opportunity to open myself in Congress, and most earnestly to entreat the serious attention of all the members, and of all the continent, to the measures which the times demanded. For my part, I thought there was great wisdom in the adage, "When the sword is drawn, throw away the scabbard." Whether we threw it away voluntarily or not, it was useless now, and would be useless forever. The pride of Britain, flushed with late triumphs and conquests, their infinite contempt of all the power of America, with an insolent, arbitrary Scotch faction, with a Bute and Mansfield at their head for a ministry, we might depend upon it, would force us to call forth every energy and resource of the country, to seek the friendship of England's enemies; and we had no rational hope, but from the *ratio ultima regum et rerum-publicarum*. These efforts could not be made without government; and, as I supposed no man would think of consolidating this vast

[1] See Ante, pp. 137–142.

continent under one national government, we should probably, after the example of the Greeks, the Dutch, and the Swiss, form a confederacy of States, each of which must have a separate government. That the case of Massachusetts was most urgent, but that it could not be long before every other colony must follow her example. . . . . That it was my opinion that Congress ought now to recommend to the people of every colony to call conventions immediately, and set up governments of their own, under their own authority; for the people were the source of all authority and original of all power. These were new, strange, and terrible doctrines to the greatest part of the members; but not a very small number heard them with apparent pleasure, and none more than Mr. John Rutledge, of South Carolina, and Mr. John Sullivan, of New Hampshire.'[1]

On the following day, and after further discussion, Rutledge, Johnson, Jay, Wilson, and Lee, were chosen, by ballot, a committee, to report to the Congress what, in their opinion, was the proper advice to be given to the Massachusetts Convention. They brought in their report on the 7th of June. It was 'in a great degree conformable to the New York and Pennsylvania system,' says Adams, 'or, in other words, to the system of Mr. Dickinson and Mr. Duane.'[2] However, he thought it an acquisition; for it was a precedent of advice to the separate states, to institute governments, and he doubted not they would soon have more occasions to follow that example. The resolution of Congress which embodied the report of the committee, declared that no obedience was due to the Act of Parliament, for altering the charter of Massachusetts, and that the powers of government should be exercised by the Assembly, elected acccording to the forms of the old charter, or by a council elected by the Assembly,

---

[1] Adams' Works, vol. iii., pp. 15, 16.

[2] Ibid., p. 17.

'until a governor of his majesty's appointment will consent to govern the colony according to its charter.'[1]

The labors of this Congress, to accomplish the great objects before them, were incessant. 'The whole Congress is taken up, almost, in different committees,' wrote Adams to his wife, at a later period in the session, 'from seven to ten in the morning. From ten to four, or sometimes five, we are in Congress, and from six to ten in committees again.'[2] It frequently happened, from the multiplicity of business, and the urgency of the occasion, that a member was appointed, at the same time, on distinct committees, and each charged with duties demanding immediate action. Thus, on the 23d of June, Rutledge was appointed chairman of a committee to draw up a declaration, to be published by Washington, upon his arrival at the camp before Boston. On the same day he was appointed one of a committee, to get proper plates engraved, to provide paper, and to agree with printers, to print the bills of credit, which Congress, on the previous day, had resolved to emit, to an amount not exceeding two millions of Spanish milled dollars. Of the declaration Jefferson gives the following account: 'On the 24th of June,' he says, 'a committee, which had been appointed to prepare a declaration of the causes of taking up arms, brought in their report (drawn, I believe, by J. Rutledge), which, not being liked, the House recommitted it, on the 26th, and added Mr. Dickinson and myself to the committee. . . . . I prepared a draught of the declaration committed to us. It was too strong for Mr. Dickinson. He still retained the hope of reconciliation with the mother-country, and was unwilling it should be lessened by offensive statements. He was so honest a man, and so able a one, that he was greatly indulged, even by those who could not feel his scruples.

[1] Ante, p. 142.

[2] Adams' Letters, vol. i., p. 77; Dec. 3, 1775.

We therefore requested him to take the paper, and put it into a form he could approve. He did so, preparing an entire new statement, and preserving of the former only the last four paragraphs, and half of the preceding one. We approved and reported it to Congress, who accepted it.'[1]

We cannot claim for Rutledge the honors of written eloquence; the art of composition he seems never to have cultivated. His name is not connected with any of the memorable state-papers, that did honor to this and the previous Congress. These, more durable than brass and marble, will carry down the names of their authors to the last syllable of recorded time. In action and speech Rutledge won his distinction; his deeds are recorded on the page of history.

On the first of August, Congress adjourned until the fifth of the following September. They did not re-assemble, however, in sufficient numbers to enter upon business, until the 13th of that month. Georgia now united with her sister colonies, and sent delegates to the Congress. The situation of both Georgia and South Carolina was critical. They had powerful tribes of Indians on their frontiers; an alarming division of sentiment had appeared among the people of the interior districts, while the disposition of the negroes was a source of apprehension. 'In the evening,' says Adams' Diary, of Sunday, the 24th of September, 'Mr. Bullock and Mr. Houston, two gentlemen from Georgia, came into our room, and smoked and chatted the whole evening. . . . These gentlemen give a melancholy account of the state of Georgia and South Carolina. They say, that if one thousand regular troops should land in Georgia, and their commander be provided with arms and clothes enough,

[1] Jefferson's Correspondence, vol. i., p. 89. Mr. Force has inserted the declaration in the second volume of his Archives (4th series).

and proclaim freedom to all the negroes who would join his camp, twenty thousand negroes would join it from the two provinces in a fortnight. The negroes have a wonderful art of communicating intelligence among themselves; it will run several hundreds of miles in a week or a fortnight. They say their only security is this: that all the king's friends, and tools of government, have large plantations and property in negroes; so that the slaves of the Tories would be lost, as well as those of the Whigs.'[1] To estimate fairly the virtue and fortitude of the men of the Revolution, we must understand the dangers that menaced them, and the situation of their respective communities.

On the 22d of September, Congress resolved, that a committee of seven be appointed, to take into consideration the state of the trade of America. This committee was elected by ballot, and consisted of Dr. Franklin, Rutledge, Jay, Randolph, Johnson, Deane, and Willing. On the 30th instant, they brought in their report. The non-exportation agreement had taken effect on the 10th instant; so that now, there could be neither importation from, nor exportation to, Great Britain, Ireland, and the British West Indies. By the restraining acts, the trade of the colonies, except the trade of New York, North Carolina, the lower counties on the Delaware, and Georgia, was prohibited elsewhere than to Great Britain, Ireland, etc. The question now was, whether the excepted colonies should be exempted from the operation of the association agreement, and be permitted to obtain from Great Britain such supplies as the situation of the country obviously required.[2] It occasioned an earnest discussion. 'The question is,' said Rutledge, 'whether we shall shut our ports entirely, or adhere to the associa-

[1] Adams' Works, vol. ii., p. 428.

[2] See Ante, pp. 144–148; also Adams' Notes of the debates upon this subject, Works, vol. ii., p. 452, *et seq.*

tion. The resolutions we come to ought to be final.'[1] He insisted that they should postpone the subject, rather than not come to a decisive resolution. 'Shall we act like the dog in the manger,' asked Willing; 'not suffer New York and the lower counties and North Carolina to export, because we can't? We may get salt and ammunition by those ports.' 'The end of administration,' replied Lee, 'will be answered by the gentleman's plan; jealousies and dissensions will arise, and disunion and division. We shall become a rope of sand.' 'I look upon Britain, Ireland, and the West Indies, as our enemies,' said Chase, 'and would not trade with them while at war. . . . . I am against these colonies trading according to the restraining act. It will produce division. . . . . I have not absolutely discarded every glimpse of a hope of a reconciliation; our prospect is gloomy. . . . When you once offer your trade to foreign nations, away with all hopes of reconciliation.' Edward Rutledge was opposed to any relaxation of the non-exportation agreement, or to carrying on any trade at all.

The subject engaged the attention of Congress, in committee of the whole, several weeks. To put New York, North Carolina, the lower counties, and Georgia, upon the same footing with the other colonies, and thus remove jealousies and divisions, Lee moved that all the custom-houses be shut, and the officers discharged. Rutledge expressed his surprise that a subject so clear had taken up so much time. 'I was for a general non-exportation. Is it not surprising that there should so soon be a motion for breaking the association? We have been reproached for our breach of faith in breaking the non-importation. I have the best authority to say that if we had abided by a former non-importation, we should have had redress. We may be obliged hereafter to break the

[1] We quote Adams' Notes, *supra*.

association; but why should we break it before we feel it? I expected the delegates from the exempted colonies would have moved to be put upon the same footing. Don't like shutting the custom-houses, but moves that the resolve be, that people in New York, North Carolina, and lower counties, dont apply to the custom-house.' 'I look upon it,' replied Zubly, 'the association altogether will be the ruin of the cause. We have ten thousand fighting Indians near us. Carolina has already smuggled goods from Georgia.' To this Chase retorted, with great severity. 'I will undertake to prove,' he said, 'that if the reverend gentleman's positions are true, and his advice followed, we shall all be made slaves. If he speaks the opinion of Georgia, I sincerely lament that they ever appeared in Congress. They cannot, they will not comply! Why did they come here? Sir, we are deceived! Sir, we are abused! Why do they come here? . . . Did they come here to ruin America? The gentleman's advice will bring destruction upon all North America.' 'Where the protection of this room did not extend, I would not sit very tamely,' replied Houston, Zubly's colleague. Houston was inferior to Zubly, in learning and abilities; but in honor and truth, greatly surpassed him.

On the day following Lee's motion, Livingston moved that the subject be postponed. Rutledge thought this motion extraordinary. 'It is really trifling,' he said. 'The committee may have time allowed to clear vessels for powder; but I had rather the continent should run the risk of sending vessels without clearances.[1] What confusion would ensue, if Congress should break up with-

[1] This discussion occurred Oct. 13th. On the 6th of Oct., Congress had resolved, that the committee appointed for the importation of powder, be directed to export, agreeable to the continental association, as much provisions, or other produce of these colonies, as they should judge expedient, for the purchase of arms and ammunition.

out any resolution of this sort! The motion seems intended to defeat the resolution entirely. Those who are against it are for postponing.' On a subsequent day, he declared that he was for adhering to the association, and going no further; 'the non-export *in terrorem*, and generally agreed.' The views of Rutledge coincided with the prevailing ones of Congress; and, it was finally resolved, that the exempted colonies ought not to avail themselves of the benefit allowed to them by the restraining acts.

It would contribute little to our knowledge, either of Rutledge's character, or the history of the times, to specify the various committees upon which he served during this Congress. It is his connection with measures that indicate the progression of opinion, that more immediately invites our attention. We may observe, however, that the journals of Congress, as well as the brief notes of the debates in that body, preserved by Adams, afford abundant evidence of his constant employment.[1]

The delegates from New Hampshire were instructed to use their utmost endeavors to obtain the advice and direction of the Congress, as to what method that colony should adopt, to administer justice and regulate their civil police. They laid this instruction before Congress on the 18th of October. Adams says it might have been

---

[1] Thus, on the 13th of Oct., he was appointed Chairman of a Committee of five, to take into consideration the memorials of sundry merchants of New York and Philadelphia, respecting a quantity of tea, imported prior to the 1st of the preceding March. Oct. 16th, Chairman of a Committee to consider and report an answer to two letters from the Convention of New Jersey. On the same day, one of a committee of five, to consider further ways and means of promoting the manufacture of saltpetre. Oct. 17th, Chairman of a Committee to take into consideration the disputes between the people of Connecticut and Pennsylvania, and report what, in their opinion, is proper to be done by Congress. The labors of this Congress were incessant and exhausting, and the demands on Rutledge various and constant.

obtained by Langdon or Whipple, but he always supposed it was General Sullivan who suggested the measure, because he left Congress with a stronger impression upon his mind of its importance, than he had observed in either of the others.[1]

Whoever suggested it, there could be no doubt that it was a question of moment. The necessity of forming governments in the several colonies, and thus, in the most solemn manner, superseding the royal authority, began to be apparent; but 'the opposition,' says Adams, 'was still inveterate.'[2] The subject was postponed. On the 26th, it was again brought on the carpet. 'After a long discussion,' (we again quote Adams,) 'in which Mr. John Rutledge, Mr. Ward, Mr. Lee, Mr. Gadsden, Mr. Sherman, Mr. Dyer, and some others had spoken on the same side with me, Congress resolved, that a committee of five members be appointed to take into consideration the instructions given to the delegates of New Hampshire, and report their opinion thereon. The members chosen, — Mr. John Rutledge, Mr. J. Adams, Mr. Ward, Mr. Lee, and Mr. Sherman.

'Although this committee was entirely composed of members as well disposed to encourage the enterprise as could have been found in Congress, yet they could not be brought to agree upon a report and to bring it forward in Congress, till Friday, November 3d, when Congress, taking into consideration the report of the committee on the New Hampshire instructions, after another long deliberation and debate, Resolved, That it be recommended to the Provincial Convention of New Hampshire, to call a full and free representation of the people, and that the representatives, if they think it necessary, establish such a form of government as in their judgment will best produce the happiness of the people, and most effectually

[1] Adams' Works, vol. iii., p. 18. [2] Ibid., p. 14.

secure peace and good order in the Province, during the continuance of the present dispute between Great Britain and the colonies.

'By this time, I mortally hated the words 'Province,' 'Colonies,' and 'Mother Country,' and strove to get them out of the report. The last was indeed left out, but the other two were retained even by this committee, who were all as high Americans as any in the house, unless Mr. Gadsden be excepted. Nevertheless, I thought this resolution a triumph, and a most important point gained.'[1]

It should be here observed, that the difference between Rutledge and Gadsden, at this stage of the controversy, consisted in this: the former still cherished the hope of reconciliation; the latter had renounced it forever. Both stood firmly for the rights of the colonies, and would neglect no means to vindicate and defend them.

'Mr. John Rutledge,' says Adams, 'was now completely with us in our desire of revolutionizing all the governments; and he brought forward immediately some representations from his own State, when Congress, then taking into consideration the State of South Carolina, and sundry papers relative thereto being read and considered, Resolved, That a committee of five be appointed to take the same into consideration, and report what, in their opinion, is necessary to be done.'[2]

This committee consisted of Harrison, Bullock, Hooper, Chase, and S. Adams. They were appointed on the 3d of November, and on the following day brought in their report, which led to the adoption of several resolutions, and among others, one containing a recommendation to the Convention of South Carolina, (should they find it necessary to establish a form of government in that

---

[1] Adams' Works, vol. iii., p. 20, 21.

[2] Ibid. The committee reported on the New Hampshire instructions, Nov. 3.

colony,) in the precise language employed in the recommendation to the convention of New Hampshire.

'Although Mr. John Rutledge united with me and others in persuading the committee to report this resolution,' says Adams, 'and the distance of Carolina made it convenient to furnish them with this discretionary recommendation, I doubt whether Mr. Harrison or Mr. Hooper were, as yet, sufficiently advanced to agree to it. Mr. Bullock, Mr. Chase, and Mr. Samuel Adams, were very ready for it.' [1]

In addition to this recommendation, Congress resolved, that three battalions of Foot be kept up in South Carolina, at the Continental expense; that Charleston be defended against any attempt to take it; and for this purpose, that the Convention or Council of Safety, should immediately erect such fortifications and batteries, in or near that town, as would best conduce to its security.

The condition of affairs in that colony called Rutledge thither. He appears to have returned home immediately upon the adoption of these resolutions. Adams conveys the erroneous impression that he left Congress at an earlier period. Speaking of the advice, given by Congress on the 9th of June, to the Convention of Massachusetts,[2] he says: 'Not long after this, Mr. John Rutledge returned to South Carolina, and Mr. Sullivan went with General Washington to Cambridge; so that I lost two of my able coadjutors. But we soon found the benefit of their co-operation at a distance.'

I am happy, while thus correcting a mistake, to record this tribute to Rutledge's services and ability. In the next chapter we shall contemplate the part he performed in the affairs of his native State.

---

[1] Adams' Works, vol. iii., p. 22.

[2] Ante, p. 512.

CHAPTER IX.

1775—1776.

GOVERNMENT INSTITUTED IN SOUTH CAROLINA.

THE second Provincial Congress of South Carolina assembled at Charleston on the 1st day of November, 1775. It does not appear from the journals of that body, at what precise time Rutledge took his seat among them. On the 28th of November, however, he was appointed, together with Rawlins Lowndes, and Arthur Middleton, a committee to consider and report what measures were proper to be adopted, respecting the persons confined in the several jails of the State. On the following day, the Congress adjourned to the 1st of February, but not without evincing their continued confidence in the delegates to the Continental Congress, by reappointing them to represent the colony in that body.

When the Provincial Congress came together again in February, Rutledge and Middleton, being present, received the thanks of the Congress for their late important services. 'Your constituents,' said the President, in his address to them, 'sensible of the propriety of your conduct, and of the benefits which, with the blessing of the Almighty, it is calculated to shed upon America, have constituted me their instrument, as well to signify to you their approbation, as to present to you their thanks; and it is in the discharge of these duties that I now have the honor to address you. In an important crisis like the present, to receive the public thanks of a free people, is to receive the most honorable recompense for past services; and to deserve such thanks, is to be truly great. I know that it is with pain such men hear their commendations . . . . and lest I wound your delicacy, when I mean only to do justice to your merit, I forbear to particularize what is already well known.'[1]

Rutledge had been appointed a member of the Council of Safety; the business before the Congress was various and pressing; forces were to be raised, the means of defence to be provided and organized; and a form of government established. Hence, he deemed his services more important at home, than in the Continental Congress. He addressed the Congress upon this subject, on the 15th of February. He said, it was with the utmost concern he found himself obliged to request that they would dispense with his attendance in the Continental Congress in future; that he had many weighty reasons which rendered his request proper; but, above all, as the American dispute was now agitated by arms, he was certain that he could be of more service to his country, and the common cause, at home than abroad; and, therefore, he earnestly desired they would grant his request.[2] This, however, was not done. On the day following his application, the Congress resolved to choose five delegates to serve for the ensuing year; that a majority of them, when present at Philadelphia, should be a quorum; and that when, by sickness or accident, only one delegate should be in attendance, such delegate might fully represent the colony.

Doubtless this arrangement was made in consequence of Rutledge's request, and to secure his services at home, during the present emergency, without the necessity of his withdrawal from the Continental Congress. On the same day, Lynch, the two Rutledges, Arthur Middleton,[3] and Thomas Heyward, Jun., were duly elected to repre-

[1] Force's Archives, (4th series,) vol. v., p. 566. [2] Ibid., p. 572.
[3] See Ante, p. 509—note.

sent South Carolina for the ensuing year, in the Congress at Philadelphia.

Wherever the Royal authority was overthrown, the powers of government were assumed and exercised by committees and conventions. The necessity of a more stable authority, an authority strictly defined, and exercised according to law, was soon felt. The subject had early occupied the attention of Rutledge. We have seen in the preceding chapter, that he was among the foremost to urge the institution of governments in the several colonies. The forms which those governments should assume, he had made a topic of reflection and conversation.[1] Hence, he was prepared to take an efficient part in framing the Constitution of South Carolina.

On the 8th of February, he was appointed one of a committee to consider the resolution of the Continental Congress, adopted the previous November, and recommending the mode of establishing a form of government in that colony.[2] On the 10th, this committee made their report. It was immediately taken into consideration. Many members of the Congress were opposed to establishing an independent Constitution. Some there were, who were not yet sufficiently advanced for so decisive a step; while others contended that their constituents had not clothed them with the requisite authority.[3] Gadsden had returned from Philadelphia on the 8th instant, and brought with him the first copy of Paine's pamphlet, called *Common Sense;* 'written in vindication of doctrines,' said Adams, in a letter to his wife, dated the 18th instant, 'which there is reason to expect, that the further encroachments of tyranny and depredations of oppression will soon make the common faith,' &c.[4] Gadsden avowed himself, not only in favor of an independent

---

[1] See Adams' Works, vol. iii., pp. 16–21. [2] Ante, p. 520.
[3] Drayton, vol. ii., p. 172. [4] Adams' Letters, vol. i., p. 84.

government, but of the absolute independence of the United Colonies.

'This last sentiment,' says Drayton, 'came like an explosion of thunder upon the members of Congress; as the resolution of the Continental Congress, upon which the report for a form of government was grounded, had by no means led them to anticipate so decisive a step: neither had the majority of the members, at that time, any thoughts of aspiring at independence. A distinguished member, in particular, declared he abhorred the idea; and that he was willing to ride post, by day and night, to Philadelphia, in order to assist in reuniting Great Britain and America; and another called the author of *Common Sense* —— ——. Even the few who wished for independence thought Colonel Gadsden imprudent in thus suddenly declaring for it, when the house was unprepared for considering a matter of such great importance.' [1]

It has been assumed, but upon what authority does not appear, that the distinguished member to whom Drayton alludes in this extract, was Rutledge.[2] However, there is nothing, in the supposition, inconsistent with his position at this time; while there is much to support it. In the first place, the person in question was evidently a member of the Continental Congress;

[1] Drayton's Memoirs, vol. ii., p. 172.

[2] See Johnson's Traditions of the Revolution, p. 41. 'It must not be forgotten,' says Drayton, 'that the citizens of South Carolina did not lead, but followed, the American Revolution. They had been mildly treated by the Royal Government, and therefore did not hastily lose sight of British protection. Hence, the public mind weighed how far it should support violent measures against the ancient government; and did not give way until the revolutionary troubles, and revolutionary principles thence arising, led them, step by step, to concede points as proper and patriotic, which, a short time before, they had thought disloyal and unadvisable.' Vol. ii., p. 89. As to the anxiety, 'approaching to despondency,' at this time 'prevailing through the Southern Colonies,' see Adams' Letters, vol. i., p. 81.

and, of Gadsden's colleagues in that body, only Rutledge and Middleton were now in attendance upon the Provincial Congress. In the second place, the language used in denunciation of Gadsden's sentiment, is characteristic of Rutledge, and would seem to indicate him as its author.

Notwithstanding the diversity of opinion that appeared in the Congress, and the excitement occasioned by Gadsden's bold and unexpected avowal of obnoxious sentiments, the report of the committee, declaring that the present mode of conducting public affairs was inadequate to the well-governing the good people of the colony; and that many regulations were wanting to secure peace and good order, during the unhappy disputes between Great Britain and the colonies, was agreed to, without any alteration. On the following day,[1] a committee of eleven was chosen, by ballot, to prepare and report to the Congress a plan or form of government. This committee consisted of C. C. Pinckney, John Rutledge, Charles Pinckney, Henry Laurens, Christopher Gadsden, Rawlins Lowndes, Arthur Middleton, Henry Middleton, Thomas Bee, Thomas Lynch, Jun., and Thomas Heyward, Jun.

On the 4th of March, they brought in their report. Its consideration was postponed until the following day; and, in the meantime, all members of the Congress, who were absent, and within sixty miles of Charleston, were sent for by special messengers, and at their own expense. The form of government, reported by the committee, engaged the earnest attention of the Congress; it was considered by sections, and, after several amendments, was finally adopted on the 26th of March, 1776.[2]

This result, however, was not attained without much opposition and controversy. The moderate men urged

[1] Sunday, Feb. 11.

[2] Drayton's Memoirs, vol. ii., p. 178, and Journals of the Provincial Congress.

every objection, and interposed every obstacle, that might prevent so decisive a step. But while the discussion was going on, there arrived at Charleston, by express from Savannah, the act of Parliament of December 21st, 1775, declaring the Colonies in a state of Rebellion, and authorizing the capture of their vessels and property. 'This silenced, in a great measure, the moderate men, who wished a reconciliation with Great Britain — put down attempts of postponement and opposition—and greatly advanced the public measures which were then in hand.'[1]

Three days after its reception, namely on the 24th of March, Rutledge, on behalf of the committee, reported a Preamble to the Constitution. It was drawn by him, and recites, in strong and forcible language, the causes of the war, the wrongs of the colonies, and the necessity of establishing a mode for regulating the internal polity of the colony.

The general features of the South Carolina Constitution are worthy of observation.

The Legislative authority was vested in a President, General Assembly, and Legislative Council.

The Congress was to constitute the General Assembly until the ensuing October, when members were to be chosen, and afterwards biennially, from the respective districts and parishes of the State. The number thus chosen was to be equal to the representation in the present Congress.

The Legislative Council consisted of thirteen members, elected biennially by the General Assembly, out of their own body.

The President was chosen by the General Assembly and the Legislative Council, either from among themselves or the people at large. He was vested with the

---

[1] Drayton's Memoirs, vol. ii., p. 180.

Executive authority of the State, and allowed a salary of nine thousand pounds per annum.

The Judicial power was vested in a Court of Chancery and Courts of Law.

The Court of Chancery was composed of the Vice-President and Privy Council, who were chosen by the General Assembly and Legislative Council; and whose ordinary duty was to advise the President when required. The Chief Justice and Assistant Judges were chosen in the same manner, and commissioned during good behavior.

All money-bills originated in the General Assembly, and could not be altered or amended by the Legislative Council, though they might reject them. Bills of a different character could be initiated in either branch, and be altered or rejected by the other. The President had a negative upon their acts.

No change was made in the laws of the State; and all pending suits could be prosecuted, if either party desired it, to a final termination, in the courts originating under this Constitution, without being obliged to commence *de novo*.

This Constitution was hailed by the people with great satisfaction. It virtually extinguished all authority under the crown. It professed to be temporary. It was carried after a long debate, that it should only continue 'until an accommodation of the unhappy differences between Great Britain and America could be obtained.'[1] But sagacious minds perceived, that independent governments, once established, the people would never consent to give them up.

'I have reasons to believe,' wrote John Adams on the 17th of May, 'that no colony, which shall assume a

[1] Ramsay's Revolution of South Carolina, vol. i., p. 83.

government under the people, will give it up. There is something very unnatural and odious in a government a thousand leagues off. A whole government of our own choice, managed by persons whom we love, revere, and can confide in, has charms in it for which men will fight.'[1]

---

[1] Adams' Letters, vol. i., p. 109, 110.

CHAPTER X.

PRESIDENT OF SOUTH CAROLINA.

1776—1778.

THE Congress, now acting as the General Assembly, proceeded, on the very day the Constitution was adopted, to organize a government, agreeably to its provisions. Rutledge was chosen President.[1] When the Assembly convened the next morning, he thus addressed them.[2] 'The very great, unsolicited, and unexpected honor which you have been pleased to confer on me, has overwhelmed me with gratitude and concern. Permit me to return you my most sincere thanks for so distinguishing and

---

[1] March 26th, 1776. He was elected on the second ballot. See Journals, Force's Archives, vol. v., p. 615.

[2] I observe that Ramsay, (Revolution of S. C., vol. i., p. 94,) speaks of this address as being delivered immediately upon Rutledge's election. So does Moultrie, Memoirs, vol. i., p. 130. This is a mistake. The Journals of the Assembly show otherwise. Ramsay frequently errs in details, though accurate in substance. Drayton, on the other hand, relates details as if he were writing under the obligations of an oath, and seldom is erroneous. He conforms to the journals and public documents, the only safe guides in matters of fact. Drayton, vol. ii., p. 241.

'The Colonies to the South,' wrote Adams to his wife, 'are pursuing the same maxims which have heretofore governed those to the north. In constituting their new governments, their plans are remarkably popular, more so than I could ever have imagined; . . . and, in the choice of their rulers, capacity, spirit, and zeal in the cause, supply the place of fortune, family, and every other consideration which used to have weight with mankind. My friend, Archibald Bullock, Esquire, is Governor of Georgia; John Rutledge, Esquire, is Governor of South Carolina; Patrick Henry, Esquire, is Governor of Virginia; Dr. Franklin will be Governor of Pennsylvania,' &c. July 10th, 1776. Letters of Adams, vol. i., p. 135.

unmerited a mark of your confidence and esteem. I have the deepest sense of this honor. The being called by the free suffrages of a brave and generous people to preside over their welfare, is, in my opinion, the highest any man can receive. But, dreading the weighty and arduous duties of this station, I really wish that your choice had fallen upon one better qualified to discharge them; for, though in zeal and integrity I will yield to no man, in abilities to serve you I know my inferiority to many. Since, however, this, gentlemen, is your pleasure, although I foresee that, by submitting to it, I shall be ranked by your enemies amongst ambitious and designing men, (by whom they say the people have been deceived and misled,) yet, as I have always thought every man's best services due to his country, no fear of slander, or of difficulty or danger, shall deter me from yielding mine. In so perilous a season as the present I will not withhold them; but in her cause every moment of my time shall be devoted. Happy, indeed, shall I be, if those services answer your expectations, or my own wishes. On the candor of my worthy countrymen I rely to put the most favorable construction, as they hitherto have done, upon my actions. I assure myself of receiving, in the faithful discharge of my duty, the support and assistance of every good man in the colony; and my most fervent prayer to the Omnipotent Ruler of the Universe is, that, under his Providence, the liberties of America may be forever preserved.'

The Vice-President, Judges, and other officers, being chosen and qualified to act, the oath of office, previously framed and adopted, was administered to the President in the General Assembly on the 28th instant.[1] It was

[1] The following is the form of oath administered to him on that occasion: 'I solemnly promise and swear to preside over the people of this colony according to the Constitution, or form of government, agreed to,

deemed appropriate to distinguish so interesting an occasion as the inauguration of a government, emanating from the people, and instituted for the defence and protection of their liberties, by imposing ceremonies. Accordingly, the troops and citizens were formed in Broad street, when 'His Excellency, preceded by the Sheriff bearing the Sword of State, and the officers of the Legislative Council,'[1] and accompanied by the two Houses, 'made a

and resolved upon by the Representatives of South Carolina, on the 26th day of March, 1776; that I will cause law and justice in mercy to be executed; and to the utmost of my power maintain and defend the laws of God, the Protestant Religion, and the liberties of America. So help me God.' It is observable, that, in the Constitution of '76, no provision was made to equalize the religious rights of the people. The establishment was continued as before.

[1] Journals of the S. C. General Assembly. Force's Archives, (4th series,) vol. v., p. 618. In our day, office confers but little distinction, and official titles are but little respected. At the era of the Revolution a different sentiment prevailed. Then, office was a post of respect and dignity; it was also a post of danger. Accustomed to the English mode, persons engaged in the public service were abundantly distinguished by appellations of honor. In addition to the recognized titles, which were never to be omitted, such as Excellency and Honorable, others were occasionally employed, so extravagant as to become ridiculous. 'In writing letters,' says Sparks, 'the uninitiated sometimes made ludicrous mistakes, and interlarded Worship, Worshipful, and the like, out of all time and measure, and were guilty of strange transpositions and misplacings of the recognized titles. Letters to Washington frequently began, 'Illustrious Sir;' and petitions were prefaced with a string of lofty and sonorous epithets.' Life of Gouverneur Morris, vol. i., p. 85.

The tendency to extravagance in this regard did not escape the notice of that remarkable but eccentric genius, General Charles Lee. 'There is a barbarism,' thus he wrote Patrick Henry, 'crept in among us that extremely shocks me; I mean those tinsel epithets with which (I come in for my share) we are so beplastered—His Excellency and his Honor, the Honorable President of the Honorable Congress, or the Honorable Convention. This fulsome, nauseating cant, may be well enough adapted to barbarous monarchies, or to gratify the adulterated pride of the *magnifici* in pompous aristocracies; but in a great, free, manly, equal Commonwealth, it is quite abominable; for my own part, I would as lief

solemn procession from the State-house to the Exchange, in front of the line of troops.'[1] Here, the preamble, and a portion of the Constitution being read by the Sheriff, the President was formally proclaimed, 'amidst the heart-cheering plaudits of the people.' These were responded to, 'by thirteen discharges from the cannon of the artillery — a *feu de joye* from the line of troops — and the cannon of the Prosper ship-of-war, and other armed vessels in the harbor. The procession then returned to the State-house, and each branch of the government entered on the performance of its respective duties.'[2]

'Two young gentlemen from South Carolina in this city,' thus wrote John Adams from Philadelphia, 'who were in Charlestown when their new Constitution was promulgated, and when their new Governor and Council and Assembly walked out in procession, attended by the guards, company of cadets, light-horse, &c., told me, that they were beheld by the people with transports and tears of joy. The people gazed at them with a kind of rapture. They both told me, that the reflection that these were gentlemen whom they all loved, esteemed and revered, gentlemen of their own choice, whom they could trust, and whom they could displace, if any of them should behave amiss, affected them so, that they could not help crying. They say, their people will never give up this government.'[3]

On the 3d of April, the two Houses presented a joint

---

they would put ratsbane in my mouth, as the Excellency with which I am daily crammed. How much more true dignity was there in the simplicity of address among the Romans! Marcus Tullius Cicero, Decimo Bruto Imperatori, or Caio Marcello Consuli, than to his Excellency Major-General *Noodle*, or to the Honorable John *Doodle*. My objections are perhaps trivial and whimsical; but for my soul I cannot help starting them.' Memoirs of Lee, p. 323. Force's Archives, (5th series,) vol. i., p. 630.

[1] Drayton, vol. ii., p. 243. [2] Ibid.

[3] Adams' Letters, vol. i., p. 109, 110. May 17th, 1776.

address to the President, congratulating him upon holding the reins of government, and assuring him that they would support him with their lives and fortunes. 'Be persuaded,' was the language of his reply, 'that no man would embrace a just and equitable accommodation with Great Britain more gladly than myself; but until so desirable an object can be obtained, the defence of my country, and preservation of that Constitution, which, from a perfect knowledge of the rights, and a laudable regard to the happiness of the people, you have so wisely framed, shall engross my whole attention. To this country I owe all that I hold dear and valuable, and would, with the greatest pleasure, sacrifice every temporal felicity, to establish and perpetuate her freedom.' [1]

The Assembly, having perfected various acts for the defence of the colony, and for regulating its internal polity, adjourned on the 11th of April to the first day of the ensuing October. On that occasion, the President, after giving his assent to several bills presented to him for that purpose by the two Houses, addressed them in a written speech, which 'was received with much applause,' and was ordered to be 'forthwith printed, as well in the newspapers as otherwise.' [2]

From this speech, thus praised, we can make but a single extract. Having referred to the mutual oaths they had taken — on his part, for the faithful discharge of his duty — on theirs, to support him therein, he proceeded as follows: — 'And now, gentlemen, let me intreat that you will, in your several parishes and districts, use your influence and authority to keep peace and good order, and procure strict observance of, and ready obedience to the law. If any persons therein are still strangers to the

---

[1] Journals of Assembly, Force's Archives, vol. v., p. 630.

[2] Drayton, vol. ii., p. 253. Force's Archives, vol. v., (4th series,) p. 652.

nature and merits of the dispute between Great Britain and the colonies, you will explain it to them fully, and teach them, if they are so unfortunate as not to know their inherent rights. Prove to them, that the privileges of being tried by a jury of the vicinage, acquainted with the parties and witnesses; of being taxed only with their own consent, given by their representatives, freely chosen by and sharing the burden equally with themselves—not for aggrandizing a rapacious minister and his dependent favorites, and for corrupting the people and subverting their liberties, but for such wise and salutary purposes as they themselves approve; and of having their internal polity regulated only by laws consented to by competent judges of what is best adapted to their situation and circumstances—equally bound, too, by those laws which are inestimable, and derived from that Constitution which is the birthright of the poorest man, and the best inheritance of the most wealthy. . . . To the most illiterate it must appear that no power on earth can of right deprive them of the hard-earned fruits of their honest industry, toil, and labor; even to them the impious attempt to prevent many thousands from using the means of subsistence provided for man by the bounty of his Creator, and to compel them, by famine, to surrender their rights, will seem to call for divine vengeance. The endeavors, by deceit and bribery, to engage barbarous nations to imbrue their hands in the innocent blood of helpless women and children; and the attempt by fair, but false promises, to make the ignorant domestics subservient to the most wicked purposes, are acts at which humanity must revolt. Show your constituents, then, the indispensable necessity which there was for establishing some mode of government in this colony; the benefits of that which a full and free representation has established; and that the consent of the people is the origin, and their happiness the end, of government. . . . Let it be known that this Constitution is but temporary, till an accommodation of the unhappy differences between Great Britain and America can be obtained; and that such an event is still desired by men who still remember former friendships and intimate connections, though, for defending their persons and properties, they are stigmatized and treated as rebels.

'Truth, being know, will prevail over artifice and misrepresentation — conviction must follow its discovery. . . . . Although superior force may, by the permission of Heaven, lay waste our towns and ravage our country, it can never eradicate from the hearts of freemen those principles which are ingrafted in their very nature. Such men will do their duty, neither knowing or regarding consequences, but submitting them, with humble confidence, to the omniscient and omnipotent Arbiter and Director of the fate of Empires, and trusting that His Almighty arm, which has been so signally stretched out for our defence, will deliver them in a righteous cause.'

With a regular system of government, acting within prescribed limits, the affairs of South Carolina were soon redeemed from the confusion into which they had fallen, in consequence of the disagreements in the Council of Safety, and conducted with order and uniformity. The courts of law were opened with great solemnity on the 23d of April, 1776; justice was regularly administered; and the new system, in all its branches, fully asserted its value and efficiency.—'What every one once dreaded as the greatest misery,' said the Presentment of the Grand Jury, for Cheraw's District, 'they now unexpectedly find their greatest advantage. . . . . When we consider the public officers of our present form of government, how appointed, as well as the method and duration of their appointment, we cannot but declare our entire satisfaction and comfort; as well in the characters of such men, who are justly esteemed for every virtue, as their well-known abilities to execute the important trusts which they now hold.'[1]

The President and privy council, after the adjournment of the General Assembly, were constantly employed in putting the colony in a state of defence. 'They continued to carry on the fortifications, issue money; to examine accounts, and to pay all liquidated demands.'[2] News arrived at Charleston, the latter part of April, that a British fleet and army were preparing at New York, for the invasion of South Carolina. This intelligence occasioned increased activity in the public councils; the laborers on the public works were multiplied; 'every one seemed to be busy, and everything went on with great spirit.'[3] On the 31st of May, the President was informed by expresses sent from Christ Church Parish, that a fleet of British vessels were seen off Dewees' Island, about twenty miles to the northward of the Charleston bar; and on the following day, about fifty sail, men-of-war and transports, appeared before the town.

'The sight of these vessels,' says Moultrie, 'alarmed us very much; all was hurry and confusion; the President with his council busy in sending expresses to every part of the country, to hasten down the militia,'[4] and using every exertion demanded by the imminence of the crisis. Military works were thrown up at every exposed point, lead was taken from the windows of churches and dwelling-houses, and cast into musket-balls, and everything was called into requisition to repel an attack, 'which appeared certain and immediate.'[5] In company with General Armstrong, who had arrived from the North a few days before, Rutledge visited the fortifi-

---

[1] Force's Archives, vol. vi., (4th series) p. 514. This Presentment was made the 20th of May, 1776.

[2] Moultrie's Memoirs, vol. i., p. 138.

[3] Ibid.

[4] Ibid., vol. i., p. 140.

[5] Dayton's Memoirs, vol. ii., p. 279.

cations, and in a variety of ways evinced his extreme anxiety for the public welfare.

General Lee had been appointed by Congress, several months before, to the command in the Southern department; and when the British fleet sailed from Cape Fear,[1] where General Clinton and Sir Peter Parker had joined their forces, he was at Wilmington. He was quite uncertain as to their destination, whether it was Virginia or South Carolina. As the latter, however, was weaker than the former, he immediately ordered Muhlenburg's regiment, at a venture, to Charleston, together with a detachment of seven hundred men from Wilmington. This was on the first day of June. 'I shall myself set out for Charleston to-morrow,' he wrote on the same day, 'but at the same time confess I know not whether I shall go to or from the enemy.'[2] Rutledge received a letter from him at five o'clock in the afternoon of June 4th, and immediately replied. 'I wish,' he said, 'you and a powerful reinforcement were now here. For *God's* sake, lose not a moment. There are fifty sail of vessels at anchor off the bar, within sight of the town, which will, I suppose, come in with to-morrow's tide, if the wind is not unfavorable. Bring us all the forces you can collect to cope with this armament, either from North Carolina, Virginia, or any part of this Province you pass through. I send this express to you, and send on the roads and at the several

---

[1] The British squadron arrived at Cape Fear the first of May, after a voyage of three months. 'Upon our arrival in Cape Fear,' wrote Lieutenant Falconer to his brother, the Hon. Anthony Falconer, of Montrose, Scotland, 'we disembarked, and were encamped in the woods until the 27th of May, when we went on board again, and sailed for this infernal place.

'Camp Long Island, near Charleston, July 13, 1776.'—[Force's Archives, vol. i., (5th series,) p. 250.

[2] Lee to Edmund Pendleton, June 6, 1776. Force's Archives, vol. vi., (4th series,) p. 721.

ferries to facilitate your march.'[1] Lee arrived at Charleston on the 6th.[2] 'His presence gave us great spirits,' says Moultrie, ... 'it was thought by many that his coming among us was equal to a reinforcement of one thousand men, and I believe it was, because he taught us to think lightly of the enemy, and gave a spur to all our actions.'[3] 'He is the first officer in military knowledge and experience we have in the whole army,' wrote Washington to his brother; 'he is zealously attached to the cause, honest and well meaning, but rather fickle and violent, I fear, in his temper. However, as he possesses an uncommon share of good sense and spirit, I congratulate my countrymen upon his appointment to that department.'[4] As the troops raised by South Carolina had not been put upon the Continental establishment, Lee had no control over them.[5] They were subject to the orders of Rutledge, as Commander-in-chief. But he knew too well the dangers of a divided authority, and had too much confidence in Lee to insist on his prerogative. He accordingly invested that officer with the command of the militia, acting in conjunction with the regular forces, and directed that

---

[1] Rutledge to Lee, June 4th, 5 o'clock, P. M. Force's Archives, vol. vi., (4th series,) p. 720.

[2] Moultrie speaks of his arrival on the 4th; but Rutledge's letter, quoted above, proves the contrary. Besides, Lee addressed a letter to the President of Congress on the 6th, from "Little River, on the road to Charleston."—Ibid.

[3] Moultrie, vol. i., p. 141.

[4] Letter to John Augustine Washington, March 31, 1776. Force's Archives, vol. v., (4th series).

This letter was written soon after Lee's appointment to the Southern department. Washington's brief delineation of his character is accurate and just. Lee was a remarkable man, and in some respects a great one. The decision of the court-martial upon his conduct at Monmouth was absurd and indefensible. See Lee's Memoirs, vol. i., p. 60–64; also Sparks's Life of Lee, American Biography, vol. xviii.

[5] They had not been put upon the Continental establishment because South Carolina disliked the Continental regulations.

orders issued by him should be obeyed. When Lee first visited Sullivan's Island, only the front and one side of the fort were finished. As an immediate attack was apprehended, he thought the place indefensible. Besides, he had little confidence in the officers and men who were to maintain it.[1] He said 'that it could not hold out half an hour, and that the platform was but a slaughtering-stage.'[2] He proposed to Rutledge to abandon it. 'General Lee wishes you to evacuate the fort,' wrote the latter to Moultrie, who had the command. 'You will not without an order from me; I would sooner cut off my hand than write one!'[3] This letter is characteristic of Rutledge, and exhibits his energy and decision in a very conspicuous light.

Though Lee deemed the fort indefensible, he left no endeavors unessayed to hasten its completion. His letters to Moultrie all indicate his vigilance and untiring activity. That officer, beloved for his personal qualities, a man of honor, courage, and good abilities, was, nevertheless, negligent and immethodical in his habits, and easy and yielding in his temper. Lee perceived that if the British ships should pass the fort, and take a position in Rebellion Road towards the cove of Sullivan's Island, their guns would enfilade the fort, and make it, as he had pronounced it, 'a slaughter-pen.' To protect the men from the anticipated destructive fire, he had directed Moultrie to raise screens of planks upon the front platforms of the south-east curtain and its two bastions. But Lee's orders were not attended to; the day before the action, he found the screens were not raised. He then determined to supersede Moultrie, and place the command of the fort in the hands of Colonel Nash of the

---

[1] See Letter to Washington, post, pp. 542, 544.

[2] Drayton, vol. ii., p. 282. Drayton writes with a strong bias against Lee.

[3] Ramsay's History of South Carolina, vol. ii., p. 516.

North Carolina line. The night before the action took place, he told Nash of his intention, and directed him to come in the morning for his written orders. While Nash was on his way to Lee for that purpose, the movement of the ships to the attack rendered a change improper, and Moultrie retained his command.[1] However, the very manœuvre Lee had foreseen, was attempted by three of the enemy's vessels, the Acteon, Sphinx, and Syren; 'but Almighty Providence,' says Drayton, 'confounded the plan, and frustrated the attempt. For, while the detached frigates were standing well over towards the lower middle-ground opposite the fort, ... they got entangled in the shoal, when the Sphinx and Acteon ran foul of each other. The Syren got off, as did the Sphinx, with the loss of her bowsprit; but the Acteon was left immovably fixed in the sand.'[2] Had it not been for this fortunate accident, it is highly probable that the fate of the day would have been different, and the military judgment of Lee been justified.

The brilliant action at Sullivan's Island was fought on the 28th of June. The British land forces, commanded by General Clinton, were stationed on a sand-bank, called Long Island,[3] and amounted to about 3000 men. The

---

[1] Drayton, vol. ii., p. 298, 312. See also Lee's Letters to Moultrie, Moultrie's Memoirs, vol. i., pp. 149–168.

[2] Drayton, *supra*. Moultrie himself says, if the ships had effected their purpose, they would have been enfiladed, and thus driven from their guns. Moultrie's Memoirs, vol. i., p. 178.

[3] 'We have been encamped on this island for this month past,' wrote Lieutenant Falconer to his brother, on the 13th of July, 'and have lived upon nothing else but salt pork and peas. We sleep upon the sea-shore, nothing to shelter us from the violent rains but our coats and miserable paltry blankets. There is nothing that grows upon this island, it being a mere sand-bank, and a few bushes, which harbor millions of moschitoes—a greater plague than there can be in hell itself. . . . . The oldest of the officers do not remember of ever undergoing such hardships as we have done since our arrival here.'—Force's Archives (5th series), vol. i. p 249. This letter was found on Long Island, forwarded to Congress, and made public by their order.

attack was to be made by the army and fleet conjointly. While Sir Peter Parker, with the ships, should engage the fort in front, Clinton was to cross over from Long Island to Sullivan's Island, and make an assault on the land side, where the works were unfinished and unprotected by cannon. To repel Clinton, Lee had made a judicious disposition of the South Carolina militia, and the Virginia and North Carolina regulars. Clinton was deceived upon two points. He had been informed that the depth of the channel between the two islands, and at the point he had selected for crossing, was but eighteen inches. At flood tide, it proved to be upwards of seven feet. He acted too, upon the erroneous idea, that the Americans had several thousand men to dispute his passage, supported by a strong battery. The result was, that he remained an inactive spectator of the ineffectual efforts of the fleet. Lee described the naval attack, in the following letter to Washington, written on the 1st of July:

'I shall not trouble you with a detail of their manœuvres or delays,' he said, 'but defer it to another time, when I have more leisure to write, and you to attend; let it suffice that, having lost an opportunity . . . . of taking the town, which, on my arrival, was utterly defenceless, the Commodore thought proper, on Friday last, with his whole squadron, consisting of two fifties, six frigates and a bomb, . . . to attack our fort on Sullivan's Island. They dropped their anchors about eleven in the forenoon, at the distance of 300 or 400 yards before the front battery. I was myself at this time in a boat, endeavouring to make the island, but the wind and tide being violently against us, drove us on the main. They immediately commenced the most furious fire that I ever heard or saw. I confess I was in pain from the little confidence I reposed in our troops, the officers being all boys, and the men raw recruits. What augmented my anxiety was, that we had no bridge finished for retreat or communication, and the creek or cove which separated it from the continent, is near a mile wide. I had received, likewise, intelligence that their land troops intended at the same time to land and assault. I never in my life felt myself so uneasy; and what added to my uneasiness was, that I knew our stock of ammunition was miserably low. I had once thoughts of ordering the commanding officer to spike his guns, and when his ammunition was spent to retreat with as little loss as possible.[1] However, I thought proper previous, to send to town for a fresh supply, if it could possibly be procured, and ordered my Aid-de-camp, Mr. Byrd (who is a lad of magnanimous courage), to pass over in a small canoe and report the state of the spirit of the garrison; if it had been low, I should have abandoned all thoughts of defence. His report was flattering. I then determined to maintain the post at all risks, and passed the creek or cove in a small boat, in order to animate the garrison *in propria persona;* but I found they had no occasion for such encouragement. They were pleased with my visit, and assured me they never would abandon the post but with their lives. The cool courage they displayed astonished and enraptured me; for I do assure you, my dear General, I never experienced a hotter fire—twelve full hours it was continued without intermission. The noble fellows who were mortally wounded, conjured their brethren never to abandon the standard of liberty. Those who lost their limbs deserted not their posts. Upon the whole, they acted like Romans in the third century. However, our works were so good and solid, that we lost but few

[1] He did order Moultrie, *if* he should unfortunately expend his ammunition without beating off the enemy or driving them on ground, to spike his guns and retreat with all the order possible; 'but I know,' he added, 'you will be careful not to throw away your ammunition,'—Moultrie's Memoirs, vol. i., p. 166.

—only ten killed on the spot, and twenty-two wounded, some of whom lost their legs or arms."[1]

In the beginning of the action, Moultrie wrote to Lee for more powder. When his note reached Charleston, Lee had gone to Haddrell's Point; as the occasion was urgent, it was delivered to Rutledge. The terms employed by Moultrie, did not seem to imply that his deficiency of powder was so great as it really was. Rutledge, accordingly, sent him but 500 pounds. It was accompanied with the following laconic letter, written with a pencil, on a small slip of paper: 'I send you 500 pounds of powder. I should think you may be supplied well from Haddrell's . . . You know our collection is not very great. Honor and victory, my good Sir, to you, and our worthy countrymen with you.' The

[1] Lee to Washington, July 1, 1776. Force's Archives (4th series), vol. iv., p. 1183. Lee thus frankly states his doubts and difficulties, and thus highly extols the conduct of the garrison at Fort Sullivan. But because he entertained those doubts and difficulties, (justified by the situation of affairs,) certain writers have endeavored to deprive him of any share in the glories of that day. Such was not the opinion at the time of the citizens of Charleston, nor of Congress, nor of the country at large. The day after the action, Lee wrote Gates a very characteristic letter. 'Our troops,' he said, 'though raw, behaved most nobly; the fire was extremely hot and incessant . . . . My two young aids-de-camp, Byrd and A. Morris, stand fire most nobly. Young, old Jenifer,[1] and little Nourse,[2] strutted like crows in a gutter. The fire was, I assure you, very hot. I am much pleased with the troops, men and officers, and really believe them braver than the enemy. . . . . Enclosed is a return of our strength: apropos, I cannot send it just now, for the Adjutant-General (who is in love) has forgotten a whole regiment.'[3] Ibid., p. 1128.

[1] 'Mr. Jenifer, of Maryland, a gentleman of fortune, and not of the age when the blood of men flows heroically, has shown not less spirit than these youngsters.' Lee to Washington, *supra.*

[2] Lee's secretary.

[3] Two days later, Lee wrote Washington that he had ordered the Adjutant-General to send him a return. 'I suppose it will be imperfect,' he added, 'for it is an Herculean labor to a South Carolina officer to make any detail.'

postscript is characteristic: 'P. S. Do not make too free with your cannon. Cool, and do mischief.'[1]

The day after the action, Rutledge wrote Moultrie as follows: 'My very particular thanks are due to you, and the brave officers and men in your garrison for their heroic behaviour of yesterday. I beg that you will receive them yourself, and make them acceptable to the gentlemen, officers, and soldiers. Seeing the necessity of supporting you properly, I will strain every nerve to supply you with ammunition; no man would go a greater length than myself in this matter; but, my good Sir, you know the scantiness of our stock. I send you 1500 pounds, I think more cannot be spared ..... We must not wholly exhaust ourselves for the forts; small arms must decide the matter at last ...... If those gentry think proper to revisit you, after saying what I have done, you will not need any caution to spare your powder.'[2] Rutledge's gratitude for the heroic exertions of the garrison did not expend itself solely in thanks and congratulations. He accompanied his letter to Moultrie with a hogshead of rum, as a present to the men. In those days, total abstinence had not been elevated to the rank of a cardinal virtue.

On the 4th of July, the memorable day when the form of the Declaration of Independence was agreed to, Rutledge visited Fort Moultrie, and returned his thanks to the garrison for their gallant conduct. 'It was my good fortune,' says Garden, 'many years after this celebrated victory, to meet Governor Rutledge on the spot where the action of the 28th of June was fought, when the recollection of the triumphs of the day, filling his soul with enthusiastic delight, he exclaimed: 'I remember the engagement as if it were fought but yesterday! I remember my perfect confidence in Moultrie! I have all the scenes before me,

[1] Moultrie's Memoirs, vol. i., p. 167. See also Drayton, vol. ii., p. 311.
[2] Moultrie, *supra*, p. 168, June 29th, 1776.

too, when I visited the fort to express the thanks of the country to the heroes who had defended it. *There* stood Moultrie, *there* Motte, *there* Marion, Horry, and the intrepid band whom they commanded. I addressed them with an energy of feeling that I had never before experienced, and if ever I had pretension to eloquence, it was at that moment.'

'I will not dwell on a subject,' continues Garden, 'to which it is impossible for me to do justice, but briefly state, that inspired by it, and animated as if the objects of his commendation were immediately before him, he delivered him, self in an eloquent and impressive strain of eulogy, so perfectly fascinating, that had his first address but borne a shadow of resemblance to it, there could not have been a man among his auditors who would not have been proud to die for liberty and his country. I have often heard of the strong impression made at the moment of delivery by this celebrated harangue. Certain it is, that under its animating influence, new honors crowned the valiant defenders of the fort, and to the last, the gallant second regiment were covered with glory.'[1]

Whilst the attempted invasion of the British was happily repelled, a different, but not less alarming danger,

[1] Garden's Anecdotes, p. 11. This work of Garden's is interesting, and in some respects, valuable. Its greatest defect is exaggeration and over-statement. Many of the honest fellows whose names he has recorded and blazoned, if they could reappear on earth, would be amazed at the grand and swelling proportions they have assumed in the eyes of their posterity. The exciting scenes of the Revolution seem to have imparted a wonderful fertility of language to the actors in them. Early in the year 1775, two British officers, who went through the counties of Suffolk and Worcester, disguised like countrymen, to sketch the roads for General Gage, saw a company of Militia exercised, and listened to the speech of one of their commanders, — 'Very eloquent . . . quotes Cæsar and Pompey, Brigadiers Putnam and Ward, and all such great men.' American Archives, vol. i., p. 1265. In this vein were written many of the books put forth just after the Revolution. Garden did not escape the contagion.

menaced the State on the frontiers. 'That detestable villain, Stuart,[1] has prevailed upon the Cherokees to take up the hatchet against our countrymen,'[2] wrote a gentleman in Charleston, on the 21st of July. When the Indians heard that the British fleet had arrived off Charleston, 'they poured down upon the frontiers, . . . massacreing without distinction of age or sex, all persons who fell into their power.'[3] When this intelligence reached Charleston, Rutledge lost not a moment in taking such steps as the peril of the inhabitants in the exposed districts suggested and required. 'I have given orders to Major Williamson,' thus he wrote to the President of the Virginia Convention, requesting aid in this emergency, 'to proceed with what men he has embodied and can raise, which I suppose may amount to about 1100 men, and march . . . . . . against the lower Cherokees, and then to carry on a war against them, unless they will submit to reasonable terms.'[4] The success of Williamson's expedition is a part of the general history of the country, and does not need repetition.[5]

With the repulse of the British attack, it occurred to Rutledge that an act of clemency and magnanimity would make a favourable impression upon the loyalists, and crown the triumphs of the day. Accordingly, he directed that such of them as had been apprehended and confined in the jails of Charleston should be set at liberty. This act, proceeding from a liberal policy, was not received in the country districts with the satisfaction

---

[1] John Stuart, the British Indian Agent.

[2] American Archives, vol. i. (5th series), p. 481. See also Stedman's American War, vol. i., p. 248, 249. Drayton, vol. ii., p. 338.

[3] Drayton, *supra*. They commenced hostilities on the 15th of July.

[4] July 7, 1776. American Archives, vol. i. (5th series), p. 611.

[5] 'In less than three months, viz., from the 15th of July, to the 11th of October, 1776, the business was completed, and the nation of the Cherokees so far subdued as to be incapable of annoying the settlements.' Ramsey's Revolution in S. C., vol. i., p. 159.

and forbearance that had been anticipated. When the intelligence reached the camp of Williamson it nearly occasioned a mutiny. 'It is really a measure,' wrote Salvador to Drayton, on the 18th of July, 'which, though certainly intended for the best, is very alarming to all ranks of people. The ignorant look upon it as turning their enemies loose on their backs in the day of their distress; the sensible part consider it as a dangerous exercise of a dispensing power, assumed contrary to the express determination of Congress, and a corroborating resolve of the succeeding House of Assembly.'[1] In a short time, however, the discontent subsided; 'and the returned prisoners were permitted to remain peaceably at home, in the enjoyment of their several rights and privileges.'[2]

While the delegates of South Carolina to the Continental Congress voted for the Declaration of Independence with reluctance, and only for the sake of unanimity,[3] their constituents were prepared to hail that measure with unfeigned satisfaction. This crowning act of Congress was received at Charleston on the 2d of August. It was welcomed with the greatest joy. On the 5th, it was officially proclaimed; 'the President, accompanied by all the officers, civil and military, making a grand procession on the occasion.'[4] On the 17th of September,

---

[1] American Archives, (fifth series) vol. i., p. 406. Salvador was with Williamson, whose camp was near Dewett's corner.

[2] Drayton, vol. ii., p. 316. The alarms of the people sprung from no adequate cause. Several of the tories wrote to Rutledge, 'and told him that they never dreamt the King would descend to such low and diabolical designs;[1] that they were now willing to do everything in their power to assist their brethren in America.' American Archives, *supra*, 481.

[3] Jefferson's Correspondence, vol. i., p. 15.

[4] Drayton, vol. ii., p. 315. See also Johnson's Traditions. Ramsay's Revolution of South Carolina, vol. i., p. 174.

---

[1] Meaning, the employment of the Indians.

the General Assembly met at Charleston.[1] They received the President's announcement of the Declaration of Independence 'with transports of joy.'[2] The dissolution of the political connection between the two countries was 'an event,' said Rutledge, on that occasion, 'which necessity had rendered not only justifiable, but unavoidable.'[3] 'It is a decree now worthy of America,' replied the legislative council. 'We thankfully receive the notification of, and rejoice at it; and we are determined at every hazard to endeavor to maintain it, that so, after we have departed, our children and their latest posterity may have cause to bless our memory.'[4] 'It is with unspeakable pleasure,' said the General Assembly, 'we embrace this opportunity of expressing our satisfaction in the declaration of the Continental Congress, constituting the United Colonies free and independent States, ... and totally dissolving all political union between them and Great Britain.'[5]

The legislature continued in session until the 20th of October. As the political connection between Great Britain and the colonies was now dissolved, certain changes in the Constitution were obviously proper. But changes of a more radical character were contemplated, which resulted in a division of sentiment, and Rutledge's resignation. A few days before the adjournment of the General Assembly, a committee was appointed to revise the Constitution. They brought in their report; but the subject, for the present, was postponed The next Legislature, however, at once addressed themselves to the task of reforming their constitution. They had not been elected for that purpose, and were not clothed with the

---

[1] They had been called together by the President's proclamation, issued the 5th of the preceding August.

[2] Ramsay, *supra*.

[3] American Archives, vol. ii. (5th series), p. 392.

[4] Ibid.

[5] Ibid., p. 394.

requisite authority, by the Constitution itself. But, as more than a year elapsed before they gave to their deliberations a final sanction, the people had an opportunity to consider the proposed changes, and indicate their sentiments with regard to them.

The new Constitution substituted State for Colony, and Governor for President. It reduced the legislative authority from three to two branches, and established a rotation in the public offices, so that the Governor, for instance, could not serve more than two years out of six. Instead of the Legislative Council chosen by the Assembly, it substituted a Senate of twenty-eight members, elected by the people, distributed into districts. The church establishment was abolished; and all Protestant sects put on a footing of equality.

These changes were very generally approved by the people; not, indeed, that there was entire unanimity of sentiment. On the contrary, the new Constitution had warm and influential opponents, both in the Legislature and out of it. The clergy declaimed against the abolition of the establishment, and seemed to regard the security of their stipends, and the safety of the commonwealth, as mutually dependent. The Legislative Council struggled hard against any change in the mode of their election. The leading men of Charleston were averse to the new order of things (as was thought), from a persuasion that the control of affairs would be transferred from the city to the country. But in the face of all obstacles, and with the implied consent of their constituents, the new Constitution was finally adopted by both branches of the Legislature, and early in March, 1778, was presented to the President for his sanction. He vetoed it. His reasons were three-fold. First, he deemed it impossible, consistently with his oath, to sanction the establishment of a mode of government different from that which he had sworn to support. Secondly, he was of opinion that they had not lawful authority to annihilate one branch of the Legislature, and transfer the right of electing another branch from the General Assembly to the people. 'The legislative authority being fixed and limited,' he said, 'cannot change or destroy itself without subverting the Constitution from which it is derived . . . . Experience teaches, that it is the indispensible duty of every lover of his country to adhere inflexibly to its Constitution, not admitting any innovation of it, though specious and plausible, lest the first making way for others, they rush forward like an impetuous torrent, bearing down all before it.' Thirdly, he deemed the causes assigned for abandoning the old constitution insufficient. Admitting it to be temporary, it was, nevertheless, to continue until peace or an accommodation with Great Britain should take place; 'an event,' he said, 'as desirable now as it ever was, so that the situation of public affairs is, in this respect, the same as when the constitution was established.' He preferred the present mode of electing a Legislative Council, to the mode proposed for electing a Senate. In a word, he preferred a compounded or mixed government, to a simple democracy, or one verging towards it. 'However unexceptionable democratic power may appear at the first view,' such was his language, 'its effects have been found arbitrary, severe and destructive.'

Having stated his objections to the new Constitution in frank, manly language, and the reasons that compelled him to reject it, he thus concluded. 'I am not so vain as to imagine that what I have said can influence your minds in a matter which has been so lately the subject of debate. But having delivered my sincere and real sentiments, with a freedom which I hope is neither unbecoming nor offensive, I confide in your candor to regard them as such. And now, I think proper to resign the office of President and Commander-in-chief of this State.' The Assembly accepted his resignation, and elected

Arthur Middleton to the vacant post. But Middleton had the same objections to the new Constitution as Rutledge, and declined the office. Rawlins Lowndes was then elected, and on the 19th of March, 1778, gave his assent to the new Constitution, which henceforth became the rule of government.

Rutledge's administration had been eminently prosperous. Victory marked its outset, and order and harmony attended it to its conclusion. 'During this period South Carolina felt very few of the inconveniences which were then grinding their brethren to the northward. They were in possession of a lucrative commerce, and comparatively happy . . . . . At no period of peace were fortunes more easily or more rapidly acquired.'[1]

---

[1] Ramsey's Revolution of S. C., vol. i., p. 176.

CHAPTER XI.

GOVERNOR OF SOUTH CAROLINA.

1778—1782.

THE gallant defence of Fort Moultrie preserved Georgia and South Carolina from the ravages of war, nearly three years. The repose and comparative happiness of those States was now to be interrupted. Foiled in their efforts against the northern States, the British Ministry projected the conquest of the southern. Late in the year 1778, Sir Henry Clinton detached Lieutenant-Colonel Campbell, with 3000 men, for the reduction of Georgia. Orders had been previously despatched to General Prevost, who commanded the British troops in East Florida, to effect a junction with Campbell, and assume the direction of their united force. Campbell landed his troops below Savannah, on the 29th of December, and immediately advanced towards that city. General Howe, who commanded the American force in Georgia, had less than a thousand men to resist the invader.[1] These he posted on advantageous ground, about half a mile from the town, and across the main road leading to it. But the enemy gained his rear, and a complete and disastrous defeat was the result. Taking possession of Savannah, Campbell, who was both brave and humane, conciliated the good-will of the inhabitants, by sparing their property, and protecting their persons. He

[1] Moultrie says, only 600 or 700; while the British force was 2000. Moultrie's Memoirs, vol. i., p. 254.

was soon after joined by General Prevost, who took the command, and detached Campbell to Augusta. He gained possession of that town without opposition; the different posts upon the Savannah river were all secured, and in the short space of one month, Georgia was restored to the British crown. 'The affections of the people were enlisted on the side of the conqueror; and the youth flocked to the British standard.'[1]

With Georgia in possession of the enemy, it was obvious that South Carolina was in a situation of imminent danger. At the request of her delegates in the Continental Congress, General Lincoln, the friend of Washington, and the second to Gates at the battle of Saratoga, had been appointed to the command in the Southern department. 'Upright, mild, and amiable,' says Lee, 'he was universally respected and beloved; a truly good man, and a brave and prudent, but not consummate, soldier.'[2] He arrived at Charleston on the 6th of December, and was engaged in perfecting his arrangements for the defence of the South, when the disastrous defeat of General Howe hurried him to the field. He established himself at Purysburg, about fifteen miles above Savannah, on the Carolina side. Here, on the first of February, he found himself in command of about 3700 men. Prevost's force amounted to nearly 4000, distributed, in different posts, from Savannah to Augusta.

The Legislature of South Carolina was now in session, and fully impressed with the necessity of vigorous action.

---

[1] Lee's Memoirs, vol. i., p. 71. Stedman's American War, vol. ii., p. 72. Moultrie to C. C. Pinckney, Jan. 14th, 1779. Moultrie's Memoirs, vol. i., p. 261–263.

[2] Lee's Memoirs, *supra*, p. 75. 'General Lincoln,' says Moultrie, 'was a brave, active, and very vigilant officer, and always so very cautious that he would take no step of any consequence without first calling a council of officers, to advise with them on the measures.' Moultrie's Memoirs, vol. i., p. 476.

They made provision for filling the Continental regiments, revived the law for impressing boats, wagons, &c., for the public service, and authorized the imprisonment of suspected persons. Mr. Lowndes, having retired from the chair of State, they recalled to that responsible post, the man, whose firm, manly conduct, in the face of the previous invasion, won universal applause. On the 5th of February, 1779, John Rutledge was again elected Governor of South Carolina. 'An accomplished gentleman,' says Lee, 'a profound statesman, a captivating orator, decisive in his measures, and inflexibly firm, he infused his own lofty spirit into the general mass.'[1]

To Rutledge and his Council, the Legislature delegated the extraordinary power 'to do everything that appeared to him and them necessary for the public good.' The affairs of the State now began to wear a different aspect. Every exertion was made to strengthen the Continental forces, while the militia were increased, and a severe law passed for their government.[2] The State was exposed to attack on several sides, by the savages and disaffected from the west, by Prevost from Georgia, and by a British fleet from sea. To be at hand to relieve any threatened point, Rutledge determined to form a camp in a central position, and there concentrate the militia.[3] 'The Governor has signified his intention of taking the field,'

---

[1] Lee's Memoirs, vol. i., p. 80. Lee fixes the election of Rutledge, after the total rout of General Ash, at Brier-creek, which occurred March 3d, 1779. Ramsay has fallen into the same error. Revolution of South Carolina, vol. ii., p. 19. 'In this time of general alarm,' says Ramsay, 'John Rutledge, Esquire, by the almost unanimous voice of his countrymen, was called to the chair of government.' Ibid.

[2] They had, hitherto, given a great deal of trouble. They 'were so discordant,' says Moultrie, 'that they disobeyed every order which was disagreeable to them, and left their posts and guards whenever they pleased, and that with impunity.' Memoirs, vol. i., p. 313.

[3] 'My opinion is not yet settled as to time, place, numbers, &c.,' wrote Rutledge to Moultrie, Feb. 22d. Ibid., p. 317.

wrote one of the Council to Moultrie, March 9th, 'and joining the camp at Orangeburgh; which, I believe, will have a good effect to increase our numbers there. We propose to raise two or three companies of artillery of some excellent seamen and mariners now in town, who have offered their services to attend the camp, with half-a-dozen field-pieces. His Excellency is so sanguine in this business, that he thinks they will be ready to march and act in a very few days, from the assurances he has received on this head.'[1]

Rutledge joined the camp at Orangeburgh the 24th of March. 'His Excellency has been obliged to postpone his setting off for his camp until to-morrow noon,' wrote Pinckney on the 22d. 'I am told that there are not above 1000 men in that camp, but that their number, in a few days, will be increased to double; and in due time, if orders are complied with, the given number (5000) fixed on, may be there.'[2] The contemplated number were never assembled; but with the aid Rutledge could afford from Orangeburgh, Lincoln determined to resume his original plan, of driving the enemy from the upper part of Georgia.[3] He sent Moultrie to Orangeburgh to confer with Rutledge respecting it. He approved the plan, and immediately detached 1000 men to co-operate in it. Three days after his return, Moultrie thus wrote his friend Pinckney: 'We were (Mr. Kinlock and myself) gone six days; one day we staid with the Governor, the others in travelling. We expect Colonel Simons here to-morrow, with 1000 men of all ranks. This will be a reinforcement to us that will be very acceptable. The Governor has promised more as soon

[1] Charles Pinckney to Moultrie. Moultrie's Memoirs, vol. i., p. 328.

[2] Pinckney to Moultrie, March 22d, 1779. Moultrie's Memoirs, vol. i., p. 359.

[3] This plan had been interrupted by the unfortunate defeat of General Ashe, at Brier-creek, the 3d ult.

as they can be collected. I was sorry to see so few[1] left at Orangeburgh after this detachment marched off; though Colonel Neal lay about four miles off, with 280 men of his regiment, and was to march in that morning. Whilst I was there, I could see the Governor had a great deal of trouble, and I wish his zeal may not cause him to commit some improprieties.'[2]

The improprieties, to which Moultrie alludes, he thus explains: 'I think I see matters brewing that may bring on misunderstandings between the Governor and General Lincoln, such as orders issued from two commanders, which may perhaps run retrograde to each other.'[3] This actually occurred. Rutledge had directed General Williamson to make incursions into Georgia, whenever an opportunity offered, and destroy all the cattle, horses, provisions, and carriages, he might meet with in that State.[4] He hoped in this manner to distress the enemy, and cut off their sources of supply. But Lincoln, in order to prevent the Georgians from joining the British standard, had privately sent word to them, that if they would remain quiet until he could relieve them, they should not be molested. Williamson's fulfilment of Rutledge's orders would be a direct violation of this assurance. But when the Governor was informed that his directions

---

[1] Three or four hundred.

[2] Moultrie to Pinckney, April 16th, 1779. Moultrie's Memoirs, vol. i., p. 370.

[3] Ibid.

[4] After Williamson had received Rutledge's instructions, Lieutenant-Colonel Prevost proposed to him to suffer a certain portion of the people of Georgia to remain unmolested by either side. Williamson sent this proposition to Rutledge, for his determination upon it. He received this characteristic reply: 'Sir, Lieutenant-Colonel Prevost's proposition of a temporary neutrality for a part of Georgia is really too absurd and ridiculous to require a moment's consideration; indeed it scarce merits an answer. However, as you have promised, I presume you will give him one, which need be nothing more than that you are expressly enjoined not to agree to it.' Rutledge to Williamson, April 11th, 1779. Ibid., p. 372.

conflicted with Lincoln's, rising superior to the pride of command, and looking only to the good of the service, he countermanded them.

Reinforced by the detachment from the camp at Orangeburgh, Lincoln, on the 20th of April, put his troops in motion towards Augusta. He left Moultrie, with 1000 men, at Purysburg and Black-swamp, to guard that part of the country, and hold the enemy in check, should they pass the Savannah river. Prevost at once comprehended the full danger to which Lincoln's plan of operations exposed his divided force, and acted with becoming resolution. But instead of hastening to the relief of Augusta, he sought to recall Lincoln from that point by crossing into Carolina, and threatening Charleston. Driving Moultrie from his posts at Purysburg and Black-swamp, Prevost advanced rapidly into the country. His force consisted of 2400 regular troops, and 100 Indians. Moultrie determined to make a stand at Tullifiny-hill. Accordingly, he sent Colonel Laurens with a small force to bring in his rear guard from Coosawhatchie; but Laurens, whom Moultrie describes as 'a young man of great merit, and a brave soldier, but an imprudent officer, too rash and impetuous,'[1] instead of bringing off the guard, as he was directed, engaged the enemy, and was soon compelled to retreat. 'Well, Colonel, what do you think of it?' said Moultrie. 'Why, sir,' said Laurens, 'your men won't stand.' 'If that be the case I will retreat,' replied Moultrie.[2]

'I soon found myself under the necessity of retreating,' thus he wrote Lincoln the following day.[3] 'I have had good information . . . that they intend for Charleston. I must beg you would hasten to our assistance, or I fear

---

[1] Moultrie's Memôirs, vol. i., p. 404. [2] Ibid., 403.

[3] May 5th.

the town is in danger. My little army decreases. Every one running to look after his family and property. The enemy carry everything before them with fire and sword.'[1] The next day, he wrote Rutledge from Jacksonborough. 'I hope your excellency will be here; the people are very much alarmed in town. Your presence seems absolutely necessary.'[2] 'There is a strange consternation in town;' thus he wrote two days later. 'People frightened out of their wits.'[3] The panic along the line of the enemy's march was universal. The terror inspired by the savages who accompanied the royal army, seemed to paralyze the energies of the inhabitants. Many applied for British protection; and then, with parricidal aim, encouraged the conqueror to advance towards the capital. Informed of its defenceless state, and urged on by the representations of the apostate inhabitants, who joined him on his march, Prevost converted a feint into a fixed invasion, and conceived the purpose of reducing Charleston, before Lincoln could hasten to its relief.

When Moultrie commenced his retreat, he had 1200 men. When he entered Charleston, on the 9th of May, he had but 600. 'At this time,' he says, 'there never was a country in greater confusion and consternation.'[4] Lincoln, made aware of the altered purpose of the British General, was advancing rapidly to Moultrie's aid; while Rutledge, 'the father of the State,' as Lee terms him, with 600 militia, was hastening down from Orangeburgh. He arrived in Charleston on the 10th of May. He would have been shut out, as well as a detachment from Lincoln's force, of 250 continentals, had not Prevost, inexplicably and fatuitously made a halt, at Salt Ketcher bridge, of forty-eight hours. 'Forty-eight hours lost in his situation, gave

[1] Moultrie to Lincoln, May 15th, 1779. Moultrie's Memoirs, vol. i., p. 407. [2] May 6th, Ibid, p. 410. [3] Moultrie to Lincoln.

[4] Memoirs, vol. i., p. 412.

a finishing blow to his grand project. . . . Rutledge joined Moultrie; and Charleston became safe. . . . . . The time gained by the Americans had been most advantageously used. Defences on the land side had been pushed with increasing exertion, and though not complete, were formidable. Masters and servants, boys and girls, mixed in the honorable work of self-defence. The beloved Governor and heroic defender of Fort Moultrie, by their dictation and their example, re-inspired effort, even when drooping nature begged repose.'[1]

As displaying the lights and shades of character, the following anecdote will not be uninteresting to the reader. It was in one of his visits of inspection, that Rutledge 'discovered some of the militia inattentive to their duty, and to the danger of their situation. He rode up to them, and not only reproved them in a tone of irritation, but actually struck one of them with his ratan or twig whip. . . . . On the day after this occurrence, he rode back again to the same place, and addressed those who were on the station; stated, with much dignity and propriety, that in his extreme anxiety for the public welfare, he had hastily struck a citizen at that station. He did not know who, but that he had come publicly to express his regret for having done so, and to hope that nothing more might be thought of it.'[2]

In the afternoon of the 11th of May, General Prevost's army appeared before the gates of the town. An immediate attack was apprehended. The command was not well settled; but all confusion from that cause was obviated by Rutledge yielding the general direction of the militia to Moultrie. The troops stood to their arms all night. 'About three o'clock in the morning,' says Moultrie, 'it being still very dark, I heard some person

[1] Lee's Memoirs, vol. i., p. 83, 85.

[2] Johnson's Traditions of the Revolution, p. 224.

inquiring for me; I rode up, and was then told the Governor wanted to see me; upon which I rode up to him. He then took me aside, and asked me 'whether we had not best have a parley with the enemy, and whether we were able to resist their force;' and asked about our number. I assured him that they were upwards of 2200 men. He replied, 'he did not think we had more than 1800 men, and that the enemy's force, as he was informed, was 7000 or 8000 men, at least,[1] and should they force the lines, a great number of citizens would be put to death.' He represented to me the horrors of a storm; he told me that the States' Engineer (Col. Senf), had represented to him the lines to be in a very weak state. After some conversation, he proposed to me the sending out a flag, to know what terms we could obtain.'[2] Moultrie thought they could stand against the enemy, and declined sending a flag in his own name. However, at the request of the Governor and Council, he sent a message to General Prevost, desiring to know on what terms he would grant a capitulation. The reply was, that peace and protection would be granted to such of the inhabitants as chose to accept them, while all others would be received as prisoners of war, and their fate be determined by that of the other Colonies.[3]

Rutledge immediately summoned his Council. They met at his house. Moultrie, Count Pulaski, Col. Laurens, and Col. Cambray, were also present. The terms offered by the enemy, and the propriety of accepting them, were the topics of discussion. Moultrie advised against giving up the town, and insisted that they had force enough to defend it. He was supported by Pulaski and Laurens. He stated the number of the troops, as

---

[1] The American force was about 3300; the British, about 2400.

[2] Moultrie's Memoirs, vol. i., p. 427.

[3] Prevost's reply was sent in about 11 o'clock, A. M. He allowed four hours for an answer.

exhibited by the returns. They amounted to 3180, at the lowest computation. Rutledge, however, thought there must be some mistake, and that there were not more than 2500 on the lines. A gentleman who was present on this occasion, and who had reconnoitred the enemy, stated their number, according to the information he had received, to be nearly 3700, exclusive of a great many tories. However, the Governor and Council instructed Moultrie to reject Prevost's proposal; but as it was important to gain time, 'things were so contrived,' says Stedman, 'that the whole day was spent in sending and receiving messages.'[1] The correspondence closed with a message from the Governor and Council, proposing a neutrality during the war, the peace to determine whether South Carolina should belong to Great Britain, or remain one of the United States.[2]

This transaction has been the subject of severe animadversion. Professor Bowen, in his life of General Lincoln, has denounced it as little short of treason.[3] But while I do not vindicate it, neither do I admit that it deserves such severity of censure. The circumstances must be considered, and the motives that determined the decision. It must be recollected, that the enemy had thus far been successful. Georgia had submitted to the invader. The disposition of the inhabitants of South Carolina, as manifested in the country through which General Prevost had just passed, was unfavorable. Three years of peace and unprecedented prosperity seem to have relaxed their spirit. Moultrie had been deserted,

---

[1] History of the American War, vol. ii. p. 112.

[2] The Council consisted of eight members; and of these, General Gadsden, Mr. Ferguson, and Mr. John Edwards, a merchant of Charleston, were opposed to the offer of neutrality. It has been suggested, that the offer of neutrality, like the previous offers, was intended to gain time. The suggestion, however, is wholly unsupported by a tittle of evidence.

[3] Sparks' American Biography, vol. xxiii., p. 285.

instead of reinforced, and an eagerness exhibited to accept British protection. The number too, of the army before the town, was represented to be much larger than the force within it. In the character of his troops, and the quality of his arms, the enemy, beyond all doubt, was superior. Does it deserve the imputation of treason, that, with such facts confronting them, the Governor and Council, seeing in the fate of Georgia the image of their own, should make a proposal that might avert the impending blow for the present, and possibly forever?

To the offer of neutrality, General Prevost replied, that he did not come in a legislative capacity, that his business was not with the Governor, but with General Moultrie, and as the garrison were in arms, they must surrender prisoners of war. 'Upon this, the Governor and Council,' says Moultrie, 'looked very grave and steadfastly on each other and on me, not knowing what I would say. After a little pause, I said to the Governor and Council, 'Gentlemen, you see how the matter stands, the point is this, I am to deliver you up prisoners of war, or not.' Some replied 'Yes.' I then said, 'I am determined not to deliver you up prisoners of war; we will fight it out.' Upon saying this, Colonel Laurens, who was in the tent, jumped up, and said, 'Thank God! we are upon our legs again.'[1]

Negotiation being at an end, an assault was now expected; but, on the following morning, 'to the great joy of the citizens, it was cried out along the line, "the enemy is gone."'[2] An intercepted letter from Lincoln to Moultrie, saying, that he was marching to the relief of the town, was the cause of this sudden decampment.

'What train of reasoning,' says Lee, 'could have produced the rejection of the proposition to surrender the town on condition of neutrality by a General situated as

---

[1] Moultrie's Memoirs, vol. i., p. 434. [2] Ibid.

was Prevost, I confess myself incapable of discerning. The moment he found that the works could not be carried, he ought to have exerted himself to procure possession by negotiation; and certainly the condition of neutrality was in itself eligible. It disarmed South Carolina for the war, the effect of which upon her infant sister, already strangled, would have been conclusive; and Congress would have soon found that her army, unaided by South Carolina, could not be maintained in Georgia. No British force would have been retained from the field to preserve the neutral State; and the sweets of peace, with the allurements of the British commerce, would probably have woven a connexion with Great Britain, fatal in its consequences, to the independence of the Southern States.'[1]

'The only real advantage gained by this irruption into South Carolina,' says Stedman, 'was a supply of provisions for the troops, the want of which had begun to be felt in Georgia, and the establishing a post at Beaufort.'[2] The British army gained other advantages, but of a different character. In their retreat along the sea-coast, towards Savannah, they disgraced themselves, and the British name, by their rapacity, their indiscriminate plunderings, and devastations. They did not escape, however, without molestation; and in the various attempts that were made to engage and annoy them, including the attack at Stono Ferry, General Lincoln had the active aid and co-operation of Governor Rutledge.

---

[1] Lee's Memoirs, vol. i., p. 85. See also, to the same effect, Stedman's History of the American War, vol. ii., p. 112.

[2] Ibid. Eight hundred men were left at Beaufort, under Colonel Maitland. So long as the British held their posts in the lower parts of Georgia, and maintained their position at Beaufort, South Carolina was constantly exposed to incursions. So long as the British preserved their superiority at sea, Beaufort was secure from attack; and so long as they preserved Beaufort, General Lincoln was *hors de combat*.

The Legislature assembled at Charleston in July. Moultrie, and many officers of the army, were members. The reorganization of the militia, and measures for the general defence of the State, were the chief subjects of deliberation. The result was not favorable. 'I am sorry to inform you,' wrote Lincoln, at a later period, 'that little may be expected from this State, unless they rescind their late resolutions; for after solemn debate in the Assembly, it was resolved that the militia should not be drafted to fill up the Continental battalions; that the black troops recommended by Congress should not be raised;[1] and that the militia, while in the field, should not be subject to the Continental articles of war.'[2]

While the Legislature was yet in session, and early in the month of September, Count D'Estaing, who commanded the French squadron on the West India station, arrived off the American coast. He had been urged by Rutledge and Lincoln, in conjunction with M. Plombard, the French Consul at Charleston, to unite his force with that of the Americans in the South, take advantage of the weak and divided condition of General Prevost's army, and overwhelm it by a *coup-de-main*. The Count, ambitious of fame, and anxious to atone for his ineffectual efforts the previous year, promptly responded to the call thus made upon him;[3] and when precluded, by the hurricane season, from further naval operations in the West Indies, he set sail for Tybee, a small island at the mouth of Savannah river. His armament consisted of forty-one sail, mostly of the line, having on board ten regiments,

---

[1] This was a pet project of Colonel Laurens. He went to Philadelphia to urge it upon the attention of Congress. He secured the co-operation of Colonel Hamilton, who wrote a very able letter to Jay, then the President of Congress, recommending the measure of arming the blacks. See Writings of Jay.

[2] Life of Lincoln. Sparks' Am. Biog., vol. xxiii., p. 321.

[3] He had discretionary orders to co-operate with the Americans.

amounting to six thousand men. As soon as he had got through the windward passage, he dispatched two ships of the line, with three frigates, to announce his approach to the authorities at Charleston.[1]

This force arrived off the bar the 4th of September, and an officer, with a message for General Lincoln, was sent up to the city. The General was informed that Count D'Estaing was ready to assist in the reduction of Savannah, but despatch was necessary, as he could not, at that season of the year, remain long upon the American coast. This intelligence occasioned great joy in Charleston. It 'put us all in high spirits,' says Moultrie. 'The Legislature adjourned; the Governor and Council, and the military, joined heartily in expediting everything that was necessary. Boats were sent to Count D'Estaing's fleet, to assist in taking the cannon and stores on shore; every one cheerful, as if we were sure of success; and no one doubted but that we had nothing more to do than to march up to Savannah and demand a surrender. The militia were drafted, and a great number of volunteers joined readily, to be present at the surrender, and in hopes to have the pleasure of seeing the British march out, and deliver up their arms. But alas! it turned out a bloody affair; and we were repulsed from the lines with the loss of 800 or 900 men, killed and wounded.'[2]

---

[1] Stedman's American War, vol. ii., p. 122. Lee's Memoirs, vol. i., p. 99.

[2] Moultrie's Memoirs, vol. ii., p. 33. On the 16th of September the French and American forces united in front of Savannah. Count D'Estaing had already summoned the garrison to surrender. Prevost asked a truce for twenty-four hours, to enable him, as he suggested, to adjust the terms; but, in reality, to complete his unfinished works, and enable Maitland, 'always the source of comfort where danger reigned,' to join him with his force from Beaufort. 'Unfortunate respite,' exclaims Lee. Both the objects contemplated by Prevost were accomplished. His defences were hastened towards completion, and before the expiration of the truce, the accomplished Maitland entered the

The repulse of the allied forces before Savannah was the source of innumerable woes to South Carolina. Its immediate effect was to depress the spirits of her people, and nearly destroy the value of her currency. To add to the gloomy aspect of affairs, the small-pox now broke out in Charleston; a disease which the militia dreaded more than the enemy. Difficult, indeed, was the situation of the State; and yet she was only at the beginning of her troubles.

Sir Henry Clinton had conceived the design of her total subjugation; and no sooner was he informed of the departure of the French fleet from the American coast, than he prepared to execute it. The force intended for this expedition sailed from Sandy Hook on the 26th of December, 1779. Owing to adverse weather, it did not arrive at the mouth of Savannah river until the 30th of January. At this time the Legislature was sitting at Charleston; but, on receiving intelligence of the British armament, they immediately adjourned, but not without delegating, 'till ten days after their next session, to the Governor, John Rutledge, Esquire, and such of his Council as he could conveniently consult, a power to do everything necessary for the public good, except the taking away the life of a citizen without a legal trial.'

Armed with this dictatorial power, he exerted it judiciously, but with zeal. He immediately ordered a general rendezvous of the militia; but he ordered in vain. 'Not one militia-man at this place on duty,' thus wrote Moultrie to Rutledge, February 22d; and yet the enemy was advancing towards the capital. 'They are much averse to going to town; they are apprehensive of the small-pox breaking out.'[1]

town. The allied armies attempted to carry the place by assault on the 9th of October. They were repulsed, and on the 18th the siege was raised.

[1] Moultrie's Memoirs, vol. ii., p. 48. Moultrie was stationed at Bacon's Bridge, above Charleston Neck.

Rutledge now issued a proclamation, 'requiring such of the militia as were regularly drafted, and all the inhabitants and owners of property in the town, to repair to the American standard, and join the garrison immediately, under pain of confiscation.' But terror of the small-pox and the enemy was more prevalent than terror of confiscation, and few obeyed this summons to the defence of their country.

Clinton landed his troops on John's Island, the 10th of February. His force amounted to more than 5000, and he was soon joined by General Patterson, from Savannah, with 1400 more. He was now thirty miles from Charleston; and all accounts agree, that if he had not sacrificed time, to excessive caution, and had advanced, at once, to the town, he might have carried it, by a *coup-de-main.* Lacking, however, the enterprising spirit of Cornwallis, Clinton determined to take the place by a regular investiture. But so slow were all his movements, that it was not until the first of April, that he began to break ground before it.[1] It is unnecessary to recapitulate the incidents of the siege. The southern army ought never to have been enclosed in the untenable town; but the sound mind of General Lincoln was bent 'from its own resolve by the wishes of all the influential characters of the State, and by the confident expectation of adequate support.'[2] After a faithful effort to preserve Charleston against a force of at least 9000, the flower of

[1] 'It is possible,' says Lee, 'that the extraordinary delay, with which the movements of the British General were made, might have been intended with the double view of excluding the possibility of failure, and of seducing his enemy to continue in Charleston. If so, he succeeded completely in both objects.' Lee's Memoirs, vol. i., p. 117.

[2] Ibid. Lee expresses the opinion, that neither of the considerations mentioned in the text, would have influenced Lincoln, but for the long time that intervened between the disembarkation of the British troops and their investment of the town. If so, it was fortunate for Clinton that he moved so slowly.

the British army, and with a garrison but little exceeding 2500 men, Lincoln at length, on the 10th of May, capitulated.[1]

Early in the siege, he urged upon Rutledge and his Council, the necessity of their leaving the town. He represented, 'that their being in the country would keep up the civil authority, and be more useful than they could possibly be by staying in town. The Governor made many objections, and said the citizens would say he left them in a time of danger. At last, they fell upon an expedient, that satisfied all parties, which was, that the Governor, and three of his Council, should leave the town; and that Lieutenant-Governor Gadsden, and the five others of the Council, should remain within the lines. This being agreed to, on the 12th day of April, Governor Rutledge, the Honorable Charles Pinckney, John Lewis Gervais, and Daniel Huger, left the town, and went into the north part of the country.' 'It was very fortunate for the Province,' we are quoting from Moultrie, 'that the Governor was not made a prisoner in town. His presence in the country kept everything alive; and gave great spirits to the people, to have a man of such great abilities, firmness, and decision amongst them. He gave commissions; raised new corps; embodied the militia, and went to Philadelphia to solicit reinforcements. He returned, and joined the army. He stayed by them, enforced the laws of the Province, called the Legislature; in short, he did everything that could be done for the good of the country.'[2]

To this general summary of Rutledge's services, after he left Charleston, we must now add such details as we have been able to collect. With all his exertions, he was neither able to reinforce Lincoln, nor embody but a trifling number of the militia in the country. The fall of

---

[1] Clinton had been reinforced by Cornwallis, during the progress of the siege.

[2] Moultrie's Memoirs, vol. ii., p. 105.

Charleston, that 'sad deranging blow to the South,' and the defeat of Colonel Buford, with his 300 Virginia continentals, at Wax-haws, on the 29th of May, suspended for several weeks, all military opposition to the invader. The inhabitants, for the most part, submitted as British subjects, or remained at their homes on parole.[1] Rutledge retired into North Carolina, and thence proceeded to Richmond and Philadelphia. He urged upon the authorities of North Carolina and Virginia, as well as upon Congress, the necessity and importance of vigorous exertions, to recover South Carolina and Georgia from the hands of the invader. While thus employed, the ill-timed policy of the British commander was destroying the fruits of his conquest.

The inhabitants of South Carolina had accepted their paroles, in order to escape the calamities of war, and to pursue, unmolested, their usual employments. Great, therefore, was their astonishment and indignation, to see a proclamation from Sir Henry Clinton, issued a little more than twenty days after the capitulation of Charleston, setting aside all paroles, after the 20th of June, and calling upon the holders of them to resume the character of British subjects, and take an active part in

[1] Two hundred and ten of the principal inhabitants of Charleston, congratulated Clinton on the success of his arms, and expressed their ardent wishes, 'speedily to be re-admittted to the character and condition of British subjects.' Perhaps to ingratiate themselves with the conqueror, they denounced the government of South Carolina, as a 'rank democracy,' which had 'exhibited a system of tyrannic domination, only to be found among the uncivilized part of mankind, or in the history of the dark and barbarous ages of antiquity.' Most of those who signed this address, did so against their wishes, and under the influence of either persuasion or fear. The greater part of them had but recently borne arms against the British, and several had been leaders in the popular government. But having thus solemnly committed themselves, like all apostates, they became the instigators of every severity against their late friends. Ramsay's Revolution of S. C., vol. ii. p. 118. This conduct of his countrymen, excited Rutledge's deepest resentment, and called forth his severest denunciation.

forwarding military operations, or be considered as rebels against his Majesty's Government.[1] It was not long before a counter-revolution was produced in the minds and inclinations of the people, as complete and universal, as that which succeeded the fall of Charleston.[2] While this process of change and reaction was going on, Colonel Sumpter, at the head of a small force, composed of exiles, like himself, from South Carolina, and a number of North Carolinians, made an irruption into his native Province, and on the 12th of July, defeated a detachment of British troops and tories, assembled at a place called Williams' Plantation.[3] He was soon reinforced, and especially by a battalion of militia, under Colonel Lisle, who, having taken the oath of allegiance, obtained military rank as a King's officer. He served in that capacity just long enough to supply his men with clothes, arms and ammunition, and then led them off to Sumpter.[4]

With a force, now increased to 900 men, Sumpter, on the 30th of July, made a gallant, but unsuccessful attack on the British post at Rocky-Mount. But not at all discouraged, he recruited his corps, and on the 6th of August, led them against the post at Hanging-Rock. The enemy suffered severely, but the post remained in

[1] Stedman, who was an officer in the British army, and acted as commissary to Lord Cornwallis, condemns the course pursued by Sir Henry Clinton. 'The revolutionists complained,' he says, 'that their condition was altered without their concurrence; and the loyalists murmured because notorious rebels, by taking the oath of allegiance, and putting on a show of attachment, became entitled to the same privileges with themselves.' History of the American War, vol. ii., p. 149. [2] Ibid.

[3] Sumpter's force was but 133. The tories were commanded by an infamous, brutal wretch, by the name of Huck, who, fortunately for humanity, was killed.

[4] This conduct of Lisle's exasperated the British officers, and, in consequence, rendered the situation of the inhabitants still more uncomfortable.

their possession. The services of Sumpter, in thus recommencing hostilities, were important, and deserved grateful recognition. After Rutledge's return from Philadelphia, he promoted him to the rank of Brigadier-General in the State militia. Subsequently, he promoted Marion and Pickens to the same rank.[1]

---

[1] The distinguished part enacted by these celebrated partizan officers, constitutes a marked feature in the history of Rutledge's administration, and will justify a brief sketch of their persons and character: —

'Marion,' thus is he described by a brother soldier, 'was about forty-eight years of age, small in stature, hard in visage, healthy, abstemious and taciturn. Enthusiastically wedded to the cause of liberty, he deeply deplored the doleful condition of his beloved country. The common weal was his sole object; nothing selfish, nothing mercenary, soiled his ermine character. Fertile in stratagem, he struck unperceived; and retiring to those hidden retreats, selected by himself, in the morasses of Pedee and Black River, he placed his corps not only out of the reach of his foe, but often out of the discovery of his friends. A rigid disciplinarian, he reduced to practice the justice of his heart; and during the difficult course of warfare, through which he passed, calumny itself never charged him with violating the rights of person, property, or of humanity. Never avoiding danger, he never rashly sought it; and acting for all around him as he did for himself, he risked the lives of his troops only when it was necessary. Never elated with prosperity, nor depressed by adversity, he preserved an equanimity which won the admiration of his friends, and exacted the respect of his enemies.

'Sumpter was younger than Marion, larger in frame, better fitted in strength of body to the toils of war, and, like his compeer, devoted to the freedom of his country. His aspect was manly and stern, denoting insuperable firmness and lofty courage. He was not over scrupulous as a soldier in his use of means, and apt to make considerable allowances for a state of war. Believing it warranted by the necessity of the case, he did not occupy his mind with critical examinations of the equity of his measures, or of their bearings on individuals; but indiscriminately pressed forward to his end—the destruction of his enemy and liberation of his country. In his military character he resembled Ajax; relying more upon the fierceness of his courage than upon the results of unrelaxing vigilance and nicely adjusted combination. Determined to deserve success, he risked his own life and the lives of his associates without reserve. Enchanted with the splendour of victory, he would wade in torrents of blood to attain it. . . . . .

The renewal of hostilities by Sumpter, and the approach of a Continental army, cherished the spirit of resistance among the inhabitants of South Carolina, and inspired them with hope. 'They began to rear their heads and look forward to a recovery of their country.'[1]

On the 27th of July General Gates overtook De Kalb with the Continental force, at Deep River, and was 'hailed to the command of the army with universal gratulations.'[2] The confident expectations of victory that were entertained from Gates' great reputation, were all sadly disappointed by his total rout at Camden, on the 16th of August. That disastrous defeat sunk still lower the fortunes of South Carolina. The conqueror seemed determined to crush the spirit and ensure the submission of her people, by a system of severity as unrelenting as it proved impolitic.

Rutledge, at this season of gloom and suffering, was at Philadelphia, invoking Congress, and the Commander-in-Chief, to make a great effort, and restore South Carolina and Georgia to the Confederacy. 'I fully intended,' thus he wrote Washington from that city, on the 27th of August, 'for several weeks past, to pay my respects in person to your Excellency, but am obliged to deny myself that pleasure, having been detained here

'Andrew Pickens, younger than either of them, inexperienced in war, with a sound head, a virtuous heart, and a daring spirit, joined in the noble resolve to burst the chains of bondage rivetted upon the two southern States, and soon proved himself worthy of being ranked with his illustrious precursors. This gentleman was also promoted by the Governor to the station of Brigadier-General; and having assembled his associates, of the same bold and hardy cast, distinguished himself and corps in the progress of the war, by the patience and cheerfulness with which every privation was borne, and the gallantry with which every danger was confronted.' Lee's Memoirs, vol. i., pp. 164–166.

[1] Moultrie's Memoirs, vol. ii., p. 220.

[2] Lee's Memoirs, vol. i., p. 160.

much longer than I expected, and being anxious to return to Carolina. . . . I cannot forbear representing that the state of South Carolina and Georgia is such as demonstrates the absolute necessity of expelling the enemy from those countries as speedily as possible, and that this cannot be done without a considerable naval force, and a large number of regular troops.'[1]

On his return to the South, he appears to have remained, for the most part, and, until the resumption of hostilities, at Hillsborough, in North Carolina.[2] Here Gates retired, after his defeat, to collect his scattered forces, and gather reinforcements. He acted, throughout this disagreeable period, with intelligence, assiduity, and zeal.[3] But Congress having directed that a court of inquiry should examine into his conduct, and that Washington should, in the interim, appoint a successor, he was soon superseded.

General Greene, whom Washington nominated to the command of the Southern army, arrived at Charlotte, to which place General Gates had advanced, on the 2d of December. 'The appearance of the troops,' he says, 'was wretched beyond description; and their distress, on account of provisions, was little less than their sufferings for want of clothing and other necessaries. General Gates had lost the confidence of the officers, and the troops all their discipline, and so addicted to plundering, that they were a terror to the inhabitants.'[4]

---

[1] Correspondence of the Revolution, vol. iii., p. 64.

[2] He writes to Horry from this place, Oct. 3, 1780. 'Am very sorry,' he says, 'to hear of your indisposition; I hope, however, you will soon be able to join Colonel Marion, and continue your services to our country.' Documentary History of South Carolina, p. 12.

[3] Lee's Memoirs, *supra*, p. 226. He seems, however, to have wanted sufficient firmness to inspire respect and enforce discipline.

[4] Greene to Joseph Reed, Jan. 9th, 1781. Life of Reed, vol. ii., p. 344. Greene was not among the censurers of Gates. 'From all I can learn,' thus he wrote in the letter above quoted, 'if General Gates had

A few days after Greene's arrival, Rutledge thus wrote to the delegates in Congress from South Carolina: 'I was shocked,' he says, 'to see the ragged, shabby condition of our brave and virtuous men, who would not remain in the power of the enemy, but have taken to arms. This, however, is but a faint description of the sufferings of our country; for it is beyond a doubt the enemy have hanged many of our people, who, from fear, and the impracticability of removing, had given paroles, and from attachment to our side, joined it. Nay, Tarleton has, since the action at Black-stocks,[1] hung one Johnson, a magistrate of respectable character. They have also burnt a prodigious number of houses, and turned a vast many women, formerly of affluent and easy fortunes, with their children, almost naked into the woods. . . . In short, the enemy seem determined, if they can, to break every man's spirit, if they cannot ruin him; engagements of capitulations and proclamations are no security against their oppressions and cruelties.'[2]

Such were the sufferings of the people, and such the condition of the army, when Greene appeared on the scene of action. 'Capable of doing much with little, he was not discouraged by this unfavorable prospect. His vivid plastic genius soon operated on the latent elements of martial capacity in his army, invigorated its weak-

---

stopped at Charlotte, little more disgrace would have fallen to his share than is common to the unfortunate.' His not stopping at Charlotte, but pushing on to Hillsborough, is applauded by Lee, as doing him honor. Lee's Memoirs, vol. i., p. 192.

[1] In this action Sumpter was victorious, though Tarleton, upon very insufficient grounds, asserted the contrary.

[2] Dec. 8th, 1780. Moultrie's Memoirs, vol. ii., p. 239. It must be confessed that there was a great deal of cruelty on both sides. 'The whigs and tories,' wrote Greene, 'pursue each other with little less than savage fury.' Greene to Reed, Jan. 9th, 1781. Life of Reed, vol. ii., p. 345. 'The whigs and tories,' he again wrote to the same correspondent, May 4th, 'are butchering one another hourly.' Ibid., p. 351.

ness, turned its confusion into order, and its despondency into ardor. A wide sphere of intellectual resource enabled him to inspire confidence, to rekindle courage, to decide hesitation, and infuse a spirit of exalted patriotism in the citizens of the State. By his own example he showed the incalculable value of obedience, of patience, of vigilance and temperance. Dispensing justice, with an even hand, to the citizen and soldier; benign in heart, and happy in manners; he acquired the durable attachment and esteem of all.' [1]

Advancing towards South Carolina, he took post on the Pedee. 'This camp,' thus he wrote on the 9th of January, 'I mean as a camp of repose, for the purpose of repairing our wagons, recruiting our horses, and disciplining our troops.' [2] Rutledge appears to have accompanied the army; and we have the testimony of Greene to the value of his services.[3] 'The situation of these States is wretched,' he writes, just after the defeat of the enemy at the Cowpens, on the 17th of January, 1781, 'and the distress of the inhabitants beyond all description. . . . . We are obliged to subsist ourselves by our own industry, aided by the influence of Governor Rutledge, who is one of the first characters I ever met with.' [4]

The entire rout of Tarleton at the Cowpens raised the spirits and inspired the hopes of the people. That his captive friends in Charleston might share the general joy, Rutledge sent in a person on some pretence with a flag; but the object was to inform the American prisoners of the success of their countrymen. 'The person,' says Moultrie, 'informed me of the whole affair, which I communicated to the officers at Haddrell's-point, on my return in the evening. The news gave great joy, and

[1] Lee's Memoirs, vol. i., p. 244. [2] Life of Reed, vol. ii., p. 346.

[3] See a letter from Rutledge to Washington, of Dec. 28th, written from Cheraw. Correspondence of the Revolution, vol. iii., p. 64.

[4] American Review, vol. vi., p. 278. Simms' Life of Rutledge.

put us all in high spirits.'[1] The immediate value of that victory, however, was much overrated. 'Our force was so small,' says Greene, 'and Lord Cornwallis's movements were so rapid, that we got no reinforcements of militia, and therefore were obliged to retire out of the State, upon which the spirits of the people sunk, and almost all classes of the inhabitants gave themselves up for lost.'[2]

It is uncertain whether Rutledge followed the army in the masterly retreat through North Carolina; but he writes to Marion, from the camp at Haw River, on the 8th of March. 'The present situation of affairs,' he says, 'rendering it impracticable for me to return into South Carolina, not seeing any prospect of being able to go thither very soon, and it being impossible, if we could penetrate that country, to re-establish the civil government for some time, and my remaining here being of no service to the State, I have determined to set off in a few days for Philadelphia, with a view of procuring, if possible, some supplies of clothing for our militia, (whose distress for want of it gives me great concern,) and of obtaining such effectual aid as may soon restore both the town and country to our possession. My utmost endeavors for these purposes shall be executed, and I flatter myself that I may succeed by personal applications.'[3]

Rutledge repaired to Philadelphia, obtained a large supply of clothing, and returned to South Carolina about the first of August.[4] Meanwhile, the condition of affairs had totally changed; the British were dispossessed of all their posts in the upper country, and their interest was fast declining. The tories now began to suffer from the

[1] Moultrie's Memoirs, vol. ii., p. 257.

[2] Greene to Reed, March 18th, 1781. Life of Reed, *supra*, p. 348.

[3] Rutledge to Marion. Documentary History of South Carolina, p. 32.

[4] It was unfortunately captured by the enemy while on its progress to the army.

unsparing vengeance of their exasperated countrymen. They had plundered and murdered while the Royal cause was in the ascendant, and now, the whigs, to reimburse their losses and gratify revenge, began to plunder and murder in turn.[1] To put a stop to this barbarous state of things, Rutledge issued his proclamation on the 5th of August, denouncing speedy and effectual punishment against all persons guilty of violence and rapine. He appointed magistrates, and wherever it was practicable, re-established civil government.[2]

'I think of appointing immediately,' thus he wrote Marion, the 13th of August, 'an ordinary in each district, by whom wills may be proved, and letters testamentary and administration granted, and other business within the ordinary jurisdiction transacted. The Con-

[1] Ramsay's Revolution of South Carolina, vol. ii., p. 271. Another species of depredation, to which both whigs and tories were subjected, is thus denounced in a letter from Rutledge to Marion: 'The Captains of several vessels, with Commissions or Letters of Marque from Congress, having some time ago made a practice of landing on our islands and sea-coast, and others of coming up the rivers and taking away from plantations negroes and other property, under pretence of their owners being tories, though several persons whose property has been so taken are well known to be friends of the United States; and this practice being highly illegal and unwarrantable, even as to tories, whose property (if they have been guilty of a capital offence) is forfeited to the State, and not plunder to any freebooter who can lay hold on it, I desire that you will be pleased to give the necessary orders, and have the most effectual means taken (within the district of your brigade) for having all masters of vessels, and their crews, who shall commit, or attempt to commit the offence above described, apprehended and sent under a sufficient guard to me, with the witnesses to prove the fact, that they may be properly tried for it.' Documentary History of South Carolina, Oct. 12th, p. 188.

[2] Two days after issuing his proclamation, viz., August 7th, 1781, Rutledge writes to Marion, 'that if a little hard money, thirty or thirty-five guineas, would be useful for getting intelligence or other services,' he has that sum ready for him. This shows the slender means with which operations were carried on in the Southern department.

stitution directs that this shall be done, and I think it a measure absolutely necessary for a number of reasons.'[1] In a subsequent letter, he directs Marion to appoint justices of the peace, immediately, in every district.[2]

Rutledge, as Commander-in-Chief, claimed and exercised the general direction of the militia of the State. 'You will put your men in two divisions,' he writes Marion, a few days before the battle of Eutaw, 'the first to serve one month, and be relieved by the second. . . . You will punish any man who shall take, destroy, or waste any provisions; and such men who may be found spoiling the property of any persons must be taken up and prosecuted as felons. Every man who refuses serving when called upon must be deemed an enemy, and taken prisoner and sent to the British . . . and must not be permitted to return. All their property must be taken care of for the use of the State, and no part suffered to be conveyed away on any pretence whatever. Any persons who go to town or the enemy without a permit from you or an officer, must be treated as carrying intelligence to the enemy, and suffer accordingly. Any woman who will go to town, or in the enemy's post without leave, must not be permitted to return. . . . Whenever the enemy march in your district in force, you will call out the whole of your militia to oppose them; and if too weak you will let me know, and I will march to your assistance.'[3]

Of those who signed the address to Clinton on the fall of Charleston, several now ventured out among their countrymen. Hearing that one of this class was at Georgetown, Rutledge thus wrote to Marion. 'I really am amazed at the impudence of these people, to dare, after such an atrocious act, to come out and reside

---

[1] Documentary History of South Carolina, p. 126.

[2] Ibid., p. 131. Sept. 2d, 1781.

[3] Ibid.

amongst us, without making their application to proper authority, and knowing whether they would be received or not, as if they had really been guilty of no offence whatever; though, in my opinion, they have acted in the most criminal manner. For my part, I don't desire to have any of them with us, and will not receive any of them; for I should not believe them to be sincere, even if they pretended to conversion. They only came out to serve their own or the enemy's purpose; and even if they be sincere, I would not have them, for we can do very well without them. Every one of us should lose all his property for such infamous conduct. I therefore desire that you will immediately have this Mr. W. taken and sent up to me under an appropriate guard, and that you will make the necessary enquiries, and having discovered what property he has with him, or which may be come at, take the whole of it, let it consist of what it may,—money, goods, negroes, boats, or any other article whatever, and send to me all such as may be recovered hither, and dispose of all the rest for public account.'[1] This, it must be admitted, was rather a summary mode of dealing with an offender.

In May a general exchange of prisoners was effected; and a large number of South Carolinians, who had been languishing in confinement, were delivered at the American posts, in Virginia, and Pennsylvania. But this happy event was clouded by the distress it brought upon their families. For on the 25th of June, the military commandant of Charleston issued an order, directing that the wives and families of the exchanged prisoners should quit the town and province before the first day of the ensuing August. More than 1000 persons were thus exiled from their homes, and thrown on the charity

---

[1] Sept. 2d, 1781. Documentary History of South Carolina, p. 132.

of strangers for their support.[1] Rutledge resolved on retaliation, and accordingly directed, that the wives and families of such men as were then with, and adhered to the enemy, should, without delay or exception, be sent into Charleston. 'I lament the distress,' he wrote Marion, 'which many innocent women and children may probably suffer by this measure, but they must follow the fate of their husbands and parents, and blame can only be imputed to them and to the British commanders, whose conduct, on the principles of retaliation, justifies this step, which, all circumstances considered, is an indispensable one.'[2]

The action at Eutaw Springs, which Lord Mahon characterizes as the last, and one of the sharpest in this American war, was fought on the 8th of September.[3] Though Greene's success was chiefly owing to the vigorous use of the bayonet, by the continental troops of Virginia and Maryland,[4] yet on no field, perhaps, did the militia ever show greater steadiness and courage. Rutledge, who was anxiously attending the event of this battle, a few miles in the rear, wrote to the South Carolina delegates, that the militia fired seventeen rounds before they retired.[5] The result of this action was fatal to British ascendency in South Carolina. Gradually falling back, before the close of the year, the enemy had no foothold in the State, except Charleston, and the adjacent country.

The generous foe heightens the hour of triumph, by

---

[1] Ramsay's Revolution of S. C., vol. ii., p. 300. The wives and families of such persons as had long chosen to reside in the Colonies, 'now in rebellion,' were included in this order.

[2] Documentary History of S. C., p. 134. Sept. 3.

[3] History of England, vol. vii., p. 110.

[4] Greene's Official Letter to the President of Congress. Documentary History of S. C., p. 141.

[5] From the account of the battle, furnished by Col. Otho Williams. Ibid. p. 141–148.

forbearance and mercy. But in indulging the feelings of his heart, he does not forget the paramount claims of his country. 'I think, after the glorious victory at Eutaw,' wrote Rutledge to Marion, 'it would be expedient to issue a proclamation, offering to all who have joined and are now with the enemy, excepting such as signed the congratulatory addresses to Clinton and Cornwallis, or have held, or hold commissions under the British government, a free pardon, and permission for their wives and families to return and re-occupy their possessions, on condition that such men, appearing at our head-quarters, or before a Brigade or the Colonel of any regiment, and there subscribing an engagement to serve the State faithfully, as militia men, for six months, and declaring, in case of their deserting in that time, their wives and families shall be sent into Charleston or the enemy's lines. I apprehend such a measure would be well-timed at this juncture, and might induce some, perhaps many, to return to their allegiance and behave well; which would not only deprive the British of their services, but turn those services to our account.'[1]

Accordingly, on the 27th of September, he issued his proclamation, offering pardon to the tories, upon certain conditions. There were several classes of persons, however, whom he excepted from the proffered pardon. Among others, 'all those,' such is the language of the proclamation, 'whose conduct has been so infamous, as that they cannot (consistently with justice or policy), be admitted to partake of the privileges of America; notwithstanding which last mentioned exception, such persons, if they be deemed by me, or the Governor and

[1] Sept. 15, 1781. Ibid, p. 162. Rutledge did not determine to offer pardon to the tories without a good deal of reflection. 'I have been very much puzzled,' he again wrote Marion, 'about a proclamation to offer pardon to the tories. I have, however, determined, upon the whole, to issue one with certain exceptions.' Ibid, p. 175.

Commander-in-chief (for the time being), inadmissible to the rights and privileges of subjects, will not be detained as prisoners, but shall have full and free liberty, and a pass or permit to return.'

In the endeavor to re-establish order and promote the public good, Rutledge exercised his dictatorial authority judiciously, but at the same time efficiently. He suspended the acts of the Legislature, which made Continental and State money a legal tender, until ten days after their next meeting; and made all fines payable in specie.[1] He ordered impressments of indigo, specie, and horses, in cases where the owners would not part with them on the public security.[2] He empowered Horry to impress horses for his corps; but complaints being made that this authority was abused, he took effectual steps to remedy the evil.[3] 'I think Colonel Horry's conduct very extraordinary,' thus he wrote Marion. . . . 'He is not yet a Continental officer, and his regiment is not yet on Continental establishment; but if he was, I know of no authority that any Continental officer, or any other person (whomsoever he may be) has, to impress in this State without a power from me.'[4]

---

[1] See this Proclamation in Documentary History of South Carolina, p. 165. It was dated Sept. 13th, 1781. The great depreciation of paper rendered this step a very necessary one.

[2] See letter to Marion of Sept. 1st, 1781. Ibid., p. 130. Captain Richardson's letter to Marion of Sept. 12th. Ibid., p. 158. And Rutledge to Horry, Sept. 25th. Ibid., p. 173.

[3] 'I assure you,' thus he wrote Horry, 'that if I ever hear another complaint of the abuse of the press-warrant, which, confiding in your discreet exercise of it, I gave you, I will instantly revoke it, and never let you have another.' Oct. 27th, 1781. Ibid., p. 198.

Horry replied on the 30th instant,—'Reprimands,' said he, 'I am not accustomed to, and such your Excellency's letter appears to me to be; and so severe a one, that in the course of near seven years' service, I never received from any of my superior officers; and it hurts me much to receive this unmerited one from your Excellency.' Ibid., p. 201.

[4] Ibid., p 186.

Hearing that several persons liable to do militia duty found substitutes, he issued an order against it. 'It is illegal and unwarrantable,' he said; 'such conduct never did, nor will receive my sanction or approbation.'[1] He insisted on every man's full performance of the duty which the law required of him; and was prompt in forbidding all practices inconsistent with judicious police regulations.

His letters during this period, though written amid the hurry of business, all indicate sagacity, foresight, and knowledge of mankind. He writes Marion, that it is an old trick of men coming to camp, to pretend that they have no arms, and cautions him to be on his guard against deception. He tells him too, that in impressing horses, he must select such as are fit for dragoon service. 'I am afraid,' he adds, 'if all plough-horses were exempted, an exclusion would prevent our getting any horses at all; for all may be brought under the description.'[2] Nevertheless, he said it would be very oppressive to take such horses, and a thing that ought not to be suffered.

His superintending care extended to matters of small as well as grave importance; and, while promoting the public service, he guarded the rights of the people. 'It would give me pleasure,' he said, 'to restore every encroachment on the liberties of the people, and shall certainly do so as far as my power extends,' &c.[3]

It was while thus actively employed, that Rutledge was prostrated, for a time, by a severe attack of fever. He was not long confined; but the effects of the illness were afterwards visible.[4]

As the greater portion of the State was now recovered,

---

[1] Rutledge to Marion, Sept. 26th, 1781. Ibid., p. 173.

[2] Oct. 10th, 1781. Ibid., p. 185. [3] Ibid., p. 187.

[4] See letters to Marion and Horry, of Oct. 2d and 27th. Ibid., pp. 178–194. 'This illness,' writes a valued correspondent, 'was the fatal fever of the swamps, taken during great exposure, at an unhealthy season.'

Rutledge issued writs of election for members of the Legislature. The time fixed for the meeting of that body was the 8th of January, 1782. Many of the citizens, who had been exchanged, and sent to Philadelphia and Virginia, had returned to South Carolina. Among them were most of the civil officers of the State, as well as members of the former Legislature. All those who had taken British protection, or having taken it, had not rejoined their countrymen on or before the 27th of September, 1781, were excluded from voting or being elected.

As it would be difficult, in the present exhausted state of the country, to obtain a supply of provisions for a body of 200 or 300 men from the resources of a small inland town like Jacksonborough, Rutledge, on the 15th of December, thus wrote to Marion: 'I wish to procure twelve barrels of rice for the use of the Assembly, at their intended meeting on the 8th of next month. Be pleased to have that quantity procured as high up Santee as it can be got, and let me know as soon as possible where it is, that I may order wagons down to fetch it from thence to Camden in time.'[1]

The Legislature assembled at Jacksonborough, but not in sufficient numbers to form a quorum, until the 18th of January. On that day the Governor delivered his message: — 'Since the last meeting of a General Assembly,' he said, 'the good people of this State have not only felt the common calamities of war, but, from the wanton and savage manner in which it has been prosecuted, they have experienced such severities as are un-

[1] Documentary History of South Carolina, p. 223. Notwithstanding the success of the American arms, there was a great deal of distress in the country from want of provisions and clothes. Greene wrote to Horry on the 14th of December, that near one-half of his soldiers had not a shoe to their feet, and not a blanket to ten men through the line, and that they had not received a shilling of pay since they came to the State. Ibid., p. 222.

precedented, and will scarcely be credited by civilized nations. The enemy, unable to make any impression on the Northern States, the number of whose inhabitants and the strength of whose country had baffled their repeated efforts, turned their views towards the Southern, which a difference of circumstances afforded some expectation of conquering, or at least of greatly distressing. . . . . Regardless, therefore, of the sacred ties of honor, destitute of the feelings of humanity, and determined to extinguish, if possible, every spark of freedom in this country, they, with the insolent pride of conquerors, gave unbounded scope to the excess of their tyrannical dispositions, infringed their public engagements, and violated the most solemn capitulations. Many of our worthiest citizens were without cause long and closely confined; some on board of prison-ships, and others in the town and castle of St. Augustine; their properties disposed of at the will and caprice of the enemy, and their families sent to a different and distant part of the continent, without the means of support; many who had surrendered as prisoners of war were killed in cold blood; several suffered death in the most ignominious manner, and others were delivered up to savages and put to tortures, under which they expired. Thus the lives, liberties, and properties of the people were dependent solely on the pleasure of British officers, who deprived them of either or all on the most frivolous pretences. Indians, slaves, and a desperate banditti of the most profligate characters, were caressed and employed by the enemy to execute their infamous purposes. Devastation and ruin marked their progress and that of their adherents; nor were their violences restrained by the charms or influence of beauty and innocence; even the fair sex, whom it is the duty of all, and the pleasure and pride of the brave, to protect, they and their tender offspring were victims to the inveterate malice of an unrelenting foe; neither the tears of mothers nor the cries of infants could excite in their breasts pity or compassion. Not only the peaceful habitations of the widow, the aged, and the infirm, but the holy temples of the Most High were consumed in flames, kindled by their sacrilegious hands. They tarnished the glory of the British army, disgraced the profession of a British soldier, and fixed indelible stigmas of rapine, cruelty, perfidy, and profaneness on the British name. But I can now congratulate you, and do so most cordially, on the pleasing change of affairs, which, under the blessing of God, the wisdom, prudence, address, and bravery, of the great and gallant General Greene, and the intrepidity of the officers and men under his command, have happily effected — a General who is justly entitled, from his many special services, to honorable and singular marks of your approbation and gratitude. His successes have been more rapid and complete than the most sanguine could have expected. The enemy, compelled to surrender or evacuate every post which they held in this country, frequently defeated and driven from place to place, are obliged to seek refuge under the walls of Charleston and on islands in its vicinity. We have now the full and absolute possession of every other part of the State; and the legislative, executive, and judicial powers are in the free exercise of their respective authorities.'

This address, the perusal of which even at the present day will gratify and reward the reader, is perhaps the most favorable specimen extant of Rutledge's eloquence. His earnestness, sincerity, and warm feelings are manifest in every line of it. That the men to whom it was addressed, all of them sufferers from the excesses so vividly portrayed, should have felt indignation against such of their countrymen as had joined the enemy, and assisted in perpetrating them, is not surprising. Nor is it surprising that they should have passed the confiscation, banishment, and amercement laws, afterwards so severely censured as unjust and cruel. Those upon whom these laws operated, had taken protection, then arms, and then treated their countrymen worse and with more rigor than enemies themselves.[1] Rutledge both approved and counselled the measures adopted for their punishment.[2]

In answer to the Governor's address, both the Senate and House of Representatives testified, in warm, heartfelt language, the grateful sense they entertained of his unwearied zeal and attention to the interests and welfare of the State. The auspicious change in the condition of its affairs they attributed in a great degree to his prudence, firmness, and good conduct. 'If any thing,' said the House of Representatives, 'can add to the sublime and refined enjoyment which must arise from your Excellency's own reflections on your persevering, unabated, and successful exertions towards rescuing your country from the iron hand of oppression, be pleased, sir, to accept the most sincere and unfeigned thanks of your grateful fellow-citizens.'

The period for which Rutledge was elected had now expired; and by the rotation established, it became necessary to choose a new Governor. On the 29th of January, John Matthews was elected his successor, and he descended from his high position blest with the wishes and crowned with the grateful homage of his countrymen. Though clothed with dictatorial authority, and in times requiring the utmost exertion of it, 'the justice

---

[1] Moultrie, who considered the taking protection and remaining quiet as no great offence, says the conduct described in the text was unpardonable. Memoirs, vol. ii., p. 235, 236.

[2] It is well known, that after the peace, and, under a different condition of affairs, past offences, if not forgotten, were forgiven. In the course of a few years, most of those whose names were on the confiscation, banishment, and amercement lists, were received as fellow-citizens, and their property was restored to them.

and equitable current of his administration never engendered the slightest murmur, nor gave birth to a single complaint. So mild, indeed, and conciliating were all his actions, that obedience went hand in hand with command, and the ardor of zeal seemed rather to solicit service than seek the means of avoiding it.'[1]

[1] Garden's Anecdotes.

CHAPTER XII.

SERVICES IN CONGRESS.

1782—1783.

DEPRIVED of his services as Governor, the Legislature now returned Rutledge to the scene of his earlier labors. On the 31st of January, 1782, he was elected a delegate to Congress. He took his seat in that body May 2d. Nearly seven years had elapsed since he retired from the councils of the Confederacy. Then, the Congress was animated by high resolves, and supported by the ardent exertions of the people. Now, the resources of the States were well-nigh exhausted, and their energies relaxed. The surrender of Cornwallis at Yorktown,[1] and the resolution of the House of Commons against any further attempts to reduce the insurgent colonies,[2] had induced the opinion that the war was virtually concluded. The absence of vigor and exertion on the part of the States left Congress unsupplied with money, and the army without pay, provisions, or clothing.[3] Apprehensions begun to be entertained that the enemy, seeing the unprepared state of the country, might renew hostilities.

In order to explain the condition of public affairs to the States, and to urge the necessity of complying with the requisitions of Congress, that body determined to depute two members to visit the Eastern States, and two

[1] Oct. 19, 1781.

[2] Feb. 27, 1782.

[3] Letter of Baron Steuben, May 25. See Gordon's History, vol. iv., p. 292.

the Southern.[1] Rutledge and Clymer were selected for the latter mission, and in a few days set off. On the 14th of June they were permitted to make a personal address to the Virginia Assembly. 'In the execution of this duty,' says Ramsay, who at this time was one of his colleagues in Congress, 'John Rutledge drew such a picture of the United States, and of the danger to which they were exposed by the backwardness of the particular States to comply with the requisitions of Congress, as produced a very happy effect. The addresser acquitted himself with so much ability that the Virginians, who, not without reason, are proud of their statesmen and orators, began to doubt whether their Patrick Henry or the Carolina Rutledge was the most accomplished public speaker.'[2]

But a higher tribute to the abilities of Rutledge, as a public speaker, than any general expression of praise, was the effect produced in Congress by his speech respecting the exchange of Lord Cornwallis. The impolitic severities of that commander in South Carolina had greatly exasperated the people against him. Their delegates in Congress shared the general feeling; and Arthur Middleton made a formal motion that Charles Earl Cornwallis ought not to be exchanged, not from any apprehension of his influence or superior abilities, but because he was looked upon, not in the light of a British general, but as a barbarian. This motion was very properly rejected.[3] Subsequently, Mr. Laurens was enlarged and discharged from all engagements without any condition whatever. He then declared of his own accord, that he considered Lord Cornwallis as freed from his parole.

---

[1] May 22, 1782. Congress had made a requisition for eight millions of dollars, but as yet had not received a penny of it.

[2] Ramsay's South Carolina, vol. ii., p. 517. He returned and resumed his seat in Congress the 27th of June.

[3] This motion was made Feb. 23.

This information was communicated to Washington by Sir Guy Carleton, and by him transmitted to Congress. Lee, Witherspoon, and Rutledge, were appointed a committee to consider and report upon it. They proposed and reported that the General should be directed to empower his commissioners (for negotiating a cartel) to release Earl Cornwallis from his parole, in return for the indulgence granted to Mr. Laurens; but Mr. Rutledge, one of the committee, inveighed against this with so much warmth and indignation, that it was rejected with a loud and general *No!* from all parts of the House.'[1]

The effect of oratory is the test of the orator's powers. In this instance, the eloquence of Rutledge, arousing and exciting the feelings of his auditors, communicating to their breasts the emotion that swelled his, produced a decision which, in a calmer hour, they must have condemned. For, as Washington justly demanded, 'is it reasonable that Mr. Laurens should be at full liberty, and acting as a commissioner in Europe, while Lord Cornwallis, for whose liberation he pledged his own honor, and consequently, as a public man, that of the States, is held bound by his parole? Either disavow the propriety of Mr. Laurens' conduct, and let him be remanded by the British ministry, or set Lord Cornwallis at equal liberty.'[2]

But if Rutledge cherished resentment towards Cornwallis, he did a grateful service to the wounded feelings of General Gates, by introducing and supporting a motion to repeal the resolution of Congress, directing a court of

---

[1] Charles Thomson's MS. Sketch of the Debate in Congress, August 12th. See Writings of Washington, vol. viii., p. 334.

[2] Ibid., p. 333. It will be observed, that Mr. Laurens, notwithstanding his unconditional release, chose to consider himself as exchanged for Cornwallis. Hence, the propriety of Washington's strictures. See, as to further discussion of this subject, Madison Papers, vol. i., pp. 202, 206, 479.

inquiry on his conduct at the battle of Camden. This motion prevailed, and Gates was assigned by Washington to the command of the right wing of the army. The journals of Congress furnish abundant evidence of the leading part Rutledge took in their proceedings. The time of that body was occupied with questions relating to the public lands, and military and financial arrangements. Upon all these subjects, on committees, and in debate, the mind of Rutledge was actively employed. It would serve no useful purpose at this day, to recite, in detail, the labors that engaged this portion of his life. We shall, therefore, only glance at the more prominent features of his Congressional career. How to provide means to pay the pressing debts of the Confederacy, was a subject of anxious deliberation. The army was in a state bordering on mutiny, in consequence of the large arrears of pay due to it, while the national character and credit were suffering abroad, from the debility of the Federal government, and the unwillingness of the States to support and invigorate it.

Madison suggested as practicable objects of a general revenue, first, an impost on trade; secondly, a poll-tax, under certain qualifications; thirdly, a land-tax, also under qualifications.[1] Rutledge was in favor of an impost on trade, and introduced a resolution that it be earnestly recommended to the several States, to impose and levy a duty of five per cent., *ad valorem*, at the time and place of importation, on all goods, wares, and merchandizes of foreign growth and manufacture, which may be imported into the said States, respectively, except goods of the United States or any of them, and a like duty on all prizes and prize-goods condemned in the Court of Admiralty of said States; that the money arising from such duties be paid into the Continental Treasury, to be appro-

[1] Madison Papers, vol. i., p. 300.

priated and applied to the payment of the interest, and to sink the principal, of the money which the United States have borrowed in Europe, and of what they may borrow; for discharging the arrears due to the army, and for the future support of the war, and to no other use or purpose whatsoever; that the said duties be continued for twenty-five years, unless the debts abovementioned be discharged in the meantime, in which case they shall cease and determine; that the money arising from the said duties, and paid by any State, be passed to the credit of such State on account of its quota of the debt of the United States. On a subsequent day, he proposed to change, whenever it was practicable, *ad valorem* for specific duties. This, he said, would lessen the opportunity of collusion between collector and importer, and would be more equal among the States.[1]

In levying a land-tax, Rutledge supported the rule of apportionment prescribed by the Articles of Confederation.[2] It was objected to this rule, that it could not be applied without the intervention of the several States, and if they intervened, all confidence in an impartial distribution of the tax would be at an end.[3] Congress, it was said, would not undertake to determine the value of the lands in each State, and if the States were permitted to fix the valuation, doubt and suspicion would ensue as to its justness. Rutledge, on the other hand, advocated the propriety of the constitutional rule, and was willing to trust to the honor of the States, should Congress refer the valuation of the lands to them. The plan adopted but subsequently abandoned is thus described by Mr. Madison. 'It proposes,' thus he wrote Edmund

[1] Madison Papers, vol. i., pp. 308, 340.

[2] Namely, that the tax should be paid by the respective States, in proportion to the value of all land within each State.

[3] Madison to Randolph, Jan. 14th, 1783. Madison Papers, vol. i., p. 498. See also Journals of Congress, vol. viii., p. 132.

Randolph, 'that the States shall return to Congress, before January next, their respective quantities of land, the number of houses thereon, distinguishing dwelling-houses from others, the number of inhabitants, distinguishing whites from blacks. These data are to be referred to a grand committee, by whom a report, in which nine voices must unite, is to be made to Congress; which report is to settle the proportions of each State, to be ratified or rejected by Congress without alteration.'[1] But this plan, conforming in principle to Rutledge's opinion, was at length superseded. 'A change of valuation of lands for the number of inhabitants,' Madison again wrote to the same correspondent, 'deducting two-fifths of the slaves, has received a tacit sanction; and, unless hereafter expugned, will go forth in the general recommendation as material to future harmony and justice among the members of the Confederacy. The deduction of two-fifths was a compromise between the wide opinions and demands of the southern and other States.'[2] This change was adhered to, and submitted to the States for their sanction.[3]

With respect to a revenue from imposts, to be applied to the payment of the interest of the national debt, it was recommended to the several States to invest Congress with a power to levy, for the use of the United States, specific duties on rum, wines, teas, sugars, molasses, cocoa, and coffee, and upon all other goods a duty of five *per cent., ad valorem.* The whole to be collected by persons amenable to Congress, but appointed by the States. It was also recommended to the States to establish, for a term of twenty-five years, substantial and effectual reve-

---

[1] Feb. 18, 1783. Ibid, p. 506. This plan was adopted, Feb. 17.

[2] April 8, 1783. Ibid, p. 522.

[3] Journals of Congress, vol. viii., p. 188. That is, the States were requested to authorize their delegates to subscribe and ratify an alteration in the articles of confederation, such as are mentioned in the text.

nues, of such nature as they might judge most convenient, to discharge their proportion of the annual interest. The whole interest amounted to $2,415,956. A million and a half of this sum was referred to the States to be provided for. For the discharge of the principal, Congress relied on the natural increase of the revenue from commerce, in requisitions to be made from time to time, and on the prospect of vacant lands.

These measures, though not in all respects consonant to the ideas of Rutledge, as expressed in the frequent discussions that arose, and briefly reported by Madison, nevertheless received his support. Justice, good faith, and national honor were at stake, and he advocated what seemed the most practicable scheme to preserve them untarnished.

It will be recollected that Congress, in the previous year, instructed their Commissioners in Europe 'to undertake nothing in the negotiations for peace or truce' without the knowledge and concurrence of France. The letters of Jay, and the intercepted one from Marbois, convinced Rutledge that the essential interests of the country would be endangered by thus subjecting the American ministers to the will of our ally. He therefore advocated a motion to exempt them from the obligation imposed by their instructions. Those instructions, he contended, were inconsistent with the national dignity, and of dangerous tendency; as it was obvious that France had separate views.[1] Congress, however, did not concur with him; and the instructions remained unreversed. It is well known that the Commissioners violated them, and concluded a treaty, not only without the concurrence, but without the knowledge of the French Court.[2] This conduct subjected them to a good deal of unfriendly criticism in Congress. Mercer of Virginia

---

[1] Madison Papers, vol. i., p. 240.

[2] Ante, pp. 338–344.

denounced the course which they had pursued as a mixture of follies which had no example, as a tragedy to America, and a comedy to all the world beside. He said he felt inexpressible indignation at their meanly stooping, as it were, to lick the dust from the feet of a nation whose hands were still dyed with the blood of their fellow-citizens.

Rutledge replied to these denunciations. He hoped, he said, the character of our ministers would not be affected, much less their recall produced, by declamations against them; and that facts would be ascertained and stated, before any decision should be passed. He was of opinion, that the separate article did not concern France, and therefore there was no necessity for communicating it to her; and, as to Spain, she deserved nothing at our hands; she had treated us in a manner that forfeited all claim to our good offices or our confidence. She had not, as had been supposed, entered into the war as an ally to our ally, for our support; but, as she herself had declared, as a principal, and on her own account. He said he was for adhering religiously to the spirit and letter of the treaty with France; that our ministers had done so; and, if recalled or censured for the part they had acted, he was sure no man of spirit would take their place.[1]

On the 24th of March, 1783, intelligence was communicated to Congress, that the preliminaries for a general peace had been signed on the 20th of the previous January.[2] This information again brought upon the carpet the conduct of the American ministers. Rutledge, however, contended that Congress had no occasion to meddle with the subject; that the ministers had done right; that they had maintained the honor of the United

---

[1] Madison Papers, vol. i., p. 391. See also Madison's comments on the instructions, &c. Ibid, p. 398, 399.

[2] Ante, p. 354.

States after Congress had given it up; that the manœuvre practised by them was common in all courts, and was justifiable against Spain, who alone was affected by it; that instructions ought to be disregarded whenever the public good required it; and that he himself would never be bound by them when he thought them improper.[1]

We have thus presented to the reader the prominent features of Rutledge's services in the Congress of 1782 and 1783. He 'brought into this assembly,' says the son and biographer of Hamilton, 'all the weight of an established reputation, the influence of inflexible determination, great experience, and high eloquence.'[2] His sagacity, his knowledge of men, his sensibility to justice, his lofty spirit, his invincible courage, his penetrating judgment, together with his bold, unhesitating avowal of opinions, could not fail to secure to him a high position in the councils of the Confederacy. He retired from Congress in June, 1783, and in the next chapter we shall witness the exhibition of his talents on a different theatre.

---

[1] Madison Papers, *supra*, p. 410.

[2] Life of Hamilton, vol. ii., p. 14.

CHAPTER XIII.

CHANCELLOR OF SOUTH CAROLINA, AND MEMBER OF THE FEDERAL CONVENTION.

1783—1791.

THE Revolutionary contest gave to the country independence; but that object was not attained without immense sacrifices. All descriptions of the people had suffered from the calamities of the war. Industry in all its branches had been interrupted, property pillaged, and affluence reduced to beggary. Rutledge did not escape the common misfortune. On his return to South Carolina, he found his affairs deranged, and his fortune wasted. Even his library, I am informed, had been destroyed by the enemy.

He was now relieved for a space of all public employments, and seems to have formed a resolution to devote himself to private pursuits. But, in the following year, when the new Court of Chancery was created, he was elected by the Legislature its senior Judge.[1] As this honorable position would not withdraw him from the circle of his family or affairs, he accepted it. He resisted, however, all attempts to bring him back again into the service of the Confederacy. He declined the appointment of a Judge of the Federal Court, to determine the con-

[1] The bill for erecting and organizing that court, is said to have been drawn by him. It was adopted by the Legislature, the 21st of March, 1784; and on the same day John Rutledge, Richard Hutson, and John Matthews, were elected Judges.

troversies between New York and Massachusetts;[1] and the mission to the United Netherlands, to which he was elected by the unanimous vote of Congress.[2] In his letter declining this latter appointment, he said he would with great pleasure accept it, if he could with any degree of convenience; but that having been for a long time wholly engrossed in public business, his own affairs now required attention, and would not for some years admit of his residing in Europe.[3]

Highly as Rutledge's cotemporaries rated his forensic and political abilities, and much as they commended the vigor and wisdom that distinguished his executive career, they still regarded his administration of the law as among his first titles to the public respect and confidence. He possessed a well-digested stock of legal learning, and a native vigor of mind, that enabled him to comprehend its spirit and foundations. He yielded all proper deference to authority; but he consulted reason as well as precedent, and made their blended light the guide of his judicial career. His penetrating mind readily discerned the bearings and relations of the causes brought before him; and he seldom failed to place his decisions on grounds obvious and satisfactory to all parties. He had on the Bench, as elsewhere, all the advantages of what is termed *presence*. He was tall, grave, and uncommonly dignified. His demeanor repressed familiarity, and insured respect. He exercised his authority with much rigor when he thought the occasion required it; and though ordinarily patient, and always impartial, his temper sometimes took fire, and broke out without much check or restraint. 'I have heard,' writes a friend, 'some

[1] He was elected Dec. 24th, 1784. He declined the appointment March 26th, 1785.

[2] July 5th, 1785.

[3] Secret Journals of Congress, vol. iii., p. 585. This letter was dated Aug. 1st, 1785.

of our old lawyers describe the manner in which court, jury, and audience quailed before him, when he assumed his gubernatorial air.'

The first term of the new Court of Chancery was held at Charleston on the 14th of June, 1784. No causes were heard; and during the first terms of the Court no decisions were made involving important principles. Indeed, none of the judgments reported by Desaussure, while Rutledge remained on the Equity Bench, possess much of interest or information.[1] Upon the re-organization of the Courts of Law and Equity, in February, 1791, Rutledge was elected Chief Justice of the Court of Common Pleas, and thereby vacated his seat in the Court of Chancery. Before tracing this portion of his career, however, we must contemplate the part he acted, and the opinions he expressed, in the Convention that framed the Constitution of the United States.

The federal authority, feeble and inefficient, had neither respect abroad, nor credit or confidence at home. All the efforts of Congress to procure from the States an adequate power to provide means for the payment of the public debt had failed. The want of a general authority over commerce led to conflicting and irritating regulations on the part of the several States. 'Illiberality, jealousy, and local policy,' wrote Washington, in a letter of October, 1785, 'mix too much in our public councils for the good government of the Union. In a word, the Confederation appears to me to be little more than a shadow without the substance; and Congress a nugatory body, their ordinances being little attended to. . . . . By such policy as this, the wheels of government are clogged, and our brightest prospects, and that high expectation which was entertained of us by the wondering world, are turned

[1] Much business was transacted by the court, but as their judgments were pronounced *in banc*, they do not enable us to determine the precise share Rutledge had in them.

into astonishment; and from the high ground on which we stood, we are descending into the vale of confusion and darkness.'

As time advanced the public affairs grew worse. The political condition of the United States, when the Federal Convention met at Philadelphia, in May, 1787, was both distracted and disheartening.[1] Nothing relieved the ominous gloom but a hope that so distinguished a body might devise a remedy for the evils from which the country was suffering. The day fixed for the meeting of the Convention was the 14th of May. Seven States, however, were not convened until the 25th. John Rutledge, C. C. Pinckney, Charles Pinckney, and Pierce Butler, represented South Carolina.[2] Robert Morris, in behalf of the delegation from Pennsylvania, proposed Washington for President of the Convention. Rutledge seconded the proposal, and observed that Washington's presence forbade any observations which might otherwise be proper.

Rutledge's speculative opinions respecting forms of government can only be inferred from the part he took, and the sentiments he expressed, in the discussions of the Convention. No letters of his, written at this period, and touching the interesting subject that now engaged the attention of the whole country, have been preserved. The debates of the Convention are the only depository of his sentiments, and to those we must turn to ascertain what features of the Constitution he favored and what

---

[1] Ante, pp. 373–376.

[2] The general history of this Convention is well known. See the Madison Papers, Yates' Secret Debates, and Journal of the Federal Convention. It would be superfluous, therefore, to reproduce here the details of their proceedings. We have sought only to lay before the reader the sentiments expressed by Rutledge; and to briefly state the part, the important part, he took in the deliberations of that distinguished assembly.

opposed. It would be unjust, however, to the individual members of that body, to regard the various propositions they introduced or supported, as in all cases indicating their final opinions. Rutledge was not among those who, from pride or obstinacy, blindly and irrationally cling to their preconceived sentiments against all the lights of experience, and all the deductions of reason. When there appeared a reluctance on the part of members to commit themselves on the question touching the constitution of the executive department, he animadverted upon their shyness, not only on this, but other subjects. He said it looked as if they supposed themselves precluded, by having frankly disclosed their opinions, from afterwards changing them, which he did not take to be at all the case.

Rutledge proposed that the executive authority should be exercised by one person. The reasons in favor of one, he said, were so obvious and conclusive, that he presumed no member of the Convention would oppose his motion. A single man would feel the greatest responsibility, and administer the public affairs best.

He deemed it prudent to connect the tie of property with that of reputation; and when Charles Pinckney brought forward a proposition that the President, Judges of the Supreme Court, and Members of Congress, should be required to possess a clear, unincumbered estate, the amount to be fixed by the Convention, he supported it.[1] Dr. Franklin opposed it. 'If honesty,' he said, 'was often the companion of wealth, and if poverty was exposed to peculiar temptation, it was not less true that the possession of property increased the desire of more property. Some of the greatest rogues he was ever acquainted with were

[1] Mr. Pinckney said, were he to fix the quantum of property which should be required, he should not think of less than $100,000 for the President, half of that sum for each of the Judges, and in like proportion for the members of the National Legislature.

the richest rogues. We should remember the character which Scripture requires in rulers, that they should be men hating covetousness. This Constitution will be much read and attended to in Europe; and if it should betray a great partiality to the rich, will not only hurt us in the esteem of the most liberal and enlightened men there, but discourage the common people from removing to this country.' Pinckney's motion was rejected by so general a *no*, that the States were not called.[1]

It was proposed, and the proposition was earnestly supported by several of the leading members of the Convention, by Madison, Mason, Gouverneur Morris, and Ellsworth, to associate the Judges of the Supreme Court with the Executive in the revisionary power. Rutledge, on the other hand, thought the judges, of all men, the most unfit to be concerned in a revisionary council. The judges ought never to give their opinion on a law, he said, till it comes before them. He thought it equally unnecessary. The Executive could advise with the officers of state, as of War, Finance, &c., and avail himself of their information and opinions. Rutledge was opposed to a popular election of the Chief Magistrate. He should be appointed, he said, by the National Legislature, and declared ineligible to a second term.

He contended, too, that the members of the lower House of Congress ought to be chosen by the State Legislatures. He said he could not admit the solidity of the distinction between a mediate and immediate election by the people. It was the same thing to act by one's self and to act by another. An election by the Legislature would be more refined than an election immediately by the people; and would be more likely to correspond with the sense of the whole community. If this Convention had been chosen by the people in districts, it is

---

[1] Madison Papers, vol. iii., p. 1285.

not to be supposed that such proper characters would have been preferred. The delegates to Congress, he thought, had also been fitter men than would have been appointed by the people at large. He proposed, too, that the proportion of representation in this branch of Congress should be according to the quotas of contribution, and not according to numbers. He thought property ought to be taken into the estimate as well as the number of inhabitants. Property, he said, was certainly the principal object of society; and if numbers should be made the rule of representation, the Atlantic States would be subjected to the Western. Rutledge proposed that the representatives should be elected biennially; and was in favor of declaring them ineligible, during their term of service, and for one year after, to all offices that should be established;—or the emoluments augmented by Congress, while they were members. He would preserve, he said, the legislature as pure as possible, by shutting the door against the appointment of its own members to office, which was one source of its corruption.

He favored a representation of the States in the Senate according to their importance. He proposed to divide the States into three classes—the first class to have three members, the second two, and the third one member each. But the little States insisted upon an equality of representation, and would yield to no compromise. Rutledge would not risk a failure of the great objects of the Convention by inflexibly opposing their wishes. The little States, he said, were fixed. They had repeatedly and solemnly declared themselves to be so. All that the larger States then had to do was, to decide whether to yield or not. For his part, he conceived that although we could not do what we thought best in itself, we ought to do something. Had we not better keep the government up a little longer, hoping that another Convention will supply our omissions, than abandon everything to hazard? Our constituents will be very little satisfied with us if we take the latter course.

He was opposed to giving the House of Representatives the exclusive right to originate money bills. Those who would confide this privilege to that branch of the legislature alone were not, he said, consistent in their reasoning. 'They tell us,' thus he proceeded, 'that we ought to be guided by the long experience of Great Britain, and not our own experience of eleven years; and yet they themselves propose to depart from it. The House of Commons have not only the exclusive right of originating, but the Lords are not allowed to alter or amend a money bill. Will not the people say that this restriction is but a mere tub to the whale? They cannot but see that it is of no real consequence; and will be more likely to be displeased with it as an attempt to bubble them, than to impute it to a watchfulness over their rights. For his part, he would prefer giving the exclusive right to the Senate, if it was to be given exclusively at all. The Senate being more conversant in business, and having more leisure, will digest the bills much better, and as they are to have no effect till examined and approved by the House of Representatives, there can be no possible danger. These clauses in the Constitutions of the States had been put in through a blind adherence to the British model. If the work was to be done over now, they would be omitted. The experiment in South Carolina, where the Senate cannot originate or amend money bills, has shown that it answers no good purpose; and produces the very bad one of continually dividing and heating the two Houses.'

We have seen that it was a favorite dogma of our first Chief Justice, that those who own the country ought to govern it.[1] Rutledge was of a different opinion. When

---

[1] Ante, p. 212.

it was proposed, in elections for representatives, to restrict the right of suffrage to freeholders, he was among those who opposed it. He said the idea of restraining the right of suffrage to freeholders was a very unadvised one. It would create division among the people; and make enemies of all those who should be excluded. Dr. Franklin maintained the same opinion. It was of great consequence, he said, not to depress the virtue and public spirit of the common people, whose exertions contributed chiefly to the favorable issue of the war. The sons of a substantial farmer, not being themselves freeholders, would not be pleased at being disfranchised, and that class was numerous.

In constituting the Judicial department, Rutledge objected to any national tribunal, except a single supreme one. The State tribunals, he said, were most proper to decide in all cases in the first instance. The right of appeal, he contended, would be adequate to secure the national rights and uniformity of judgments. Dispersing inferior tribunals throughout the Republic he thought was an unnecessary encroachment on the rights of the States, and interposing an unnecessary obstacle to their adoption of the new system.

It was deemed important, by many of the leading members of the Convention, to confer on the National Government, a negative, in all cases whatsoever, on the legislative acts of the States. This was a favorite scheme of Madison's. It received the cordial support of Charles Pinckney. Wilson considered it as the key-stone wanted to complete the wide arch of government they were raising. It found many advocates; and the votes on it were more than once equally divided. Rutledge viewed the proposition with indignation, and thus denounced it. 'If nothing else, this alone would damn, and ought to damn, the Constitution. Will any State ever agree to be bound hand and foot in this manner? It is worse than making mere corporations of them, whose by-laws would not be subject to this shackle.' He was equally opposed to investing the National Government with power to erect new States, within, as well as without, the territory of the several States. 'Is it to be supposed,' he demanded, 'that the States are to be cut up without their own consent?' Luther Martin urged the unreasonableness of compelling the people of Virginia beyond the mountains, the western people of North Carolina and Georgia, and the people of Maine, to continue under the States then governing them, until those States thought proper to consent to their separation. It may be superfluous to add that the views of Rutledge prevailed.

Whether the Constitution should prohibit the slave-trade, and restrict the power of making commercial regulations, were questions of a very interesting character, and elicited much discussion. Virginia and Maryland, to their honor be it said, furnished the most distinguished opponents of the slave-trade. Its leading advocates were the delegates from South Carolina and Connecticut. Luther Martin said slaves weakened one part of the Union which the other parts were bound to protect; the privilege was therefore unreasonable. Besides, he declared, that it was inconsistent with the principles of the Revolution, and dishonorable to the American character, to have such a feature in the Constitution. Rutledge replied. He was not apprehensive of insurrections, and would readily exempt the other States from the obligation to protect the Southern against them. 'Religion and humanity,' he said, 'had nothing to do with this question. Interest alone is the governing principle with nations. The true question at present is, whether the Southern States shall or shall not be parties to the Union. If the Northern States consult their interest, they will not oppose the increase of slaves, which will increase the commodities of which they will become the carriers.'

'Let every State import what it pleases,' responded Ellsworth. 'The morality or wisdom of slavery are considerations belonging to the States themselves. What enriches a part enriches the whole; and the States are the best judges of their particular interest. The old Confederation had not meddled with this point; and he did not see any greater necessity for bringing it within the policy of the new one.'

'This infernal traffic,' said Mason of Virginia, 'originated in the avarice of British merchants. The British government constantly checked the attempts of Virginia to put a stop to it. The present question concerns not the importing States alone, but the whole Union. The evil of having slaves was experienced during the last war. Had slaves been treated as they might have been by the enemy, they would have proved dangerous instruments in their hands. But their folly dealt by the slaves as it did by the tories. . . . Slavery discourages arts and manufactures. The poor despise labor when performed by slaves. They prevent the emigration of whites, who really enrich and strengthen a country. They produce the most pernicious effect on manners. Every master of slaves is born a petty tyrant. They bring the judgment of heaven on a country. As nations cannot be rewarded or punished in the next world, they must be in this. By an inevitable chain of causes and effects, Providence punishes national sins by national calamities. He lamented that some of our Eastern brethren had, from a lust of gain, embarked in this nefarious traffic. As to the States being in possession of the right to import, this was the case with many other rights, now to be properly given up. He held it essential, in every point of view, that the General Government should have power to prevent the increase of slavery.'

'If the Convention thinks,' said Rutledge, 'that North Carolina, South Carolina, and Georgia, will ever agree to the plan, unless their right to import slaves be untouched, the expectation is vain. The people of those States will never be such fools as to give up so important an interest.'

The subject was referred to a committee of one member from each State; and to this committee was also referred the proposition, which had been reported by the committee of detail, that no navigation act should be passed without the assent of two-thirds of the members present in each house. This feature of the system the staple and commercial States were solicitous to retain, lest their commerce should be placed too much under the power of the Eastern States. The latter were equally anxious to reject it. Here, then, was a convenient basis for a compromise. An understanding soon took place, and the committee, by a great majority, agreed on a report, by which the General Government was to be prohibited from preventing the importation of slaves for a limited time; and the restrictive clause relative to navigation acts was to be omitted.[1]

Charles Pinckney was not satisfied with this compromise, and renewed the proposition requiring a vote of two-thirds to pass a navigation act. But General Pinckney, who was one of the committee, considering the loss brought on the commerce of the Eastern States by the Revolution, their liberal conduct towards the views of South Carolina, and the interest the weak Southern States had in being united with them, thought it proper that no fetters should be imposed on the power of making commercial regulations, and that his constituents, though prejudiced against the Eastern States, would be reconciled to this liberality. He had, himself, he said, prejudices against those States before he came to the Convention;

[1] Luther Martin's 'genuine information,' laid before the Maryland Legislature.

but would acknowledge that he had found them as liberal and candid as any men whatever.

Rutledge, also, opposed the motion of his colleague. 'It did not follow from a grant of the power to regulate trade, that it would be abused. At the worst, a navigation act could bear hard a little while only on the Southern States. As we are laying the foundation for a great Empire, we ought to take a permanent view of the subject, and not look at the present moment only.' He reminded the Convention of the necessity of securing the West India trade to this country. That was the great object; and a navigation act was necessary for obtaining it.

For the protection of individual liberty, Rutledge was for declaring the *habeas corpus* inviolate. He did not conceive that its suspension could ever be necessary, at the same time, through all the States.

We have now put the reader in possession of the more prominent opinions expressed by Rutledge in the Federal Convention. He approved parts of the Constitution and objected to others. Nevertheless, he gave to the whole his assent. He acted as did most of the members, and sacrificed his opinions to the public good. 'I confess,' said Dr. Franklin, and he spoke the general feeling, 'that there are several parts of this Constitution which I do not at present approve, but I am not sure I shall never approve them. For, having lived long, I have experienced many instances of being obliged, by better information or fuller consideration, to change opinions even on important subjects, which I once thought right, but found to be otherwise. It is, therefore, that the older I grow, the more apt I am to doubt my own judgment, and to pay more respect to the judgment of others. Most men, indeed, as well as most sects in religion, think themselves in possession of all truth, and that wherever others differ from them, it is so far error. Steele, a Protestant, in a dedication, tells the Pope that the only difference between our churches in their opinions of the certainty of their doctrines is, "the Church of Rome is infallible, and the Church of England is never in the wrong." But though many private persons think as highly of their own infallibility as that of their sect, few express it so naturally as a certain French lady who, in a dispute with her sister, said, "I don't know how it happens, sister, but I meet with nobody but myself that is always in the right —*il n'y a que moi qui a toujours raison.*" . . . . Thus I consent, sir, to this Constitution, because I expect no better, and because I am not sure that it is not the best. The opinions I have had of its errors I sacrifice to the public good. I have never whispered a syllable of them abroad. Within these walls they were born, and here they shall die. . . . . On the whole, sir, I cannot help expressing a wish that every member of the Convention who may still have objections to it, would with me, on this occasion, doubt a little of his own infallibility, and to make manifest our unanimity, put his name to this instrument.' Rutledge signed the Constitution, and heartily recommended it to his constituents.

CHAPTER XIV.

MEMBER OF THE STATE CONVENTION.

1788.

THE Federal Convention adjourned on the 17th of September, 1787, after a session of nearly four months. The plan of government they had devised was laid before the Legislature of South Carolina on the 10th of January, 1788. It met with strong opposition. Rutledge was present, and participated in the discussions. Rawlins Lowndes, a gentleman of good abilities, but never in advance of public opinion, and seldom keeping pace with it, was the leading opponent of the new system. Reading that article which declares the Constitution, and the laws made in pursuance of it, together with treaties made under the authority of the United States, the supreme law of the land, he demanded if there was an instance in the history of the known world, of the rulers of a republic being allowed to go so far? 'Even the most arbitrary kings,' he said, 'possessed nothing like it.' Rutledge replied. Every treaty was law paramount, he said, and must operate. It was so under the Articles of Confederation. As a proof of it, he instanced the treaty with France, which secured to that country certain privileges. 'Now,' thus he continued, 'supposing any law had passed taking those privileges away, would not the treaty be a sufficient bar to any local or municipal laws? What sort of power is that which leaves individuals in full power to reject or approve? Suppose a treaty was unexpectedly concluded between nations at war, would individual subjects ravage and plunder under letters of marque and reprisal? Certainly not. The treaty concluded, even secretly, would be a sufficient bar to the establishment. Pray, what solid reasons could be urged to support gentlemen's fears, that our new governors would wish to promote measures injurious to their native land? Was it not more reasonable, that if every State in the Union had a negative voice, a single State might be tampered with, and defeat every good intention?' Adverting to the objection relative to the instalment law being done away,[1] he asked, supposing a person gave security conformable to that law, whether, judging from precedent, the judges would permit any further proceedings contrary to it. He scouted the idea that only ten members would ever be left to manage the business of the Senate; yet, even if so, our delegates might be part of that ten, and consequently our interest secured. He described difficulties experienced in Congress in 1781 and '82. In those times business of vast importance stood still because nine States could not be kept together. Having said that the laws would stand just as they did before, the chancellor asked whether gentlemen seriously could suppose that a President, who has a character at stake, would be such a fool and knave as to join with ten others to tear up liberty by the roots, when a full Senate was competent to impeach him.[2]

Most of the men who had gained distinction in the revolutionary contest were members of the Legislature, and most of them were friendly to the Constitution.

---

[1] A law for the relief of debtors.

[2] We have followed the Reporter's notes, printed in Elliot's Debates, vol. iv., p. 268.

The objections raised by Lowndes brought into the arena of debate the best political talents of the State. He was not, however, to be driven from his purpose; and he defended his positions with zeal and pertinacity. Differing with his constituents respecting the Constitution, and therefore not expecting to be returned to the Convention, should the Legislature decide to call one, Lowndes availed himself of his present position fully to declare his sentiments. 'Let us not,' he said, 'receive this proffered system with implicit confidence, as carrying with it the stamp of superior perfection; rather let us compare what we already possess with what we are offered for it. We are now under the government of a most excellent Constitution, one that had stood the test of time, and carried us through difficulties generally supposed insurmountable; one that had raised us high in the eyes of all nations, and given to us the enviable blessings of liberty and independence; a Constitution sent like a blessing from heaven; yet we are impatient to change it for another that vested power in a few men to pull down that fabric which we had raised at the expense of our blood. . . . It has been said that this new government was to be considered as an experiment. . . . So far from having any expectation of success from such experiments, he sincerely believed that, when this new Constitution should be adopted, the sun of the Southern States would set, never to rise again.' South Carolina would dwindle, he said, into a mere skeleton of what it was, 'its legislative powers would be pared down to little more than those now vested in the corporation; and he should value the honor of a seat in the Legislature in no higher estimation than a seat in the city council.' He observed, that he had been accused of obstinacy in standing out against such a formidable opposition; but he assured the House that he was as open to conviction as any gentleman on the floor, yet would not be mislead by specious arguments.[1]

Rutledge replied. He said he had often heard the honorable gentleman with much pleasure; but, on the present occasion, he was astonished at his perseverance. 'Well might he apologize for taking up the time of gentlemen when, in the very outset, he declared that this Constitution must necessarily be submitted to a future Convention of the people. Why, then, enter so largely in argument on its merits, when the ultimate decision depended on another body? . . . . The gentleman had declared that his sentiments were so much in contradiction to the voice of his constituents, that he did not expect to be appointed a member of the Convention. Rutledge hoped he would be appointed, and did not hesitate to pledge himself to prove, demonstrably, that all those grounds on which he dwelt so much amounted to nothing more than mere declamation; that this boasted Confederation was not worth a farthing; and that, if Mr. Chairman was intrenched in such instruments up to his chin, they would not shield him from one single national calamity. So far from thinking that the sun of this country was obscured by the new Constitution, he did not doubt but that, whenever it was adopted, the sun of this State, united with twelve other suns, would exhibit a meridian radiance astonishing to the world. The gentleman's obstinacy brought to his recollection a friend to this country, once a member of that house, who said, "It is generally imputed to me that I am obstinate. This is a mistake. I am not so, but sometimes hard to be convinced."'

The debates continued three days. On the 19th of

[1] Mr. Lowndes spoke several times, and the extracts in the text are taken from different speeches.

January it was unanimously resolved to call a Convention to consider the Constitution, and either ratify or reject it. But on the question, whether the Convention should assemble as early as the 12th of May, opinions were nearly equally divided. It was resolved in the affirmative, but only by a majority of one. Those who favored a later day for the meeting of the Convention wished to know the result in other States, particularly in Virginia, before South Carolina determined to accept the Constitution.

The Convention assembled at Charleston on the 12th of May, 1788. It consisted of 236 members.[1] Rutledge was among the number. The friends of the Constitution do not appear to have taken an active part in the debates. Rutledge did not address the Convention at all.[2] His opinions, however, were well known; and his high character, his long services, his admitted abilities, without the aid of public speech, supported and enforced them. Besides, a large majority of the members were Federalists, and no discussion was necessary to ensure their suffrages for the Constitution. To gain time till the determination of Virginia could be known, General Sumpter, on the 21st instant, brought forward a motion for an adjournment to the 20th of the ensuing October. After an animated debate, it was rejected by a majority of forty-six. This vote was considered decisive in favor of the Constitution. 'When the result of the vote was announced,' says Ramsay, 'an event unexampled in the annals of Carolina took place. Strong and involuntary expressions of applause and joy burst forth from the numerous transported spectators. The minority loudly complained of disrespect—unpleasant consequences were anticipated. The majority joined with the complaining

---

[1] 236 members were appointed to the Convention, but only 222 attended.

[2] If he did, no record of his speech has been preserved.

members in clearing the house, and in the most delicate manner soothed their feelings.'[1]

On the 23d of May, the Convention assented to and ratified the Constitution, by a majority of sixty-seven. In the next chapter we shall see, that, on the organization of the Government, Rutledge was appointed to one of its most honorable departments.

[1] History of South Carolina, vol. ii., p. 432.

CHAPTER XV.

ASSOCIATE JUSTICE OF THE SUPREME COURT.— CHIEF JUSTICE OF SOUTH CAROLINA.

1789—1795.

As the Constitution originally stood, the person having the highest number, and a majority of the whole number of electoral votes, was to be President.[1] 'Hence,' says Hamilton, 'it was deemed an essential point of caution to take care that accident or an intrigue of the officers of the government, should not raise Mr. Adams, instead of General Washington, to the first place. . . . . It was, therefore, agreed that a few votes should be diverted from Mr. Adams to other persons, so as to insure to General Washington a plurality. Great was my astonishment, and equally great my regret, when afterwards I learned from persons of unquestionable veracity, that Mr. Adams had complained of unfair treatment, in not having been permitted to take an equal chance with General Washington, by leaving the votes to an uninfluenced current.'[2]

---

[1] But if there should be more than one having such majority, and also an equal number of votes, then the election devolved on the House of Representatives. The House were to choose one of the persons thus having a majority and equality of votes. If no person had a majority, then they were to choose from the five highest on the list. In every case, after the choice of the President, the person having the greatest number of electoral votes was to be the Vice-President.

[2] Hamilton's Works, vol. vii, p. 692.

'What Mr. Adams complained of, and very reasonably too,' says his grandson, 'was the secret effort made to reduce the votes for him everywhere, to such a degree as to leave him the representative of a minority.'[1] We do not think such was Hamilton's design. He wished merely to guard against the possibility of Adams receiving a plurality of votes. The latter, at this time, stood high in the affections of his countrymen. In weight and popularity he was second to Washington alone. The public voice, almost unanimously, designated him for the second position in the government. Hamilton could have no motive to act an unfriendly part towards him. They had never come into collision; indeed, they were, personally, strangers to each other. Mr. Adams' feelings, however, were deeply wounded in consequence of the large number of votes withheld from him; and he seems to have entertained the belief that Hamilton's object was to prevent his being chosen even Vice-President.[2]

---

[1] Works of John Adams, vol. viii., p. 484.

[2] In his Review of Hillhouse's propositions for amending the Constitution, submitted to the Senate of the United States in 1808, Mr. Adams thus refers to this irritating subject. 'Caucuses of patricians, and caucuses of plebeians, always prevailed in Rome, and in all other free countries. Our Revolution was effected by caucuses. The Federal Constitution was formed by caucuses; and the Federal Administrations, for twenty years, have been supported or subverted by caucuses. There is little more of the kind now than there was twenty years ago. Alexander Hamilton was the greatest organist that ever played upon this instrument. He made all the use he could of these bodies of Cincinnati and others, to prevent Mr. Adams from being chosen Vice-President. The reason of his antipathy I know not; for he had never seen him. He caused it to be propagated in the Northern States that Virginia would not vote for Washington; and in the Southern States, that New England would not vote for Washington; or, at least, that their votes would not be unanimous; at the same time, that there was a great probability there would be a unanimous vote for Adams; that, therefore, the electors must throw away so many of their votes that Adams could not have a majority, and, consequently, could not be President. If he believed one word of the apprehensions he propagated, it is very unaccountable; for there was a

South Carolina withheld her electoral votes from Adams, and bestowed them upon her own distinguished son, John Rutledge.[1]

We have seen elsewhere,[2] that the Judiciary bill was approved the 24th of September, 1789, and provided for the appointment of a Chief Justice, and five Associate Justices, who were to constitute the Supreme Court of the United States. John Rutledge, James Wilson, William Cushing, Robert Harrison, and John Blair, were nominated as Associate Justices. They were confirmed on the same day, but were appointed in the order we have mentioned, and took precedence accordingly.[3] 'Some of these gentlemen,' says Marshall, 'had filled the highest law-offices in their respective States; and all of them had received distinguished marks of the public confidence.'[4]

Rutledge, notwithstanding his acceptance of this appointment, retained his seat on the equity bench of South Carolina; though he does not appear to have taken any part in the proceedings of that court after the December term, 1789.[5] The first term of the Supreme Court was held at New York, in February, 1790. Rutledge was not

---

very great certainty in the public opinion that Washington would have a unanimous vote. At the second election, he was pleased to permit Mr. Adams to have a considerable majority as Vice-President.' Adams' Works, vol. vi., p. 543.

[1] 'I find, on inquiry,' wrote Gerry to Adams, March 4th, 1789, 'that you are elected Vice-President, having three or four times the number of votes of any other candidate. Maryland threw away their votes on Colonel Harrison, and South Carolina on Governor Rutledge; being, with some other States which were not unanimous for you, apprehensive that this was a necessary step to prevent your election to the chair. In this point they were mistaken; for the President, as I am informed from pretty good authority, has a unanimous vote.' Adams' Works, vol. viii., p. 484.

[2] Ante, p. 383.

[3] They were confirmed Sept. 26th.

[4] Life of Washington, vol. ii., p. 170. Second Edition, 1834.

[5] See Desaussure's Reports, vol. i.

present. On the 16th of February, 1791, he was elected by the Legislature of South Carolina Chief Justice of the Court of Common Pleas and Sessions. He accepted this post, and resigned his seat on the Federal bench.[1]

He presided in the Common Pleas, for the first time, on the 9th of March. The case of the State *versus* Washington, indicted for forgery, was before the Court, on a motion in arrest of judgment. It was very elaborately argued, both on the part of the prosecution and the prisoner. Rutledge delivered the opinion of the Court. The indictment charged the prisoner with having forged and uttered as true, an indented certificate, called a general indent of the State of South Carolina. He was also charged with having forged on the back of such indent, and uttered as true, a receipt for the accruing annual interest, which appeared from the face of the instrument to be payable. The Chief Justice said the arguments for the prisoner rested on three grounds: — First, that the receipt was not given with intention to defraud. Secondly, that if it was not felony to counterfeit the indent, it could not be felony to forge the receipt. Thirdly, that the receipt was not given for money or goods. 'Although these arguments,' said he, 'may at first view appear ingenious and plausible, yet, on examination, they will be found altogether destitute of solidity. The only point in which we agree with the prisoner's counsel is, that to make forgery felony under this act, it must be done with intention to defraud. It surely must. It is the essence of the crime. But they say these receipts were not intended to defraud either the treasurers or Vale. But the jury have found that it was with intent to defraud both. They were the judges of that fact. We cannot say they were mistaken. It is of no consequence whether any

[1] Writings of Washington, vol. x., p. 164. Washington visited South Carolina, in May, 1791, and while there, offered the vacant post to Edward Rutledge and C. C. Pinckney. Both declined it. Ibid.

person was actually defrauded or not; if the forgery was done with intention to defraud, it is sufficient, and that is found.' After citing several leading cases to sustain this opinion, he thus proceeded: — 'The counsel for the prisoner contended farther, that if the counterfeiting the indent was not felony, counterfeiting the receipts could not be felony; for it cannot be more criminal to counterfeit the receipt than the indent; and unconnected with the indent, the receipt is perfectly innocent. But this we conceive to be false and inconclusive reasoning; and that the transactions of counterfeiting the indent, and forging the receipt, may be considered and determined upon, as totally independent of each other. The charge with respect to the receipt is, for forging a receipt for money, with intention to defraud certain persons. And it is of no consequence on what those receipts were written; whether on the back of an indent, on the back of a lottery ticket, on a sheet of paper, or on the margin of a newspaper. If the receipt was for money—if it was forged — if it was forged with intention to defraud any person, that is sufficient to constitute it felony under the act. . . . . It is immaterial to consider any of the other objections which have been offered; because the first and last objection being overruled, it follows that the prisoner is lawfully convicted of having forged a receipt for money, with intention to defraud the persons mentioned in the indictment; and that such a forgery is, by the act of assembly, felony without benefit of clergy.'

I infer from the Chief Justice's address to the prisoner, before pronouncing the sentence of death against him, that he was quite insensible to the total disproportion between the offence and the punishment, and was not sufficiently in advance of his time, to perceive the atrocity of the penal code which he was administering. 'His honor,' says the reporter, 'dilated upon the enormity and ruinous tendency of this crime, in all countries, and especially in a commercial community, and strongly painted the heinousness of the guilt in a civil, a moral, and a religious view. That as a citizen he had grossly infringed the public rights; as a man, he had broken through the obligations of honor and integrity; and as a Christian, he had violated the most wholsome precepts of religion. That from a person of his education and habits, better things were to have been expected. That the Court pitied his condition, and hoped that he felt on that solemn occasion as he ought to feel; recommending to him, in a very pathetic manner, to employ that little interval of life which remained in making his peace with that God whose law he had offended; and suggesting, as an additional motive, that, from the malignity of his offence, the Court could not flatter him with any hope of pardon.'[1]

In Eden *v.* Legare,[2] the Chief Justice held that calling a man a mulatto is actionable; 'because,' said he, 'if true, the party would be deprived of all civil rights; and, moreover, would be liable to be tried in all cases, under the negro act, without the privilege of a trial by jury. Any words, therefore, which tended to subject a citizen to such disabilities, were actionable.'

He gave full weight to the dictates of reason and justice in a case that came before him involving a question of personal freedom. The master of a negro girl had given her permission to work or hire herself out, in any manner she pleased, upon paying him a certain monthly sum. By her industry and frugality, she was enabled to pay the stipulated amount, and save a part of her wages besides. Having an affection for another negro girl, she bought her, with the money she had thus accumulated, and set her free. In the course of time, the master claimed this girl whose freedom had been thus meritoriously acquired, as his property. Rutledge delivered the

---

[1] Bay's Reports, vol. i., pp. 120, 157.

[2] Ibid, p. 171.

opinion of the Court; and, in his charge to the jury, observed, 'that although the case was a new one, yet the Court found no difficulty whatever in forming an opinion on it; for if the master got the labor of his wench, or what he agreed to receive for her monthly wages, (which was the same thing,) he would not be injured: on the contrary, he was completely satisfied, and all that she earned over ought to be at her own disposal; and if the wench chose to appropriate the savings of her extra labor to the purchase of this girl, in order afterwards to set her free, would a jury of the country say, No? He trusted not. They were too humane and upright, he hoped, to do such manifest violence to so singular and extraordinary an act of benevolence.'[1]

In Hall *v.* Smith,[2] which was an action against the endorser of a promissory note, the question arose whether the holder of the note had used due diligence in endeavoring to recover the money from the drawer. 'This is a matter,' said the Chief Justice, 'which turns upon the use or neglect of due diligence; which is a subject very proper for the consideration of merchants, in which the course and usage of trade in this country, as well as its local situation, ought to be brought into view, and duly weighed. In England, where there are great monied capitals and banking establishments, from whence money can at all times be easily drawn to answer the purposes of trade by men in good and solvent circumstances, a greater degree of strictness is observed than can easily be established in this country; especially among planters, who can only bring their crops to market at one season of the year, and who are often obliged to sell them on a credit to the merchants; who are, on the other hand, obliged, from the nature of trade, to give large credits to the planters. In this kind of mutual intercourse, then,

---

[1] Guardian of Sally *v.* Beaty, 1 Bay, p. 260. [2] Ibid, p. 330.

the strict rules observed in England with regard to promissory notes are not altogether applicable to the local situation of Carolina. The great question for the jury, therefore, in this case, is, whether a reasonable diligence has been used or not: such as a prudent man, in his ordinary affairs, would observe, where his own interest only was immediately concerned. But it must be recollected, also, that this note was endorsed over after it was due; and, therefore, the law presumes, in such case, that the endorsee took it upon the credit of the endorser, and not upon the credit of the drawer. It is in such case considered as a new-drawn note by the endorser. Under these circumstances, therefore, although the endorsee may recover against the drawer, it is not subject to such strict rules as a note would be which was endorsed before due. In every such case, the endorser himself must have given indulgence to the drawer before he negotiated it; and it would be hard indeed if the holder should suffer for a further reasonable indulgence afterward, which the endorser himself had shown before he endorsed it. . . . Upon the whole, I am clearly of opinion that, instead of an unreasonable delay, very unusual diligence has been used. Of this, however, the jury are to judge.'

The creditors of Scott *v.* Scott[1] was a case of a different character from the others we have cited, and shows that Rutledge was well imbued with juridical learning. The question was, whether dower must be assigned out of each separate tract or parcel of land, or whether a portion might be given in lieu of the whole. Rutledge delivered the opinion of the Court. 'The Act of Assembly,' he said, 'makes no alteration as to the mode of assigning dower; because the words of the act follow the words and form of the judgment, and *habere facias* in dower at common law. The act, indeed, gives the commissioners

---

[1] Bay's Rep., vol. i., pp. 504–506.

a power to relinquish the admeasurement of dower altogether, and of assessing a sum of money in lieu thereof. But one or the other must be pursued solely; and no other composition can be made unless by consent. The commissioners then, if they undertook to admeasure dower at all, stand in the place of the sheriff at common law. At common law, where the husband is sole-seized, dower must be admeasured off, *per metas et bundas*. But it may be otherwise assigned by consent. So also a bad assignment may be rectified; and a *scire facias* will lie to assign, *de novo*. The latter shows that the Court has an equitable power of directing the apportionment of dower. . . . Common right gives the widow but one-third of each tract. *De quocunque tenemento tertia pars*. In 3 *Comy*. tit. *Dower*, it is said the widow shall not be endowed of entire tenements. If there be several feoffees, and one assign dower for all, the others cannot take advantage of it. If the thing out of which the widow be dowable at common law be divisible, her dower must be set out *per metas et bundas;* but if it be indivisible, then she must be endowed specially — as of the third presentation of a church—the third toll-dish of a mill—the third part of the profits of an office. The Act of Assembly in this State was made, not to vary the right to dower, but to institute a more easy and certain mode of obtaining it. From the peculiar situation of this country, and the great disadvantage sometimes to all parties that may attend the dividing of a plantation, the commissioners are vested with powers to assess a sum of money, not as dower, but in lieu of dower. Where they do this, their return is indeed final, because they are made the judges of the value of the property. But it would be exceedingly dangerous, if they possessed the power of giving a part of land in lieu of all the rest. Dangerous to the widow; for they might assign her an entire tract in some remote and uncultivated part of the State.

Dangerous to purchasers; for they might lay the burthen of all her dower upon the lands only which had been sold by her husband, and exonerate the heir from all incumbrance. In such case, it would be impossible for any man to know, or for counsel to advise him, how far the claim of dower might, at a future day, affect the lands he was purchasing. Instead of the widow taking her life-estate in one-third, the commissioners might assign her two-thirds; perhaps a larger portion still. With regard to the competency of the creditors in the present case to be admitted as parties, it is certain that lands being subject to judgments and executions, the creditors stand in the place of the heir, and possess his interest, which is always subject to their debts. If this were not so, the heir and widow colluding together might always defeat the remedy of creditors. They might get dower assigned in those lands only which are subject to the debts, and the creditors would have no remedy against the lands that had been antecedently sold by her husband, though they might be equally subject to her dower.'

Chief Justice Rutledge continued in the Court of Common Pleas a little more than four years. When he retired, it was to preside as Chief Justice in the Supreme Court of the United States. But before we view him in this latter position, and attend him to the sad conclusion of his judicial career, I must relate several passages, connected with that period of his life, which it was the design of this chapter to illustrate.

In 1792, he had the misfortune to lose his wife, 'after an illness so slight and short,' writes one of his descendants, 'that her death might almost be called sudden.' This was an event in the course and order of Providence, but it touched the very deepest feelings of his heart. He was a man of strong and concentrated affections, and his unexpected loss was one of the sharpest and rudest trials to which he had been subjected. He was remarkably domestic, and sought relaxation from the weight of public employments at his own fireside. It was in the midst of his family that he unbent and gave full play to all the gentler feelings of his nature.

The events of the Revolution had left upon the mind of Rutledge a deep and abiding impression. His hatred of Great Britain was intense. It influenced his politics; in a certain degree it influenced his fortunes. He viewed the efforts of that country to check and confound the Revolution in France, with unrepressed indignation and abhorrence. He deemed that Revolution, despite all the excesses that marked and marred it, a blessing to France and the world; and his soul was fired with enthusiasm by the unsurpassed energy, spirit and abilities, with which the French combatted in defence of their principles. When the news reached Charleston that the National Convention had abolished the regal government, and declared France a Republic, Consul Mangourit appointed a day to celebrate these 'auspicious events.'[1] The several military corps of Charleston paraded on the occasion, and the civil authorities of the State participated in the pageant. A procession, with fifty French sailors, chaunting the *Marsellois* hymn, proceeded to Williams' Coffee-house in Tradd street, where they were joined by the Governor, the Speaker of the Senate, Chief Justice Rutledge, the other Judges, and a large number of the most respectable citizens. When the procession was passing the French Protestant church, it was halted by the Consul, who took off his hat and saluted it with the

[1] In a contemporary account of this affair, printed in the Aurora newspaper, the day on which it occurred is stated to have been the 11th of November, 1792. The account in the Aurora was evidently taken from a Charleston paper. In the 'Reminiscences of Charleston,' by Mr. Frazer, it is said to have been the 11th of January, 1793. See p. 40. The events that were celebrated took place the 21st of September, 1792.

National colors, as an expiation for the persecution of that church, by Louis XIV. On arriving at St. Philip's church, two salutes were fired by the regiment of infantry. 'The Rev. Mr. Coste,' such is the account, 'delivered an animated and eloquent oration, to a numerous and splendid audience of ladies and gentlemen. *Te Deum* was sung, and the church-service closed by the hymn *des Marsellois*, accompanied with the organ.' The company then returned to Williams' Coffee-house, where the Consul received the Governor and other distinguished guests, and presented them with branches of laurel. On presenting one to General Gadsden, the Consul politely bowed, and said, 'General, you have been long acquainted with this tree.' The General replied, that such was his satisfaction on the cause of the day, that 'if he had not been able to walk on his feet, he would have ordered himself to be carried to the procession.'[1]

With a warm affection for the French Republic, with a still warmer aversion to Great Britain, the reader will

---

[1] Mr. Frazer thus describes 'the extravagant and enthusiastic sympathy in behalf of the French Revolution,' at this time prevailing in Charleston. 'The tri-colored cockade was generally worn. The American and French colors waved together at public entertainments. Civic feasts were given by the privateers'-men, and patronized by some of our most distinguished inhabitants, who did not hesitate, when the *bonnet rouge* was circulated round the table, to put it on, and then pass it to their neighbor. The cognomen of *citoyen* was the order of the day. Their cards of invitation were always addressed to citizen *such-a-one*. On occasion of one of these civic festivals, given by citizen Boutelle, Captain of the little privateer *Sanspareille*, a guinea was placed under each plate as a pledge of fraternity. But finding that this offering was unpalatable to his guests, on the next occasion he changed it for a play-ticket. I remember the privateers'-men parading our streets with long sabres at their sides, and assuming quite an ascendency in our community. They even had rendezvous opened in Charleston for volunteers, which the Governor, by an order of April, 1793, directed to be closed. They had also their Jacobin clubs, *and public gambling houses.*' Reminiscences of Charleston, p. 39.

not be surprised that Rutledge manifested vehement opposition to Jay's treaty. Giving the whole length to the reins of his aroused and excited feelings, he denounced both the negotiator and his work in unmeasured language. In the next chapter we shall put the reader in possession of an abstract of his speech on that occasion. It was the last exhibition of his oratory. The light of his genius was soon to be extinguished. Clouds had already gathered on his mind. His long and incessant labors had impaired his constitution, and begun to unchain his faculties. The calamity that robbed his home of its chief happiness hastened the development of his malady; and the unhappy event, which we shall relate in the next chapter, completed it. And if among the symptoms of his disorder there occasionally appeared, at this period of his life, those follies of the wise, or those frailties that are common to mankind, it is no part of my duty to draw them from their dread abode.

CHAPTER XVI.

CHIEF JUSTICE OF THE UNITED STATES.

1795.

We have seen that during Jay's absence in England he was chosen Governor of New York.[1] Anticipating his resignation of the Chief Justiceship, Washington inquired of Rutledge whether, in that event, he would accept the vacant post. He replied in the affirmative. 'Your private letter of the 18th ultimo,' thus wrote Washington, July 1st, 1795, 'and Mr. Jay's resignation of the office of Chief Justice of the United States, both came to my hands yesterday. The former gave me much pleasure; and without hesitating a moment, after knowing you would accept the latter, I directed the Secretary of State to make you an official offer of this honorable appointment; to express to you my wish that it may be convenient and agreeable to you to accept it; to intimate, in that case, my desire and the advantages that would attend your being in this city the first Monday in August, at which time the next session of the Supreme Court will commence; and to inform you that your commission as Chief Justice will take date on this day, July 1st, when Mr. Jay's will cease; but that it would be detained here, to be presented to you on your arrival.'[2]

This letter of the President's, and the British treaty,

[1] Ante, p. 415.

[2] Washington to Rutledge. Writings of Washington, vol. xi., p. 34.

must have reached Rutledge about the same time.[1] If the former gave him satisfaction, the latter excited his deepest indignation. With John Langdon, he considered the treaty 'a damned thing made to plague the French.' The excitement and ferment in Charleston were tremendous. Nowhere were the popular proceedings more violent and indecorous. Jay and his treaty were burnt in effigy; the British flag was dragged through the streets, and finally burnt before the doors of the British Consul.[2]

A public meeting was called by notifications published in the Gazettes, and on the 16th of July a large concourse of citizens convened in the Exchange. General Gadsden presided, so far as to adjourn the meeting to St. Michael's church, which promised better accommodation, but declined the chair on account of his age. It was then taken by Judge Matthews. Chief Justice Rutledge addressed the excited assemblage. He commenced by saying that the title was a perversion of terms — that it was styled a treaty of amity, commerce, and navigation; but in fact

---

[1] The latter was printed in a Philadelphia paper, July 2. Ante, p. 412.

[2] The following are copies of handbills printed on this occasion, and posted up at the public corners. 'This evening, at 8 o'clock, will be burnt by the public executioner, near the old market in Broad street, the treaty proposed to be established between Great Britain and America, to show the disapprobation of the citizens of Charleston.

'REPUBLICANS BE VIGILANT!

'As it is in contemplation to burn the effigy of John Jay, and the treaty which he signed, derogatory to the National character of America; and rumor tells us, that persons inimical to liberty, who wish to subvert the ties existing between America and France, mean to try to repel the execution of this just action; it is hoped that the spirit which ever characterized true friends to a democratical government will be prevalent on the occasion, and show these *satellites of anarchy* that *tar and feathers* will be the recompense of their good intentions.' Signed *Ca. Ira. Ca. Ira* See Reminiscences of Charleston, p. 45, for a further account of the popular proceedings on this occasion.

it was an humble acknowledgment of our dependence upon his Majesty; a surrender of our rights and privileges, for so much of his gracious favor as he should be pleased to grant. That the first article securing friendship and peace to people of every degree, was extending favor to all those who were under banishment or amercement, which was improper. He adverted to the frequent inattention to the proper use of words throughout this puerile production. Diplomatic characters were generally particular in this respect; and it was inconceivable how such perversion of terms should take place. 'His Majesty *will* withdraw his troops, &c., within the boundaries *assigned* by the treaty of peace,' &c. *Will*, he contended, implied it as a favor. It should have been *shall* withdraw his troops. It is not impossible to conceive it a matter of will, even in his most gracious Majesty. But the whole of this clause, he contended, was improperly introduced. Mr. Jay should have demanded an unconditional relinquishment of those posts as a right; till which was granted, and until Lord Grenville had given orders to Lord Dorchester to that effect, open, to be sent to our President, to be by him forwarded, he should not have opened his lips upon the treaty. It was prostituting the dearest rights of freemen, and laying them prostrate at the feet of Royalty. 'Assigned by the treaty of peace,' was an expression that ought not to have been admitted by one who knew the territory to have been fought for, to have been attained with our freedom, and who should have insisted upon the possession of it.

He adverted to the tricks, easy to be discovered in every article and clause of the treaty, that were put upon our envoy. But his admitting that 'it is uncertain whether the river Mississippi extends so far northward as the Lake of the Woods, as to be intersected by a line drawn due west from the Lake of the Woods in the manner mentioned in the treaty of peace,' and 'whereas doubts had arisen what river was truly intended under the name of the river St. Croix,' are the grossest absurdities; particularly when assented to by a man who absolutely signed that treaty, and had before him maps that excluded both uncertainty and doubt. To be diplomatically chaste, it should have been 'as we are uncertain,' and 'whereas doubts have arisen with us,' &c.

The appointment of the Commissioners was a measure that could operate to the advantage of but one party — the British — in case it should be properly conducted; but he asserted that the chance was greatly against fairness, and he doubted not that it would be little better than a direct relinquishment of all it was intended they should decide upon. After observing that he hoped a full discussion would take place this day, he insisted that there was but one article or clause in the whole that had the appearance of reciprocity — an idea requisite in the inception of a treaty — or conferring advantage on the United States; and that was the one allowing us the West India trade—a deception; a trick that added insult to the injury.

In pointing out the improprieties of negotiations of any kind with England, the Chief Justice was led to the state of the French successes. He lavished the highest encomiums on that brave and heroic nation. The Alexanders, the Cæsars, and the Charles of antiquity, gave place to a whole nation of heroes. Their deeds of heroism were great; but nobler ones were daily enacted in all parts of France. As a nation, she had conquered all her opposers. Holland owned her conquest, Prussia felt her energy, Germany retired from her arms, Spain was suing for peace, and the perfidious, boasting, assuming nation, Great Britain, that had arrogated for ages power never possessed, that assumed the sovereignty of the sea, and monopolized the commerce of the whole world, was hoping for peace upon whatever terms France might grant it.

To negotiate she could not hope. She was reduced to the last gasp; and were America to seize her by the throat, she would expire in agonies at her feet.

One thing appeared to him right — it was justice, and he hoped his country would always maintain it — he alluded to the intent of the articles that secure to British creditors their debts in the United States. He would allow them their just demands, but we ought not to be bound to do it by treaty. To take the power of deciding upon those claims from our State Courts; to manifest a want of confidence in the Supreme Court of the United States, and submit them to a few Commissioners, was ridiculous and inadmissible.

Such is the abstract of Rutledge's speech on this occasion, as published in the Philadelphia papers. 'To attempt to do justice to the energy and eloquence, the decided and manly firmness of this sage republican,' says the reporter, 'is a rashness that we disclaim. We only seek to sketch the outlines; not without some hopes, however, of extending the rays of his patriotism by even our humble efforts.' Whatever the merits of Rutledge's oratory on this occasion — and we do not doubt they were great — it must be confessed that his objections to the treaty were the suggestions of feeling rather than reason — the offspring of verbal criticism rather than of comprehensive views. The recollection of the misery inflicted on his country during the revolutionary struggle still rankled in his heart; and his hatred of Great Britain, as we have already observed, was intense and unconquerable. He spoke to an audience that shared and sympathized with his feelings.

In addition to the causes that elsewhere inflamed opposition to the treaty, there was one peculiar to Charleston alone. Here, many persons 'were displeased with Mr. Jay's appointment because it superseded Mr. Pinckney, and they were resolved beforehand to reprobate this treaty.'[1] Thus wrote William Smith, a federal member of Congress from South Carolina, to Oliver Wolcott; and though he may have misconceived the purpose of those who resented the displacement of Mr. Pinckney, there can be no doubt that they were predisposed to regard the treaty with disfavor. Mr. Pinckney, however, uninfluenced by personal considerations, endeared himself to the administration and the friends of the administration by the wholly disinterested part he acted on this occasion. He witnessed and appreciated all the difficulties Jay had to encounter; and his sentiments, greatly influential at the time, may serve as a guide to correct conclusions even now. 'Altho' some points'—thus he wrote to the Secretary of State—'might have been arranged more beneficial for us if the treaty had been dictated entirely by the United States, yet, when it is considered as a composition of difference, where mutual complaints had rendered mutual concessions necessary to establish good understanding, I think it may be fairly said, that as little has been conceded by Mr. Jay, and as much obtained for the United States, as, all circumstances considered, could be expected. The business, upon the whole, has been concluded more beneficially for us than I had any hope we would obtain by negotiation six months ago; and, in my opinion, places us in a more advantageous situation than we should have been by becoming parties to the war.'[2]

Rutledge's speech was hailed by the enemies of the administration and the opponents of the treaty, with an eager approbation. By his friends of the Federal party it was read with surprise and indignation. The sensation it created testifies very strongly to the weight Rutledge had in the country, and the importance that was attached to his opinions. Hamilton, writing under the signature

[1] Sept. 8th, 1795. Gibbs' Federal Administrations, vol. i., p. 230.
[2] Written Nov. 16th, 1794.

of Camillus, deemed it necessary to counteract the tendency of his sentiments, by a brief but severe rejoinder. 'No man in the habit of thinking well, either of Mr. Rutledge's head or heart,' he added in a note, 'but must have felt, at reading the passages of his speech which have been published, pain, surprise, and mortification. I regret the occasion and the necessity of animadversion.'[1]

Wolcott, the Secretary of the Treasury, though by no means the compeer of his predecessor in abilities, was nevertheless a man of generous temper and kindly feelings. The comments that appear in his published correspondence upon Rutledge's appointment, show in a very conspicuous light in what an inflamed state were the politics of the time.[2]

Nor was Wolcott singular in the feelings he expressed. The leading Federalists, uninformed that Rutledge had been virtually Chief Justice since the 1st of July, and before his sentiments respecting the treaty could have been divined, for its contents were then unknown to the public, were sadly puzzled at his appointment. His speech, and the rumor of his promotion, went abroad about the same time. If the former occasioned surprise and indignation, the latter was the subject of very general speculation.

'Many of the warmest advocates of the present measures,' wrote Chauncey Goodrich, 'are hurt by Mr. Rutledge's appointment, and are unable to account for it, but impute it to want of information of his hostility to the government, or some hidden cause which justifies the measure. We shall be loth to find faction is to be courted at so great a sacrifice of consistency.'[3]

'N. E. (New England) is tolerably quiet,' wrote Oliver

---

[1] Hamilton's Works, vol. vii., p. 206.

[2] Wolcott to Hamilton, July 28th, 1795. Gibbs' Federal Administrations, vol. i., p. 219. To Oliver Wolcott, Sen., Aug. 10th. Ibid., p. 224.

[3] Goodrich to Wolcott, July 30th, 1795. Ibid., p. 220.

Ellsworth, whom we shall view, in a subsequent volume, as one of Rutledge's successors on the Bench, 'and will be more so as the subject becomes more understood; but I am to be responsible only for Connecticut. That E. R. (Edward Rutledge) should not act at all, is less surprising than that J. R. (John Rutledge) should act like the *devil.* I wait for the unravelling, when more is to be known.'[1]

Rutledge sailed from Charleston for Baltimore, on his way to Philadelphia, the 31st of July. He was accompanied by one of his sons. He was present at the opening of the August term of the Supreme Court.[2] His commission, which was read, bore date, as Washington had written him it should, the 1st of July, 1795. The case of Talbot *v.* Janson[3] was before the Court, on a writ of error, in the nature of an appeal from the Circuit Court for the District of South Carolina. The material facts in the case were, that Ballard, the commander of a vessel, which was fitted out in the United States, cruised in company with Talbot, who alleged that he was a French citizen, and produced a French commission. Ballard captured the Magdalena, a Dutch prize; he was then joined by Talbot, and the prize was brought into the harbor of Charleston. The questions for the Court were, whether the capture, under such circumstances, was a violation of the treaty between the United States and Holland? and whether it was such a case of prize that the Courts of the United States could take cognizance of it?

Rutledge, Chief Justice.—'The merits of the case are so obvious, that I do not conceive there is much difficulty in pronouncing a fair and prompt decision for affirming the decree of the Circuit Court. The doctrine of expatriation is certainly of great magnitude; but it is not

---

[1] Ellsworth to Wolcott, Aug. 15th, 1795 Ibid., p. 225.

[2] August 21st, 1795.

[3] 3 Dallas, 133.

necessary to give an opinion upon it in the present cause, there being no proof that Captain Talbot's admission as a citizen of the French Republic, was with a view to relinquish his native country; and a man may, at the same time, enjoy the rights of citizenship under two governments. It appears, upon the whole, that Ballard's vessel was illegally fitted out in the United States; and the weight of evidence satisfies my mind, that Talbot's vessel, which was originally American property, continued so at the time of the capture, notwithstanding all the fraudulent attempts to give it a different complexion. The capture, therefore, was a violation of the law of nations, and of the treaty with Holland. The Court has a clear jurisdiction of the cause, upon the express authority of Pelaches' case.[1] And every motive of good faith and justice must induce us to concur with the Circuit Court in awarding restitution.'

Of his judicial bearing, while presiding at this term of the Court, 'enough has come down,' says Mr. Wharton, 'to enable us to say, that, though tinged with that haughtiness which in later years had marked him, it was graceful and courtly, and that his natural impetuosity had been subdued by the approach of age, the weight of long public service, and the anxiety of a position' which he could not but regard as too insecure.[2] No trace of his disorder was discernible during his stay in Philadelphia. 'He was perfectly himself; but the excitement of the times was too much; and it soon became evident that he never could assume the high office to which he had been called.' [3]

It is with a feeling of pity and sadness, that we now approach the conclusion of a public life, passed in the service of the public, distinguished for high and generous qualities, and presenting strong and varied claims to our

---

[1] 4th Inst.

[2] Wharton's State Trials, p. 36.

[3] MS. letter to the Author.

gratitude and respect. On the adjournment of the Supreme Court, after a session of a few days, the Chief Justice returned to Charleston. In November, he proceeded to Augusta, to hold a term of the Circuit Court. But the records were in Savannah, the clerk of the court had recently died, and the Associate Justice was not in attendance. The court was accordingly adjourned until the next term. The Chief Justice then set out to hold the circuit in North Carolina; but he was attacked with sickness on his way, and I am not informed whether he was able to continue his journey.[1]

When Congress met in December, the feelings of the federal members towards him had softened; and we think it apparent, from the published correspondence of the period, that if there was nothing in the case but what Hamilton terms 'his imprudent sally upon a certain occasion,'[2] he would have been confirmed. But the condition of his intellect had become known, and his rejection, however much we may lament the occasion, was doubtless the dictate of prudence. We could well conceive, even in the absence of authentic information, how this action of the Senate affected his proud spirit. He had sat at the very cradle of our liberties.[3] From the meeting of the

[1] 'By a gentleman who left Camden on Wednesday last, we are informed that the Chief Justice of the United States left that place on the Saturday preceding, on his way to hold the Circuit Court in North Carolina; that on the evening of that day he reached Evans' tavern, on Lynch's creek, which he left the next morning. A few hours after, he was taken so unwell, that he was obliged to return to Mr. Evans'. When the account came away, he was so much indisposed as to make it doubtful whether he would be able to proceed in time to hold the Court in North Carolina.'

The above paragraph appeared in a Charleston Gazette, Dec. 1st, 1795.

[2] Hamilton to Rufus King, Dec. 14th, 1795. Hamilton's Works, vol. vi., p. 76.

[3] "I sat at its cradle, I followed its hearse," was Grattan's celebrated reference to the extinction of the Irish Parliament; justly described by Lord Brougham as among the finest passages of figurative eloquence.

Stamp-Act Congress, in 1765, down to this inauspicious day,[1] his name had been identified with the history of his country. In that long interval he had occupied stations of dignity and high responsibility. In a gloomy period of the war he had been invested with dictatorial authority over the affairs of his native commonwealth, and exercised it in a manner to secure the gratitude of friends, and extort even the homage of foes. He had taken a conspicuous part in forming that very government, one of whose branches now fixed upon him what he must have deemed a stigma; but which impartial history, taking note of all the circumstances, explains and rectifies. The very contrast between his past services and honors, and his present fortunes, must have heightened and exalted his distress. 'The Senate's refusal to confirm his appointment, extinguished the last spark of sanity,'[2] and closed his public career.

---

[1] He was rejected by the Senate, Dec. 15th, 1795.

[2] MS. letter to the author.

CHAPTER XVII.

CONCLUSION.

1795—1800.

The remaining portion of Rutledge's life is brief, and its story is quickly told. He languished under the weight and oppression of disease until the 18th of July, 1800, when he was summoned to other scenes. His death occurred while at the house of his friend, Bishop Smith, and was the wearing out of an exhausted frame rather than the result of positive illness. 'His bed of lingering languor was attended by his two daughters and two of his sons: his other children were absent. There are yet a few survivors of those who attended the funeral from Bishop Smith's house. They have described it to me as most solemn and sad, but unaccompanied by any parade.'[1] He was buried in St. Michael's church-yard, in the city of Charleston. A modest grave-stone marks the place of his interment. He left eight children — six sons and two daughters. The elder daughter married Mr. Francis Kinloch; the younger, Mr. Henry Laurens. None of these children of Rutledge survive; but their descendants are numerous.

The portrait of Rutledge by Trumbull gives us a pretty accurate idea of his personal appearance. He was tall, his frame well formed and robust. His forehead was

[1] MS. letter to the author.

broad and full; his eyes dark and piercing. His mouth was compressed, and, together with the lower part of his face, indicated firmness and decision. His hair was combed back from his forehead, and, according to the fashion of the times, was powdered and tied behind. His aspect was *resolute*—almost stern, and wore an expression of blended thought and determination.

The personal and intellectual qualities of Rutledge, so far as they are discoverable from the acts of his life, have been presented to the reader in the preceding pages. We have concealed nothing, and nothing extenuated. No human life is perfect, and seldom altogether uniform. It is only by viewing the lights and shades of character that we can form a just judgment of its real merits. It will be found, we think, on thus contemplating Rutledge, that the high position he held in the opinion of his cotemporaries was the result of qualities equally high and rare. Though his feelings were warm and ardent, they seldom controlled his judgment. Vigorous common sense, and an impulsive energy that forthwith executed its dictates, were his greatest excellencies as a public man. He had nothing in common with that class of politicians who are governed by metaphysical niceties and logical distinctions, unrepressed and uncorrected by broad views and extensive generalizations. He saw things in their practical relations, and formed his judgment accordingly. He had one quality which, even unallied with high abilities, will always have great weight in the affairs of mankind—he was always in earnest. His opinions were not suspended in doubt, nor his inspirations and original impulses neutralized and confounded by refined speculations. Energetic and ardent, he pressed forward to his objects with unfailing and unfaltering resolution. Earnestness was the characteristic of his eloquence and the secret of its power.

Of the literary character of Rutledge, I can say but

little. His pursuits were so entirely those of law and politics, that he bestowed, I infer, small attention upon the *literæ humaniores*. His written style bore the impress neither of grace nor art. He seemed intent only upon expressing his meaning, regardless of the form in which he clothed it. His spoken eloquence, on the contrary, was direct, manly, and elegant.

From this imperfect analysis of his merits, the reader must recur to the long and varied public career of Rutledge, to obtain a more adequate conception of him than it is in the power of criticism to unfold. Though his life was passed in the public service, and 'in the very eye of public inspection,' but little has been transmitted that exhibits those personal traits and qualities which, after all, are the most reliable indicia of character. I have spared, however, no pains to acquire such facts and information as would serve to illustrate the man himself; with what success the preceding pages will disclose.

www.ingramcontent.com/pod-product-compliance
Lightning Source LLC
LaVergne TN
LVHW021053110826
845150LV00001B/63

9781425567552